Teaching Composition

Background Readings

T. R. Johnson

University of New Orleans

Shirley Morahan

Northeast Missouri State University

Bedford/St. Martin's   Boston   ◆   New York

For Bedford/St. Martin's

Developmental Editors: Erin Durkin, Michelle Clark
Production Editor: Deborah Baker
Production Supervisor: Maria Gonzalez
Marketing Manager: Brian Wheel
Copyeditor: Paula Woolley
Text Design: Claire Seng-Niemoeller
Cover Design: Donna Lee Dennison
Composition: Karla Goethe, Orchard Wind Graphics
Printing and Binding: Haddon Craftsmen, Inc., an R. R. Donnelley & Sons Company

President: Charles H. Christensen
Editorial Director: Joan E. Feinberg
Editor in Chief: Karen S. Henry
Director of Marketing: Karen Melton
Director of Editing, Design, and Production: Marcia Cohen
Managing Editor: Elizabeth M. Schaaf

Manufactured in the United States of America.

6   5   4   3   2   1
f   e   d   c   b   a

For information, write: Bedford/St. Martin's, 75 Arlington Street, Boston, MA 02116
(617-399-4000)

ISBN: 0–312–39711–9

Acknowledgments

Arnetha Ball and Ted Lardner. "Dispositions Toward Language: Teacher Constructs of Knowledge and the Ann Arbor Black English Case." *College Composition and Communication* 48 (1997).

David Bartholomae. "Inventing the University." From *When a Writer Can't Write: Studies in Writer's Block and Other Composing-Process Problems* edited by Mike Rose. Guilford Press (1985): 135–165. Reprinted with permission.

James A. Berlin. "Rhetoric and Ideology in the Writing Class." *College English,* September 1988. Copyright © 1988 by the National Council of Teachers of English. Reprinted with permission.

Lynn Z. Bloom. "Why I (Used to) Hate to Give Grades." *College Composition and Communication* 48.3 (1997) pp. 360–371. Copyright © 1997 by the National Council of Teachers of English. Reprinted with permission.

Wayne C. Booth. "The Rhetorical Stance." *College Composition and Communication,* October 1963. Copyright © 1963 by the National Council of Teachers of English. Reprinted with permission.

Acknowledgments and copyrights are continued at the back of the book on pages 579–80, which constitute an extension of the copyright page. It is a violation of the law to reproduce these selections by any means whatsoever without the written permission of the copyright holder.

Preface

This selection of readings is designed to help you acquire or broaden a theoretical and practical background as you prepare to teach college-level composition. Although we've selected the readings with first-time instructors in mind, we also hope that veteran instructors in community colleges and four-year institutions will find helpful perspectives, important ideas, and practical suggestions.

Our discipline's conversations have always been spirited, whether about philosophical issues, learning and writing theory, or pedagogical assumptions that influence our work with writers. From such conversations — public and private, in scholarly journals, faculty lounges, and on listservs — and from our own classroom experience and reflection, we gain confidence and clarity in our vision of the nature and purpose of writing courses. We hope your "conversation" with these readings will help you to become an adept and creative teacher of writing.

The readings in this volume address major concerns of composition theory and practice. Chapter 1, "Teaching Writing: Key Concepts and Philosophies for Reflective Practice," examines, describes, and reflects on the beliefs and assumptions that inform writing pedagogies. The readings in Chapter 2, "Thinking about the Writing Process," discuss ways that writers shape thought into words when they explore ideas, plan, draft, consider (or ignore) audiences, and revise. This chapter contains a subsection on the increasingly important topic of integrating technology into the writing classroom, as well as new material on the evolving principles and concerns of visual literacy as it applies to the teaching of composition. Chapter 3, "Responding to and Evaluating Student Writing," presents teachers' strategies for responding to writers' needs and working with students at diverse writing sites. Chapter 4, "Issues in Writing Pedagogy: Institutional Politics and the Other," focuses on classroom and faculty diversity. Throughout this volume, many of the readings include helpful citations, and an annotated bibliography lists other relevant and important articles that could not be included here. These pieces offer the opportunity for further reflection and research on composition and its artful teaching.

You can, of course, jump in anywhere and read the article that best suits your needs at the moment. Know, however, that there are rich interconnections among the readings that build a recursivity into the collection. If you are reading Juanita Rodgers Comfort's "Becoming a Writerly Self," you might find yourself dropping back to follow up her reference to Bartholomae's "Inventing the University" and his views on academic discourse. The articles by Peter Elbow and Nancy Sommers are referenced frequently in other readings in this collection, so you may find yourself stopping in the middle of one reading to refer to them. The readings have also been thoughtfully organized to logically build upon, and segue into, important concepts.

Because each writer in this collection has teachers as his or her primary audience, you will find very practical recommendations about teaching strategies. A headnote to each reading focuses on its writer's key assumptions and consistent themes. Two kinds of reflective question sets follow each selection: "The Writer's Insights as a Resource for Your Teaching" and "The Writer's Insights as a Resource for Your Writing Classroom." We wrote the first set of recommendations to prompt you into reflective practice as a writing teacher. We based these recommendations on our experience working with writers, our training and supervision of novice writing instructors, and our work with colleagues across the curriculum. The second set of suggestions describes strategies that have worked for professors and graduate writing instructors alike as we apply the insights of a reading to our actual practice in the classroom.

Teaching Composition: Background Readings — written to accompany composition texts — includes both theoretical background and practical advice for writing instructors. Each Bedford/St. Martin's composition text is also accompanied by its own instructor's manual, which provides such practical resources as chapter overviews, sample syllabi, teaching tips, discussion prompts, additional assignments, and recommendations about using the electronic ancillary package. We recommend that you use this volume of background readings in tandem with the instructor's manual for the text you and your students are using to take best advantage of the information and possibilities offered by the textbook.

Contents

"A reflective practitioner will analyze a new idea in light of its appropriateness to the students and their present knowledge; its fit with available theory, experience, and the goals of teaching; and its probability for success as judged from the teacher's experience and knowledge."

"If you're a working-class kid in the vocational track, the options you'll have to deal with this will be constrained in certain ways: You're defined by your school as 'slow'; you're placed in a curriculum that isn't designed to liberate you but to occupy you, or, if you're lucky, train you, though the training is for work the society does not esteem."

"When we look at writing instruction from the perspective of underlife, it appears that the purpose of our courses is to allow students to substitute one kind of underlife for another. Instead of the naïve, contained form they normally employ, we're asking them to take on a disruptive form — a whole stance towards their social world that questions it, explores it, writes about it."

"[S]ince language is a social phenomenon that is a product of a particular historical moment, our notions of the observing self, the communities in which the self functions, and the very structures of the material world are social constructions — all specific to a particular time and culture. These social constructions are thus inscribed in the very language we are given to inhabit in responding to our experience."

"[The student] has to invent the university by assembling and mimicking its language while finding some compromise between idiosyncrasy, a personal history, on the one hand, and the requirements of convention, the history of a discipline, on the other hand."

"[I]nstead of thinking bigger and wider, as composition has typically done — using large imagined geographies to situate and validate composition studies as a discipline — now it is time to think smaller and more locally."

"What teachers teach in [collaborative learning] is how to establish and maintain intellectually productive rapport and ways to negotiate that rapport when the task is done. They help students learn to negotiate boundaries between the communities they belong to and the communities their fellow students may belong to. They allow students latitude to define their individuality not as a stark and lonesome independence, isolated or alienated from others, but as a function of interdependence among peers."

"All the writers I have observed, skilled and unskilled alike, use the process of retrospective structuring while writing. Yet the degree to which they do so varies and seems, in fact, to depend upon the model of the writing process that they have internalized. Those who realize that writing can be a recursive process have an easier time with waiting, looking, and discovering."

"This paper, too, treats writing as a problem-solving process, focusing, however, on what happens when the process dead-ends in writer's block. It will further suggest that [. . .] blockers may well be stymied by possessing rigid or inappropriate rules, or inflexible or confused plans. Ironically enough, these are occasionally instilled by the composition teacher or gleaned from the writing textbook."

"The common ingredient that I find in all of the writing I admire [. . .] is something that I shall reluctantly call the rhetorical stance, a stance which depends on discovering and maintaining in any writing situation a proper balance among the three elements that are at work in any communicative effort: the available arguments about the subject itself, the interests and peculiarities of the audience, and the voice, the implied character, of the speaker."

"[U]nless the writer is composing a diary or journal entry, intended only for the writer's own eyes, the writing process is not complete unless another person, someone other than the writer, reads the text also. The second assertion thus emphasizes the creative, dynamic duality of the process of reading and writing, whereby writers create readers and readers create writers. In the meeting of these two lies meaning, lies communication."

"An audience is a field of force. The closer we come — the more we think about these readers — the stronger the pull they exert on the contents of our minds. The practical question, then, is always whether a particular audience functions as a helpful field of force or one that confuses or inhibits us."

"But student writers constantly struggle to bring their essays into congruence with a predefined meaning. The experienced writers do the opposite: They seek to discover (to create) meaning in the engagement with their writing, in revision."

"[I]ntentions are shaped by the community the writer wants to make his or her way into, and the revision process is not a simple matter of making a text 'better' or 'clearer.' Revision is instead the very complicated matter of struggle between a full, excess-ive life and the seemingly strict limits of what can be written and understood within a particular discourse community."

"Will the on-line classroom be the end of our teaching? Certainly we lose face-to-face contact. But might we not generate another relationship, a different intimacy that might have its own virtues? Might the virtual classroom foster new relationships and new kinds of learning?"

Patricia R. Webb
Narratives of Self in Networked Communications   289

"Although network technologies can offer us opportunities to challenge traditional notions of self, we must first understand how strongly entrenched those narratives are and what shape they take before we can begin to consider disrupting them. Merely introducing technology into the classroom is not, as I found, a guarantee that these narratives will be disrupted."

TEACHING VISUAL LITERACY   309

Sandra E. Moriarty
A Conceptual Map of Visual Communication   309

"[T]here is an evolving and well-recognized body of visual communication theory and literature that crosses a variety of disciplines that could provide some sense of a coherent conceptual base. Such work clusters in the area of visual literacy, visual thinking, visual perception, imagery and representation."

Robert Kramer and Stephen Bernhardt
Teaching Text Design   324

"In all corners of our culture, visually informative texts are on the ascendancy, and it is crucial that we continue to map the principles of visual design and that we pursue principled methods for learning to become text designers. In this essay, we suggest a scope and sequence of text design skills and knowledge as a contribution toward a curriculum that helps writers become text designers."

3 Responding to and Evaluating Student Writing   351

Nancy Sommers
Responding to Student Writing   351

"Instead of finding errors or showing students how to patch up parts of their texts, we need to sabotage our students' conviction that the drafts they have written are complete and coherent. Our comments need to offer students revision tasks of a different order of complexity and sophistication from the ones that they themselves identify, by forcing students back into the chaos, back to the point where they are shaping and restructuring their meaning."

"Writing instruction should enable students to recognize the writerly self as a *persuasive instrument* that can be strategically deployed and to learn to make effective use of their own multiple locations to take personal stands on public issues *that transcend the confessional.*"

"[O]ur writing classes do become the setting for argument about capital punishment, euthanasia, abortion, women's rights. If we regard these discussions as having at most only 'situational' weight — a 'this time and place' payoff — then the dynamics of shared ideas is not allowed its proper role in the *necessary directionality* for the human condition and the condition of the planet we inhabit — that of alleviating suffering and cruelty."

"In this essay I set out a case for why the concept of sponsorship is so richly suggestive for exploring economies of literacy and their effects. Then, through use of extended case examples, I demonstrate the practical application of this approach for interpreting current conditions of literacy teaching and learning, including persistent stratification of opportunity and escalating standards for literacy achievement."

Teaching Writing: Key Concepts and Philosophies for Reflective Practice

I n this chapter, you will find readings that encourage you to reflect on your practice as a writing teacher. These readings have been chosen for two reasons: to illuminate major assumptions — implicit and explicit — about why and how we teach students to grow as writers; and to illustrate important pedagogic strategies used by writing instructors, such as viewing writing as a recursive process, using writing as a tool for critical thinking, developing evaluative criteria for revision, and so on. We recommend that you begin your research into composition theory and pedagogy with these readings and that you return to them when you want to reflect on the experiences of the writing community that you foster.

Every choice you make as a writing instructor is informed by some philosophy of composition and of teaching composition, even if you're not fully aware of the philosophy you hold. The more aware you become of your assumptions and premises, the more you can rethink and improve your teaching. Each of the writers in this section challenges us to examine the assumptions that govern the ways we teach. To begin this process of reflection, we recommend that — before you start to teach a writing course or early in the semester — you sit down and freewrite or brainstorm for about fifteen minutes, listing your "I believes" about writing and about the teaching of writing. Periodically shape those beliefs into a coherent format that you can refer to as you plan assignments, structure sequences of assignments, build or redesign a syllabus, ponder a writing curriculum, propose support services for writers across the curriculum, or discuss your pedagogy with colleagues.

Many first-year instructors keep a reflective journal in which they log and reflect on what occurs in class and how students respond to assignments. Those instructors use the journal to describe their own reactions and responses to the class dynamic, to the process of building a writing community, and to the connections they are making between what they are reading outside the classroom and actual events within their classroom. Two or three times a semester they read over their entries and chart their own learning and growth as instructors. By the end of the first semester, most new instructors can see some dramatic changes in confidence, attitudes about writing communities and student writing, use of teaching strategies, and understanding of how the parts of the syllabus or the course connect.

The reflective journal is a very useful resource for writing about teaching, for developing a final draft of a philosophy for teaching writing, and for designing syllabi for second-semester or second-year courses. It could be an important part of a teaching portfolio, a collection of products that demonstrate your practice and improvement as an instructor. That portfolio could include assignments given, copies of student responses, syllabi, descriptions of classroom activities, notes on reading journal entries, student feedback, printouts of e-mail and e-conference conversations of student writers, copies of the summative comments you write students, and hypertext documents. From that collection, you might on occasion select representative materials for others to view, read, hear, and evaluate. Your teaching portfolio both fosters and illustrates your reflective practice as a writing instructor, and you should use it to assess your progress as a professional educator. You can also use it to identify strengths, areas for improvement, and new visions and goals for your writing community; it will be helpful in your construction of knowledge about writing and about teaching writers. The portfolio is a primary document to use when you apply for teaching positions, fellowships, research grants, tenure, and promotions.

Some Basics for Thinking about Teaching Writing

George Hillocks

The college writing classroom can seem disarmingly complex, especially for new teachers. How does one formulate a flexible approach that will evolve and improve as it must in order to succeed? This chapter from George Hillocks's Teaching Writing as Reflective Practice *offers a concrete, step-by-step strategy for making the classroom a viable place to learn more about the teaching of writing. Hillocks begins by discussing in broad terms the nature of "theory" and how it provides our classrooms with coherence, purpose, and a meaningful way to gauge our success.*

Hillocks distinguishes practice-as-routine from practice-as-reflective-inquiry and sets up a six-phase model for improving our teaching: first, we evaluate a particular practice; next, we project a desired change in student performance; third, we devise strategies that might bring about the desired change; fourth, we implement the strategies; fifth, we evaluate the results; and finally, we consider the incidental or unexpected results that derive from the new practice. By making reflective inquiry a part of our daily practice as teachers, we transform our classrooms into dynamic spaces of constant change and growth — for teachers as well as students.

In various projects that my students and I have been conducting to discover how teachers think about their teaching, one distinct profile has emerged so far that hinges on a common set of attitudes toward students, teaching, and learning. While our sample is drawn from teachers in a large urban community college system, experience indicates that the same profile appears at other levels. I present this profile as representative of beliefs shared by several teachers in the sample, but certainly not all.

This representative professor holds a Ph.D. in English from a prestigious university. He believes that the primary task of his freshman composition class is to teach the "modes of writing." Of his students, he says, "I'm always surprised at how little the students do know about a given subject or a given approach to writing about something." He believes that, after mechanics and editing, "Perhaps their second weakest area . . . is what I would loosely call reading between the lines, thinking for oneself, thinking, using analogy, being creative."

Classes observed begin with the professor making an assignment followed by a presentation of information about the mode of writing represented in the assignment. This complete, he turns to the previous assignment and asks several students to read their papers aloud. After each reading the professor comments. This goes on until class ends. In one class he presents the mode of writing he calls "extended example." He explains at some length that it will not be the same as classification or narrative.

The essay that I am about to put on the board, where we use example as a way of developing a paper, will be somewhat closer to the classification one, but not the same. There will never be a paper that is exactly like the last one. Don't you see? Don't think that just because you did that last time, that somehow you've got to do it this way this time and if you can't fit it, there is a problem. Don't *try* to fit it. It's a different assignment. It has an entirely different set of problems that you have to work on solving. When you tell your story, it's just like if I turn on the television and I had missed the commercial. I am seeing characters developing some conflict. I'm seeing them change as a result of the pressures they are under. It's a *story*. I'm trying to say that over and over again, it is a story. It is not a classification of anything. You are telling a story. So there's no first, second, and finally. There is a plot, which may have a beginning, a middle, and an end. That is not first, second, and finally. There is no conclusion; there is an ending.

He continues for thirty lines of transcript, talking more about narrative, which students have already written and will read aloud later, and contrasting it with news commentaries on TV. He says he wants to "take a minute and throw some things on the board so you have a sense of where we're going." He says, "Do not hesitate to ask questions if the assignment is still not clear to you. I'm not trying to rush you. I thought it was fairly well understood, but if it's not, I can only know unless, you know, you ask me questions and indicate what's not been made clear. OK. Just copy what's on the board, but don't copy anything yet. Some of this is just a reminder, which you probably already know." Perhaps not surprisingly, no one asks questions. He writes several assignments in abbreviated form, including one for "theme three," the next composition that students will write.

> Theme 3 (extended example)
> Choose only one:
> (1) What are three dangerous drugs?
> (2) What are three situations where we should not drink and drive?
> (3) What are three jobs for the future?
> (4) Who are three well-known illiterates?

After thirty-nine lines of transcript and a period for role taking, he turns to theme three:

> Now the expository mode, we call an example. Really, example is not an expository mode, but I'll make it one anyway. Secondly, example is used in all the various modes to get the point across. And we are concentrating on using example very explicitly this time, so I think we will just say the expository mode is example. You have to decide who the audience is and who you are as a speaker, what your attitude is, and if you're having some difficulty with that, we can discuss it on Thursday. Give it some thought before Thursday. For number six I have given you four questions which will force you to write a paper in which you have an introductory paragraph, three developmental paragraphs, each of which will have one example in the second form, and then you will have a fifth paragraph, which is a conclusion. Now this time you are *not* telling a story. You are explaining something. You must use one of the four, only one. If you choose number one, I'll see your topic is drugs.

The professor continues for sixty-five lines of transcript, which include a lecture on famous illiterate athletes, before asking volunteers to read their narratives.

The Basics of Practice

Any teacher of writing is faced with a wide variety of possibilities for teaching that range from the imposition of little or no structure to very tight constraints on students, from teacher lecture to free-flowing class discussion with no limits on topics students may wish to mention, from daily free writing to daily drill on usage, from the use of computers to the use of chalkboards, from curricula based on the writing types of current traditional rhetoric to those that seem to admit to no important differences among writing tasks and sometimes no curricula at all. In this welter of possibilities how can we know how to proceed in making decisions about both curriculum and specific classroom practice? What prevents classrooms from becoming a hodge-podge of activities: ten minutes of free writing, five of sentence combining, fifteen of lecture about "description," twelve on vocabulary, and, assuming a fifty-minute class, eight minutes of small-group discussion on a topic of the students' choice?

What is it that renders the classroom process coherent? What can be the basis of future practice with particular students? I think the answer to both these questions is *theory*. Every teacher of writing has a set of theories that provide a coherent view of the field and means of approaching the task of teaching. Leon Lederman, the physicist and Nobel laureate, says simply that theory is "the best explanation of the data," taken to include their nature and relationships. Theories may be based on a combination of assumptions, constructions derived from empirical research, and argument. They vary in quality with the care exercised in establishing each component. One such "explanation" for writing teachers has to do with written discourse, some explanation of the features of writing, their occurrence, and relationships.

The profile with which this chapter opens illustrates several theories. Let us look at four. The most obvious is the explanation of discourse that leads to the teacher's opening discussion about how "extended example" differs from "classification" and "narrative." In this teacher's theory, written discourse includes many such "types." He will teach ten of them in the course of the semester. Each is characterized by a structure that he endeavors to explain to his students, contrasting it with others that may be similar in certain ways. Thus, he says, of narrative: "There is a plot, which may have a beginning, a middle, and an end. That is not first, second, and finally. There is no conclusion; there is an ending." Further, he believes that the central features of each type are adequately represented in his chalkboard outline of the assignment. He believes that if students understand these features, they will be able to generate an example of the type.

The second theory underlying this profile is pedagogical and quite straightforward. Simply stated, it holds that teaching is tantamount to telling. It is based on the assumption, which Lindley Murray states in the 1795 preface to his venerable grammar, that people can, using appropriate language, "transfuse . . . sentiments into the minds of one another" (5). In the classes of these teachers, observations reveal that their talk dominates the available time by wide margins, not infrequently 100 to 1. In the class transcript excerpted above, the teacher has 229 lines while one student speaks for two lines up to the point that students read their essays aloud.

A third theory, one of epistemology or knowing, appears to underlie both of the above. It appears to be what postmodern critics would call a "positivist" epistemology, one that holds reality and knowledge to be directly apprehensible by the senses without interpretation, almost without ambiguity. Such a theory endorses teaching as telling. The professor simply needs to "infuse" his ideas of "extended example" into the minds of students. Further, those ideas can be adequately represented simply by means of the outline on the chalkboard. The same epistemology is implicated in the theory of representational discourse the professor holds. He seems to believe that the substance of at least some kinds of discourse may be directly apprehended without the filters of persuasion on the part of the writer or interpretation on the part of the reader. Thus, he says, "example is used in all the various modes to get the point across." For him, the import of an example is self-evident.

These three theories are closely tied together so as to support one another. Their interlocking results in the smooth functioning of the class, which rolls along under the professor's direction without any apparent difficulty.

The fourth theory is based on the assumption that students have weak backgrounds that render them unlikely to learn. This assumption is taken as fact, as the epistemology might lead us to expect, and statements about student weakness tend to the absolute; for example, "No matter what I do, there is very little improvement." Because they perceive students as very weak, they adopt the corollary that whatever is taught must be simplified and "highly structured." That simplification and structure should enable them to "transfuse" the necessary information directly into the minds of students who cannot think for themselves and "want to be force fed." They say, "The more structure they have, the more comfortable they are with an assignment." Note the simple structure of the five-paragraph theme assignment above.

The basic assumption about students and the theory of teaching in this profile, taken together, form a very tight syllogistic system for thinking about teaching. If teaching is telling, then proper teaching has taken place when the proper basic formulas about writing have been presented. If students do not learn much even when proper teaching has taken place, it is not surprising because they are weak and cannot be expected to learn. The teaching has not failed; the students have. Therefore there is no reason to change the method of teaching. Teaching writing becomes a protected activity. There is no need to call assumptions about methods into question, no need to try something new, no reason to doubt oneself as a teacher. Of course, not all teachers in our sample conform to this profile. Many believe that students can learn, and this belief appears to influence what they do. The point is that *the assumptions we make and the theories we hold have a powerful effect on what and how we teach*.

I believe that teachers of written composition must work from at least four major, interconnected sets of theories: (1) composing processes, (2) written discourse, (3) invention or inquiry, and (4) learning and teaching. These theories will necessarily be the basis for the content and organization of students' experiences in any program intended for helping people learn to write.

This is not to say that theory is the only source of what we do as teachers. Two other sources are equally important: what has been called reflective practice, and the teacher's general fund of life experience.

The Nature of Reflective Practice

Many people believe that research and theory govern practice. The relationships, however, seem far more complex than that, particularly if we think of "practice" in more than the simplest sense of the word as, according to the *Oxford English Dictionary (OED)*, "the action of doing something." What I intend here is more akin to the third and fifth definitions offered by the *OED*: "the doing of something repeatedly or continuously by way of study; exercise in any art, handicraft, etc. for the purpose or with the result of attaining proficiency" (3) and "the carrying on or exercise of a profession or occupation" (5). Taken together, these suggest a kind of practice that is reflective, that permits the practitioner to learn through practice, not simply through *trial and error*, an expression that suggests a kind of randomness that does not allow for the building of knowledge. Others suggest that practice is essentially routine.

Practice as Routine

Stephen North writes of the knowledge of practitioners as a body of lore that he characterizes as "the accumulated body of traditions, practices, and beliefs in terms of which practitioners understand how writing is done, learned, and taught" (22). He argues that "practice is largely a matter of routine. . . . Practitioners operate within the bounds of lore's known: they approach the matter of what to do by reducing the infinite number of new situations into familiar terms, then handling them with familiar strategies" (33).

North allows, however, that under three conditions "practice becomes inquiry" but only

- (a) when the situation cannot be framed in familiar terms, so that any familiar strategies will have to be adapted for use;
- (b) when, although the situation is perceived as familiar, standard approaches are no longer satisfactory, and so new approaches are created for it; or
- (c) when both situation and approach are nonstandard. (33)

North speculates that, judged by these standards, with the normal freshman composition teaching load, "practice qualifies as inquiry less than ten percent of the time" (34).

These guidelines for thinking about what constitutes inquiry in practice are useful. To use them for the analysis of inquiry in the practice of teaching writing would require definitions of the key terms, of course. What constitutes standard and nonstandard situations? What constitutes "an approach" in the teaching of writing? When is an approach standard or nonstandard? North's examples suggest that a nonstandard situation represents a shift in circumstances comparable to the advent of the open admissions policy that brought underprepared students into Mina Shaughnessy's classroom, prompting the inquiry that resulted in *Errors and Expectations*. In the same way, a nonstandard approach is one that leaves behind most, if not all, of the teaching tactics previously used.

Reflective Practice as Inquiry

It seems to me, however, that inquiry occurs in practice on a far less grand scale. Assume that a teacher who has been using a story from the classroom anthology to exemplify specificity in writing has decided to dump it because she feels her students are unenthusiastic about it and do not seem to care about its specific imagery. Instead she selects a passage by a ninth-grader from the student magazine, *Merlyn's Pen*, as a model of effective, specific writing, asks a ninth-grade class to read and respond to it, and examines students' responses to it in some way to determine its impact on students' understanding of what specific prose is. Does that sequence constitute inquiry? The sequence will not allow the teacher to explain the kind of cause-and-effect relationship that North talks about. She will not know if there is a more or less effective passage. And if she uses other activities to promote specific imagery in the writing of her ninth-graders, she will not be able to judge how important her prose model was in that effort.

Her evaluation of the impact of the passage is likely to sound something like this: "I think the kids liked the passage a lot. They were very attentive while I read it aloud, they had lots to say about it when I asked what they liked about it, and they were able to find many examples of specific details. I think it has given them a better idea of what it means to be specific in their own writing." Clearly, the teacher has engaged in a kind of practical inquiry that includes the identification of a problem (an ineffective model), the hypothesis of a reasoned solution (that a piece written by a student might have greater appeal), the informal testing of the hypothesis, and an arrival at some resolution of the problem. In Dewey's terms, this process that originates in doubt and moves in a rational way to resolution constitutes inquiry.

If the teacher uses the same model with many ninth-grade classes over a period of several years, does the practice become what North calls routine? The *OED* defines *routine* as "of a mechanical or unvaried character; performed by rule." To say that teaching is routine is to suggest its comparability to operating a punch press, without having to set the press up. If our teacher is aware that no two groups of students are the same and uses the selection in an interactive way, monitoring responses, responding to students as individuals, and evaluating the effectiveness of the selection, then the teaching cannot be mechanical, unvaried, or performed by rule. (By the same definition, the kind of teaching represented in the profile that opens this chapter is routine.)

If the teacher remains open to the possibility that the piece of writing may not have the desired effect for one reason or another, if she monitors student response to determine how it is or is not working, then the teacher maintains the basic posture of inquiry in teaching, regarding actions as hypotheses to be assessed. If, on the other hand, the teacher presents material without regard to any student response and makes no attempt to assess student understanding as teaching proceeds prior to grading assignments at the end of teaching sequences, then the teaching must be regarded as routine: mechanical and unvarying. We may call the former by Donald A. Schön's term: reflective practice. And such reflective practice is the basis for inquiry in teaching. Indeed, reflective practice becomes inquiry, in North's sense, as it becomes more formal and systematic.

The Priority of Reflective Practice

Quite clearly, in the case of teaching writing (and perhaps in other cases as well), research and theory would not exist if practice were entirely unreflective. More than creating a need, however, reflective practice can provide the foundation for research. A number of research projects, for example, seem to have been instigated by classroom practice. Teachers have noticed something interesting, curious, or unexpected in the process of interacting with students and have developed and examined those possibilities with great care, using a variety of research strategies from case studies to quasi-experiments designed to examine hypotheses (e.g., Atwell; Cochran-Smith and Lytle; Hillocks, "Effects," "Interaction"; Olson; Sager; Troyka).

At the same time, practice appears to generate important ideas for theory. For example, some teachers were using small student-led group discussions long before Vygotsky was translated into English. The success of small-group collaborative learning has a potential for adding to Vygotskian theory. The success of the practice drives a need to develop an explanatory theory.

Further, practice may give us cause to question theory. For example, I recently witnessed a teacher attempting to capture the interest of what had been designated by the school as one of its lowest-level ninth-grade groups. She had asked them to write journal entries about their own personal experiences or whatever concerned them, to share entries they liked with others, to revise them, and so forth. So far as I could see, she was doing everything she could to follow Donald Graves's recommendations. Nonetheless, these African American inner-city youngsters were not buying it. They saw no value, at the time, in writing about their own personal experience. Several students had even asked the teacher if they could go back to doing fill-in-the-blank exercises. This they regarded as "real" English. What does one do if the theoretical stance recommends an open approach to topics and structures but the students view such an approach as silly? Such situations wrestle us into rethinking theory.

If practice can lead us to reexamine theory, it must be the case that practice may take a theoretical stance. Reflective teachers develop a stance based on sets of ideas about their students and their subject, ideas that may be more or less systematically developed but that are able to provide tentative hypotheses about how students will react and what they are likely to learn under certain conditions. As the initial profile of this chapter indicates, even the least reflective teachers operate on the basis of some theories of learning and subject matter.

Frame Experiments

When teachers move beyond the automatic and begin to consider the effects of their actions on students and to devise alternatives, they find that, as Schön points out, they "deal often with uncertainty, uniqueness, and conflict. The non-routine situations of practice are at least partly indeterminate and must somehow be made coherent" (157). To do that, Schön argues, they "frame" the "messy" problem by attending selectively to certain features, organizing them, and setting "a direction for action" (4), which becomes a "frame experiment."

Between the body of knowledge and theory available in a field and its skillful application in a concrete situation, there is always a "gap of knowledge." Bridging that gap requires "a thoughtful invention of new trials based on appreciation of the results of earlier moves. The application of such a rule to a concrete case must be mediated by an art of reflection-in-action" (158). "Skillful practitioners learn to conduct frame experiments in which they impose a kind of coherence on messy situations and thereby discover consequences and implications of their chosen frames" (157). For Schön, the "frame experiment" is the essence of reflective practice. I argue that it is also the basis of inquiry in teaching.

What would such a frame experiment look like in the teaching of composition? Over thirty years ago, well before the current popularity of "process instruction," my friend and colleague, James F. McCampbell, was teaching a class of ninth-graders, mostly boys, whose reading in a remedial reading class had improved enough to move into a regular English class. Because other students making this shift had experienced so much difficulty in expressing themselves in writing, we had decided to keep them together as a group to try to help them become more fluent as writers. At the time, no one was doing much of anything about the teaching of writing, let alone with students who were particularly weak as writers. The automatic response to weak writing for most teachers at the time was to go for the grammar book, reasoning that if only students knew their parts of speech, their syntax, and usage, they would be able to write adequately. Making this assumption required ignoring the fact that these means did not bring about the desired end, not even with students who did not experience inordinate difficulty with writing (Braddock, Lloyd-Jones, and Schoer; Hillocks, *Research*).

Jim McCampbell noted that the papers attempted by these students were characterized not so much by poor spelling and lack of proper punctuation as by brevity. Most students in this group would not write much more than three or four lines for any assignment, no matter how much time had been involved in what we would call "prewriting" today. Jim was using our normal literature program, one that had been developed by the faculty over a period of several years (Hillocks and McCampbell). Generally, writing activities grew out of unit activities. For example, in a unit on the "Outcast," students wrote about their own feelings of being ostracized, their responses to and interpretations of events and situations in stories and poems, and a story in newspaper format about a case of ostracism.

Normally, our instructional emphasis was on the development of content as students wrote, shared drafts, provided feedback in small groups, and revised. Because these students normally wrote so little, McCampbell decided to jettison the usual emphasis and adopt one that concentrated on encouraging students to write more. After a classroom discussion that began with student reaction to a recent news story about a child who had been locked away in a trunk for many months and ended with students telling about how at one time or another they had felt left out, if not ostracized, he asked his students to write whatever they wished as long as it related somehow to the topic they had been discussing. As he circulated among the class as they wrote, he complimented students on what they had written and asked them to write more. He reported that students did produce more. In fact, after a few weeks, they were producing ten to fifteen times the amount they had prior to his beginning this "frame experiment." At the time, we all thought this appeared to be a remarkable result, one that we could attribute to Jim's having simplified the task and reinforced students as they wrote more.

Six Dimensions of Frame Experiments

What Jim did in this instance exemplifies at least six basic dimensions of the "frame experiment" essential to reflective teaching: (1) analyzing current student progress in relation to general course goals; (2) positing some change or range of possible changes sought in the writing of students; (3) selecting or devising a teaching strategy or set of strategies to implement the desired change; (4) devising a plan for implementing the teaching strategies; (5) assessing the impact of the teaching strategy in order to "discover consequences and implications of [the] chosen frames"; and, perhaps most important, (6) confirmation or change of the strategies used. For it is easy to imagine a teacher who, while noting the failure of students to learn what was taught, simply proceeds with more of the same, assuming that the "consequences and implications" of the "chosen frame" are the students' problems, not the teacher's. Let us examine each of these six in somewhat more detail.

The first dimension of reflective teaching appears to be an ongoing analysis of student progress in terms of the course goals. By *ongoing* I mean the daily consideration of student progress as indicated in responses during teacher-led discussions, participation in small groups, and the full variety of writing that is part of an active composition class. Most of these judgments will be informal, concerned with the quantity and character of individual responses in classroom talk and signs of understanding and change in pieces of writing at various stages of development; fewer will be formal, based on fully developed, final pieces of writing.

In reflective practice, assessment asks the extent to which the teaching and goals have been appropriate and effective for the students. Such assessments will be generated from the teacher's store of relevant theory and ideas garnered from practice and life experience. For assessment to be reflective, it must grow out of theory related to the particular teaching problem and students. In that sense, testing programs mandated by states and school districts or college English departments have nothing to do with reflective practice; nor do teacher-made tests that are administered without regard to specific teaching or learning problems.

In the example above, Jim McCampbell assessed the character of student writing in a way not foreseen by the existing course and unit structures. Those structures had assumed that students would have the ability or disposition to develop more extended pieces of writing. When Jim realized that his students did not, rather than simply bewailing the luck of the draw as others might well have done, he assumed that his students could move beyond their present stage and asked himself what he might do to help them. He also assumed that the problem was not one of intelligence or knowledge, but one of disposition. These students, he knew, had met with anything but success in the English classroom. Therefore he concluded that the ordinary goal of the unit (elaboration of ideas in different writing tasks) was inappropriate for his students. He adopted a modified goal. Students would still elaborate ideas, but developing a disposition to write would take priority.

The second dimension of reflective teaching is the envisionment of some desired change in light of the teacher's available theory. It requires deciding *in advance* what will be taken as evidence of success and generally means that the teacher can let the students know the purpose of instruction so that they can work toward the goal thoughtfully. To begin a personal narrative in the middle of an event (*in me-*

dias res) might be such a goal, one that is based on a reasoned conception of personal-experience writing, an understanding of what students can already do, and some idea of how to help students reach that goal.

In the teaching of writing it is not possible, nor would it be desirable, to specify in advance precisely what success entails for any given piece of writing, certainly not with the precision engineers expect in specifying the characteristics and tolerances, let us say, for the construction of a bridge. Such standardization is antithetical to what most of us regard as good writing. At the same time, that we have and use criteria for judging writing is evident in a variety of settings. In Jim McCampbell's case above, the problem was rather a simple one, to write more words in connected discourse, at least loosely connected. . . .

The third feature of reflective teaching is selecting or inventing particular strategies for particular purposes and particular students. Jim McCampbell's strategy above, though simple, is a good example of reflection-in-action. Jim assessed the students' writing, brought to bear his knowledge of what life in classrooms is like for students who have difficulty, recalled a study or two reported at National Council of Teachers of English meetings that indicated focusing on "correctness" resulted in shorter and simpler sentences, and decided that what he really wanted was to encourage students to write more. He decided to allow students to write what they wanted following class discussions and to encourage them, however he could, to write more.

Many strategies that teachers adopt are quite complex. Often, they seem simply to work from a good idea, an insight into what students might enjoy and could do with some support in the form of a model, a special activity, perhaps simply clear directions and support from the teacher during the process. When teachers have the support of theory, they can invent many "good ideas." Processes of inventing, sequencing, and validating activities will be examined in later chapters.

Because Jim's strategy was so simple, the plan for implementing it (the fourth dimension) was also simple: (1) Circulate among students while they worked in class and make such statements as, "That's great! You've written a lot. Try to write some more." (2) Write comments on papers in the same vein: "Terrific! You have written more than you usually do. Keep it up!" Unfortunately most plans for implementation are not so simple.

The fifth and sixth dimensions involve assessing the impact of the strategies and deciding whether the plan might be worth using again. As with the first dimension, judging the impact of the teaching strategies on students' learning will be based on the goals and the theory underlying them. But to focus only on the goals and nothing more is to ignore too much that may occur incidentally. For example, research suggests that a focus on "correctness" may result in a general degradation of writing including fewer words and simpler sentences as students strive to avoid error (Adams; Hillocks, *Research*). Teachers who focus on "correctness" tend to ignore decreases in complexity of thought and syntax in favor of their selected goal.

On the other hand, unexpected benefits can be ignored as a result of the excessive myopia that a mechanical adherence to goals might foster. My students and I discovered that about twenty-one of the twenty-nine African American seventh-graders assigned to what is called in Chicago a "low-level" language arts class began to produce interesting and lively figurative language when they were involved in writing descriptions of sea shells so that one of their classmates could pick out the shell described from the whole batch of twenty-nine shells. Serendipity at its best. All we had hoped for was concrete detail.

In McCampbell's case, assessment was relatively simple. There was certainly no need for elaborate counting. A glance at earlier and later papers told the story clearly. Volume had increased enormously. Several students were producing between two hundred and three hundred words at each writing. The strategy was confirmed. Quality would be another question.

Frame Experiments and Theory

At the time of this success, we attributed the change in student production to Jim's having simplified the task and provided positive reinforcement on a regular schedule. These moves made good pedagogical sense, simply on the basis of our experience with students who had difficulty with reading. At the time, we thought of this as an essentially Skinnerian interpretation, one that is out of fashion now, rejected as mechanistic and shallow. But it is interesting that other, more recent theories also make use of the idea of positive reinforcement, for example, Csikszentmihalyi's *Flow: The Psychology of Optimal Experience.*

In retrospect, we can add a layer of interpretation. Bereiter and Scardamalia's studies of young children writing reveal that they knew a great deal more about given topics than they use in writing. In one study, students wrote about as many words as they would say in a conversational turn (Bereiter and Scardamalia). In a second study, the researchers urged the youngsters to write as much as they could, and they wrote about three times more than the students in the first study. When a researcher asked them simply to write more, they wrote about as much again as they had after the initial prompt. Additional requests to "write some more" yielded more (Scardamalia, Bereiter, and Goelman). These researchers reason that children have learned a schema for conversation but not one for writing. In their responses to assignments, they are fulfilling what they see as a conversational turn. It is possible that Jim's promptings to write more were serving the same function as that of the researcher in Bereiter and Scardamalia's studies.

Whatever the case, the point is that the act of considering such reasons in relation to experimental frames provides the theoretical base for reflective teaching. When teachers reason about choices, plan in light of those reasons, implement those plans, examine their impact on students, and revise and reformulate reasons and plans in light of all that experience, that conjunction constitutes theory-driven teaching. Such teachers are engaged in reflective practice and inquiry.

By definition, then, teachers who try new ideas, whether their own or those of others, without considering them in light of some organized body of assumptions and knowledge (including their own experience) that acts as a kind of preliminary testing ground for those ideas, cannot be considered reflective. A reflective practitioner will analyze a new idea in light of its appropriateness to the students and their present knowledge; its fit with available theory, experience, and the goals of teaching; and its probability for success as judged from the teacher's experience and knowledge. All parts of these theories may not be explicit, and those that are may not be fully tested or examined critically. But for reflective practitioners, the working or action theories they hold continue to grow as they conduct new "frame experiments."

Life Experience and Teaching

Our ideas and beliefs about teaching come not only from theory, practice, and research, but from a variety of perhaps disparate sources. Ideas for some of my activities that have been most popular with students came from watching my own children at play. Many have come from news stories of various kinds. Some I have been able to tie to theory; others have seemed atheoretical in their early uses but aided in the development of theories that I have worked with over the years. My students report similar experiences. Some have said that they seem always on the lookout for materials that will be irresistible to their students. That kind of search appears to become part of the life pattern of teachers who invent materials and activities. It is habit forming.

Other influences on teaching come from sources that we can no longer identify: values, attitudes, beliefs. Sometimes it seems important to take stock of these, to say "What is it I believe and why?" These personal beliefs are difficult to explain and even more difficult to pass on to another. One of the most important beliefs for my teaching comes, at least in part, from my father's firm faith in the value of struggling to succeed even in the face of defeat. It is embodied in his favorite story of Robert the Bruce. Legend says that after suffering six defeats at the hands of the English, the Bruce lay in a cave one night, discouraged, even considering giving up the struggle against the English. He watched a spider as it painstakingly climbed a fine thread to its web, only to fall back and start over again. Six times the spider made its way slowly up the thread. Six times it fell back. But on the seventh try, the spider succeeded. The Bruce took this lesson to heart, gathered his forces, and began a successful campaign against King Edward crowned by the Battle of Bannockburn, where Bruce succeeded in crushing the English even though he was outnumbered three to one.

No doubt the story of the spider is apocryphal. The Bruce did not keep a journal, after all. But there is truth in it. Though someone has failed any number of times, there is no evidence that the next try will not succeed. For with every trial we reinvent ourselves. Only the failure to try assures failure.

Works Cited

Adams, V. A. "A Study of the Effects of Two Methods of Teaching Composition to Twelfth Graders." Unpublished doctoral dissertation. University of Illinois at Urbana-Champaign.

Atwell, N. *In the Middle: Writing, Reading, and Learning with Adolescents.* Portsmouth, NH: Heinemann, 1987.

Bereiter, C., and M. Scardamalia. "From Conversation to Composition: The Role of Instruction in a Developmental Process." *Advances in Instructional Psychology.* Ed. R. Glaser. Vol. 2. Hillsdale, NJ: Erlbaum, 1982. 1–64.

Braddock, R., R. Lloyd-Jones, and L. Schoer. *Research in Written Composition.* Champaign, IL: NCTE, 1963.

Cochran-Smith, M., and S. L. Lytle. *Inside/Outside: Teacher Research and Knowledge.* New York: Teachers College, 1993.

Csikszentmihalyi, M. *Flow: The Psychology of Optimal Experience.* New York: Harper, 1990.

Dewey, J. *Logic, the Theory of Inquiry.* New York: Holt, 1938.

Graves, D. *Writing: Teachers and Children at Work.* Portsmouth, NH: Heinemann, 1983.

Hillocks, G., Jr. "The Effects of Observational Activities on Student Writing." *Research in the Teaching of English* (Feb. 1979): 23–35.

Hillocks, G., Jr. "The Interaction of Instruction, Teacher Comment, and Revision in Teaching the Composing Process." *Research in the Teaching of English* (Oct. 1982): 261–78.

Hillocks, G., Jr. *Research on Written Composition: New Directions for Teaching.* Urbana, IL: National Conference on Research in English/ERIC Clearinghouse on Reading and Communication Skills, 1986.

Hillocks, G., Jr., and J. F. McCampbell. *An Introduction to a Curriculum: Grades 7–9.* Euclid, OH: Project English Demonstration Center/Euclid Central Junior High School and Western Reserve University, 1964.

Lederman, L. "Scientific Literacy." Lecture presented at the Workshop on Dimensions of Literacy and Numeracy, University of Chicago, 15 March 1991.

Murray, L. *English Grammar.* New York: Raynor, 1849.

North, S. *The Making of Knowledge in Composition: Portrait of an Emerging Field.* Portsmouth, NH: Heinemann, 1987.

Olson, C. B. *Thinking Writing: Fostering Critical Thinking through Writing.* Irvine, CA: HarperCollins, 1992.

Sager, C. "Improving the Quality of Written Composition through Pupil Use of Rating Scale." Diss. Boston U, 1973.

Scardamalia, M., C. Bereiter, and H. Goelman. "The Role of Production Factors in Writing Ability." *What Writers Know: The Language, Process, and Structure of Written Discourse.* Ed. M. Nystrand. New York: Academic P, 1982. 173–210.

Schön, D. A. *Educating the Reflective Practitioner: Toward a New Design for Teaching and Learning in the Professions.* San Francisco: Jossey-Bass, 1987.

Shaughnessy, M. *Errors and Expectations.* New York: Oxford UP, 1977.

Troyka, L. Q. "A Study of the Effect of Simulation-Gaming on Expository Prose Competence of Remedial English Composition Students." Diss. New York U, 1973.

Hillocks's Insights as a Resource for Your Teaching

1. Off the top of your head, list the key assumptions that shape your approach to teaching writing. Study the list, and pinpoint a pattern of connection among the key assumptions. Draft a statement that links and organizes these assumptions into a theory — a kind of mission statement for your classroom. What are the sources for your beliefs about writing pedagogy? Do you see gaps in these sources or perhaps conflicts between them? How have you been negotiating your way through these gaps in your daily practice of teaching? Do they suggest windows into possible areas of growth and improvement for either your theory or your practice?

2. In your journal, describe a classroom situation in which a particular pedagogic "routine" is not working. Describe exactly what comprises your practice, and, as closely as you can, pinpoint how and why it is missing the mark. Using what Hillocks calls the "six dimensions of frame experiments," try to explore ways to improve the situation you have described.

Hillocks's Insights as a Resource for Your Writing Classroom

1. Share Hillocks's ideas about the teaching of writing as a reflective practice with your students. Explain in your terms how you might see the classroom as a scene of ongoing inquiry, adjustment, and improvement. Have the students write a brief account in their journals of classroom routines that they have experienced in the past that have fallen short of the instructors' intended goals. Ask the students why they thought the routine was less than successful. Discuss with them your own thoughts about what they have described.

2. Share your own theory of writing pedagogy with your students. Discuss the particular ways it informs your classroom practice — from the overall structure of your syllabus to the details of your briefest assignments. Discuss with them the ways you hope to fine-tune this theory — the dimensions of it that you hope to explore further with them via particular assignments. Most importantly, invite them to comment on your plans, and listen to their feedback.

I Just Wanna Be Average

Mike Rose

In this powerful memoir of his years in the "vocational track" and the teacher who helped him progress beyond the expectations others held, Mike Rose argues that students will "float to the mark you set." The ways students come to see themselves and their potential, having been cued and prompted to this perception by their teachers, has an overwhelming influence on their faith in their ability to learn. Rose also describes a particular teaching style that has an optimal effect on self-perception.

Between 1880 and 1920, well over four million Southern Italian peasants immigrated to America. Their poverty was extreme and hopeless — twelve hours of farm labor would get you one lira, about twenty cents — so increasing numbers of desperate people booked passage for the United States, the country where, the steamship companies claimed, prosperity was a way of life. My father left Naples before the turn of the century; my mother came with her mother from Calabria in 1921. They met in Altoona, Pennsylvania, at the lunch counter of Tom and Joe's, a steamy diner with twangy-voiced waitresses and graveyard stew.

For my mother, life in America was not what the promoters had told her father it would be. She grew up very poor. She slept with her parents and brothers and sisters in one room. She had to quit school in the seventh grade to care for her sickly younger brothers. When her father lost his leg in a railroad accident, she began working in a garment factory where women sat crowded at their stations, solitary as penitents in a cloister. She stayed there until her marriage. My father had found a freer route. He was closemouthed about his past, but I know that he had been a salesman, a tailor, and a gambler; he knew people in the mob and had, my uncles whisper, done time in Chicago. He went through a year or two of Italian elementary school and could write a few words — those necessary to scribble measurements for a suit — and over the years developed a quiet urbanity, a persistence, and a slowly debilitating arteriosclerosis.

When my father proposed to my mother, he decided to open a spaghetti house, a venture that lasted through the war and my early years. The restaurant collapsed in bankruptcy in 1951 when Altoona's major industry, the Pennsylvania Railroad, had to shut down its shops. My parents managed to salvage seven hundred dollars and, on the advice of the family doctor, headed to California, where the winters would be mild and where I, their seven-year-old son, would have the possibility of a brighter future.

At first we lived in a seedy hotel on Spring Street in downtown Los Angeles, but my mother soon found an ad in the *Times* for cheap property on the south side of town. My parents contacted a woman named Mrs. Jolly, used my mother's engagement ring as a down payment, and moved to 9116 South Vermont Avenue, a house about one and one-half miles northwest of Watts. The neighborhood was poor, and it was in transition. Some old white folks had lived there for decades and were retired. Younger black families were moving up from Watts and settling by working-class white families newly arrived from the South and the Midwest. Immigrant Mexican families were coming in from Baja. Any such demographic mix is potentially volatile, and as the fifties wore on, the neighborhood would be marked by outbursts of violence.

I have many particular memories of this time, but in general these early years seem a peculiar mix of physical warmth and barrenness: a gnarled lemon tree, thin rungs, a dirt alley, concrete in the sun. My uncles visited a few times, and we went to the beach or to orange groves. The return home, however, left the waves and spray, the thick leaves and split pulp far in the distance. I was aware of my parents watching their money and got the sense from their conversations that things could quickly take a turn for the worse. I started taping pennies to the bottom of a shelf in the kitchen.

My father's health was bad, and he had few readily marketable skills. Poker and pinochle brought in a little money, and he tried out an idea that had worked in Altoona during the war: He started a "suit club." The few customers he could scare up would pay two dollars a week on a tailor-made suit. He would take the measurements and send them to a shop back East and hope for the best. My mother took a job at a café in downtown Los Angeles, a split shift 9:00 to 12:00 and 5:00 to 9:00, but her tips were totaling sixty cents a day, so she quit for a night shift at Coffee Dan's. This got her to the bus stop at one in the morning, waiting on the same street where drunks were urinating and hookers were catching the last of the bar crowd. She made friends with a Filipino cook who would scare off the advances of old men aflame with the closeness of taxi dancers. In a couple of years, Coffee Dan's would award her a day job at the counter. Once every few weeks my father and I would take a bus downtown and visit with her, sitting at stools by the window, watching the animated but silent mix of faces beyond the glass.

My father had moved to California with faint hopes about health and a belief in his child's future, drawn by that far edge of America where the sun descends into green water. What he found was a city that was warm, verdant, vast, and indifferent as a starlet in a sports car. Altoona receded quickly, and my parents must have felt isolated and deceived. They had fallen into the abyss of paradise — two more poor settlers trying to make a go of it in the City of the Angels.

Let me tell you about our house. If you entered the front door and turned right you'd see a small living room with a couch along the east wall and one along the west wall — one couch was purple, the other tan, both bought used and both well worn. A television set was placed at the end of the purple couch, right at arm level. An old Philco radio sat next to the TV, its speaker covered with gold lamé. There was a small coffee table in the center of the room on which sat a murky fishbowl occupied by two listless guppies. If, on entering, you turned left you would see a green Formica dinner table with four chairs, a cedar chest given as a wedding present to my mother by her mother, a painted statue of the Blessed Virgin Mary, and a black trunk. I also had a plastic chaise lounge between the door and the table. I would lie on this and watch television.

A short hallway leading to the bathroom opened on one side to the kitchen and, on the other, to the bedroom. The bedroom had two beds, one for me and one for my parents, a bureau with a mirror, and a chest of drawers on which we piled old shirt boxes and stacks of folded clothes. The kitchen held a refrigerator and a stove, small older models that we got when our earlier (and newer) models were repossessed by two silent men. There was one white wooden chair in the corner beneath wall cabinets. You could walk in and through a tiny pantry to the backyard and to four one-room rentals. My father got most of our furniture from a secondhand store on the next block; he would tend the store two or three hours a day as payment on our account.

As I remember it, the house was pretty dark. My mother kept the blinds in the bedroom drawn — there were no curtains there — and the venetian blinds in the living room were, often as not, left closed. The walls were bare except for a faded picture of Jesus and a calendar from the *Altoona Mirror*. Some paper carnations bent out of a white vase on the television. There was a window on the north side of the kitchen that had no blinds or curtains, so the sink got good light. My father would methodically roll up his sleeves and show me how to prepare a sweet potato or avocado seed so it would sprout. We kept a row of them on the sill above the sink, their shoots and vines rising and curling in the morning sun.

The house was on a piece of land that rose about four feet up from heavily trafficked Vermont Avenue. The yard sloped down to the street, and three steps and a short walkway led up the middle of the grass to our front door. There was a similar house immediately to the south of us. Next to it was Carmen's Barber Shop. Carmen was a short, quiet Italian who, rumor had it, had committed his first wife to the crazy house to get her money. In the afternoons, Carmen could be found in the lot behind his shop playing solitary catch, flinging a tennis ball high into the air and running under it. One day the police arrested Carmen on charges of child molesting. He was released but became furtive and suspicious. I never saw him in the lot again. Next to Carmen's was a junk store where, one summer, I made a little money polishing brass and rewiring old lamps. Then came a dilapidated real estate office, a Mexican restaurant, an empty lot, and an appliance store owned by the father of Keith Grateful, the streetwise, chubby boy who would become my best friend.

Right to the north of us was a record shop, a barber shop presided over by old Mr. Graff, Walt's Malts, a shoe repair shop with a big Cat's

Paw decal in the window, a third barber shop, and a brake shop. It's as I write this that I realize for the first time that three gray men could have had a go at your hair before you left our street.

Behind our house was an unpaved alley that passed, just to the north, a power plant the length of a city block. Massive coils atop the building hissed and cracked through the day, but the doors never opened. I used to think it was abandoned — feeding itself on its own wild arcs — until one sweltering afternoon a man was electrocuted on the roof. The air was thick and still as two firemen — the only men present — brought down a charred and limp body without saying a word.

The north and south traffic on Vermont was separated by tracks for the old yellow trolley cars, long since defunct. Across the street was a huge garage, a tiny hot dog stand run by a myopic and reclusive man named Freddie, and my dreamland, the Vermont Bowl. Distant and distorted behind thick lenses, Freddie's eyes never met yours; he would look down when he took your order and give you your change with a mumble. Freddie slept on a cot in the back of his grill and died there one night, leaving tens of thousands of dollars stuffed in the mattress.

My father would buy me a chili dog at Freddie's, and then we would walk over to the bowling alley where Dad would sit at the lunch counter and drink coffee while I had a great time with pinball machines, electric shooting galleries, and an ill-kept dispenser of cheese corn. There was a small, dark bar abutting the lanes, and it called to me. I would devise reasons to walk through it: "'Scuse me, is the bathroom in here?" or "Anyone see my dad?" though I can never remember my father having a drink. It was dark and people were drinking and I figured all sorts of mysterious things were being whispered. Next to the Vermont Bowl was a large vacant lot overgrown with foxtails and dotted with car parts, bottles, and rotting cardboard. One day Keith heard that the police had found a human head in the brush. After that we explored the lot periodically, coming home with stickers all the way up to our waists. But we didn't find a thing. Not even a kneecap.

When I wasn't with Keith or in school, I would spend most of my day with my father or with the men who were renting the one-room apartments behind our house. Dad and I whiled away the hours in the bowling alley, watching TV, or planting a vegetable garden that never seemed to take. When he was still mobile, he would walk the four blocks down to St. Regina's Grammar School to take me home to my favorite lunch of boiled wieners and chocolate milk. There I'd sit, dunking my hot dog in a jar of mayonnaise and drinking my milk while Sheriff John tuned up the calliope music on his "Lunch Brigade." Though he never complained to me, I could sense that my father's health was failing, and I began devising child's ways to make him better. We had a box of rolled cotton in the bathroom, and I would go in and peel off a long strip and tape it around my jaw. Then I'd rummage through the closet, find a sweater of my father's, put on one of his hats — and sneak around to the back door. I'd knock loudly and wait. It would take him a while to get there. Finally, he'd open the door, look down, and quietly say, "Yes,

Michael?" I was disappointed. Every time. Somehow I thought I could fool him. And, I guess, if he had been fooled, I would have succeeded in redefining things: I would have been the old one, he much younger, more agile, with strength in his legs.

The men who lived in the back were either retired or didn't work that much, so one of them was usually around. They proved to be, over the years, an unusual set of companions for a young boy. Ed Gionotti was the youngest of the lot, a handsome man whose wife had run off and who spoke softly and never smiled. Bud Hall and Lee McGuire were two out-of-work plumbers who lived in adjacent units and who weekly drank themselves silly, proclaiming in front of God and everyone their undying friendship or their unequivocal hatred. Old Cheech was a lame Italian who used to hobble along grabbing his testicles and rolling his eyes while he talked about the women he claimed to have on a string. There was Lester, the toothless cabbie, who several times made overtures to me and who, when he moved, left behind a drawer full of syringes and burnt spoons. Mr. Smith was a rambunctious retiree who lost his nose to an untended skin cancer. And there was Mr. Berryman, a sweet and gentle man who eventually left for a retirement hotel only to be burned alive in an electrical fire.

Except for Keith, there were no children on my block and only one or two on the immediate side streets. Most of the people I saw day to day were over fifty. People in their twenties and thirties working in the shoe shop or the garages didn't say a lot; their work and much of what they were working for drained their spirits. There were gang members who sauntered up from Hoover Avenue, three blocks to the east, and occasionally I would get shoved around, but they had little interest in me either as member or victim. I was a skinny, bespectacled kid and had neither the coloring nor the style of dress or carriage that marked me as a rival. On the whole, the days were quiet, lazy, lonely. The heat shimmering over the asphalt had no snap to it; time drifted by. I would lie on the couch at night and listen to the music from the record store or from Walt's Malts. It was new and quick paced, exciting, a little dangerous (the church had condemned Buddy Knox's "Party Doll"), and I heard in it a deep rhythmic need to be made whole with love, or marked as special, or released in some rebellious way. Even the songs about lost love — and there were plenty of them — lifted me right out of my socks with their melodious longing:

> Came the dawn,
> and my heart and her love and the night
> were gone.
> But I know I'll never forget
> her kiss in the moonlight Oooo . . .
> such a kiss Oooo Oooo such a night . . .

In the midst of the heat and slow time the music brought the promise of its origins, a promise of deliverance, a promise that, if only for a moment, life could be stirring and dreamy.

But the anger and frustration of South Vermont could prove too strong for music's illusion; then it was violence that provided deliverance of a different order. One night I watched as a guy sprinted from Walt's to toss something on our lawn. The police were right behind, and a cop tackled him, smashing his face into the sidewalk. I ducked out to find the packet: a dozen glassine bags of heroin. Another night, one August midnight, an argument outside the record store ended with a man being shot to death. And the occasional gang forays brought with them some fated kid who would fumble his moves and catch a knife.

It's popular these days to claim you grew up on the streets. Men tell violent tales and romanticize the lessons violence brings. But, though it was occasionally violent, it wasn't the violence in South L.A. that marked me, for sometimes you can shake that ugliness off. What finally affected me was subtler, but more pervasive: I cannot recall a young person who was crazy in love or lost in work or one old person who was passionate about a cause or an idea. I'm not talking about an absence of energy — the street toughs and, for that fact, old Cheech had energy. And I'm not talking about an absence of decency, for my father was a thoughtful man. The people I grew up with were retired from jobs that rub away the heart or were working hard at jobs to keep their lives from caving in or were anchorless and in between jobs and spouses or were diving headlong into a barren tomorrow: junkies, alcoholics, and mean kids walking along Vermont looking to throw a punch. I developed a picture of human existence that rendered it short and brutish or sad and aimless or long and quiet with rewards like afternoon naps, the evening newspaper, walks around the block, occasional letters from children in other states. When, years later, I was introduced to humanistic psychologists like Abraham Maslow and Carl Rogers, with their visions of self-actualization, or even Freud with his sober dictum about love and work, it all sounded like a glorious fairy tale, a magical account of a world full of possibility, full of hope and empowerment. Sindbad and Cinderella couldn't have been more fanciful.

Some people who manage to write their way out of the working class describe the classroom as an oasis of possibility. It became their intellectual playground, their competitive arena. Given the richness of my memories of this time, it's funny how scant are my recollections of school. I remember the red brick building of St. Regina's itself, and the topography of the playground: the swings and basketball courts and peeling benches. There are images of a few students: Erwin Petschaur, a muscular German boy with a strong accent; Dave Sanchez, who was good in math; and Sheila Wilkes, everyone's curly-haired heartthrob. And there are two nuns: Sister Monica, the third-grade teacher with beautiful hands for whom I carried a candle and who, to my dismay, had wedded herself to Christ; and Sister Beatrice, a woman truly crazed, who would sweep into class, eyes wide, to tell us about the Apocalypse.

All the hours in class tend to blend into one long, vague stretch of time. What I remember best, strangely enough, are the two things I couldn't understand and over the years grew to hate: grammar lessons and mathematics. I would sit there watching a teacher draw her long horizontal line and her short, oblique lines and break up sentences and put adjectives here and adverbs there and just not get it, couldn't see the reason for it, turned off to it. I would hide by slumping down in my seat and page through my reader, carried along by the flow of sentences in a story. She would test us, and I would dread that, for I always got Cs and Ds. Mathematics was a bit different. For whatever reasons, I didn't learn early math very well, so when it came time for more complicated operations, I couldn't keep up and started daydreaming to avoid my inadequacy. This was a strategy I would rely on as I grew older. I fell further and further behind. A memory: The teacher is faceless and seems very far away. The voice is faint and is discussing an equation written on the board. It is raining, and I am watching the streams of water form patterns on the windows.

I realize now how consistently I defended myself against the lessons I couldn't understand and the people and events of South L.A. that were too strange to view head-on. I got very good at watching a blackboard with minimum awareness. And I drifted more and more into a variety of protective fantasies. I was lucky in that although my parents didn't read or write very much and had no more than a few books around the house, they never debunked my pursuits. And when they could, they bought me what I needed to spin my web.

One early Christmas they got me a small chemistry set. My father brought home an old card table from the secondhand store, and on that table I spread out my test tubes, my beaker, my Erlenmeyer flask, and my gas-generating apparatus. The set came equipped with chemicals, minerals, and various treated papers — all in little square bottles. You could send away to someplace in Maryland for more, and I did, saving pennies and nickels to get the substances that were too exotic for my set, the Junior Chemcraft: Congo red paper, azurite, glycerine, chrome alum, cochineal — this from female insects! — tartaric acid, chameleon paper, logwood. I would sit before my laboratory and play for hours. My father rested on the purple couch in front of me watching wrestling or *Gunsmoke* while I measured powders or heated crystals or blew into solutions that my breath would turn red or pink. I was taken by the blends of names and by the colors that swirled through the beaker. My equations were visual and phonetic. I would hold a flask up to the hall light, imagining the veils of a million atoms dancing. Sulfur and alcohol hung in the air. I wanted to shake down the house.

One day my mother came home from Coffee Dan's with an awful story. The teenage brother of one of her waitress friends was in the hospital. He had been fooling around with explosives in his garage "where his mother couldn't see him," and something happened, and "he blew away part of his throat. For God's sake, be careful," my mother said. "Remember poor Ada's brother." Wow! I thought. How neat! Why couldn't my experiments be that dangerous? I really lost heart when I realized that you could probably eat the chemicals spread across my table.

I knew what I had to do. I saved my money for a week and then walked with firm resolve past Walt's Malts, past the brake shop, across Ninetieth Street, and into Palazolla's market. I bought a little bottle of Alka-Seltzer and ran home. I chipped up the wafers and mixed them into a jar of white crystals. When my mother came home, dog tired, and sat down on the edge of the couch to tell me and Dad about her day, I gravely poured my concoction into a beaker of water, cried something about the unexpected, and ran out from behind my table. The beaker foamed ominously. My father swore in Italian. The second time I tried it, I got something milder — in English. And by my third near-miss with death, my parents were calling my behavior cute. Cute! Who wanted cute? I wanted to toy with the disaster that befell Ada Pendleton's brother. I wanted all those wonderful colors to collide in ways that could blow your voice box right off.

But I was limited by the real. The best I could do was create a toxic antacid. I loved my chemistry set — its glassware and its intriguing labels — but it wouldn't allow me to do the things I wanted to do. St. Regina's had an all-purpose room, one wall of which was lined with old books — and one of those shelves held a row of plastic-covered space novels. The sheen of their covers was gone, and their futuristic portraits were dotted with erasures and grease spots like a meteor shower of the everyday. I remember the rockets best. Long cylinders outfitted at the base with three slick fins, tapering at the other end to a perfect conical point, ready to pierce out of the stratosphere and into my imagination: X-15s and Mach 1, the dark side of the moon, the Red Planet, Jupiter's Great Red Spot, Saturn's rings — and beyond the solar system to swirling wisps of galaxies, to stardust.

I would check out my books two at a time and take them home to curl up with a blanket on my chaise longue, reading, sometimes, through the weekend, my back aching, my thoughts lost between galaxies. I became the hero of a thousand adventures, all with intricate plots and the triumph of good over evil, all many dimensions removed from the dim walls of the living room. We were given time to draw in school, so, before long, all this worked itself onto paper. The stories I was reading were reshaping themselves into pictures. My father got me some butcher paper from Palazolla's, and I continued to draw at home. My collected works rendered the Horsehead Nebula, goofy space cruisers, robots, and Saturn. Each had its crayon, a particular waxy pencil with mood and meaning: rust and burnt sienna for Mars, yellow for the Sun, lime and rose for Saturn's rings, and bright red for the Jovian spot. I had a little sharpener to keep the points just right. I didn't write any stories; I just read and drew. I wouldn't care much about writing until late in high school.

The summer before the sixth grade, I got a couple of jobs. The first was at a pet store a block or so away from my house. Since I was still small, I could maneuver around in breeder cages, scraping the heaps of parakeet crap from the tin floor, cleaning the water troughs and seed trays. It was pretty awful. I would go home after work and fill the tub and soak until all the fleas and bird mites came floating to the surface, little Xs in their multiple eyes. When I heard about a job selling strawberries door-to-door, I jumped at it. I went to work for a white-haired Chicano named Frank. He would carry four or five kids and dozens of crates of strawberries in his ramshackle truck up and down the avenues of the better neighborhoods: houses with mowed lawns and petunia beds. We'd work all day for seventy-five cents, Frank dropping pairs of us off with two crates each, then picking us up at preassigned corners. We spent lots of time together, bouncing around on the truck bed redolent with strawberries or sitting on a corner, cold, listening for the sputter of Frank's muffler. I started telling the other kids about my books, and soon it was my job to fill up that time with stories.

Reading opened up the world. There I was, a skinny bookworm drawing the attention of street kids who, in any other circumstances, would have had me for breakfast. Like an epic tale-teller, I developed the stories as I went along, relying on a flexible plot line and a repository of heroic events. I had a great time. I sketched out trajectories with my finger on Frank's dusty truck bed. And I stretched out each story's climax, creating cliffhangers like the ones I saw in the Saturday serials. These stories created for me a temporary community.

It was around this time that fiction started leading me circuitously to a child's version of science. In addition to the space novels, St. Regina's library also had half a dozen books on astronomy — *The Golden Book of the Planets* and stuff like that — so I checked out a few of them. I liked what I read and wheedled enough change out of my father to enable me to take the bus to the public library. I discovered star maps, maps of lunar seas, charts upon charts of the solar system and the planetary moons: Rhea, Europa, Callisto, Miranda, Io. I didn't know that most of these moons were named for women — I didn't know classical mythology — but I would say their names to myself as though they had a woman's power to protect: Europa, Miranda, Io . . . The distances between stars fascinated me, as did the sizes of the big telescopes. I sent away for catalogs. Then prices fascinated me too. I wanted to drape my arm over a thousand-dollar scope and hear its motor drive whirr. I conjured a twelve-year-old's life of the astronomer: sitting up all night with potato chips and the stars, tracking the sky for supernovas, humming "Earth Angel" with the Penguins. What was my mother to do but save her tips and buy me a telescope?!

It was a little reflecting job, and I solemnly used to carry it out to the front of the house on warm summer nights, to find Venus or Alpha Centauri or trace the stars in Orion or lock onto the moon. I would lay out my star maps on the concrete, more for their magic than anything else, for I had trouble figuring them out. I was no geometer of the constellations; I was their balladeer. Those nights were very peaceful. I was far enough away from the front door and up enough from the sidewalk to make it seem as if I rested on a mound of dark silence, a mountain in Arizona, perhaps, watching the sky alive with points of light. Poor Freddie, toothless Lester whispering promises about making me feel good, the flat days, the gang fights — all this receded, for it was now me, the star child, lost in an eyepiece focused on a reflecting mirror that cradled, in its center, a shimmering moon.

The loneliness in Los Angeles fosters strange arrangements. Lou Minton was a wiry man with gaunt, chiseled features and prematurely gray hair, combed straight back. He had gone to college in the South for a year or two and kicked around the country for many more before settling in L.A. He lived in a small downtown apartment with a single window and met my mother at the counter of Coffee Dan's. He had been alone too long and eventually came to our house and became part of the family. Lou repaired washing machines, and he had a car, and he would take me to the vast, echoing library just west of Pershing Square and to the Museum of Science and Industry in Exposition Park. He bought me astronomy books, taught me how to use tools, and helped me build model airplanes from balsa wood and rice paper. As my father's health got worse, Lou took care of him.

My rhapsodic and prescientific astronomy carried me into my teens, consumed me right up till high school, losing out finally, and only, to the siren call of pubescence — that endocrine hoodoo that transmogrifies nice boys into gawky flesh fiends. My mother used to bring home *Confidential* magazine, a peep-show rag specializing in the sins of the stars, and it beckoned me mercilessly: Jayne Mansfield's cleavage, Gina Lollobrigida's eyes, innuendos about deviant sexuality, ads for Frederick's of Hollywood — spiked heels, lacy brassieres, the epiphany of silk panties on a mannequin's hips. Along with Phil Everly, I was through with counting the stars above.

Budding manhood. Only adults talk about adolescence budding. Kids have no choice but to talk in extremes; they're being wrenched and buffeted, rabbit-punched from inside by systemic thugs. Nothing sweet and pastoral here. Kids become ridiculous and touching at one and the same time: passionate about the trivial, fixed before the mirror, yet traversing one of the most important rites of passage in their lives — liminal people, silly and profoundly human. Given my own expertise, I fantasized about concocting the fail-safe aphrodisiac that would bring Marianne Bilpusch, the cloakroom monitor, rushing into my arms or about commanding a squadron of bosomy, linguistically mysterious astronauts like Zsa Zsa Gabor. My parents used to say that their son would have the best education they could afford. Maybe I would be a doctor. There was a public school in our neighborhood and several Catholic schools to the west. They had heard that quality schooling meant private, Catholic schooling, so they somehow got the money together to send me to Our Lady of Mercy, fifteen or so miles southwest of Ninety-first and Vermont. So much for my fantasies. Most Catholic secondary schools then were separated by gender.

It took two buses to get to Our Lady of Mercy. The first started deep in South Los Angeles and caught me at midpoint. The second drifted through neighborhoods with trees, parks, big lawns, and lots of flowers. The rides were long but were livened up by a group of South L.A. veterans whose parents also thought that Hope had set up shop in the west end of the county. There was Christy Biggars, who, at sixteen, was dealing and was, according to rumor, a pimp as well. There were Bill Cobb and Johnny Gonzales, grease-pencil artists extraordinaire, who left Nembutal-enhanced swirls of "Cobb" and "Johnny" on the corrugated walls of the bus. And then there was Tyrrell Wilson. Tyrrell was the coolest kid I knew. He ran the dozens like a metric halfback, laid down a rap that outrhymed and outpointed Cobb, whose rap was good but not great — the curse of a moderately soulful kid trapped in white skin. But it was Cobb who would sneak a radio onto the bus, and thus underwrote his patter with Little Richard, Fats Domino, Chuck Berry, the Coasters, and Ernie K. Doe's mother-in-law, an awful woman who was "sent from down below." And so it was that Christy and Cobb and Johnny G. and Tyrrell and I and assorted others picked up along the way passed our days in the back of the bus, a funny mix brought together by geography and parental desire.

Entrance to school brings with it forms and releases and assessments. Mercy relied on a series of tests, mostly the Stanford-Binet, for placement, and somehow the results of my tests got confused with those of another student named Rose. The other Rose apparently didn't do very well, for I was placed in the vocational track, a euphemism for the bottom level. Neither I nor my parents realized what this meant. We had no sense that Business Math, Typing, and English–Level D were dead ends. The current spate of reports on the schools criticizes parents for not involving themselves in the education of their children. But how would someone like Tommy Rose, with his two years of Italian schooling, know what to ask? And what sort of pressure could an exhausted waitress apply? The error went undetected, and I remained in the vocational track for two years. What a place.

My homeroom was supervised by Brother Dill, a troubled and unstable man who also taught freshman English. When his class drifted away from him, which was often, his voice would rise in paranoid accusations, and occasionally he would lose control and shake or smack us. I hadn't been there two months when one of his brisk, face-turning slaps had my glasses sliding down the aisle. Physical education was also pretty harsh. Our teacher was a stubby ex-lineman who had played old-time pro ball in the Midwest. He routinely had us grabbing our ankles to receive his stinging paddle across our butts. He did that, he said, to make men of us. "Rose," he bellowed on our first encounter; me standing geeky in line in my baggy shorts. "'Rose'? What the hell kind of name is that?"

"Italian, sir," I squeaked.

"Italian! Ho. Rose, do you know the sound a bag of shit makes when it hits the wall?"

"No, sir."

"Wop!"

Sophomore English was taught by Mr. Mitropetros. He was a large, bejeweled man who managed the parking lot at the Shrine Auditorium. He would crow and preen and list for us the stars he'd brushed against. We'd ask questions and glance knowingly and snicker, and all that fueled the poor guy to brag some more. Parking cars was his night job. He had little training in English, so his lesson plan for his day work had us reading the district's required text, *Julius Caesar*, aloud for the semester. We'd finish the play way before the twenty weeks was up, so he'd have us switch parts again and again and start again: Dave Snyder, the fastest guy at Mercy, muscling through Caesar to the breathless squeals of Calpurnia, as interpreted by Steve Fusco, a surfer who owned the school's most envied paneled wagon. Week ten and Dave and Steve would take on new roles, as would we all, and render a water-logged Cassius and a Brutus that are beyond my powers of description.

Spanish I — taken in the second year — fell into the hands of a new recruit. Mr. Montez was a tiny man, slight, five foot six at the most, soft-spoken and delicate. Spanish was a particularly rowdy class, and Mr. Montez was as prepared for it as a doily maker at a hammer throw. He would tap his pencil to a room in which Steve Fusco was propelling spitballs from his heavy lips, in which Mike Dweetz was taunting Billy Hawk, a half-Indian, half-Spanish, reed-thin, quietly explosive boy. The vocational track at Our Lady of Mercy mixed kids traveling in from South L.A. with South Bay surfers and a few Slavs and Chicanos from the harbors of San Pedro. This was a dangerous miscellany: surfers and hodads and South-Central blacks all ablaze to the metronomic tapping of Hector Montez's pencil.

One day Billy lost it. Out of the corner of my eye I saw him strike out with his right arm and catch Dweetz across the neck. Quick as a spasm, Dweetz was out of his seat, scattering desks, cracking Billy on the side of the head, right behind the eye. Snyder and Fusco and others broke it up, but the room felt hot and close and naked. Mr. Montez's tenuous authority was finally ripped to shreds, and I think everyone felt a little strange about that. The charade was over, and when it came down to it, I don't think any of the kids really wanted it to end this way. They had pushed and pushed and bullied their way into a freedom that both scared and embarrassed them.

Students will float to the mark you set. I and the others in the vocational classes were bobbing in pretty shallow water. Vocational education has aimed at increasing the economic opportunities of students who do not do well in our schools. Some serious programs succeed in doing that, and through exceptional teachers — like Mr. Gross in Horace's Compromise — students learn to develop hypotheses and troubleshoot, reason through a problem, and communicate effectively — the true job skills. The vocational track, however, is most often a place for those who are just not making it, a dumping ground for the disaffected. There were a few teachers who worked hard at education; young Brother Slattery, for example, combined a stern voice with weekly quizzes to try to pass along to us a skeletal outline of world history. But mostly the teachers had no idea of how to engage the imaginations of us kids who were scuttling along at the bottom of the pond.

And the teachers would have needed some inventiveness, for none of us was groomed for the classroom. It wasn't just that I didn't know things — didn't know how to simplify algebraic fractions, couldn't identify different kinds of clauses, bungled Spanish translations — but that I had developed various faulty and inadequate ways of doing algebra and making sense of Spanish. Worse yet, the years of defensive tuning out in elementary school had given me a way to escape quickly while seeming at least half alert. During my time in Voc. Ed., I developed further into a mediocre student and a somnambulant problem solver, and that affected the subjects I did have the wherewithal to handle: I detested Shakespeare; I got bored with history. My attention flitted here and there. I fooled around in class and read my books indifferently — the intellectual equivalent of playing with your food. I did what I had to do to get by, and I did it with half a mind.

But I did learn things about people and eventually came into my own socially. I liked the guys in Voc. Ed. Growing up where I did, I understood and admired physical prowess, and there was an abundance of muscle here. There was Dave Snyder, a sprinter and halfback of true quality. Dave's ability and his quick wit gave him a natural appeal, and he was welcome in any clique, though he always kept a little independent. He enjoyed acting the fool and could care less about studies, but he possessed a certain maturity and never caused the faculty much trouble. It was a testament to his independence that he included me among his friends — I eventually went out for track, but I was no jock. Owing to the Latin alphabet and a dearth of *R*s and *S*s, Snyder sat behind Rose, and we started exchanging one-liners and became friends.

There was Ted Richard, a much-touted Little League pitcher. He was chunky and had a baby face and came to Our Lady of Mercy as a seasoned street fighter. Ted was quick to laugh and he had a loud, jolly laugh, but when he got angry he'd smile a little smile, the kind that simply raises the corner of the mouth a quarter of an inch. For those who knew, it was an eerie signal. Those who didn't found themselves in big trouble, for Ted was very quick. He loved to carry on what we would come to call philosophical discussions: What is courage? Does God exist? He also loved words, enjoyed picking up big ones like *salubrious* and *equivocal* and using them in our conversations — laughing at himself as the word hit a chuckhole rolling off his tongue. Ted didn't do all that well in school — baseball and parties and testing the courage he'd speculated about took up his time. His textbooks were *Argosy* and *Field and Stream*, whatever newspapers he'd find on the bus stop — from *The Daily Worker* to pornography — conversations with uncles or hobos or businessmen he'd meet in a coffee shop, *The Old Man and the Sea*. With hindsight, I can see that Ted was developing into one of those rough-hewn intellectuals whose sources are a mix of the learned and the apocryphal, whose discussions are both assured and sad.

And then there was Ken Harvey. Ken was good-looking in a puffy way and had a full and oily ducktail and was a car enthusiast . . . a hodad. One day in religion class, he said the sentence that turned out to be one of the most memorable of the hundreds of thousands I heard in those Voc. Ed. years. We were talking about the parable of the talents, about achievement, working hard, doing the best you can do, blah-blah-blah, when the teacher called on the restive Ken Harvey for an opinion. Ken thought about it, but just for a second, and said (with studied, minimal affect), "I just wanna be average." That woke me up. Average?! Who wants to be average? Then the athletes chimed in with the clichés that make you want to laryngectomize them, and the exchange became a platitudinous melee. At the time, I thought Ken's assertion was stupid, and I wrote him off. But his sentence has stayed with me all these years, and I think I am finally coming to understand it.

Ken Harvey was gasping for air. School can be a tremendously disorienting place. No matter how bad the school, you're going to encounter notions that don't fit with the assumptions and beliefs that you grew up with — maybe you'll hear these dissonant notions from teachers, maybe from the other students, and maybe you'll read them. You'll also be thrown in with all kinds of kids from all kinds of backgrounds, and that can be unsettling — this is especially true in places of rich ethnic and linguistic mix, like the L.A. basin. You'll see a handful of students far excel you in courses that sound exotic and that are only in the curriculum of the elite: French, physics, trigonometry. And all this is happening while you're trying to shape an identity, your body is changing, and your emotions are running wild. If you're a working-class kid in the vocational track, the options you'll have to deal with this will be constrained in certain ways: You're defined by your school as "slow"; you're placed in a curriculum that isn't designed to liberate you but to occupy you, or, if you're lucky, train you, though the training is for work the society does not esteem; other students are picking up the cues from your school and your curriculum and interacting with you in particular ways. If you're a kid like Ted Richard, you turn your back on all this and let your mind roam where it may. But youngsters like Ted are rare. What Ken and so many others do is protect themselves from such suffocating madness by taking on with a vengeance the identity implied in the vocational track. Reject the confusion and frustration by openly defining yourself as the Common Joe. Champion the average. Rely on your own good sense. Fuck this bullshit. Bullshit, of course, is everything you — and the others — fear is beyond you: books, essays, tests, academic scrambling, complexity, scientific reasoning, philosophical inquiry.

The tragedy is that you have to twist the knife in your own gray matter to make this defense work. You'll have to shut down, have to reject intellectual stimuli or diffuse them with sarcasm, have to cultivate stupidity, have to convert boredom from a malady into a way of confronting the world. Keep your vocabulary simple, act stoned when you're not or act more stoned than you are, flaunt ignorance, materialize your dreams. It is a powerful and effective defense — it neutralizes the insult and the frustration of being a vocational kid and, when perfected, it drives teachers up the wall, a delightful secondary effect. But like all strong magic, it exacts a price.

My own deliverance from the Voc. Ed. world began with sophomore biology. Every student, college prep to vocational, had to take biology, and unlike the other courses, the same person taught all sections. When teaching the vocational group, Brother Clint probably slowed down a bit or omitted a little of the fundamental biochemistry, but he used the same book and more or less the same syllabus across the board. If one class got tough, he could get tougher. He was young and powerful and very handsome, and looks and physical strength were high currency. No one gave him any trouble.

I was pretty bad at the dissecting table, but the lectures and the textbook were interesting: plastic overlays that, with each turned page, peeled away skin, then veins and muscle, then organs, down to the very bones that Brother Clint, pointer in hand, would tap out on our hanging skeleton. Dave Snyder was in big trouble, for the study of life — versus the living of it — was sticking in his craw. We worked out a code for our multiple-choice exams. He'd poke me in the back: once for the answer under *A*, twice for *B*, and so on; and when he'd hit the right one, I'd look up to the ceiling as though I were lost in thought. Poke: cytoplasm. Poke, poke: methane. Poke, poke, poke: William Harvey. Poke, poke, poke, poke: islets of Langerhans. This didn't work out perfectly, but Dave passed the course, and I mastered the dreamy look of a guy on a record jacket. And something else happened. Brother Clint puzzled over this Voc. Ed. kid who was racking up 98s and 99s on his tests. He checked the school's records and discovered the error. He recommended that I begin my junior year in the College Prep program. According to all I've read since, such a shift, as one report put it, is virtually impossible. Kids at that level rarely cross tracks. The telling thing is how chancy both my placement into and exit from Voc. Ed. was; neither I nor my parents had anything to do with it. I lived in one world during spring semester, and when I came back to school in the fall, I was living in another.

Switching to College Prep was a mixed blessing. I was an erratic student. I was undisciplined. And I hadn't caught onto the rules of the game: Why work hard in a class that didn't grab my fancy? I was also hopelessly behind in math. Chemistry was hard; toying with my chemistry set years before hadn't prepared me for the chemist's equations. Fortunately, the priest who taught both chemistry and second-year algebra was also the school's athletic director. Membership on the track team covered me; I knew I wouldn't get lower than a C. U.S. history was taught pretty well, and I did okay. But civics was taken over by a football coach who had trouble reading the textbook aloud — and reading aloud was the centerpiece of his pedagogy. College Prep at Mercy was certainly an improvement over the vocational program — at least it carried some status — but the social science curriculum was weak, and the mathematics and physical sciences were simply beyond me. I had a miserable quantitative background and ended up copying some assignments and finessing the rest as best I could. Let me try to explain how it feels to see again and again material you should once have learned but didn't.

You are given a problem. It requires you to simplify algebraic fractions or to multiply expressions containing square roots. You know this is pretty basic material because you've seen it for years. Once a teacher took some time with you, and you learned how to carry out these operations. Simple versions, anyway. But that was a year or two or more in the past, and these are more complex versions, and now you're not sure. And this, you keep telling yourself, is ninth- or even eighth-grade stuff.

Next it's a word problem. This is also old hat. The basic elements are as familiar as story characters: trains speeding so many miles per hour or shadows of buildings angling so many degrees. Maybe you know enough, have sat through enough explanations, to be able to begin setting up the problem: "If one train is going this fast . . ." or "This shadow is really one line of a triangle . . . ." Then: "Let's see . . ." "How did Jones do this?" "Hmmmm." "No." "No, that won't work." Your attention wavers. You wonder about other things: a football game, a dance, that cute new checker at the market. You try to focus on the problem again. You scribble on paper for a while, but the tension wins out and your attention flits elsewhere. You crumple the paper and begin daydreaming to ease the frustration.

The particulars will vary, but in essence this is what a number of students go through, especially those in so-called remedial classes. They open their textbooks and see once again the familiar and impenetrable formulas and diagrams and terms that have stumped them for years. There is no excitement here. *No* excitement. Regardless of what the teacher says, this is not a new challenge. There is, rather, embarrassment and frustration and, not surprisingly, some anger in being reminded once again of long-standing inadequacies. No wonder so many students finally attribute their difficulties to something inborn, organic: "That part of my brain just doesn't work." Given the troubling histories many of these students have, it's miraculous that any of them can lift the shroud of hopelessness sufficiently to make deliverance from these classes possible.

Through this entire period, my father's health was deteriorating with cruel momentum. His arteriosclerosis progressed to the point where a simple nick on his shin wouldn't heal. Eventually it ulcerated and widened. Lou Minton would come by daily to change the dressing. We tried renting an oscillating bed — which we placed in the front room — to force blood through the constricted arteries in my father's legs. The bed hummed through the night, moving in place to ward off the inevitable. The ulcer continued to spread, and the doctors finally had to amputate. My grandfather had lost his leg in a stockyard accident. Now my father too was crippled. His convalescence was slow but steady, and the doctors placed him in the Santa Monica Rehabilitation Center, a sun-bleached building that opened out onto the warm spray of the Pacific. The place gave him some strength and some color and some training in walking with an artificial leg. He did pretty well for a year or so until he slipped and broke his hip. He was confined to a wheelchair after that, and the confinement contributed to the diminishing of his body and spirit.

I am holding a picture of him. He is sitting in his wheelchair and smiling at the camera. The smile appears forced, unsteady, seems to quaver, though it is frozen in silver nitrate. He is in his mid-sixties and looks eighty. Late in my junior year, he had a stroke and never came out of the resulting coma. After that, I would see him only in dreams, and to this day that is how I join him. Sometimes the dreams are sad and grisly and primal: my father lying in a bed soaked with his suppuration, holding me, rocking me. But sometimes the dreams bring him back to me healthy: him talking to me on an empty street, or buying some pictures to decorate our old house, or transformed somehow into someone strong and adept with tools and the physical.

Jack MacFarland couldn't have come into my life at a better time. My father was dead, and I had logged up too many years of scholastic indifference. Mr. MacFarland had a master's degree from Columbia and decided, at twenty-six, to find a little school and teach his heart out. He never took any credentialing courses, couldn't bear to, he said, so he had to find employment in a private system. He ended up at Our Lady of Mercy teaching five sections of senior English. He was a beatnik who was born too late. His teeth were stained, he tucked his sorry tie in between the third and fourth buttons of his shirt, and his pants were chronically wrinkled. At first, we couldn't believe this guy, thought he slept in his car. But within no time, he had us so startled with work that we didn't much worry about where he slept or if he slept at all. We wrote three or four essays a month. We read a book every two to three weeks, starting with the *Iliad* and ending up with Hemingway. He gave us a quiz on the reading every other day. He brought a prep school curriculum to Mercy High.

MacFarland's lectures were crafted, and as he delivered them he would pace the room jiggling a piece of chalk in his cupped hand, using it to scribble on the board the names of all the writers and philosophers and plays and novels he was weaving into his discussion. He asked questions often, raised everything from Zeno's paradox to the repeated last line of Frost's "Stopping by Woods on a Snowy Evening."

He slowly and carefully built up our knowledge of Western intellectual history — with facts, with connections, with speculations. We learned about Greek philosophy, about Dante, the Elizabethan world view, the Age of Reason, existentialism. He analyzed poems with us, had us reading sections from John Ciardi's *How Does a Poem Mean?*, making a potentially difficult book accessible with his own explanations. We gave oral reports on poems Ciardi didn't cover. We imitated the styles of Conrad, Hemingway, and *Time* magazine. We wrote and talked, wrote and talked. The man immersed us in language.

Even MacFarland's barbs were literary. If Jim Fitzsimmons, hung over and irritable, tried to smart-ass him, he'd rejoin with a flourish that would spark the indomitable Skip Madison — who'd lost his front teeth in a hapless tackle — to flick his tongue through the gap and opine, "good chop," drawing out the single "o" in stinging indictment. Jack MacFarland, this tobacco-stained intellectual, brandished linguistic weapons of a kind I hadn't encountered before. Here was this *egghead*, for God's sake, keeping some pretty difficult people in line. And from what I heard, Mike Dweetz and Steve Fusco and all the notorious Voc. Ed. crowd settled down as well when MacFarland took the podium. Though a lot of guys groused in the schoolyard, it just seemed that giving trouble to this particular teacher was a silly thing to do. Tomfoolery, not to mention assault, had no place in the world he was trying to create for us, and instinctively everyone knew that. If nothing else, we all recognized MacFarland's considerable intelligence and respected the hours he put into his work. It came to this: The troublemaker would look foolish rather than daring. Even Jim Fitzsimmons was reading *On the Road* and turning his incipient alcoholism to literary ends.

There were some lives that were already beyond Jack MacFarland's ministrations, but mine was not. I started reading again as I hadn't since elementary school. I would go into our gloomy little bedroom or sit at the dinner table while, on the television, Danny McShane was paralyzing Mr. Moto with the atomic drop, and work slowly back through *Heart of Darkness*, trying to catch the words in Conrad's sentences. I certainly was not MacFarland's best student; most of the other guys in College Prep, even my fellow slackers, had better backgrounds than I did. But I worked very hard, for MacFarland had hooked me. He tapped my old interest in reading and creating stories. He gave me a way to feel special by using my mind. And he provided a role model that wasn't shaped on physical prowess alone, and something inside me that I wasn't quite aware of responded to that. Jack MacFarland established a literacy club, to borrow a phrase of Frank Smith's, and invited me — invited all of us — to join.

There's been a good deal of research and speculation suggesting that the acknowledgment of school performance with extrinsic rewards — smiling faces, stars, numbers, grades — diminishes the intrinsic satisfaction children experience by engaging in reading or writing or problem solving. While it's certainly true that we've created an educational system that encourages our best and brightest to become cynical grade collectors and, in general, have developed an obsession with evaluation and assessment, I must tell you that venal though it may have been, I loved getting good grades from MacFarland. I now know how subjective grades can be, but then they came tucked in the back of essays like bits of scientific data, some sort of spectroscopic readout that said, objectively and publicly, that I had made something of value. I suppose I'd been mediocre for too long and enjoyed a public redefinition. And I suppose the workings of my mind, such as they were, had been private for too long. My linguistic play moved into the world; like the intergalactic stories I told years before on Frank's berry-splattered truck bed, these papers with their circled, red B-pluses and A-minuses linked my mind to something outside it. I carried them around like a club emblem.

One day in the December of my senior year, Mr. MacFarland asked me where I was going to go to college. I hadn't thought much about it. Many of the students I teach today spent their last year in high school with a physics text in one hand and the Stanford catalog in the other, but I wasn't even aware of what "entrance requirements" were. My folks would say that they wanted me to go to college and be a doctor, but I don't know how seriously I ever took that; it seemed a sweet thing to say, a bit of supportive family chatter, like telling a gangly daughter she's graceful. The reality of higher education wasn't in my scheme of things: No one in the family had gone to college; only two of my uncles had completed high school. I figured I'd get a night job and go to the local junior college because I knew that Snyder and Company were going there to play ball. But I hadn't even prepared for that. When I finally said, "I don't know," MacFarland looked down at me — I was seated in his office — and said, "Listen, you can write."

My grades stank. I had A's in biology and a handful of B's in a few English and social science classes. All the rest were C's — or worse. MacFarland said I would do well in his class and laid down the law about doing well in the others. Still, the record for my first three years wouldn't have been acceptable to any four-year school. To nobody's surprise, I was turned down flat by USC and UCLA. But Jack MacFarland was on the case. He had received his bachelor's degree from Loyola University, so he made calls to old professors and talked to somebody in admissions and wrote me a strong letter. Loyola finally accepted me as a probationary student. I would be on trial for the first year, and if I did Okay, I would be granted regular status. MacFarland also intervened to get me a loan, for I could never have afforded a private college without it. Four more years of religion classes and four more years of boys at one school, girls at another. But at least I was going to college. Amazing.

In my last semester of high school, I elected a special English course fashioned by Mr. MacFarland, and it was through this elective that there arouse at Mercy a fledgling literati. Art Mitz, the editor of the school newspaper and a very smart guy, was the kingpin. He was joined by me and by Mark Dever, a quiet boy who wrote beautifully and who would die before he was forty. MacFarland occasionally invited us to his apartment, and those visits became the high point of our apprenticeship: We'd clamp on our training wheels and drive to his salon.

He lived in a cramped and cluttered place near the airport, tucked away in the kind of building that architectural critic Reyner Banham calls a *dingbat*. Books were all over: stacked, piled, tossed, and crated, underlined and dog eared, well worn and new. Cigarette ashes crusted with coffee in saucers or spilled over the sides of motel ashtrays. The little bedroom had, along two of its walls, bricks and boards loaded with notes, magazines, and oversized books. The kitchen joined the living room, and there was a stack of German newspapers under the sink. I had never seen anything like it: a great flophouse of language furnished by City Lights and Café le Metro. I read every title. I flipped through paperbacks and scanned jackets and memorized names: Gogol, *Finnegan's Wake*, Djuna Barnes, Jackson Pollock, *A Coney Island of the Mind*, F. O. Matthiessen's *American Renaissance*, all sorts of Freud, *Troubled Sleep*, Man Ray, *The Education of Henry Adams*, Richard Wright, *Film as Art*, William Butler Yeats, Marguerite Duras, *Redburn*, *A Season in Hell*, *Kapital*. On the cover of Alain-Fournier's *The Wanderer* was an Edward Gorey drawing of a young man on a road winding into dark trees. By the hotplate sat a strange Kafka novel called *Amerika*, in which an adolescent hero crosses the Atlantic to find the Nature Theater of Oklahoma. Art and Mark would be talking about a movie or the school newspaper, and I would be consuming my English teacher's library. It was heady stuff. I felt like a Pop Warner athlete on steroids.

Art, Mark, and I would buy stogies and triangulate from MacFarland's apartment to the Cinema, which now shows X-rated films but was then L.A.'s premiere art theater, and then to the musty Cherokee Bookstore in Hollywood to hobnob with beatnik homosexuals — smoking, drinking bourbon and coffee, and trying out awkward phrases we'd gleaned from our mentor's bookshelves. I was happy and precocious and a little scared as well, for Hollywood Boulevard was thick with a kind of decadence that was foreign to the South Side. After the Cherokee, we would head back to the security of MacFarland's apartment, slaphappy with hipness.

Let me be the first to admit that there was a good deal of adolescent passion in this embrace of the avant-garde: self-absorption, sexually charged pedantry, an elevation of the odd and abandoned. Still it was a time during which I absorbed an awful lot of information: long lists of titles, images from expressionist paintings, new wave shibboleths, snippets of philosophy, and names that read like Steve Fusco's misspellings — Goethe, Nietzsche, Kierkegaard. Now this is hardly the stuff of deep understanding. But it was an introduction, a phrase book, a Baedeker to a vocabulary of ideas, and it felt good at the time to know all these words. With hindsight I realize how layered and important that knowledge was.

It enabled me to do things in the world. I could browse bohemian bookstores in far-off, mysterious Hollywood; I could go to the Cinema and see events through the lenses of European directors; and, most of all, I could share an evening, talk that talk, with Jack MacFarland, the man I most admired at the time. Knowledge was becoming a bonding agent. Within a year or two, the persona of the disaffected hipster would prove too cynical, too alienated to last. But for a time it was new and exciting: It provided a critical perspective on society, and it allowed me to act as though I were living beyond the limiting boundaries of South Vermont.

Rose's Insights as a Resource for Your Teaching

1. Consider the ways in which Rose characterizes Jack MacFarland. What are the essential features of MacFarland's teaching, and why are they so effective?

2. Rose offers an implicit theory of how and why students "resist" our pedagogies. Trace this theory and check it against your own experience.

Rose's Insights as a Resource for Your Writing Classroom

1. Ask your students to read Rose's essay. How do students' own experiences in a tracked or untracked educational system concur with or differ from Rose's? What does Rose's assertion that "students will float to the mark [the teachers] set" then imply about the legitimacy of the widely used practice of tracking? Under what circumstances might tracking be valid or beneficial?

2. In reflecting on their past educational experiences, do students recognize instances in which the teachers' setting of standards affected their learning, either positively or negatively? How did a positive experience differ from a negative one in terms of self-perception and the students' expectations of their teachers?

3. Ask students to think about the many factors that influence educational success and opportunity. In what ways might tracking contain socially and culturally embedded biases? Was Rose victim to such biases in these early years?

Underlife and Writing Instruction

Robert Brooke

Though published in the late 1980s, this article anticipates the major preoccupations of composition theory today in its focus on how students imagine and inhabit their identities in our classrooms and, more particularly, how certain conflicts in their senses of identity manifest themselves in the moment-to-moment experiences of our teaching. Brooke shows how these conflicts, which we've traditionally understood as disruptive problems, can actually be examined to provide powerful focal points for our teaching and for the assignments we create.

This article uses the sociological concept of underlife to explain several aspects of writing instruction. In sociological theory, "underlife" refers to those behaviors which undercut the roles expected of participants in a situation — the ways an employee, for example, shows she is not just an employee, but has a more complex personality outside that role.

In contemporary writing instruction, both students and teachers undercut the traditional roles of the American educational system in order to substitute more complex identities in their place. On the one hand, students disobey, write letters instead of taking notes, and whisper with their peers to show they are more than just students and can think independently of classroom expectations. On the other, writing teachers develop workshop methods, use small groups, and focus on students' own "voices" in order to help students see themselves as writers first and students second. Both sets of behaviors are underlife behaviors, for they seek to provide identities that go beyond the roles offered by the normal teacher-as-lecturer, student-as-passive-learner educational system.

These forms of underlife, moreover, are connected to the nature of writing itself. Writing, in the rich sense of interactive knowledge creation advocated by theorists like Ann Berthoff in *The Making of Meaning* and Janet Emig in *The Web of Meaning*, necessarily involves standing outside the roles and beliefs offered by a social situation — it involves questioning them, searching for new connections, building ideas that may be in conflict with accepted ways of thinking and acting. Writing involves being able to challenge one's assigned roles long enough that one can think originally; it involves living in conflict with accepted (expected) thought and action.

This article will explore student and teacher behavior in writing instruction as the underlife of the current educational system, and will suggest that the identities which may be developing for students in writing classrooms are more powerful for real academic success than the traditional identity of the successful student. It may be that the process of allowing a particular kind of identity to develop is what contemporary writing instruction is all about.

The Concept of Underlife

My understanding of "underlife" stems from Erving Goffman's books *Asylums* and *Stigma*, although the concept has long been accepted in sociology. As presented in these books, the concept of underlife rests on three assumptions about social interaction. First, a person's identity is assumed to be a function of social interaction. Second, social interaction is assumed to be a system of information games. Third, social organizations are assumed to provide roles for individuals which imply certain kinds of identities. With these assumptions in mind, "underlife" can be understood as the activities (or information games) individuals engage in to show that their identities are different from or more complex than the identities assigned them by organizational roles. In this section, I will describe these assumptions and the concept of underlife that emerges from them.

Identity as Social Interaction

In *Stigma*, Goffman explains that we understand another person's identity as a product of (1) how they immediately appear to us through dress, bearing, accent, physical features, and the like; (2) what we know about their history; and (3) the stances they take towards the groups we assume they belong to. We may initially assume, for example, that the young man in the front row of a new class is a typical "fraternity boy" because of (1) his haircut, his polo shirt, and his brand name tennis shoes. As we get to know (2) his history, we may find out that he comes from a wealthy family, that his parents hope he will become a doctor, and that he struggles with this because he has a hard time keeping up his grades. We will also begin to get a sense of him as a unique individual when we find out (3) he is troubled by his relationship to his family, more interested in English than in medicine, and feels in conflict because he would like to drop medicine, reject the family, and go into graduate school, but also wants to marry his sorority sweetheart, keep the family fortune, and lead a "successful" life. We (and he) use all three forms of information in assigning to him a particular identity.

Information Games

The identity we assign such a young man is greatly determined, however, by the kinds of information he chooses to give us. If he dressed differently, we would see him differently. Perhaps if we knew more of his history we would see him in a different light. Perhaps we may think that his choice to tell us of his interest in English is a calculated choice, intended to get us to grade easier. The identity assigned an individual by other people is largely the product of the "information games" people play when interacting with each other. By what each person chooses to reveal about himself in each context, we develop a sense of that person's identity. Central to Goffman's conception of the human person, then, is a sense of the "information games" nature of interaction — people are assumed to attempt to develop the best defensible portrait for themselves in social interactions.

Organizational Roles

The kind of portrait a person can develop for herself, however, is a function of the organizations (businesses, families, clubs, hospitals, etc.) she operates in. As Goffman explains, social organizations are places where individuals are placed into certain roles. Appropriate activity in these roles carries with it implications about identity. In a school classroom, for example, prompt and accurate completion of tasks set by the teacher carries with it a "good student" identity, and a student who always complies pleasantly will be understood as smart, well-mannered, possibly a teacher's pet.

Underlife

Exactly because organizations offer definitions of identity, they also offer individuals the opportunity to respond to the definitions in creative ways. Because definitions of self exist in organizations, individuals can give information about how they see themselves by rejecting the definition offered. Institutional underlife is exactly such a case: actors in an institution develop behaviors which assert an identity different from the one assigned them.

In *Asylums*, Goffman studies the underlife of a major American mental hospital, and comes to the conclusion that underlife activities take two primary forms. First, there are *disruptive* forms of underlife, like those engaged in by union organizers, "where the realistic intentions of the participants are to abandon the organization or radically alter its structure." Second, there are *contained* forms of underlife, which attempt to fit into "existing institutional structures without introducing pressure for radical change" (199). Most forms of underlife are of the second kind — they work around the institution to assert the actor's difference from the assigned role, rather than working for the elimination of the institution. In the mental hospital, Goffman finds many examples of such contained underlife patterns, including identity jokes and challenges (where staff and inmates would kid each other about having attributes of the other class), attempts to "get around" established procedures (such as dumping dinner in the garbage and having a friend who works in the kitchen smuggle out a plateful of boiled eggs), and explicit attempts to express rejection of inmate status (like withdrawing from interaction with other patients, parodying psychological theory, claiming it was all a mistake, and engaging in violent behavior). The point of each of these behaviors, claims Goffman, is to show that one has a self different from the patient-self assigned by the hospital.

The prevalence of such behaviors throughout the hospital and other institutions leads Goffman to conclude that underlife behaviors are a normal part of institutional life. All members of the institution — staff, patients, technicians, janitors, doctors — engaged in such behaviors. Consequently, Goffman claims, institutional underlife must be understood as an activity closely related to individual identity. "I want to argue," he writes, "that this recalcitrance is not an incidental mechanism of defense but rather an essential constituent of the self" (319). For Goffman, looking at those activities through which individuals resist or reject the identity assigned them by institutions is a way of looking at how individuals form their sense of identity. No one but the complete fanatic completely associates herself with only one role — instead, the self is formed in the distance one takes from the roles one is assigned. In such an analysis, activities which aren't "on task" become as important as activities which are, for besides the task itself there is also always the formation of identity.

Underlife in a Writing Class

Underlife activities, as Goffman describes them, are the range of activities people develop to distance themselves from the surrounding institution. By so doing they assert something about their identity. Underlife allows individuals to take stances towards the roles they are expected to play, and to show others the stances they take. When the kinds of student behaviors normally seen as misbehavior are examined in writing classrooms, what appears is exactly this sort of constructive, individual stance-taking. It is exactly in these underlife behaviors that students are developing their individual stances towards classroom experience.

I would like to discuss several examples of underlife in the writing classroom from this perspective. The examples all come from a semester-long participant-observation study of a freshmen writing class in spring 1986. As a participant-observer, I was able to hear and record many behaviors I am unable to attend to while teaching my own courses. These behaviors include the private conversations students have with one another, the notes they write to themselves and then scratch out, the things they're writing when the teacher thinks they're taking notes, and other such activities. What surprised me was the extent and content of these activities — even in the most docile class hour, such activities are constantly going on, and (significantly) they are usually connected to the class activities in some way. The students are developing their own stances towards class activity, not whispering about unrelated subjects like parties and dates as I had always assumed.

In the classroom I observed, the students' underlife activities divided fairly cleanly into four major types, which I will discuss in order of frequency.

First, students tend to find creative uses for classroom activities and materials which are purposefully different from those the teacher intended. Usually, these creative uses show that classroom ideas could be used outside of class in ways more interesting to the students. During a class period devoted to using Young, Becker, and Pike's tagmemic matrix in *Rhetoric: Discovery and Change*, for example, two male students found ways of thinking about the subject that asserted their own interests. The teacher had brought in a bag of potatoes to serve as an example, and was having the class use the tagmemic matrix to explore "how many ways they could think about something as simple as a potato." While the class was discussing how a potato might change over time and in what contexts this change would be interesting, these students began a private discussion of how to ferment the potato to get vodka. When asked by the teacher what they were talking about, one of the two (looking nervous) explained that the process of fermentation was obviously a "change over time" and that this process was interesting "in the context of alcohol production." In this example, the students had openly ceased to participate in class, and seemed (from their giggles) to be "telling jokes" behind the teacher's back. But the content of their "jokes" was actually a way of applying the class concepts to their own late-adolescent interests in alcohol. Their retreat from class participation was a retreat which took a class concept with it, and which applied that concept in a highly creative and accurate way.

In the classroom I studied, this kind of creative use of classroom ideas was the most frequent form of underlife behavior. Most of the private conversations I heard applied a class concept to the students' world. In fact, particularly striking images or ideas frequently sparked several private conversations throughout the room. When the class discussed Annie Dillard's "Lenses," for example, a student pointed out Dillard's comparison of feeling disoriented to the shock of coming out of a really good movie and realizing you'd forgotten where you parked the car. Immediately, several private conversations started up throughout the room — the ones I could hear focused on how that feeling had happened to them too, in situations they could share with their peers.

To a teacher thinking only of how well her point is getting across, what seems to be going on in these cases is disruptive: students aren't paying attention, but are talking to one another about things that don't have to do with class. But to a teacher thinking about how students are using classroom information, these diversions should seem positive. In them, no matter how jokingly, students are actively connecting ideas in the classroom to their own lives outside the classroom, and are discovering ways in which classroom knowledge seems useful even when (or especially when) it isn't used for classroom purposes.

The second most frequent kind of underlife was student comments on the roles people were taking in the classroom, or the roles the classroom was asking them to take. Students, for example, frequently focused on the "games-playing" nature of student participation in college courses. Consider, for example, the following interaction which occurred during a small group discussion of a chapter from Margaret Laurence's

A Bird in the House:

> *Mick*: You know, everyone in the story tries to make themselves seem better than they are, you know, but Vanessa finds out every one of them is worse than they seem. It's like *all* of them are lying.
>
> *Mel*: Good point. She[the teacher]'ll like that.
>
> *Chuck*: Yeah. Home run. Three strikes.
>
> *Mel*: (laughing): Big bucks.
>
> *Chuck*: Yeah, big bucks, no whammies.
>
> General laughter, and the conversation immediately turned to discussion of a TV game show called "Press Your Luck!" On this show, contestants played a form of roulette to get "big bucks," but lost everything if they landed on a "whammie." The whammies, incidentally, were animated cartoon characters which would ramble across the screen and devour the hapless contestant's earnings. The group's discussion (which went on for several minutes, the assigned task having been forgotten) focused on how "lucky" players had to be to win anything on "Press Your Luck!" and how in general the game was a rip-off — as a contestant, nine times out of ten you got to get humiliated for nothing.

What struck me most about this interaction was not that students were avoiding the official task, nor that they were avoiding my presence enough to feel comfortable avoiding the task, but that the interaction highlighted (and sprung from) a deep-rooted sense of their experience with classrooms. Their comments, and the quick shift from doing a classroom exercise to discussing a game show, pointed out that they thought of the classroom as a "games-playing" environment, where "points" accumulated "big bucks," where one might get "whammied," where you always had to "press your luck." They thought of themselves as contestants in a game of luck, nerves, and skill, in which those who scored the most points survived, and those who didn't went home humiliated. They were aware, in short, that the classroom environment demanded certain actions of them which were as formal and arbitrary as the actions demanded in games-playing. The purpose of their interaction was to show each other that they all recognized this, that they as individuals were different from the roles they were being asked to play, and that they were all aware of each other as fellow games-players.

As a consequence of this mutual recognition of each other as games-players, students frequently engaged in conversations about how to "get by" effectively in the classroom. Especially in the few minutes before class when the teacher was not yet in the room, students would openly discuss strategies they'd used to succeed in the classroom. One woman told another, for example, that she'd written in her journal (which the teacher would see) an entry describing how hard the last paper was to write and how long it took her because that was the sort of thing the teacher wanted — even though she'd actually written the paper in an hour and a half after midnight the night before. Similarly, students would often share the comments they received on papers, and discuss what in the papers might have sparked the teacher to make these comments. These conversations occurred especially when one student had done well on a paper, and another hadn't, as if the students were together trying to pinpoint what was expected of them for success in this classroom. In all these activities, it was clear that students were not immediately evaluating each other on their success and honesty in embracing the classroom roles, but were instead mutually helping each other to succeed in "getting by" in the classroom without losing themselves in its expectations.

Such "role-recognition" activities on the part of students seem very similar to the "identity jokes" Goffman found in the hospital he studied. The purpose for commenting on the roles that exist in the classroom is the same purpose for kidding a staff member for acting like an inmate — such comments show that the speaker is aware of and different from the roles assigned in the situation, that there is more to the speaker than that. The quantity of such comments in the classroom I studied suggests that students are highly aware of the roles the classroom asks them to play, and highly defensive of their differences from these roles.

A third major category of underlife activities involves evaluations of what is going on in the classroom. In these comments, students explicitly took a stance towards some aspect of the classroom, and evaluated it as good or bad. Often, these evaluations focused on their own performance:

> *Chuck*: Did you bring your paper?
>
> *Ben*: That damn thing —
>
> *Chuck*: Pretty "damn," huh?
>
> *Ben*: It's so "damn" I keep forgetting it.

or on the course materials:

> *Jane*: (holding up book): Did you think this was all right?
>
> *Holly*: Dumb.
>
> *Jane*: Dumb?
>
> *Holly*: I hated it. Let me read your journal.
>
> *Jane*: No, it's stupid. — No, don't take it. — Give it back. (whispers) Teacher! Teacher! (Teacher comes into the classroom, and both students straighten in their seats.)

or on the day's activity:

Nellie: (to those around her during potato description day): I can't believe this! (She closes her book and starts writing a letter to a friend.)

These activities, also relatively common, allow the individual students to claim explicitly whether or not they accept the activity going on around them. Interestingly, most of these in-class comments expressed negative evaluations, even though formal student evaluations of the course showed most students thought this was the best writing course they'd ever taken. The purpose of these evaluative comments, it seems, is the same purpose as the other underlife activities — to assert one's fundamental distance from the classroom roles. Negative evaluations show that one can think independently; positive evaluations would show compliance with the course expectations. The purpose of such an evaluative comment has nothing to do with what the student really thinks of the class when comparing it to other classes. Instead, it has to do with asserting the student's ability to think in ways other than those expected in the classroom.

The last major category of underlife activity involved those private activities whereby an individual divides her attention between the class activity and something else. The most common example of divided attention was reading the student newspaper while the teacher was beginning class, but more interesting examples occurred. In this class, students were required to turn in a one-page journal entry every day — in a typical class period, four or five students could be observed writing their journals. Sometimes they would write these in such a way that the teacher would think they were taking notes. Sometimes they would write them as they were participating in small group discussions. In each case, however, they would be dividing their attention between the journal page and the activity that the teacher had set up. Both activities, of course, were connected to class demands; what was rebellious about writing the journal in class was that it took full and undivided attention away from the prescribed activity in the classroom.

The point of all these underlife activities is clearly to distance oneself from the demands of the classroom while hopefully remaining successful within it. All would be considered examples of "contained" underlife by Erving Goffman. The point is not to disrupt the functioning of the classroom, but to provide the other participants in the classroom with a sense that one has other things to do, other interests, that one is a much richer personality than can be shown in this context. All these activities, in short, allow the student to take a stance towards her participation in the classroom, and show that, while she can succeed in this situation, her self is not swallowed up by it. The interesting parts of herself, she seems to say, are being held in reserve.

Underlife and the Writing Teacher

If student underlife within the writing classroom is "contained" underlife, then the writing teacher's position can only be considered "disruptive." Students merely try to gain a little psychic distance from the roles they must inhabit in the classroom, but writing teachers clearly see themselves as engaged in the process of changing classroom roles. In fact, many writing teachers explain their position as one of "struggle" against the prevailing educational institution because the goals of writing are finally different from the goals of traditional education. Adrienne Rich, for example, claims in "Teaching Language in Open Admissions" that her goal of helping underprivileged writers find ways of writing powerfully in their own contexts comes into conflict with large social institutions which would prefer these individuals remained inarticulate. Mike Rose's article, "The Language of Exclusion," describes the writing teacher's plight, aware of the importance of writing for learning and thinking on the one hand, but forced by institutional administrators to test, remediate, and exclude students because of their poor writing "skills" on the other, and claims teachers must strive for the first while combating the second. In "Reality, Consensus, and Reform," Greg Myers shows how wanting to teach writing as a freeing process has historically been in conflict with (and undercut by) the ideological purposes of the educational institution, and argues that writing teachers need to recognize that "our interests are not the same as those of the institutions that employ us, and that the improvement of our work will involve social changes" (170). Similarly, Pamela Annas's "Style as Politics" shows how, for writers who are disadvantaged within the current social structure, writing is always a complex political act of finding language to express other possibilities than those offered by the current sociopolitical climate, and that this finding of language is in conflict with the standards of accepted writing. In each case, these writing teachers feel themselves to be after something different from what the traditional education system produces — instead of traditional "good students," they want students who will come to see themselves as unique, productive writers with influence on their environment.

They would like their students to see themselves as writers rather than as students, and their pedagogical changes are attempts to facilitate this shift in roles. Writing teachers change the classroom to help students extend their identities.

Writing teachers, however, are more likely to speak of "voice" than of "identity," for the first is a rhetorical concept and the second a sociological concept. But the two are very closely related, since both have to do with the stance an individual takes towards experience. In writing theory, a writer's "voice" is most often described as the unique stance she takes towards experience, and the unique way she relates herself to her context. In sociological theory, as we have seen, "identity" develops out of the individual's stance towards experience and out of the way she relates herself to the roles assigned her in the context. The ideas are closely connected: when a writing teacher worries about her student's "voice," she is also worrying about her student's "identity."

In writing classrooms, "voice" is often felt to be the paradox that prompts pedagogical change — as teachers, we want students to write in their own voices, but how can they when we *assign* them to? And how can their voices really be their own when they are evaluated by us? Knoblauch and Brannon explain in their *Rhetorical Traditions and the Teaching of Writing*:

> How can teachers hope to encourage engaged writing, particularly given the fact that classroom composing is, to a degree, inevitably artificial since the impulse to write comes from outside the writers? . . . Any school writing alters the normal circumstances in which a writer takes initiative to communicate to some reader, and in which the reader is interested in the substance of that particular text but not especially interested in the writer's overall ability or continuing maturation. (108)

If our goal as writing teachers is to enable students to see themselves as and to act as writers, then our role as teachers making assignments and evaluating their performance can only get in the way. In the classroom, students write to comply with our demands — they don't write because they see themselves as writers. The need for writers to develop their own voices is the central place where writing pedagogy comes into conflict with itself. If students really are to develop their own voices, they will need to ignore the requirements set for them by outsiders and write instead as they want — they would need, in short, to engage in a kind of underlife in relation to the classroom.

What's at stake, it seems, is a part of their "identity" — we would like them to think of themselves as *writers* rather than as *students*. We would hope they see purposes for writing beyond the single purpose of getting us to give them good grades. We would like them to take initiative to communicate with readers, to use writing to help better their world, to use writing to help them understand their world. Instead, we worry that they may see themselves only as games-players, as individuals forced to play the student role and who consequently distance themselves from that role as anyone working in an organization does. As writing teachers, we want them to *own* their writing, rather than attributing it only to the classroom — rather than claiming it's only a game we play in class.

If we wish them to see themselves as writers, we must help both them and ourselves to see our interaction in writing classrooms as cut from a different mold than "regular" classrooms. The roles must be different.

In fact, it is exactly such problems with classroom roles that lurk behind current calls to change writing pedagogy. The range of such suggested changes is staggering. Janet Emig's "Non-Magical Thinking" and Peter Elbow's *Writing Without Teachers* both argue that the teacher should become "a writer among writers," and that the first requirement of the writing teacher is that she must write herself, often and in many modes. Knoblauch and Brannon's *Rhetorical Traditions* suggests changing the structure of the classroom to a "writing workshop" where students and teacher can really talk to one another "as members of the same community of learners" (111). Donald Murray's *A Writer Teaches Writing* argues for one-on-one conferences between writer and teacher, in which the teacher takes a secondary place to the writer's own talk about her work and acts mainly as a fellow writer-editor and not as a teacher. Alongside these suggestions for classroom reform are powerful indictments of the traditional writing classroom for being teacher-centered rather than student-centered, focused on the product rather than process, being oppressive rather than liberating.

The whole call for pedagogical shift is most powerfully a call for a shift in the identity roles offered in the classroom. In other words, although we haven't clearly articulated it, the organizing assumption of composition instruction, in theory and practice, is that the primary function of the composition classroom is to foster a particular identity or stance towards the world. Writing teachers want to produce writers, not students, and consequently we seek to change our pedagogy to allow the possibility of the writer's identity.

Conclusion: Writing, Autonomy, and Action

The reasons writing teachers seek to alter normal classroom practice and the reasons students express their distance as individuals from classroom roles thus seem intimately connected: both have to do with a concern for the student's identity. Neither writing teacher no student is content to rely on the expected roles of teacher and student. Both want there to be more to the self, and both show this desire — the student by distancing herself from classroom expectations, the teacher by structuring the course so that normal classroom expectations are only partly in effect.

What is at stake, in other words, is who the individuals in the classroom will be. Student underlife primarily attempts to assert that the individuals who play the role of students are not only students, that there is more to them than that. It is thus a *contained* form of underlife, a form which (as Goffman would say) attempts to exist within the existing structure without introducing too much friction. But writing teachers would have students go further — thcy would havc students see themselves as writers, as people who use the processes writing offers to explore, question, and change elements of their social lives. Writing instruction is thus a *disruptive* form of underlife, a form which tries to undermine the nature of the institution and posit a different one in its place.

When we look at writing instruction from the perspective of underlife, it appears that the purpose of our courses is to allow students to substitute one kind of underlife for another. Instead of the naïve, contained form they normally employ, we're asking them to take on a disruptive form — a whole stance towards their social world that questions it, explores it, writes about it. We ask them to stand apart from the roles they normally play, and instead to try exploring what they normally think and what they'd normally do through writing. We would like them to become distanced from their experience, and consider it. As their underlife behavior shows, they are of course already distanced, already posing as "different from" the roles they play every day. They *are* different from these roles. But they aren't conscious of how they are different, and how they work to maintain their difference. And that, it seems, is what writing instruction tries to do — get them to become conscious of their differences from their normal roles, get them to accept that they are different, get them to explore and write out of these differences. Writing, finally, asks individuals to accept their own underlife, to accept the fact that they are never completely subsumed by their roles, and instead can stand apart from them and contemplate. Writing instruction seeks to help the learner see herself as an original thinker, instead of as a "student" whose purpose is to please teachers by absorbing and repeating information.

It is in this desire to shift roles, from student to writer, from teacher-pleaser to original thinker, that writing instruction comes into greatest conflict with the existing educational system, and also has the most to offer to it. For the shift begun in writing classrooms is a shift that would improve education in other classrooms as well. If the student in a chemistry class grew to think of herself as someone who thinks in certain ways to solve certain problems rather than as someone who must "learn" equations to pass tests, then the student would begin to see herself as a chemist, and to act accordingly. In other words, if all our classrooms were to focus on fostering the identities of students as thinkers in our disciplines rather than merely on transmitting the knowledge of our fields, then students might easily see the purpose for these particular "information games." But for students to see themselves as chemists, or social scientists, or writers, they must first see themselves as more than just students in our classrooms, as real thinkers with power and ability in this area. To help students make this change, of course, would require just as far-reaching pedagogical changes in other areas as writing teachers have begun to make in theirs. It would need much that is now only offered in writing classes — small class size, student-directed projects, peer interaction, chances for revising work and ideas as the course progresses. In all these changes, writing teachers could lead the way. For the student's identity of writer as original thinker, as able to step outside expectations and think creatively on one's own, may be the identity that would make the other identities possible, in the same way that the identity of "good student" (complete with study skills and time management behaviors) is now what makes traditional academic learning possible. Such a shift in education would be a far-reaching and beneficial shift, focusing on the identity and abilities of the student as an original thinker, rather than on the student's ability to comply with classroom authority.

Writing, in short, is "about" autonomy and action — to really learn to write means becoming a certain kind of person, a person who accepts, explores, and uses her differences from assigned roles to produce new knowledge, new action, and new roles. The concept of underlife shows us this process, a process at work in every classroom and at the core of our discipline. It suggests we think carefully about the identities we have, the identities we model, and the identities we ask students to take on, for the process of building identity is the business we are in.

Works Cited

Annas, Pamela. "Style as Politics." *College English* 47 (1985): 360–71.

Berthoff, Ann. *The Making of Meaning*. Upper Montclair, NJ: Boynton/Cook, 1983.

Dillard, Annie. "Lenses." *The Bedford Reader*. Ed. X. J. Kennedy and Dorothy Kennedy. 2nd ed. New York: St. Martin's Press, 1985. 101–05.

Elbow, Peter. *Writing Without Teachers*. New York: Oxford UP, 1973.

Emig, Janet. "Non-Magical Thinking: Presenting Writing Developmentally in Schools." *Writing: The Nature, Development, and Teaching of Written Communication, Vol. 2; Writing: Process, Development and Communication*. Ed. Carl Frederiksen and Joseph Dominic. Hillsdale, NJ: Erlbaum, 1981. 21–30.

———. *The Web of Meaning*. Upper Montclair, NJ: Boynton/Cook, 1983.

Goffman, Erving. *Asylums: Essays on the Social Situation of Mental Patients and Other Inmates*. New York: Anchor, 1961.

———. *Stigma: Notes on the Management of Spoiled Identity*. Englewood Cliffs, NJ: Prentice-Hall, 1963.

Knoblauch, C. H., and Lil Brannon. *Rhetorical Traditions and the Teaching of Writing*. Upper Montclair, NJ: Boynton/Cook, 1984.

Laurence, Margaret. *A Bird in the House*. Toronto: Seal, 1978.

Murray, Donald. *A Writer Teaches Writing*. 2nd ed. Boston: Houghton Mifflin, 1982.

Myers, Greg. "Reality, Consensus, and Reform in the Rhetoric of Composition Teaching." *College English* 48 (1986): 154–74.

Rich, Adrienne. "Teaching Language in Open Admissions." *On Lies, Secrets, and Silence: Selected Prose 1966–1978*. New York: Norton, 1979. 51–68.

Rose, Mike. "The Language of Exclusion." *College English* 47 (1985): 341–59.

Young, Richard, Alton Becker, and Kenneth Pike. *Rhetoric: Discovery and Change*. New York: Harcourt Brace Jovanovich, 1970.

Afterword

Rereading "Underlife and Writing Instruction" in 1998, I notice the focus on identity and conflict. "Writing involves being able to challenge one's assigned roles long enough that one can think originally; it involves living in conflict," I wrote then. Now, in 1998, these ideas resonate with many of the movements energizing composition: cultural studies viewing identity as a product of cultural literacies; critical pedagogies asking students to critique their cultural places; postcolonial and feminist compositionists describing the self as torn between opposing discourses. All these movements developed independently, yet I note the resonance now and can't help thinking this article would have been richer had I access to such material then.

But beyond that, the difference in myself as a reader/writer of this article involves exactly the kind of identity shift I was struggling to articulate. In 1987, I was a beginning assistant professor, fresh from graduate school, fascinated by the "disruptive" side of underlife. Goffman's concept helped me articulate something I was feeling: skepticism about the coercive forces of power that pushed all of us (students, teachers, administrators) into institutional roles. I wanted to find and name my own individual stance amongst these forces. But now, in 1998, my identity has shifted as my relations to power and institutions have changed. Now, I'm a full professor working with the National Writing Project and several state agencies to develop programs which might help revitalize Nebraska's rural communities. I still see the coercive force of power (it's hard not to in a world as inequitable as ours), but I focus more on the productive possibilities of institutions and communities, the roles they create. I watch an oral history project develop in Aurora, Nebraska, through which high school students create web pages to record the wisdom of elderly community members, or I watch elementary teachers in Albion, Nebraska, pair students and community members to adopt local buildings, find their archives, interview any surviving past owners. Such school projects are, of course, necessarily coercive in their reading, writing, and research requirements. But at the same time they produce new roles and relationships. Teenagers and the elderly get to know each other, value each other's stories. Kids and businesses become jointly interested in their town's past, perhaps seeing themselves as part of ongoing rural change in relation to American history. These emerging programs create identity options for rural people that weren't fully there before. They enrich the range of roles we all might choose.

"The process of building identity is the business we are in," I write in 1987. Much of the work of compositionists in the 1990s, by minds far better than my own, has been to develop deep connections and conflicts between identity and discourse and community. Now that we, as a field, understand this, perhaps the task of the next ten years will be to imagine programs which increase the self's possible roles, widening the ways literacy is used in the celebration and establishment of viable, sustainable communities.

— Robert Brooke
University of Nebraska–Lincoln

Brooke's Insights as a Resource for Your Teaching

1. Think about your own experience of underlife in the classroom and the ways you usually respond to it. Having read Brooke's essay, how might you now respond differently to these moments?

2. Brooke ends his essay with the claim, "the process of building identity is the business we are in." How does such a definition of our mission ask us to fundamentally reconsider the strategies we will use in the classroom? Consider the types of discussion you guide your students in, the ways in which you react to students' questions and responses, and the ways in which you assess or grade your students.

Brooke's Insights as a Resource for Your Writing Classroom

1. Ask your students to discuss characteristics that define the "ideal" student, and list these characteristics on the board. Next, generate a second — honest and realistic — list of characteristics of actual students. Explore the tension between the real and the ideal. You might have students develop their findings as the basis for a paper topic.

2. At the beginning of class, ask your students to pair off and discuss anything other than schoolwork for a few moments. Stop them and ask them to make a quick list of the topics that came up. After listing several on the board, challenge the class as a whole to draw connections between these items and the actual themes of the class's discussions so far. Have them draft paper topics that draw links between some of these items, themselves, and the recent readings from class.

Rhetoric and Ideology in the Writing Class

James A. Berlin

This classic essay provides an introduction to the theories that Berlin developed fully in Rhetoric and Reality: Writing Instruction in American Colleges, 1900–1985. *According to Berlin, an ideology addresses three questions: What exists? What is good? What is possible? Berlin suggests that there are three competing ideologies of writing instruction in our time: (1) cognitivist, (2) expressionist, and (3) social-epistemic. Each of these three ideologies carries its own notion of what writing is, what good writing and teaching are, and what we should aspire to accomplish with our students. Each of the three also represents a political stance, a take on the power relations that exist among author, audience, and text, as well as between teacher and student. This valuable essay can be used as a bibliography for further reading about these different approaches.*

The question of ideology has never been far from discussions of writing instruction in the modern American college. It is true that some rhetorics have denied their imbrication in ideology, doing so in the name of a disinterested scientism — as seen, for example, in various manifestations of current-traditional rhetoric. Most, however, have acknowledged the role of rhetoric in addressing competing discursive claims of value in the social, political, and cultural. This was particularly evident during the sixties and seventies, for example, as the writing classroom became one of the public areas for considering such strongly contested issues as Vietnam, civil rights, and economic equality. More recently the discussion of the relation between ideology and rhetoric has taken a new turn. Ideology is here foregrounded and problematized in a way that situates rhetoric within ideology, rather than ideology within rhetoric. In other words, instead of rhetoric acting as the transcendental recorder or arbiter of competing ideological claims, rhetoric is regarded as always already ideological. This position means that any examination of a rhetoric must first consider the ways its very discursive structure can be read so as to favor one version of economic, social, and political arrangements over other versions. A rhetoric then considers competing claims in these three realms from an ideological perspective made possible both by its constitution and by its application — the dialectical interaction between the rhetoric as text and the interpretive practices brought to it. A rhetoric can never be innocent, can never be a disinterested arbiter of the ideological claims of others because it is always already serving certain ideological claims. This perspective on ideology and rhetoric will be discussed in greater detail later. Here I merely wish to note that it has been forwarded most recently by such figures as Patricia Bizzell, David Bartholomae, Greg Myers, Victor Vitanza, and John Clifford and John Schilb. I have also called upon it in my monograph on writing instruction in twentieth-century American colleges. I would like to bring the discussion I began there up to date, focusing on ideology in the three rhetorics that have emerged as most conspicuous in classroom practices today: the rhetorics of cognitive psychology, of expressionism, and of a category I will call social-epistemic.

Each of these rhetorics occupies a distinct position in its relation to ideology. From the perspective offered here, the rhetoric of cognitive psychology refuses the ideological question altogether, claiming for itself the transcendent neutrality of science. This rhetoric is nonetheless easily preempted by a particular ideological position now in ascendancy because it encourages discursive practices that are compatible with dominant economic, social, and political formations. Expressionistic rhetoric, on the other hand, has always openly admitted its ideological predilections, opposing itself in no uncertain terms to the scientism of current-traditional rhetoric and the ideology it encourages. This rhetoric is, however, open to appropriation by the very forces it opposes in contradiction to its best intentions. Social-epistemic rhetoric is an alternative that is self-consciously aware of its ideological stand, making the very question of ideology the center of classroom activities, and in so doing providing itself a defense against preemption and a strategy for self-criticism and self-correction. This third rhetoric is the one I am forwarding here, and it provides the ground of my critique of its alternatives. In other words, I am arguing from ideology, contending that no other kind of argument is possible — a position that must first be explained.

Ideology is a term of great instability. This is true whether it is taken up by the Left or Right — as demonstrated, for example, by Raymond Williams in *Keywords* and *Marxism and Literature* and by Jorge Larrain in *The Concept of Ideology*. It is thus necessary to indicate at the outset the formulation that will be followed in a given discussion. Here I will rely on Göran Therborn's usage in *The Ideology of Power and the Power of Ideology*. Therborn, a Marxist sociologist at the University of Lund, Sweden, calls on the discussion of ideology found in Louis Althusser and on the discussion of power in Michel Foucault. I have chosen Therborn's adaptation of Althusser rather than Althusser himself because Therborn so effectively counters the ideology-science distinction of his source, a stance in which ideology is always false consciousness while a particular version of Marxism is defined as its scientific alternative in possession of objective truth. For Therborn, no position can lay claim to absolute, timeless truth, because finally all formulations are historically specific, arising out of the material conditions of a particular time and place. Choices in the economic, social, political, and cultural are thus always based on discursive practices that are interpretations, not mere transcriptions of some external, verifiable certainty. The choice for Therborn then is never between scientific truth and ideology, but between competing ideologies, competing discursive interpretations. Finally, Therborn calls upon Foucault's "micropolitics of power" (7) without placing subjects within a seamless web of inescapable, wholly determinative power relations. For Therborn, power can be identified and resisted in a meaningful way.

Therborn offers an especially valuable discussion for rhetoricians because of his emphasis on the discursive and dialogic nature of ideology. In other words, Therborn insists that ideology is transmitted through language practices that are always the center of conflict and contest:

> The operation of ideology in human life basically involves the constitution and patterning of how human beings live their lives as conscious,

> reflecting initiators of acts in a structured, meaningful world. Ideology operates as discourse, addressing or, as Althusser puts it, interpellating human beings as subjects. (15)

Conceived from the perspective of rhetoric, ideology provides the language to define the subject (the self), other subjects, the material world, and the relation of all of these to each other. Ideology is thus inscribed in language practices, entering all features of our experience.

Ideology for Therborn addresses three questions: "What exists? What is good? What is possible?" The first deals with epistemology, as Therborn explains: "what exists, and its corollary, what does not exist: that is, who we are, what the world is, what nature, society, men and women are like. In this way we acquire a sense of identity, becoming conscious of what is real and true; the visibility of the world is thereby structured by the distribution of spotlights, shadows, and darkness." Ideology thus interpellates the subject in a manner that determines what is real and what is illusory, and, most important, what is experienced and what remains outside the field of phenomenological experience, regardless of its actual material existence. Ideology also provides the subject with standards for making ethical and aesthetic decisions: "*what is good,* right, just, beautiful, attractive, enjoyable, and its opposites. In this way our desires become structured and normalized." Ideology provides the structure of desire, indicating what we will long for and pursue. Finally, ideology defines the limits of expectation: "*what is possible* and impossible; our sense of the mutability of our being-in-the-world and the consequences of change are hereby patterned, and our hopes, ambitions, and fears given shape" (18). This last is especially important since recognition of the existence of a condition (poverty, for example) and the desire for its change will go for nothing if ideology indicates that a change is simply not possible (the poor we have always with us). In other words, this last mode of interpellation is especially implicated in power relationships in a group or society, in deciding who has power and in determining what power can be expected to achieve.

Ideology always carries with it strong social endorsement, so that what we take to exist, to have value, and to be possible seems necessary, normal and inevitable — in the nature of things. Ideology also, as we have seen, always includes conceptions of how power should — again, in the nature of things — be distributed in a society. Power here means political force but covers as well social forces in everyday contacts. Power is an intrinsic part of ideology, defined and reinforced by it, determining, once again, who can act and what can be accomplished. These power relationships, furthermore, are inscribed in the discursive practices of daily experience — in the ways we use language and are used (interpellated) by it in ordinary parlance. Finally, it should be noted that ideology is always pluralistic, a given historical moment displaying a variety of competing ideologies and a given individual reflecting one or another permutation of these conflicts, although the overall effect of these permutations tends to support the hegemony of the dominant class.

Cognitive Rhetoric

Cognitive rhetoric might be considered the heir apparent of current-traditional rhetoric, the rhetoric that appeared in conjunction with the new American university system during the final quarter of the last century. As Richard Ohmann has recently reminded us, this university was a response to the vagaries of competitive capitalism, the recurrent cycles of boom and bust that characterized the nineteenth-century economy. The university was an important part of the strategy to control this economic instability. Its role was to provide a center for experts engaging in "scientific" research designed to establish a body of knowledge that would rationalize all features of production, making it more efficient, more manageable, and, of course, more profitable. These experts were also charged with preparing the managers who were to take this new body of practical knowledge into the marketplace. The old nineteenth-century college had prepared an elite to assume its rightful place of leadership in church and state. The economic ideal outside the college was entirely separate, finding its fulfillment in the self-made, upwardly mobile entrepreneur who strikes it rich. The academic and the economic remained divided and discrete. In the new university, the two were joined as the path to success became a university degree in one of the new scientific specialities proven to be profitable in the world of industry and commerce. The new middle class of certified meritocrats had arrived. As I have indicated in my monograph on the nineteenth century, current-traditional rhetoric with its positivistic epistemology, its pretensions to scientific precision, and its managerial orientation was thoroughly compatible with the mission of this university.

Cognitive rhetoric has made similar claims to being scientific, although the method called upon is usually grounded in cognitive psychology. Janet Emig's *The Composing Process of Twelfth Graders* (1971), for example, attempted an empirical examination of the way students compose, calling on the developmental psychology of Jean Piaget in guiding her observations. In studying the cognitive skills observed in the composing behavior of twelve high school students, Emig was convinced that she could arrive at an understanding of the entire rhetorical context — the role of reality, audience, purpose, and even language in the composing act. Richard Larson was equally ambitious as throughout the seventies he called upon the developmental scheme of Jerome Bruner (as well as other psychologists) in proposing a problem-solving approach to writing, once again focusing on cognitive structures in arriving at an understanding of how college students compose. James Moffett and James Britton used a similar approach in dealing with the writing of students in grade school. For cognitive rhetoric, the structures of the mind correspond in perfect harmony with the structures of the material world, the minds of the audience, and the units of language (see my *Rhetoric and Reality* for a fuller discussion of this history). This school has been the strongest proponent of addressing the "process" rather than the "product" of writing in the classroom — although other theories have also supported this position even as they put forward a different process. Today the cognitivists continue to be a strong force in composition studies. The leading experimental research in this area is found in the work of Linda Flower and John Hayes, and I would like to focus the discussion of the relation of ideology and cognitive rhetoric on their contribution.

There is no question that Flower considers her work to fall within the domain of science, admitting her debt to cognitive psychology (Hayes's area of specialization), which she describes as "a young field — a reaction, in part, against assumptions of behaviorism" (vii). Her statements about the composing process of writing, furthermore, are based on empirical findings, on "data-based" study, specifically the analysis of protocols recording the writing choices of both experienced and inexperienced writers. This empirical study has revealed to Flower and Hayes — as reported in "A Cognitive Process Theory of Writing" — that there are three elements involved in composing: the task environment, including such external constraints as the rhetorical problem and the text so far produced; the writer's long-term memory, that is, the knowledge of the subject considered and the knowledge of how to write; and the writing processes that go on in the writer's mind. This last is, of course, of central importance to them, based as it is on the invariable structures of the mind that operate in a rational, although not totally predictable, way.

The mental processes of writing fall into three stages: the planning stage, further divided into generating, organizing, and goal setting; the translating stage, the point at which thoughts are put into words; and the reviewing stage, made up of evaluating and revising. This process is hierarchical, meaning that "components of the process [are] imbedded within other components" (Flower and Hayes 375), and it is recursive, the stages repeating themselves, although in no predetermined order. In other words, the elements of the process can be identified and their functions described, but the order of their operation will vary from task to task and from individual to individual, even though the practices of good writers will be very similar to each other (for a rich critique, see Bizzell). The "keystone" of the cognitive process theory, Flower and Hayes explain, is the discovery that writing is a goal-directed process: "In the act of composing, writers create a hierarchical network of goals and these in turn guide the writing process." Because of this goal-directedness, the protocols of good writers examined consistently "reveal a coherent underlying structure" (377).

It is clear from this brief description that Flower and Hayes focus on the individual mind, finding in the protocol reports evidence of cognitive structures in operation. Writing becomes, as Flower's textbook indicates, just another instance of "problem-solving processes people use every day," most importantly the processes of experts, such as "master chess players, inventors, successful scientists, business managers, and artists" (Flower 2–3). Flower's textbook says little about artists, however, focusing instead on "real-world" writing. She has accordingly called upon the help of a colleague from the School of Industrial Management (vi), and she includes a concern for consulting reports and proposals as well as ordinary academic research reports — "the real world of college and work" (4). This focus on the professional activity of experts is always conceived in personal and managerial terms: "In brief, the goal of this book is to help you gain more control of your own composing process: to become more efficient as a writer and more effective with your readers" (2). And the emphasis is on self-made goals, "on your own goals as a writer, on what you want to do and say" (3).

As I said at the outset, the rhetoric of cognitive psychology refuses the ideological question, resting secure instead in its scientific examination of the composing process. It is possible, however, to see this rhetoric as being eminently suited to appropriation by the proponents of a particular ideological stance, a stance consistent with the modern college's commitment to preparing students for the world of corporate capitalism. And as we have seen above, the professional orientation of *Problem-Solving Strategies for Writing* — its preoccupation with "analytical writing" (4) in the "real world" of experts — renders it especially open to this appropriation.

For cognitive rhetoric, the real is the rational. As we observed above, for Flower and Hayes the most important features of composing are those which can be analyzed into discrete units and expressed in linear, hierarchical terms, however unpredictably recursive these terms may be. The mind is regarded as a set of structures that performs in a rational manner, adjusting and reordering functions in the service of the goals of the individual. The goals themselves are considered unexceptionally apparent in the very nature of things, immediately identifiable as worthy of pursuit. Nowhere, for example, do Flower and Hayes question the worth of the goals pursued by the manager, scientist, or writer. The business of cognitive psychology is to enable us to learn to think in a way that will realize goals, not deliberate about their value: "I have assumed that, whatever your goals, you are interested in discovering better ways to achieve them" (Flower and Hayes 1). The world is correspondingly structured to foreground goals inherently worth pursuing — whether these are private or professional, in writing or in work. And the mind is happily structured to perceive these goals and, thanks to the proper cognitive development of the observer — usually an expert — to attain them. Obstacles to achieving these goals are labelled "problems," disruptions in the natural order, impediments that must be removed. The strategies to resolve these problems are called "heuristics," discovery procedures that "are the heart of problem solving" (36). Significantly, these heuristics are not themselves rational, are not linear and predictable — "they do not come with a guarantee" (37). They appear normally as unconscious, intuitive processes that problem solvers use without realizing it, but even when formulated for conscious application they are never foolproof. Heuristics are only as good or bad as the person using them, so that problem solving is finally the act of an individual performing in isolation, solitary and alone (see Brodkey). As Flower explains: "Good writers not only have a large repertory of powerful strategies, but they have sufficient self-awareness of their own process to draw on these alternative techniques as they need them. In other words, they guide their own creative process" (37). The community addressed enters the process only after problems are analyzed and solved, at which time the concern is "adapting your writing to the needs of the reader" (1). Furthermore, although the heuristics used in problem solving are not themselves rational, the discoveries made through them always conform to the mensurable nature of reality, displaying "an underlying hierarchical organization" (10) that reflects the rationality of the world. Finally, language is regarded as a system of rational signs that is compatible with the mind and the external world, enabling the "translating" or "transforming" of the nonverbal intellectual operations into the verbal. There is thus a beneficent correspondence between the structures of the mind, the structures of the world, the structures of the minds of the audience, and the structures of language.

This entire scheme can be seen as analogous to the instrumental method of the modern corporation, the place where members of the meritocratic middle class, the 20 percent or so of the work force of certified college graduates, make a handsome living managing a capitalist economy (see Braverman ch. 18). Their work life is designed to turn goal-seeking and problem-solving behavior into profits. As we have seen in Flower, the rationalization of the writing process is specifically designated an extension of the rationalization of economic activity. The pursuit of self-evident and unquestioned goals in the composing process parallels the pursuit of self-evident and unquestioned profit-making goals in the corporate marketplace: "whatever your goals are, you are interested in achieving better ways to achieve them" (Flower 12). The purpose of writing is to create a commodified text (see Clines) that belongs to the individual and has exchange value — "problem solving turns composing into a goal-directed journey — writing my way to where I want to be" (4) — just as the end of corporate activity is to create a privately-owned profit. Furthermore, while all problem solvers use heuristic procedures — whether in solving hierarchically conceived writing problems or hierarchically conceived management problems — some are better at using them than are others. These individuals inevitably distinguish themselves, rise up the corporate ladder, and leave the less competent and less competitive behind. The class system is thus validated since it is clear that the rationality of the universe is more readily detected by a certain group of individuals. Cognitive psychologists specializing in childhood development can even isolate the environmental features of the children who will become excellent problem solvers, those destined to earn the highest grades in school, the highest college entrance scores, and, finally, the highest salaries. Middle-class parents are thus led to begin the cultivation of their children's cognitive skills as soon as possible — even in utero — and of course there are no shortage of expert-designed commodities that can be purchased to aid in the activity. That the cognitive skills leading to success may be the product of the experiences of a particular social class rather than the perfecting of inherent mental structures, skills encouraged because they serve the interests of a ruling economic elite, is never considered in the "scientific" investigation of the mind.

Cognitive rhetoric can be seen from this perspective as compatible with the ideology of the meritocratic university described in Bowles and Gintis's *Schooling in Capitalist America.* Power in this system is relegated to university-certified experts, those individuals who have the cognitive skills and the training for problem solving. Since social, political, and cultural problems are, like the economic, the result of failures in rational goal-seeking behavior, these same experts are the best prepared to address these matters as well. Furthermore, the agreement of experts in addressing commonly shared problems in the economic and political arenas is additional confirmation of their claim to power: all trained observers, after all, come to the same conclusions. Once again, the possibility that this consensus about what is good and possible is a product of class interest and class experience is never seriously entertained. Cognitive rhetoric, then, in its refusal of the ideological question leaves itself open to association with the reification of technocratic science characteristic of late capitalism, as discussed, for example, by Georg Lukács, Herbert Marcuse, and Jürgen Habermas (see Larrain ch. 6). Certain structures of the material world, the mind, and language, and their correspondence with certain goals, problem-solving heuristics, and solutions in the economic, social, and political are regarded as inherent features of the universe, existing apart from human social intervention. The existent, the good, and the possible are inscribed in the very nature of things as indisputable scientific facts, rather than being seen as humanly devised social constructions always remaining open to discussion.

Expressionistic Rhetoric

Expressionistic rhetoric developed during the first two decades of the twentieth century and was especially prominent after World War I. Its earliest predecessor was the elitist rhetoric of liberal culture, a scheme arguing for writing as a gift of genius, an art accessible only to a few, and then requiring years of literary study. In expressionistic rhetoric, this gift is democratized, writing becoming an art of which all are capable. This rhetoric has usually been closely allied with theories of psychology that argued for the inherent goodness of the individual, a goodness distorted by excessive contact with others in groups and institutions. In this it is the descendant of Rousseau on the one hand and of the romantic recoil from the urban horrors created by nineteenth-century capitalism on the other. Left to our own devices, this position maintains, each of us would grow and mature in harmony. Unfortunately, hardly anyone is allowed this uninhibited development, and so the fallen state of society is both the cause and the effect of its own distortion, as well as the corrupter of its individual members. In the twenties, a bowdlerized version of Freud was called upon in support of this conception of human nature. More recently — during the sixties and after — the theories of such figures as Carl Rogers, Abraham Maslow, Eric Fromm, and even Carl Jung have been invoked in its support. (For a fuller discussion of the history and character of expressionistic rhetoric offered here, see my "Contemporary Composition," and *Rhetoric and Reality* 43–46, 73–81, 159–65.)

For this rhetoric, the existent is located within the individual subject. While the reality of the material, the social, and the linguistic are never denied, they are considered significant only insofar as they serve the needs of the individual. All fulfill their true function only when being exploited in the interests of locating the individual's authentic nature. Writing can be seen as a paradigmatic instance of this activity. It is an art, a creative act in which the process — the discovery of the true self — is as important as the product — the self discovered and expressed. The individual's use of the not-self in discovering the self takes place in a specific way. The material world provides sensory images that can be used in order to explore the self, the sensations leading to the apprehending-source of all experience. More important, these sense impressions can be coupled with language to provide metaphors to express the experience of the self, an experience which transcends ordinary non-metaphoric language but can be suggested through original figures and tropes. This original language in turn can be studied by others to understand the self and can even awaken in readers the experience of their selves. Authentic self-expression can thus lead to authentic self-experience for both the writer and the reader. The most important measure of authenticity, of genuine self-discovery and self-revelation, furthermore, is the presence of originality in expression; and this is the case whether the writer is creating poetry or writing a business report. Discovering the true self in writing will simultaneously enable the individual to discover the truth of the situation which evoked the writing, a situation that, needless to say, must always be compatible with the development of the self, and this leads to the ideological dimension of the scheme.

Most proponents of expressionistic rhetoric during the sixties and seventies were unsparingly critical of the dominant social, political, and cultural practices of the time. The most extreme of these critics demanded that the writing classroom work explicitly toward liberating students from the shackles of a corrupt society. This is seen most vividly in the effort known as "composition as happening." From this perspective, the alienating and fragmenting experience of the authoritarian institutional setting can be resisted by providing students with concrete experiences that alter political consciousness through challenging official versions of reality. Writing in response to such activities as making collages and sculptures, listening to the same piece of music in different settings, and engaging in random and irrational acts in the classroom was to enable students to experience "structure in unstructure; a random series of ordered events; order in chaos; the logical illogicality of dreams" (Lutz 35). The aim was to encourage students to resist the "interpretations of experience embodied in the language of others [so as] to order their own experience" (Paull and Kligerman 150). This more extreme form of political activism in the classroom was harshly criticized by the moderate wing of the expressionist camp, and it is this group that eventually became dominant. The names of Ken Macrorie, Walker Gibson, William Coles, Jr., Donald Murray, and Peter Elbow were the most visible in this counter effort. Significantly, these figures continued the ideological critique of the dominant culture while avoiding the overt politicizing of the classroom. In discussing the ideological position they encouraged, a position that continues to characterize them today, I will focus on the work of Murray and Elbow, both of whom explicitly address the political in their work.

From this perspective, power within society ought always to be vested in the individual. In Elbow, for example, power is an abiding concern — apparent in the title to his recent textbook *(Writing with Power)*, as well as in the opening pledge of his first to help students become "less helpless, both personally and politically" by enabling them to get "control over words" *(Writing without Teachers* vii). This power is consistently defined in personal terms: "power comes from the words somehow fitting the *writer* (not necessarily the reader) . . . power comes from the words somehow fitting *what they are about*" *(Writing with Power* 280). Power is a product of a configuration involving the individual and her encounter with the world, and for both Murray and Elbow this is a function of realizing one's unique voice. Murray's discussion of the place of politics in the classroom is appropriately titled "Finding Your Own Voice: Teaching Composition in an Age of Dissent," and Elbow emphasizes, "If I want power, I've got to use *my* voice" *(Embracing Contraries* 202). This focus on the individual does not mean that no community is to be encouraged, as expressionists repeatedly acknowledge that communal arrangements must be made, that, in Elbow's words, "the less acceptable hunger for participation and merging is met" (98). The community's right to exist, however, stands only insofar as it serves all of its members as individuals. It is, after all, only the individual, acting alone and apart from others, who can determine the existent, the good, and the possible. For Murray, the student "must hear the contradictory counsel of his readers, so that he learns when to ignore his teachers and his peers, listening to himself after evaluating what has been said about his writing and considering what he can do to make it work" ("Finding Your Own Voice" 144–45). For Elbow, the audience can be used to help improve our writing, but "the goal should be to move toward the condition where we don't necessarily need it in order to speak or write well." Since audiences can also inhibit us, Elbow continues, "we need to learn to write what is true and what needs saying even if the whole world is scandalized. We need to learn eventually to find in *ourselves* the support which — perhaps for a long time — we must seek openly from others" (*Writing with Power* 190).

Thus, political change can only be considered by individuals and in individual terms. Elbow, for example, praises Freire's focus on the individual in seeking the contradictions of experience in the classroom but refuses to take into account the social dimension of this pedagogy, finally using Freire's thought as an occasion for arriving at a personal realization of a "psychological contradiction, not an economic one or political one," at the core of our culture (*Embracing Contraries* 98). The underlying conviction of expressionists is that when individuals are spared the distorting effects of a repressive social order, their privately determined truths will correspond to the privately determined truths of all others: my best and deepest vision supports the same universal and eternal laws as everyone else's best and deepest vision. Thus, in *Writing without Teachers* Elbow admits that his knowledge about writing was gathered primarily from personal experience, and that he has no reservations about "making universal generalizations upon a sample of one" (16). Murray is even more explicit in his first edition of *A Writer Teaches Writing*: "the writer is on a search for himself. If he finds himself he will find an audience, because all of us have the same common core. And when he digs deeply into himself and is able to define himself, he will find others who will read with a shock of recognition what he has written" (4).

This rhetoric thus includes a denunciation of economic, political, and social pressures to conform — to engage in various forms of corporate-sponsored thought, feeling, and behavior. In indirectly but unmistakably decrying the dehumanizing effects of industrial capitalism, expressionistic rhetoric insists on defamiliarizing experience, on getting beyond the corruptions of the individual authorized by the language of commodified culture in order to re-experience the self and through it the external world, finding in this activity possibilities for a new order. For expressionistic rhetoric, the correct response to the imposition of current economic, political, and social arrangements is thus resistance, but a resistance that is always construed in individual terms. Collective retaliation poses as much of a threat to individual integrity as do the collective forces being resisted, and so is itself suspect. The only hope in a society working to destroy the uniqueness of the individual is for each of us to assert our individuality against the tyranny of the authoritarian corporation, state, and society. Strategies for doing so must of course be left to the individual, each lighting one small candle in order to create a brighter world.

Expressionistic rhetoric continues to thrive in high schools and at a number of colleges and universities. At first glance, this is surprising, unexpected of a rhetoric that is openly opposed to establishment practices. This subversiveness, however, is more apparent than real. In the first place, expressionistic rhetoric is inherently and debilitatingly divisive of political protest, suggesting that effective resistance can only be offered by individuals, each acting alone. Given the isolation and incoherence of such protest, gestures genuinely threatening to the establishment are difficult to accomplish. Beyond this, expressionistic rhetoric is easily co-opted by the very capitalist forces it opposes. After all, this rhetoric can be used to reinforce the entrepreneurial virtues capitalism most values: individualism, private initiative, the confidence for risk taking, the right to be contentious with authority (especially the state). It is indeed not too much to say that the ruling elites in business, industry, and government are those most likely to nod in assent to the ideology inscribed in expressionistic rhetoric. The members of this class see their lives as embodying the creative realization of the self, exploiting the material, social, and political conditions of the world in order to assert a private vision, a vision which, despite its uniqueness, finally represents humankind's best nature. (That this vision in fact represents the interests of a particular class, not all classes, is of course not acknowledged.) Those who have not attained the positions which enable them to exert this freedom have been prevented from doing so, this ideology argues, not by economic and class constraints, but by their own unwillingness to pursue a private vision, and this interpretation is often embraced by those excluded from the ruling elite as well as by the ruling elite itself. In other words, even those most constrained by their positions in the class structure may support the ideology found in expressionistic rhetoric in some form. This is most commonly done by divorcing the self from the alienation of work, separating work experience from other experience so that self-discovery and -fulfillment take place away from the job. For some this may lead to the pursuit of self-expression in intellectual or aesthetic pursuits. For most this quest results in a variety of forms of consumer behavior, identifying individual self-expression with the consumption of some commodity. This separation of work from authentic human activity is likewise reinforced in expressionistic rhetoric, as a glance at any of the textbooks it has inspired will reveal.

Social-Epistemic Rhetoric

The last rhetoric to be considered I will call social-epistemic rhetoric, in so doing distinguishing it from the psychological-epistemic rhetoric that I am convinced is a form of expressionism. (The latter is found in Kenneth Dowst and in Cyril Knoblauch and Lil Brannon, although Knoblauch's recent *College English* essay displays him moving into the social camp. I have discussed the notion of epistemic rhetoric and these two varieties of it in *Rhetoric and Reality* 145–55, 165–77, and 184–85.) There have been a number of spokespersons for social-epistemic rhetoric over the last twenty years: Kenneth Burke, Richard Ohmann, the team of Richard Young, Alton Becker and Kenneth Pike, Kenneth Bruffee, W. Ross Winterowd, Ann Berthoff, Janice Lauer, and, more recently, Karen Burke Lefevre, Lester Faigley, David Bartholomae, Greg

Myers, Patricia Bizzell, and others. In grouping these figures together I do not intend to deny their obvious disagreements with each other. For example, Myers, a Leftist, has offered a lengthy critique of Bruffee, who — along with Winterowd and Young, Becker and Pike — is certainly of the Center politically. There are indeed as many conflicts among the members of this group as there are harmonies. They are brought together here, however, because they share a notion of rhetoric as a political act involving a dialectical interaction engaging the material, the social, and the individual writer, with language as the agency of mediation. Their positions, furthermore, include an historicist orientation, the realization that a rhetoric is an historically specific social formation that must perforce change over time; and this feature in turn makes possible reflexiveness and revision as the inherently ideological nature of rhetoric is continually acknowledged. The most complete realization of this rhetoric for the classroom is to be found in Ira Shor's *Critical Teaching and Everyday Life.* Before considering it, I would like to discuss the distinguishing features of a fully articulated social-epistemic rhetoric.

For social-epistemic rhetoric, the real is located in a relationship that involves the dialectical interaction of the observer, the discourse community (social group) in which the observer is functioning, and the material conditions of existence. Knowledge is never found in any one of these but can only be posited as a product of the dialectic in which all three come together. (More of this in a moment.) Most important, this dialectic is grounded in language: the observer, the discourse community, and the material conditions of existence are all verbal constructs. This does not mean that the three do not exist apart from language: they do. This does mean that we cannot talk and write about them — indeed, we cannot know them — apart from language. Furthermore, since language is a social phenomenon that is a product of a particular historical moment, our notions of the observing self, the communities in which the self functions, and the very structures of the material world are social constructions — all specific to a particular time and culture. These social constructions are thus inscribed in the very language we are given to inhabit in responding to our experience. Language, as Raymond Williams explains in an application of Bakhtin (*Marxism and Literature* 21–44), is one of the material and social conditions involved in producing a culture. This means that in studying rhetoric — the ways discourse is generated — we are studying the ways in which knowledge comes into existence. Knowledge, after all, is an historically bound social fabrication rather than an eternal and invariable phenomenon located in some uncomplicated repository — in the material object or in the subject or in the social realm. This brings us back to the matter of the dialectic.

Understanding this dialectical notion of knowledge is the most difficult feature of social-epistemic rhetoric. Psychological-epistemic rhetoric grants that rhetoric arrives at knowledge, but this meaning-generating activity is always located in a transcendent self, a subject who directs the discovery and arrives through it finally only at a better understanding of the self and its operation — this self-comprehension being the end of all knowledge. For social-epistemic rhetoric, the subject is itself a social construct that emerges through the linguistically circumscribed interaction of the individual, the community, and the material world. There is no universal, eternal, and authentic self that beneath all appearances is at one with all other selves. The self is always a creation of a particular historical and cultural moment. This is not to say that individuals do not ever act as individuals. It is to assert, however, that they never act with complete freedom. As Marx indicated, we make our own histories, but we do not make them just as we wish. Our consciousness is in large part a product of our material conditions. But our material conditions are also in part the products of our consciousness. Both consciousness and the material conditions influence each other, and they are both imbricated in social relations defined and worked out through language. In other words, the ways in which the subject understands and is affected by material conditions is circumscribed by socially devised definitions, by the community in which the subject lives. The community in turn is influenced by the subject and the material conditions of the moment. Thus, the perceiving subject, the discourse communities of which the subject is a part, and the material world itself are all the constructions of an historical discourse, of the ideological formulations inscribed in the language-mediated practical activity of a particular time and place. We are lodged within a hermeneutic circle, although not one that is impervious to change.

This scheme does not lead to an anarchistic relativism. It does, however, indicate that arguments based on the permanent rational structures of the universe or on the evidence of the deepest and most profound personal intuition should not be accepted without question. The material, the social, and the subjective are at once the producers and the products of ideology, and ideology must continually be challenged so as to reveal its economic and political consequences for individuals. In other words, what are the effects of our knowledge? Who benefits from a given version of truth? How are the material benefits of society distributed? What is the relation of this distribution to social relations? Do these relations encourage conflict? To whom does our knowledge designate power? In short, social-epistemic rhetoric views knowledge as an arena of ideological conflict: there are no arguments from transcendent truth since all arguments arise in ideology. It thus inevitably supports economic, social, political, and cultural democracy. Because there are no "natural laws" or "universal truths" that indicate what exists, what is good, what is possible, and how power is to be distributed, no class or group or individual has privileged access to decisions on these matters. They must be continually decided by all and for all in a way appropriate to our own historical moment. Finally, because of this historicist orientation, social-epistemic rhetoric contains within it the means for self-criticism and self-revision. Human responses to the material conditions of existence, the social relations they encourage, and the interpellations of subjects within them are always already ideological, are always already interpretations that must be constantly revised in the interests of the greater participation of all, for the greater good of all. And this of course implies an awareness of the ways in which rhetorics can privilege some at the expense of others, according the chosen few an unequal share of power, perquisites, and material benefits.

Social-epistemic rhetoric thus offers an explicit critique of economic, political, and social arrangements, the counterpart of the implicit critique found in expressionistic rhetoric. However, here the source and the solution of these arrangements are described quite differently. As Ira Shor explains, students must be taught to identify the ways in which control over their own lives has been denied them, and denied in such a way that they have blamed themselves for their powerlessness. Shor thus situates the individual within social processes, examining in detail the interferences to critical thought that would enable "students to be their own agents for social change, their own creators of democratic culture" (48). Among the most important forces preventing work toward a social order supporting the student's "full humanity" are forms of false consciousness — reification, pre-scientific thought, acceleration, mystification — and the absence of democratic practices in all areas of experience. Although Shor discusses these forms of false consciousness in their relation to working-class students, their application to all students is not hard to see, and I have selected for emphasis those features which clearly so apply.

In falling victim to reification, students begin to see the economic and social system that renders them powerless as an innate and unchangeable feature of the natural order. They become convinced that change is impossible, and they support the very practices that victimize them — complying in their alienation from their work, their peers, and their very selves. The most common form of reification has to do with the preoccupation with consumerism, playing the game of material acquisition and using it as a substitute for more self-fulfilling behavior. In pre-scientific thinking, the student is led to believe in a fixed human nature, always and everywhere the same. Behavior that is socially and self-destructive is then seen as inevitable, in the nature of things, or can be resisted only at the individual level, apart from communal activity. Another form of pre-scientific thinking is the belief in luck, in pure chance, as the source of social arrangements, such as the inequitable distribution of wealth. The loyalty to brand names, the faith in a "common sense" that supports the existing order, and the worship of heroes, such as actors and athletes, are other forms of this kind of thought, all of which prevent "the search for rational explanations to authentic problems" (66). Acceleration refers to the pace of everyday experience — the sensory bombardment of urban life and of popular forms of entertainment — which prevents critical reflection. Mystifications are responses to the problems of a capitalist society which obscure their real sources and solutions, responses based on racism, sexism, nationalism, and other forms of bigotry. Finally, students are constantly told they live in the most free, most democratic society in the world, yet they are at the same time systematically denied opportunities for "self-discipline, self-organization, collective work styles, or group deliberation" (70), instead being subjected at every turn to arbitrary authority in conducting everyday affairs.

Shor's recommendations for the classroom grow out of an awareness of these forces and are intended to counter them. The object of this pedagogy is to enable students to *"extraordinarily reexperience the ordinary"* (93), as they critically examine their quotidian experience in order to externalize false consciousness. (Shor's use of the term "critical" is meant to recall Freire as well as the practice of the Hegelian Marxists of the Frankfurt School.) The point is to "address self-in-society and social-relations-in-self" (95). The self then is regarded as the product of a dialectical relationship between the individual and the social, each given significance by the other. Self-autonomy and self-fulfillment are thus possible not through becoming detached from the social, but through resisting those social influences that alienate and disempower, doing so, moreover, in and through social activity. The liberatory classroom begins this resistance process with a dialogue that inspires "a democratic model of social relations, used to problematize the undemocratic quality of social life" (95). This dialogue — a model inspired by Paulo Freire — makes teacher and learner equals engaged in a joint practice that is "[l]oving, humble, hopeful, trusting, critical" (95). This is contrasted with the unequal power relations in the authoritarian classroom, a place where the teacher holds all power and knowledge and the student is the receptacle into which information is poured, a classroom that is "[l]oveless, arrogant, hopeless, mistrustful, acritical" (95). Teacher and student work together to shape the content of the liberatory classroom, and this includes creating the materials of study in the class — such as textbooks and media. Most important, the students are to undergo a conversion from "manipulated objects into active, critical subjects" (97), thereby empowering them to become agents of social change rather than victims. Shor sums up these elements: "social practice is studied in the name of freedom for critical consciousness; democracy and awareness develop through the form of dialogue; dialogue externalizes false consciousness, changing students from re-active objects into society-making subjects: the object-subject switch is a social psychology for empowerment; power through study creates the conditions for reconstructing social practice" (98).

This approach in the classroom requires interdisciplinary methods, and Shor gives an example from the study of the fast-food hamburger: "Concretely my class's study of hamburgers not only involved English and philosophy in our use of writing, reading, and conceptual analysis, but it also included economics in the study of the commodity relations which bring hamburgers to market, history and sociology in an assessment of what the everyday diet was like prior to the rise of the hamburger, and health science in terms of the nutritional value of the ruling burger" (114). This interdisciplinary approach to the study of the reproduction of social life can also lead to "the unveiling of hidden social history" (115), the discovery of past attempts to resist self-destructive experience. This in turn can lead to an examination of the roots of sexism and racism in our culture. Finally, Shor calls upon comedy to reunite pleasure and work, thought and feeling, and upon a resourceful use of the space of the classroom to encourage dialogue that provides students with information withheld elsewhere on campus — "informational, conceptual, personal, academic, financial" (120) — ranging from the location of free or inexpensive services to the location of political rallies.

This survey of the theory and practice of Ira Shor's classroom is necessarily brief and reductive. Still, it suggests the complexity of the behavior recommended in the classroom, behavior that is always open-ended, receptive to the unexpected, and subversive of the planned. Most important, success in this classroom can never by guaranteed. This is a place based on dialectical collaboration — the interaction of student, teacher, and shared experience within a social, interdisciplinary framework — and the outcome is always unpredictable. Yet, as Shor makes clear, the point of this classroom is that the liberated consciousness of students is the only educational objective worth considering, the only objective worth the risk of failure. To succeed at anything else is no success at all.

It should now be apparent that a way of teaching is never innocent. Every pedagogy is imbricated in ideology, in a set of tacit assumptions about what is real, what is good, what is possible, and how power ought to be distributed. The method of cognitive psychology is the most likely to ignore this contention, claiming that the rhetoric it recommends is based on an objective understanding of the unchanging structures of mind, matter, and language. Still, despite its commitment to the empirical and scientific, as we have seen, this rhetoric can easily be made to serve specific kinds of economic, social, and political behavior that works to the advantage of the members of one social class while disempowering others — doing so, moreover, in the name of objective truth. Expressionistic rhetoric is intended to serve as a critique of the ideology of corporate capitalism, proposing in its place an ideology based on a radical individualism. In the name of empowering the individual, however, its naivete about economic, social, and political arrangements can lead to the marginalizing of the individuals who would resist a dehumanizing society, rendering them ineffective through their isolation. This rhetoric also is easily co-opted by the agencies of corporate capitalism, appropriated and distorted in the service of the mystifications of bourgeois individualism. Social-epistemic rhetoric attempts to place the question of ideology at the center of the teaching of writing. It offers both a detailed analysis of dehumanizing social experience and a self-critical and overtly historicized alternative based on democratic practices in the economic, social, political, and cultural spheres. It is obvious that I find this alternative the most worthy of emulation in the classroom, all the while admitting that it is the least formulaic and the most difficult to carry out. I would also add that even those who are skeptical of the Marxian influence found in my description of this rhetoric have much to learn from it. As Kenneth Burke has shown, one does not have to accept the Marxian premise in order to realize the value of the Marxian diagnosis (109). It is likewise not necessary to accept the conclusions of Ira Shor about writing pedagogy in order to learn from his analysis of the ideological practices at work in the lives of our students and ourselves. A rhetoric cannot escape the ideological question, and to ignore this is to fail our responsibilities as teachers and as citizens.

Works Cited

Bartholomae, David. "Inventing the University." *When a Writer Can't Write: Research on Writer's Block and Other Writing Problems.* Ed. Mike Rose. New York: Guilford, 1986.

Berlin, James A. "Contemporary Composition: The Major Pedagogical Theories." *College English* 44 (1982): 765–77.

———. *Rhetoric and Reality: Writing Instruction in American Colleges, 1900–1985.* Carbondale: Southern Illinois UP, 1987.

———. *Writing Instruction in Nineteenth-Century American Colleges.* Carbondale: Southern Illinois UP, 1984.

Bizzell, Patricia. "Cognition, Convention, and Certainty: What We Need to Know about Writing." *PRETEXT* 3 (1982): 213–43.

Bowles, Samuel, and Herbert Gintis. *Schooling in Capitalist America.* New York: Basic, 1976.

Braverman, Harry. *Labor and Monopoly Capital: The Degradation of Work in the Twentieth Century.* New York: Monthly Review P, 1974.

Brodkey, Linda. "Modernism and the Scene of Writing." *College English* 49 (1987): 396–418.

Bruner, Jerome S. *The Process of Education.* Cambridge: Harvard UP, 1960.

Burke, Kenneth. *A Rhetoric of Motives.* Berkeley: U of California P, 1969.

Clifford, John, and John Schilb. "A Perspective on Eagleton's Revival of Rhetoric." *Rhetoric Review* 6 (1987): 22–31.

Clines, Ray. "Composition and Capitalism." *Progressive Composition* 14 (Mar. 1987): 4–5.

Dowst, Kenneth. "The Epistemic Approach: Writing, Knowing, and Learning." *Eight Approaches to Teaching Composition.* Ed. Timothy Donovan and Ben W. McClelland. Urbana: NCTE, 1980.

———. "An Epistemic View of Sentence Combining: A Rhetorical Perspective." *Sentence Combining: A Rhetorical Perspective.* Eds. Donald A. Daiker, Andrew Kerek, and Max Morenberg. Carbondale: Southern Illinois UP, 1986. 321–33.

Elbow, Peter. *Embracing Contraries: Explorations in Learning and Teaching.* New York: Oxford, 1981.

———. *Writing without Teachers.* New York: Oxford UP, 1973.

———. *Writing with Power: Techniques for Mastering the Writing Process.* New York: Oxford UP, 1981.

Emig, Janet. *The Composing Process of Twelfth Graders.* Research Report No. 13. Urbana: NCTE, 1971.

Flower, Linda. *Problem-Solving Strategies for Writing.* 2nd ed. San Diego: Harcourt, 1985.

Flower, Linda, and John R. Hayes. "A Cognitive Process Theory of Writing." *College Composition and Communication* 32 (1981): 365–87.

Knoblauch, C. H. "Rhetorical Constructions: Dialogue and Commitment." *College English* 50 (1988): 125–40.

Knoblauch, C. H., and Lil Brannon. *Rhetorical Traditions and the Teaching of Writing.* Upper Montclair: Boynton, 1984.

Larrain, Jorge. *The Concept of Ideology.* Athens: U of Georgia P, 1979.

Larson, Richard. "Discovery through Questioning: A Plan for Teaching Rhetorical Invention." *College English* 30 (1968): 126–34.

———. "Invention Once More: A Role for Rhetorical Analysis." *College English* 32 (1971): 665–72.

———. "Problem-Solving, Composing, and Liberal Education." *College Composition and Communication* 23 (1972): 208–10.

Lutz, William D. "Making Freshman English a Happening." *College Composition and Communication* 22 (1971): 35–38.

Murray, Donald. "Finding Your Own Voice: Teaching Composition in an Age of Dissent." *College Composition and Communication* 20 (1969): 118–23.

———. *A Writer Teaches Writing.* Boston: Houghton, 1968.

Myers, Greg. "Reality, Consensus, and Reform in the Rhetoric of Composition Teaching." *College English* 48 (1986): 154–74.

Ohmann, Richard. "Literacy, Technology, and Monopoly Capital." *College English* 47 (1985): 675–89.

Paull, Michael, and Jack Kligerman. "Invention, Composition, and the Urban College." *College English* 33 (1972): 651–59.

Shor, Ira. *Critical Teaching and Everyday Life.* 1980. Chicago: U of Chicago P, 1987.

Therborn, Göran. *The Ideology of Power and the Power of Ideology.* London: Verso, 1980.

Vitanza, Victor. "'Notes' towards Historiographies of Rhetorics; or, Rhetorics of the Histories of Rhetorics: Traditional, Revisionary, and Sub/Versive." *PRETEXT* 8 (1987): 63–125.

Williams, Raymond. *Keywords: A Vocabulary of Culture and Society.* Rev. ed. New York: Oxford UP, 1977.

———. *Marxism and Literature.* New York: Oxford UP, 1977.

Berlin's Insights as a Resource for Your Teaching

1. Make some notes on the ideology that dominates your own teaching. Which moments in your classroom practice most clearly illustrate your commitment to this ideology? What moments suggest that your classroom practice incorporates more than one ideology? While Berlin's tripartite model is a powerful tool for organizing our sense of what goes on in our classroom, actual practice is far too "messy" to be contained and fully delineated by such a simplistic model. Explore ways in which certain aspects of

your teaching advance more than one ideology. Are some of your assignments driven by all three modes?

2. Which of Berlin's approaches to writing instruction do your students seem most inclined to accept? Do you have some budding expressionists in your classroom? Do you have any cognitivists on board? Consider ways of using ideological differences among your students as the basis for class discussion, even for writing.

Berlin's Insights as a Resource for Your Writing Classroom

1. Classroom reality is always more complex than any clear-cut taxonomy or model. Monitor your teaching for a few weeks to see how the more successful moments in class discussion are grounded in ideology. If you find that you get the best results when you are an expressivist, then examine what within this approach causes the success. Can it be combined with the more appealing elements of other ideologies?

2. Have students write brief, informal accounts of how they see themselves as writers. Read through these accounts with Berlin's taxonomy in mind. Which ideologies rule your students' self-conceptions? Do ideological patterns emerge in the accounts of strong students as opposed to weak students? How might you use Berlin's thinking to address weaker students?

Inventing the University

David Bartholomae

In this classic statement about the overall aims of the composition classroom, David Bartholomae argues that we must, above all, enable our students to participate in the discourses of the academy. These discourses embody the "conventional" ideals of skepticism and critique and require those who participate in them to move beyond what have traditionally been considered, by comparison, naive clichés and commonplaces that more often characterize personal writing. Bartholomae is chiefly interested in bringing students to share in the authority that the academic institution makes available; in order to do so, he argues, we must teach students to acquire those particular habits of mind that are the mark of that authority.

Education may well be, as of right, the instrument whereby every individual, in a society like our own, can gain access to any kind of discourse. But we well know that in its distribution, in what it permits and in what it prevents, it follows the well-trodden battle-lines of social conflict. Every educational system is a political means of maintaining or of modifying the appropriation of discourse, with the knowledge and the powers it carries with it.

— Foucault, *The Discourse on Language*

. . . the text is the form of the social relationships made visible, palpable, material.

— Bernstein, *Codes, Modalities and the Process*
of Cultural Reproduction: A Model

I

Every time a student sits down to write for us, he has to invent the university for the occasion — invent the university, that is, or a branch of it, like history or anthropology or economics or English. The student has to learn to speak our language, to speak as we do, to try on the peculiar ways of knowing, selecting, evaluating, reporting, concluding, and arguing that define the discourse of our community. Or perhaps I should say the *various* discourses of our community, since it is in the nature of a liberal arts education that a student, after the first year or two, must learn to try on a variety of voices and interpretive schemes — to write, for example, as a literary critic one day and as an experimental psychologist the next; to work within fields where the rules governing the presentation of examples or the development of an argument are both distinct and, even to a professional, mysterious.

The student has to appropriate (or be appropriated by) a specialized discourse, and he has to do this as though he were easily and comfortably one with his audience, as though he were a member of the academy or an historian or an anthropologist or an economist; he has to invent the university by assembling and mimicking its language while finding some compromise between idiosyncrasy, a personal history, on the one hand, and the requirements of convention, the history of a discipline, on the other hand. He must learn to speak our language. Or he must dare to speak it or to carry off the bluff, since speaking and writing will most certainly be required long before the skill is "learned." And this, understandably, causes problems.

Let me look quickly at an example. Here is an essay written by a college freshman.

In the past time I thought that an incident was creative was when I had to make a clay model of the earth, but not of the classical or your everyday model of the earth which consists of the two cores, the mantle and the crust. I thought of these things in a dimension of which it would be unique, but easy to comprehend. Of course, your materials to work with were basic and limited at the same time, but thought help to put this limit into a right attitude or frame of mind to work with the clay.

In the beginning of the clay model, I had to research and learn the different dimensions of the earth (in magnitude, quantity, state of matter, etc.) After this, I learned how to put this into the clay and come up with something different than any other person in my class at the time. In my opinion, color coordination and shape was the key to my creativity of the clay model of the earth.

Creativity is the venture of the mind at work with the mechanics relay to the limbs from the cranium, which stores and triggers this action. It can be a burst of energy released at a precise time a thought is being transmitted. This can cause a frenzy of the human body, but it depends on the characteristics of the individual and how they can relay the message clearly enough through mechanics of the body to us as an observer. Then we must determine if it is creative or a learned process varied by the individuals thought process. Creativity is indeed a tool which has to exist, or our world will not succeed into the future and progress like it should.

I am continually impressed by the patience and goodwill of our students. This student was writing a placement essay during freshman orientation. (The problem set to him was: "Describe a time when you did something you felt to be creative. Then, on the basis of the incident you have described, go on to draw some general conclusions about 'creativity.'") He knew that university faculty would be reading and evaluating his essay, and so he wrote for them.

In some ways it is a remarkable performance. He is trying on the discourse even though he doesn't have the knowledge that would make the discourse more than a routine, a set of conventional rituals and gestures. And he is doing this, I think, even though he *knows* he doesn't have the knowledge that would make the discourse more than a routine. He defines himself as a researcher working systematically, and not as a kid in a high school class: "I thought of these things in a dimension of . . ."; "I had to research and learn the different dimensions of the earth (in magnitude, quantity, state of matter, etc.)." He moves quickly into a specialized language (his approximation of our jargon) and draws both a general, textbook-like conclusion — "Creativity is the venture of the mind at work . . ." — and a resounding peroration — "Creativity is indeed a tool which has to exist, or our world will not succeed into the future and progress like it should." The writer has even picked up the rhythm of our prose with that last "indeed" and with the qualifications and the parenthetical expressions of the opening paragraphs. And through it all he speaks with an impressive air of authority.

There is an elaborate but, I will argue, a necessary and enabling fiction at work here as the student dramatizes his experience in a "setting" — the setting required by the discourse — where he can speak to us as a companion, a fellow researcher. As I read the essay, there is only one moment when the fiction is broken, when we are addressed differently. The student says, "Of course, your materials to work with were basic and limited at the same time, but thought help to put this limit into a right attitude or frame of mind to work with the clay." At this point, I think, we become students and he the teacher giving us a lesson (as in, "You take your pencil in your right hand and put your paper in front of you"). This is, however, one of the most characteristic slips of basic writers. (I use the term "basic writers" to refer to university students traditionally placed in remedial composition courses.) It is very hard for them to take on the role — the voice, the persona — of an authority whose authority is rooted in scholarship, analysis, or research. They slip, then, into a more immediately available and realizable voice of authority, the voice of a teacher giving a lesson or the voice of a parent lecturing at the dinner table. They offer advice or homilies rather than "academic" conclusions. There is a similar break in the final paragraph, where the conclusion that pushes for a definition ("Creativity is the venture of the mind at work with the mechanics relay to the limbs from the cranium") is replaced by a conclusion that speaks in the voice of an elder ("Creativity is indeed a tool which has to exist, or our world will not succeed into the future and progress like it should").

It is not uncommon, then, to find such breaks in the concluding sections of essays written by basic writers. Here is the concluding section of an essay written by a student about his work as a mechanic. He had been asked to generalize about work after reviewing an on-the-job experience or incident that "stuck in his mind" as somehow significant.

> How could two repairmen miss a leak? Lack of pride? No incentive? Lazy? I don't know.

At this point the writer is in a perfect position to speculate, to move from the problem to an analysis of the problem. Here is how the paragraph continues, however (and notice the change in pronoun reference).

> From this point on, I take *my* time, do it right, and don't let customers get under *your* skin. If they have a complaint, tell them to call your boss and he'll be more than glad to handle it. Most important, worry about yourself, and keep a clear eye on everyone, for there's always someone trying to take advantage of you, anytime and anyplace. (Emphasis added)

We get neither a technical discussion nor an "academic" discussion but a Lesson on Life.[1] This is the language he uses to address the general question, "How could two repairmen miss a leak?" The other brand of conclusion, the more academic one, would have required him to speak of his experience in our terms; it would, that is, have required a special vocabulary, a special system of presentation, and an interpretive scheme (or a set of commonplaces) he could have used to identify and talk about the mystery of human error. The writer certainly had access to the range of acceptable commonplaces for such an explanation: "lack of pride," "no incentive," "lazy." Each commonplace would dictate its own set of phrases, examples, and conclusions; and we, his teachers, would know how to write out each argument, just as we know how to write out more specialized arguments of our own. A "commonplace," then, is a culturally or institutionally authorized concept or statement that carries with it its own necessary elaboration. We all use commonplaces to orient ourselves in the world; they provide points of reference and a set of "prearticulated" explanations that are readily available to organize and interpret experience. The phrase "lack of pride" carries with it its own account of the repairman's error, just as at another point in time a reference to "original sin" would have provided an explanation, or just as in certain university classrooms a reference to "alienation" would enable writers to continue and complete the discussion. While there is a way in which these terms are interchangeable, they are not all permissible: A student in a composition class would most likely be turned away from a discussion of original sin. Commonplaces are the "controlling ideas" of our composition textbooks, textbooks that not only insist on a set form for expository writing but a set view of public life.[2]

When the writer says, "I don't know," then, he is not saying that he has nothing to say. He is saying that he is not in a position to carry on this discussion. And so we are addressed as apprentices rather than as teachers or scholars. In order to speak as a person of status or privilege, the writer can either speak to us in our terms — in the privileged language of university discourse — or, in default (or in defiance) of that, he can speak to us as though we were children, offering us the wisdom of experience.

I think it is possible to say that the language of the "Clay Model" paper has come *through* the writer and not from the writer. The writer has located himself (more precisely, he has located the self that is represented by the "I" on the page) in a context that is finally beyond him, not his own and not available to his immediate procedures for inventing and arranging text. I would not, that is, call this essay an example of "writer-based" prose. I would not say that it is egocentric or that it represents the "interior monologue or a writer thinking and talking to himself" (Flower, 1981, p. 63). It is, rather, the record of a writer who has lost himself in the discourse of his readers. There is a context beyond the intended reader that is not the world but a way of talking about the world, a way of talking that determines the use of examples, the possible conclusions, acceptable commonplaces, and key words for an essay on the construction of a clay model of the earth. This writer has entered the discourse without successfully approximating it.

Linda Flower (1981) has argued that the difficulty inexperienced writers have with writing can be understood as a difficulty in negotiating the transition between "writer-based" and "reader-based" prose. Expert writers, in other words, can better imagine how a reader will respond to a text and can transform or restructure what they have to say around a goal shared with a reader. Teaching students to revise for readers, then, will better prepare them to write initially with a reader in mind. The success of this pedagogy depends on the degree to which a writer can imagine and conform to a reader's goals. The difficulty of this act of imagination and the burden of such conformity are so much at the heart of the problem that a teacher must pause and take stock before offering revision as a solution. A student like the one who wrote the "Clay Model" paper is not so much trapped in a private language as he is shut out from one of the privileged languages of public life, a language he is aware of but cannot control.

II

Our students, I've said, have to appropriate (or be appropriated by) a specialized discourse, and they have to do this as though they were easily or comfortably one with their audience. If you look at the situation this way, suddenly the problem of audience awareness becomes enormously complicated. One of the common assumptions of both composition research and composition teaching is that at some "stage" in the process of composing an essay a writer's ideas or his motives must be tailored to the needs and expectations of his audience. Writers have to "build bridges" between their point of view and the reader's. They have to anticipate and acknowledge the reader's assumptions and biases. They must begin with "common points of departure" before introducing new or controversial arguments. Here is what one of the most popular college textbooks says to students.

> Once you have your purpose clearly in mind, your next task is to define and analyze your audience. A sure sense of your audience — knowing who it is and what assumptions you can reasonably make about it — is crucial to the success of your rhetoric. (Hairston, 1978, p. 107)

It is difficult to imagine, however, how writers can have a purpose before they are located in a discourse, since it is the discourse with its projects and agendas that determines what writers can and will do. The writer who can successfully manipulate an audience (or, to use a less pointed language, the writer who can accommodate her motives to her reader's expectations) is a writer who can both imagine and write from a position of privilege. She must, that is, see herself within a privileged discourse, one that already includes and excludes groups of readers. She must be either equal to or more powerful than those she would address. The writing, then, must somehow transform the political and social relationships between students and teachers.

If my students are going to write for me by knowing who I am — and if this means more than knowing my prejudices, psyching me out — it means knowing what I know; it means having the knowledge of a professor of English. They have, then, to know what I know and how I know what I know (the interpretive schemes that define the way I would work out the problems I set for them); they have to learn to write what I would write or to offer up some approximation of that discourse. The problem of audience awareness, then, is a problem of power and finesse. It cannot be addressed, as it is in most classroom exercises, by giving students privilege and denying the situation of the classroom — usually, that is, by having students write to an outsider, someone excluded from their privileged circle: "Write about 'To His Coy Mistress,' not for your teacher but for the students in your class"; "Describe Pittsburgh to someone who has never been there"; "Explain to a high school senior how best to prepare for college"; "Describe baseball to an Eskimo." Exercises such as these allow students to imagine the needs and goals of a reader, and they bring those needs and goals forward as a dominant constraint in the construction of an essay. And they argue, implicitly, what is generally true about writing — that it is an act of aggression disguised as an act of charity. What these assignments fail to address is the central problem of academic writing, where a student must assume the right of speaking to someone who knows more about baseball or "To His Coy Mistress" than the student does, a reader for whom the general commonplaces and the readily available utterances about a subject are inadequate.

Linda Flower and John Hayes, in an often quoted article (1981), reported on a study of a protocol of an expert writer (an English teacher) writing about his job for readers of *Seventeen* magazine. The key moment for this writer, who seems to have been having trouble getting started, came when he decided that teenage girls read *Seventeen*; that some teenage girls like English because it is tidy ("some of them will have wrong reasons in that English is good because it's tidy — can be a neat tidy little girl"); that some don't like it because it is "prim" and that, "By God, I can change that notion for them." Flower and Hayes's conclusion is that this effort of "exploration and consolidation" gave the writer "a new, relatively complex, rhetorically sophisticated working goal, one which encompasses plans for topic, a persona, and the audience" (p. 383).[3]

Flower and Hayes give us a picture of a writer solving a problem, and the problem as they present it is a cognitive one. It is rooted in the way the writer's knowledge is represented in the writer's mind. The problem resides there, not in the nature of knowledge or in the nature of discourse but in a mental state prior to writing. It is possible, however, to see the problem as (perhaps simultaneously) a problem in the way subjects are located in a field of discourse.

Flower and Hayes divide up the composing process into three distinct activities: "planning or goal-setting," "translating," and "reviewing." The last of these, reviewing (which is further divided into two subprocesses, "evaluating" and "revising"), is particularly powerful, for as a writer continually generates new goals, plans, and text, he is engaging in a process of learning and discovery. Let me quote Flower and Hayes's conclusion at length.

> If one studies the process by which a writer uses a goal to generate ideas, then consolidates those ideas and uses them to revise or regenerate new, more complex goals, one can see this learning process in action.

> Furthermore, one sees why the process of revising and clarifying goals has such a broad effect, since it is through setting these new goals that the fruits of discovery come back to inform the continuing process of writing. In this instance, some of our most complex and imaginative acts can depend on the elegant simplicity of a few powerful thinking processes. We feel that a cognitive process explanation of discovery, toward which this theory is only a start, will have another special strength. By placing emphasis on the inventive power of the writer, who is able to explore ideas, to develop, act on, test, and regenerate his or her own goals, we are putting an important part of creativity where it belongs — in the hands of the working, thinking writer. (1981, p. 386)

While this conclusion is inspiring, the references to invention and creativity seem to refer to something other than an act of writing — if writing is, finally, words on a page. Flower and Hayes locate the act of writing solely within the mind of the writer. The act of writing, here, has a personal, cognitive history but not a history as a text, as a text that is made possible by prior texts. When located in the perspective afforded by prior texts, writing is seen to exist separate from the writer and his intentions; it is seen in the context of other articles in *Seventeen*, of all articles written for or about women, of all articles written about English teaching, and so on. Reading research has made it possible to say that these prior texts, or a reader's experience with these prior texts, have bearing on how the text is read. Intentions, then, are part of the history of the language itself. I am arguing that these prior texts determine not only how a text like the *Seventeen* article will be read but also how it will be written. Flower and Hayes show us what happens in the writer's mind but not what happens to the writer as his motives are located within our language, a language with its own requirements and agendas, a language that limits what we might say and that makes us write and sound, finally, also like someone else. If you think of other accounts of the composing process — and I'm thinking of accounts as diverse as Richard Rodriguez's *Hunger of Memory* (1983) and Edward Said's *Beginnings* (1975) — you get a very different account of what happens when private motive enters into public discourse, when a personal history becomes a public account. These accounts place the writer in a history that is not of the writer's own invention; and they are chronicles of loss, violence, and compromise.

It is one thing to see the *Seventeen* writer making and revising his plans for a topic, a persona, and an audience; it is another thing to talk about discovery, invention, and creativity. Whatever plans the writer had must finally have been located in language and, it is possible to argue, in a language that is persistently conventional and formulaic. We do not, after all, get to see the *Seventeen* article. We see only the elaborate mental procedures that accompanied the writing of the essay. We see a writer's plans for a persona; we don't see that persona in action. If writing is a process, it is also a product; and it is the product, and not the plan for writing, that locates a writer on the page, that locates him in a text and a style and the codes or conventions that make both of them readable.

Contemporary rhetorical theory has been concerned with the "codes" that constitute discourse (or specialized forms of discourse). These codes determine not only what might be said but also who might be speaking or reading. Barthes (1974), for example, has argued that the moment of writing, where private goals and plans become subject to a public language, is the moment when the writer becomes subject to a language he can neither command nor control. A text, he says, in being written passes through the codes that govern writing and becomes "'de-originated,' becomes a fragment of something that has always been *already* read, seen, done, experienced" (p. 21). Alongside a text we have always the presence of "off-stage voices," the oversound of all that has been said (e.g., about girls, about English). These voices, the presence of the "already written," stand in defiance of a writer's desire for originality and determine what might be said. A writer does not write (and this is Barthes's famous paradox) but is, himself, written by the languages available to him.

It is possible to see the writer of the *Seventeen* article solving his problem of where to begin by appropriating an available discourse. Perhaps what enabled that writer to write was the moment he located himself as a writer in a familiar field of stereotypes: Readers of *Seventeen* are teenage girls; teenage girls think of English (and English teachers) as "tidy" and "prim," and, "By God, I can change that notion for them." The moment of eureka was not simply a moment of breaking through a cognitive jumble in that individual writer's mind but a moment of breaking into a familiar and established territory — one with insiders and outsiders; one with set phrases, examples, and conclusions.

I'm not offering a criticism of the morals or manners of the teacher who wrote the *Seventeen* article. I think that all writers, in order to write, must imagine for themselves the privilege of being "insiders" — that is, the privilege both of being inside an established and powerful discourse and of being granted a special right to speak. But I think that right to speak is seldom conferred on us — on any of us, teachers or students — by virtue of the fact that we have invented or discovered an original idea. Leading students to believe that they are responsible for something new or original, unless they understand what those words mean with regard to writing, is a dangerous and counterproductive practice. We do have the right to expect students to be active and engaged, but that is a matter of continually and stylistically working against the inevitable presence of conventional language; it is not a matter of inventing a language that is new.

When a student is writing for a teacher, writing becomes more problematic than it was for the *Seventeen* writer (who was writing a version of the "Describe baseball to an Eskimo" exercise). The student, in effect, has to assume privilege without having any. And since students assume privilege by locating themselves within the discourse of a particular community — within a set of specifically acceptable gestures and commonplaces — learning, at least as it is defined in the liberal arts curriculum, becomes more a matter of imitation or parody than a matter of invention and discovery.

To argue that writing problems are also social and political problems is not to break faith with the enterprise of cognitive science. In a recent paper reviewing the tremendous range of research directed at identifying general cognitive skills, David Perkins (1985) has argued that "the higher the level of competence concerned," as in the case of adult learning, "the fewer *general* cognitive control strategies there are." There comes a point, that is, where "field-specific" or "domain-specific" schemata (what I have called "interpretive strategies") become more important than general problem-solving processes. Thinking, learning, writing — all these become bound to the context of a particular discourse. And Perkins concludes:

> Instruction in cognitive control strategies tends to be organized around problem-solving tasks. However, the isolated problem is a creature largely of the classroom. The nonstudent, whether operating in scholarly or more everyday contexts, is likely to find himself or herself involved in what might be called "projects" — which might be anything from writing a novel to designing a shoe to starting a business.

It is interesting to note that Perkins defines the classroom as the place of artificial tasks and, as a consequence, has to place scholarly projects outside the classroom, where they are carried out by the "nonstudent." It is true, I think, that education has failed to involve students in scholarly projects, projects that allow students to act as though they were colleagues in an academic enterprise. Much of the written work that students do is test-taking, report, or summary — work that places them outside the official discourse of the academic community, where they are expected to admire and report on what we do, rather than inside that discourse, where they can do its work and participate in a common enterprise.[4] This, however, is a failure of teachers and curriculum designers, who speak of writing as a mode of learning but all too often represent writing as a "tool" to be used by an (hopefully) educated mind.

It could be said, then, that there is a bastard discourse peculiar to the writing most often required of students. Carl Bereiter and Marlene Scardamalia (1985) have written about this discourse (they call it "knowledge-telling"; students who are good at it have learned to cope with academic tasks by developing a "knowledge-telling strategy"), and they have argued that insistence on knowledge-telling discourse undermines educational efforts to extend the variety of discourse schemata available to students.[5] What they actually say is this:

> When we think of knowledge stored in memory we tend these days to think of it as situated in three-dimensional space, with vertical and horizontal connections between sites. Learning is thought to add not

> only new elements to memory but also new connections, and it is the richness and structure of these connections that would seem . . . to spell the difference between inert and usable knowledge. On this account, the knowledge-telling strategy is educationally faulty because it specifically avoids the forming of connections between previously separated knowledge sites.

It should be clear by now that when I think of "knowledge" I think of it as situated in the discourse that constitutes "knowledge" in a particular discourse community, rather than as situated in mental "knowledge sites." One can remember a discourse, just as one can remember an essay or the movement of a professor's lecture; but this discourse, in effect, also has a memory of its own, its own rich network of structures and connections beyond the deliberate control of any individual imagination.

There is, to be sure, an important distinction to be made between learning history, say, and learning to write as an historian. A student can learn to command and reproduce a set of names, dates, places, and canonical interpretations (to "tell" somebody else's knowledge); but this is not the same thing as learning to "think" (by learning to write) as an historian. The former requires efforts of memory; the latter requires a student to compose a text out of the texts that represent the primary materials of history and in accordance with the texts that define history as an act of report and interpretation.

Let me draw on an example from my own teaching. I don't expect my students to *be* literary critics when they write about *Bleak House*. If a literary critic is a person who wins publication in a professional journal (or if he or she is one who could), the students aren't critics. I do, however, expect my students to be, themselves, invented as literary critics by approximating the language of a literary critic writing about *Bleak House*. My students, then, don't invent the language of literary criticism (they don't, that is, act on their own) but they are, themselves, invented by it. Their papers don't begin with a moment of insight, a "by God" moment that is outside of language. They begin with a moment of appropriation, a moment when they can offer up a sentence that is not theirs as though it were their own. (I can remember when, as a graduate student, I would begin papers by sitting down to write literally in the voice — with the syntax and the key words — of the strongest teacher I had met.)

What I am saying about my students' essays is that they are approximate, not that they are wrong or invalid. They are evidence of a discourse that lies between what I might call the students' primary discourse (what the students might write about *Bleak House* were they not in my class or in any class, and were they not imagining that they were in my class or in any class — if you can imagine any student doing any such thing) and standard, official literary criticism (which is imaginable but impossible to find). The students' essays are evidence of a discourse that lies between these two hypothetical poles. The writing is limited as much by a student's ability to imagine "what might be said" as it is by cognitive control strategies.[6] The act of writing takes the student away from where he is and what he knows and allows him to imagine something else. The approximate discourse, therefore, is evidence of a change, a change that, because we are teachers, we call "development." What our beginning students need to learn is to extend themselves, by successive approximations, into the commonplaces, set phrases, rituals and gestures, habits of mind, tricks of persuasion, obligatory conclusions and necessary connections that determine the "what might be said" and constitute knowledge within the various branches of our academic community.[7]

Pat Bizzell is, I think, one of the most important scholars writing now on "basic writers" (and this is the common name we use for students who are refused unrestrained access to the academic community) and on the special characteristics of academic discourse. In a recent essay, "Cognition, Convention, and Certainty: What We Need to Know about Writing" (1982a), she looks at two schools of composition research and the way they represent the problems that writing poses for writers.[8] For one group, the "inner-directed theorists," the problems are internal, cognitive, rooted in the way the mind represents knowledge to itself. These researchers are concerned with discovering the "universal, fundamental structures of thought and language" and with developing pedagogies to teach or facilitate both basic, general cognitive skills and specific cognitive strategies, or heuristics, directed to serve more specialized needs. Of the second group, the "outer-directed theorists," she says that they are "more interested in the social processes whereby language-learning and thinking capacities are shaped and used in particular communities."

> The staple activity of outer-directed writing instruction will be analysis of the conventions of particular discourse communities. For example, a main focus of writing-across-the-curriculum programs is to demystify the conventions of the academic discourse community. (1982a, p. 218)

The essay offers a detailed analysis of the way the two theoretical camps can best serve the general enterprise of composition research and composition teaching. Its agenda, however, seems to be to counter the influence of the cognitivists and to provide bibliography and encouragement to those interested in the social dimension of language learning.

As far as basic writers are concerned, Bizzell argues that the cognitivists' failure to acknowledge the primary, shaping role of convention in the act of composing makes them "particularly insensitive to the problems of poor writers." She argues that some of those problems, like the problem of establishing and monitoring overall goals for a piece of writing, can be

> better understood in terms of the unfamiliarity with the academic discourse community, combined, perhaps, with such limited experience outside their native discourse communities that they are unaware that there is such a thing as a discourse community with conventions to be

mastered. What is underdeveloped is their knowledge both of the ways experience is constituted and interpreted in the academic discourse community and of the fact that all discourse communities constitute and interpret experience. (1982a, p. 230)

One response to the problems of basic writers, then, would be to determine just what the community's conventions are, so that those conventions could be written out, "demystified" and taught in our classrooms. Teachers, as a result, could be more precise and helpful when they ask students to "think," "argue," "describe," or "define." Another response would be to examine the essays written by basic writers — their approximations of academic discourse — to determine more clearly where the problems lie. If we look at their writing, and if we look at it in the context of other student writing, we can better see the points of discord that arise when students try to write their way into the university.

The purpose of the remainder of this chapter will be to examine some of the most striking and characteristic of these problems as they are presented in the expository essays of first-year college students. I will be concerned, then, with university discourse in its most generalized form — as it is represented by introductory courses — and not with the special conventions required by advanced work in the various disciplines. And I will be concerned with the difficult, and often violent accommodations that occur when students locate themselves in a discourse that is not "naturally" or immediately theirs.

III

I have reviewed 500 essays written, as the "Clay Model" essay was, in response to a question used during one of our placement exams at the University of Pittsburgh: "Describe a time when you did something you felt to be creative. Then, on the basis of the incident you have described, go on to draw some general conclusions about 'creativity.'" Some of the essays were written by basic writers (or, more properly, those essays led readers to identify the writers as basic writers); some were written by students who "passed" (who were granted immediate access to the community of writers at the university). As I read these essays, I was looking to determine the stylistic resources that enabled writers to locate themselves within an "academic" discourse. My bias as a reader should be clear by now. I was not looking to see how a writer might represent the skills demanded by a neutral language (a language whose key features were paragraphs, topic sentences, transitions, and the like — features of a clear and orderly mind). I was looking to see what happened when a writer entered into a language to locate himself (a textual self) and his subject; and I was looking to see how, once entered, that language made or unmade the writer.

Here is one essay. Its writer was classified as a basic writer and, since the essay is relatively free of sentence-level errors, that decision must have been rooted in some perceived failure of the discourse itself.

> I am very interested in music, and I try to be creative in my interpretation of music. While in high school, I was a member of a jazz ensemble. The members of the ensemble were given chances to improvise and be creative in various songs. I feel that this was a great experience for me, as well as the other members. I was proud to know that I could use my imagination and feelings to create music other than what was written.
>
> Creativity to me, means being free to express yourself in a way that is unique to you, not having to conform to certain rules and guidelines. Music is only one of the many areas in which people are given opportunities to show their creativity. Sculpting, carving, building, art, and acting are just a few more areas where people can show their creativity.
>
> Through my music I conveyed feelings and thoughts which were important to me. Music was my means of showing creativity. In whatever form creativity takes, whether it be music, art, or science, it is an important aspect of our lives because it enables us to be individuals.

Notice the key gesture in this essay, one that appears in all but a few of the essays I read. The student defines as his own that which is a commonplace. "Creativity, *to me*, means being free to express yourself in a way that is unique to you, not having to conform to certain rules and guidelines." This act of appropriation constitutes his authority; it constitutes his authority as a writer and not just as a musician (that is, as someone with a story to tell). There were many essays in the set that told only a story — where the writer established his presence as a musician or a skier or someone who painted designs on a van, but not as a person at a remove from that experience interpreting it, treating it as a metaphor for something else (creativity). Unless those stories were long, detailed, and very well told — unless the writer was doing more than saying, "I am a skier" or a musician or a van-painter — those writers were all given low ratings.

Notice also that the writer of the "Jazz" paper locates himself and his experience in relation to the commonplace (creativity is unique expression; it is not having to conform to rules or guidelines) regardless of whether the commonplace is true or not. Anyone who improvises "knows" that improvisation follows rules and guidelines. It is the power of the commonplace — its truth as a recognizable and, the writer believes, as a final statement — that justifies the example and completes the essay. The example, in other words, has value because it stands within the field of the commonplace.[9] It is not the occasion for what one might call an "objective" analysis or a "close" reading. It could also be said that the essay stops with the articulation of the commonplace. The following sections speak only to the power of that statement. The reference to "sculpting, carving, building, art, and acting" attests to the universality of the commonplace (and it attests the writer's nervousness with the status he has appropriated for himself — he is saying, "Now, I'm not the only one here who has done something unique"). The commonplace stands by itself. For this writer, it does not need to be elaborated. By virtue of having written it, he has completed the essay and established the contract by which we may be spoken to as equals:

"In whatever form creativity takes, whether it be music, art, or science, it is an important aspect of *our* lives because it enables *us* to be individuals." (For me to break that contract, to argue that *my* life is not represented in that essay, is one way for me to begin as a teacher with that student in that essay.)

All of the papers I read were built around one of three commonplaces: (1) creativity is self-expression, (2) creativity is doing something new or unique, and (3) creativity is using old things in new ways. These are clearly, then, key phrases from the storehouse of things to say about creativity. I've listed them in the order of the students' ratings: A student with the highest rating was more likely to use number three than number one, although each commonplace ran across the range of possible ratings. One could argue that some standard assertions are more powerful than others, but I think the ranking simply represents the power of assertions within our community of readers. Every student was able to offer up an experience that was meant as an example of "creativity"; the lowest range of writers, then, was not represented by students who could not imagine themselves as creative people.[10]

I said that the writer of the "Jazz" paper offered up a commonplace regardless of whether it was true or not; and this, I said, was an instance of the power of a commonplace to determine the meaning of an example. A commonplace determines a system of interpretation that can be used to "place" an example within a standard system of belief. You can see a similar process at work in this essay.

> During the football season, the team was supposed to wear the same type of cleats and the same type socks, I figured that I would change this a little by wearing my white shoes instead of black and to cover up the team socks with a pair of my own white ones. I thought that this looked better than what we were wearing, and I told a few of the other people on the team to change too. They agreed that it did look better and they changed their combination to go along with mine. After the game people came up to us and said that it looked very good the way we wore our socks, and they wanted to know why we changed from the rest of the team.
>
> I feel that creativity comes from when a person lets his imagination come up with ideas and he is not afraid to express them. Once you create something to do it will be original and unique because it came about from your own imagination and if any one else tries to copy it, it won't be the same because you thought of it first from your own ideas.

This is not an elegant paper, but it seems seamless, tidy. If the paper on the clay model of the earth showed an ill fit between the writer and his project, here the discourse seems natural, smooth. You could reproduce this paper and hand it out to a class, and it would take a lot of prompting before the students sensed something fishy and one of the more aggressive ones said something like, "Sure he came up with the idea of wearing white shoes and white socks. Him and Billy 'White-

Shoes' Johnson. Come on. He copied the very thing he said was his own idea, 'original and unique.'"

The "I" of this text — the "I" who "figured," "thought," and "felt" — is located in a conventional rhetoric of the self that turns imagination into origination (I made it), that argues an ethic of production (I made it and it is mine), and that argues a tight scheme of intention (I made it because I decided to make it). The rhetoric seems invisible because it is so common. This "I" (the maker) is also located in a version of history that dominates classrooms, the "great man" theory: History is rolling along (the English novel is dominated by a central, intrusive narrative presence; America is in the throes of a Great Depression; during football season the team was supposed to wear the same kind of cleats and socks) until a figure appears, one who can shape history (Henry James, FDR, the writer of the "White Shoes" paper), and everything is changed. In the argument of the "White Shoes" paper, the history goes "I figured . . . I thought . . . I told . . . They agreed . . ." and, as a consequence, "I feel that creativity *comes from when* a person lets his imagination come up with ideas and he is not afraid to express them." The act of appropriation becomes a narrative of courage and conquest. The writer was able to write that story when he was able to imagine himself in that discourse. Getting him out of it will be a difficult matter indeed.

There are ways, I think, that a writer can shape history in the very act of writing it. Some students are able to enter into a discourse but, by stylistic maneuvers, to take possession of it at the same time. They don't originate a discourse, but they locate themselves within it aggressively, self-consciously. Here is another essay on jazz, which for sake of convenience I've shortened. It received a higher rating than the first essay on jazz.

> Jazz has always been thought of as a very original creative field in music. Improvisation, the spontaneous creation of original melodies in a piece of music, makes up a large part of jazz as a musical style. I had the opportunity to be a member of my high school's jazz ensemble for three years, and became an improvisation soloist this year. Throughout the years, I have seen and heard many jazz players, both professional and amateur. The solos performed by these artists were each flavored with that particular individual's style and ideas, along with some of the conventional premises behind improvisation. This particular type of solo work is creative because it is done on the spur of the moment and blends the performer's ideas with basic guidelines.
>
> I realized my own creative potential when I began soloing. . . .
>
> My solos, just as all the solos generated by others, were original because I combined and shaped other's ideas with mine to create something completely new. Creativity is combining the practical knowledge and guidelines of a discipline with one's original ideas to bring about a new, original end result, one that is different from everyone else's. Creativity is based on the individual. Two artists can interpret the same scene differently. Each person who creates something does so by bringing out something individual in himself.

The essay is different in some important ways from the first essay on jazz. The writer of the second is more easily able to place himself in the context of an "academic" discussion. The second essay contains an "I" who realized his "creative potential" by soloing; the first contained an "I" who had "a great experience." In the second essay, before the phrase, "I had the opportunity to be a member of my high school's jazz ensemble," there is an introduction that offers a general definition of improvisation and an acknowledgment that other people have thought about jazz and creativity. In fact, throughout the essay the writer offers definitions and counterdefinitions. He is placing himself in the context of what has been said and what might be said. In the first paper, before a similar statement about being a member of a jazz ensemble, there was an introduction that locates jazz solely in the context of this individual's experience: "I am very interested in music." The writer of this first paper was authorized by who he is, a musician, rather than by what he can say about music in the context of what is generally said. The writer of the second essay uses a more specialized vocabulary; he talks about "conventional premises," "creative potential," "musical style," and "practical knowledge." And this is not just a matter of using bigger words, since these terms locate the experience in the context of a recognizable interpretive scheme — on the one hand there is tradition and, on the other, individual talent.

It could be said, then, that this essay is also framed and completed by a commonplace: "Creativity is combining the practical knowledge and guidelines of a discipline with one's original ideas to bring about a new, original end result, one that is different from everyone else's." Here, however, the argument is a more powerful one; and I mean "powerful" in the political sense, since it is an argument that complicates a "naïve" assumption (it makes scholarly work possible, in other words), and it does so in terms that come close to those used in current academic debates (over the relation between convention and idiosyncrasy or between rules and creativity). The assertion is almost consumed by the pleas for originality at the end of the sentence; but the point remains that the terms "original" and "different," as they are used at the end of the essay, are problematic, since they must be thought of in the context of "practical knowledge and guidelines of a discipline."

The key distinguishing gesture of this essay, that which makes it "better" than the other, is the way the writer works against a conventional point of view, one that is represented within the essay by conventional phrases that the writer must then work against. In his practice he demonstrates that a writer, and not just a musician, works within "conventional premises." The "I" who comments in this paper (not the "I" of the narrative about a time when he soloed) places himself self-consciously within the context of a conventional discourse about the subject, even as he struggles against the language of that conventional discourse. The opening definition of improvisation, where improvisation is defined as spontaneous creation, is rejected when the writer begins talking about "the conventional premises behind improvisation."

The earlier definition is part of the conventional language of those who "have always thought" of jazz as a "very original creative field in music." The paper begins with what "has been said" and then works itself out against the force and logic of what has been said, of what is not only an argument but also a collection of phrases, examples, and definitions.

I had a teacher who once told us that whenever we were stuck for something to say, we should use the following as a "machine" for producing a paper: "While most readers of _____ have said _____, a close and careful reading shows that _____." The writer of the second paper on jazz is using a standard opening gambit, even if it is not announced with flourish. The essay becomes possible when he sets himself against what must become a "naïve" assumption — what "most people think." He has defined a closed circle for himself. In fact, you could say that he has laid the groundwork for a discipline with its own key terms ("practical knowledge," "disciplinary guidelines," and "original ideas"), with its own agenda and with its own investigative procedures (looking for common features in the work of individual soloists).

The history represented by this student's essay, then, is not the history of a musician and it is not the history of a thought being worked out within an individual mind; it is the history of work being done within and against conventional systems.

In general, as I reviewed essays for this study, I found that the more successful writers set themselves in their essays against what they defined as some more naïve way of talking about their subject — against "those who think that . . ." — or against earlier, more naïve versions of themselves — "once I thought that. . . ." By trading in one set of commonplaces at the expense of another, they could win themselves status as members of what is taken to be some more privileged group. The ability to imagine privilege enabled writing. Here is one particularly successful essay. Notice the specialized vocabulary, but notice also the way in which the text continually refers to its own language and to the language of others.

> Throughout my life, I have been interested and intrigued by music. My mother has often told me of the time, before I went to school, when I would "conduct" the orchestra on her records. I continued to listen to music and eventually started to play the guitar and the clarinet. Finally, at about the age of twelve, I started to sit down and to try to write songs. Even though my instrumental skills were far from my own high standards, I would spend much of my spare time during the day with a guitar around my neck, trying to produce a piece of music.
>
> Each of these sessions, as I remember them, had a rather set format. I would sit in my bedroom, strumming different combinations of the five or six chords I could play, until I heard a series of which sounded particularly good to me. After this, I set the music to a suitable rhythm, (usually dependent on my mood at the time), and ran through the tune until I could play it fairly easily. Only after this section was complete did I go on to writing lyrics, which generally followed along the lines of the current popular songs on the radio.

At the time of the writing, I felt that my songs were, in themselves, an original creation of my own; that is, I, alone, made them. However, I now see that, in this sense of the word, I was not creative. The songs themselves seem to be an oversimplified form of the music I listened to at the time.

In a more fitting sense, however, I *was* being creative. Since I did not purposely copy my favorite songs, I was, effectively, originating my songs from my own "process of creativity." To achieve my goal, I needed what a composer would call "inspiration" for my piece. In this case the inspiration was the current hit on the radio. Perhaps, with my present point of view, I feel that I used too much "inspiration" in my songs, but, at that time, I did not.

Creativity, therefore, is a process which, in my case, involved a certain series of "small creations" if you like. As well, it is something, the appreciation of which varies with one's point of view, that point of view being set by the person's experience, tastes, and his own personal view of creativity. The less experienced tend to allow for less originality, while the more experienced demand real originality to classify something a "creation." Either way, a term as abstract as this is perfectly correct and open to interpretation.

This writer is consistently and dramatically conscious of herself forming something to say out of what has been said *and* out of what she has been saying in the act of writing this paper. "Creativity" begins in this paper as "original creation." What she thought was "creativity," however, she now says was imitation; and, as she says, "in a sense of the word" she was not "creative." In another sense, however, she says that she *was* creative, since she didn't purposefully copy the songs but used them as "inspiration."

While the elaborate stylistic display — the pauses, qualifications, and the use of quotation marks — is in part a performance for our benefit, at a more obvious level we as readers are directly addressed in the first sentence of the last paragraph: "Creativity, therefore, is a process which, in my case, involved a certain series of 'small creations' if you like." We are addressed here as adults who can share her perspective on what she has said and who can be expected to understand her terms. If she gets into trouble after this sentence, and I think she does, it is because she doesn't have the courage to generalize from her assertion. Since she has rhetorically separated herself from her younger "self," and since she argues that she has gotten smarter, she assumes that there is some developmental sequence at work here and that, in the world of adults (which must be more complete than the world of children) there must be something like "real creativity." If her world is imperfect (if she can only talk about creation by putting the word in quotation marks), it must be because she is young. When she looks beyond herself to us, she cannot see our work as an extension of her project. She cannot assume that we too will be concerned with the problem of creativity and originality. At least she is not willing to challenge us on those grounds, to generalize her argument, and to argue that even for adults creations are really only "small creations." The sense of privilege that has allowed her to expose her own language cannot be extended to expose ours.

The writing in this piece — that is, the work of the writer within the essay — goes on in spite of, or against, the language that keeps pressing to give another name to her experience as a songwriter and to bring the discussion to closure. (In comparison, think of the quick closure of the "White Shoes" paper.) Its style is difficult, highly qualified. It relies on quotation marks and parody to set off the language and attitudes that belong to the discourse (or the discourses) that it would reject, that it would not take as its own proper location.

David Olson (1981) has argued that the key difference between oral language and written language is that written language separates both the producer and the receiver from the text. For my student writers, this means that they had to learn that what they said (the code) was more important than what they meant (the intention). A writer, in other words, loses his primacy at the moment of writing and must begin to attend to his and his words' conventional, even physical presence on the page. And, Olson says, the writer must learn that his authority is not established through his presence but through his absence — through his ability, that is, to speak as a god-like source behind the limitations of any particular social or historical moment; to speak by means of the wisdom of convention, through the oversounds of official or authoritative utterance, as the voice of logic or the voice of the community. He concludes:

> The child's growing competence with this distinctive register of language in which both the meaning and the authority are displaced from the intentions of the speaker and lodged "in the text" may contribute to the similarly specialized and distinctive mode of thought we have come to associate with literacy and formal education. (1981, p. 110)

Olson is writing about children. His generalizations, I think I've shown, can be extended to students writing their way into the academic community. These are educated and literate individuals, to be sure, but they are individuals still outside the peculiar boundaries of the academic community. In the papers I've examined in this chapter, the writers have shown an increasing awareness of the codes (or the competing codes) that operate within a discourse. To speak with authority they have to speak not only in another's voice but through another's code; and they not only have to do this, they have to speak in the voice and through the codes of those of us with power and wisdom; and they not only have to do this, they have to do it before they know what they are doing, before they have a project to participate in, and before, at least in terms of our disciplines, they have anything to say. Our students may be able to enter into a conventional discourse and speak, not as themselves, but through the voice of the community; the university, however, is the place where "common" wisdom is only of negative values — it is something to work against. The movement toward a more specialized discourse begins (or, perhaps, best begins) both when a student can define a position of privilege, a position that sets him against a "common" discourse, and when he or she can work self-consciously, critically, against not only the "common" code but his or her own.

IV

Pat Bizzell, you will recall, argues that the problems of poor writers can be attributed both to their unfamiliarity with the conventions of academic discourse and to their ignorance that there are such things as discourse communities with conventions to be mastered. If the latter is true, I think it is true only in rare cases. All the student writers I've discussed (and, in fact, most of the student writers whose work I've seen) have shown an awareness that something special or something different is required when one writes for an academic classroom. The essays that I have presented in this chapter all, I think, give evidence of writers trying to write their way into a new community. To some degree, however, all of them can be said to be unfamiliar with the conventions of academic discourse.

Problems of convention are both problems of finish and problems of substance. The most substantial academic tasks for students, learning history or sociology or literary criticism, are matters of many courses, much reading and writing, and several years of education. Our students, however, must have a place to begin. They cannot sit through lectures and read textbooks and, as a consequence, write as sociologists or write literary criticism. There must be steps along the way. Some of these steps will be marked by drafts and revisions. Some will be marked by courses, and in an ideal curriculum the preliminary courses would be writing courses, whether housed in an English department or not. For some students, students we call "basic writers," these courses will be in a sense the most basic introduction to the language and methods of academic writing.

Our students, as I've said, must have a place to begin. If the problem of a beginning is the problem of establishing authority, of defining rhetorically or stylistically a position from which one may speak, then the papers I have examined show characteristic student responses to that problem and show levels of approximation or stages in the development of writers who are writing their way into a position of privilege.

As I look over the papers I've discussed, I would arrange them in the following order: the "White Shoes" paper; the first "Jazz" essay; the "Clay Model" paper; the second "Jazz" essay; and, as the most successful paper, the essay on "Composing Songs." The more advanced essays for me, then, are those that are set against the "naïve" codes of "everyday" life. (I put the terms "naïve" and "everyday" in quotation marks because they are, of course, arbitrary terms.) In the advanced essays one can see a writer claiming an "inside" position of privilege by rejecting the language and commonplaces of a "naïve" discourse, the language of "outsiders." The "I" of those essays locates itself against the specialized language of what is presumed to be a more powerful and more privileged community. There are two gestures present then — one imitative and one critical. The writer continually audits and pushes against a language that would render him "like everyone else" and mimics the language and interpretive systems of the privileged community.

At a first level, then, a student might establish his authority by simply stating his own presence within the field of a subject. A student, for example, writes about creativity by telling a story about a time he went skiing. Nothing more. The "I" on the page is a skier, and skiing stands as a representation of a creative act. Neither the skier nor skiing are available for interpretation; they cannot be located in an essay that is not a narrative essay (where skiing might serve metaphorically as an example of, say, a sport where set movements also allow for a personal style). Or a student, as did the one who wrote the "White Shoes" paper, locates a narrative in an unconnected rehearsal of commonplaces about creativity. In both cases, the writers have finessed the requirement to set themselves against the available utterances of the world outside the closed world of the academy. And, again, in the first "Jazz" paper, we have the example of a writer who locates himself within an available commonplace and carries out only rudimentary procedures for elaboration, procedures driven by the commonplace itself and not set against it. Elaboration, in this latter case, is not the opening up of a system but a justification of it.

At a next level I would place student writers who establish their authority by mimicking the rhythm and texture, the "sound," of academic prose, without there being any recognizable interpretive or academic project under way. I'm thinking, here, of the "Clay Model" essay. At an advanced stage, I would place students who establish their authority as *writers*; they claim their authority, not by simply claiming that they are skiers or that they have done something creative, but by placing themselves both within and against a discourse, or within and against competing discourses, and working self-consciously to claim an interpretive project of their own, one that grants them their privilege to speak. This is true, I think, in the case of the second "Jazz" paper and, to a greater degree, in the case of the "Composing Songs" paper.

The levels of development that I've suggested are not marked by corresponding levels in the type or frequency of error, at least not by the type or frequency of sentence-level error. I am arguing, then, that a basic writer is not necessarily a writer who makes a lot of mistakes. In fact, one of the problems with curricula designed to aid basic writers is that they too often begin with the assumption that the key distinguishing feature of a basic writer is the presence of sentence-level error. Students are placed in courses because their placement essays show a high frequency of such errors, and those courses are designed with the goal of making those errors go away. This approach to the problems of the basic writer ignores the degree to which error is less often a constant feature than a marker in the development of a writer. A student who can write a reasonably correct narrative may fall to pieces when faced with a more unfamiliar assignment. More important, however, such courses fail to serve the rest of the curriculum. On every campus there is a significant number of college freshmen who require a course to introduce them to the kinds of writing that are required for a university education. Some of these students can write correct sentences and some cannot; but, as a group, they lack the facility other freshmen possess when they are faced with an academic writing task.

The "White Shoes" essay, for example, shows fewer sentence-level errors than the "Clay Model" paper. This may well be due to the fact that the writer of the "White Shoes" paper stayed well within safe, familiar territory. He kept himself out of trouble by doing what he could easily do. The tortuous syntax of the more advanced papers on my list is a syntax that represents a writer's struggle with a difficult and unfamiliar language, and it is a syntax that can quickly lead an inexperienced writer into trouble. The syntax and punctuation of the "Composing Songs" essay, for example, shows the effort that is required when a writer works against the pressure of conventional discourse. If the prose is inelegant (although I confess I admire those dense sentences) it is still correct. This writer has a command of the linguistic and stylistic resources — the highly embedded sentences, the use of parentheses and quotation marks — required to complete the act of writing. It is easy to imagine the possible pitfalls for a writer working without this facility.

There was no camera trained on the "Clay Model" writer while he was writing, and I have no protocol of what was going through his mind, but it is possible to speculate on the syntactic difficulties of sentences like these: "In the past time I thought that an incident was creative was when I had to make a clay model of the earth, but not of the classical or your everyday model of the earth which consists of the two cores, the mantle and the crust. I thought of these things in a dimension of which it would be unique, but easy to comprehend." The syntactic difficulties appear to be the result of the writer's attempt to use an unusual vocabulary and to extend his sentences beyond the boundaries of what would have been "normal" in his speech or writing. There is reason to believe, that is, that the problem was with *this* kind of sentence, in this context. If the problem of the last sentence is that of holding together the units "I thought," "dimension," "unique," and "easy to comprehend," then the linguistic problem was not a simple matter of sentence construction. I am arguing, then, that such sentences fall apart not because the writer lacked the necessary syntax to glue the pieces together but because he lacked the full statement within which these key words were already operating. While writing, and in the thrust of his need to complete the sentence, he had the key words but not the utterance. (And to recover the utterance, I suspect, he would need to do more than revise the sentence.) The invisible conventions, the prepared phrases remained too distant for the statement to be completed. The writer would have needed to get inside of a discourse that he could in fact only partially imagine. The act of constructing a sentence, then, became something like an act of transcription in which the voice on the tape unexpectedly faded away and became inaudible.

Shaughnessy (1977) speaks of the advanced writer as one who often has a more facile but still incomplete possession of this prior discourse. In the case of the advanced writer, the evidence of a problem is the presence of dissonant, redundant, or imprecise language, as in a sentence such as this: "No education can be *total*, it must be *continuous*."

Such a student, Shaughnessy says, could be said to hear the "melody of formal English" while still unable to make precise or exact distinctions. And, she says,

> the pre-packaging feature of language, the possibility of taking over phrases and whole sentences without much thought about them, threatens the writer now as before. The writer, as we have said, inherits the language out of which he must fabricate his own messages. He is therefore in a constant tangle with the language, obliged to recognize its public, communal nature and yet driven to invent out of this language his own statements. (1977, pp. 207–208)

For the unskilled writer, the problem is different in degree and not in kind. The inexperienced writer is left with a more fragmentary record of the comings and goings of academic discourse. Or, as I said above, he or she often has the key words without the complete statements within which they are already operating.

Let me provide one final example of this kind of syntactic difficulty in another piece of student writing. The writer of this paper seems to be able to sustain a discussion only by continually repeating his first step, producing a litany of strong, general, authoritative assertions that trail quickly into confusion. Notice how the writer seems to stabilize his movement through the paper by returning again and again to recognizable and available commonplace utterances. When he has to move away from them, however, away from the familiar to statements that would extend those utterances, where he, too, must speak, the writing — that is, both the syntax and the structure of the discourse — falls to pieces.

> Many times the times drives a person's life depends on how he uses it. I would like to think about if time is twenty-five hours a day rather than twenty-four hours. Some people think it's the boaring or some people might say it's the pleasure to take one more hour for their life. But I think the time is passing and coming, still we are standing on same position. We should use time as best as we can use about the good way in our life. Everything we do, such as sleep, eat, study, play and doing

something for ourselves. These take the time to do and we could find the individual ability and may process own. It is the important for us and our society. As time going on the world changes therefor we are changing, too. When these situation changes we should follow the suitable case of own. But many times we should decide what's the better way to do so by using time. Sometimes like this kind of situation can cause the success of our lives or ruin. I think every individual of his own thought drive how to use time. These affect are done from environmental causes. So we should work on the better way of our life recognizing the importance of time.

There is a general pattern of disintegration when the writer moves off from standard phrases. This sentence, for example, starts out coherently and then falls apart: "*We should use time as best as we can* use about the good way in our life." The difficulty seems to be one of extending those standard phrases or of connecting them to the main subject reference, "time" (or "the time," a construction that causes many of the problems in the paper). Here is an example of a sentence that shows, in miniature, this problem of connection: "*I think every individual* of his own thought drive how to use *time*."

One of the remarkable things about this paper is that, in spite of all the syntactic confusion, there is the hint of an academic project here. The writer sets out to discuss how to creatively use one's time. The text seems to allude to examples and to stages in an argument, even if in the end it is all pretty incoherent. The gestures of academic authority, however, are clearly present, and present in a form that echoes the procedures in other, more successful papers. The writer sets himself against what "some people think"; he speaks with the air of authority: "But I think. . . . Everything we do. . . . When these situation changes. . . ." And he speaks as though there were a project underway, one where he proposes what he thinks, turns to evidence, and offers a conclusion: "These affect are done from environmental causes. So we should work. . . ." This is the case of a student with the ability to imagine the general outline and rhythm of academic prose but without the ability to carry it out, to complete the sentences. And when he gets lost in the new, in the unknown, in the responsibility of his own commitment to speak, he returns again to the familiar ground of the commonplace.

The challenge to researchers, it seems to me, is to turn their attention again to products, to student writing, since the drama in a student's essay, as he or she struggles with and against the languages of our contemporary life, is as intense and telling as the drama of an essay's mental preparation or physical production. A written text, too, can be a compelling model of the "composing process" once we conceive of a writer as at work within a text and simultaneously, then, within a society, a history, and a culture.

It may very well be that some students will need to learn to crudely mimic the "distinctive register" of academic discourse before they are prepared to actually and legitimately do the work of the discourse, and before they are sophisticated enough with the refinements of tone and gesture to do it with grace or elegance. To say this, however, is to say that our students must be our students. Their initial progress will be marked by their abilities to take on the role of privilege, by their abilities to establish authority. From this point of view, the student who wrote about constructing the clay model of the earth is better prepared for his education than the student who wrote about playing football in white shoes, even though the "White Shoes" paper is relatively error-free and the "Clay Model" paper is not. It will be hard to pry loose the writer of the "White Shoes" paper from the tidy, pat discourse that allows him to dispose of the question of creativity in such a quick and efficient manner. He will have to be convinced that it is better to write sentences he might not so easily control, and he will have to be convinced that it is better to write muddier and more confusing prose (in order that it may sound like ours), and this will be harder than convincing the "Clay Model" writer to continue what he has already begun.

Acknowledgments

Preparation of this chapter was supported by the Learning Research and Development Center of the University of Pittsburgh, which is supported in part by the National Institute of Education.

Notes

1. David Olson (1981) has made a similar observation about school-related problems of language learning in younger children. Here is his conclusion: "Hence, depending upon whether children assumed language was primarily suitable for making assertions and conjectures or primarily for making direct or indirect commands, they will either find school texts easy or difficult" (p. 107).

2. For Aristotle, there were both general and specific commonplaces. A speaker, says Aristotle, has a "stock of arguments to which he may turn for a particular need."

   > If he knows the *topoi* (regions, places, lines of argument) — and a skilled speaker will know them — he will know where to find what he wants for a special case. The general topics, or *common*places, are regions containing arguments that are common to all branches of knowledge. . . . But there are also special topics (regions, places, *loci*) in which one looks for arguments appertaining to particular branches of knowledge, special sciences, such as ethics or politics. (1932, pp. 154–155)

   And, he says, "the topics or places, then, may be indifferently thought of as in the science that is concerned, or in the mind of the speaker." But the question of location is "indifferent" *only* if the mind of the speaker is in line with set opinion, general assumption. For the speaker (or writer) who is not situated so comfortably in the privileged public realm, this is indeed not an indifferent matter at all. If he does not have the commonplace at hand, he will not, in Aristotle's terms, know where to go at all.

3. Pat Bizzell has argued that the *Seventeen* writer's process of goal-setting

> can be better understood if we see it in terms of writing for a discourse community. His initial problem . . . is to find a way to include these readers in a discourse community for which he is comfortable writing. He places them in the academic discourse community by imagining the girls as students. . . . Once he has included them in a familiar discourse community, he can find a way to address them that is common in the community: he will argue with them, putting a new interpretation on information they possess in order to correct misconceptions. (1982a, p. 228)

4. See Bartholomae (1979, 1983) and Rose (1983) for articles on curricula designed to move students into university discourse. The movement to extend writing "across the curriculum" is evidence of a general concern for locating students within the work of the university; see Bizzell (1982a) and Maimon *et al.* (1981). For longer works directed specifically at basic writing, see Ponsot and Deen (1982) and Shaughnessy (1977). For a book describing a course for more advanced students, see Coles (1978).

5. In spite of my misgivings about Bereiter and Scardamalia's interpretation of the cognitive nature of the problem of "inert knowledge," this is an essay I regularly recommend to teachers. It has much to say about the dangers of what seem to be "neutral" forms of classroom discourse and provides, in its final section, a set of recommendations on how a teacher might undo discourse conventions that have become part of the institution of teaching.

6. Stanley Fish (1980) argues that the basis for distinguishing novice from expert readings is the persuasiveness of the discourse used to present and defend a given reading. In particular, see the chapter, "Demonstration vs. Persuasion: Two Models of Critical Activity" (pp. 356–373).

7. Some students, when they come to the university, can do this better than others. When Jonathan Culler says, "the possibility of bringing someone to see that a particular interpretation is a good one assumes shared points of departure and common notions of how to read," he is acknowledging that teaching, at least in English classes, has had to assume that students, to be students, were already to some degree participating in the structures of reading and writing that constitute English studies (quoted in Fish, 1980, p. 366).

Stanley Fish tells us "not to worry" that students will violate our enterprise by offering idiosyncratic readings of standard texts:

> The fear of solipsism, of the imposition by the unconstrained self of its own prejudices, is unfounded because the self does not exist apart from the communal or conventional categories of thought that enable its operations (of thinking, seeing, reading). Once we realize that the conceptions that fill consciousness, including any conception of its own status, are culturally derived, the very notion of an unconstrained self, of a consciousness wholly and dangerously free, becomes incomprehensible. (1980, p. 335)

He, too, is assuming that students, to be students (and not "dangerously free"), must be members in good standing of the community whose

immediate head is the English teacher. It is interesting that his parenthetical catalogue of the "operations" of thought, "thinking, seeing, reading," excludes writing, since it is only through written records that we
have any real indication of how a student thinks, sees, and reads. (Perhaps "real" is an inappropriate word to use here, since there is certainly a
"real" intellectual life that goes on, independent of writing. Let me say
that thinking, seeing, and reading are valued in the academic community
only as they are represented by extended, elaborated written records.)
Writing, I presume, is a given for Fish. It is the card of entry into this
closed community that constrains and excludes dangerous characters.
Students who are excluded from this community are students who do poorly
on written placement exams or in freshman composition. They do not,
that is, move easily into the privileged discourse of the community, represented by the English literature class.

8. My debt to Bizzell's work should be evident everywhere in this essay. See
   also Bizzell (1978, 1982b) and Bizzell and Herzberg (1980).

9. Fish says the following about the relationship between student and an
   object under study:

   > we are not to imagine a moment when my students "simply see" a
   > physical configuration of atoms and *then* assign that configuration a
   > significance, according to the situation they happen to be in. To be in
   > the situation (this or any other) is to "see" with the eyes of its
   > interests, its goals, its understood practices, values, and norms, and
   > so to be conferring significance *by* seeing, not after it. The categories
   > of my students' vision are the categories by which they understand
   > themselves to be functioning as students . . . and objects will appear
   > to them in forms related to that way of functioning rather than in
   > some objective or preinterpretive form. (1980, p. 334)

10. I am aware that the papers given the highest rankings offer arguments
    about creativity and originality similar to my own. If there is a conspiracy
    here, that is one of the points of my chapter. I should add that my reading
    of the "content" of basic writers' essays is quite different from Lunsford's
    (1980).

References

Aristotle. (1932). *The Rhetoric of Aristotle* (L. Cooper, Trans.). Englewood Cliffs,
NJ: Prentice-Hall.

Barthes, R. (1974). S/Z (R. Howard, Trans.). New York: Hill & Wang.

Bartholomae, D. (1979). Teaching basic writing: An alternative to basic skills.
Journal of Basic Writing, 2, 85–109.

Bartholomae, D. (1983). Writing assignments: Where writing begins. In P. Stock
(Ed.), *Forum* (pp. 300–312). Montclair, NJ: Boynton/Cook.

Bereiter, C., & Scardamalia, M. (1985). Cognitive coping strategies and the
problem of "inert knowledge." In S. S. Chipman, J. W. Segal, & R. Glaser
(Eds.), *Thinking and learning skills: Research and open questions* (Vol. 2).
Hillsdale, NJ: Erlbaum.

Bizzell, P. (1978). The ethos of academic discourse. *College Composition and
Communication*, 29, 351–355.

Bizzell, P. (1982a). Cognition, convention, and certainty: What we need to know
about writing. *Pre/text*, 3, 213–244.

Bizzell, P. (1982b). College composition: Initiation into the academic discourse community. *Curriculum Inquiry*, 12, 191–207.

Bizzell, P., & Herzberg, B. (1980). "Inherent" ideology, "universal" history, "empirical" evidence, and "context-free" writing: Some problems with E. D. Hirsch's *The Philosophy of Composition. Modern Language Notes*, 95, 1181–1202.

Coles, W. E., Jr. (1978). *The plural I.* New York: Holt, Rinehart & Winston.

Fish, S. (1980). *Is there a text in this class? The authority of interpretive communities.* Cambridge, MA: Harvard University Press.

Flower, L. S. (1981). Revising writer-based prose. *Journal of Basic Writing*, 3, 62–74.

Flower, L., & Hayes, J. (1981). A cognitive process theory of writing. *College Composition and Communication*, 32, 365–387.

Hairston, M. (1978). *A contemporary rhetoric.* Boston: Houghton Mifflin.

Lunsford, A. A. (1980). The content of basic writers' essays. *College Composition and Communication*, 31, 278–290.

Maimon, E. P., Belcher, G. L., Hearn, G. W., Nodine, B. F., & O'Conner, F. X. (1981). *Writing in the arts and sciences.* Cambridge, MA: Winthrop.

Olson, D. R. (1981). Writing: The divorce of the author from the text. In B. M. Kroll & R. J. Vann (Eds.), *Exploring speaking–writing relationships: Connections and contrasts.* Urbana, IL: National Council of Teachers of English.

Perkins, D. N. (1985). General cognitive skills: Why not? In S. S. Chipman, J. W. Segal, & R. Glaser (Eds.), *Thinking and learning skills: Research and open questions* (Vol. 2). Hillsdale, NJ: Erlbaum.

Ponsot, M., & Deen, R. (1982). *Beat not the poor desk.* Montclair, NJ: Boynton/Cook.

Rodriguez, R. (1983). *Hunger of memory.* New York: Bantam.

Rose, M. (1983). Remedial writing courses: A critique and a proposal. *College English*, 45, 109–128.

Said, E. W. (1975). *Beginnings: Intention and method.* Baltimore: The Johns Hopkins University Press.

Shaughnessy, M. (1977). *Errors and expectations.* New York: Oxford University Press.

Bartholomae's Insights as a Resource for Your Teaching

1. Make a brief list of the particular features of academic discourse. How does academic discourse differ from the sorts of mental and verbal habits that characterize students who are new to the university?

2. Think back on your own gradual initiation into academic authority. What processes were involved? How might you duplicate these for your students?

3. Consider the social and political implications of Bartholomae's argument. Will some students be at a distinct advantage or disadvantage in terms of appropriating "authoritative discourse" because of their social or cultural background? How might you level the playing field for your students?

Bartholomae's Insights as a Resource for Your Writing Classroom

1. Share with your students the student essays that Bartholomae uses as examples. After they have had time to think and form their own opinions about the essays, share with them Bartholomae's ideas about the essays. Ask students to compare and contrast their own sense of what's interesting about this student work with Bartholomae's ideas. What do they like or dislike about Bartholomae's vision of the composition classroom?

2. Explore the implications of Bartholomae's theory by asking students to imagine what a wholly opposed theory might value and emphasize. In other words, are there important factors that Bartholomae's theory implicitly leaves out or suppresses? Is this an important loss in terms of their own writing and meaning-making? Why or why not?

3. Have students explore the social implications of Bartholomae's theory. Will certain groups be excluded from appropriating this discourse, or at least face significant barriers to doing so? Ask students whether they feel that Bartholomae's views of helping students master this academic discourse are pragmatic, laden with cultural values, or both? What do they feel should be standards for valid discourse? Valued discourse?

Composition's Imagined Geographies: The Politics of Space in the Frontier, City, and Cyberspace

Nedra Reynolds

Certain spatial metaphors have figured prominently in the ways composition has come to understand itself. As the world shrinks and we hear more and more talk of a "global village," we need to reflect carefully on these terms rather than persist uncritically in thinking that space is merely neutral or transparent or devoid of powerful social significance. We initially thought of our discipline in terms of the frontier; later, we came to see it more and more as a contact zone or a city; as we look to the future, we find ourselves increasingly concerned with our work in cyberspace. In this essay, Nedra Reynolds argues that we should be especially alert to the actual material conditions of our working lives and those of our students, for these contexts inform our process of making and communicating meaning and self-understanding quite powerfully and with considerable complexity — complexity that is often masked by a too-casual reliance on abstract, general metaphors.

We must be insistently aware of how space can be made to hide consequences from us, how relations of power and discipline are inscribed into the apparently innocent spatiality of social life, how human geographies become filled with politics and ideology.

— Edward W. Soja (6)

It is helpful to remind ourselves that one of the things a university does is alter one's sense of geography.

— Mary N. Muchiri et al. (178)

In their recent article on "Importing Composition: Teaching and Researching Academic Writing Beyond North America," Mary N. Muchiri and her coauthors challenge our assumptions that composition is "universal" in its uses and applications, and that writing instructors and writing students do not occupy particular geographic locations. Muchiri et al. remind readers that composition is very much a product of North America and of capitalism and illustrate what happens to composition research when it is exported — how it changes in a different, delocalized context of its origination. "Importing Composition" highlights some of the assumptions that form the basis of U.S. research on academic writing — assumptions that sometimes seem "bizarre" in a new context (176). In our limited notions of geography, we make assumptions about serving the world in our writing classes: "The teacher in New York or Los Angeles may look out over a classroom and think, 'The whole world is here.' It isn't" (195).

In its analysis of contemporary writing instruction — informed by imports and exports, journeys, the local and the global — "Importing Composition" contributes to a geographic study of composition that asks us to confront many of our assumptions about place and space. My purpose here is to extend that contribution by using concepts from postmodern geography to explore how spaces and places are socially produced through discourse and how these constructed spaces can then deny their connections to material reality or mask material conditions.[1] Cultural geography invites us to question the relationships between material conditions and imagined territories, a relationship I identify here as the politics of space, and asks us to attend to the negotiations of power that take place across and within a number of spaces: regional or topographical, domestic or institutional, architectural or electronic, real or imagined. Making a geographic turn enables me to examine the politics of space in composition with three general aims: (1)

to interpret some of composition's most enduring spatial metaphors as "imagined geographies" responsible, in part, for composition's disciplinary development and identity; (2) to illustrate the effects of time-space compression on composition's workers; (3) and to argue for a spatial politics of writing instruction that denies transparent space and encourages the study of neglected places where writers work.

Attending to the politics of space can begin with simple observations about where writers and writing instructors work — in a variety of institutional, public, and private spaces (some of them difficult to categorize as either public or private): the academic buildings of our offices, computer labs, and writing centers; the cafeterias, libraries, and classrooms of our campuses; the large conference hotels where we meet to exchange ideas and socialize; the kitchen table, desks, or computer corners in our homes. These actual locations for the work of writing and writing instruction coexist with several metaphorical or imaginary places where we write, study writing, or create theories about writing: webs of meaning, research paradigms, home departments, discourse communities, frontiers, cities, and cyberspaces.

Composition workers have long had to deal with the politics of space, whether this has involved trying to reduce section sizes, find a room to establish a writing center, or stake our disciplinary territory. In carving out areas to call its own, composition has created imagined geographies that hold a number of implications. A writing center, for example, occupies a certain number of square feet in a campus building, but it also occupies an imaginary place where writing is taught, learned, or talked about very differently than in a lecture hall or around a seminar table. Edward Soja, in *Postmodern Geographies: The Reassertion of Space in Critical Social Theory*, defines postmodern geography as the study of the social production of spaces or studying the linkages among space, knowledge, and power (20). The social production of spaces takes place in all discourse arenas, wherever rhetors are "inventing" the boundaries of inquiry, the agendas of research, or the languages of arguments. How have composition theorist-practitioners imagined the spaces of writing, writers, and writing instruction? "Where" have they placed the work of composition studies as a field or discipline, and what implications do these real or imaginary placements hold? After demonstrating the endurance of one of composition's most important imagined geographies, the *frontier*, and the emergence of two more, the *city* and *cyberspace*, I argue that these imaginary places for writing and writing instruction have been rendered benign, or anesthetized by the influence of transparent space; that we have neglected the relationship between material spaces and actual practices; and that we need to attend to the effects of time-space compression on composition's workers.

Spatial Metaphors in the Discourses of Composition Studies

Spatial metaphors have long dominated our written discourse in this field ("field" being one of the first spatial references we can name) because, first, writing itself is spatial, or we cannot very well conceive of writing in ways other than spatial. In "The Limits of Containment: Text-as-Container in Composition Studies," Darsie Bowden asserts that composition "is especially rife with metaphors because composing involves complex cognitive activities . . . that are difficult to talk about and understand" (364). As Bowden's analysis suggests, many of our metaphors in writing and composition studies involve or depend on imaginary conceptions of space. From bound texts to pages to paragraphs, sentences, and words, we read and write in distinctly spatial ways. We read from left to right (in most languages), and we scan pages up and down or rifle through a stack of pages from top to bottom. We are accustomed to margins and borders that frame texts for us and page numbers or arrow icons that mark our place. (How often have you found a remembered passage by its placement on a page, its position in the text?) Academic and professional writers are comfortable with manipulating textual spaces and now that the tasks of organizing and presenting information — with spatial constraints all around — constitute one of a writer's biggest challenges. Techno-revolutions are changing our notions of texts on pages, most of us realize, and the days of container metaphors for texts may be numbered.

Jay David Bolter's *Writing Space: The Computer, Hypertext, and the History of Writing* thoroughly demonstrates that writing specialists would be hard pressed to imagine or explain writing in terms other than spatial. From *topoi* to transitions, we make decisions throughout the writing process based on spatial relationships; for example, where an example goes or what point connects to what claim. To control textual space *well* is to be a good writer; in fact, controlling textual spaces is very much tied to both literacy and power. Chris Anson identifies some commonly-accepted practices that are really about writing teachers' efforts to assert control over textual space — rules about margins and double-spacing, about where the staple or paper clip goes, about where the writer's name and the date belong — all of these practices or rules are about control, which as he points out, might slip away from us in the age of electronic writing.

When created via computer interfaces, texts burst out of their containers, as Cynthia Selfe and Richard Selfe have argued. One of the reasons that word processing has been so revolutionary to writers is that it allows for easier, faster manipulation of space: sentences, chunks, or paragraphs can be deleted or moved in seconds. Because readers orient themselves spatially within printed texts — "How many more pages?" — Bolter explains that spatial disorientation is, in fact, one of the problems or challenges of electronic writing, where "the reader seldom has a sense of where he or she is in the book" (87).

Because writing teachers recognize both the spatial nature of writing and the importance of controlling textual as well as disciplinary space, compositionists have developed a rich repertoire of memorable spatial images and referents, everything from webs of meaning to turf wars. Spatial metaphors have served to establish what composition should be or to lament what composition has become. For example, claims of composition as a discipline have called on the lofty spatial metaphors of paradigms and "domains" (Phelps) or on the more mundane: inside Stephen North's sprawling, junky house of lore resides a group of sad occupants who live in the basement (Miller). Feminist readings of the field have concentrated on the domestic spaces of composition, where underpaid women are assigned primarily chores and housekeeping tasks (Slagle and Rose; Neel). In our discussions of economic and political issues about composition, we refer to heavy courseloads as teaching "in the trenches" because composition occupies the "low" position in the academy, akin to a carnival (Miller).

Generally, as composition has encountered postmodernism, metaphors of inside and outside, margin and center, boundaries and zones have become increasingly familiar, appealing, even comfortable. Mike Rose's *Lives on the Boundary;* Carolyn Ericksen Hill's *Writing on the Margins;* and Mary Louise Pratt's "Arts of the Contact Zone" identify three of the most popular spatial metaphors for discussing issues of difference and diversity or for asserting where the work of composition studies should concentrate. Perhaps the most appealing spatial metaphor right now is Gloria Anzaldúa's "borderlands" (*La Frontera*), where cultures are mixed and mingled and where geographic borders do not hold. Imagining spaces where differences mingle is important to a field characterized by interdisciplinarity and populated with some of the most marginalized members of the academy: per-course instructors, teaching assistants, and first-year students.

Despite composition's affinity for spatial metaphors, and despite rhetoric's attention to spaces for public discourse, there has not yet been a concerted effort to examine composition's geographies, nor have composition scholars typically looked to the disciplinary area of geography studies. Composition and geography have undergone similar changes in recent decades due to the impact of new technologies, and both fields are pursuing a growing interest in spatial theories.[2]

Geographic Literacy: Yet Another Crisis

Geography is, literally or etymologically, *writing the earth*, yet composition studies has not drawn much from it, exploring instead the terrains of history, philosophy, linguistics, and cognitive psychology. The lack of engagement so far between composition and geography is particularly striking in light of the fact that both fields remain so marginalized among academic disciplines and that both have been targeted by media-driven campaigns regarding literacy, composition in the mid-1970s and geography in the mid-1980s.

Like composition studies, geography has experienced the national media attention of a declared "literacy crisis." Approximately a decade after the claims that schoolchildren could not read or write, the media began reporting on survey and test results showing that college students guessed wildly on geography tests and were unable to read a map, identify important countries, or name boundary rivers or mountains.[3] With the collapse of several subjects into "social studies," American students had become geographically illiterate. Surveys confirmed that nearly 70% of all secondary students had no formal course work in geography, and the media were eager to report the most egregious examples of ignorance; for example, the belief that Canada was a state ("Teachers Lament").

In 1985, in response to "deterioration of geographic knowledge," two professional organizations set forth new guidelines for the teaching of geography in elementary and secondary schools, and Congress designated a "National Geography Awareness Week" in 1988 "to combat a widespread ignorance of geography" ("Redoubling"). The National Geographic Society pumped over two million dollars into the D.C. public school system alone, for teacher-training, a high-tech classroom, atlases, maps, and software (Horwitz A8).

Now, just ten years after the nationwide concern with geographic ignorance, interest in geography is said to be soaring, with a declared "Renaissance" in geographic education (ABC World News). From inflatable globes to such popular programs and games as "Where in the World is Carmen Sandiego?," American schoolchildren have improved test scores. Geography's fortunes are changing because of a new push towards geographic education — complete with corporate sponsorship — and because of near-revolutionary changes in map-making technology (Hitt).

A driving force behind geography's renaissance is economics: the interest in geography aligns sharply with the expansion of multinational capitalism across the globe. Satellites, cable, NAFTA, and the information superhighway — all of these developments have motivated politicians and educators to argue that American students need to be able to navigate these new horizons for commercialism. Functional illiteracy is bad for the goals of capitalism, and educators recognize the urgency of knowing more about other places and cultures in order to be competitive in the world market. A new urgency about geographic literacy accompanies other signs of the impact of time-space compression, or the belief that the planet is shrinking, with a general speed-up in the pace of everyday life.

Time-Space Compression

> Our daily life, our psychic experience, our cultural languages, are today dominated by categories of space rather than by categories of time
> — Fredric Jameson (16)

The huge campaign to remedy the geography literacy crisis gained momentum, in part, by changing conceptions of space in our late-capitalist economy. With technologies that allow the rapid, almost instantaneous, transmission of information and ever-faster modes of transportation, our world is perceived to be "smaller" than it used to be, a phenomenon known as *time-space compression*. First named by Marx as the annihilation of space through time, time-space compression means more time to work and thus more profit (Massey 146; Harvey 293; Soja 126). As spaces seem to shrink, time seems to expand — and the illusion that there is more time would allow capitalists to get more out of workers. "Time-space compression refers to movement and communication across space, to the geographical stretching-out of social relations, and to our experience of all this" (Massey 147). The perception that the earth is shrinking to the size of a "global village" — a perception that benefits the expansion of capitalism — is important to contemporary geography studies and to any examination of the spatial turn in postmodernism.

The general sensations of a shrinking planet — busier, noisier, and more crowded — triggers the temptation to look out over urban classrooms and think "the whole world is here." Other examples of time-space compression include: (1) satellites beaming events "around the globe"; (2) the weird sense of mobility that comes from "surfing the net" or from exchanging e-mail with someone in Johannesburg or Berlin or Seoul; (3) the "really there" feeling enhanced by big-screen televisions or expensive sound systems in theaters; (4) Microsoft's slogan "Where do you want to go today?" and (5) the IBM slogan "solutions for a small planet." Notably, these examples are from business, the media, and technology — forces that have combined to give us an onslaught of everyday images about how small our world is and how easily traversed.

In *The Condition of Postmodernity*, geographer David Harvey claims that the history of capitalism has been characterized by this speed-up in the pace of life. Harvey explains that time-space compression forces us "to alter, sometimes in quite radical ways, how we represent the world to ourselves" (240), the consequences of which "have particular bearing on postmodern ways of thinking, feeling, and doing" (285). These postmodern effects have by now become quite familiar: a dominance of images, where the images themselves become more real than reality: "reality gets created rather than interpreted under conditions of stress and time-space compression" (306). We get the false sense of going somewhere when we log on and having been somewhere after we log off. Through the ability of technology to simulate travel, we think we're "experiencing" a different culture, otherness, or diversity, but we're not even leaving the comfortable (or crowded) confines of our homes or offices.

As technology and capitalism have combined to make time-space compression more common and familiar, one alarming result has been the idea that space is negligible or transparent. This consequence is related to what Jameson identifies as "a new kind of flatness or depthlessness, a new kind of superficiality, . . . perhaps the most supreme formal feature of all the postmodernisms" (9). As space flattens out, time becomes both harder to notice *and* more important; the masking of *time* through the changing boundaries for *space* has consequences for workers, students, women, for all of us. Time-space compression masks the politics of space by producing the illusion that, for example, electronic gadgets can overcome space and create more time. There are distinct dangers in believing that space does not matter, and a number of geographers or spatial theorists have named this threat *transparent space*.

Transparent Space

> Transparent space assumes that the world can be seen as it really is and that there can be unmediated access to the truth of objects it sees; it is a space of mimetic representation.
> — Alison Blunt and Gillian Rose (5)

It is easy to take space and time for granted because they are such an obvious part of our everyday existence; they become routine because there doesn't seem to be anything we can do about them. However, it is important to challenge the idea of a single and objective sense of time or space, against which we attempt to measure the diversity of human conceptions and perceptions. Time-space compression leads us to believe that space is no big deal, that every divide is smaller than it seems, but feminist and other cultural geographers insist that divides are real, that differences are material and concrete, and that space cannot be treated as transparent or "innocent."

In *Space, Place, and Gender,* Doreen Massey explains that the "usual" explanation for time-space compression is internationalized capitalism, but that such an explanation is "insufficient" for women:

> The degree to which we can move between countries, or walk about the streets at night, or venture out of hotels in foreign cities, is not just influenced by 'capital.' Survey after survey has shown how women's mobility . . . is restricted — in a thousand different ways, from physical violence to being ogled at or made to feel quite simply 'out of place' — not by 'capital,' but by men. (147–48)

Time-space compression is a "high theory" concept that feminist geographers have tried to make more practical and more concerned with the everyday. As Elizabeth Wilson notes, feminists are more interested in policy issues related to space — women's safety, street lighting, or the dearth of public transport — than in theoretical or conceptual considerations (148). Massey and other feminist geographers are working towards notions of space as paradoxical, provisional, contradictory, fragmented. A notion of paradoxical spaces helps feminists to resist "transparent space," which is a particularly dangerous notion for women and other minorities because it denies differences or neglects the politics of space, especially in domestic or everyday environments. Documenting women's relationships to space has resulted in numerous studies of the home or neighborhoods — locales particularly important for women. Whether women find themselves in public space or private homes, real or imagined communities, they often experience those spaces as oppressive (Gillian Rose 143–50). Their experiences and emotions in domestic spaces are so geographically-rooted, they can vary with the floor plan — women can get angry in the kitchen, for example, but not in the bedroom (Blunt and Rose 2).

Even spaces presumed to be safe are often a threat to women. College campuses provide a good example of this image, especially as they are represented in typical media shots (especially recruitment or fundraising videos or photographs). The stately buildings, wide green lawns, and gatherings of people, presumably engaged in collegial exchanges, give the impression of harmonious intellectual activity in a tranquil environment. I spent four years on one of the most attractive college campuses ever to appear in a brochure, Miami University of Oxford, Ohio. The buildings match. Framed in buildings of southern Georgian architecture, red brick with large windows trimmed in the (exact) same shade of creamy yellow, the campus is famous for its gardens and landscaping. The serene appearance, however, masks the politics of space; for example, the numerous "keep off the grass" signs that dot the lush green lawns or the threat to women who dare to walk alone at night.

I began to think more about the politics of space after Jane Marcus visited Miami University and, struck by its wealth and privilege, spoke about the material conditions at her institution, City College, where instructors were lucky to have an office with a desk at all; forget about photocopying, a phone, chalk, or paper. If your walls weren't covered with graffiti and you had a chair, you were truly lucky. Then I read Jonathan Kozol's *Savage Inequalities* with an undergraduate course, a book which details the educational injustices done to students in cold, damp, dark classrooms, with falling plaster and trashy playgrounds. Place does matter; surroundings do have an effect on learning or attitudes towards learning, and material spaces have a political edge. In short, *where* writing instruction takes place has everything to do with *how*. When, for example, open admissions' policies went into effect, writing-center directors found themselves fighting for the most modest of spaces. Hard-won writing centers were often located in basements or tiny rooms, far from the heart of campus activity.

Some composition scholars *have* recognized issues of transparent space. In the February 1996 *CCC*, Ellen Cushman uses photographs and community history to show how "the Approach," a granite walkway leading up the hill to RPI in Troy, NY, illustrates "deeply rooted sociological distances" between the university and the community (8). The Approach is not simply a set of steps and pillars in disrepair — not transparent space — but a symbol of the wide gap between town and gown, a gap that is economic and political. Cushman's material analysis of a physical location resists the notion of transparent space. It is more typical in composition texts, however, to find notions of space that reach beyond the physical confines of classrooms or campuses, to think bigger and wider, to imagine frontiers, cities, and cyberspaces.

Imagined Geographies: Frontier, City, and Cyberspace

In what follows, I offer three extended examples of sites where time-space compression and transparent space have played out in the discourses of composition studies. While I hesitate to make the argument that time-space compression "causes" the creation of these imagined geographies, these three sites offer powerful examples of the social production of spaces in composition. In addition, their features and metaphors illustrate how material conditions can be ignored when a pioneering spirit takes hold.

The Frontier of Basic Writing

As composition workers struggled with the impact of open admissions and the demands of an expanding population, they faced working in crowded, inadequate building space populated by speakers and writers of many languages or dialects, few of them closely resembling traditional academic discourse. The feeling of "foreignness" and claustrophobia led to the construction, in discursive terms, of spaces where their struggles could be enacted. The only space big enough for such a struggle was a *frontier.*

From the first day of Open Admissions at City College, more space was needed for writing instruction. *The New York Times* reported in October of 1970 that tutoring was taking place in coat rooms while classes were being held in former ice skating rinks and supermarkets. At John Jay College, the square feet per student shrunk from 93 in 1969 to 31 the following year. "With lounge space scarce and college cafeterias jammed, many students study, do homework and eat their lunches sitting on corridor floors and stairways," and this crowding was reported in October, before the weather forced all students inside (Buder). Nearly everyone associated with the Open Admissions program has commented on the overcrowded conditions; Adrienne Rich's famous essay on "Teaching Language in Open Admissions" refers to the "overcrowded campus where in winter there is often no place to sit between classes" (60), and she gives another account to Jane Maher: "the overcrowding was acute. In the fall of 1970 we taught in open plywood cubicles set up in Great Hall [where] you could hear the noise from other cubicles; concentration was difficult for the students" (109).

The crowded and otherwise inadequate material conditions at City College led to composition's first imagined geography — and perhaps its most enduring spatial metaphor for arguing composition's legitimacy as a discipline. Mina Shaughnessy's *Errors and Expectations* opens with pointed attention to the local environment and to a very concrete physical space: she sits "alone in [a] worn urban classroom," reading with shock and dismay the folder of "alien" student essays (*vii*). The worn urban classroom, however, is soon replaced by a metaphoric location, larger and more romantic — the frontier: "the territory I am calling basic writing . . . is still very much of a frontier, unmapped, except for . . . a few blazed trails" (4). Instead of concentrating on the worn urban classroom as a site for the study of basic writing, Shaughnessy creates a guide for teachers "heading to [a] pedagogical West" (4). She admits the flaws of her map — "it is certain to have the shortcomings of other frontier maps, with doubtless a few rivers in the wrong place and some trails that end nowhere" — but what is important here is that she does not map the classroom, or the urban college spaces, or the city of New York (4). A concrete physical location, then, is erased by the more powerful American metaphor of the frontier.

Shaughnessy's early reviewers eagerly picked up on this frontier imagery because it allowed inexperienced, tentative, even resistant writing teachers to feel like brave, noble conquerors. Harvey Wiener, for example, describes Shaughnessy's book as the map, compass, and guide for those who dare to venture — or who would be sent — into the "jungle of trial and error" where teachers must "hack branches" through students' tortuous prose (715).

One way to read Shaughnessy's construction of the frontier metaphor is to see it romantically as desire for the open space of the frontier, in reaction to the crowded, chaotic conditions of City College in an Open Admissions system. Shaughnessy was undoubtedly, surrounded by overwhelming needs and demands, and all of her biographers or reviewers connect her frontier imagery to her regional identity, formed in the Black Hills of South Dakota. For example, Janet Emig writes in her eulogy for Shaughnessy, "Mina could not be understood without understanding that she came from the West" (37). To read Shaughnessy's work through the lens of the Western motif is tempting not only because of her family roots in the West, but also because of the contrast provided by her move to New York City and her major life's work spent in crowded, urban classrooms. Imagining her homeland and her own identity as a strong prairie-dweller gave her a form of escape from the multiple and oppressive institutional structures of City College. In this version, sustaining her practical, perhaps even vocational, emphasis can be draining and frustrating because of the enormity of the task; thus, Shaughnessy looks to the West for energy and a sense of mission.

Others have interpreted Shaughnessy's frontier metaphor through the realities of her workload and the crowded material spaces of City College. Robert Lyons claims that "her frequent allusions to the pioneer role of basic writing teachers and to the 'frontier' experience of such work had more to do with her sense of taxing workloads than with nostalgia for her Western past" (175). Indeed, Shaughnessy worked herself to exhaustion, suffering a brief physical collapse in 1971 (Lyons 175). For teachers in the trenches, hard work defines their experience more accurately than large expanses of hope and possibility.

Metaphors of the frontier result from dominant ideologies of space, place, and landscape in the United States: the more the better; own as much as possible; keep trespassers off; if it looks uninhabited, it must be. Canonical in American studies, F. J. Turner's thesis, "The Significance of the Frontier in American History" (1893), claimed that pushing west into the frontier was the most defining aspect of the American spirit, that the social, political, and intellectual development of the United States can be traced along the line of Western expansion. Settling the frontier, according to Turner, reenacted the history of social evolution. Turner's thesis, along with more recent studies from literature and film, can help to explain the power of the frontier metaphor in composition studies. As critics have shown, Western films capture the harshness and supposed "emptiness" of the landscape. One cinematic shot of rock and desert puts into place "an entire code of values," especially the lure of "infinite access": "the openness of the space means that domination can take place . . . . The blankness of the plain implies — without ever stating — that this is a field where a certain kind of mastery is possible" (Tompkins 74–75).

The frontier metaphor appears again and again in the literature of composition studies, often as a way of establishing or confirming composition's disciplinary status. Janice Lauer, for example, in an article which begins by asking, "Is this study a genuine discipline?" reinscribes Shaughnessy's frontier imagery. Lauer traces "the field's pioneer efforts" as it "staked out [the] territory [of writing] for investigation" (21). She characterizes composition's early theorists in "their willingness to take risks, to go beyond the boundaries of their traditional training into foreign domains" (21). According to Lauer, composition's "dappled" character as a discipline holds both advantages and risks: composition can be a "rich field of inquiry" or "a terrain of quicksand":

> The immensity of unexplored land presents a subtle seduction, drawing newcomers by promising not to relegate them to tiny plots in which to work out the arcane implications of already established scholarship. But once committed, some individuals have difficulty finding entries or end up losing their way because the role of pathfinder is challenging and thus ill-suited to everyone. The field's largely unmapped territory, therefore, has rewarded some handsomely but been fatal to others. (25)

To construct composition as a risky venture, not for the fainthearted, as Lauer does, gives composition studies a tough image: if only the fittest can survive, then it must be worthy of the status of a discipline. Joseph Harris has argued that Shaughnessy mistakenly assumed the frontier of basic writing was unoccupied, and the frontier metaphor has problematic colonialist echoes that are fairly obvious (79). Harris also makes the case that the frontier metaphor is actually quite innocuous; it gave teachers of literature a dose of missionary zeal about teaching writing to underprepared students, but also allowed them to imagine that they were not changing but simply extending the reach of the curriculum (80). Naming basic writing a frontier served to mask the politics of space — the real material conditions that crowded students into classrooms with overworked and underpaid teachers.

The frontier metaphor endures because composition's professional development was dependent on sounding "new," bold, untamed and exciting without really changing the politics of space at all. Frontier was an important imaginary space for the early days of open admissions because it seemed to invite "vision," hope, and wide expanses of possibility, but the frontier metaphor was also a reaction against the overwhelming work and responsibility that went along with educating larger, more diverse populations of college writers. Composition's development and growth meant changes in its imagined geographies, and after a brief investment in the geography of "community," composition needed a more powerful and diverse space in which to imagine its work, subjects, and practices — the *city*.

Composition as City: Postmodern and Rhetorical Spaces

As composition grew and developed, different settlements sprang up all across the wide frontier, communities characterized by differences in philosophy, political allegiances, or research methods. Acknowledgment of the diverse communities within composition was one way of demonstrating its legitimacy, but the appeal of the community metaphor soon wore thin, replaced by evocations of the city. Naming composition a city marks a moment of maturity in its history, but there are consequences to any imagined geography, and the politics of space can be either illuminated or disguised by images of the modern city.

As a second generation imagined geography, "community" offered tremendous rhetorical power. As Joseph Harris explicates, the metaphor of community is "both seductive and powerful" and "makes a claim on us that is hard to resist" (99). However, like the notion of frontier, community too often assumed transparent space — where there are clear insiders or outsiders; where differences may not be so welcomed or encouraged; or where the goal of consensus silences productive dissensus (Trimbur 608–10).

Composition scholars were quick to recognize that a warm, fuzzy notion of composition — where like-minded peoples cooperate harmoniously — would not serve the diverse populations of composition dwellers. If the frontier metaphor characterized composition as a tough field, community sounded too "wimpy," and composition continued to need authority or legitimacy within the academy. "Community" was also not geographically loaded enough to be appealing and enduring, not in the ways that frontier and city are geographically expansive and symbolically romantic. In other words, community did not last long as an imagined geography in composition because its spaces were just too limited. An imagined geography big enough to hold composition's ambitions was that of the city. Cities offer diversity of peoples and places, models of cooperation, more sites for public gathering, and more feelings of exhilaration, sometimes a keen sense of "survival of the fittest." A city metaphor seems richer and more exciting; the bustle of a city implies that work is getting done.

Seeing composition as a city also invokes the places where rhetoric flourishes — the agora, marketplace, theater, or coffeehouse. The city, therefore, offers at least two ideologies or dominant sets of images and metaphors: 1) city as an embodiment of postmodernism; 2) city as a reflection of democratic ideals. The material conditions of the city are more "in your face" than those of the frontier, which assumes a blank plain; the politics of space, therefore, seem more obvious in the city or less difficult to identify. Still, notions of the city differ ideologically, and too many views of the city glamorize its appeal.

Contemporary geographers often turn to the city to illustrate their claims about postmodernism. Edward Soja reads Los Angeles as the perfect example of "the dynamics of capitalist spatialization"; L.A. is *the* capitalist city (191). One view of the city emphasizes simultaneous stimulation and terror, where postmodern subjects feel most keenly a kind of twenty-first-century panic: the fear of being crowded; that all the space is being taken up; that the planet is overpopulated and toxic. Simultaneously, however, caught between contradictory desires, we also want the excitement and exhilaration of a city. The goal of postmodern city life is not to achieve stable orientation, but to accept disorientation as a way of life.

To invoke a city is, on one hand, to identify composition with postmodernism since crowded urban streets, like busy visual images, are more postmodern. On the other hand, unlike postmodern geographers, Harris and Lester Faigley want to claim the democratic, rhetorical, or public images of the city; for example, the idea that cities revolve around a center (Soja 234–35). In contrast to the frontier, cities have a central location, a "polis," or a "heart" (as in "in the heart of the city"). Thus, the city seems a more appropriate, more invigorating site for the exchange of ideas: there is a central place to meet, an especially appealing notion for rhetorical scholars interested in the gathering places of ancient cultures and in public spheres for communication.[4]

The city seems a more sophisticated image for composition's maturity than that of the frontier because it invites a more paradoxical notion of space and represents a different kind of work. Composition as a city invites more diversity because many different activities can go on simultaneously and, following the logic of traffic lights, no one will cause accidents or pile-ups; everyone cooperates. To navigate a city requires more experience, skill, or wits than to navigate a small community, and the alienation or anonymity are outweighed by the opportunities or stimulation. The frontier signifies the hard physical labor of sod-busting and planting and harvesting, with a landscape of plains or rolling hills, capped by big skies. The city holds bolder or more complicated signifiers, but corporate work images come to mind: high-rise office buildings, with photocopiers and air conditioning and water coolers, where the politics of space are both enhanced and complicated by modern architecture and technologies.

In representing the city as a place of either postmodern exhilaration or democratic participation, scholars and theorists may be glamorizing the city and overlooking some of the material realities — the same problem that exists with the frontier metaphor. Visitors to cities almost never see the ghettos, for example, and tourists are herded — through promotional materials, transportation routes, and hotel locations — to the most attractive sites. In addition, time-space compression works to make city-dwellers believe that technologies to shrink space have actually resulted in more time. As most commuters will attest, however, "having more time" is not exactly their experience. As cultural geographer Peter Jackson points out, ideologies of city and frontier do not differ all that much: "frontier ideologies are extraordinarily persistent even in the contemporary city, where they reappear as ideologies of 'pioneering' or 'homesteading' in the urban 'wilderness'" (111). Thus, Turner's thesis is once again reinforced — that the pioneering spirit is deeply American, and that American ideologies celebrate pioneering myths.

While the appeal of frontier turns on the American fantasies of space and place (that it is endless; the more the better; that space can be mastered), the appeal of the city turns on busy visual images, heightened adrenaline, movement, and a desire for public space or mutual co-existence with others. As Shaughnessy found out, however, work in the city was just as hard and taxing. Both of these appeals are present in a potent geographic site — *cyberspace.* Cyberspace is an imagined geography where visitors or homesteaders can be simultaneously stimulated and terrified, where order and disorder co-exist, and where the frontier metaphor continues its hold over our collective imagination. Cyberspace and its attendant electronic technologies also offer the most representative example of time-space compression, where space seems to shrink as time seems to expand.

Cyberspace and the New Frontier

> Space is not a scientific object removed from ideology and politics; it has always been political and strategic
>
> — Henri Lefebvre (qtd. in Soja 80)

As electronic writing technologies radicalize the work of our field once again, with an impact probably as large as that of Open Admissions, the pattern repeats itself: in the face of some confusion and an overwhelming sense of responsibility, the frontier beckons. It is tempting to call cyberspace "the new frontier" because it offers a sense of excitement and possibility in the face of otherwise frightening changes, and those influences combine to make cyberspace the latest imagined geography.

The frontier metaphor served well during the Kennedy Administration to justify the space program; now the frontier extends beyond space, into new imaginary territory called cyberspace. Without NASA-level technology and equipment — with only a PC and Internet access — "anyone" can go there, making it far more accessible. It is not difficult to illustrate the dominance of the frontier metaphor in discourses of electronic technologies. A core course in the telecommunications MA at George Mason University is titled "Taming the Electronic Frontier" (Cox). The Electronic Frontier Foundation lobbies to stop legislation limiting the freedom of computer users. Howard Rheingold's *The Virtual Community: Homesteading on the Electronic Frontier* addresses the idea of domesticating space — making a home in unfamiliar territory, staking a claim, naming it ours. Even the moral code of the frontier is reproduced: "The Internet has been like the Wild West before law and order was brought to it" (Vitanza 133). When two hackers meet in the OK corral for a shoot-out, the good guy usually wins (Markoff 121).

Composition, like *Star Trek* and NASA, is so completely "American," as the Muchiri essay argues, that the temptation to claim a new final frontier is strong and appealing. Despite the attractiveness of naming cyberspace a new frontier, cyberspace is not transparent space, as several scholars have recognized. Emily Jessup says it quite succinctly: "The land of computing is a frontier country, and, as in the development of most frontier countries, there are many more men than women" (336). Women and other disenfranchised groups will have to follow the maps, tracks, and instructional manuals written by the techies, mostly men who got to the colony first. Concerns of colonialism have been addressed by invoking democracy — claims that cyberspace offers more opportunities for voices to be heard, that "anyone" can participate. This view has its critics, too; for example, Mark Poster claims that promotions of Internet news groups and other virtual communities as "nascent public spheres that will renew democracy" are "fundamentally misguided" because they "overlook the profound differences between Internet 'cafes' and the agoras of the past" (135). Cyberspace is not transparent space, and dominant sexual-social politics are reproduced on the Net (Tannen, Bruckman): crimes have been committed in MUDs and MOOs, with rape and death in "the Bungle case" on Lambdamoo (Dibbell).

Granted, much about cyberspace is hugely inviting: chat rooms and emoticons and a "web" of access to information (and to "community"). The notion of the web, familiar to composition through both Janet Emig and Marilyn Cooper, touches on ecological metaphors that many writing teachers found more inviting than other mechanistic metaphors for the writing process. The World Wide Web has the same inviting ecological tenor, and the implication is that strands seem to connect the whole world, stretching across and enveloping many sites. At odds with these "warm and fuzzy" notions of the WWW are some material realities: the whole world is *not* in the Web. Issues of access aside, the metaphor of a web also evokes entrapment. Webs, as any fly knows, can be sticky traps for the negligent or gullible; not all of us are safe in a web. A web has thousands, if not millions, of intersecting strands. What I want to know is, how do I get around in here? And how do I get out when I want to leave? (If it weren't for the "Back" and "Home" icons on the newer Web browsers, I would still be lost in cyberspace!)

A lot of Net users find it hard to leave — not only from confusion but from a sense that virtual spaces are more inviting or attractive. When they devote themselves to screens and keyboards, online participants are removing their actual bodies from physical spaces, and that creates another set of problems for geopolitics. As Stephen Doheny-Farina argues in *The Wired Neighborhood*, participation in online communities removes people from their geophysical communities — the streets and schools, sidewalks and shops that make up a neighborhood. People have understandably turned to virtual communities to fulfill some of their needs not being met by physical communities, but Doheny-Farina critiques claims that the Internet's chat rooms are new public spaces. Admitting his own fascination with MediaMOO, in one chapter, Doheny-Farina shows how the supposedly public spaces are more accurately a maze of private rooms, where one's participation ("socialization") is dependent upon one's technical expertise, including one's skill as a typist (61). Settling upon the analogy of virtual communities being like airport bars, Doheny-Farina admits to the compelling nature of these online enterprises, but repeatedly notes the seduction, even the danger, of ignoring the politics of space in our daily environments.

While I am no expert on computers and writing or electronic technologies, my lack of expertise is precisely the point: Most people aren't, and we are the ones entering frontierland well behind the first settlers. The material spaces have changed but the challenges and responsibilities have not. Much as Shaughnessy sat in her worn urban classroom wondering how to help her stunningly unskilled students through the tangle of academic discourse, I sit in a new, well-equipped computer classroom and wonder how I can guide my students through the maze of electronic writing technologies — or if I should turn my composition classes into Computer Literacy 101, Advanced Word Processing, or Introduction to the Internet. Our field is beginning to feel very keenly the responsibility for educating students about electronic writing technologies, and that creates a new level of anxiety (and stimulation) akin to city life. From my experience at a fairly large state university in the Northeast, most of my first-year students are not computer-literate or computer-comfortable. Their high schools in this and surrounding states did not exactly pass out laptops as students walked through the security terminals. Most literacy workers are more affected by budget constraints than by a technology explosion, so expectations to educate students in electronic discourses and computer technologies — while also helping them to think more critically, write more fluently and persuasively, and edit more carefully — becomes an overwhelming responsibility.

The frontier, city, and cyberspace are three imagined geographies that illustrate how composition's socially produced spaces have served to give composition vision and a sense of mission but have also served to mask the politics of space. In the concluding section below, I want to turn to more unfamiliar material places that need our attention, especially in their implications for workers and working conditions.

Between Spaces and Practices: Geographic Possibilities for Studying Composition

As this section suggests, time-space compression affects composition's workers on a daily basis, in concrete ways that need our attention. A spatial politics of writing instruction works to deny transparent space and to attend to neglected places, in their material rather than their imaginary forms, where writers and writing teachers work, live, talk, daydream, or doodle. I'm particularly interested in the increased demands on *time* because technologies have shifted *space*, along with the ways in which technology has increased responsibilities and workloads while material spaces for writing instruction continue to crowd or deteriorate. Composition needs to develop ways to study space differently that might close the gap between imagined geographies and material conditions for writing, between the spaces and practices, or that might confront the way that time-space compression creates illusions about "more time" and "overcoming" spatial barriers.

First, instead of thinking bigger and wider, as composition has typically done — using large imagined geographies to situate and validate composition studies as a discipline — now it is time to think smaller and more locally. And while there have been plenty of studies of classrooms or writing centers or writing programs, a geographic emphasis would insist on more attention to the connection between spaces and practices, more effort to link the material conditions to the activities of particular spaces, whether those be campuses, classrooms, office, computer labs, distance-learning sites, or hotels.

The material spaces of campuses, schoolyards, and classrooms across the country — especially those in economically devastated areas — are marked by ceiling tiles falling onto unswept floors, in rooms with graffiti, trash, and no chalk, or no chalkboard. Classrooms are crowded and too hot or too cold, or with badly filtered air. Certain buildings on many campuses are said to be "poison," where a disproportionate number of illnesses develop, including cancer.[5] To neglect these material realities in qualitative studies of writing instruction is to ignore the politics of space, the ways in which our surroundings or location affect the work that is done there. In research studies of all types, there is scant attention to the conditions and context affecting participants and researchers alike: the weather, the room, the amount or quality of space.

To illustrate, the teaching assistant offices at my institution are referred to, variously, as the pit, the rat's nest, or the hole, where the walls are paper-thin dividers; where there's only one phone for roughly twenty-four instructors; and where occupants last winter had to dodge buckets and trash cans strategically placed to catch rain leaks and falling plaster. Any outsider would immediately recognize the status of the teaching assistants based only on the appearance of their office space. Moving beyond a "thick description," a qualitative study of this space would have to account, in the fullest possible ways, for the material conditions of this office which have everything to do with the work that gets done there. Even newcomers to the academy recognize that the larger or nicer the office, the more senior its occupant, and they don't need a member of a space allocation committee to tell them that.

Perhaps more important than a spatial-politics approach to qualitative research, understanding more about how time-space compression works would enable us to both acknowledge and address working conditions in writing instruction, an issue of the 1990s that will not go away in the new century. Time-space compression creates the illusion that we have "shrunk" space or overcome wide distances; with such a notion comes the conclusion that without travel time, workers can produce more. The capitalist equation — less space equals more time — makes issues of worker exploitation even more complicated for writing instruction.

Issues of working conditions are near the top of the agendas of our professional organizations, with CCCC and MLA having passed or considering resolutions committed to the improvement of the status of non–tenure-track faculty in composition studies. Given the complexity of trying to make any concrete or measurable changes, it seems that one way to improve the status of non–tenure-track faculty in composition is to examine closely the spaces in which we ask them to work, the conditions of those spaces, and the assumptions about time and space that control workers' daily environments.

With laptop computers, around-the-clock access, and the option of asynchronous dialogue, the idea that workers can be productive from "anywhere" at "any time" permeates our culture. Composition workers are just now beginning to recognize how new technologies have affected our workdays, as this passage illustrates:

> In theory, email should create more time. But even though readers can chug along at their own paces, individual paces may not always be in sync. . . . [In participating in Portnet, an online discussion], I was desperate for time. Because of my teaching and professional schedule, my email communication had to wait until evening — late evening. My commitment to Portnet faltered somewhat the first time I turned on my computer at eleven o'clock p.m. and discovered more than forty Portnet messages waiting for me. The next night over eighty Portnet messages appeared on the screen. . . . between . . . more than twenty posts from my students . . . and another ten from local colleagues on various matters. (Dickson, qtd. in Allen et al. 377)

Questions about working conditions multiply, too, when considering the impact of distance-learning, the latest rage in the competitive world of higher education, especially in areas of the West and Midwest where towns and cities are far apart. Questions should arise for composition programs about how distance-learning changes our ideas about writing instruction and our common practices involving, as just one example, peer response groups (that is, f2f meetings between writers). What happens to classrooms, libraries, "memorial unions," or lecture halls, especially on some already-deteriorating campuses, many built on the cheap in the late 1960s and early 70s? Should colleges invest more in electronic technologies than in buildings that invite gatherings? Some colleges, in an effort to combine community outreach, distance-learning, and keen competitiveness, have all but eliminated central campuses. For example, Rio Salado Community College in Tempe, Arizona, "has no campus and educates 34,000 students in places like churches and shopping malls, and, increasingly, at home on their computers" (Applebome 24). What happens, then, to the geopolitical spaces of university campuses, especially in light of Doheny-Farina's concerns?

Despite the growing attention to new spaces for the work of our profession, the material sites for composition extend beyond offices, classrooms, computer labs, or cyberspaces. Many of the debates, discussions and conversations about writing instruction take place in hotels or on conference sites distinguished by huge buildings in the downtown areas of major cities, and these sites are especially prone to being treated as transparent space. With the growth of CCCC in the last fifty years, our meeting sites have had to expand and change to accommodate the growing numbers, and site selection for our annual meetings has become the most highly charged, time-consuming, and hotly politicized issue of the CCCC Executive Committee in recent years.

First, on a very practical level, CCCC's annual meeting, held in the spring months of every year, requires thirty-five contiguous meeting rooms and 1,500 sleeping rooms for a four-day gathering of over 3,000 members. Those numbers and needs alone make it difficult to find cities that can serve our membership, and the equation is complicated by the desire to represent fairly or sensitively every diverse constituency within CCCC — to attend to a complicated variety of geographic, economic, and political concerns. While the effort to rotate the locations by region has been in place for years, increasing efforts to accommodate political concerns have made the process of site selection fraught with difficult decisions about "whose" interests count more or which cities have the least offensive laws or statutes. An inept process of site selection was finally challenged after the Executive Committee decided to go to Atlanta for the 1999 convention. Some members of the Gay and Lesbian Caucus announced, in response, that they would boycott that convention, citing in particular their exclusion from the process of selecting convention cities. Since then, the CCCC Officers and Executive Committee have worked to institutionalize the voices and concerns of various caucuses within the organization, making communication across the membership a more integral part of the site selection process (culminating in a recently named "Convention Concerns Committee").

What does it matter where we meet? First, convention sites are tangible examples of the politics of space in composition — where discourses, practices, and people meet in a geopolitical space — and convention hotels and cities also represent some of the neglected places where the work of writing instruction is impacted by geophysical factors. Second, beyond the large concerns about the personal safety of CCCC members, there are many small material realities that affect many things about the success of a conference site. For example, when we are occupied with transportation woes, the cost of a meal in a hotel, or the lack of women's bathroom stalls, time and energy are taken away from conversation about writing, about students, about our programs and ideas. When hotels don't have a central meeting place, or the main lobby is hard to find, or the levels are oddly numbered, members waste time finding each other and sacrifice time talking or listening or engaging.

Imagined geographies have served their purpose in composition's identity-formation and will continue to shape a sense of vision and possibility for writing teachers and researchers. However, the imaginary visions must be more firmly grounded in material conditions: traveling through cyberspace, for example, does require hardware and software, and meeting in hotels does mean that workers must serve and clean up after us.

A spatial politics of writing instruction would not call for a new frontier but for a more paradoxical sense of space to inform our research and practices and to approach the study of the social production of spaces in a field already committed to examining the production of discourse. Most importantly, a spatial politics of writing instruction would resist notions of transparent space that deny the connections to material conditions and would account for the various ways in which time-space compression affects composition's workers.

Acknowledgments

Thanks to those who read, responded, and made me think harder: Kristen Kennedy, Arthur Riss, Nancy Cook, and the two *CCC* reviewers, John Trimbur and Gregory Clark.

Notes

1. Many of the geographers I have been reading have been influenced by Henri Lefebvre and by Foucault's later writings, particularly "Questions on Geography" and "Of Other Spaces." Michel de Certeau's *The Practice of Everyday Life* has been tremendously helpful in thinking about the rhetoric of negotiating space (see esp. "Walking in the City" 91–110) and the connection between spaces and practices. Feminist geographers draw from a range

of landscape studies, women's travel writing, and colonialist theories, and urban geographers are likely to frame their work with postmodernist architecture; the fascination with Los Angeles is particularly striking (Jameson; Soja; Harvey). My turn to geography is one response to John Schilb's challenge to rhetoricians: that we should be explaining and illustrating postmodernism for those who cannot (or will not) read Fredric Jameson. In an RSA presentation in May, 1994, Schilb demonstrated this claim through a reading of a Clint Eastwood film, set at the Hotel Bonaventure in Los Angeles.

2. Composition scholarship is increasingly interested in spatial theories and the importance of locations. A quick review of the program for the 1998 CCCC Annual Convention yields at least a dozen panel or forum titles with such keywords as space, place, landscapes, the politics of space, the public sphere, postmodern geography, or travel. See also Gregory Clark's 1998 *CCC* essay, "Writing as Travel, or Rhetoric on the Road."

3. For example, a 1988 Gallup survey showed that 75% of Americans age 18–24 couldn't locate the Persian Gulf on a world map and 25% couldn't find the Pacific Ocean (Horwitz A8).

4. Most recently, Harris has offered *public* as a better keyword than *community*. See *A Teaching Subject*, pp. 107–10.

5. The campus building I work in is just plain filthy, one result of severe budget cuts, and the conditions do affect the morale of workers. The state of the bathroom, while it may "bond" the women on my floor, does not exactly promote worker loyalty or productivity.

Works Cited

Allen, Michael, et al. "Portfolios, WAC, Email, and Assessment: An Inquiry on Portnet." *Situating Portfolios*. Ed. Kathleen Blake Yancey and Irwin Weiser. Logan: Utah State UP, 1997. 370–84.

Anson, Chris. "Assigning and Responding to Student Writing." Colgate U, Hamilton, NY, August 1995.

Anzaldúa, Gloria. *Borderlands/La Frontera*. San Francisco: Aunt Lute, 1987.

Applebome, Peter. "Community Colleges at the Crossroads: Which Way Is Up?" *New York Times* 3 August 1997: 4A; 24–26; 30.

Blunt, Alison, and Gillian Rose, eds. *Writing Women and Space: Colonial and Postcolonial Geographies*. NY: Guilford, 1994.

Bolter, Jay David. *Writing Space: The Computer, Hypertext, and the History of Writing*. Mahwah: Erlbaum, 1991.

Bowden, Darsie. "The Limits of Containment: Text-as-Container in Composition Studies." *CCC* 44 (1993): 364–79.

Bruckman, Amy S. "Gender Swapping on the Internet." Vitanza. 441–47.

Buder, Leonard. "Open-Admissions Policy Taxes City U. Resources." *New York Times* 12 October 1970: A1+.

Certeau, Michel de. *The Practice of Everyday Life*. Berkeley: U of California P, 1984.

Clark, Gregory. "Writing as Travel, or Rhetoric on the Road." *CCC* 49 (1998): 9–23.

Cooper, Marilyn M. "The Ecology of Writing." *College English* 48 (1986): 364–75.

Cox, Brad. "Taming the Electronic Frontier." http://gopher.gmu.edu/bcox/LRN6372/00LRNG572.html.

Cushman, Ellen. "Rhetorician as Agent of Social Change." *CCC* 47 (1996): 7–28.

Dibbell, Julian. "A Rape in Cyberspace." Vitanza. 448–65.

Doheny-Farina, Stephen. *The Wired Neighborhood*. New Haven: Yale UP, 1996.

Emig, Janet. "Mina Pendo Shaughnessy." *CCC* 30 (1979): 37–8.

Faigley, Lester. *Fragments of Rationality: Postmodernity and the Subject of Composition*. U of Pittsburgh P, 1992.

Harris, Joseph. *A Teaching Subject: Composition since 1966*. Upper Saddle River: Prentice, 1997.

Harvey, David. *The Condition of Postmodernity: An Enquiry into the Origins of Cultural Change*. Cambridge: Blackwell, 1989.

Hill, Carolyn Ericksen. *Writing from the Margins: Power and Pedagogy for Teachers of Composition*. New York: Oxford UP, 1990.

Hitt, Jack. "Atlas Shrugged: The New Face of Maps." *Lingua Franca* 5.5 (1995): 24–33.

Horwitz, Sari. "No Longer a World Apart: Grant Brings Geography Home to District Students." *Washington Post* 19 March 1994: A1; A8.

Jackson, Peter. *Maps of Meaning: An Introduction to Cultural Geography*. New York: Routledge, 1989.

Jameson, Fredric. *Postmodernism, or, The Cultural Logic of Late Capitalism*. Durham: Duke UP, 1991.

Jessup, Emily. "Feminism and Computers in Composition Instruction." *Evolving Perspectives on Computers and Composition Studies: Questions for the 1990s*. Ed. Gail E. Hawisher and Cynthia L. Selfe. Urbana: NCTE, 1991. 336–55.

Kozol, Jonathan. *Savage Inequalities: Children in America's Schools*. New York: Crown, 1991.

Lauer, Janice M. "Composition Studies: A Dappled Discipline." *Rhetoric Review* 3 (1984): 20–29.

Lyons, Robert. "Mina Shaughnessy." *Traditions of Inquiry*. Ed. John Brereton. New York: Oxford UP, 1985. 171–89.

Maher, Jane. *Mina P. Shaughnessy: Her Life and Work*. Urbana: NCTE, 1997.

Markoff, John. "Hacker and Grifter Duel on the Net." Vitanza. 119–21.

Massey, Doreen. *Space, Place, and Gender*. Minneapolis: U of Minnesota P, 1994.

Miller, Susan. *Textual Carnivals: The Politics of Composition*. Southern Illinois UP, 1991.

Muchiri, Mary N., Nshindi G. Mulamba, Greg Myers, and Deoscorous B. Ndoloi. "Importing Composition: Teaching and Researching Academic Writing beyond North America." *CCC* 46 (1995): 175–98.

Nash, Catherine. "Remapping the Body/Land: New Cartographies of Identity, Gender, and Landscape in Ireland." *Writing Women and Space: Colonial and Postcolonial Geographies*. Ed. Alison Blunt and Gillian Rose. 227–50.

Neel, Jasper. "The Degradation of Rhetoric; Or, Dressing Like a Gentleman, Speaking Like a Scholar." *Rhetoric, Sophistry, Pragmatism*. Ed. Steven Mailloux. New York: Cambridge UP, 1995. 61–81.

North, Stephen M. *The Making of Knowledge in Composition: Portrait of an Emerging Field*. Upper Montclair: Boynton, 1987.

Phelps, Louise Wetherbee. "The Domain of Composition." *Rhetoric Review* 4 (1986): 182–95.

Poster, Mark. "The Net as a Public Sphere?" *Wired* Nov. 1995: 135–36.

Pratt, Mary Louise. "Arts of the Contact Zone." *Profession 91* (1991): 33–40.

"Redoubling the Efforts at Teaching Geography." *New York Times* 19 Nov. 1993: C, 11:1.

Rheingold, Howard. *The Virtual Community: Homesteading on the Electronic Frontier.* New York: Harper, 1993.

Rich, Adrienne. "Teaching Language in Open Admissions." *On Lies, Secrets, and Silence: Selected Prose 1966–1978.* New York: Norton, 1979. 51–68.

Rose, Gillian. *Feminism and Geography: The Limits of Geographical Knowledge.* Minneapolis: U of Minnesota P, 1993.

Rose, Mike. *Lives on the Boundary.* New York: Free P, 1989.

Schilb, John. "Articulating the Discourses of Postmodernism." Rhetoric Society of America, Norfolk, VA, May 1994.

Selfe, Cynthia, and Richard J. Selfe, Jr. "The Politics of the Interface: Power and Its Exercise in Electronic Contact Zones." *CCC* 45 (1994): 480–504.

Shaughnessy, Mina. *Errors and Expectations.* New York: Oxford UP, 1977.

Slagle, Diane Buckles, and Shirley K. Rose. "Domesticating English Studies." *Journal of Teaching Writing* 13 (1994): 147–68.

Soja, Edward W. *Postmodern Geographies: The Reassertion of Space in Critical Social Theory.* New York: Verso, 1989.

Tannen, Deborah. "Gender Gap in Cyberspace." Vitanza. 141–43.

"Teachers Lament Geography Scores." *New York Times* 12 March 1985: III, 11:1.

Tompkins, Jane. *West of Everything: The Inner Life of Westerns.* New York: Oxford UP, 1992.

Trimbur, John. "Consensus and Difference in Collaborative Learning." *College English* 51 (1989): 602–16.

Turner, Frederick Jackson. "The Significance of the Frontier in American History (1893)." *History, Frontier, and Section.* Albuquerque: U of New Mexico P, 1993. 59–91.

Vitanza, Victor, ed. *CyberReader.* Boston: Allyn, 1996.

Wiener, Harvey S. Rev. of *Errors and Expectations,* by Mina P. Shaughnessy. *College English* 38 (1977): 715–17.

Wilson, Elizabeth. "The Rhetoric of Urban Space." *New Left Review* 209 (1995): 146–60.

Reynolds's Insights as a Resource for Your Teaching

1. After reading Reynolds's essay, the question "Where do you work?" resonates with particular complexity. Try brainstorming some distinguishing features of the student body at the institution where you teach. What sorts of regional influences or economic factors shape their experience in your classroom? In what ways do these influences shape the administration under which you work?

2. While the essay's three dominant metaphors (frontier, city, cyberspace) have a certain value, they also are undoubtedly loaded with myths and assumptions that mask key aspects of your distinctive environment. Explore the limitations of these

metaphors as models for understanding your classroom. Can you identify actual moments or imagine possible scenarios where this masking proceeds with particularly destructive results?

Reynolds's Insights as a Resource for Your Writing Classroom

1. Summarize Reynolds's ideas about the metaphor of the frontier and the city for your students. What concerns do they have about this way of looking at the classroom? What potential problems do they envision?

2. Ask your students to share their thoughts about the way in which communications technology is making the world an ever smaller place. What do they feel this means for the particular corner or corners of the world where their lives have unfolded so far?

3. In considering the increased accessibility that telecommunications technology offers to regions and people on a global scale, do students think that this access emphasizes the perception and understanding of cultural, social, and regional differences, or do they think that it is contributing to an increasingly homogenized worldview?

Toward Reconstructing American Classrooms: Interdependent Students, Interdependent World

Kenneth Bruffee

Kenneth Bruffee researched and reflected on collaborative learning, writers, and writing in the 1970s and structured his book A Short Course in Writing *with peer tutoring and collaborative activities. The full title of the fourth edition shows the scope of his assumptions about the purpose of a writing course:* A Short Course in Writing: Composition, Collaborative Learning, and Constructive Reading. *Bruffee has written extensively about processes of collaboration and the social construction of knowledge in American classrooms; his extensive analysis and discussion in* Collaborative Learning *(Baltimore: Johns Hopkins UP, 1993) addresses the role of college and university teachers across the curriculum in helping "students converse with increasing facility in the language of the communities they want to join." The following article is Chapter 4 from this book.*

Bruffee, too, counsels instructors to identify and question their assumptions about the nature and authority of knowledge. Because collaborative learning contrasts markedly with the conventions of tradi-

tional teaching, Bruffee carefully defines terms and traces the philosophi-cal history of collaborative learning. In particular, he emphasizes the distinctive role of assisting groups of students in classrooms or "transi-tion communities"; all the students are leaving one community of knowl-edge to join a community that is new to them. Writing instructors can easily perceive connections among Bruffee's discussion of "translation" and "linguistic improvisation," their classrooms, and their reflective practice. They are likely to check out the volume to follow his references back to Chapter 3, where he specifically discusses teaching writing, or forward to Chapter 10, to eavesdrop on the translation groups William Perry reported in his study of sociocognitive development over college careers.

C ollege and university teachers are likely to be successful in orga-nizing collaborative learning to the degree that they understand the three kinds of negotiation that occur in the nonfoundational social construction of knowledge: negotiation among the members of a com-munity of knowledgeable peers, negotiation at the boundaries among knowledge communities, and negotiation at the boundaries between knowledge communities and outsiders who want to join them.[1]

These three kinds of negotiation define both the practice of college and university teaching and the nature of college and university teach-ing as a profession. In Chapter 8 I will examine some of the profes-sional implications of this distinguishing expertise. In the present chap-ter, after explaining the three kinds of negotiation in some detail, I will address some of their pedagogical and educational implications for col-leges and universities and their teachers. In doing so, I will answer two questions: How does collaborative learning differ from foundational innovations in teaching? and, How does the thinking of college and university teachers about teaching have to change if change in college and university education is not to be superficial and ephemeral?

The first kind of negotiation that occurs in the nonfoundational social construction of knowledge is within a community of knowledge-able peers, among its members. Members of academic or professional knowledge communities such as law, medicine, and the academic disci-plines negotiate with other members of the same community in order to establish and maintain the beliefs that constitute that community. Biochemists, for example (as we saw at the beginning of Chapter 3), review each other's work over the lab bench, and they read and re-spond to each other's published articles. This conversation within knowl-edge communities is what Thomas Kuhn calls *normal science* and, fol-lowing Kuhn, what Richard Rorty calls *normal discourse*. As members of disciplinary and other kinds of knowledge communities, college and university teachers are fluent in the normal discourse of these commu-nities.

The second kind of negotiation involved in constructing knowledge understood nonfoundationally occurs between different knowledge com-munities and is carried on at the boundaries where communities meet.

Members of different academic and professional knowledge communities negotiate with one another in order to translate the language of one community into the language of another. They may do this so as to neutralize threats that one community seems to pose to the established beliefs of another, or they may do it to assimilate and normalize options that one knowledge community seems to offer to the other. Paleobotanists try to reconcile what they know with what the microbiologists are coming up with; New Critics defend themselves against what the deconstructionists have to say; physicists find themselves talking with historians, biologists with lawyers, ethnographers with literary critics. Kuhn and Rorty call this boundary negotiation *abnormal science* and *abnormal discourse,* respectively. Clifford Geertz calls it, somewhat less prejudicially if not necessarily more accurately, *nonstandard discourse.*

Nonstandard discourse is a demanding and uncertain kind of conversation. It is "nonstandard" because, in negotiation between two different knowledge communities, the language and ideas that one community accepts without resistance — for example, what they agree to count as a "real question" and an interesting answer to that question — is not likely to be accepted without resistance by another community. The standard that will prevail between two communities, if their boundary negotiation is successful, is a major part of what they have to negotiate. College and university teachers, as active members of their professional or academic communities, have to be able to engage in this nonstandard discourse of boundary negotiation between communities that they belong to and those that their colleagues belong to.

College and university teachers have to be especially adept at nonstandard, boundary discourse, because they have to engage in it professionally on two fronts. The third kind of negotiation involved in knowledge understood nonfoundationally occurs at community boundaries that may be even more difficult to negotiate than the boundaries that separate academic or professional communities. Teachers have to be able to translate at the community boundaries between the academic or professional knowledge communities that they belong to and uncountable numbers of nonacademic, nonprofessional communities that their students belong to. That is, they have to be able to translate the languages of academics and professionals into the languages of people who are not (yet) members of any academic or professional community, but who aspire to become members: from biologists to biology students, philosophers to philosophy students, literary critics to naive readers, and so on.

Mastering the linguistic improvisation involved in this third kind of nonstandard discourse — negotiation at the boundaries between knowledge communities and outsiders who want to join them — distinguishes a knowledge community's teachers from its ordinary members. More than anything else, this facility in negotiating what Mary Louise Pratt calls "contact zones . . . social spaces where cultures meet, clash, and grapple with each other, often in contexts of highly asymmetrical relations of power," defines the classroom authority of college and university teachers.[2] It also defines the cultural importance and cultural authority of college and university teachers outside the classroom and beyond the campus.

What makes boundary negotiation especially challenging is that people who are not yet members of the community of, say, chemists, philosophers, or literary critics are not simply members of no knowledge community at all. On the contrary, they are already stalwart, long-time, loyal members of an enormous array of other, mostly nonacademic, nonprofessional knowledge communities.

That is why negotiation between members of academic or professional communities and nonmembers is difficult. College and university students are decidedly not a *tabula rasa*. The language of caring, of counting to ten, of belligerence, or of baseball may be anybody's mother or father tongue, as the language of chemistry, say, can never be. So, although mere chemists have to be able to talk comprehensively as chemists with other chemists and, on occasion, perhaps, to a physicist, astronomer, biologist, or lawyer, college and university chemistry *teachers* have to be able to talk comprehensively as chemists also with all the Trekkies, romance-novel readers, canoeists, computer hackers, fast-food restaurant assistant managers, and football players who aspire to become chemists or at least to learn something about chemistry.

Of these three kinds of negotiation, the most important to college and university teachers *as* teachers is of course the third. Skill in negotiating between knowledge communities of which the teacher is a member and those who aspire to join them — students — requires understanding first of all that every college and university classroom — indeed, every college and university — is a community that, like all communities, has its own set of rules, mores, values, and goals, all of them accepted, more or less, by everyone in the community. They regulate everyone's deportment, relationships, and expectations. They are appropriate to the assumptions, shared by everyone in the community, about human nature, the human mind, and the nature and authority of knowledge. The depth and persistence of these conventions and assumptions result in one of the quiet, nagging truths of college and university education: we tend to forget much of the subject matter of the courses we have taken shortly after we complete them, but we do not easily forget the conventions that govern those courses and the values implicit in them.

The foundational conventions that govern traditional college and university classrooms assume (as we shall see in Chapter 12) that the authority of teachers lies in their function as curators of acknowledged touchstones of value and truth above and beyond themselves, such as treasured artifacts of art, literature, science, mathematics, and the universals of sound reasoning. The authority of college and university teachers from this point of view rests on the understanding that knowledge is a kind of substance contained in and given form by the vessel we call the mind. Teachers transfer knowledge from their own fuller vessels to the less full vessels of their students. Teachers impart knowledge that was imparted to them, as it was imparted to them.

The classroom social structure and conventions implicit in these foundational assumptions — what Pratt aptly calls "pupiling" — are familiar to everyone who has attended an American college or university.[3] They prevail with few exceptions today the world over, from the two Cambridges to Tokyo, from first grade to Ph.D. They are so familiar that we take them for granted. Like the curatorial role of college and university teachers, they have an ancient and honorable history, they remain educationally valuable under certain local circumstances today, and they probably will always remain so.

The social structure and conventions of foundational college and university education assume a one-to-one relationship between student and teacher. Students talk to the teacher, write to the teacher, and determine their fate in relation to the teacher, individually. This is true no matter how many students there may be in a class: three, thirty, or three hundred. There is no recognized, validly institutionalized, productive relationship among students. More accurately, traditional teaching assumes and maintains a negative competitive relationship among students. They are officially anonymous to one another, and isolated. Classroom learning is an almost entirely individual process. It is not just that most foundational teaching does not encourage students to collaborate. Most foundational teaching does not recognize collaboration as educationally valid. In fact, in traditional teaching collaboration is highly suspect. In some forms it is the worst possible academic sin: plagiarism.

The conventions of traditional teaching can be classified under two headings, the Lecture Conventions and the Recitation Conventions. Lecture Convention teachers tend to talk and perform; their students listen and watch. Recitation Convention teachers tend to listen and watch; their students talk and perform. Most college and university teachers combine these conventions in some proportion or other. For example, Lecture-Recitation teachers may choose students who talk and perform particularly well to talk and perform in place of the teacher. Then the teacher listens and watches along with the rest of the class.

The normal goal of Lecture Convention teaching is to provide answers, promote the authority of those answers, and enhance the authority of the lecturer providing them. Since answers imply questions, it would seem that the role that questions play in Lecture Convention teaching must be particularly interesting and varied. In most cases, however, it is not. Most lecturers answer the questions that they are prepared and willing to answer. They may or may not accept questions raised by students, or they may answer some and finesse others.

The most common Lecture Convention in which questions do play a major role is Socratic Dialogue. The conventions of this form of teaching derive from Plato's *Meno,* in which Socrates teaches a slave. In Socratic Dialogue, students do not ask the questions. Teachers ask them, and the role that questions play in teaching is tightly controlled. Teachers approve or disapprove the answers students offer in response to questions. They try to lead students to say what teachers might as well have said themselves, had they chosen to. The line of reasoning taken during the dialogue is the teacher's own, leading to a point that the teacher has decided on beforehand.

Recitation Convention teaching differs from Lecture Convention teaching by shifting to students the burden of filling class time. In outlining the requirements of the course, the teacher makes it clear that students will do most of the talking and performing, specifies what they will perform and talk about, and explains what kind of talk it should be. The teacher retains the privilege of interrupting recitations at will in order to evaluate what students say, correct it, or elaborate on it.

Forms of Recitation Convention adapted to special circumstances include the Tutorial Convention, the Seminar Convention, the Writing Course Convention, and the Teamwork Convention. In each of these, students present their work individually, in written or oral form. Then they discuss their work with the teacher or answer questions that the teacher asks them about it. In turn, the teacher evaluates, corrects, or elaborates upon the student's work.

The Seminar Convention is a cost-efficient version of the Tutorial Convention. In tutorials, teachers meet students one at a time. In seminars, they meet them five to fifteen at a time. Tutorials and seminars both allow for considerable debate between students and the teacher and, in seminars under the teacher's direction and observation, among students. At issue is the quality of each student's live performance before the teacher in competition with other students. In a seminar a student sometimes replaces the teacher as the discussion moderator, but performance quality before the teacher is still the main criterion of judgment. Students who "take over the class" in this way become teacher surrogates. If they are wise and well adapted, they read a paper and field questions about their work in a way that is calculated to receive maximum approval from the teacher.

In the Writing Course Convention and its subgenre, the Creative Writing Course Convention, the teacher prompts students to comment on one another's essays, stories, poems, or plays. But in these classes, which are usually described publicly as being about writing, not about reading or criticism, teachers seldom instruct students in how to engage helpfully in the intellectually demanding, aesthetically sophisticated, and socially delicate process of commenting helpfully on the work of peers. As a result, students understand that their comments on one another's work are made not primarily for the benefit of fellow students. They are a performance before an audience of one, the teacher. In these comments students tend to become (as we noticed in Chapter 1) alternately sharks and teddy bears, providing cutting insult or effusive praise depending on their interpretation of "what the teacher wants."

The Teamwork Convention is most often found in engineering and the sciences, where it takes the form of research teams, and in music, theater, and film in the form of ensembles and production units. It is the most nearly collaborative of all traditional forms of teaching. Assigned to a team, students work together on a project under the teacher's supervision. In some cases, all the members of the team are equally responsible for the quality of the work they do together. In other cases, the teacher evaluates a report written by each student on the team. At issue in most cases is what students accomplish together, the product of their cooperative effort. In educational teamwork at its best, the nature and quality of what students internalize and carry away from the experience is also at issue.

All four forms of the Recitation Convention allow teachers the prerogative of lecturing when they choose, a prerogative that many teachers frequently exercise. Science course laboratory work, for example, is a kind of recitation in which the student's response takes the form of actively manipulating material and instruments and then reporting that work in writing. But many labs are like the introductory undergraduate astronomy lab described by one of Sheila Tobias's informants, in which students saw no stars. The instructor spent every class hour working problems on the blackboard — in effect, lecturing. Some creative writing teachers fill large portions of class time reading their own work to their students. Some seminar teachers (the philosopher Edmund Husserl is reputed to have been a particularly egregious example) lecture incessantly, believing all the while that they are "leading discussion."

A student's responsibility, according to these traditional classroom conventions, is to "absorb" what the teacher, in one way or another, imparts. The teacher's responsibility is to impart knowledge to students and evaluate students' retention of it. Teachers evaluate students in the same way their own teachers evaluated them, and as the college or university in which they teach is likely to evaluate teachers, in terms of their "product."

Dissatisfaction with the conventions of foundational teaching is hardly new. It has grown throughout this century. John Dewey voiced it in the 1920s and 1930s. It reached a peak in the late 1960s and early 1970s, when leading college and university teachers made well-known and widely discussed attempts to change the nature of college and university teaching. Since that heyday of experimentation, widespread interest in innovation has waned, except for scattered recent attempts to repackage science education (discussed in Chapter 9); politically motivated efforts to change or enlarge the literary "canon"; efforts to "personalize" teaching in the manner of Roland Barthes; and a few largely speculative poststructuralist ventures (discussed in Chapter 11).[4]

Most of these recent attempts are likely to fail for the same reason that similar teaching innovations of the sixties failed, because their foundational assumptions about the nature and authority of knowledge remain unquestioned. The innovations of the sixties tended to be of two types, corresponding to the inner-outer polarity of the foundational understanding of knowledge. Both hoped to improve students' grasp of subject matter. One of the two alternatives was objectivist in approach, influenced by behaviorist notions of positive reinforcement, while the other was subjectivist, influenced by loosely thought-through notions borrowed from Rogerian group psychology.

One of the best known of the objectivist efforts to change the way college and university courses are traditionally taught was somewhat misleadingly called the personalized system of instruction, or PSI. In PSI, teachers determined procedures that students should follow and the results they should attain. Then they trained selected students to act as "proctors." Proctors reinforced both the procedures and the results achieved by those procedures. Thus, although PSI seemed to change the social relationship among students and between students and teachers by placing intermediaries between teachers and individual students, in fact it did not. It was a rigorously controlled "monitor" tutorial system of the sort described in Chapter 5. Proctors were, unequivocally for all involved, the teacher's agents — teachers writ small. Nor did PSI provide a vehicle for questioning the foundational assumptions that underlay it or in any way encourage such questions to be raised.

Taking the opposite tack from this objectivist approach, the motivating hope in subjectivist efforts to change college and university teaching was that students' emotional dependence on established authority could be overcome by giving them "complete freedom," defined as absence of direction from the teacher. These attempts at innovation equated freedom with individual enterprise. Their individualist emphasis reveals how deeply rooted these innovations were in traditional assumptions about the nature and authority of knowledge. The bottom line remained the individual student's "cognition." Lacking direction from the teacher and constructive relations with each other, a very few students — those who had already internalized the mores and practices favored by their teachers and who were comfortable in social isolation — showed themselves able to "handle" their "new-found freedom" by asserting their individuality. All the rest took one or another of the four alternatives that students typically have in traditional education: plodding acquiescence, cut-throat competition, self-destructive rebellion, or withdrawal.

The failure of these attempts to innovate without challenging the traditional understanding of knowledge tends to confirm John Dewey's observation that "the mere removal of external control" cannot guarantee "the production of self-control":

> It may be a loss rather than a gain to escape from the control of another person only to find one's conduct dictated by immediate whim and caprice; that is, at the mercy of impulses into whose formation intelligent judgment has not entered. A person whose conduct is controlled in

this way has at most only the illusion of freedom. Actually he is directed by forces over which he has no command.[5]

Learning results, Dewey argues, when teachers exercise control indirectly through "work done as a social enterprise in which all individuals have an opportunity to contribute and to which all feel a responsibility." Productive community life of this sort, he insists, "does not organize itself in an enduring way spontaneously. It requires thought and planning ahead." Careful thought given to the social enterprise that controls the work is what the experimental teaching innovations of the sixties lacked. They rejected the tidy, reliable, well-understood, time-refined social conventions of traditional learning and the forms of schoolroom community life appropriate to the foundational understanding of knowledge. But they did not replace those conventions and forms with others appropriate to an alternative understanding of knowledge. Leaving the traditional understanding of knowledge implicitly in place and in many cases leaving students without guidance under stress, these honest efforts to innovate set themselves up to fail.[6]

Collaborative learning differs from these failed teaching innovations. It replaces the traditional social conventions of schoolroom community life with other conventions that students are, for the most part, already familiar with and can rely on for support under conditions of stress and that are appropriate to a clearly defined alternative understanding of knowledge. The social conventions of collaborative learning, which regulate deportment, relationships, and expectations, are of course not yet so time-refined as those of traditional teaching. Many college and university teachers are unfamiliar with them and with the understanding of knowledge appropriate to them. A good deal of conscious "thought and planning ahead" therefore still has to go into implementing them.

This thought and planning has to be directed toward organizing a classroom in which, as Dewey puts it, "all individuals have an opportunity to contribute something, and in which the activities in which all participate are the chief carrier of control."[7] In traditional classrooms, the teacher's intelligent judgment is exclusively in control. In collaborative learning, students, acting collaboratively, also exercise intelligent judgment, so their collaborative activities together with the teacher's become the chief carriers of control.

That is, the social structure and conventions of a collaborative classroom assume not a one-to-one relationship between student and teacher but, rather, a collaborative relationship among small groups of students and between the teacher and those groups functioning as classroom subunits. Students talk and write to the teacher and determine their fate in relation to the teacher. They do so, however, not as isolated individuals anonymous to one another, but organized in recognized, validly institutionalized, positive, productive relationships with other students.

Changing classroom social structure in this way changes not just how teachers exercise their authority but the very nature of the authority they exercise. It is therefore not the kind of change that teachers and students can merely acquiesce to. It has to be effected by thinking through and planning classroom social relationships in which authority is understood differently by teachers and students alike. It is classroom social relationships of this sort that collaborative learning establishes. In a collaborative learning classroom, no one's conduct is dictated by "impulses into whose formation intelligent judgment has not entered," and yet (as we saw in Chapters 2 and 3) a central issue is the locus of that intelligent judgment: the source of the prevailing authority of knowledge. By shifting the "activities" that are "the chief carrier of control" from those of a presiding individual to those of people working collaboratively, control is systematically reconstructed and relocated. It is located variously in student working groups of various sizes and complexity and in the knowledge communities that the teacher represents. The authority of the knowledge that each of these communities constructs varies according to the size and complexity of the community. That is, the authority of knowledge varies according to the intelligent judgment of the knowledge community that is at that moment in control in the classroom.

Collaborative learning therefore implies that teachers have to rethink what they have to do to get ready to teach and what they are doing when they are actually teaching. According to the traditional, foundational understanding of knowledge, teachers tend to think that the most important thing they have to do to prepare for teaching is to fill their own heads to overflowing with disciplinary knowledge and expertise so that they will have plenty in reserve with which to fill the heads of their students. Teachers stock up their own minds by reflecting reality as accurately as they can with their cognitive mental equipment, the mirror of nature we are all supposed to have built into our heads. Teachers read, do their research, and consult their notes. The mind's mirror collects images of the miscellaneous, unrelated elements that reality offers and presents those images to the other piece of mental equipment we are supposed to have in there, our inner eye. The teacher's inner eye discerns these images as coherently as it can, making sense of them by examining, interpreting, and synthesizing them according to some variety of mental structure, conceptual framework, or procedure of critical thinking and higher-order reasoning.

Once they have prepared themselves to teach, what teachers do when they actually set about teaching, understood foundationally, is reflect outward what their own inner eye has perceived, so that other people, their students, can reflect it in their mental mirrors and discern it with their inner eyes. Teachers reflect their knowledge outward by lecturing and leading students through their paces in recitation in ways outlined earlier in this chapter.

Throughout this process, the best teachers and the best students, we say, have insight. Theirs is "higher order" reasoning, because they have the clearest, most highly polished mental mirrors giving (when good teachers teach and when good students take tests) the most accurate, most all-encompassing reflection of reality, and they have the best trained, most sensitive, most discerning inner eyes to comprehend that reflection. In contrast, poor teachers, and students who learn slowly or inadequately are, as we say, "blind." Their mirrors don't reflect much reality, and the little bit they do reflect is inaccurate. Their inner eyes are insensitive and poorly trained. Theirs is "lower-order" reasoning. The reasoning of teachers must of course be of a "higher order," because their task is to "elevate" reasoning that we regard as being of a "lower order." Otherwise education would be a case, as we say, of "the blind leading the blind."

In contrast to this foundational view of what teachers do when they prepare and when they teach, the nonfoundational social constructionist understanding of knowledge implies that preparing to teach is not a process by which teachers stock up their own minds, and teaching is not a process by which they stock up others' in turn. Preparing to teach involves learning the languages of the relevant communities and creating social conditions in which students can become reacculturated into those communities by learning the languages that constitute them. That is, from this perspective, college and university teaching involves helping students converse with increasing facility in the language of the communities they want to join.

Thus, to teach mathematics, sociology, or classics is to create conditions in which students learn to converse as nearly as possible in the ways that, in their own communities, mathematicians converse with one another, sociologists converse with one another, and classicists converse with one another. To teach writing (as we saw in Chapter 3) is to create conditions in which students learn to converse with one another about writing as writers do, and it is also to create conditions in which students learn to write to each other as do the members of the community of literate people.

Setting out to teach this way leads teachers to ask themselves a set of questions that are quite different from the questions they ordinarily ask themselves. According to the foundational or cognitive understanding of knowledge, teachers ask themselves questions such as

- What's going on inside my students' heads?
- How can I get in there and change what's going on?
- What's the best way to impart to them what I know?

These questions arise when teachers believe that their job is to "reach" students and to empty into students' heads what teachers believe is filling their own. When teachers begin to think of their job instead as undertaking to reacculturate students into communities they are not yet members of, they tend to ask a wholly different set of questions. They no longer ask themselves subject-object questions about getting into other people's heads or teaching "how" *vs.* teaching "what." Instead, they ask themselves questions about what Thomas Kuhn calls "the special characteristics of the groups that create and use" the knowledge in question:

> How does one elect and how is one elected to membership in a particular community, scientific or not? What is the process and what are the stages of socialization to the group? What does the group collectively see as its goals; what deviations, individual or collective, will it tolerate; and how does it control the impermissible aberration?[8]

For college and university teachers, these questions have to be unpacked to reveal further questions about the social conditions in which students are most likely to gain fluency in the language of the disciplinary knowledge community that the teacher belongs to:

- What are those conditions and how can I best create them?

- How do the community languages my students already know reinforce or interfere with learning the language I am teaching?

- How can I help students renegotiate the terms of membership in the communities they already belong to?

- How can I make joining a new, unfamiliar community as unthreatening and fail-safe as possible?

In asking such questions as these, college and university teachers assume that learning is what Richard Rorty has called it. Learning, Rorty says, is not "a shift inside the person which now *suits* him to enter . . . new relationships" with "reality" and with other people. It is "a shift in a person's relations with others," period.[9] Teachers assume that their responsibility, as agents of educational reacculturation, is to help students make that shift. The best teachers, by this token, are those who mobilize students to work together in ways that make reacculturation possible. The best students are those who help effect constructive consensus by drawing both themselves and their peers into relevant conversation.

The most important tool that college and university teachers have at hand to help students reacculturate themselves into the knowledge communities they aspire to join is transition communities. Transition communities are small, new, temporary communities made up of people who want to make the same change. A teacher's role, besides helping students form transition communities, is (as we have seen in earlier chapters) to provide them with the tasks and occasions that will help them negotiate the transition they want to make.

Educational transition communities are sometimes misleadingly called support groups. This useful term was devised in the sixties by the women's liberation movement and the self-help mutual-aid movement to describe a basic reacculturative tool. Support groups are small autonomous or semiautonomous coalitions of people who recognize in each other similar needs and problems and learn to depend on one another to help fulfill those needs and solve those problems. Collaborative learning groups — for example, classroom consensus groups — are similar to support groups and in fact were first devised on the support-group model.[10]

Useful as it is, however, the term "support group" suggests that what is going on in the group is ancillary to something more important that those involved are doing somewhere else and which their work in the support group "supports." To call a "support group" a "transition community" has the advantage of suggesting that the most important thing going on — making a transition between established communities or constructing new communities yet to be established — is going on right there in that small local group, not somewhere else.

A close look at what goes on in transition communities suggests that what they really are is *translation* communities. They organize students into social relationships involving a "temporary fusion of interests" that allow them to relinquish dependence on their fluency in one community-constituting language (their "old" one) and acquire fluency in the language that constitutes the community of which they are now becoming members (their "new" one).[11] Enrolled in transition communities, students have a chance to learn and practice, relative to substantive issues, linguistic improvisation, that is, negotiation of the second kind listed at the beginning of this chapter. They carry on this nonstandard boundary discourse between the knowledge communities they belong to and one they do not belong to (the one in this case that they are trying to join), in order to reacculturate themselves to the standards — the language, mores, and goals — of that unfamiliar community.

The groups for learning medical judgment that Abercrombie reorganized students into were translation communities. In these groups, students translated the diverse languages they brought with them into the unfamiliar language of medical diagnosis that they were learning — the language of the new community that they aspired to join. The consensus groups that Harvard's New Pathways program plunges first-year medical students into and Uri Treisman's math and science study groups are translation communities in the same sense.

Many of the students William Perry interviewed had organized translation, or transition, communities in their residence houses (as we shall see in Chapter 10), but Perry thought it beneath the dignity of an instructor at Harvard College to help organize them.[12] Like Abercrombie's and Treisman's students but outside the institution's curricular framework, Perry's undergraduates negotiated among themselves the diverse languages they brought with them from their homes, and they negotiated between these languages and the new languages provided by the liberal education they were undertaking.

Such subcultural transitional social units as these maintain the coherence of students' lives in transit. They give their lives — and their language — a measure of stability as they loosen or give up their loyalties to the communities they are already members of, give up the comforts and sense of identity pertaining to those communities, form loyalties to communities that are new to them, and experience the comforts and sense of identity pertaining to those communities.

A transition community is therefore an odd, unstable, ephemeral social entity. Instability is of course entirely appropriate to communities of fence-sitters gathered on the boundary or "contact zone" between (probably) quite incompatible communities, engaged in what Thomas Kuhn correctly describes as the "threatening process" of translation.[13] The language and paralinguistic symbol systems that constitute transition communities — conversation across community boundaries — is nonstandard discourse in a number of respects. As we shall see in the next section, some of its language, some of its conventions, and some of the beliefs, values, traditions, interests, and goals that its members maintain are those of the communities its members are leaving. Some are those of the community they hope to join. Still others are common only to the conversation of transition communities. Furthermore, this unstable mix is itself undergoing constant change.

As a result, membership in a transition community may often be, as reacculturation always is, stressful and uncertain. The conversation of transition-community members is dominated by talk about these stresses and uncertainties of reacculturation. Much of it is in-the-same-boat talk. Members talk about what it was like to be a member of the old community, what it may be like to be a member of the new, unfamiliar community, and what a pain in the neck it is to change: nostalgia, anxious anticipation, and complaint.

Transition community members also talk a lot about coping. They trade hints and tips, some accurate, many apocryphal, about how a person is expected to behave and talk as a member of the community they hope to join. As Abercrombie noticed, they refute and cancel out each other's presuppositions and biases. They practice using the unfamiliar community's constituting language — sometimes accurately and appropriately, sometimes not, under as many different conditions, some relevant and some not, and in many different settings, some relevant and some not — so as gradually to become fluent in it.

To say that through collaborative learning nonfoundational teaching teaches the "languages" that constitute established knowledge communities, such as the academic disciplines and the professions, does not mean, however, that what it teaches is fluency in the jargon and methodological consensus of those communities. That is precisely the purpose of foundational teaching and jigsaw-puzzle tasks (described in Chapter 2). Foundational teaching inculcates students with disciplinary jargon and well-established methods. As my wife, Anthea, once put it while she was in law school (and in most law schools legal study is a foundational exercise if there ever was one), what she was doing there was learning how to quack.

In contrast, the purpose of collaborative learning is not primarily to teach students how to quack. Collaborative learning tasks are designed to generate conversation in which students learn to "speak differently" (in Rorty's phrase), to speak in ways unlike their former habits of speaking. So students almost inevitably pick up a good deal of disciplinary jargon along the way. But in collaborative learning the route to fluency in the language of a new community is paved with ad hoc intermediary languages that students devise themselves to serve their own purposes as they work through the assigned task. Like foundational teaching, nonfoundational teaching will almost certainly teach students to quack. But on the way they will also learn to gobble, honk, peep, and squawk.

Some of this ad hoc language sticks. It is this measure of residual nondisciplinary vocabulary, however small, that helps distinguish the results of nonfoundational teaching from the results of foundational teaching. It represents a precious resource: the grain of newly constructed knowledge that collaboratively educated students take away from the course with them.

The process of ad hoc translation that goes on in a transition group was illustrated in detail for me once during a class in which I had asked students organized collaboratively to subdivide a paragraph and describe how the parts are related, in order to write a "descriptive outline" of it. This is a nonfoundational constructive tool-making task appropriate to collaborative learning for two reasons. First, there is no "right answer," although there may be some clear options, the merits of which can be negotiated. Second, students undertake the task at first without a prescribed, disciplinary vocabulary to work with. They have to root around in their own collective experience and make use of whatever language they find there.

During this particular class, I (unintentionally) overheard a student explaining something to the other members of his consensus group about the paragraph I had asked them to outline. It contained, he said, a "transition between the whoosie-whatsis and the other thing." No one would call these terms elegant or professional. But for the time being, the expression served this student's purposes and the purposes of the group he was working with. It negotiated the boundary between languages that he and his fellow students knew and the one they were just beginning to learn, by cobbling together a variety of terms that every student in the group understood. To use a term of the Russian critic Bakhtin that has been fashionable recently among American literary academics, the expression was "heteroglossic." It drew on informal street-corner or beauty-parlor lingo ("whoosie-whatsis") and the plain, unvarnished speech of home, shop, and playground ("the other thing"), combining these with a new bit of classroom jargon ("transition").

Eventually, of course, these students replaced their rough-hewn, ad hoc linguistic tools with more efficient and appropriate terms as they explored further the nuances of the complex task they had been assigned. In fact, in any course taught collaboratively, adopting and culling linguistic tools to establish a transitional critical language is implicitly as much the point of the assigned task as the point that the task explicitly targets. In collaborative learning, college and university students learn to lift themselves by their own verbal bootstraps, making new language by borrowing from, renovating, and reconstructing the old. Their transitional terms emerge from the conversational history they share with one another and with their teacher, as they identify the task before them, formulate it, and do it.

The kind of translation at community boundaries that students do in collaborative learning is translation of an especially "thick" and complex kind. Students translate the languages that they bring to the task into a composite working vocabulary common to the particular small group they are working in. That's where, for example, my students working on descriptive outlines got the phrases "whoosie-whatsis" and "the other thing." While students are translating among each other's languages in this way, furthermore, they are also translating into their own new composite vocabulary the language in which the teacher posed the task, which is the language of the community they aspire to join. That's where my writing students picked up the word "transition."

To turn classrooms into arenas in which students can negotiate their way into new knowledge communities in this way, college and university teachers have to discover points of access or ports of entry to the relevant community that are appropriate to the varieties of nonmembers in their charge. They have to discover ways to help those nonmembers loosen their loyalty to some of the communities they are already members of — to "divorce" themselves from those communities, as Perry puts it — and marry instead into the knowledge community that the teacher represents.[14]

What teachers teach in this way is how to establish and maintain intellectually productive rapport and ways to renegotiate that rapport when the task is done. They help students learn to negotiate boundaries between the communities they belong to and communities their fellow students may belong to. They allow students latitude to define their individuality not as a stark and lonesome independence, isolated or alienated from others, but as a function of interdependence among peers.

For college and university teachers to adapt themselves to teaching of this sort, however, may require (as Chapter 1 suggests) a depth of change that is difficult if not impossible for individuals to accomplish on their own. It is a process of reacculturation best undertaken, and perhaps only undertaken with success, collaboratively. In this chapter we found William Perry's confused undergraduates undertaking it by working together to construct new speech, lifting themselves by their own verbal bootstraps with a transitional language constructed for the purpose. In Chapter 7 we will find engaged in the same process Thomas Kuhn's scientists facing a theory crisis and Bruno Latour's example of a mother and child negotiating the name of birds.

Collaborative learning is most likely to fulfill its promise when faculty members of whole institutions, or of coherent subdivisions within them, build transitional conversational units similarly committed to this painful, painstaking collaborative talking-through. The next chapter will explore the most promising way to begin this process of institutionalizing collaborative learning. It uses leverage gained through a form of collaborative learning that I have alluded to but not discussed so far: peer tutoring.

Notes

1. For a general discussion of negotiation see Roger Fisher, William Ury, and Bruce Patton, *Getting to Yes: Negotiating Agreement without Giving In,* 2nd ed. (New York: Penguin, 1991); and Roger Fisher and Scott Brown, *Getting Together: Building a Relationship That Gets to Yes* (New York: Houghton, 1988). Although we know a lot about how negotiation works in political, legal, and economic situations, we are only beginning to learn (from studies such as those of Latour and Knorr-Cetina) how it works in epistemological or educational ones. Perhaps more to the point, as Fisher and Ury put it, we normally think of negotiation in any context as "positional bargaining." The craft of interdependence, involving what Fisher calls "principled negotiation," is a good deal more complex than that. It almost goes without saying that nothing like principled negotiation has yet been systematically applied to learning and to constructing knowledge.
2. Mary Louise Pratt, "Arts of the Contact Zone," *Profession* 91 (New York: MLA, 1991) 33–40; 34, her emphasis.
3. Pratt 38.
4. On Roland Barthes, see Steve Ungar, "The Professor of Desire," *The Pedagogical Imperative: Teaching as a Literary Genre. Yale French Studies* 63, ed. Barbara Johnson (1982): 81–97.
5. John Dewey, *Experience and Education* (1938; New York: Collier, 1963) 64–65.
6. Dewey 55–56.
7. Dewey 56.
8. Thomas S. Kuhn, "Second Thoughts on Paradigms," *The Structure of Scientific Theories*, ed. Frederick Suppe, 2nd ed. (Urbana: U of Illinois P, 1977) 209–10.
9. Richard Rorty, *Contingency, Irony, and Solidarity* (Cambridge: Cambridge UP, 1989) 187, his emphasis.
10. On support groups see, for example, Glen Evans, *The Family Circle Guide to Self-Help* (New York: Ballantine, 1979).
11. Karen D. Knorr-Cetina, *The Manufacture of Knowledge: An Essay on the Constructivist and Contextual Nature of Science* (Oxford: Pergamon, 1981)

131. In this passage Knorr-Cetina describes the process of enrollment in translation (or transition) communities, and the "process of conversion" involved, as it occurs in scientific research.

12. William G. Perry, Jr., *Forms of Intellectual and Ethical Development in the College Years: A Scheme* (New York: Holt, 1968) 214.
13. Kuhn 203.
14. Perry 65.

Bruffee's Insights as a Resource for Your Teaching

1. Notice Bruffee's frequent references to "conscious thought and planning ahead" and the list of questions about the characteristics of groups of students who will construct and use the knowledge generated through collaboration. In your reflective journal, it is useful to note what you think may be true about the writer you will work with, based on your own experiences and your observations of others as students and writers in "transition." As you work with the "writing community," detail what you observe and learn about the students in large-class discussions, in small group projects, and in peer critique workshops. In a similar manner, write down your plans and processes for class activities; later jot down notes about what happened — by design or serendipity — and ways that students collaborated effectively. Use these data in your feedback to groups and individuals and in your planning for later activities and for later semesters.

2. If you are a new instructor, you may have recognized yourself in the descriptions of what learners do in their transition communities: conversing with others about such things as becoming a "real" writing teacher; coping with something new or different in the surrounding academic culture; and managing the stress of planning, responding, teaching, evaluating, facilitating collaborative learning, and "learning how to do it as you do it." Imitate those students who organized translation or transition communities to negotiate the languages you brought with you and the new languages you met — even in this set of readings — in the community of writing teachers. In addition, you can benefit from the exchange of what Stephen North in *The Making of Knowledge in Composition* defines as "practitioner's lore."

Bruffee's Insights as a Resource for Your Writing Classroom

1. Using Bruffee's distinctions, think about your course as a large transition community within which smaller groups often con-

verse and advise each other about writing for their readers. In the large writing community, these early journal prompts are very useful to many students: the nature of the "old communities" writers left; how it feels to become a member of the college community or of the writing community; and shifts in perspectives and changes in identities.

In a similar manner, many writers will respond to the "writing from recall" prompt with personal narratives about significant events from other knowledge communities. Encourage members of invention groups and critique workshops to ask and talk about the language and conventions specific to those communities; this will help the writer write specifically for readers who don't know his or her story.

2. Organize small groups to work collaboratively on a "glossary": the language of writing classes, of other disciplines, of the campus culture, and so on. Small groups will negotiate both contributions and meanings for what will become a class publication on "speaking differently" than they had before college.

3. When you become concerned about writers who restrict themselves to the five-paragraph theme or other writing strategies they mastered in earlier coursework, organize small groups to read and discuss alternative thinking and organizing patterns that are used successfully by class members. Bruffee explains why some students will accept the authority of peers more than that of an English teacher.

4. Bruffee indicates that the process of "adopting and culling linguistic tools to establish a transitional critical language is implicitly as much the point of the assigned task as the point that the task explicitly targets." Give students opportunities to talk and write about the collaborative skills and processes they are learning and refining: during class discussions, in journal entries, during one-on-one conferences, and in self-evaluations when the course concludes. Let groups practice evaluating their joint and individual participation in collaborative projects while you provide feedback from your observations as well.

5. If you have access to a networked classroom or can build an electronic conference, set up chat topics so class members can talk about coping, complain about difficulties with roommates, ask how others in the class interpret a reading, ask for reactions to ideas for essays, critique recent films, and so on. Cyberspace conversations frequently turn into collaborative inquiry; participants practice collaborative skills without thinking about being part of a group.

2

Thinking about the Writing Process

The readings in this chapter all proceed from good teaching practice: carefully observing writers at work, reflecting on what was observed, posing research questions (whether for personal, classroom, or empirical research), and speculating from the data about the practices of developing, novice, and experienced writers. A habit of thinking about writers and their processes leads to creative design of prompts, syllabi, and collaborative learning activities; it also influences how writing teachers respond to and evaluate impromptu drafts, peer criticism, finished drafts, and portfolios. The following readings are organized under headings that describe issues writers face when they approach writing tasks. As with all the readings in this volume, the essays interconnect: They may modify, challenge, or confirm the insights of other essays. The series on audience, for example, particularly demonstrates such a "conversation" about what writers do when they consider the possible needs of their audiences. "Teaching Writing with Computers" presents two different yet ultimately complementary viewpoints about the integration of technology into the classroom and its potential to change the classroom writing community, while the readings on visual literacy work in tandem by first offering a conceptual map and, in the second article, offering practical and concrete teaching techniques. In each case, the readings were carefully sequenced to unfold in a logical progression.

Generating a Draft

As a result of the paradigm shift in composition studies from viewing writing as product to viewing writing as process, we now know much more about what writers do when they generate texts. This section is designed to address the individual and complex nature of the multiple processes of getting started (prewriting, invention, discovery, planning, considering audience); drafting (composing by hand or keyboard, planning, scanning, considering audience, using invention, assessing, revising); and revising (rereading and goal-setting, re-visioning, considering audience, discovery, reorganizing, editing). Each writer's highly individualized and recursive processes of composing and constructing meaning cannot be fit easily or appropriately into a neat definition of "the writing process." Composition research and theory centering on "sustained drafting" — an extensive field of study — is helpful in focusing our thinking about writers in process.

Understanding Composing

Sondra Perl

Most writing teachers and theorists share Sondra Perl's belief that writing is a recursive process and that writers engage in "retrospective structuring" as they generate drafts. Perl uses her own observations of the composing processes of a variety of writers to analyze the significance of those processes. She defines a "felt sense" that may be a very rich and necessary resource for the writer even as it may be one that the writer (and his or her audience) has difficulty describing and consciously triggering.

Perl believes that "skilled writers" rely on a felt sense even when they don't know it, and she implies that "unskilled writers" might come to use this felt sense and to engage in "retrospective structuring" more productively. She theorizes that writers who have internalized a model of writing as a recursive process rather than a linear process may have an easier time attending to their inner reflections.

You may well find "new thoughts" about composing as you read Perl's conjectures about "felt sense." In particular, you may be interested in the link of "felt sense" with "projective structuring," Perl's name for the process in which writers make what they intend to say intelligible to others.

> Any psychological process, whether the development of thought or voluntary behavior, is a process undergoing changes right before one's eyes. . . . Under certain conditions it becomes possible to trace this development.[1]
>
> — L. S. Vygotsky

> It's hard to begin this case study of myself as a writer because even as I'm searching for a beginning, a pattern of organization, I'm watching myself, trying to understand my behavior. As I sit here in silence, I can see lots of things happening that never made it onto my tapes. My mind leaps from the task at hand to what I need at the vegetable stand for tonight's soup to the threatening rain outside to ideas voiced in my writing group this morning, but in between "distractions" I hear myself trying out words I might use. It's as if the extraneous thoughts are a counterpoint to the more steady attention I'm giving to composing. This is all to point out that the process is more complex than I'm aware of, but I think my tapes reveal certain basic patterns that I tend to follow.
> — Anne, New York City teacher

Anne is a teacher of writing. In 1979, she was among a group of twenty teachers who were taking a course in research and basic writing at New York University.[2] One of the assignments in the course was for the teachers to tape their thoughts while composing aloud on the topic "My Most Anxious Moment as a Writer." Everyone in the group was given the topic in the morning during class and told to compose later on that day in a place where they would be comfortable and relatively free from distractions. The result was a tape of composing aloud and a written product that formed the basis for class discussion over the next few days.

One of the purposes of this assignment was to provide teachers with an opportunity to see their own composing processes at work. From the start of the course, we recognized that we were controlling the situation by assigning a topic and that we might be altering the process by asking writers to compose aloud. Nonetheless we viewed the task as a way of capturing some of the flow of composing and, as Anne later observed in her analysis of her tape, she was able to detect certain basic patterns. This observation, made not only by Anne, then leads me to ask "What basic patterns seem to occur during composing?" and "What does this type of research have to tell us about the nature of the composing process?"

Perhaps the most challenging part of the answer is the recognition of recursiveness in writing. In recent years, many researchers including myself have questioned the traditional notion that writing is a linear process with a strict plan-write-revise sequence.[3] In its stead, we have advocated the idea that writing is a recursive process, that throughout the process of writing, writers return to substrands of the overall process, or subroutines (short successions of steps that yield results on which the writer draws in taking the next set of steps); writers use these to keep the process moving forward. In other words, recursiveness in writing implies that there is a forward-moving action that exists by virtue of a backward-moving action. The questions that then need to be answered are "To what do writers move back?" "What exactly is being repeated?" "What recurs?"

To answer these questions, it is important to look at what writers do while writing and what an analysis of their processes reveals. The descriptions that follow are based on my own observations of the composing processes of many types of writers including college students, graduate students, and English teachers like Anne.

Writing does appear to be recursive, yet the parts that recur seem to vary from writer to writer and from topic to topic. Furthermore, some recursive elements are easy to spot while others are not.

1. The most visible recurring feature or backward movement involves rereading little bits of discourse. Few writers I have seen write for long periods of time without returning briefly to what is already down on the page.

For some, like Anne, rereading occurs after every few phrases; for others, it occurs after every sentence; more frequently, it occurs after a "chunk" of information has been written. Thus, the unit that is reread is not necessarily a syntactic one, but rather a semantic one as defined by the writer.

2. The second recurring feature is some key word or item called up by the topic. Writers consistently return to their notion of the topic throughout the process of writing. Particularly when they are stuck, writers seem to use the topic or a key word in it as a way to get going again. Thus many times it is possible to see writers "going back," rereading the topic they were given, changing it to suit what they have been writing or changing what they have written to suit their notion of the topic.

3. There is also a third backward movement in writing, one that is not so easy to document. It is not easy because the move, itself, cannot immediately be identified with words. In fact, the move is not to any words on the page nor to the topic but to feelings or nonverbalized perceptions that *surround* the words, or to what the words already present evoke in the writer. The move draws on sense experience, and it can be observed if one pays close attention to what happens when writers pause and seem to listen or otherwise react to what is inside of them. The move occurs inside the writer, to what is physically felt. The term used to describe this focus of writers' attention is *felt sense*. The term "felt sense" has been coined and described by Eugene Gendlin, a philosopher at the University of Chicago. In his words, felt sense is

> the soft underbelly of thought . . . a kind of bodily awareness that . . . can be used as a tool . . . a bodily awareness that . . . encompasses everything you feel and know about a given subject at a given time. . . . It is felt in the body, yet it has meanings. It is body *and* mind before they are split apart.[4]

This felt sense is always there, within us. It is unifying, and yet, when we bring words to it, it can break apart, shift, unravel, and become something else. Gendlin has spent many years showing people how to work with their felt sense. Here I am making connections between what he has done and what I have seen happen as people write.

When writers are given a topic, the topic itself evokes a felt sense in them. This topic calls forth images, words, ideas, and vague fuzzy feelings that are anchored in the writer's body. What is elicited, then, is not solely the product of a mind but of a mind alive in a living, sensing body.

When writers pause, when they go back and repeat key words, what they seem to be doing is waiting, paying attention to what is still vague and unclear. They are looking to their felt experience, and waiting for an image, a word, or a phrase to emerge that captures the sense they embody.

Usually, when they make the decision to write, it is after they have a dawning awareness that something has clicked, that they have enough of a sense that if they begin with a few words heading in a certain direction, words will continue to come which will allow them to flesh out the sense they have.

The process of using what is sensed directly about a topic is a natural one. Many writers do it without any conscious awareness that that is what they are doing. For example, Anne repeats the words "anxious moments," using these key words as a way of allowing her sense of the topic to deepen. She asks herself, "Why are exams so anxiety provoking?" and waits until she has enough of a sense within her that she can go in a certain direction. She does not yet have the words, only the sense that she is able to begin. Once she writes, she stops to see what is there. She maintains a highly recursive composing style throughout and she seems unable to go forward without first going back to see and to listen to what she has already created. In her own words, she says:

> My disjointed style of composing is very striking to me. I almost never move from the writing of one sentence directly to the next. After each sentence I pause to read what I've written, assess, sometimes edit and think about what will come next. I often have to read the several preceding sentences a few times as if to gain momentum to carry me to the next sentence. I seem to depend a lot on the sound of my words and . . . while I'm hanging in the middle of this uncompleted thought, I may also start editing a previous sentence or get an inspiration for something which I want to include later in the paper.

What tells Anne that she is ready to write? What is the feeling of "momentum" like for her? What is she hearing as she listens to the "sound" of her words? When she experiences "inspiration," how does she recognize it?

In the approach I am presenting, the ability to recognize what one needs to do or where one needs to go is informed by calling on felt sense. This is the internal criterion writers seem to use to guide them when they are planning, drafting, and revising.

The recursive move, then, that is hardest to document but is probably the most important to be aware of is the move to felt sense, to what is not yet *in words* but out of which images, words, and concepts emerge.

The continuing presence of this felt sense, waiting for us to discover it and see where it leads, raises a number of questions.

Is "felt sense" another term for what professional writers call their "inner voice" or their feeling of "inspiration"?

Do skilled writers call on their capacity to sense more readily than unskilled writers?

Rather than merely reducing the complex act of writing to a neat formulation, can the term "felt sense" point us to an area of our experience from which we can evolve even richer and more accurate descriptions of composing?

Can learning how to work with felt sense teach us about creativity and release us from stultifyingly repetitive patterns?

My observations lead me to answer "yes" to all four questions. There seems to be a basic step in the process of composing that skilled writers rely on even when they are unaware of it and that less skilled writers can be taught. This process seems to rely on very careful attention to one's inner reflections and is often accompanied with bodily sensations.

When it's working, this process allows us to say or write what we've never said before, to create something new and fresh, and occasionally it provides us with the experience of "newness" or "freshness," even when "old words" or images are used.

The basic process begins with paying attention. If we are given a topic, it begins with taking the topic in and attending to what it evokes in us. There is less "figuring out" an answer and more "waiting" to see what forms. Even without a predetermined topic, the process remains the same. We can ask ourselves, "What's on my mind?" or "Of all the things I know about, what would I most like to write about now?" and wait to see what comes. What we pay attention to is the part of our bodies where we experience ourselves directly. For many people, it's the area of their stomachs; for others, there is a more generalized response and they maintain a hovering attention to what they experience throughout their bodies.

Once a felt sense forms, we match words to it. As we begin to describe it, we get to see what is there for us. We get to see what we think, what we know. If we are writing about something that truly interests us, the felt sense deepens. We know that we are writing out of a "centered" place.

If the process is working, we begin to move along, sometimes quickly. Other times, we need to return to the beginning, to reread, to see if we captured what we meant to say. Sometimes after rereading we move on again, picking up speed. Other times by rereading we realize we've gone off the track, that what we've written doesn't quite "say it," and we need to reassess. Sometimes the words are wrong and we need to change them. Other times we need to go back to the topic, to call up the sense it initially evoked to see where and how our words led us astray. Sometimes in rereading we discover that the topic is "wrong," that the direction we discovered in writing is where we really want to go. It is important here to clarify that the terms "right" and "wrong" are not necessarily meant to refer to grammatical structures or to correctness.

What is "right" or "wrong" corresponds to our sense of our intention. We intend to write something, words come, and now we assess if those words adequately capture our intended meaning. Thus, the first question we ask ourselves is "Are these words right for me?" "Do they capture what I'm trying to say?" "If not, what's missing?"

Once we ask "what's missing?" we need once again to wait, to let a felt sense of what is missing form, and then to write out of that sense.

I have labeled this process of attending, of calling up a felt sense, and of writing out of that place, the process of *retrospective structuring*. It is retrospective in that it begins with what is already there, inchoately, and brings whatever is there forward by using language in structured form.

It seems as though a felt sense has within it many possible structures or forms. As we shape what we intend to say, we are further structuring our sense while correspondingly shaping our piece of writing.

It is also important to note that what is there implicitly, without words, is not equivalent to what finally emerges. In the process of writing, we begin with what is inchoate and end with something that is tangible. In order to do so, we both discover and construct what we mean. Yet the term "discovery" ought not lead us to think that meaning exists fully formed inside of us and that all we need do is dig deep enough to release it. In writing, meaning cannot be discovered the way we discover an object on an archeological dig. In writing, meaning is crafted and constructed. It involves us in a process of coming-into-being. Once we have worked at shaping, through language, what is there inchoately, we can look at what we have written to see if it adequately captures what we intended. Often at this moment discovery occurs. We see something new in our writing that comes upon us as a surprise. We see in our words a further structuring of the sense we began with and we recognize that in those words we have discovered something new about ourselves and our topic. Thus when we are successful at this process, we end up with a product that teaches us something, that clarifies what we know (or what we knew at one point only implicitly), and that lifts out or explicates or enlarges our experience. In this way, writing leads to discovery.

All the writers I have observed, skilled and unskilled alike, use the process of retrospective structuring while writing. Yet the degree to which they do so varies and seems, in fact, to depend upon the model of the writing process that they have internalized. Those who realize that writing can be a recursive process have an easier time with waiting, looking, and discovering. Those who subscribe to the linear model find themselves easily frustrated when what they write does not immediately correspond to what they planned or when what they produce leaves them with little sense of accomplishment. Since they have relied on a formulaic approach, they often produce writing that is formulaic as well, thereby cutting themselves off from the possibility of discovering something new.

Such a result seems linked to another feature of the composing process, to what I call *projective structuring,* or the ability to craft what one intends to say so that it is intelligible to others.

A number of concerns arise in regard to projective structuring; I will mention only a few that have been raised for me as I have watched different writers at work.

1. Although projective structuring is only one important part of the composing process, many writers act as if it is the whole process. These writers focus on what they think others want them to write rather than looking to see what it is they want to write. As a result, they often ignore their felt sense and they do not establish a living connection between themselves and their topic.

2. Many writers reduce projective structuring to a series of rules or criteria for evaluating finished discourse. These writers ask, "Is what I'm writing correct?" and "Does it conform to the rules I've been taught?" While these concerns are important, they often overshadow all others and lock the writer in the position of writing solely or primarily for the approval of readers.

Projective structuring, as I see it, involves much more than imagining a strict audience and maintaining a strict focus on correctness. It is true that to handle this part of the process well, writers need to know certain grammatical rules and evaluative criteria, but they also need to know how to call up a sense of their reader's needs and expectations.

For projective structuring to function fully, writers need to draw on their capacity to move away from their own words, to decenter from the page, and to project themselves into the role of the reader. In other words, projective structuring asks writers to attempt to become readers and to imagine what someone other than themselves will need before the writer's particular piece of writing can become intelligible and compelling. To do so, writers must have the experience of being readers. They cannot call up a felt sense of a reader unless they themselves have experienced what it means to be lost in a piece of writing or to be excited by it. When writers do not have such experiences, it is easy for them to accept that readers merely require correctness.

In closing, I would like to suggest that retrospective and projective structuring are two parts of the same basic process. Together they form the alternating mental postures writers assume as they move through the act of composing. The former relies on the ability to go inside, to attend to what is there, from that attending to place words upon a page, and then to assess if those words adequately capture one's meaning. The latter relies on the ability to assess how the words on that page will affect someone other than the writer, the reader. We rarely do one without the other entering in; in fact, again in these postures we can see the shuttling back-and-forth movements of the composing process, the move from sense to words and from words to sense, from inner experience to outer judgment and from judgment back to experience. As we move through this cycle, we are continually composing and recomposing our meanings and what we mean. And in doing so, we display some of the basic recursive patterns that writers who observe themselves closely seem to see in their own work. After observing the process for a long time we may, like Anne, conclude that at any given moment the process is more complex than anything we are aware of; yet such insights, I believe, are important. They show us the fallacy of reducing the composing process to a simple linear scheme and they leave us with the potential for creating even more powerful ways of understanding composing.

Notes

1. L. S. Vygotsky, *Mind in Society,* trans. M. Cole, V. John-Steiner, S. Scribner, and E. Souberman (Cambridge: Harvard UP, 1978) 61.
2. [I team-taught this course with] Gordon Pradl, Associate Professor of English Education at New York University.
3. See Janet Emig, *The Composing Processes of Twelfth-Graders,* NCTE Research Report No. 13 (Urbana: NCTE, 1971); Linda Flower and J. R. Hayes, "The Cognition of Discovery," *CCC* 31 (Feb. 1980): 21–32; Nancy Sommers, "The Need for Theory in Composition Research," *CCC* 30 (Feb. 1979): 46–49.
4. Eugene Gendlin, *Focusing* (New York: Everest, 1978) 35, 165.

Perl's Insights as a Resource for Your Teaching

1. Perl models a "holistic perspective" on the composing process and pays careful attention to the composing processes of the students she teaches. As you read this article and reflect on it, jot down your own memories of this experience of a "felt sense" as well as statements your students have made about such experiences. Save those notes for use in your discussions of getting started with a writing task.

2. Many generating strategies — those used by individual writers as well as the more formally described heuristics like freewriting, brainstorming, and the reporter's questions — help students start to pay attention to inner reflections and accompanying physical sensations. After they have practiced with several formal heuristics, ask your students to describe, either in journal

entries or in fifteen-minute writing sessions, what they notice about their "getting started" and their "beginning again."

3. Journal entries that ask writers simply to list "what I'm thinking now about this assignment" or "things I feel I need to say sometime this year" often provoke students to "listen in" on their inner reflections. The double-entry journal format assists writers, as they are retrospective in second entries, to become more aware of the "felt sense" Perl describes. Assignments that allow students to write from imagination give them license to work from "retrospective structuring"; some students will surprise themselves with their composing for such assignments.

4. Be sure to ask students periodically, particularly at the end of the term, to tell you about times they surprised themselves by composing from "inspiration." Let students know, because you discuss it, that composing often has this basic process of calling on "felt sense." Be careful to respect the comments writers make in conferences (such as "It isn't right yet") and not to appropriate their texts with your judgment about their drafts.

Perl's Insights as a Resource for Your Writing Classroom

1. Perl insists that to craft writing to be accessible and intelligible to others, writers have to project themselves as readers of the work. They must anticipate the needs of readers even before and while the writing is in process. This sort of "decentering" is difficult for many students. Perl recommends reading as a major resource for such positive structuring. To assist students in calling up a felt sense of their readers, ask them to discuss, in journals or in small groups, experiences they have had of being excited by something they read.

   Organize a class discussion of a "difficult" reading. Ask students to discuss any experiences of feeling overwhelmed by the reading, or "lost" in parts of it. Ask them to use sensory description, if appropriate to their experience.

   In helping students to recognize an awareness of themselves as critical readers, this discussion also encourages students to think about the particular readers' needs that they may have anticipated in the essays that they are currently drafting.

2. Ask students to write for five minutes, listing moments when they felt exhilarated by "inspiration" while reading, writing, or participating in class discussion. Then ask each student to choose one instance and to describe it to the class, ending the description with some explanation of "effect." If students say they can't recall such events, tell them to listen carefully to other class

members; someone will describe an event that will jar their memories. This exercise could prompt responses that might surprise students who heretofore have never considered their creative lives or learning experiences as viable topics for discussion, reading, and writing.

Rigid Rules, Inflexible Plans, and the Stifling of Language: A Cognitivist Analysis of Writer's Block

Mike Rose

What's really going on when a student writer can't write, even when an assignment's deadline looms closer and closer? In this study, Mike Rose finds ten students at UCLA who struggle with writer's block and compares their composing processes with those of students who do not have writer's block. Students are often blocked by very specific cognitive objects: They are stifled by rigid "dos and don'ts" that they have internalized from past teachers and textbooks, and what they finally, painstakingly produce inevitably never matches their inflexible plans. Writers who do not struggle with writer's block, on the other hand, are unimpeded by any such hypersensitivity to rules and plans: they just write, knowing that they can revise or retract later. In the next section of this chapter, Considering Audience, Peter Elbow focuses on how writers' concerns about audience — particularly in the generating and drafting stages — can inhibit or "block" writing (see "Closing My Eyes As I Speak"), in that students may feel bound by their preconceived ideas of audience expectation and thus conform their writing to "fit" these. It is when we try to fit our writing into predetermined molds that we become stymied by self-consciousness, making it nearly impossible to tap the resources of our imagination.

Ruth will labor over the first paragraph of an essay for hours. She'll write a sentence, then erase it. Try another, then scratch part of it out. Finally, as the evening winds on toward ten o'clock and Ruth, anxious about tomorrow's deadline, begins to wind into herself, she'll compose that first paragraph only to sit back and level her favorite exasperated interdiction at herself and her page: "No. You can't say that. You'll bore them to death."

Ruth is one of ten UCLA undergraduates with whom I discussed writer's block, that frustrating, self-defeating inability to generate the next line, the right phrase, the sentence that will release the flow of words once again. These ten people represented a fair cross-section of the UCLA student community: lower-middle-class to upper-middle-class backgrounds and high schools, third-world and Caucasian origins, biology to fine arts majors, C+ to A– grade point averages, enthusiastic to blasé attitudes toward school. They were set off from the community by the twin facts that all ten could write competently, and all were currently enrolled in at least one course that required a significant amount of writing. They were set off among themselves by the fact that five of them wrote with relative to enviable ease while the other five experienced moderate to nearly immobilizing writer's block. This blocking usually resulted in rushed, often late papers and resultant grades that did not truly reflect these students' writing ability. And then, of course, there were other less measurable but probably more serious results: a growing distrust of their abilities and an aversion toward the composing process itself.

What separated the five students who blocked from those who didn't? It wasn't skill; that was held fairly constant. The answer could have rested in the emotional realm — anxiety, fear of evaluation, insecurity, etc. Or perhaps blocking in some way resulted from variation in cognitive style. Perhaps, too, blocking originated in and typified a melding of emotion and cognition not unlike the relationship posited by Shapiro between neurotic feeling and neurotic thinking.[1] Each of these was possible. Extended clinical interviews and testing could have teased out the answer. But there was one answer that surfaced readily in brief explorations of these students' writing processes. It was not profoundly emotional, nor was it embedded in that still unclear construct of cognitive style. It was constant, surprising, almost amusing if its results weren't so troublesome, and, in the final analysis, obvious: the five students who experienced blocking were all operating either with writing rules or with planning strategies that impeded rather than enhanced the composing process. The five students who were not hampered by writer's block also utilized rules, but they were less rigid ones, and thus more appropriate to a complex process like writing. Also, the plans these non-blockers brought to the writing process were more functional, more flexible, more open to information from the outside.

These observations are the result of one to three interviews with each student. I used recent notes, drafts, and finished compositions to direct and hone my questions. This procedure is admittedly non-experimental, certainly more clinical than scientific; still, it did lead to several inferences that lay the foundation for future, more rigorous investigation: (a) composing is a highly complex problem-solving process[2] and (b) certain disruptions of that process can be explained with cognitive psychology's problem-solving framework. Such investigation might include a study using "stimulated recall" techniques to validate or disconfirm these hunches. In such a study, blockers and non-blockers would write essays. Their activity would be videotaped and, immediately after writing, they would be shown their respective tapes and questioned about the rules, plans, and beliefs operating in their writing behavior. This procedure would bring us close to the composing process (the writers' recall is stimulated by their viewing the tape), yet would not interfere with actual composing.

In the next section I will introduce several key concepts in the problem-solving literature. In section three I will let the students speak for themselves. Fourth, I will offer a cognitivist analysis of blockers' and non-blockers' grace or torpor. I will close with a brief note on treatment.

Selected Concepts in Problem Solving: Rules and Plans

As diverse as theories of problem solving are, they share certain basic assumptions and characteristics. Each posits an *introductory period* during which a problem is presented, and all theorists, from Behaviorist to Gestalt to Information Processing, admit that certain aspects, stimuli, or "functions" of the problem must become or be made salient and attended to in certain ways if successful problem-solving processes are to be engaged. Theorists also believe that some conflict, some stress, some gap in information in these perceived "aspects" seems to trigger problem-solving behavior. Next comes a *processing period,* and for all the variance of opinion about this critical stage, theorists recognize the necessity of its existence — recognize that man, at the least, somehow "weighs" possible solutions as they are stumbled upon and, at the most, goes through an elaborate and sophisticated information-processing routine to achieve problem solution. Furthermore, theorists believe — to varying degrees — that past learning and the particular "set," direction, or orientation that the problem solver takes in dealing with past experience and present stimuli have critical bearing on the efficacy of solution. Finally, all theorists admit to a *solution period,* an end-state of the process where "stress" and "search" terminate, an answer is attained, and a sense of completion or "closure" is experienced.

These are the gross similarities, and the framework they offer will be useful in understanding the problem-solving behavior of the students discussed in this paper. But since this paper is primarily concerned with the second stage of problem-solving operations, it would be most useful to focus this introduction on two critical constructs in the processing period: rules and plans.

Rules

Robert M. Gagné defines "rule" as "an inferred capability that enables the individual to respond to a class of stimulus situations with a class of performances."[3] Rules can be learned directly[4] or by inference through experience.[5] But, in either case, most problem-solving theorists would affirm Gagné's dictum that "rules are probably the major organizing factor, and quite possibly the primary one, in intellectual functioning."[6] As Gagné implies, we wouldn't be able to function without rules; they guide response to the myriad stimuli that confront us daily, and might even be the central element in complex problem-solving behavior.

Dunker, Polya, and Miller, Galanter, and Pribram offer a very useful distinction between two general kinds of rules: algorithms and heuristics.[7] Algorithms are precise rules that will always result in a specific answer if applied to an appropriate problem. Most mathematical rules, for example, are algorithms. Functions are constant (e.g., pi), procedures are routine (squaring the radius), and outcomes are completely predictable. However, few day-to-day situations are mathematically circumscribed enough to warrant the application of algorithms. Most often we function with the aid of fairly general heuristics or "rules of thumb," guidelines that allow varying degrees of flexibility when approaching problems. Rather than operating with algorithmic precision and certainty, we search, critically, through alternatives, using our heuristic as a divining rod — "if a math problem stumps you, try working backwards to solution"; "if the car won't start, check X, Y, or Z," and so forth. Heuristics won't allow the precision or the certitude afforded by algorithmic operations; heuristics can even be so "loose" as to be vague. But in a world where tasks and problems are rarely mathematically precise, heuristic rules become the most appropriate, the most functional rules available to us: "a heuristic does not guarantee the optimal solution or, indeed, any solution at all; rather, heuristics offer solutions that are good enough most of the time."[8]

Plans

People don't proceed through problem situations, in or out of a laboratory, without some set of internalized instructions to the self, some program, some course of action that, even roughly, takes goals and possible paths to that goal into consideration. Miller, Galanter, and Pribram have referred to this course of action as a plan: "A plan is any hierarchical process in the organism that can control the order in which a sequence of operations is to be performed" (16). They name the fundamental plan in human problem-solving behavior the TOTE, with the initial T representing a *test* that matches a possible solution against the perceived end-goal of problem completion. O represents the clearance to *operate* if the comparison between solution and goal indicates that the solution is a sensible one. The second T represents a further, post-operation, *test* or comparison of solution with goal, and if the two mesh and problem solution is at hand the person *exits* (E) from problem-solving behavior. If the second test presents further discordance between solution and goal, a further solution is attempted in TOTE-fashion. Such plans can be both long-term and global and, as problem solving is underway, short-term and immediate.[9] Though the mechanicality of this information-processing model renders it simplistic and, possibly, unreal, the central notion of a plan and an operating procedure is an important one in problem-solving theory; it at least attempts to metaphorically explain what earlier cognitive psychologists could not — the mental procedures . . . underlying problem-solving behavior.

Before concluding this section, a distinction between heuristic rules and plans should be attempted; it is a distinction often blurred in the literature, blurred because, after all, we are very much in the area of gestating theory and preliminary models. Heuristic rules seem to function with the flexibility of plans. Is, for example, "If the car won't start, try X, Y, or Z" a heuristic or a plan? It could be either, though two qualifications will mark it as heuristic rather than plan. (A) Plans subsume and sequence heuristic and algorithmic rules. Rules are usually "smaller," more discrete cognitive capabilities; plans can become quite large and complex, composed of a series of ordered algorithms, heuristics, and further planning "sub-routines." (B) Plans, as was mentioned earlier, include criteria to determine successful goal-attainment and, as well, include "feedback" processes — ways to incorporate and use information gained from "tests" of potential solutions against desired goals.

One other distinction should be made: that is, between "set" and plan. Set, also called "determining tendency" or "readiness,"[10] refers to the fact that people often approach problems with habitual ways of reacting, a predisposition, a tendency to perceive or function in one way rather than another. Set, which can be established through instructions or, consciously or unconsciously, through experience, can assist performance if it is appropriate to a specific problem,[11] but much of the literature on set has shown its rigidifying, dysfunctional effects.[12] Set differs from plan in that set represents a limiting and narrowing of response alternatives with no inherent process to shift alternatives. It is a kind of cognitive habit that can limit perception, not a course of action with multiple paths that directs and sequences response possibilities.

The constructs of rules and plans advance the understanding of problem solving beyond that possible with earlier, less developed formulations. Still, critical problems remain. Though mathematical and computer models move one toward more complex (and thus more real) problems than the earlier research, they are still too neat, too rigidly sequenced to approximate the stunning complexity of day-to-day (not to mention highly creative) problem-solving behavior. Also, information-processing models of problem solving are built on logic theorems, chess strategies, and simple planning tasks. Even Gagné seems to feel more comfortable with illustrations from mathematics and science rather than with social science and humanities problems. So although these complex models and constructs tell us a good deal about problem-solving behavior, they are still laboratory simulations, still invoked from the outside rather than self-generated, and still founded on the mathematico-logical.

Two Carnegie-Mellon researchers, however, have recently extended the above into a truly real, amorphous, unmathematical problem-solving process — writing. Relying on protocol analysis (thinking aloud while solving problems), Linda Flower and John Hayes have attempted to tease out the role of heuristic rules and plans in writing behavior.[13] Their research pushes problem-solving investigations to the real and complex and pushes, from the other end, the often mysterious process of writing toward the explainable. The latter is important, for at least since Plotinus many have viewed the composing process as unexplainable, inspired, infused with the transcendent. But Flower and Hayes are beginning, anyway, to show how writing generates from a problem-solving process with rich heuristic rules and plans of its own. They show, as well, how many writing problems arise from a paucity of heuristics and suggest an intervention that provides such rules.

This paper, too, treats writing as a problem-solving process, focusing, however, on what happens when the process dead-ends in writer's block. It will further suggest that, as opposed to Flower and Hayes's students who need more rules and plans, blockers may well be stymied by possessing rigid or inappropriate rules, or inflexible or confused plans. Ironically enough, these are occasionally instilled by the composition teacher or gleaned from the writing textbook.

"Always Grab Your Audience" — The Blockers

In high school, *Ruth* was told and told again that a good essay always grabs a reader's attention immediately. Until you can make your essay do that, her teachers and textbooks putatively declaimed, there is no need to go on. For Ruth, this means that beginning bland and seeing what emerges as one generates prose is unacceptable. The beginning is everything. And what exactly is the audience seeking that reads this beginning? The rule, or Ruth's use of it, doesn't provide for such investigation. She has an edict with no determiners. Ruth operates with another rule that restricts her productions as well: if sentences aren't grammatically "correct," they aren't useful. This keeps Ruth from toying with ideas on paper, from the kind of linguistic play that often frees up the flow of prose. These two rules converge in a way that pretty effectively restricts Ruth's composing process.

The first two papers I received from *Laurel* were weeks overdue. Sections of them were well written; there were even moments of stylistic flair. But the papers were late and, overall, the prose seemed rushed. Furthermore, one paper included a paragraph on an issue that was never mentioned in the topic paragraph. This was the kind of mistake that someone with Laurel's apparent ability doesn't make. I asked her about this irrelevant passage. She knew very well that it didn't fit, but believed she had to include it to round out the paper. "You must always make three or more points in an essay. If the essay has less, then it's not strong." Laurel had been taught this rule both in high school and in her first college English class; no wonder, then, that she accepted its validity.

As opposed to Laurel, *Martha* possesses a whole arsenal of plans and rules with which to approach a humanities writing assignment, and, considering her background in biology, I wonder how many of them were formed out of the assumptions and procedures endemic to the physical sciences.[14] Martha will not put pen to first draft until she has spent up to two days generating an outline of remarkable complexity. I saw one of these outlines and it looked more like a diagram of protein synthesis or DNA structure than the time-worn pattern offered in composition textbooks. I must admit I was intrigued by the aura of process (vs. the static appearance of essay outlines) such diagrams offer, but for Martha these "outlines" only led to self-defeat: the outline would become so complex that all of its elements could never be included in a short essay. In other words, her plan locked her into the first stage of the composing process. Martha would struggle with the conversion of her outline into prose only to scrap the whole venture when deadlines passed and a paper had to be rushed together.

Martha's "rage for order" extends beyond the outlining process. She also believes that elements of a story or poem must evince a fairly linear structure and thematic clarity, or — perhaps bringing us closer to the issue — that analysis of a story or poem must provide the linearity or clarity that seems to be absent in the text. Martha, therefore, will bend the logic of her analysis to reason ambiguity out of existence. When I asked her about a strained paragraph in her paper on Camus' "The Guest," she said, "I didn't want to admit that it [the story's conclusion] was just hanging. I tried to force it into meaning."

Martha uses another rule, one that is not only problematical in itself, but one that often clashes directly with the elaborate plan and obsessive rule above. She believes that humanities papers must scintillate with insight, must present an array of images, ideas, ironies gleaned from the literature under examination. A problem arises, of course, when Martha tries to incorporate her myriad "neat little things," often inherently unrelated, into a tightly structured, carefully sequenced essay. Plans and rules that govern the construction of impressionistic, associational prose would be appropriate to Martha's desire, but her composing process is heavily constrained by the non-impressionistic and nonassociational. Put another way, the plans and rules that govern her exploration of text are not at all synchronous with the plans and rules she uses to discuss her exploration. It is interesting to note here, however, that as recently as three years ago Martha was absorbed in creative writing and was publishing poetry in high school magazines. Given what we know about the complex associational, often nonneatly-sequential nature of the poet's creative process, we can infer that Martha was either free of the plans and rules discussed earlier or they were not as intense. One wonders, as well, if the exposure to three years of university physical science either established or intensified Martha's concern with structure. Whatever the case, she now is hamstrung by conflicting rules when composing papers for the humanities.

Mike's difficulties, too, are rooted in a distortion of the problem-solving process. When the time of the week for the assignment of writing topics draws near, Mike begins to prepare material, strategies, and plans that he believes will be appropriate. If the assignment matches his expectations, he has done a good job of analyzing the professor's intentions. If the assignment *doesn't* match his expectations, however, he cannot easily shift approaches. He feels trapped inside his original plans, cannot generate alternatives, and blocks. As the deadline draws near, he will write something, forcing the assignment to fit his conceptual procrustean bed. Since Mike is a smart man, he will offer a good deal of information, but only some of it ends up being appropriate to the assignment. This entire situation is made all the worse when the time between assignment of topic and generation of product is attenuated further, as in an essay examination. Mike believes (correctly) that one must have a plan, a strategy of some sort in order to solve a problem. He further believes, however, that such a plan, once formulated, becomes an exact structural and substantive blueprint that cannot be violated. The plan offers no alternatives, no "sub-routines." So, whereas Ruth's, Laurel's, and some of Martha's difficulties seem to be rule-specific ("always catch your audience," "write grammatically"), Mike's troubles are more global. He may have strategies that are appropriate for various writing situations (e.g., "for this kind of political science assignment write a compare/contrast essay"), but his entire approach to formulating plans and carrying them through to problem solution is too mechanical. It is probable that Mike's behavior is governed by an explicitly learned or inferred rule: "Always try to 'psych out' a professor." But in this case this rule initiates a problem-solving procedure that is clearly dysfunctional.

While Ruth and Laurel use rules that impede their writing process and Mike utilizes a problem-solving procedure that hamstrings him, *Sylvia* has trouble deciding which of the many rules she possesses to use. Her problem can be characterized as cognitive perplexity: some of her rules are inappropriate, others are functional; some mesh nicely with her own definitions of good writing, others don't. She has multiple rules to invoke, multiple paths to follow, and that very complexity of choice virtually paralyzes her. More so than with the previous four students, there is probably a strong emotional dimension to Sylvia's blocking, but the cognitive difficulties are clear and perhaps modifiable.

Sylvia, somewhat like Ruth and Laurel, puts tremendous weight on the crafting of her first paragraph. If it is good, she believes the rest of the essay will be good. Therefore, she will spend up to five hours on the initial paragraph: "I won't go on until I get that first paragraph down." Clearly, this rule — or the strength of it — blocks Sylvia's production. This is one problem. Another is that Sylvia has other equally potent rules that she sees as separate, uncomplementary injunctions: one achieves "flow" in one's writing through the use of adequate transitions; one achieves substance to one's writing through the use of evidence. Sylvia perceives both rules to be "true," but several times followed one to the exclusion of the other. Furthermore, as I talked to Sylvia, many other rules, guidelines, definitions were offered, but none with conviction. While she *is* committed to one rule about initial paragraphs, and that rule is dysfunctional, she seems very uncertain about the weight and hierarchy of the remaining rules in her cognitive repertoire.

"If It Won't Fit My Work, I'll Change It" — The Non-blockers

Dale, Ellen, Debbie, Susan, and Miles all write with the aid of rules. But their rules differ from blockers' rules in significant ways. If similar in content, they are expressed less absolutely — e.g., "*Try* to keep audience in mind." If dissimilar, they are still expressed less absolutely, more heuristically — e.g., "I can use as many ideas in my thesis paragraph as I need and then develop paragraphs for each idea." Our non-blockers do express some rules with firm assurance, but these tend to be simple injunctions that free up rather than restrict the composing process, e.g., "When stuck, write!" or "I'll write what I can." And finally, at least three of the students openly shun the very textbook rules that some blockers adhere to: e.g., "Rules like 'write only what you know about' just aren't true. I ignore those." These three, in effect, have formulated a further rule that expresses something like: "If a rule conflicts with what is sensible or with experience, reject it."

On the broader level of plans and strategies, these five students also differ from at least three of the five blockers in that they all possess problem-solving plans that are quite functional. Interestingly, on first exploration these plans seem to be too broad or fluid to be useful and, in some cases, can barely be expressed with any precision. Ellen, for example, admits that she has a general "outline in [her] head about how a topic paragraph should look" but could not describe much about its structure. Susan also has a general plan to follow, but, if stymied, will quickly attempt to conceptualize the assignment in different ways: "If my original idea won't work, then I need to proceed differently." Whether or not these plans operate in TOTE-fashion, I can't say. But they do operate with the operate-test fluidity of TOTEs.

True, our non-blockers have their religiously adhered-to rules: e.g., "When stuck, write," and plans, "I couldn't imagine writing without this pattern," but as noted above, these are few and functional. Otherwise, these non-blockers operate with fluid, easily modified, even easily discarded rules and plans (Ellen: "I can throw things out") that are sometimes expressed with a vagueness that could almost be interpreted as ignorance. There lies the irony. Students that offer the least precise rules and plans have the least trouble composing. Perhaps this very lack of precision characterizes the functional composing plan. But perhaps this lack of precision simply masks habitually enacted alternatives and sub-routines. This is clearly an area that needs the illumination of further research.

And then there is feedback. At least three of the five non-blockers are an Information-Processor's dream. They get to know their audience, ask professors and T.A.s specific questions about assignments, bring half-finished products in for evaluation, etc. Like Ruth, they realize the importance of audience, but unlike her, they have specific strategies for obtaining and utilizing feedback. And this penchant for testing writing plans against the needs of the audience can lead to modification of rules and plans. Listen to Debbie:

In high school I was given a formula that stated that you must write a thesis paragraph with *only* three points in it, and then develop each of those points. When I hit college I was given longer assignments. That stuck me for a bit, but then realized that I could use as many ideas in my thesis paragraph as I needed and then develop paragraphs for each one. I asked someone about this and then tried it. I didn't get any negative feedback, so I figured it was o.k.

Debbie's statement brings one last difference between our blockers and non-blockers into focus; it has been implied above, but needs specific formulation: the goals these people have, and the plans they generate to attain these goals, are quite mutable. Part of the mutability comes from the fluid way the goals and plans are conceived, and part of it arises from the effective impact of feedback on these goals and plans.

Analyzing Writer's Block

Algorithms Rather Than Heuristics

In most cases, the rules our blockers use are not "wrong" or "incorrect" — it is good practice, for example, to "grab your audience with a catchy opening" or "craft a solid first paragraph before going on." The problem is that these rules seem to be followed as though they were algorithms, absolute dicta, rather than the loose heuristics that they were intended to be. Either through instruction, or the power of the textbook, or the predilections of some of our blockers for absolutes, or all three, these useful rules of thumb have been transformed into near-algorithmic urgencies. The result, to paraphrase Karl Dunker, is that these rules do not allow a flexible penetration into the nature of the problem. It is this transformation of heuristic into algorithm that contributes to the writer's block of Ruth and Laurel.

Questionable Heuristics Made Algorithmic

Whereas "grab your audience" could be a useful heuristic, "always make three or more points in an essay" is a pretty questionable one. Any such rule, though probably taught to aid the writer who needs structure, ultimately transforms a highly fluid process like writing into a mechanical lockstep. As heuristics, such rules can be troublesome. As algorithms, they are simply incorrect.

Set

As with any problem-solving task, students approach writing assignments with a variety of orientations or sets. Some are functional, others are not. Martha and Jane (see note 14), coming out of the life sciences and social sciences respectively, bring certain methodological orientations with them — certain sets or "directions" that make composing for the humanities a difficult, sometimes confusing, task. In fact, this orientation may cause them to misperceive the task. Martha has formulated a planning strategy from her predisposition to see processes in terms of linear, interrelated steps in a system. Jane doesn't realize that she can revise the statement that "committed" her to the direction her essay has taken. Both of these students are stymied because of formative experiences associated with their majors — experiences, perhaps, that nicely reinforce our very strong tendency to organize experiences temporally.

The Plan That Is Not a Plan

If fluidity and multi-directionality are central to the nature of plans, then the plans that Mike formulates are not true plans at all but, rather, inflexible and static cognitive blueprints.[15] Put another way, Mike's "plans" represent a restricted "closed system" (vs. "open system") kind of thinking, where closed system thinking is defined as focusing on "a limited number of units or items, or members, and those properties of the members which are to be used are known to begin with and do not change as the thinking proceeds," and open system thinking is characterized by an "adventurous exploration of multiple alternatives with strategies that allow redirection once 'dead ends' are encountered."[16] Composing calls for open, even adventurous thinking, not for constrained, no-exit cognition.

Feedback

The above difficulties are made all the more problematic by the fact that they seem resistant to or isolated from corrective feedback. One of the most striking things about Dale, Debbie, and Miles is the ease with which they seek out, interpret, and apply feedback on their rules, plans, and productions. They "operate" and then they "test," and the testing is not only against some internalized goal, but against the requirements of external audience as well.

Too Many Rules — "Conceptual Conflict"

According to D. E. Berlyne, one of the primary forces that motivate problem-solving behavior is a curiosity that arises from conceptual conflict — the convergence of incompatible beliefs or ideas. In *Structure and Direction in Thinking*,[17] Berlyne presents six major types of conceptual conflict, the second of which he terms "perplexity":

> This kind of conflict occurs when there are factors inclining the subject toward each of a set of mutually exclusive beliefs. (257)

If one substitutes "rules" for "beliefs" in the above definition, perplexity becomes a useful notion here. Because perplexity is unpleasant, people are motivated to reduce it by problem-solving behavior that can result in "disequalization":

> Degree of conflict will be reduced if either the number of competing . . . [rules] or their nearness to equality of strength is reduced. (259)

But "disequalization" is not automatic. As I have suggested, Martha and Sylvia hold to rules that conflict, but their perplexity does *not* lead to curiosity and resultant problem-solving behavior. Their perplexity, contra Berlyne, leads to immobilization. Thus "disequalization" will have to be effected from without. The importance of each of, particularly, Sylvia's rules needs an evaluation that will aid her in rejecting some rules and balancing and sequencing others.

A Note on Treatment

Rather than get embroiled in a blocker's misery, the teacher or tutor might interview the student in order to build a writing history and profile: How much and what kind of writing was done in high school? What is the student's major? What kind of writing does it require? How does the student compose? Are there rough drafts or outlines available? By what rules does the student operate? How would he or she define "good" writing? etc. This sort of interview reveals an incredible amount of information about individual composing processes. Furthermore, it often reveals the rigid rule or the inflexible plan that may lie at the base of the student's writing problem. That was precisely what happened with the five blockers. And with Ruth, Laurel, and Martha (and Jane) what was revealed made virtually immediate remedy possible. Dysfunctional rules are easily replaced with or counter-balanced by functional ones if there is no emotional reason to hold onto that which simply doesn't work. Furthermore, students can be trained to select, to "know which rules are appropriate for which problems."[18] Mike's difficulties, perhaps because plans are more complex and pervasive than rules, took longer to correct. But inflexible plans, too, can be remedied by pointing out their dysfunctional qualities and by assisting the student in developing appropriate and flexible alternatives. Operating this way, I was successful with Mike. Sylvia's story, however, did not end as smoothly. Though I had three forty-five minute contacts with her, I was not able to appreciably alter her behavior. Berlyne's theory bore results with Martha but not with Sylvia. Her rules were in conflict, and perhaps that conflict was not exclusively cognitive. Her case keeps analyses like these honest; it reminds us that the cognitive often melds with, and can be overpowered by, the affective. So while Ruth, Laurel, Martha, and Mike could profit from tutorials that explore the rules and plans in their writing behavior, students like Sylvia may need more extended, more affectively oriented counseling sessions that blend the instructional with the psychodynamic.

Notes

1. David Shapiro, *Neurotic Styles* (New York: Basic, 1965).
2. Barbara Hayes-Ruth, a Rand cognitive psychologist, and I are currently developing an information-processing model of the composing process. A good deal of work has already been done by Linda Flower and John Hayes (see note 13 and surrounding text). I have just received — and recommend — their "Writing as Problem Solving" (paper presented at American Educational Research Association, April 1979).
3. Robert M. Gagné, *The Conditions of Learning* (New York: Holt, 1970) 193.
4. E. James Archer, "The Psychological Nature of Concepts," *Analysis of Concept Learning*, ed. H. J. Klausmeirer and C. W. Harris (New York: Academic P, 1966), 37–44; David P. Ausubel, *The Psychology of Meaningful Verbal Behavior* (New York: Grune, 1963); Robert M. Gagné, "Problem Solving," *Categories of Human Learning*, ed. Arthur W. Melton (New York: Academic P, 1964) 293–317; George A. Miller, *Language and Communication* (New York: McGraw, 1951).
5. George Katona, *Organizing and Memorizing* (New York: Columbia UP, 1940); Roger N. Shepard, Carl I. Hovland, and Herbert M. Jenkins, "Learning and Memorization of Classifications," *Psychological Monographs*, 75.13 (1961) (entire no. 517); Robert S. Woodworth, *Dynamics of Behavior* (New York: Holt, 1958) chs. 10–12.
6. Gagné, *The Conditions of Learning*, 190–91.
7. Karl Dunker, "On Problem Solving," *Psychological Monographs*, 58.5 (1945) (entire no. 270); George A. Polya, *How to Solve It* (Princeton: Princeton UP, 1945); George A. Miller, Eugene Galanter, and Karl H. Pribram, *Plans and the Structure of Behavior* (New York: Holt, 1960).
8. Lyle E. Bourne, Jr., Bruce R. Ekstrand, and Roger L. Dominowski, *The Psychology of Thinking* (Englewood Cliffs: Prentice, 1971).
9. John R. Hayes, "Problem Topology and the Solution Process," *Thinking: Current Experimental Studies*, ed. Carl P. Duncan (Philadelphia: Lippincott, 1967) 167–81.
10. Hulda J. Rees and Harold E. Israel, "An Investigation of the Establishment and Operation of Mental Sets," *Psychological Monographs*, 46 (1925) (entire no. 210).
11. Ibid.; Melvin H. Marx, Wilton W. Murphy, and Aaron J. Brownstein, "Recognition of Complex Visual Stimuli as a Function of Training with Abstracted Patterns," *Journal of Experimental Psychology* 62 (1961): 456–60.
12. James L. Adams, *Conceptual Blockbusting* (San Francisco: Freeman, 1974); Edward DeBono, *New Think* (New York: Basic, 1958); Ronald H. Forgus, *Perception* (New York: McGraw, 1966) ch. 13; Abraham Luchins and Edith Hirsch Luchins, *Rigidity of Behavior* (Eugene: U of Oregon Books, 1959); N. R. F. Maier, "Reasoning in Humans. I. On Direction," *Journal of Comparative Psychology* 10 (1920): 115–43.
13. Linda Flower and John Hayes, "Plans and the Cognitive Process of Writing," paper presented at the National Institute of Education Writing Conference, June 1977; "Problem-Solving Strategies and the Writing Process," *College English* 39 (1977): 449–61. See also note 2.
14. Jane, a student not discussed in this paper, was surprised to find out that a topic paragraph can be rewritten after a paper's conclusion to make that paragraph reflect what the essay truly contains. She had gotten so indoc-

trinated with Psychology's (her major) insistence that a hypothesis be formulated and then left untouched before an experiment begins that she thought revision of one's "major premise" was somehow illegal. She had formed a rule out of her exposure to social science methodology, and the rule was totally inappropriate for most writing situations.

15. Cf. "A plan is flexible if the order of execution of its parts can be easily interchanged without affecting the feasibility of the plan . . . the flexible planner might tend to think of lists of things he had to do; the inflexible planner would have his time planned like a sequence of cause-effect relations. The former could rearrange his lists to suit his opportunities, but the latter would be unable to strike while the iron was hot and would generally require considerable 'lead-time' before he could incorporate any alternative sub-plans" (Miller, Galanter, and Pribram, 120).

16. Frederic Bartlett, *Thinking* (New York: Basic, 1958) 74–76.

17. *Structure and Direction in Thinking* (New York: Wiley, 1965) 255.

18. Flower and Hayes, "Plans and the Cognitive Process of Writing" 26.

Rose's Insights as a Resource for Your Teaching

1. Consider the risks in teaching students how to write: Invariably, a few students will be cowed by your authority and will internalize even the most idle and perfunctory observations that you make. Worse yet, they will treat them not simply as useful tips but as some sort of holy edict. When they do, their ability to compose will be curtailed. In a journal, reflect on ways to prevent your overly earnest students from damaging themselves this way. What are some strategies you might devise to teach in a way that minimizes this risk?

2. How do you help students who have come into your classroom blocked by mishandled writing advice? What can you say to them? Can you use some of Rose's theory when giving advice to students who have already mishandled the advice given them in the past?

Rose's Insights as a Resource for Your Writing Classroom

1. After reading "The Phenomenology of Error" by Joseph Williams (see Chapter 3), explore the juxtaposition of these two essays. Could the thorough marking of "incorrect" spots in a paper contribute to what Rose identifies as an overly zealous conscientiousness about following the rules? How might these two essays modify the ways you comment on student writing?

2. Ask students to meet in small groups and make a list of the five

most important dos and don'ts of writing. Then have them write their lists on the board. As you discuss these rules, emphasize their tentative nature, and encourage students to take all of them with a grain of salt. Explain to them that to be overly concerned with such matters can undermine the process of getting thoughts down on paper.

Considering Audience

From Aristotle on, teachers have questioned how they might best assist apprentice writers to recognize audience as a critical part of any communication process. Arguably, purpose and audience are the main factors in shaping a piece of writing, and one cannot be considered without the other. "Assignments" in both the academic community and the professional world will require writers to pay close attention to the needs and discourse expectations of their audience in order to effectively achieve the desired effect with their writing. A student writer should first conceive of the audience as himself or herself; depending on writing goals, this audience will probably extend to the instructor, classmates, or another targeted group.

The decision to identify the audience, beginning with the self, is pragmatic; writers must write to and from the self to be authentic, whether in public or private discourse. Fellow writers can provide immediate response to the success of a draft and can tell a writer what needs they still have as readers; the writing instructor can role-play other kinds of readers in addition to clearly describing his or her own response to a draft. Through the support of this writing community, individual writers increase their awareness of the reader-writer relationship. They become more confident about envisioning the nature and needs of the reader in new writing situations.

Throughout the writing process, but especially during revision, the writing instructor should ask questions to help focus the writer's attention on anticipating and meeting the needs of the audience. The readings here provide an overview of the discussion of audience in contemporary composition theory and pedagogy along with practical recommendations for how and when to consider the reader.

The Rhetorical Stance

Wayne C. Booth

Although this essay was written nearly thirty-five years ago, it continues to enjoy frequent reprinting and much discussion among those who teach writing. Booth mixes casual anecdotes about his classroom practice with a sophisticated study of traditional rhetoric. Booth's central insight is that the success or failure of a piece of writing hinges on how the writer stages the author-audience relationship within the text. He suggests that the best writing alternates between utter disregard for the audience and a regard for the audience that is overbearing. The former stance he calls the pedant's stance, for such writers are more interested in the information they're presenting than in the audience's need to process this information. He defines the latter as the advertiser's stance: Writers who take this stance offer little by way of substantial content and try to woo the audience through flashy, and sometimes vapid, devices. The ideal stance is one that floats half-way between these two, which Booth calls the rhetorical stance.

Last fall I had an advanced graduate student, bright, energetic, well-informed, whose papers were almost unreadable. He managed to be pretentious, dull, and disorganized in his paper on *Emma,* and pretentious, dull, and disorganized on *Madame Bovary.* On *The Golden Bowl* he was all these and obscure as well. Then one day, toward the end of term, he cornered me after class and said, "You know, I think you were all wrong about Robbe-Grillet's *Jealousy* today." We didn't have time to discuss it, so I suggested that he write me a note about it. Five hours later I found in my faculty box a four-page polemic, unpretentious, stimulating, organized, convincing. Here was a man who had taught freshman composition for several years and who was incapable of committing any of the more obvious errors that we think of as characteristic of bad writing. Yet he could not write a decent sentence, paragraph, or paper until his rhetorical problem was solved — until, that is, he had found a definition of his audience, his argument, and his own proper tone of voice.

The word *rhetoric* is one of those catch-all terms that can easily raise trouble when our backs are turned. As it regains a popularity that it once seemed permanently to have lost, its meanings seem to range all the way from something like "the whole art of writing on any subject," as in Kenneth Burke's *The Rhetoric of Religion,* through "the special arts of persuasion," on down to fairly narrow notions about rhetorical figures and devices. And of course we still have with us the meaning of "empty bombast," as in the phrase "merely rhetorical."

I suppose that the question of the role of rhetoric in the English course is meaningless if we think of rhetoric in either its broadest or its narrowest meanings. No English course could avoid dealing with rhetoric in Burke's sense, under whatever name, and on the other hand nobody would ever advocate anything so questionable as teaching "mere rhetoric." But if we settle on the following, traditional, definition, some real questions are raised: "Rhetoric is the art of finding and employing the most effective means of persuasion on any subject, considered independently of intellectual mastery of that subject." As the students say, "Prof. X knows his stuff but he doesn't know how to put it across." If rhetoric is thought of as the art of "putting it across," considered as quite distinct from mastering an "it" in the first place, we are immediately landed in a bramble bush of controversy. Is there such an art? If so, what does it consist of? Does it have a content of its own? Can it be taught? Should it be taught? If it should, how do we go about it, head on or obliquely?

Obviously it would be foolish to try to deal with many of these issues in twenty minutes. But I wish that there were more signs of our taking all of them seriously. I wish that along with our new passion for structural linguistics, for example, we could point to the development of a rhetorical theory that would show just how knowledge of structural linguistics can be useful to anyone interested in the art of persuasion. I wish there were more freshman texts that related every principle and every rule to functional principles of rhetoric, or, where this proves impossible, I wish one found more systematic discussion of why it is impossible. But for today, I must content myself with a brief look at the charge that there is nothing distinctive and teachable about the art of rhetoric.

The case against the isolability and teachability of rhetoric may look at first like a good one. Nobody writes rhetoric, just as nobody ever writes writing. What we write and speak is always *this* discussion of the decline of railroading and *that* discussion of Pope's couplets and the other argument for abolishing the poll-tax or for getting rhetoric back into English studies.

We can also admit that like all the arts, the art of rhetoric is at best very chancy, only partly amenable to systematic teaching; as we are all painfully aware when our 1:00 section goes miserably and our 2:00 section of the same course is a delight, our own rhetoric is not entirely under control. Successful rhetoricians are to some extent like poets, born, not made. They are also dependent on years of practice and experience. And we can finally admit that even the firmest of principles about writing cannot be taught in the same sense that elementary logic or arithmetic or French can be taught. In my first year of teaching, I had a student who started his first two essays with a swear word. When I suggested that perhaps the third paper ought to start with something else, he protested that his high school teacher had taught him always to catch the reader's attention. Now the teacher was right, but the application of even such a firm principle requires reserves of tact that were somewhat beyond my freshman.

But with all of the reservations made, surely the charge that the art of persuasion cannot in any sense be taught is baseless. I cannot think that anyone who has ever read Aristotle's *Rhetoric* or, say, Whateley's *Elements of Rhetoric* could seriously make the charge. There is more than enough in these and the other traditional rhetorics to provide structure and content for a year-long course. I believe that such a course, when planned and carried through with intelligence and flexibility, can be one of the most important of all educational experiences. But it seems obvious that the arts of persuasion cannot be learned in one year, that a good teacher will continue to teach them regardless of his subject matter, and that we as English teachers have a special responsibility at all levels to get certain basic rhetorical principles into all of our writing assignments. When I think back over the experiences which have had any actual effect on my writing, I find the great good fortune of a splendid freshman course, taught by a man who believed in what he was doing, but I also find a collection of other experiences quite unconnected with a specific writing course. I remember the instructor in psychology who pencilled one word after a peculiarly pretentious paper of mine: *bull.* I remember the day when P. A. Christensen talked with me about my Chaucer paper, and made me understand that my failure to use effective transitions was not simply a technical fault but a fundamental block in my effort to get him to see my meaning. His off-the-cuff pronouncement that I should never let myself write a sentence that was not in some way explicitly attached to preceding and following sentences meant far more to me at that moment, when I had something I wanted to say, than it could have meant as part of a pattern of such rules offered in a writing course. Similarly, I can remember the devastating lessons about my bad writing that Ronald Crane could teach with a simple question mark on a graduate seminar paper, or a pencilled "Evidence for this?" or "Why this section here?" or "Everybody says so. Is it true?"

Such experiences are not, I like to think, simply the result of my being a late bloomer. At least I find my colleagues saying such things as "I didn't learn to write until I became a newspaper reporter," or "The most important training in writing I had was doing a dissertation under old *Blank.*" Sometimes they go on to say that the freshman course was useless; sometimes they say that it was an indispensable preparation for the later experience. The diversity of such replies is so great as to suggest that before we try to reorganize the freshman course, with or without explicit confrontations with rhetorical categories, we ought to look for whatever there is in common among our experiences, both of good writing and of good writing instruction. Whatever we discover in such an enterprise ought to be useful to us at any level of our teaching. It will not, presumably, decide once and for all what should be the content of the freshman course, if there should be such a course. But it might serve as a guideline for the development of widely different programs in the widely differing institutional circumstances in which we must work.

The common ingredient that I find in all of the writing I admire — excluding for now novels, plays and poems — is something that I shall reluctantly call the rhetorical stance, a stance which depends on discovering and maintaining in any writing situation a proper balance among the three elements that are at work in any communicative effort: the available arguments about the subject itself, the interests and peculiarities of the audience, and the voice, the implied character, of the speaker. I should like to suggest that it is this balance, this rhetorical stance, difficult as it is to describe, that is our main goal as teachers of rhetoric. Our ideal graduate will strike this balance automatically in any writing that he considers finished. Though he may never come to the point of finding the balance easily, he will know that it is what makes the difference between effective communication and mere wasted effort.

What I mean by the true rhetorician's stance can perhaps best be seen by contrasting it with two or three corruptions, unbalanced stances often assumed by people who think they are practicing the arts of persuasion.

The first I'll call the pedant's stance; it consists of ignoring or underplaying the personal relationship of speaker and audience and depending entirely on statements about a subject — that is, the notion of a job to be done for a particular audience is left out. It is a virtue, of course, to respect the bare truth of one's subject, and there may even be some subjects which in their very nature define an audience and a rhetorical purpose so that adequacy to the subject can be the whole art of presentation. For example, an article on "The relation of the ontological and teleological proofs," in a recent *Journal of Religion,* requires a minimum of adaptation of argument to audience. But most subjects do not in themselves imply in any necessary way a purpose and an audience and hence a speaker's tone. The writer who assumes that it is enough merely to write an exposition of what he happens to know on the subject will produce the kind of essay that soils our scholarly journals, written not for readers but for bibliographies.

In my first year of teaching I taught a whole unit on "exposition" without ever suggesting, so far as I can remember, that the students ask themselves what their expositions were *for.* So they wrote expositions like this one — I've saved it, to teach me toleration of my colleagues: the title is "Family Relations in More's *Utopia.*" "In this theme I would like to discuss some of the relationships with the family which Thomas More elaborates and sets forth in his book, *Utopia.* The first thing that I would like to discuss about family relations is that overpopulation, according to More, is a just cause of war." And so on. Can you hear that student sneering at me, in this opening? What he is saying is something like "you ask for a meaningless paper, I give you a meaningless paper." He knows that he has no audience except me. He knows that I don't want to read his summary of family relations in *Utopia,* and he knows that I know that he therefore has no rhetorical purpose. Because he has not been led to see a question which he considers worth answering, or an audience that could possibly care one way or the other, the paper is worse than no paper at all, even though it has no grammatical or spelling errors and is organized right down the line, one, two, three.

An extreme case, you may say. Most of us would never allow ourselves that kind of empty fencing? Perhaps. But if some carefree foundation is willing to finance a statistical study, I'm willing to wager a month's salary that we'd find at least half of the suggested topics in our freshman texts as pointless as mine was. And we'd find a good deal more than half of the discussions of grammar, punctuation, spelling, and style totally divorced from any notion that rhetorical purpose to some degree controls all such matters. We can offer objective descriptions of levels of usage from now until graduation, but unless the student discovers a desire to say something to somebody and learns to control his diction for a purpose, we've gained very little. I once gave an assignment asking students to describe the same classroom in three different statements, one for each level of usage. They were obedient, but the only ones who got anything from the assignment were those who intuitively imported the rhetorical instructions I had overlooked — such purposes as "Make fun of your scholarly surroundings by describing this classroom in extremely elevated style," or "Imagine a kid from the slums accidentally trapped in these surroundings and forced to write a description of this room." A little thought might have shown me how to give the whole assignment some human point, and therefore some educative value.

Just how confused we can allow ourselves to be about such matters is shown in a recent publication of the Educational Testing Service, called "Factors in Judgments of Writing Ability." In order to isolate those factors which affect differences in grading standards, ETS set six groups of readers — businessmen, writers and editors, lawyers, and teachers of English, social science and natural science — to reading the same batch of papers. Then ETS did a hundred-page "factor analysis" of the amount of agreement and disagreement, and of the elements which different kinds of graders emphasized. The authors of the report express a certain amount of shock at the discovery that the median correlation was only .31 and that 94 percent of the papers received either seven, eight, or nine of the nine possible grades.

But what *could* they have expected? In the first place, the students were given no purpose and no audience when the essays were assigned. And then all these editors and businessmen and academics were asked to judge the papers in a complete vacuum, using only whatever intuitive standards they cared to use. I'm surprised that there was any correlation at all. Lacking instructions, some of the students undoubtedly wrote polemical essays, suitable for the popular press; others no doubt imagined an audience, say, of *Reader's Digest* readers, and others wrote with the English teachers as implied audience; an occasional student with real philosophical bent would no doubt do a careful analysis of the pros and cons of the case. This would be graded low, of course, by the magazine editors, even though they would have graded it high if asked to judge it as a speculative contribution to the analysis of the problem. Similarly, a creative student who has been getting A's for his personal essays will write an amusing colorful piece, failed by all the social scientists present, though they would have graded it high if asked to judge it for what it was. I find it shocking that tens of thousands of dollars and endless hours should have been spent by students, graders, and professional testers analyzing essays and grading results totally abstracted from any notion of purposeful human communication. Did nobody protest? One might as well assemble a group of citizens to judge students' capacity to throw balls, say, without telling the students or the graders whether altitude, speed, accuracy or form was to be judged.

The judges would be drawn from football coaches, jai-lai experts, lawyers, and English teachers, and asked to apply whatever standards they intuitively apply to ball throwing. Then we could express astonishment that the judgments did not correlate very well, and we could do a factor analysis to discover, lo and behold, that some readers concentrated on altitude, some on speed, some on accuracy, some on form — and the English teachers were simply confused.

One effective way to combat the pedantic stance is to arrange for weekly confrontations of groups of students over their own papers. We have done far too little experimenting with arrangements for providing a genuine audience in this way. Short of such developments, it remains true that a good teacher can convince his students that he is a true audience, if his comments on the papers show that some sort of dialogue is taking place. As Jacques Barzun says in *Teacher in America,* students should be made to feel that unless they have said something to someone, they have failed; to bore the teacher is a worse form of failure than to anger him. From this point of view we can see that the charts of grading symbols that mar even the best freshman texts are not the innocent time savers that we pretend. Plausible as it may seem to arrange for more corrections with less time, they inevitably reduce the student's sense of purpose in writing. When he sees innumerable W13s and P19s in the margin, he cannot possibly feel that the art of persuasion is as important to his instructor as when he reads personal comments, however few.

This first perversion, then, springs from ignoring the audience or overreliance on the pure subject. The second, which might be called the advertiser's stance, comes from *under*valuing the subject and overvaluing pure effect: how to win friends and influence people.

Some of our best freshman texts — Sheridan Baker's *The Practical Stylist,* for example — allow themselves on occasion to suggest that to be controversial or argumentative, to stir up an audience is an end in itself. Sharpen the controversial edge, one of them says, and the clear implication is that one should do so even if the truth of the subject is honed off in the process. This perversion is probably in the long run a more serious threat in our society than the danger of ignoring the audience. In the time of audience-reaction meters and pre-tested plays and novels, it is not easy to convince students of the old Platonic truth that good persuasion is honest persuasion, or even of the old Aristotelian truth that the good rhetorician must be master of his subject, no matter how dishonest he may decide ultimately to be. Having told them that good writers always to some degree accommodate their arguments to the audience, it is hard to explain the difference between justified accommodation — say changing *point one* to the final position — and the kind of accommodation that fills our popular magazines, in which the very substance of what is said is accommodated to some preconception of what will sell. "The publication of *Eros* [magazine] represents a major breakthrough in the battle for the liberation of the human spirit."

At a dinner about a month ago I sat between the wife of a famous civil rights lawyer and an advertising consultant. "I saw the article on your book yesterday in the *Daily News*," she said, "but I didn't even finish it. The title of your book scared me off. Why did you ever choose such a terrible title? Nobody would buy a book with a title like that." The man on my right, whom I'll call Mr. Kinches, overhearing my feeble reply, plunged into a conversation with her, over my torn and bleeding corpse. "Now with my *last* book," he said, "I listed twenty possible titles and then tested them out on four hundred businessmen. The one I chose was voted for by 90 percent of the businessmen." "That's what I was just saying to Mr. Booth," she said. "A book title ought to grab you, and *rhetoric* is not going to grab anybody." "Right," he said. "My *last* book sold fifty thousand copies already; I don't know how this one will do, but I polled two hundred businessmen on the table of contents, and. . . ."

At one point I did manage to ask him whether the title he chose really fit the book. "Not quite as well as one or two of the others," he admitted, "but that doesn't matter, you know. If the book is designed right, so that the first chapter pulls them in, and you *keep* 'em in, who's going to gripe about a little inaccuracy in the title?"

Well, rhetoric is the art of persuading, not the art seeming to persuade by giving everything away at the start. It presupposes that one has a purpose concerning a subject which itself cannot be fundamentally modified by the desire to persuade. If Edmund Burke had decided that he could win more votes in Parliament by choosing the other side — as he most certainly could have done — we would hardly hail this party-switch as a master stroke of rhetoric. If Churchill had offered the British "peace in our time," with some laughs thrown in, because opinion polls had shown that more Britishers were "grabbed" by these than by blood, sweat, and tears, we could hardly call his decision a sign of rhetorical skill.

One could easily discover other perversions of the rhetorician's balance — most obviously what might be called the entertainer's stance — the willingness to sacrifice substance to personality and charm. I admire Walker Gibson's efforts to startle us out of dry pedantry, but I know from experience that his exhortations to find and develop the speaker's voice can lead to empty colorfulness. A student once said to me, complaining about a colleague, "I soon learned that all I had to do to get an A was imitate Thurber."

But perhaps this is more than enough about the perversions of the rhetorical stance. Balance itself is always harder to describe than the clumsy poses that result when it is destroyed. But we all experience the balance whenever we find an author who succeeds in changing our minds. He can do so only if he knows more about the subject than we do, and if he then engages us in the process of thinking — and feeling — it through. What makes the rhetoric of Milton and Burke and Churchill great is that each presents us with the spectacle of a man passionately involved in thinking an important question through, in the company of an audience. Though each of them did everything in his power to make his point persuasive, including a pervasive use of the many emotional appeals that have been falsely scorned by many a freshman composition text, none would have allowed himself the advertiser's stance; none would have polled the audience in advance to discover which position would get the votes. Nor is the highly individual personality that springs out at us from their speeches and essays present for the sake of selling itself. The rhetorical balance among speakers, audience, and argument is with all three men habitual, as we see if we look at their non-political writings. Burke's work on the Sublime and Beautiful is a relatively unimpassioned philosophical treatise, but one finds there again a delicate balance: though the implied author of this work is a far different person, far less obtrusive, far more objective, than the man who later cried *sursum corda* to the British Parliament, he permeates with his philosophical personality his philosophical work. And though the signs of his awareness of his audience are far more subdued, they are still here: every effort is made to involve the *proper* audience, the audience of philosophical minds, in a fundamentally interesting inquiry, and to lead them through to the end. In short, because he was a man engaged with men in the effort to solve a human problem, one could never call what he wrote dull, however difficult or abstruse.

Now obviously the habit of seeking this balance is not the only thing we have to teach under the heading of rhetoric. But I think that everything worth teaching under that heading finds its justification finally in that balance. Much of what is now considered irrelevant or dull can, in fact, be brought to life when teachers and students know what they are seeking. Churchill reports that the most valuable training he ever received in rhetoric was in the diagramming of sentences. Think of it! Yet the diagramming of a sentence, regardless of the grammatical system, can be a live subject as soon as one asks not simply "How is this sentence put together," but rather "Why is it put together in this way?" or "Could the rhetorical balance and hence the desired persuasion be better achieved by writing it differently?"

As a nation we are reputed to write very badly. As a nation, I would say, we are more inclined to the perversions of rhetoric than to the rhetorical balance. Regardless of what we do about this or that course in the curriculum, our mandate would seem to be, then, to lead more of our students than we now do to care about and practice the true arts of persuasion.

Booth's Insights as a Resource for Your Teaching

1. Read any piece of writing by a student, and track the ways the author appeals to you as a reader. Where does the author adopt the pedant's stance? The advertiser's stance? How might these terms help you to comment on student work that needs improvement?

2. Consider the stance that you "model" for your students. Do you alternate between pedant and advertiser, or do you strike a rhetorical stance most of the time? How do the students respond to the various stances we model for them?

Booth's Insights as a Resource for Your Writing Classroom

1. Assign Booth's essay to your students. Once they've read it, have them explore it according to the terms Booth himself presents. Is Booth's essay characterized by a subtle balance between the pedant and the advertiser? If so, how and where does he manage to strike this balance? Are there any places where the stance seems imbalanced and starts to lean in one direction or another?

2. Ask students to examine their own work or each other's in light of Booth's essay. Have them focus on passages in their own writing that were less than successful. Can they use Booth's terms to diagnose and fix problems?

Audience Addressed/Audience Invoked: The Role of Audience in Composition Theory and Pedagogy

Lisa Ede and Andrea Lunsford

Lisa Ede and Andrea Lunsford skillfully demonstrate two major, and seemingly opposed, perspectives on whether and how to emphasize audience in writing courses. They characterize as "audience addressed" the assumptions of many writing teachers and theorists that writers must know — or learn about — the attitudes, beliefs, and expectations of their readers. The authors focus on the theory of Ruth Mitchell and Mary Taylor, who base a writing pedagogy on the concept of addressing the "real" reader. The classification could also include other theorists like Linda Flower, who discusses "reader-based prose" and presents planning strategies for deciding how to address the reader.

Ede and Lunsford contrast the concept of audience addressed with that of "audience invoked." This theory states that the writer invokes an audience by providing "cues" that tell the reader what role the writer wants the reader to play. The authors discuss Walter Ong's "The Writer's Audience Is Always a Fiction," but your students may invoke their audience most clearly in papers they write that take a stand or propose a solution. In each type of persuasive writing, the successful student not only shapes a persona that readers will trust or respect but also creates a character or role for the reader — perhaps that of being altruistic and humane or of being rational yet cautiously sympathetic.

Through their analysis of the two perspectives on audience, Ede and Lunsford demonstrate that writers need to have skills both to invoke readers and to anticipate and address readers, depending on the rhetorical situation. They remind us how writers redefine audience during revision and cite their own writing processes. They conclude that a "fully elaborated view of audience . . . must balance the creativity of the writer with the different, but equally important, creativity of the reader."

One important controversy currently engaging scholars and teachers of writing involves the role of audience in composition theory and pedagogy. How can we best define the audience of a written discourse? What does it mean to address an audience? To what degree should teachers stress audience in their assignments and discussions? What is the best way to help students recognize the significance of this critical element in any rhetorical situation?

Teachers of writing may find recent efforts to answer these questions more confusing than illuminating. Should they agree with Ruth Mitchell and Mary Taylor, who so emphasize the significance of the audience that they argue for abandoning conventional composition courses and instituting a "cooperative effort by writing and subject instructors in adjunct courses? The cooperation and courses take two main forms. Either writing instructors can be attached to subject courses where writing is required, an organization which disperses the instructors throughout the departments participating; or the composition courses can teach students how to write the papers assigned in other concurrent courses, thus centralizing instruction but diversifying topics."[1] Or should teachers side with Russell Long, who asserts that those advocating greater attention to audience overemphasize the role of "observable physical or occupational characteristics" while ignoring the fact that most writers actually create their audiences? Long argues against the usefulness of such methods as developing hypothetical rhetorical situations as writing assignments, urging instead a more traditional emphasis on "the analysis of texts in the classroom with a very detailed examination given to the signals provided by the writer for his audience."[2]

To many teachers, the choice seems limited to a single option — to be for or against an emphasis on audience in composition courses. In the following essay, we wish to expand our understanding of the role audience plays in composition theory and pedagogy by demonstrating that the arguments advocated by each side of the current debate oversimplify the act of making meaning through written discourse. Each side, we will argue, has failed adequately to recognize (1) the fluid, dynamic character of rhetorical situations and (2) the integrated, interdependent nature of reading and writing. After discussing the strengths and weaknesses of the two central perspectives on audience in composition — which we group under the rubrics of *audience addressed* and *audience invoked*[3] — we will propose an alternative formulation, one which we believe more accurately reflects the richness of "audience" as a concept.[4]

Audience Addressed

Those who envision audience as addressed emphasize the concrete reality of the writer's audience; they also share the assumption that knowledge of this audience's attitudes, beliefs, and expectations is not only possible (via observation and analysis) but essential. Questions concerning the degree to which this audience is "real" or imagined, and the ways it differs from the speaker's audience, are generally either ignored or subordinated to a sense of the audience's powerfulness. In their discussion of "A Heuristic Model for Creating a Writer's Audience," for example, Fred Pfister and Joanne Petrik attempt to recognize the ontological complexity of the writer-audience relationship by noting that "students, like all writers, must fictionalize their audience."[5] Even so, by encouraging students to "construct in their imagination an audience that is as nearly a replica as is possible of *those many readers who actually exist in the world of reality*," Pfister and Petrik implicitly privilege the concept of audience as addressed.[6]

Many of those who envision audience as addressed have been influenced by the strong tradition of audience analysis in speech communication and by current research in cognitive psychology on the composing process.[7] They often see themselves as reacting against the current-traditional paradigm of composition, with its arhetorical, product-oriented emphasis.[8] And they also frequently encourage what is called "real-world" writing.[9]

Our purpose here is not to draw up a list of those who share this view of audience but to suggest the general outline of what most readers will recognize as a central tendency in the teaching of writing today. We would, however, like to focus on one particularly ambitious attempt to formulate a theory and pedagogy for composition based on the concept of audience as addressed: Ruth Mitchell and Mary Taylor's "The Integrating Perspective: An Audience-Response Model for Writing." We choose Mitchell and Taylor's work because of its theoretical richness and practical specificity. Despite these strengths, we wish to note several potentially significant limitations in their approach, limitations which obtain to varying degrees in much of the current work of those who envision audience as addressed.

In their article, Mitchell and Taylor analyze what they consider to be the two major existing composition models: one focusing on the writer and the other on the written product. Their evaluation of these two models seems essentially accurate. The "writer" model is limited because it defines writing as either self-expression or "fidelity to fact" (255) — epistemologically naive assumptions which result in troubling pedagogical inconsistencies. And the "written product" model, which is characterized by an emphasis on "certain intrinsic features [such as a] lack of comma splices and fragments" (258), is challenged by the continued inability of teachers of writing (not to mention those in other professions) to agree upon the precise intrinsic features which characterize "good" writing.

Most interesting, however, is what Mitchell and Taylor *omit* in their criticism of these models. Neither the writer model nor the written product model pays serious attention to invention, the term used to describe those "methods designed to aid in retrieving information, forming concepts, analyzing complex events, and solving certain kinds of problems."[10] Mitchell and Taylor's lapse in not noting this omission is understandable, however, for the same can be said of their own model. When these authors discuss the writing process, they stress that "our first priority for writing instruction at every level ought to be certain major tactics for structuring material because these structures are the most important in guiding the reader's comprehension and memory" (271). They do not concern themselves with where "the material" comes from — its sophistication, complexity, accuracy, or rigor.

Mitchell and Taylor also fail to note another omission, one which might be best described in reference to their own model (Figure 1). This model has four components. Mitchell and Taylor use two of these, "writer" and "written product," as labels for the models they condemn. The third and fourth components, "audience" and "response," provide the title for their own "audience-response model for writing" (249).

Mitchell and Taylor stress that the components in their model interact. Yet, despite their emphasis on interaction, it never seems to occur to them to note that the two other models may fail in large part because they overemphasize and isolate one of the four elements — wrenching it too greatly from its context and thus inevitably distorting the composing process. Mitchell and Taylor do not consider this possibility, we suggest, because their own model has the same weakness.

Mitchell and Taylor argue that a major limitation of the "writer"

Figure 1. Mitchell and Taylor's "general model of writing" (250)

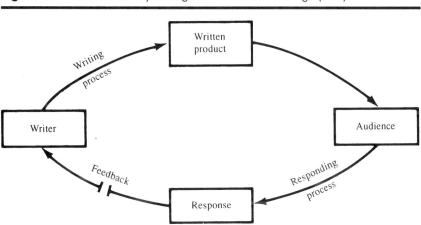

model is its emphasis on the self, the person writing, as the only potential judge of effective discourse. Ironically, however, their own emphasis on audience leads to a similar distortion. In their model, the audience has the sole power of evaluating writing, the success of which "will be judged by the audience's reaction: 'good' translates into 'effective,' 'bad' into 'ineffective.'" Mitchell and Taylor go on to note that "the audience not only judges writing; it also motivates it" (250),[11] thus suggesting that the writer has less control than the audience over both evaluation and motivation.

Despite the fact that Mitchell and Taylor describe writing as "an interaction, a dynamic relationship" (250), their model puts far more emphasis on the role of the audience than on that of the writer. One way to pinpoint the source of imbalance in Mitchell and Taylor's formulation is to note that they are right in emphasizing the creative role of readers who, they observe, "actively contribute to the meaning of what they read and will respond according to a complex set of expectations, preconceptions, and provocations" (251), but wrong in failing to recognize the equally essential role writers play throughout the composing process not only as creators but also as *readers* of their own writing.

As Susan Wall observes in "In the Writer's Eye: Learning to Teach the Rereading/Revising Process," when writers read their own writing, as they do continuously while they compose, "there are really not one but two contexts for rereading: there is the writer-as-reader's sense of what the established text is actually saying, as of this reading; and there is the reader-as-writer's judgment of what the text might say or should say. . . ."[12] What is missing from Mitchell and Taylor's model, and from much work done from the perspective of audience as addressed, is a recognition of the crucial importance of this internal dialogue, through which writers analyze inventional problems and conceptualize patterns of discourse. Also missing is an adequate awareness that, no matter how much feedback writers may receive after they have written something (or in breaks while they write), as they compose writers must rely in large part upon their own vision of the reader, which they create, as readers do their vision of writers, according to their own experiences and expectations.

Another major problem with Mitchell and Taylor's analysis is their apparent lack of concern for the ethics of language use. At one point, the authors ask the following important question: "Have we painted ourselves into a corner, so that the audience-response model must defend sociologese and its related styles?" (265). Note first the ambiguity of their answer, which seems to us to say no and yes at the same time, and the way they try to deflect its impact:

> No. We defend only the right of audiences to set their own standards and we repudiate the ambitions of English departments to monopolize that standard-setting. If bureaucrats and scientists are happy with the

way they write, then no one should interfere.
But evidence is accumulating that they are not happy. (265)

Here Mitchell and Taylor surely underestimate the relationship between style and substance. As those concerned with Doublespeak can attest, for example, the problem with sociologese is not simply its (to our ears) awkward, convoluted, highly nominalized style, but the way writers have in certain instances used this style to make statements otherwise unacceptable to laypersons, to "gloss over" potentially controversial facts about programs and their consequences, and thus violate the ethics of language use. Hence, although we support Mitchell and Taylor when they insist that we must better understand and respect the linguistic traditions of other disciplines and professions, we object to their assumption that style is somehow value free.

As we noted earlier, an analysis of Mitchell and Taylor's discussion clarifies weaknesses inherent in much of the theoretical and pedagogical research based on the concept of audience as addressed. One major weakness of this research lies in its narrow focus on helping students learn how to "continually modify their work with reference to their audience" (251). Such a focus, which in its extreme form becomes pandering to the crowd, tends to undervalue the responsibility a writer has to a subject and to what Wayne Booth in *Modern Dogma and the Rhetoric of Assent* calls "the art of discovering good reasons." [13] The resulting imbalance has clear ethical consequences, for rhetoric has traditionally been concerned not only with the effectiveness of a discourse, but with truthfulness as well. Much of our difficulty with the language of advertising, for example, arises out of the ad writer's powerful concept of audience as addressed divorced from a corollary ethical concept. The toothpaste ad that promises improved personality, for instance, knows too well how to address the audience. But such ads ignore ethical questions completely.

Another weakness in research done by those who envision audience as addressed suggests an oversimplified view of language. As Paul Kameen observes in "Rewording the Rhetoric of Composition," "discourse is not grounded in forms or experience or audience; it engages all of these elements simultaneously." [14] Ann Berthoff has persistently criticized our obsession with one or another of the elements of discourse, insisting that meaning arises out of their synthesis. Writing is more, then, than "a means of acting upon a receiver" (Mitchell and Taylor 250); it is a means of making meaning for writer *and* reader. [15] Without such a unifying, balanced understanding of language use, it is easy to overemphasize one aspect of discourse, such as audience. It is also easy to forget, as Anthony Petrosky cautions us, that "reading, responding, and composing are aspects of understanding, and theories that attempt to account for them outside of their interaction with each other run the serious risk of building reductive models of human understanding." [16]

Audience Invoked

Those who envision audience as invoked stress that the audience of a written discourse is a construction of the writer, a "created fiction" (Long 225). They do not, of course, deny the physical reality of readers, but they argue that writers simply cannot know this reality in the way that speakers can. The central task of the writer, then, is not to analyze an audience and adapt discourse to meet its needs. Rather, the writer uses the semantic and syntactic resources of language to provide cues for the reader — cues which help to define the role or roles the writer wishes the reader to adopt in responding to the text. Little scholarship in composition takes this perspective; only Russell Long's article and Walter Ong's "The Writer's Audience Is Always a Fiction" focus centrally on this issue.[17] If recent conferences are any indication, however, a growing number of teachers and scholars are becoming concerned with what they see as the possible distortions and oversimplifications of the approach typified by Mitchell and Taylor's model.[18]

Russell Long's response to current efforts to teach students analysis of audience and adaptation of text to audience is typical: "I have become increasingly disturbed not only about the superficiality of the advice itself, but about the philosophy which seems to lie beneath it" (221). Rather than detailing Long's argument, we wish to turn to Walter Ong's well-known study. Published in *PMLA* in 1975, "The Writer's Audience Is Always a Fiction" has had a significant impact on composition studies, despite the fact that its major emphasis is on fictional narrative rather than expository writing. An analysis of Ong's argument suggests that teachers of writing may err if they uncritically accept Ong's statement that "what has been said about fictional narrative applies ceteris paribus to all writing" (17).

Ong's thesis includes two central assertions: "What do we mean by saying the audience is a fiction? Two things at least. First, that the writer must construct in his imagination, clearly or vaguely, an audience cast in some sort of role. . . . Second, we mean that the audience must correspondingly fictionalize itself" (12). Ong emphasizes the creative power of the adept writer, who can both project and alter audiences, as well as the complexity of the reader's role. Readers, Ong observes, must learn or "know how to play the game of being a member of an audience that 'really' does not exist" (12).

On the most abstract and general level, Ong is accurate. For a writer, the audience is not *there* in the sense that the speaker's audience, whether a single person or a large group, is present. But Ong's representative situations — the orator addressing a mass audience versus a writer alone in a room — oversimplify the potential range and diversity of both oral and written communication situations.

Ong's model of the paradigmatic act of speech communication derives from traditional rhetoric. In distinguishing the terms audience and reader, he notes that "the orator has before him an audience which is a true audience, a collectivity. . . . Readers do not form a collectivity, acting here and now on one another and on the speaker as members of an audience do" (11). As this quotation indicates, Ong also stresses the potential for interaction among members of an audience, and between an audience and a speaker.

But how many audiences are actually collectives, with ample opportunity for interaction? In *Persuasion: Understanding, Practice, and Analysis,* Herbert Simons establishes a continuum of audiences based on opportunities for interaction.[19] Simons contrasts commercial mass media publics, which "have little or no contact with each other and certainly have no reciprocal awareness of each other as members of the same audience" with "face-to-face work groups that meet and interact continuously over an extended period of time." He goes on to note that: "Between these two extremes are such groups as the following: (1) the *pedestrian audience,* persons who happen to pass a soap box orator . . . ; (2) the *passive, occasional audience,* persons who come to hear a noted lecturer in a large auditorium . . . ; (3) the *active, occasional audience,* persons who meet only on specific occasions but actively interact when they do meet" (97–98).

Simons's discussion, in effect, questions the rigidity of Ong's distinctions between a speaker's and a writer's audience. Indeed, when one surveys a broad range of situations inviting oral communication, Ong's paradigmatic situation, in which the speaker's audience constitutes a "collectivity, acting here and now on one another and on the speaker" (11), seems somewhat atypical. It is certainly possible, at any rate, to think of a number of instances where speakers confront a problem very similar to that of writers: lacking intimate knowledge of their audience, which comprises not a collectivity but a disparate, and possibly even divided, group of individuals, speakers, like writers, must construct in their imaginations "an audience cast in some sort of role."[20] When President Carter announced to Americans during a speech broadcast on television, for instance, that his program against inflation was "the moral equivalent of warfare," he was doing more than merely characterizing his economic policies. He was providing an important cue to his audience concerning the role he wished them to adopt as listeners — that of a people braced for a painful but necessary and justifiable battle. Were we to examine his speech in detail, we would find other more subtle, but equally important, semantic and syntactic signals to the audience.

We do not wish here to collapse all distinctions between oral and written communication, but rather to emphasize that speaking and writing are, after all, both rhetorical acts. There are important differences between speech and writing. And the broad distinction between speech and writing that Ong makes is both commonsensical and particularly relevant to his subject, fictional narrative. As our illustration demonstrates, however, when one turns to precise, concrete situations, the relationship between speech and writing can become far more complex than even Ong represents.

Just as Ong's distinction between speech and writing is accurate on a highly general level but breaks down (or at least becomes less clear-cut) when examined closely, so too does his dictum about writers and their audiences. Every writer must indeed create a role for the reader, but the constraints on the writer and the potential sources of and possibilities for the reader's role are both more complex and diverse than Ong suggests. Ong stresses the importance of literary tradition in the creation of audience: "If the writer succeeds in writing, it is generally because he can fictionalize in his imagination an audience he has learned to know not from daily life but from earlier writers who were fictionalizing in their imagination audiences they had learned to know in still earlier writers, and so on back to the dawn of written narrative" (11). And he cites a particularly (for us) germane example, a student "asked to write on the subject to which schoolteachers, jaded by summer, return compulsively every autumn: 'How I Spent My Summer Vacation'" (11). In order to negotiate such an assignment successfully, the student must turn his real audience, the teacher, into someone else. He or she must, for instance, "make like Samuel Clemens and write for whomever Samuel Clemens was writing for" (11).

Ong's example is, for his purposes, well chosen. For such an assignment does indeed require the successful student to "fictionalize" his or her audience. But why is the student's decision to turn to a literary model in this instance particularly appropriate? Could one reason be that the student knows (consciously or unconsciously) that his English teacher, who is still the literal audience of his essay, appreciates literature and hence would be entertained (and here the student may intuit the assignment's actual aim as well) by such a strategy? In Ong's example the audience — the "jaded" schoolteacher — is not only willing to accept another role but, perhaps, actually yearns for it. How else to escape the tedium of reading twenty-five, fifty, seventy-five student papers on the same topic? As Walter Minot notes, however, not all readers are so malleable:

> In reading a work of fiction or poetry, a reader is far more willing to suspend his beliefs and values than in a rhetorical work dealing with some current social, moral, or economic issue. The effectiveness of the created audience in a rhetorical situation is likely to depend on such constraints as the actual identity of the reader, the subject of the discourse, the identity and purpose of the writer, and many other factors in the real world.[21]

An example might help make Minot's point concrete.

Imagine another composition student faced, like Ong's, with an assignment. This student, who has been given considerably more latitude in her choice of topic, has decided to write on an issue of concern to her at the moment, the possibility that a home for mentally retarded adults will be built in her neighborhood. She is alarmed by the strongly negative, highly emotional reaction of most of her neighbors and wishes in her essay to persuade them that such a residence might not be the disaster they anticipate.

This student faces a different task from that described by Ong. If she is to succeed, she must think seriously about her actual readers, the neighbors to whom she wishes to send her letter. She knows the obvious demographic factors — age, race, class — so well that she probably hardly needs to consider them consciously. But other issues are more complex. How much do her neighbors know about mental retardation, intellectually or experientially? What is their image of a retarded adult? What fears does this project raise in them? What civic and religious values do they most respect? Based on this analysis — and the process may be much less sequential than we describe here — she must, of course, define a role for her audience, one congruent with her persona, arguments, the facts as she knows them, etc. She must, as Minot argues, *both* analyze and invent an audience.[22] In this instance, after detailed analysis of her audience and her arguments, the student decided to begin her essay by emphasizing what she felt to be the genuinely admirable qualities of her neighbors, particularly their kindness, understanding, and concern for others. In so doing, she invited her audience to see themselves as she saw them: as thoughtful, intelligent people who, if they were adequately informed, would certainly not act in a harsh manner to those less fortunate than they. In accepting this role, her readers did not have to "play the game of being a member of an audience that 'really' does not exist" (Ong 12). But they did have to recognize in themselves the strengths the student described and to accept her implicit linking of these strengths to what she hoped would be their response to the proposed "home."

When this student enters her history class to write an examination she faces a different set of constraints. Unlike the historian who does indeed have a broad range of options in establishing the reader's role, our student has much less freedom. This is because her reader's role has already been established and formalized in a series of related academic conventions. If she is a successful student, she has so effectively internalized these conventions that she can subordinate a concern for her complex and multiple audiences to focus on the material on which she is being tested and on the single audience, the teacher, who will respond to her performance on the test.[23]

We could multiply examples. In each instance the student writing — to friend, employer, neighbor, teacher, fellow readers of her daily newspaper — would need, as one of the many conscious and unconscious decisions required in composing, to envision and define a role for the reader. But *how* she defines that role — whether she relies mainly upon academic or technical writing conventions, literary models, intimate knowledge of friends or neighbors, analysis of a particular group, or some combination thereof — will vary tremendously. At times the writer may establish a role for the reader which indeed does not "coincide with his role in the rest of actual life" (Ong 12). At other times, however, one of the writer's primary tasks may be that of analyzing the "real life" audience and adapting the discourse to it. One of the factors that makes writing so difficult, as we know, is that we have no recipes: each rhetorical situation is unique and thus requires the writer, catalyzed and guided by a strong sense of purpose, to reanalyze and reinvent solutions.

Despite their helpful corrective approach, then, theories which assert that the audience of a written discourse is a construction of the writer present their own dangers.[24] One of these is the tendency to overemphasize the distinction between speech and writing while undervaluing the insights of discourse theorists, such as James Moffett and James Britton, who remind us of the importance of such additional factors as distance between speaker or writer and audience and levels of abstraction in the subject. In *Teaching the Universe of Discourse,* Moffett establishes the following spectrum of discourse: recording ("the drama of what is happening"), reporting ("the narrative of what happened"), generalizing ("the exposition of what happens"), and theorizing ("the argumentation of what will, may happen").[25] In an extended example, Moffett demonstrates the important points of connection between communication acts at any one level of the spectrum, whether oral or written:

> Suppose next that I tell the cafeteria experience to a friend some time later in conversation. . . . Of course, instead of recounting the cafeteria scene to my friend in person I could write it in a letter to an audience more removed in time and space. Informal writing is usually still rather spontaneous, directed at an audience known to the writer, and reflects the transient mood and circumstances in which the writing occurs. Feedback and audience influence, however, are delayed and weakened. . . . *Compare in turn now the changes that must occur all down the line when I write about this cafeteria experience in a discourse destined for publication and distribution to a mass, anonymous audience of present and perhaps unborn people.* I cannot allude to things and ideas that only my friends know about. I must use a vocabulary, style, logic, and rhetoric that anybody in that mass audience can understand and respond to. I must name and organize what happened during those moments in the cafeteria that day in such a way that this mythical average reader can relate what I say to some primary moments of experience of his own. (37–38; our emphasis)

Though Moffett does not say so, many of these same constraints would obtain if he decided to describe his experience in a speech to a mass audience — the viewers of a television show, for example, or the members of a graduating class. As Moffett's example illustrates, the distinction between speech and writing is important; it is, however, only one of several constraints influencing any particular discourse.

Another weakness of research based on the concept of audience as invoked is that it distorts the processes of writing and reading by overemphasizing the power of the writer and undervaluing that of the reader. Unlike Mitchell and Taylor, Ong recognizes the creative role the writer plays as reader of his or her own writing, the way the writer uses language to provide cues for the reader and tests the effectiveness of these cues during his or her own rereading of the text. But Ong fails adequately to recognize the constraints placed on the writer, in certain situations, by the audience. He fails, in other words, to acknowledge that readers' own experiences, expectations, and beliefs do play a central role in their reading of a text, and that the writer who does not consider the needs and interests of his audience risks losing that audience. To argue that the audience is a "created fiction" (Long 225), to stress that the reader's role "seldom coincides with his role in the rest of actual life" (Ong 12), is just as much an oversimplification, then, as to insist, as Mitchell and Taylor do, that "the audience not only judges writing, it also motivates it" (250). The former view overemphasizes the writer's independence and power; the latter, that of the reader.

Rhetoric and Its Situations[26]

If the perspectives we have described as audience addressed and audience invoked represent incomplete conceptions of the role of audience in written discourse, do we have an alternative? How can we most accurately conceive of this essential rhetorical element? In what follows we will sketch a tentative model and present several defining or constraining statements about this apparently slippery concept, "audience." The result will, we hope, move us closer to a full understanding of the role audience plays in written discourse.

Figure 2 represents our attempt to indicate the complex series of obligations, resources, needs, and constraints embodied in the writer's concept of audience. (We emphasize that our goal here is *not* to depict the writing process as a whole — a much more complex task — but to focus on the writer's relation to audience.) As our model indicates, we do not see the two perspectives on audience described earlier as necessarily dichotomous or contradictory. Except for past and anomalous audiences, special cases which we describe paragraphs hence, all of the audience roles we specify — self, friend, colleague, critic, mass audience, and future audience — may be invoked or addressed.[27] It is the writer who, as writer and reader of his or her own text, one guided by a sense of purpose and by the particularities of a specific rhetorical situation, establishes the range of potential roles an audience may play. (Readers may, of course, accept or reject the role or roles the writer wishes them to adopt in responding to a text.)

Writers who wish to be read must often adapt their discourse to meet the needs and expectations of an addressed audience. They may rely on past experience in addressing audiences to guide their writing, or they may engage a representative of that audience in the writing process. The latter occurs, for instance, when we ask a colleague to read an article intended for scholarly publication. Writers may also be required to respond to the intervention of others — a teacher's comments on an essay, a supervisor's suggestions for improving a report,

Figure 2.   The concept of audience

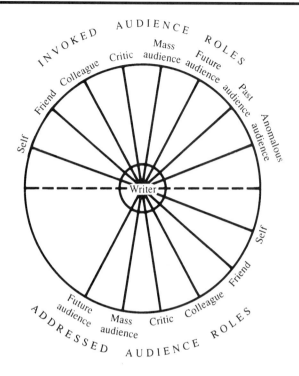

or the insistent, catalyzing questions of an editor. Such intervention may in certain cases represent a powerful stimulus to the writer, but it is the writer who interprets the suggestions — or even commands — of others, choosing what to accept or reject. Even the conscious decision to accede to the expectations of a particular addressed audience may not always be carried out; unconscious psychological resistance, incomplete understanding, or inadequately developed ability may prevent the writer from following through with the decision — a reality confirmed by composition teachers with each new set of essays.

The addressed audience, the actual or intended readers of a discourse, exists outside of the text. Writers may analyze these readers' needs, anticipate their biases, even defer to their wishes. But it is only through the text, through language, that writers embody or give life to their conception of the reader. In so doing, they do not so much create a role for the reader — a phrase which implies that the writer somehow creates a mold to which the reader adapts — as invoke it. Rather than relying on incantations, however, writers conjure their vision — a vision which they hope readers will actively come to share as they read the text — by using all the resources of language available to them to establish a broad, and ideally coherent, range of cues for the reader. Technical writing conventions, for instance, quickly formalize any of several writer-reader relationships, such as colleague to colleague or expert to lay reader. But even comparatively local semantic decisions may play an equally essential role. In "The Writer's Audience Is Always a Fiction," Ong demonstrates how Hemingway's use of definite articles in *A Farewell to Arms* subtly cues readers that their role is to be that of a "companion in arms . . . a confidant" (13).

Any of the roles of the addressed audience cited in our model may be invoked via the text. Writers may also invoke a past audience, as did, for instance, Ong's student writing to those Mark Twain would have been writing for. And writers can also invoke anomalous audiences, such as a fictional character — Hercule Poirot perhaps. Our model, then, confirms Douglas Park's observation that the meanings of audience, though multiple and complex, "tend to diverge in two general directions: one toward actual people external to the text, the audience whom the writer must accommodate; the other toward the text itself and the audience implied there: a set of suggested or evoked attitudes, interests, reactions, conditions of knowledge which may or may not fit with the qualities of actual readers or listeners."[28] The most complete understanding of audience thus involves a synthesis of the perspectives we have termed audience addressed, with its focus on the reader, and audience invoked, with its focus on the writer.

One illustration of this constantly shifting complex of meanings for "audience" lies in our own experiences writing this essay. One of us became interested in the concept of audience during an NEH Seminar, and her first audience was a small, close-knit seminar group to whom she addressed her work. The other came to contemplate a multiplicity of audiences while working on a textbook; the first audience in this case was herself, as she debated the ideas she was struggling to present to a group of invoked students. Following a lengthy series of conversations, our interests began to merge: we shared notes and discussed articles written by others on audience, and eventually one of us began a draft. Our long-distance telephone bills and the miles we travelled up and down I-5 from Oregon to British Columbia attest most concretely to the power of a coauthor's expectations and criticisms and also illustrate that one person can take on the role of several different audiences: friend, colleague, and critic.

As we began to write and rewrite the essay, now for a particular scholarly journal, the change in purpose and medium (no longer a seminar paper or a textbook) led us to new audiences. For us, the major "invoked audience" during this period was Richard Larson, editor of this journal, whose questions and criticisms we imagined and tried to anticipate. (Once this essay was accepted by *CCC*, Richard Larson became for us an addressed audience: he responded in writing with questions, criticisms, and suggestions, some of which we had, of course, failed to anticipate.) We also thought of the readers of *CCC* and those who attend the annual CCCC, most often picturing you as members of our own departments, a diverse group of individuals with widely varying degrees of interest in and knowledge of composition. Because of the generic constraints of academic writing, which limit the range of roles we may define for our readers, the audience represented by the readers of *CCC* seemed most vivid to us in two situations: (1) when we were concerned about the degree to which we needed to explain concepts or terms and (2) when we considered central organizational decisions, such as the most effective way to introduce a discussion. Another, and for us extremely potent, audience was the authors — Mitchell and Taylor, Long, Ong, Park, and others — with whom we have seen ourselves in silent dialogue. As we read and reread their analyses and developed our responses to them, we felt a responsibility to try to understand their formulations as fully as possible, to play fair with their ideas, to make our own efforts continue to meet their high standards.

Our experience provides just one example, and even it is far from complete. (Once we finished a rough draft one particular colleague became a potent but demanding addressed audience, listening to revision upon revision and challenging us with harder and harder questions. And after this essay is published, we may revise our understanding of audiences we thought we knew or recognize the existence of an entirely new audience. The latter would happen, for instance, if teachers of speech communication for some reason found our discussion useful.) But even this single case demonstrates that the term *audience* refers not just to the intended, actual, or eventual readers of a discourse, but to *all* those whose image, ideas, or actions influence a writer during the process of composition. One way to conceive of "audience," then, is as an overdetermined or unusually rich concept, one which may perhaps be best specified through the analysis of precise, concrete situations.

We hope that this partial example of our own experience will illustrate how the elements represented in Figure 2 will shift and merge, depending on the particular rhetorical situation, the writer's aim, and the genre chosen. Such an understanding is critical: Because of the complex reality to which the term audience refers and because of its fluid, shifting role in the composing process, any discussion of audience which isolates it from the rest of the rhetorical situation or which radically overemphasizes or underemphasizes its function in relation to other rhetorical constraints is likely to oversimplify. Note the unilateral direction of Mitchell and Taylor's model (5), which is unable to represent the diverse and complex role(s) audience(s) can play in the actual writing process — in the creation of meaning. In contrast, consider the model used by Edward P. J. Corbett in his *Little Rhetoric and Handbook* [see Figure 3].[29] This representation, which allows for interaction among all the elements of rhetoric, may at first appear less elegant and predictive than Mitchell and Taylor's. But it is finally more useful since it accurately represents the diverse range of potential interrelationships in any written discourse.

We hope that our model also suggests the integrated, interdependent nature of reading and writing. Two assertions emerge from this relationship. One involves the writer as reader of his or her own work. As Donald Murray notes in "Teaching the Other Self: The Writer's First

Figure 3. Corbett's model of "the rhetorical interrelationships" (5)

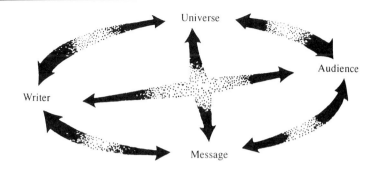

Reader," this role is critical, for "the reading writer — the map-maker and map-reader — reads the word, the line, the sentence, the paragraph, the page, the entire text. This constant back-and-forth reading monitors the multiple complex relationships between all the elements in writing."[30] To ignore or devalue such a central function is to risk distorting the writing process as a whole. But unless the writer is composing a diary or journal entry, intended only for the writer's own eyes, the writing process is not complete unless another person, someone other than the writer, reads the text also. The second assertion thus emphasizes the creative, dynamic duality of the process of reading and writing, whereby writers create readers and readers create writers. In the meeting of these two lies meaning, lies communication.

A fully elaborated view of audience, then, must balance the creativity of the writer with the different, but equally important, creativity of the reader. It must account for a wide and shifting range of roles for both addressed and invoked audiences. And, finally, it must relate the matrix created by the intricate relationship of writer and audience to all elements in the rhetorical situation. Such an enriched conception of audience can help us better understand the complex act we call composing.

Notes

1. Ruth Mitchell and Mary Taylor, "The Integrating Perspective: An Audience-Response Model for Writing," *CE* 41 (Nov. 1979): 267. Subsequent references to this article will be cited in the text.
2. Russell C. Long, "Writer-Audience Relationships: Analysis or Invention," *CCC* 31 (May 1980): 223, 225. Subsequent references to this article will be cited in the text.
3. For these terms we are indebted to Henry W. Johnstone, Jr., who refers to them in his analysis of Chaim Perelman's universal audience in *Validity and Rhetoric in Philosophical Argument: An Outlook in Transition* (University Park, PA: Dialogue of Man and World, 1978) 105.
4. A number of terms might be used to characterize the two approaches to audience which dominate current theory and practice. Such pairs as iden-

tified/envisaged, "real"/fictional, or analyzed/created all point to the same general distinction as do our terms. We chose "addressed/invoked" because the terms most precisely represent our intended meaning. Our discussion will, we hope, clarify their significance; for the present, the following definitions must serve. The "addressed" audience refers to those actual or real-life people who read a discourse, while the "invoked" audience refers to the audience called up or imagined by the writer.

5. Fred R. Pfister and Joanne F. Petrik, "A Heuristic Model for Creating a Writer's Audience," *CCC* 31 (May 1980): 213.

6. Pfister and Petrik 214; our emphasis.

7. See, for example, Lisa S. Ede, "On Audience and Composition," *CCC* 30 (Oct. 1979): 291–95.

8. See, for example, David Tedlock, "The Case Approach to Composition," *CCC* 32 (Oct. 1981): 253–61.

9. See, for example, Linda Flower's *Problem-Solving Strategies for Writers* (New York: Harcourt, 1981) and John P. Field and Robert H. Weiss's *Cases for Composition* (Boston: Little, 1979).

10. Richard E. Young, "Paradigms and Problems: Needed Research in Rhetorical Invention," *Research on Composing: Points of Departure,* ed. Charles R. Cooper and Lee Odell (Urbana: NCTE, 1978) 32n3.

11. Mitchell and Taylor do recognize that internal psychological needs ("unconscious challenges") may play a role in the writing process, but they cite such instances as an "extreme case (often that of the creative writer)" (251). For a discussion of the importance of self-evaluation in the composing process see Susan Miller, "How Writers Evaluate Their Own Writing," *CCC* 33 (May 1982): 176–83.

12. Susan Wall, "In the Writer's Eye: Learning to Teach the Rereading/Revising Process," *English Education* 14 (Feb. 1982): 12.

13. Wayne Booth, *Modern Dogma and the Rhetoric of Assent* (Chicago: U of Chicago P, 1974) xiv.

14. Paul Kameen, "Rewording the Rhetoric of Composition," *Pre/Text* 1 (Spring–Fall 1980): 82.

15. Mitchell and Taylor's arguments in favor of adjunct classes seem to indicate that they see writing instruction, wherever it occurs, as a skills course, one instructing students in the proper use of a tool.

16. Anthony R. Petrosky, "From Story to Essay: Reading and Writing," *CCC* 33 (Feb. 1982): 20.

17. Walter J. Ong, S.J., "The Writer's Audience Is Always a Fiction," *PMLA* 90 (Jan. 1975): 9–21. Subsequent references to this article will be cited in the text.

18. See, for example, William Irmscher, "Sense of Audience: An Intuitive Concept," paper delivered at the CCCC in 1981; Douglas B. Park, "The Meanings of Audience: Pedagogical Implications," paper delivered at the CCCC in 1981; and Luke M. Reinsma, "Writing to an Audience: Scheme or Strategy?" paper delivered at the CCCC in 1982.

19. Herbert W. Simons, *Persuasion: Understanding, Practice, and Analysis* (Reading: Addison, 1976).

20. Ong 12. Ong recognizes that oral communication also involves role-playing, but he stresses that it "has within it a momentum that works for the removal of masks" (20). This may be true in certain instances, such as dialogue, but does not, we believe, obtain broadly.

21. Walter S. Minot, "Response to Russell C. Long," *CCC* 32 (Oct. 1981): 337.

22. We are aware that the student actually has two audiences, her neighbors and her teacher, and that this situation poses an extra constraint for the writer. Not all students can manage such a complex series of audience constraints, but it is important to note that writers in a variety of situations often write for more than a single audience.

23. In their paper on "Student and Professional Syntax in Four Disciplines" (paper delivered at the CCCC in 1981), Ian Pringle and Aviva Freedman provide a good example of what can happen when a student creates an aberrant role for an academic reader. They cite an excerpt from a third-year history assignment, the tone of which "is essentially the tone of the opening of a television travelogue commentary" and which thus asks the reader, a history professor, to assume the role of the viewer of such a show. The result is as might be expected: "Although the content of the paper does not seem significantly more abysmal than other papers in the same set, this one was awarded a disproportionately low grade" (2).

24. One danger which should be noted is a tendency to foster a questionable image of classical rhetoric. The agnostic speaker-audience relationship which Long cites as an essential characteristic of classical rhetoric is actually a central point of debate among those involved in historical and theoretical research in rhetoric. For further discussion, see Lisa Ede and Andrea Lunsford, "On Distinctions between Classical and Modern Rhetoric," *Classical Rhetoric and Modern Discourse: Essays in Honor of Edward P. J. Corbett,* ed. Robert Connors, Lisa Ede, and Andrea Lunsford (Carbondale: Southern Illinois UP, 1984).

25. James Moffett, *Teaching the Universe of Discourse* (Boston: Houghton, 1968) 47. Subsequent references will be mentioned in the text.

26. We have taken the title of this section from Scott Consigny's article of the same title, *Philosophy and Rhetoric* 7 (Summer 1974): 175–86. Consigny's effort to mediate between two opposing views of rhetoric provided a stimulating model for our own efforts.

27. Although we believe that the range of audience roles cited in our model covers the general spectrum of options, we do not claim to have specified all possibilities. This is particularly the case since, in certain instances, these roles may merge and blend — shifting subtly in character. We might also note that other terms for the same roles might be used. In a business setting, for instance, colleague might be better termed co-worker, critic, supervisor.

28. Douglas B. Park, "The Meanings of 'Audience,'" *CE* 44 (Mar. 1982): 249.

29. Edward P. J. Corbett, *The Little Rhetoric and Handbook,* 2nd ed. (Glenview: Scott, 1982) 5.

30. Donald M. Murray, "Teaching the Other Self: The Writer's First Reader," *CCC* 33 (May 1982): 142.

Ede and Lunsford's Insights as a Resource for Your Teaching

1. Explain to your students that one element in the larger task of reading critically involves asking questions about how the writer

seems to "construct" his or her audience. Have your students make notes when they read a particular essay that enable them to keep track of the particular places in the text where the author seems to be signaling how he or she expects his or her audience to experience the essay. In a class discussion, have the students compare their notes on these crucial places where they've been able to trace the author's assumptions about the audience. Once a general outline of the author's sense of audience is complete, ask the students to write a short imitation of the author, one that duplicates as closely as possible the author's sense of audience.

2. After explaining the concepts of "audience invoked" and "audience addressed" to your students, ask them to look closely at one of their own recent compositions, to reflect on the process of writing it, and to decide if it was primarily guided by a sense of an "audience invoked" or an "audience addressed."

Ede and Lunsford's Insights as a Resource for Your Writing Classroom

1. When students keep a reading journal, ask them to record their responses to "how the writer talked to me." Have them read a short essay in class and record their responses to "how the writer considered me as the reader." Use the entries to initiate a discussion of audience from their understanding as readers of ways that writers consider audience. Ask them to "imitate" in a twenty-minute writing session one of the writers they read and to focus on "writing to the reader" in the same way that the original writer chose to write. In this exercise, content is less important than rhetorical flexibility with audience.

2. Writing instructors often ask students to write at the top of the manuscript the "audience" whom they were conscious they wrote for. Ask your students to go one step further and analyze in a short self-assessment whether they were addressing or invoking an audience. In your comments on the draft, describe your reader's response as a member of the audience addressed, as a member of the audience invoked, and as the guide in the writing classroom. Ask peer editors to also write comments from the roles of audience addressed, audience invoked, and fellow writer.

Closing My Eyes As I Speak:
An Argument for Ignoring Audience

Peter Elbow

Peter Elbow argues that writers often need simply to ignore audience. Even though he credits several arguments for audience awareness and agrees that some audiences invite and enable the writer to generate thought and feeling, he cautions that some audiences inhibit and even block writing. In particular, audience awareness in the earliest stages of writing may confuse and inhibit the writer, whereas audience awareness during revision may enlighten and liberate the writer.

    Elbow asserts that when attention to audience complicates thinking so much that student writers short out, we should suggest that the students ignore the audience and pay attention to their own thinking. Once the writers work out through drafts and "internal conversation" what they think, they can turn their attention back to audience. Elbow insists that "ignoring audience can lead to worse drafts but better revisions."

    Elbow disagrees with an interpretation of Piaget's model of cognitive development that leads some writing theorists to look at "writer-based prose," writing that ignores audience, as an indication that the writer is necessarily immature. He disagrees that writers who shape "reader-based prose" are ipso facto more cognitively mature. Instead, he insists that the ability to turn off audience awareness when it is distracting or confusing is a higher skill. Writers who can switch off audience awareness and sustain quiet, thoughtful reflection — who can in private reflection make meaning for themselves and shape a discourse from such thinking alone — are independent and mature thinkers. Elbow offers Vygotsky's cognitive model that "development in thinking is not from the individual to the socialized, but from the social to the individual" as support for his assertion that ignoring audience can lead to dialogue with self.

    Elbow insists that "private writing" that turns off and away from audience is as important to humans as public writing that addresses and invokes the audience. Writing instructors need to assist their students to discover public writing as a way of "taking part in a community of discourse" and private writing as a means for writing better reflectively. Elbow shows a symbiosis of the two kinds of discourse; each sustains the other.

    Elbow concludes with very sound and practical suggestions for how teachers can help students discover the values of both kinds of discourse. He suggests that we must counteract the reality that most schools offer little privacy for writing and little social dimension for writing by heightening both the public and private dimensions of writing. We recommend discussing how writers' various personal strategies for generating ideas and drafting — such as freewriting or keeping a journal — function as critical modes of personal discourse to develop the private dimension of their mental and emotional lives. Likewise, a discussion and practice of collaborative learning strategies and exercises will emphasize how critical public discourse is to our growth as thoughtful and creative persons.

> Very often people don't listen to you when you speak to them. It's only when you talk to yourself that they prick up their ears.
>
> — John Ashbery

When I am talking to a person or a group and struggling to find words or thoughts, I often find myself involuntarily closing my eyes as I speak. I realize now that this behavior is an instinctive attempt to blot out awareness of audience when I need all my concentration for just trying to figure out or express what I want to say. Because the audience is so imperiously present in a speaking situation, my instinct reacts with this active attempt to avoid audience awareness. This behavior — in a sense impolite or antisocial — is not so uncommon. Even when we write, alone in a room to an absent audience, there are occasions when we are struggling to figure something out and need to push aside awareness of those absent readers. As Donald Murray puts it, "My sense of audience is so strong that I have to suppress my conscious awareness of audience to hear what the text demands" (Berkenkotter and Murray 171). In recognition of how pervasive the role of audience is in writing, I write to celebrate the benefits of ignoring audience.[1]

It will be clear that my argument for writing without audience awareness is not meant to undermine the many good reasons for writing *with* audience awareness some of the time. (For example, that we are liable to neglect audience because we write in solitude; that young people often need more practice in taking into account points of view different from their own; and that students often have an impoverished sense of writing as communication because they have only written in a school setting to teachers.) Indeed I would claim some part in these arguments for audience awareness — which now seem to be getting out of hand.

I start with a limited claim: even though ignoring audience will usually lead to weak writing at first — to what Linda Flower calls "writer-based prose" — this weak writing can help us in the end to better writing than we would have written if we'd kept readers in mind from the start. Then I will make a more ambitious claim: writer-based prose is sometimes better than reader-based prose. Finally I will explore some of the theory underlying these issues of audience.

A Limited Claim

It's not that writers should never think about their audience. It's a question of when. An audience is a field of force. The closer we come — the more we think about these readers — the stronger the pull they exert on the contents of our minds. The practical question, then, is always whether a particular audience functions as a helpful field of force or one that confuses or inhibits us.

Some audiences, for example, are *inviting* or *enabling*. When we think about them as we write, we think of more and better things to say — and what we think somehow arrives more coherently structured than usual. It's like talking to the perfect listener: we feel smart and come up with ideas we didn't know we had. Such audiences are helpful to keep in mind right from the start.

Other audiences, however, are powerfully *inhibiting* — so much so, in certain cases, that awareness of them as we write blocks writing altogether. There are certain people who always make us feel dumb when we try to speak to them: we can't find words or thoughts. As soon as we get out of their presence, all the things we want to say pop back into our minds. Here is a student telling what happens when she tries to follow the traditional advice about audience:

> You know _____ [author of a text] tells us to pay attention to the audience that will be reading our papers, and I gave that a try. I ended up without putting a word on paper until I decided the hell with _____; I'm going to write to who I damn well want to; otherwise I can hardly write at all.

Admittedly, there are some occasions when we benefit from keeping a threatening audience in mind from the start. We've been putting off writing that letter to that person who intimidates us. When we finally sit down and write *to* them — walk right up to them, as it were, and look them in the eye — we may manage to stand up to the threat and grasp the nettle and thereby find just what we need to write.

Most commonly, however, the effect of audience awareness is some-where between the two extremes: the awareness disturbs or disrupts our writing and thinking without completely blocking it. For example, when we have to write to someone we find intimidating (and of course students often perceive teachers as intimidating), we often start think-ing wholly defensively. As we write down each thought or sentence, our mind fills with thoughts of how the intended reader will criticize or object to it. So we try to qualify or soften what we've just written — or write out some answer to a possible objection. Our writing becomes tangled. Sometimes we get so tied in knots that we cannot even figure out what we *think*. We may not realize how often audience awareness has this effect on our students when we don't see the writing process behind their papers: we just see texts that are either tangled or empty.

Another example. When we have to write to readers with whom we have an awkward relationship, we often start beating around the bush and feeling shy or scared, or start to write in a stilted, overly careful style or voice. (Think about the cute, too-clever style of many memos we get in our departmental mailboxes — the awkward self-conscious-ness academics experience when writing to other academics.) When students are asked to write to readers they have not met or cannot imagine, such as "the general reader" or "the educated public," they often find nothing to say except clichés they know *they* don't even quite believe.

When we realize that an audience is somehow confusing or inhibit-ing us, the solution is fairly obvious. We can ignore that audience altogether during the *early* stages of writing and direct our words only to ourselves or to no one in particular — or even to the "wrong" audience, that is, to an *inviting* audience of trusted friends or allies. This strategy often dissipates the confusion; the clenched, defensive discourse starts to run clear. Putting audience out of mind is of course a traditional practice: serious writers have long used private journals for early explorations of feeling, thinking, or language. But many writing teachers seem to think that students can get along without the private writing serious writers find so crucial — or even that students will *benefit* from keeping their audience in mind for the whole time. Things often don't work out that way.

After we have figured out our thinking in copious exploratory or draft writing — perhaps finding the right voice or stance as well — *then* we can follow the traditional rhetorical advice: Think about readers and revise carefully to adjust our words and thoughts to our intended audience. For a particular audience it may even turn out that we need to *disguise* our point of view. But it's hard to disguise something while engaged in trying to figure it out. As writers, then, we need to learn when to think about audience and when to put readers out of mind.

Many people are too quick to see Flower's "writer-based prose" as an analysis of what's wrong with this type of writing and miss the substantial degree to which she was celebrating a natural, and indeed developmentally enabling, response to cognitive overload. What she doesn't say, however, despite her emphasis on planning and conscious control in the writing process, is that we can *teach* students to notice when audience awareness is getting in their way — and when this happens, consciously to put aside the needs of readers for a while. She seems to assume that when an overload occurs, the writer-based gear will, as it were, automatically kick into action to relieve it. In truth, of course, writers often persist in using a malfunctioning *reader*-based gear despite the overload — thereby mangling their language or thinking. Though Flower likes to rap the knuckles of people who suggest a "correct" or "natural" order for steps in the writing process, she implies such an order here: When attention to audience causes an overload, start out by ignoring them while you attend to your thinking; after you work out your thinking, turn your attention to audience.

Thus if we ignore audience while writing on a topic about which we are not expert or about which our thinking is still evolving, we are likely to produce exploratory writing that is unclear to anyone else — perhaps even inconsistent or a complete mess. Yet by doing this exploratory "swamp work" in conditions of safety, we can often coax our thinking through a process of new discovery and development. In this way we can end up with something better than we could have produced if we'd tried to write to our audience all along. In short, ignoring audience can lead to worse drafts but better revisions. (Because we are professionals and adults, we often write in the role of expert: we may know what we think without new exploratory writing; we may even be able to speak confidently to critical readers. But students seldom experience this confident professional stance in their writing. And think how much richer *our* writing would be if we defined ourselves as *in*expert and allowed ourselves private writing for new explorations of those views we are allegedly sure of.)

Notice then that two pieties of composition theory are often in conflict:

1. Think about audience as you write (this stemming from the classical rhetorical tradition).

2. Use writing for *making new meaning,* not just transmitting old meanings already worked out (this stemming from the newer epistemic tradition I associate with Ann Berthoff's classic explorations).

It's often difficult to work out new meaning while thinking about readers.

A More Ambitious Claim

I go further now and argue that ignoring audience can lead to better writing — immediately. In effect, writer-based prose can be *better* than reader-based prose. This might seem a more controversial claim, but is there a teacher who has not had the experience of struggling and struggling to no avail to help a student untangle his writing, only to discover that the student's casual journal writing or freewriting is untangled and strong? Sometimes freewriting is stronger than the essays we get only because it is expressive, narrative, or descriptive writing and the student was not constrained by a topic. But teachers who collect drafts with completed assignments often see passages of freewriting that are strikingly stronger *even* when they are expository and constrained by the assigned topic. In some of these passages we can sense that the strength derives from the student's unawareness of readers.

It's not just unskilled, tangled writers, though, who sometimes write better by forgetting about readers. Many competent and even professional writers produce mediocre pieces *because* they are thinking too much about how their readers will receive their words. They are acting too much like a salesman trained to look the customer in the eye and to think at all times about the characteristics of the "target audience." There is something too staged or planned or self-aware about such writing. We see this quality in much second-rate newspaper or magazine or business writing: "good-student writing" in the awful sense of the term. Writing produced this way reminds us of the ineffective actor whose consciousness of self distracts us: he makes us too aware of his own awareness of us. When we read such prose, we wish the writer would stop thinking about us — would stop trying to "adjust" or "fit" what he is saying to our frame of reference. "Damn it, put all your attention on what you are saying," we want to say, "and forget about us and how we are reacting."

When we examine really good student or professional writing, we can often see that its goodness comes from the writer's having gotten sufficiently wrapped up in her meaning and her language as to forget all about audience needs: the writer manages to "break through." The Earl of Shaftesbury talked about writers needing to escape their audience in order to find their own ideas (Cooper 1:109; see also Griffin). It is characteristic of much truly good writing to be, as it were, on fire with its meaning. Consciousness of readers is burned away; involvement in subject determines all. Such writing is analogous to the performance of the actor who has managed to stop attracting attention to her awareness of the audience watching her.

The arresting power in some writing by small children comes from their obliviousness to audience. As readers, we are somehow sucked into a more-than-usual connection with the meaning itself because of the child's gift for more-than-usual concentration on what she is saying. In short, we can feel some pieces of children's writing as being very writer-based. Yet it's precisely that quality which makes it powerful for us as readers. After all, why should we settle for a writer's entering our point of view, if we can have the more powerful experience of being sucked out of our point of view and into her world? This is just the experience that children are peculiarly capable of giving because they are so expert at total absorption in their world as they are writing. It's not just a matter of whether the writer "decenters," but of whether the writer has a sufficiently strong focus of attention to make the *reader* decenter. This quality of concentration is what D. H. Lawrence so admires in Melville:

> [Melville] was a real American in that he always felt his audience in front of him. But when he ceases to be American, when he forgets all audience, and gives us his sheer apprehension of the world, then he is wonderful, his book [*Moby Dick*] commands a stillness in the soul, an awe. (158)

What most readers value in really excellent writing is not prose that is right for readers but prose that is right for thinking, right for language, or right for the subject being written about. If, in addition, it is clear and well suited to readers, we appreciate that. Indeed we feel insulted if the writer did not somehow try to make the writing *available* to us before delivering it. But if it succeeds at being really true to language and thinking and "things," we are willing to put up with much difficulty as readers:

> Good writing is not always or necessarily an adaptation to communal norms (in the Fish/Bruffee sense) but may be an attempt to construct (and instruct) a reader capable of reading the text in question. The literary history of the "difficult" work — from Mallarmé to Pound, Zukofsky, Olson, etc. — seems to say that much of what we value in writing we've had to learn to value by learning how to read it. (Trimbur)

The effect of audience awareness on voice is particularly striking — if paradoxical. Even though we often develop our voice by finally "speaking up" to an audience or "speaking out" to others, and even though much dead student writing comes from students not really treating their writing as a communication with real readers, nevertheless, the opposite effect is also common: we often do not really develop a strong, authentic voice in our writing till we find important occasions for *ignoring* audience — saying, in effect, "To hell with whether they like it or not. I've got to say this the way I want to say it." Admittedly, the voice that emerges when we ignore audience is sometimes odd or idiosyncratic in some way, but usually it is stronger. Indeed, teachers sometimes complain that student writing is "writer-based" when the problem is simply the idiosyncrasy — and sometimes in fact the *power* — of the voice. They would value this odd but resonant voice if they found it in a published writer (see Elbow, "Real Voice," *Writing with Power*). Usually we cannot *trust* a voice unless it is unaware of us and our needs and speaks out in its own terms (see the Ashbery epigraph). To celebrate writer-based prose is to risk the charge of *romanticism:* just warbling one's woodnotes wild. But my position also contains the austere *classic* view that we must nevertheless *revise* with conscious awareness of audience in order to figure out which pieces of writer-based prose are good as they are — and how to discard or revise the rest.

To point out that writer-based prose can be *better* for readers than reader-based prose is to reveal problems in these two terms. Does *writer-based* mean:

1. That the text doesn't work for readers because it is too much oriented to the writer's point of view?

2. Or that the writer was not thinking about readers as she wrote, although the text *may* work for readers?

Does *reader-based* mean:

3. That the text works for readers — meets their needs?

4. Or that the writer was attending to readers as she wrote although her text *may* not work for readers?

In order to do justice to the reality and complexity of what actually happens in both writers and readers, I was going to suggest four terms for the four conditions listed above, but I gradually realized that things are even too complex for that. We really need to ask about what's going on in three dimensions — in the *writer*, in the *reader*, and in the *text* — and realize that the answers can occur in virtually any combination:

Was the writer thinking about readers or oblivious to them?

Is the *text* oriented toward the writer's frame of reference or point of view, or oriented toward that of readers? (A writer may be thinking about readers and still write a text that is largely oriented toward her own frame of reference.)

Are the readers' needs being met? (The text may meet the needs of readers whether the writer was thinking about them or not, and whether the text is oriented toward them or not.)

Two Models of Cognitive Development

Some of the current emphasis on audience awareness probably derives from a model of cognitive development that needs to be questioned. According to this model, if you keep your readers in mind as you write, you are operating at a higher level of psychological development than if you ignore readers. Directing words to readers is "more mature" than directing them to no one in particular or to yourself. Flower relates writer-based prose to the inability to "decenter" which is characteristic of Piaget's early stages of development, and she relates reader-based prose to later more mature stages of development.

On the one hand, of course this view must be right. Children do decenter as they develop. As they mature they get better at suiting their discourse to the needs of listeners, particularly to listeners very different from themselves. Especially, they get better at doing so *consciously* — thinking *awarely* about how things appear to people with different viewpoints. Thus much unskilled writing is unclear or awkward *because* the writer was doing what it is so easy to do — unthinkingly taking her own frame of reference for granted and not attending to the needs of readers who might have a different frame of reference. And of course this failure is more common in younger, immature, "egocentric" students (and also more common in writing than in speaking since we have no audience present when we write).

But on the other hand, we need the contrary model that affirms what is also obvious once we reflect on it, namely that the ability to *turn off* audience awareness — especially when it confuses thinking or blocks discourse — is also a "higher" skill. I am talking about an ability to use language in "the desert island mode," an ability that tends to require learning, growth, and psychological development. Children, and even adults who have not learned the art of quiet, thoughtful, inner reflection, are often unable to get much cognitive action going in their heads unless there are other people present to have action *with*. They are dependent on live audience and the social dimension to get their discourse rolling or to get their thinking off the ground.

For in contrast to a roughly Piagetian model of cognitive development that says we start out as private, egocentric little monads and grow up to be public and social, it is important to invoke the opposite model that derives variously from Vygotsky, Bakhtin, and Meade. According to this model, we *start out* social and plugged into others and only gradually, through learning and development, come to "unplug" to any significant degree so as to function in a more private, individual and differentiated fashion: "Development in thinking is not from the individual to the socialized, but from the social to the individual" (Vygotsky 20). The important general principle in this model is that we tend to *develop* our important cognitive capacities by means of social interaction with others, and having done so we gradually learn to perform them alone. We fold the "simple" back-and-forth of dialogue into the "complexity" (literally, "foldedness") of individual, private reflection.

Where the Piagetian (individual psychology) model calls our attention to the obvious need to learn to enter into viewpoints other than our own, the Vygotskian (social psychology) model calls our attention to the equally important need to learn to produce good thinking and discourse *while alone*. A rich and enfolded mental life is something that people achieve only gradually through growth, learning, and practice. We tend to associate this achievement with the fruits of higher education.

Thus we see plenty of students who lack this skill, who have nothing to say when asked to freewrite or to write in a journal. They can dutifully "reply" to a question or a topic, but they cannot seem to *initiate* or *sustain* a train of thought on their own. Because so many adolescent students have this difficulty, many teachers chime in: "Adolescents have nothing to write about. They are too young. They haven't had significant experience." In truth, adolescents don't lack experience or material, no matter how "sheltered" their lives. What they lack is practice and help. Desert island discourse is a learned cognitive process. It's a mistake to think of private writing (journal writing and freewriting) as merely "easy" — merely a relief from trying to write right. It's also hard. Some exercises and strategies that help are Ira Progoff's "Intensive Journal" process, Sondra Perl's "Composing Guidelines," or Elbow's "Loop Writing" and "Open Ended Writing" processes (*Writing with Power* 50–77).

The Piagetian and Vygotskian developmental models (language-begins-as-private vs. language-begins-as-social) give us two different lenses through which to look at a common weakness in student writing, a certain kind of "thin" writing where the thought is insufficiently developed or where the language doesn't really explain what the writing implies or gestures toward. Using the Piagetian model, as Flower does, one can specify the problem as a weakness in audience orientation. Perhaps the writer has immaturely taken too much for granted and unthinkingly assumed that her limited explanations carry as much meaning for readers as they do for herself. The cure or treatment is for the writer to think more about readers.

Through the Vygotskian lens, however, the problem and the "immaturity" look altogether different. Yes, the writing isn't particularly clear or satisfying for readers, but this alternative diagnosis suggests a failure of the private desert island dimension: the writer's explanation is too thin because she didn't work out her train of thought fully enough *for herself*. The suggested cure or treatment is *not* to think more about readers but to think more for herself, to practice exploratory writing in order to learn to engage in that reflective discourse so central to mastery of the writing process. How can she engage readers more till she has engaged herself more?

The current emphasis on audience awareness may be particularly strong now for being fueled by *both* psychological models. From one side, the Piagetians say, in effect, "The egocentric little critters, we've got to *socialize* 'em! Ergo, make them think about audience when they write!" From the other side, the Vygotskians say, in effect, "No wonder they're having trouble writing. They've been bamboozled by the Piagetian heresy. They think they're solitary individuals with private selves when really they're just congeries of voices that derive from their discourse community. Ergo, let's intensify the social context — use peer groups and publication: make them think about audience when they write! (And while we're at it, let's hook them up with a better class of discourse community.)" To advocate ignoring audience is to risk getting caught in the crossfire from two opposed camps.

Two Models of Discourse: Discourse as Communication and Discourse as Poesis or Play

We cannot talk about writing without at least implying a psychological or developmental model. But we'd better make sure it's a complex, paradoxical, or spiral model. Better yet, we should be deft enough to use two contrary models or lenses. (Bruner pictures the developmental process as a complex movement in an upward reiterative spiral — not a simple movement in one direction.)

According to one model, it is characteristic of the youngest children to direct their discourse to an audience. They learn discourse *because* they have an audience; without an audience they remain mute, like "the wild child." Language is social from the start. But we need the other model to show us what is also true, namely that it is characteristic of the youngest children to use language in a *nonsocial* way. They use language not only because people talk to them but also because they have such a strong propensity to play and to build — often in a *nonsocial* or non-audience-oriented fashion. Thus although one paradigm for discourse is social communication, another is private exploration or solitary play. Babies and toddlers tend to babble in an exploratory and reflective way — to themselves and not to an audience — often even with no one else near. This archetypally private use of discourse is strikingly illustrated when we see a pair of toddlers in "parallel play" alongside each other — each busily talking but not at all trying to communicate with the other.

Therefore, when we choose paradigms for discourse, we should think not only about children using language to communicate, but also about children building sandcastles or drawing pictures. Though children characteristically show their castles or pictures to others, they just as characteristically trample or crumple them before anyone else can see them. Of course sculptures and pictures are different from words. Yet discourse implies more media than words; and even if you restrict discourse to words, one of our most mature uses of language is for building verbal pictures and structures for their own sake — not just for communicating with others.

Consider this same kind of behavior at the other end of the life cycle: Brahms staggering from his deathbed to his study to rip up a dozen or more completed but unpublished and unheard string quartets that dissatisfied him. How was he relating to audience here — worrying too much about audience or not giving a damn? It's not easy to say. Consider Glenn Gould deciding to renounce performances before an audience. He used his private studio to produce recorded performances for an audience, but to produce ones that satisfied *himself* he clearly needed to suppress audience awareness. Consider the more extreme example of Kerouac typing page after page — burning each as soon as he completed it. The language behavior of humans is slippery. Surely we are well advised to avoid positions that say it is "always X" or "essentially Y."

James Britton makes a powerful argument that the "making" or poesis function of language grows out of the expressive function. Expressive language is often for the sake of communication with an audience, but just as often it is only for the sake of the speaker — working something out for herself (66–67, 74ff). Note also that "writing to learn," which writing-across-the-curriculum programs are discovering to be so important, tends to be writing for the self or even for no one at all rather than for an outside reader. You throw away the writing, often unread, and keep the mental changes it has engendered.

I hope this emphasis on the complexity of the developmental process — the limits of our models and of our understanding of it — will serve as a rebuke to the tendency to label students as being at a lower stage of cognitive development just because they don't yet write well. (Occasionally they *do* write well — in a way — but not in the way that the labeler finds appropriate.) Obviously the psychologistic labeling impulse started out charitably. Shaughnessy was fighting those who called basic writers *stupid* by saying they weren't dumb, just at an earlier developmental stage. Flower was arguing that writer-based prose is a natural response to a cognitive overload and indeed developmentally enabling. But this kind of talk can be dangerous since it labels students as literally "retarded" and makes teachers and administrators start to think of them as such. Instead of calling poor writers *either* dumb or slow (two forms of blaming the victim), why not simply call them poor writers? If years of schooling haven't yet made them good writers, perhaps they haven't gotten the kind of teaching and support they need. Poor students are often deprived of the very thing they need most to write well (which is given to good students): lots of extended and adventuresome writing for self and for audience. Poor students are often asked to write only answers to fill-in exercises.

As children get older, the developmental story remains complex or spiral. Though the first model makes us notice that babies start out with a natural gift for using language in a social and communicative fashion, the second model makes us notice that children and adolescents must continually learn to relate their discourse better to an audience — must struggle to decenter better. And though the second model makes us notice that babies also start out with a natural gift for using language in a *private,* exploratory and playful way, the first model makes us notice that children and adolescents must continually learn to master this solitary, desert island, poesis mode better. Thus we mustn't think of language only as communication — nor allow communication to claim dominance either as the earliest or as the most "mature" form of discourse. It's true that language is inherently communicative (and without communication we don't develop language), yet language is just as inherently the stringing together of exploratory discourse for the self — or for the creation of objects (play, poesis, making) for their own sake.

In considering this important poesis function of language, we need not discount (as Berkenkotter does) the striking testimony of so many witnesses who think and care most about language: professional poets, writers, and philosophers. Many of them maintain that their most serious work is *making,* not *communicating,* and that their commitment is to language, reality, logic, experience, not to readers. Only in their willingness to cut loose from the demands or needs of readers, they insist, can they do their best work. Here is William Stafford on this matter:

> I don't want to overstate this . . . but . . . my impulse is to say I don't think of an audience at all. When I'm writing, the satisfactions in the process of writing are my satisfactions in dealing with the language, in being surprised by phrasings that occur to me, in finding that this miraculous kind of convergent focus begins to happen. That's my satisfaction, and to think about an audience would be a distraction. I try to keep from thinking about an audience. (Cicotello 176)

And Chomsky:

> I can be using language in the strictest sense with no intention of communicating. . . . As a graduate student, I spent two years writing a lengthy manuscript, assuming throughout that it would never be published or read by anyone. I meant everything I wrote, intending nothing as to what anyone would [understand], in fact taking it for granted that there would be no audience. . . . Communication is only one function of language, and by no means an essential one. (Qtd. in Feldman 5–6)

It's interesting to see how poets come together with philosophers on this point — and even with mathematicians. All are emphasizing the "poetic" function of language in its literal sense — "poesis" as "making." They describe their writing process as more like "getting something right" or even "solving a problem" for its own sake than as communicating with readers or addressing an audience. The task is not to satisfy readers but to satisfy the rules of the system: "[T]he writer is not thinking of a reader at all; he makes it 'clear' as a contract with *language*" (Goodman 164).

Shall we conclude, then, that solving an equation or working out a piece of symbolic logic is at the opposite end of the spectrum from communicating with readers or addressing an audience? No. To draw that conclusion would be a fall again into a one-sided position. Sometimes people write mathematics *for* an audience, sometimes not. The central point in this essay is that we cannot answer audience questions in an *a priori* fashion based on the "nature" of discourse or of language or of cognition — only in terms of the different *uses* or *purposes* to which humans put discourse, language, or cognition on different occasions. If most people have a restricted repertoire of uses for writing — if most people use writing only to send messages to readers, that's no argument for constricting the *definition* of writing. It's an argument for helping people expand their repertoire of uses.

The value of learning to ignore audience while writing, then, is the value of learning to cultivate the private dimension: the value of writing in order to make meaning to oneself, not just to others. This involves learning to free oneself (to some extent, anyway) from the enormous power exerted by society and others, to unhook oneself from external prompts and social stimuli. We've grown accustomed to theorists and writing teachers puritanically stressing the *problem* of writing: the tendency to neglect the needs of readers because we usually write in solitude. But let's also celebrate this same feature of writing as one of its glories: writing *invites* disengagement too, the inward turn of mind, and the dialogue with self. Though writing is deeply social and though we usually help things by enhancing its social dimension, writing is also the mode of discourse best suited to helping us develop the reflective and private dimension of our mental lives.

"But Wait a Minute, ALL Discourse Is Social"

Some readers who see *all* discourse as social will object to my opposition between public and private writing (the "trap of oppositional thinking") and insist that *there is no such thing as private discourse*. What looks like private, solitary mental work, they would say, is really social. Even on the desert island I am in a crowd.

> By ignoring audience in the conventional sense, we return to it in another sense. What I get from Vygotsky and Bakhtin is the notion that audience is not really out there at all but is in fact "always already" (to use that poststructuralist mannerism . . .) inside, interiorized in the conflicting languages of others — parents, former teachers, peers, prospective readers, whomever — that writers have to negotiate to write, and that we do negotiate when we write whether we're aware of it or not. The audience we've got to satisfy in order to feel good about our writing is as much in the past as in the present or future. But we experience it (it's so internalized) as *ourselves*. (Trimbur)

(Ken Bruffee likes to quote from Frost: "'Men work together, . . . / Whether they work together or apart'" ["The Tuft of Flowers"]). Or — putting it slightly differently — when I engage in what seems like private non-audience-directed writing, I am really engaged in communication with the "audience of self." For the self is multiple, not single, and discourse to self is communication from one entity to another. As Feldman argues, "The self functions as audience in much the same way that others do" (290).

Suppose I accept this theory that all discourse is really social — including what I've been calling "private writing" or writing I don't intend to show to any reader. Suppose I agree that all language is essentially communication directed toward an audience — whether some past internalized voice or (what may be the same thing) some aspect of the self. What would this theory say to my interest in "private writing"?

The theory would seem to destroy my main argument. It would tell me that there's no such thing as "private writing"; it's impossible *not* to address audience; there are no vacations from audience. But the theory might try to console me by saying not to worry, because we don't *need* vacations from audience. Addressing audience is as easy, natural, and unaware as breathing — and we've been at it since the cradle. Even young, unskilled writers are already expert at addressing audiences.

But if we look closely we can see that in fact this theory doesn't touch my central practical argument. For even if all discourse is naturally addressed to *some* audience, it's not naturally addressed to the *right* audience — the living readers we are actually trying to reach. Indeed the pervasiveness of past audiences in our heads is one more reason for the difficulty of reaching present audiences with our texts. Thus even if I concede the theoretical point, there still remains an enormous practical and phenomenological difference between writing "public" words for others to read and writing "private" words for no one to read.

Even if "private writing" is "deep down" social, the fact remains that, as we engage in it, we don't have to worry about whether it works on readers or even makes sense. We can refrain from doing all the things that audience-awareness advocates advise us to do ("keeping our audience in mind as we write" and trying to "decenter"). Therefore this social-discourse theory doesn't undermine the benefits of "private writing" and thus provides no support at all for the traditional rhetorical advice that we should "always try to think about (intended) audience as we write."

In fact this social-discourse theory reinforces two subsidiary arguments I have been making. First, even if there is no getting away from *some* audience, we can get relief from an inhibiting audience by writing to a more inviting one. Second, audience problems don't come only from *actual* audiences but also from phantom "audiences in the head" (Elbow, *Writing with Power* 186ff). Once we learn how to be more aware of the effects of both external and internal readers and how to direct our words elsewhere, we can get out of the shadow even of a troublesome phantom reader.

And even if all our discourse is *directed to* or *shaped by* past audiences or voices, it doesn't follow that our discourse is *well directed to* or *successfully shaped for* those audiences or voices. Small children *direct* much talk to others, but that doesn't mean they always *suit* their talk to others. They often fail. When adults discover that a piece of their writing has been "heavily shaped" by some audience, this is bad news as much as good: often the writing is crippled by defensive moves that try to fend off criticism from this reader.

As teachers, particularly, we need to distinguish and emphasize "private writing" in order to teach it, to teach that crucial cognitive capacity to engage in extended and productive thinking that doesn't depend on audience prompts or social stimuli. It's sad to see so many students who can reply to live voices but cannot engage in productive dialogue with voices in their heads. Such students often lose interest in an issue that had intrigued them — just because they don't find other people who are interested in talking about it and haven't learned to talk reflectively to *themselves* about it.

For these reasons, then, I believe my main argument holds force even if I accept the theory that all discourse is social. But, perhaps more tentatively, I resist this theory. I don't know all the data from developmental linguistics, but I cannot help suspecting that babies engage in *some* private poesis — or "play-language" — some private babbling in addition to social babbling. Of course Vygotsky must be right when he points to so much social language in children, but can we really trust him when he denies *all* private or nonsocial language (which Piaget and Chomsky see)? I am always suspicious when someone argues for the total nonexistence of a certain kind of behavior or event. Such an argument is almost invariably an act of definitional aggrandizement, not empirical searching. To say that *all* language is social is to flop over into the opposite one-sidedness that we need Vygotsky's model to save us from.

And even if all language is *originally* social, Vygotsky himself emphasizes how "inner speech" becomes more individuated and private as the child matures. "Egocentric speech is relatively accessible in three-year-olds but quite inscrutable in seven-year-olds: the older the child, the more thoroughly has his thought become inner speech" (Emerson 254; see also Vygotsky 134). "The inner speech of the adult represents his 'thinking for himself' rather than social adaptation. . . . Out of context, it would be incomprehensible to others because it omits to mention what is obvious to the 'speaker'" (Vygotsky 18).

I also resist the theory that all private writing is really communication with the *"audience of self."* ("When we represent the objects of our thought in language, we intend to make use of these representations at a later time. . . . [T]he speaker-self must have audience directed intentions toward a listener-self" [Feldman 289].) Of course private language often is a communication with the audience of self:

- When we make a shopping list. (It's obvious when we can't decipher that third item that we're confronting *failed* communication with the self.)

- When we make a rough draft for ourselves but not for others' eyes. Here we are seeking to clarify our thinking with the leverage that comes from standing outside and reading our own utterance as audience — experiencing our discourse as receiver instead of as sender.

- When we experience ourselves as slightly split. Sometimes we experience ourselves as witness to ourselves and hear our own words from the outside — sometimes with great detachment, as on some occasions of pressure or stress.

But there are other times when private language is not communication with audience of self:

- Freewriting to no one: for the *sake* of self but not *to* the self. The goal is not to communicate but to follow a train of thinking or feeling to see where it leads. In doing this kind of freewriting (and many people have not learned it), you don't particularly plan to come back and read what you've written. You just write along and the written product falls away to be ignored, while only the "real product" — any new perceptions, thoughts, or feelings produced in the mind by the freewriting — is saved and looked at again. (It's not that you don't experience your words *at all* but you experience them only as speaker, sender, or emitter — not as receiver or audience. To say that's the same as being audience is denying the very distinction between "speaker" and "audience.")

As this kind of freewriting actually works, it often *leads* to writing we look at. That is, we freewrite along to no one, following discourse in hopes of getting somewhere, and then at a certain point we often sense that we have *gotten* somewhere: we can tell (but not because we stop and read) that what we are now writing seems new or intriguing or important. At this point we may stop writing; or we may keep on writing, but in a new audience-relationship, realizing that we *will* come back to this passage and read it as audience. Or we may take a new sheet (symbolizing the new audience-relationship) and try to write out for ourselves what's interesting.

- Writing as exorcism is a more extreme example of private writing *not* for the audience of self. Some people have learned to write in order to get rid of thoughts or feelings. By freewriting what's obsessively going round and round in our head we can finally let it go and move on.

I am suggesting that some people (and especially poets and freewriters) engage in a kind of discourse that Feldman, defending what she calls a "communication-intention" view, has never learned and thus has a hard time imagining and understanding. Instead of always using language in an audience-directed fashion for the sake of communication, these writers unleash language for its own sake and let it function a bit on its own, without much *intention* and without much need for *communication,* to see where it leads — and thereby end up with some intentions and potential communications they didn't have before.

It's hard to turn off the audience-of-self in writing — and thus hard to imagine writing to no one (just as it's hard to turn off the audience of *outside* readers when writing an audience-directed piece). Consider "invisible writing" as an intriguing technique that helps you become less of an audience-of-self for your writing. Invisible writing prevents you from seeing what you have written: you write on a computer with the screen turned down, or you write with a spent ballpoint pen on paper with carbon paper and another sheet underneath. Invisible writing tends to get people not only to write faster than they normally do, but often better (see Blau). I mean to be tentative about this slippery issue of whether we can really stop being audience to our own discourse, but I cannot help drawing the following conclusion: just as in freewriting, suppressing the *other* as audience tends to enhance quantity and sometimes even quality of writing; so in invisible writing, suppressing the *self* as audience tends to enhance quantity and sometimes even quality.

Contraries in Teaching

So what does all this mean for teaching? It means that we are stuck with two contrary tasks. On the one hand, we need to help our students enhance the social dimension of writing: to learn to be *more* aware of audience, to decenter better and learn to fit their discourse better to the needs of readers. Yet it is every bit as important to help them learn the private dimension of writing: to learn to be *less* aware of audience, to put audience needs aside, to use discourse in the desert island mode. And if we are trying to advance contraries, we must be prepared for paradoxes.

For instance if we emphasize the social dimension in our teaching (for example, by getting students to write to each other, to read and comment on each other's writing in pairs and groups, and by staging public discussions and even debates on the topics they are to write about), we will obviously help the social, public, communicative dimension of writing — help students experience writing not just as jumping through hoops for a grade but rather as taking part in the life of a community of discourse. But "social discourse" can also help private writing by getting students sufficiently involved or invested in an issue so that they finally want to carry on producing discourse alone and in private — and for themselves.

Correlatively, if we emphasize the private dimension in our teaching (for example, by using lots of private exploratory writing, freewriting, and journal writing and by helping students realize that of course they may need practice with this "easy" mode of discourse before they can use it fruitfully), we will obviously help students learn to write better reflectively for themselves without the need for others to interact with. Yet this private discourse can also help public, social writing — help students finally feel full enough of their *own* thoughts to have some genuine desire to *tell* them to others. Students often feel they "don't have anything to say" until they finally succeed in engaging themselves in private desert island writing for themselves alone.

Another paradox: Whether we want to teach greater audience awareness or the ability to ignore audience, we must help students learn not only to "try harder" but also to "just relax." That is, sometimes students fail to produce reader-based prose because they don't *try* hard enough to think about audience needs. But sometimes the problem is cured if they just relax and write *to* people — as though in a letter or in talking to a trusted adult. By unclenching, they effortlessly call on social discourse skills of immense sophistication. Sometimes, indeed, the problem is cured if the student simply writes in a more social *setting* — in a classroom where it is habitual to share lots of writing. Similarly, sometimes students can't produce sustained private discourse because they don't try hard enough to keep the pen moving and forget about readers. They must persist and doggedly push aside those feelings of, "My head is empty, I have run out of anything to say." But sometimes what they need to learn through all that persistence is how to relax and let go — to unclench.

As teachers, we need to think about what it means to *be an audience* rather than just be a teacher, critic, assessor, or editor. If our only response is to tell students what's strong, what's weak, and how to improve it (diagnosis, assessment, and advice), we actually *undermine* their sense of writing as a social act. We reinforce their sense that writing means doing school exercises, producing for authorities what they already know — *not* actually trying to say things to readers. To help students experience us as *audience* rather than as assessment machines, it helps to respond by "replying" (as in a letter) rather than always "giving feedback."

Paradoxically enough, one of the best ways teachers can help students learn to turn off audience awareness and write in the desert island mode — to turn off the babble of outside voices in the head and listen better to quiet inner voices — is to be a special kind of private audience to them, to be a reader who nurtures by trusting and believing in the writer. Britton has drawn attention to the importance of teacher as "trusted adult" for school children (67–68). No one can be good at private, reflective writing without some *confidence and trust in self.* A nurturing reader can give a writer a kind of permission to forget about other readers or to be one's own reader. I have benefited from this special kind of audience and have seen it prove useful to others. When I had a teacher who believed in me, who was interested in me and interested in what I had to say, I wrote well. When I had a teacher who thought I was naive, dumb, silly, and in need of being "straightened out," I wrote badly and sometimes couldn't write at all. Here is an interestingly paradoxical instance of the social-to-private principle from Vygotsky and Meade: We learn to listen better and more trustingly to *ourselves* through interaction with trusting *others*.

Look for a moment at lyric poets as paradigm writers (instead of seeing them as aberrant), and see how they heighten *both* the public and private dimensions of writing. Bakhtin says that lyric poetry implies "the absolute certainty of the listener's sympathy" (113). I think it's more helpful to say that lyric poets learn to create more than usual privacy in which to write *for themselves* — and then they turn around and let *others overhear*. Notice how poets tend to argue for the importance of no-audience writing, yet they are especially gifted at being public about what they produce in private. Poets are revealers — sometimes even grandstanders or showoffs. Poets illustrate the need for opposite or paradoxical or double audience skills: on the one hand, the ability to be private and solitary and tune out others — to write only for oneself and not give a damn about readers, yet on the other hand, the ability to be more than usually interested in audience and even to be a ham.

If writers really need these two audience skills, notice how bad most conventional schooling is on both counts. Schools offer virtually no privacy for writing: everything students write is collected and read by a teacher, a situation so ingrained students will tend to complain if you don't collect and read every word they write. Yet on the other hand, schools characteristically offer little or no social dimension for writing. It is *only* the teacher who reads, and students seldom feel that in giving their writing to a teacher they are actually communicating something they really want to say to a real person. Notice how often they are happy to turn in to teachers something perfunctory and fake that they would be embarrassed to show to classmates. Often they feel shocked and insulted if we want to distribute to classmates the assigned writing they hand in to us. (I think of Richard Wright's realization that the naked white prostitutes didn't bother to cover themselves when he brought them coffee as a black bellboy because they didn't really think of him as a man or even a person.) Thus the conventional school setting for writing tends to be the least private and the least public — when what students need, like all of us, is practice in writing that is the most private and also the most public.

Practical Guidelines about Audience

The theoretical relationships between discourse and audience are complex and paradoxical, but the practical morals are simple:

1. Seek ways to heighten both the *public* and *private* dimensions of writing. (For activities, see the previous section.)

2. When working on important audience-directed writing, we must try to emphasize audience awareness *sometimes*. A useful rule of thumb is to start by putting the readers in mind and carry on as long as things go well. If difficulties arise, try putting readers out of mind and write either to no audience, to self, or to an inviting audience. Finally, always *revise* with readers in mind. (Here's another occasion when orthodox advice about writing is wrong — but turns out right if applied to revising.)

3. Seek ways to heighten awareness of one's writing process (through process writing and discussion) to get better at taking control and deciding when to keep readers in mind and when to ignore them. Learn to discriminate factors like these:

   a. The writing task. Is this piece of writing *really* for an audience? More often than we realize, it is not. It is a draft that only we will see, though the final version will be for an audience; or exploratory writing for figuring something out; or some kind of personal private writing meant only for ourselves.

   b. Actual readers. When we put them in mind, are we helped or hindered?

   c. One's own temperament. Am I the sort of person who tends to think of what to say and how to say it when I keep readers in mind? Or someone (as I am) who needs long stretches of forgetting all about readers?

   d. Has some powerful "audience-in-the-head" tricked me into talking to it when I'm really trying to talk to someone else — distorting new business into old business? (I may be an inviting teacher-audience to my students, but they may not be able to pick up a pen without falling under the spell of a former, intimidating teacher.)

   e. Is *double audience* getting in my way? When I write a memo or report, I probably have to suit it not only to my "target audience" but also to some colleagues or supervisor. When I write something for publication, it must be right for readers, but it won't be published unless it is also right for the editors — and if it's a book it won't be much read unless it's right for reviewers. Children's stories won't be bought unless they are right for editors and reviewers *and* parents. We often tell students to write to a particular "real-life" audience — or to peers in the class — but of course they are also writing for us as graders. (This problem is more common as more teachers get interested in audience and suggest "second" audiences.)

f. Is *teacher-audience* getting in the way of my students' writing? As teachers we must often read in an odd fashion: in stacks of twenty-five or fifty pieces all on the same topic; on topics we know better than the writer; not for pleasure or learning but to grade or find problems (see Elbow, *Writing with Power* 216– 36).

To list all these audience pitfalls is to show again the need for thinking about audience needs — yet also the need for vacations from readers to think in peace.

Notes

I benefited from much help from audiences in writing various drafts of this piece. I am grateful to Jennifer Clarke, with whom I wrote a collaborative piece containing a case study on this subject. I am also grateful for extensive feedback from Pat Belanoff, Paul Connolly, Sheryl Fontaine, John Trimbur, and members of the Martha's Vineyard Summer Writing Seminar.

1. There are many different entities called audience: (a) The actual readers to whom the text will be given; (b) the writer's conception of those readers — which may be mistaken (see Ong; Park; Ede and Lunsford); (c) the audience that the text implies — which may be different still (see Booth); (d) the discourse community or even genre addressed or implied by the text (see Walzer); (e) ghost or phantom "readers in the head" that the writer may unconsciously address or try to please (see Elbow, *Writing with Power* 186ff. Classically, this is a powerful former teacher. Often such an audience is so ghostly as not to show up as actually "implied" by the text). For the essay I am writing here, these differences don't much matter: I'm celebrating the ability to put aside the needs or demands of *any* or all of these audiences. I recognize, however, that we sometimes cannot fight our way free of unconscious or tacit audiences (as in b or e above) unless we bring them to greater conscious awareness.

Works Cited

Bakhtin, Mikhail. "Discourse in Life and Discourse in Poetry." Appendix. *Freudianism: A Marxist Critique.* By F. N. Volosinov. Trans. I. R. Titunik. Ed. Neal H. Bruss. New York: Academic, 1976. (Holquist's attribution of this work to Bakhtin is generally accepted.)

Berkenkotter, Carol, and Donald Murray. "Decisions and Revisions: The Planning Strategies of a Publishing Writer and the Response of Being a Rat — or Being Protocoled." *College Composition and Communication* 34 (1983): 156–72.

Blau, Sheridan. "Invisible Writing." *College Composition and Communication* 34 (1983): 297–312.

Booth, Wayne. *The Rhetoric of Fiction.* Chicago: U Chicago P, 1961.

Britton, James. *The Development of Writing Abilities, 11–18.* Urbana: NCTE, 1977.

Bruffee, Kenneth A. "Liberal Education and the Social Justification of Belief." *Liberal Education* 68 (1982): 95–114.

Bruner, Jerome. *Beyond the Information Given: Studies in the Psychology of Knowing.* Ed. Jeremy Anglin. New York: Norton, 1973.

———. *On Knowing: Essays for the Left Hand.* Expanded ed. Cambridge: Harvard UP, 1979.

Chomsky, Noam. *Reflections on Language.* New York: Random, 1975.

Cicotello, David M. "The Art of Writing: An Interview with William Stafford." *College Composition and Communication* 34 (1983): 173–77.

Clarke, Jennifer, and Peter Elbow. "Desert Island Discourse: On the Benefits of Ignoring Audience." *The Journal Book.* Ed. Toby Fulwiler. Montclair: Boynton, 1987.

Cooper, Anthony Ashley, 3rd Earl of Shaftesbury. *Characteristics of Men, Manners, Opinions, Times, Etc.* Ed. John M. Robertson. 2 vols. Gloucester, MA: Smith, 1963.

Ede, Lisa, and Andrea Lunsford. "Audience Addressed/Audience Invoked: The Role of Audience in Composition Theory and Pedagogy." *College Composition and Communication* 35 (1984): 140–54.

Elbow, Peter. *Writing with Power.* New York: Oxford UP, 1981.

———. *Writing without Teachers.* New York: Oxford UP, 1973.

Emerson, Caryl. "The Outer Word and Inner Speech: Bakhtin, Vygotsky, and the Internalization of Language." *Critical Inquiry* 10 (1983): 245–64.

Feldman, Carol Fleisher. "Two Functions of Language." *Harvard Education Review* 47 (1977): 282–93.

Flower, Linda. "Writer-Based Prose: A Cognitive Basis for Problems in Writing." *College English* 41 (1979): 19–37.

Goodman, Paul. *Speaking and Language: Defense of Poetry.* New York: Random, 1972.

Griffin, Susan. "The Internal Voices of Invention: Shaftesbury's Soliloquy." Unpublished. 1986.

Lawrence, D. H. *Studies in Classic American Literature.* Garden City: Doubleday, 1951.

Ong, Walter. "The Writer's Audience Is Always a Fiction." *PMLA* 90 (1975): 9–21.

Park, Douglas B. "The Meanings of 'Audience.'" *College English* 44 (1982): 247–57.

Perl, Sondra. "Guidelines for Composing." Appendix A. *Through Teachers' Eyes: Portraits of Writing Teachers at Work.* By Sondra Perl and Nancy Wilson. Portsmouth: Heinemann, 1986.

Progoff, Ira. *At a Journal Workshop.* New York: Dialogue, 1975.

Shaughnessy, Mina. *Errors and Expectations: A Guide for the Teacher of Basic Writing.* New York: Oxford UP, 1977.

Trimbur, John. "Beyond Cognition: Voices in Inner Speech." *Rhetoric Review* 5 (1987): 211–21.

———. Letter to the author. September 1985.

Vygotsky, L. S. *Thought and Language.* Trans. and ed. E. Hanfmann and G. Vakar. 1934. Cambridge: MIT P, 1962.

Walzer, Arthur E. "Articles from the 'California Divorce Project': A Case Study of the Concept of Audience." *College Composition and Communication* 36 (1985): 150–59.

Wright, Richard. *Black Boy.* New York: Harper, 1945.

Elbow's Insights as a Resource for Your Teaching

1. Consider the "desert island mode" that Elbow discusses. Demonstrate to your students how valuable such private writing is to you by discussing how you have kept a journal or notebook and when you have used it as a resource. Encourage your students to write a journal entry on any experience they had with writing entirely for themselves and without the distraction of a reader. A standard technique writing instructors use both to respect the "personal" in personal writing and to encourage private reflection is to require that students write daily but to give students the option of stapling together any entries that were not written with an outside reader in mind.

2. Try Elbow's recommendation to turn off the screen while writing with a computer. Report to the class what happened when you did this. Were you able to ignore audience? What effect did this have on your writing?

Elbow's Insights as a Resource for Your Writing Classroom

1. Elbow's "ghost reader" — a student's sense of an inflexible teacher-as-evaluator — surfaces frequently in early essays from first-year writers and most often in "diagnostic" essays written the first week. Photocopy a few samples of writing where the ghost reader clearly frightened the writer into dense or unclear or stuffy or inauthentic prose. Ask the class to decide where "thinking too much about the 'ghost teacher as reader' got in the way" and to suggest ways to exorcise the ghost reader.

2. Encourage the "desert island mode" by asking students to close their eyes and open their ears while you play something calming like Pachelbel's Canon in D Major or Albinoni's Adagio or some recent new age music. After five minutes, ask them to freewrite for twenty minutes. Repeat this technique several times during the semester; tell the writers that this sequence is for their private writing. Observe whether all writers are freewriting, but don't collect or read the writing. Will some students bluff you? Inevitably a few will waste the opportunity, but worry more about the writers who need some modeling of ways to move into self-discourse.

3. Ask students to describe, either in journal entries or a brainstorming session, ways that they have noticed themselves setting up their own circumstances for writing from imagination and for

self-reflection. Encourage them to think about strategies that they use or habits that they have when writing or preparing to write (which they may have dismissed as personal idiosyncrasies unrelated to writing), and how these strategies and habits are related to their personal approach to the writing process. Do these circumstances hinder or encourage the flow of ideas? How might they consciously adjust these circumstances to promote uninhibited writing?

Revising a Draft

We know that the strongest writing comes from the process of multiple drafting and serious rethinking, reordering, and rewriting. Many students have difficulty looking critically at their writing once an initial draft is completed; they are often too intimidated to generate more ideas, re-engage the draft, and substantially reshape it. Learning to truly revise and rewrite — not simply edit — may be the most dramatic experience some of your students have this semester.

Revision Strategies of Student Writers and Experienced Adult Writers

Nancy Sommers

In this landmark study of the revision strategies used by students and by "adult" writers, Nancy Sommers concludes that student writers do not work from a holistic perspective on writing or perceive revision as a recursive process. Her categories of "student" and "experienced adult" writers can be borrowed and applied to members of a first-year composition course. Many class members already understand revising as "discovery" — a repeated process of beginning over again, starting out new. Some writers, however, need to acquire this "new" perspective on revision.

Sommers cites or implies several reasons that students see revision only as a linear process attending to surface features of a manuscript: previous writing experiences, infrequent practice, traditional dicta about the nature of revising, and cognitive readiness. She asserts that writing teachers can assist student writers to mature and to acquire a perspective on writing as discovery and development. Furthermore, writing teachers can help student writers to realize, as experienced adult writers do, that "Good writing disturbs: it creates dissonance."

Sommers's discussion in "Responding to Student Writing" (Chap. 3) shows us the practical effects on student writers of our written responses to their texts. She clearly demonstrates that teacher commentary can directly affect and improve the revision strategies of writers.

A lthough various aspects of the writing process have been studied extensively of late, research on revision has been notably absent. The reason for this, I suspect, is that current models of the writing process have directed attention away from revision. With few exceptions, these models are linear; they separate the writing process into discrete stages. Two representative models are Gordon Rohman's suggestion that the composing process moves from prewriting to writing to rewriting and James Britton's model of the writing process as a series of stages described in metaphors of linear growth, conception — incubation — production.[1] What is striking about these theories of writing is that they model themselves on speech: Rohman defines the writer in a way that cannot distinguish him from a speaker ("A writer is a man who . . . puts [his] experience into words in his own mind" [15]); and Britton backs his theory of writing on what he calls (following Jakobson) the "expressiveness" of speech.[2] Moreover, Britton's study itself follows the "linear model" of the relation of thought and language in speech proposed by Vygotsky, a relationship embodied in the linear movement "from the motive which engenders a thought to the shaping of the thought, *first* in inner speech, *then* in meanings of words, and *finally* in words" (qtd. in Britton 40). What this movement fails to take into account in its linear structure — "first . . . then . . . finally" — is the recursive shaping of thought by language; what it fails to take into account is *revision*. In these linear conceptions of the writing process revision is understood as a separate stage at the end of the process — a stage that comes after the completion of a first or second draft and one that is temporally distinct from the prewriting and writing stages of the process.[3]

The linear model bases itself on speech in two specific ways. First of all, it is based on traditional rhetorical models, models that were created to serve the spoken art of oratory. In whatever ways the parts of classical rhetoric are described, they offer "stages" of composition that are repeated in contemporary models of the writing process. Edward Corbett, for instance, describes the "five parts of a discourse" — *inventio, dispositio, elocutio, memoria, pronuntiatio* — and, disregarding the last two parts since "after rhetoric came to be concerned mainly with written discourse, there was no further need to deal with them,"[4] he produces a model very close to Britton's conception [*inventio*], incubation [*dispositio*], production [*elocutio*]. Other rhetorics also follow this procedure, and they do so not simply because of historical accident. Rather, the process represented in the linear model is based on the irreversibility of speech. Speech, Roland Barthes says, "is irreversible":

> A word cannot be retracted, except precisely by saying that one retracts it. To cross out here is to add: if I want to erase what I have just said, I cannot do it without showing the eraser itself (I must say: "*or rather . . .*" "*I expressed myself badly . . .*"); paradoxically, it is ephemeral speech which is indelible, not monumental writing. All that one can do in the case of a spoken utterance is to tack on another utterance.[5]

What is impossible in speech is *revision:* like the example Barthes gives, revision in speech is an afterthought. In the same way, each stage of the linear model must be exclusive (distinct from the other stages) or else it becomes trivial and counterproductive to refer to these junctures as "stages."

By staging revision after enunciation, the linear models reduce revision in writing, as in speech, to no more than an afterthought. In this way such models make the study of revision impossible. Revision, in Rohman's model, is simply the repetition of writing; or to pursue Britton's organic metaphor, revision is simply the further growth of what is already there, the "preconceived" product. The absence of research on revision, then, is a function of a theory of writing which makes revision both superfluous and redundant, a theory which does not distinguish between writing and speech.

What the linear models do produce is a parody of writing. Isolating revision and then disregarding it plays havoc with the experiences composition teachers have of the actual writing and rewriting of experienced writers. Why should the linear model be preferred? Why should revision be forgotten, superfluous? Why do teachers offer the linear model and students accept it? One reason, Barthes suggests, is that "there is a fundamental tie between teaching and speech," while "writing begins at the point where speech becomes *impossible.*"[6] The spoken word cannot be revised. The possibility of revision distinguishes the written text from speech. In fact, according to Barthes, this is the essential difference between writing and speaking. When we must revise, when the very idea is subject to recursive shaping by language, then speech becomes inadequate. This is a matter to which I will return, but first we should examine, theoretically, a detailed exploration of what student writers as distinguished from experienced adult writers *do* when they write and rewrite their work. Dissatisfied with both the linear model of writing and the lack of attention to the process of revision, I conducted a series of studies over the past three years which examined the revision processes of student writers and experienced writers to see what role revision played in their writing processes. In the course of my work the revision process was redefined as *a sequence of changes in a composition — changes which are initiated by cues and occur continually throughout the writing of a work.*

Methodology

I used a case study approach. The student writers were twenty freshmen at Boston University and the University of Oklahoma with SAT verbal scores ranging from 450–600 in their first semester of composition. The twenty experienced adult writers from Boston and Oklahoma City included journalists, editors, and academics. To refer to the two groups, I use the terms *student writers* and *experienced writers* because the principal difference between these two groups is the amount of experience they have had in writing.

Each writer wrote three essays, expressive, explanatory, and persuasive, and rewrote each essay twice, producing nine written products in draft and final form. Each writer was interviewed three times after the final revision of each essay. And each writer suggested revisions for a composition written by an anonymous author. Thus extensive written and spoken documents were obtained from each writer.

The essays were analyzed by counting and categorizing the changes made. Four revision operations were identified: deletion, substitution, addition, and reordering. And four levels of changes were identified: word, phrase, sentence, theme (the extended statement of one idea). A coding system was developed for identifying the frequency of revision by level and operation. In addition, transcripts of the interviews in which the writers interpreted their revisions were used to develop what was called a *scale of concerns* for each writer. This scale enabled me to codify what were the writer's primary concerns, secondary concerns, tertiary concerns, and whether the writers used the same scale of concerns when revising the second or third drafts as they used in revising the first draft.

Revision Strategies of Student Writers

Most of the students I studied did not use the terms *revision* or *rewriting*. In fact, they did not seem comfortable using the word *revision* and explained that revision was not a word they used, but the word their teachers used. Instead, most of the students had developed various functional terms to describe the type of changes they made. The following are samples of these definitions:

> *Scratch Out and Do Over Again:* "I say scratch out and do over, and that means what it says. Scratching out and cutting out. I read what I have written and I cross out a word and put another word in; a more decent word or a better word. Then if there is somewhere to use a sentence that I have crossed out, I will put it there."

> *Reviewing:* "Reviewing means just using better words and eliminating words that are not needed. I go over and change words around."

> *Reviewing:* "I just review every word and make sure that everything is worded right. I see if I am rambling; I see if I can put a better word in or leave one out. Usually when I read what I have written, I say to myself, 'that word is so bland or so trite,' and then I go and get my thesaurus."

> *Redoing:* "Redoing means cleaning up the paper and crossing out. It is looking at something and saying, no that has to go, or no, that is not right."

> *Marking Out:* "I don't use the word rewriting because I only write one draft and the changes that I make are made on top of the draft. The changes that I make are usually just marking out words and putting different ones in."

Slashing and Throwing Out: "I throw things out and say they are not good. I like to write like Fitzgerald did by inspiration, and if I feel inspired then I don't need to slash and throw much out."

The predominant concern in these definitions is vocabulary. The students understand the revision process as a rewording activity. They do so because they perceive words as the unit of written discourse. That is, they concentrate on particular words apart from their role in the text. Thus one student quoted above thinks in terms of dictionaries, and, following the eighteenth-century theory of words parodied in *Gulliver's Travels,* he imagines a load of things carried about to be exchanged. Lexical changes are the major revision activities of the students because economy is their goal. They are governed, like the linear model itself, by the Law of Occam's razor that prohibits logically needless repetition: redundancy and superfluity. Nothing governs speech more than such superfluities; speech constantly repeats itself precisely because spoken words, as Barthes writes, are expendable in the cause of communication. The aim of revision according to the students' own description is therefore to clean up speech; the redundancy of speech is unnecessary in writing, their logic suggests, because writing, unlike speech, can be reread. Thus one student said, "Redoing means cleaning up the paper and crossing out." The remarkable contradiction of cleaning by marking might, indeed, stand for student revision as I have encountered it.

The students place a symbolic importance on their selection and rejection of words as the determiners of success or failure for their compositions. When revising, they primarily ask themselves: can I find a better word or phrase? A more impressive, not so clichéd, or less humdrum word? Am I repeating the same word or phrase too often? They approach the revision process with what could be labeled as a "thesaurus philosophy of writing"; the students consider the thesaurus a harvest of lexical substitutions and believe that most problems in their essays can be solved by rewording. What is revealed in the students' use of the thesaurus is a governing attitude toward their writing: that the meaning to be communicated is already there, already finished, already produced, ready to be communicated, and all that is necessary is a better word "rightly worded." One student defined *revision* as "redoing"; *redoing* meant "just using better words and eliminating words that are not needed." For the students, writing is translating: the thought to the page, the language of speech to the more formal language of prose, the word to its synonym. Whatever is translated, an original text already exists for students, one which need not be discovered or acted upon, but simply communicated.[7]

The students list repetition as one of the elements they most worry about. This cue signals to them that they need to eliminate the repetition either by substituting or deleting words or phrases. Repetition occurs, in large part, because student writing imitates — transcribes — speech: attention to repetitious words is a manner of cleaning speech.

Without a sense of the developmental possibilities of revision (and writing in general) students seek, on the authority of many textbooks, simply to clean up their language and prepare to type. What is curious, however, is that students are aware of lexical repetition, but not conceptual repetition. They only notice the repetition if they can "hear" it; they do not diagnose lexical repetition as symptomatic of problems on a deeper level. By rewording their sentences to avoid the lexical repetition, the students solve the immediate problem, but blind themselves to problems on a textual level; although they are using different words, they are sometimes merely restating the same idea with different words. Such blindness, as I discovered with student writers, is the inability to "see" revision as a process: the inability to "re-view" their work again, as it were, with different eyes, and to start over.

The revision strategies described above are consistent with the students' understanding of the revision process as requiring lexical changes but not semantic changes. For the students, the extent to which they revise is a function of their level of inspiration. In fact, they use the word *inspiration* to describe the ease or difficulty with which their essay is written, and the extent to which the essay needs to be revised. If students feel inspired, if the writing comes easily, and if they don't get stuck on individual words or phrases, then they say that they cannot see any reason to revise. Because students do not see revision as an activity in which they modify and develop perspectives and ideas, they feel that if they know what they want to say, then there is little reason for making revisions.

The only modification of ideas in the students' essays occurred when they tried out two or three introductory paragraphs. This results, in part, because the students have been taught in another version of the linear model of composing to use a thesis statement as a controlling device in their introductory paragraphs. Since they write their introductions and their thesis statements even before they have really discovered what they want to say, their early close attention to the thesis statement, and more generally the linear model, function to restrict and circumscribe not only the development of their ideas, but also their ability to change the direction of these ideas.

Too often as composition teachers we conclude that students do not willingly revise. The evidence from my research suggests that it is not that students are unwilling to revise, but rather that they do what they have been taught to do in a consistently narrow and predictable way. On every occasion when I asked students why they hadn't made any more changes, they essentially replied, "I knew something larger was wrong, but I didn't think it would help to move words around." The students have strategies for handling words and phrases and their strategies helped them on a word or sentence level. What they lack, however, is a set of strategies to help them identify the "something larger" that they sensed was wrong and work from there. The students do not have strategies for handling the whole essay. They lack procedures or heuristics to help them reorder lines of reasoning or ask questions about their purposes and readers. The students view their compositions in a linear way as a series of parts. Even such potentially useful concepts as "unity" or "form" are reduced to the rule that a composition, if it is to have form, must have an introduction, a body, and a conclusion, or the sum total of the necessary parts.

The students decide to stop revising when they decide that they have not violated any of the rules for revising. These rules, such as "Never begin a sentence with a conjunction" or "Never end a sentence with a preposition," are lexically cued and rigidly applied. In general, students will subordinate the demands of the specific problems of their text to the demands of the rules. Changes are made in compliance with abstract rules about the product, rules that quite often do not apply to the specific problems in the text. These revision strategies are teacher-based, directed towards a teacher-reader who expects compliance with rules — with pre-existing "conceptions" — and who will only examine parts of the composition (writing comments about those parts in the margins of their essays) and will cite any violations of rules in those parts. At best the students see their writing altogether passively through the eyes of former teachers or their surrogates, the textbooks, and are bound to the rules which they have been taught.

Revision Strategies of Experienced Writers

One aim of my research has been to contrast how student writers define revision with how a group of experienced writers define their revision processes. Here is a sampling of the definitions from the experienced writers:

> *Rewriting:* "It is a matter of looking at the kernel of what I have written, the content, and then thinking about it, responding to it, making decisions, and actually restructuring it."

> *Rewriting:* "I rewrite as I write. It is hard to tell what is a first draft because it is not determined by time. In one draft, I might cross out three pages, write two, cross out a fourth, rewrite it, and call it a draft. I am constantly writing and rewriting. I can only conceptualize so much in my first draft — only so much information can be held in my head at one time; my rewriting efforts are a reflection of how much information I can encompass at one time. There are levels and agenda which I have to attend to in each draft."

> *Rewriting:* "Rewriting means on one level, finding the argument, and on another level, language changes to make the argument more effective. Most of the time I feel as if I can go on rewriting forever. There is always one part of a piece that I could keep working on. It is always difficult to know at what point to abandon a piece of writing. I like this idea that a piece of writing is never finished, just abandoned."

> *Rewriting:* "My first draft is usually very scattered. In rewriting, I find the line of argument. After the argument is resolved, I am much more interested in word choice and phrasing."

Revising: "My cardinal rule in revising is never to fall in love with what I have written in a first or second draft. An idea, sentence, or even a phrase that looks catchy, I don't trust. Part of this idea is to wait a while. I am much more in love with something after I have written it than I am a day or two later. It is much easier to change anything with time."

Revising: "It means taking apart what I have written and putting it back together again. I ask major theoretical questions of my ideas, respond to those questions, and think of proportion and structure, and try to find a controlling metaphor. I find out which ideas can be developed and which should be dropped. I am constantly chiseling and changing as I revise."

The experienced writers describe their primary objective when revising as finding the form or shape of their argument. Although the metaphors vary, the experienced writers often use structural expressions such as "finding a framework," "a pattern," or "a design" for their argument. When questioned about this emphasis, the experienced writers responded that since their first drafts are usually scattered attempts to define their territory, their objective in the second draft is to begin observing general patterns of development and deciding what should be included and what excluded. One writer explained, "I have learned from experience that I need to keep writing a first draft until I figure out what I want to say. Then in a second draft, I begin to see the structure of an argument and how all the various sub-arguments which are buried beneath the surface of all those sentences are related." What is described here is a process in which the writer is both agent and vehicle. "Writing," says Barthes, unlike speech, "develops like a seed, not a line,"[8] and like a seed it confuses beginning and end, conception and production. Thus, the experienced writers say their drafts are "not determined by time," that rewriting is a "constant process," that they feel as if they "can go on forever." Revising confuses the beginning and end, the agent and vehicle; it confuses, *in order to find,* the line of argument.

After a concern for form, the experienced writers have a second objective: a concern for their readership. In this way, "production" precedes "conception." The experienced writers imagine a reader (reading their product) whose existence and whose expectations influence their revision process. They have abstracted the standards of a reader and this reader seems to be partially a reflection of themselves and functions as a critical and productive collaborator — a collaborator who has yet to love their work. The anticipation of a reader's judgment causes a feeling of dissonance when the writer recognizes incongruities between intention and execution, and requires these writers to make revisions on all levels. Such a reader gives them just what the students lacked: new eyes to "re-view" their work. The experienced writers believe that they have learned the causes and conditions, the product, which will influence their reader, and their revision strategies are geared towards creating these causes and conditions. They demonstrate a complex understanding of which examples, sentences, or phrases should be included or excluded. For example, one experienced writer decided to delete public examples and add private examples when writing about the energy crisis because "private examples would be less controversial and thus more persuasive." Another writer revised his transitional sentences because "some kinds of transitions are more easily recognized as transitions than others." These examples represent the type of strategic attempts these experienced writers use to manipulate the conventions of discourse in order to communicate to their reader.

But these revision strategies are a process of more than communication; they are part of the process of *discovering meaning* altogether. Here we can see the importance of dissonance; at the heart of revision is the process by which writers recognize and resolve the dissonance they sense in their writing. Ferdinand de Saussure has argued that meaning is differential or "diacritical," based on differences between terms rather than "essential" or inherent qualities of terms. "Phonemes," he said, "are characterized not, as one might think, by their own positive quality but simply by the fact that they are distinct."[9] In fact, Saussure bases his entire *Course in General Linguistics* on these differences, and such differences are dissonant; like musical dissonances which gain their significance from their relationship to the "key" of the composition which itself is determined by the whole language, specific language (parole) gains its meaning from the system of language (langue) of which it is a manifestation and part. The musical composition — a "composition" of parts — creates its "key" as in an overall structure which determines the value (meaning) of its parts. The analogy with music is readily seen in the compositions of experienced writers: both sorts of composition are based precisely on those structures experienced writers seek in their writing. It is this complicated relationship between the parts and the whole in the work of experienced writers which destroys the linear model; writing cannot develop "like a line" because each addition or deletion is a reordering of the whole. Explicating Saussure, Jonathan Culler asserts that "meaning depends on difference of meaning."[10] But student writers constantly struggle to bring their essays into congruence with a predefined meaning. The experienced writers do the opposite: they seek to discover (to create) meaning in the engagement with their writing, in revision. They seek to emphasize and exploit the lack of clarity, the differences of meaning, the dissonance, that writing as opposed to speech allows in the possibility of revision. Writing has spatial and temporal features not apparent in speech — words are recorded in space and fixed in time — which is why writing is susceptible to reordering and later addition. Such features make possible the dissonance that both provokes revision and promises, from itself, new meaning.

For the experienced writers the heaviest concentration of changes is on the sentence level, and the changes are predominantly by addition and deletion. But, unlike the students, experienced writers make changes on all levels and use all revision operations. Moreover, the operations the students fail to use — reordering and addition — seem to require a theory of the revision process as a totality — a theory which, in fact, encompasses the *whole* of the composition. Unlike the students, the experienced writers possess a nonlinear theory in which a sense of the whole writing both precedes and grows out of an examination of the parts. As we saw, one writer said he needed "a first draft to figure out what to say," and "a second draft to see the structure of an argument buried beneath the surface." Such a "theory" is both theoretical and strategical; once again, strategy and theory are conflated in ways that are literally impossible for the linear model. Writing appears to be more like a seed than a line.

Two elements of the experienced writers' theory of the revision process are the adoption of a holistic perspective and the perception that revision is a recursive process. The writers ask: What does my essay as a *whole* need for form, balance, rhythm, or communication? Details are added, dropped, substituted, or reordered according to their sense of what the essay needs for emphasis and proportion. This sense, however, is constantly in flux as ideas are developed and modified; it is constantly "re-viewed" in relation to the parts. As their ideas change, revision becomes an attempt to make their writing consonant with that changing vision.

The experienced writers see their revision process as a recursive process — a process with significant recurring activities — with different levels of attention and different agenda for each cycle. During the first revision cycle their attention is primarily directed towards narrowing the topic and delimiting their ideas. At this point, they are not as concerned as they are later about vocabulary and style. The experienced writers explained that they get closer to their meaning by not limiting themselves too early to lexical concerns. As one writer commented to explain her revision process, a comment inspired by the summer 1977 New York power failure: "I feel like Con Edison cutting off certain states to keep the generators going. In first and second drafts, I try to cut off as much as I can of my editing generator, and in a third draft, I try to cut off some of my idea generators, so I can make sure that I will actually finish the essay." Although the experienced writers describe their revision process as a series of different levels or cycles, it is inaccurate to assume that they have only one objective. The same objectives and sub-processes are present in each cycle, but in different proportions. Even though these experienced writers place the predominant weight upon finding the form of their argument during the first cycle, other concerns exist as well. Conversely, during the later cycles, when the experienced writers' primary attention is focused upon stylistic concerns, they are still attuned, although in a reduced way, to the form of the argument. Since writers are limited in what they can attend to during each cycle (understandings are temporal), revision strategies help balance competing demands on attention. Thus, writers can concentrate on more than one objective at a time by developing strategies to sort out and organize their different concerns in successive cycles of revision.

It is a sense of writing as discovery — a repeated process of beginning over again, starting out new — that the students failed to have. I have used the notion of dissonance because such dissonance, the incongruities between intention and execution, governs both writing and meaning. Students do not see the incongruities. They need to rely on their own internalized sense of good writing and to see their writing with their "own" eyes. Seeing in revision — seeing beyond hearing — is at the root of the word *revision* and the process itself; current dicta on revising blind our students to what is actually involved in revision. In fact, they blind them to what constitutes good writing altogether. Good writing disturbs: it creates dissonance. Students need to seek the dissonance of discovery, utilizing in their writing, as the experienced writers do, the very difference between writing and speech — the possibility of revision.

Notes

The author wishes to express her gratitude to Professor William Smith, University of Pittsburgh, for his vital assistance with the research reported in this article and to Patrick Hays, her husband, for extensive discussions and critical help.

1. D. Gordon Rohman and Albert O. Wlecke, "Pre-writing: The Construction and Application of Models for Concept Formation in Writing," Cooperative Research Project No. 2174, U.S. Office of Education, Department of Health, Education, and Welfare; James Britton, Anthony Burgess, Nancy Martin, Alex McLeod, Harold Rosen, *The Development of Writing Abilities* (11–18) (London: Macmillan, 1975).

2. Britton is following Roman Jakobson, "Linguistics and Poetics," *Style in Language,* ed. T. A. Sebeok (Cambridge: MIT P, 1960).

3. For an extended discussion of this issue see Nancy Sommers, "The Need for Theory in Composition Research," *College Composition and Communication* 30 (Feb. 1979): 46–49.

4. *Classical Rhetoric for the Modern Student* (New York: Oxford UP, 1965) 27.

5. Roland Barthes, "Writers, Intellectuals, Teachers," *Image-Music-Text,* trans. Stephen Heath (New York: Hill, 1977) 190–91.

6. Barthes 190.

7. Nancy Sommers and Ronald Schleifer, "Means and Ends: Some Assumptions of Student Writers," *Composition and Teaching* 2 (1980): 69–76.

8. *Writing Degree Zero,* in *Writing Degree Zero and Elements of Semiology,* trans. Annette Lavers and Colin Smith (New York: Hill, 1968) 20.

9. *Course in General Linguistics,* trans. Wade Baskin (New York, 1966) 119.

10. Jonathan Culler, *Saussure,* Penguin Modern Masters Series (London: Penguin, 1976) 70.

Sommers's Insights as a Resource for Your Teaching

1. In your reflective journal, reflect on the experiences that influenced you to think about revising your own texts.

2. When you work with a writer who engages in "deep revision," ask whether that writer will give you permission to use excerpts from his or her multiple drafts. With these drafts, you can demonstrate to future students what can happen when a writer moves beyond surface revision. (Any time you want to use student writing — for teaching or research or published writing — you must receive permission.)

3. Computer drafting has profoundly changed the revision process for writers by eliminating the need to start over for each change. Some writers have a stronger sense of "retrospective structuring" and of composing from the "felt sense" Sondra Perl describes in "Understanding Composing." Some writers are less conscious of revisions, major and minor, that they make on disk (rather than by hand). Encourage students to keep hard copies of drafts so they can review and reflect on their revision strategies and share the strategies with you in conferences.

Sommers's Insights as a Resource for Your Writing Classroom

1. Ask your students to reflect — in journal entries or in fifteen-minute writing sessions — on their definitions of *revision*. Have them write this definition before their first experience with peer evaluation in the course and before you hand back their first pieces of writing with your comments about revision. Ask them to think again about their definitions midway through the term, and as they near completion of the course.

2. Use the categories Sommers sets up to prompt small-group discussion about revision. Ask the groups to list what they view as characteristics of good revising. Then introduce the concept of "student" and "mature or experienced student" and ask them to classify the characteristics they described as representative of one or the other. Often students will volunteer descriptions that echo those that Sommers lists. If they don't, you should feel free to cite the "research" you read and ask the students to consider Sommers's list as categories by which they can look at their own revising strategies. If you establish with your students that a "mature" college writer views revision as a recursive process, you give them one criterion by which to assess their growth as writers.

3. Prepare a sampler of revision suggestions from completed peer editing checklists or from transcripts of workshop sessions. (Borrow such materials from a teaching colleague if you are teaching for the first time or find your students apprehensive about seeing their comments used anonymously.) Organize small groups to evaluate peer criticism. Students should be instructed to consider which comments encourage revisions to improve the form and substance of the writer's argument, which comments focus the writer's attention on the needs of multiple readers, and which comments address lexical concerns. Ask each group to list the comments they would welcome on working drafts and to define or describe specifically what makes those comments useful. Have them also explain, in as much detail as possible, what makes the other comments less useful or less accessible. Don't be surprised if some class members find the exercise challenging: Many have never been asked to reflect on their critical thinking or encouraged to regard peer criticism as a significant writing experience.

Toward an Excess-ive Theory of Revision

Nancy Welch

With its mix of immediately recognizable, real-life writing situations and powerful philosophical underpinnings, this excerpt disrupts our "contin-ued insistence on words like clarity, consistency, *and* completeness*" in describing what we want our students to achieve in their writing. More specifically, Nancy Welch questions the "dominant beliefs about revision as a one-way movement [. . .] from unruly, unsocialized first draft to socially adapted, socially meaningful final product." She describes a different idea of revision, one "in which individual identities exceed and transgress" these neat-and-tidy containers, for it is in this excess that she wants us to locate emergent identities, voices, and truly important acts of re-visioning, crafting, and shaping meaning.*

> I think there is more that I want in here. Here is where I start to feel that my ideas scatter. I feel like I need something else or that it's just missing something.
>
> — Brandie, a first-year composition
> student writing in the margins of a draft

While it's generally thought that students view revision as a me-chanical activity of correcting errors or as punishment for not getting a piece of writing right the first time, my classroom and writ-ing center experiences tell me that many of our students *do* under-stand revision as a rich, complex, and often dramatic life-changing process. They understand — and have experienced — the kind of revision Adrienne Rich (1979) describes: as a moment of awakening consciousness, as entering old texts and cherished beliefs from new critical directions, as seeing with fresh and troubled eyes how they've been led to name themselves and each other (pp. 34–35).

The problem: The students I've worked with don't always know how to take the next step of intervening in a draft's meanings and representations. Or, in the context of a composition classroom, they understand that "revision" means the very opposite of such work, the systematic suppression of all complexity and contradiction. Another problem: Composition teachers by and large haven't been asking questions like "Something missing, something else?" that promote revision as getting restless with familiar and constrictive ways of writing and being, as creating alternatives. We respond instead (so a look through recent classroom texts suggests) in ways that restrict revision to a "narrowing" of focus, the correction of an "inappropriate tone" or "awkward repetition," the changing of any passage that might "confuse, mislead, or irritate" readers.[1]

Historians and critics of rhetoric, composition, and literacy education like James Berlin (1984), Susan Miller (1994), and Frank Smith (1986) have traced numerous reasons for this emphasis on writing as the management of meaning. They've linked such emphasis to the rise and codification of English as a discipline, to the opening of universities to working-class and minority students judged "deficient" and in need of linguistic and social correction, and to the faith educators have placed in the tenets of behaviorism.[2] Teachers and researchers in composition, rhetoric, and women's studies have also been resisting and recasting this history: through the arguments of Ann Berthoff against behaviorist conceptions of composing, through the productive dissonance that collaborative writing can generate (Lunsford 1991, Trimbur 1989, the *JAC* Winter 1994 issue on collaboration), through experiments in blending or contrasting autobiographical and academic voices (Bloom 1992, Bridwell-Bowles 1995, Brodkey 1994, Fulwiler 1990, Tompkins 1987), and through critiques of static conceptions of genre and the privileging of argument over autobiography (Bleich 1989, Bridwell-Bowles 1992, Frey 1990, Lamb 1991, Tompkins 1992). Most recently compositionists have also engaged Mary Louise Pratt's (1991) metaphor of the *contact zone* and Gloria Anzaldúa's (1987) of *borderlands* in refiguring academic scenes of writing as dynamic sites for multiple, conflicting, and creative language practices that push against and redraw the bounds of particular communities and genres (Horner 1994, Lu 1994, Severino 1994). The work of these researchers and many others destabilizes set notions about what constitutes academic discourse, genre, and authority, and they open up a field of speculation about what forms, voices, audiences, and concerns might be available and valued as academic work in the future. "At stake," Gesa Kirsch (1993) writes, "is nothing less than a new vision of what constitutes reading and writing — our scholarly work — in the academy" (p. 134).

What we still need to examine, however, are how these critiques, experiments, and speculations might be brought to bear on our ideas about revision and, more specifically, ways of talking in classrooms about revision that, despite the displacements of postmodernity, continue to posit the ideal of a stable, clear, and complete text. We need to consider, too, what practices of revision — of seeing with fresh eyes, of entering old texts from new critical directions — we must figure into our speculations and in our pedagogies if we are to move beyond calls for change into enactments of change in our writing and in our classrooms both.

In this chapter I want to revisit composition's articulated theories of revision and consider another layer to their history that can help us understand this continued insistence on words like *clarity*, *consistency*, and *completeness* at a time when other cherished and problematic ideals have given way — a history that's underwritten first by readings of Sigmund Freud, later by readings of Jacques Lacan, and their narratives of the encounter between an individual and society.[3] In particular I'll examine how one offshoot of Freud, "ego psychology," along with Lacanian rereadings, shape composition's dominant beliefs about revision as a one-way movement from writer-based to reader-based prose; from unruly, unsocialized first draft to socially adapted, socially meaningful final product.[4] Then, turning to feminist rereadings of Freud and Lacan, I'll consider a different story of revision that highlights the ways in which individual identities always exceed and transgress the discursive formations available to them — always confuse, mislead, and irritate not only a text's readers, but oftentimes its writer as well. More, contemporary feminist theorists stress that it's in the pursuit of what exceeds, what transgresses, what is restless and irritated, that we can locate the beginnings of identity, voice, and revision — revision as getting restless with a first draft's boundaries, revision as asking, "Something missing, something else?" of our texts and of our lives.

My short story "The Cheating Kind" (1994) started with a memory from my teenage years: riding the backroads in an old, beat-up Cadillac that my best friend's father and his girlfriend loaned us along with a six-pack of Black Label beer because, even though we were only fifteen, without licenses, our presence wasn't wanted in the house. When I started the story, those memories seemed charged with rebellion, possibility, heady high-speed freedom; as the drafting continued, though, I grew more and more uneasy with the narrator's point of view. She seemed capable of just about anything for a taste of adventure. Her desires seemed to eclipse completely whatever Marla, her friend, might be feeling as they drove around in that Cadillac, banished from her house, banished from the narrator's house, too, since the narrator's mother didn't regard Marla as a "nice" girl. Though a cherished myth of the fiction workshop, as Mary Cain (1995) writes, is that a writer is in control of the text and meanings she creates, seeking the advice of workshop members only to make her text and meanings clear and unambiguous to others, I didn't feel at all in control of this story and the questions it raised: Where was this narrator taking my memories? How much did she have to do with me? And what did social class, power, and status — the narrator from an exceedingly quiet, exceedingly polite middle-class family; Marla from a working-class household and the part of town where "things happen" — have to do with this story, with the memory from which it came?

Then came the story's end — a minor car wreck, the old Cadillac skidding off the road and into a corn field — I thought I was "dreaming up" since I couldn't quite remember how my friendship with the real Marla ended:

> *It was only slender stalks of corn, ripe and ready for picking, that we hit. They gave way easily, and Marla, of course, didn't die.*
>
> *It would be an easier story to tell if she had — the stuff of high drama like Gatsby face down and bleeding in a pool, the romance of a steak knife shivering between two ribs. I couldn't simply walk away then, pretend it had all never happened, brush off my acquaintance with Marla like a fine layer of dirt . . .*
>
> *"We'll have to get a tow truck," Marla said, looking down at the Cadillac's front end shoved through rows of broken stalks, the tires dug into soft, rutted earth. She stepped carefully around the undamaged plants, shook her head, and said, "We'll need help."*
>
> *A drop of blood clung to her lip, and she touched a finger to it. Probably I should have asked her, "Are you hurt?" But I was already thinking ahead to the tow truck, the sheriff, the call to my mother. I saw Bob Crofton shaking his head and saying no, of course he didn't give two fourteen-year-olds his Cadillac to drive.*
>
> *"I'll go," I said. I took one step back. Crisp leaves and stalks crackled beneath my feet. I kicked into the road a crushed, empty can of Black Label. "You stay here. I'll get help."*
>
> *I took another step back, then paused for the jagged bolt of lightning to strike me dead or for Marla to read my aura and explode, "Oh, like hell I'm going to let you leave me here to take the blame." But the sky stayed the same bruised rainless gray, and Marla remained by the car and nodded as if she believed me, as if she trusted me to do this one small, honest thing.*
>
> *"You stay here," I said again, turning now to run. (p. 45)*

In the end, the narrator leaves Marla with the wreck, Marla to take the blame, back to the quiet, polite, "nothing-ever-happens-here" part of town. Though this ending isn't autobiographical, didn't actually happen, it also strikes me as true.

Let me put it this way: As I drafted and revised "The Cheating Kind," and especially its last scene, I wasn't concerned with the questions, "How can I better adapt each scene to the story's central theme?" and "How can I get my message across to readers?" — questions of craft, questions of a writer detached from and in complete control of his or her meanings. I was too caught up in the questions instead, "How much of this narrator's point of view was mine, is mine?" and "What does this story say about how I am already adapted — and to what?"

The Ethics of Excess: Three Stories

Psychoanalysis, French feminism, excess: These are words, I know, that conjure up images of uncritical celebrations of "writing the body" and lead to the protest, "But it's not responsible to invite students to write to excess, given what they're asked to do in their other classes" and "This is unethical since we're not licensed in psychology and psychiatry and aren't trained to handle what might result from encouraging the excessive."[5] Following a 1994 MLA presentation in which Wendy Bishop and Hans Ostrom (1994a) argued for "convention making" and "convention breaking" taught together in the classroom, one teacher remarked to another, "I don't think students need to be confused any more than they already are." These are concerns I will address directly at this chapter's end, as well as indirectly in revision narratives placed throughout this chapter. Here, to suggest why we need to address these issues of restlessness, confusion, and excess along the borders of convention and genre, I'll introduce three brief stories that will be on my mind throughout this chapter:

1. Brandie, a student in a first-year composition class is, like many students at this large Midwestern land-grant institution, viewing the university as a place of transition between her rural upbringing and an adulthood defined primarily by what she cannot do and where she cannot go. She knows that after graduation she can neither return to the farm her family no longer owns nor to the small town where her parents met and married; its shrinking economy can't support her and the numbers of other children raised and schooled there. Her mission at the university, as she vaguely understands and writes it, is "to get a teaching certificate so I can get a decent job somewhere or maybe to meet someone and get married which is weird since my parents always knew each other growing up and that won't be true for me and whoever 'he' may be." At the start of the semester she writes essays in a consistently upbeat tone about moving to the city and adjusting to a large university, stating, "I feel that in a huge place like the university you can very easily be just a number, but just as easily be somebody," and concluding, "I am making all I can of being a college student." As she reads this last paragraph aloud to her small group, another student, her background similar to Brandie's, begins to sing, "Be all that you can be. Get an edge on life . . ." Everyone laughs, Brandie too. "But, hey," Brandie says. "this is reality, right? We got to do it." Another student asks, "But don't you miss your old friends?" Brandie nods. "Aren't you ever homesick?" Brandie nods again and says, "But I don't want to put any of that into the story. It would take away from the positive idea I'm trying to get across. I don't want people to think I'm a mess."

2. To the writing center, Moira, a sophomore taking an intermediate writing class, brings a draft about her experience of going through a pregnancy, then placing the child up for adoption. The draft begins in the doctor's office where Moira learned she was pregnant, then proceeds through the adoption and her decision to return to school. Though the draft is seven pages long, Moira doesn't get past reading aloud in the writing center the first two paragraphs, stopping frequently to explain to me about her boyfriend, her parents, the plans she'd been making to move with her sister to another state, the uncertainty she shared with her boyfriend about whether they were really in love, her worries too that this uncertainty was created by her father who insisted she was too young for a serious relationship, how she sat on the examination table waiting for the doctor, thinking of all of this, and telling herself, "There's nothing wrong, there's nothing wrong." When I ask her if all she's telling me and jotting down in the margins has a place in the draft, Moira says, "That's the problem. I feel like it does, but then I worry about boring readers with all this background. It's all set up for the doctor to come in and tell me the news, and I don't feel like I can just leave readers hanging."

3. Lisa, a composition instructor, stops me in the hallway between classes and asks me to talk to her sometime about revision. She continues:

> I don't feel comfortable asking my students to revise because I don't really know how to revise either. I've got all these journals and papers that I don't do anything with because even though I know they're not perfect, I don't want to take the life out of them, "do this" or "do that" like people tell me I need to. So they just sit there, and it's the same with my students. Maybe what they write isn't perfect, but it's got life and maybe cleaning it up would kill that life.

As Lisa talks, I wonder how many teachers moving down the hall around us might voice the same ambivalence, how many also have stacks of journals and papers they've written and are afraid to touch. Strangely, I think too of Tillie Olsen's (1976) short story "I Stand Here Ironing" and especially its closing phrase, "helpless before the iron" (p. 21).

These stories are on my mind now because each suggests to me the start of revisionary consciousness — as Brandie and her group members recognize a troubling cultural narrative that may be writing their lives, as Moira considers aloud the relationships that shape her experiences and that don't fit into the shape of her draft, as Lisa notes the tension between her classroom's generative theories of composing and dominant ideas of revision as cleaning up, closing down, even killing off. These stories also suggest to me the kind of helplessness that Olsen's narrator voices as she stands at the ironing board. Brandie, Moira, and

Lisa aren't sure how they can intervene in these texts, they're not sure *that* they can intervene. They stand, in other words, at the intersection between full, excessive lives and the seemingly strict limits of texts that must be ironed out, made unwrinkled and smooth.

These stories also suggest that, difficult and discomforting as it is to linger at this intersection, real irresponsibility lies in denying its existence, in trying to push past this place as quickly and neatly as possible. It's here, at this intersection, that we need, first, to question the legacy of twentieth-century psychologies with their emphasis on the clear, the consistent, and the complete, and, second, to expand our understanding of the psychoanalytic frame to include what were, at least at times, Freud and Lacan's very much *plural* aims: the movement of individual desires toward social goals; the exploration too of ideas, feelings, experiences, and identities that exceed the rules of a given language, the margins of a given genre, the boundaries of the communities in which we live and write.

Sometimes it's surprisingly easy. In the writing center I ask Moira if she were to imagine writing out some of this "background," if she were to imagine that these details won't "bore" readers — including herself as reader — where would she want to begin? She takes her pencil and draws a line between one sentence about sitting on the exam table and the next in which the doctor arrives. We talk, then, about the idea of "space breaks" — a visual interruption of four spaces on the page, opening up room for writing about the relationships, questions, and hopes her first draft left out, then another space break signaling the return to the original narrative. When Moira returns to the writing center the next week, she's tried the space break and says she was surprised to realize that what she wrote within it wasn't "background" but the "heart of it all." She still feels restless, though, about one sentence, explaining, "I say here about my father being overbearing, and that's how it felt at the time but that's not always true or completely true." She pauses, then asks, "Can I take just that one sentence and write another essay from it?"

Yes. Yes, of course.

The Ego, the Id, and Revising with Freud

As Robert Con Davis (1987) observes in his introduction to *College English*'s second of two special issues on composition and psychoanalysis, we can find in the *Collected Works* not one Freud but (at least) two: the early Freud of the instinctual "drive" theory, and the later Freud of "ego" psychoanalysis from which springs mainstream American psychoanalytic and pop psychological practice. It's that later Freud who carved the mind into three not-at-all-distinct realms — the ego, the id, and the superego — giving us a three-part topography of a self at war with its selves. According to this model, the *id* is that part of agency, part of the self, that develops from the needs and impulses of the body and is inseparably bound to sensations of pain, pleasure, deprivation, and fulfillment. Out of the id develops the *ego*, that part of the self that seeks to regulate and control chaotic id impulses, and the *superego*, that part that represents parental, social, and institutional controls — the genesis of prohibition, censorship, and guilt, but also of social awareness and responsibility.

From this later Freud grew two popular versions of psychoanalytic practice. Id psychology focuses on and privileges the instinctual drives and an individual's "private" and "personal" fantasies that escape or speak in muted form through the ego's monitor. From id psychology comes the practice of dream analysis, classical Freudian readings of literature as revelations of an author's psyche, and the idea of automatic writing. Ego psychology, on the other hand, stresses the containment of id fantasy and the construction and maintenance of a social identity.[6] Defining psychoanalysis as an "instrument to enable the ego to achieve a progressive conquest of the id" (Freud 1962b, XIX, p. 56), ego psychology underwrites behaviorism (which places the superego outside the individual in external punishments and rewards that shape the ego's functioning), literature's reader-response theories (which follow an individual among others as he or she develops personal reactions into culturally shared interpretations), and, I'd like to argue, composition's dominant ideas about writing and revision.[7] Consider:

> Revision is by nature a strategic, adaptive process. . . . One revises only when the text needs to be better. (Flower, and colleagues 1986, p. 18)

> Perhaps the best definition of revising is this: revising is whatever a writer does to change a piece of writing for a particular reader or readers — whoever they may be. . . . (Elbow and Belanoff 1989, p. 166)

> [H]e must become like us. . . . He must become someone he is not. . . . The struggle of the student writer is not the struggle to bring out that which is within; it is the struggle to carry out those ritual activities that grant one entrance into a closed society. (Bartholomae 1983, p. 300)

These compositionists, usually divided into the separate realms of *cognitivist, expressivist*, and *social constructionist*, share *in common* an understanding of revision as movement from the individual (or writer-based) to the social (or reader-based), the increasingly strategized, adapted, socially integrated and socially meaningful finished product. Though Flower and colleagues have been criticized for ignoring the social dimensions of writing in their seemingly interior cognitivist model, they actually highlight the social in their definition of revision — the need for writers to reread and adapt their texts according to very much social ideas of what they should say, how a piece of writing should appear, what would make it "better." Similarly, though the pedagogy of Elbow and Belanoff has been labeled "expressivist" and might be read as a pedagogy of the id, they too construct revision (albeit with some discomfort) as changes made toward a social text and social functioning; they too (within *Community of Writers*, that is) share in common with ego psychology the belief that movement from individual to social, private fantasy to public meaning, is desirable or, at least, unavoidable.

But it's David Bartholomae especially who makes visible for me the intersections between our understandings of composing and the ideas of ego psychology, showing how Freud's tripartite model of the mind has been further codified into separate, distinct realms: the student as "id" who must not bring out that which is within — or rather, that which is formed by social languages and communities deemed unintelligible within academe, deemed "other" than academic discourse; the draft as developing, regulatory "ego"; the teacher as "superego," the embodiment of the closed society and its rituals for meaning. Bartholomae doesn't tone down this process as entirely natural and as always positive and progressive. Rather, noting that stories of learning to write in academic settings are often "chronicles of loss, violence, and compromise" (1985, p. 142), his construction of the writing scene suggests that revision has much more to do with politics than with brain biology or liberal humanism. In this construction, intentions are shaped by the community the writer wants to make his or her way into, and the revision process is not a simple matter of making a text "better" or "clearer." Revision is instead the very complicated matter of struggle between a full, excess-ive life and the seemingly strict limits of what can be written and understood within a particular discourse community. Here, Bartholomae and other social constructionists like Patricia Bizzell and Thomas Recchio share much in common with Jacques Lacan, his rereading of Freud, and his view that the making of identity and meaning are social acts from the very start.

At a midterm conference, Rachel, a student in my first-year composition course, tells me, "I'm learning a lot from your class." I cock my head, puzzled. Rachel is always in class, never late, always has a draft, neatly typed, never handwritten, for workshops. A model student. Disturbingly so. (I can't remember now, looking back, what Rachel wrote about, only that her drafts were always clear and concise, a thesis stated in the first paragraph and stuck to through the very end.) "Is there anything missing for you in class?" I ask. "Anything we're not doing that you wish we would or something we could be doing more of?" I'm fumbling about, trying to get at my sense that there's something that could be and isn't in Rachel's writing for class or that could be and isn't in the class for Rachel. But Rachel shakes her head. "No, everything's great. It really makes a lot of sense, you know: free write, think about what's at the center, free write some more, get some feedback, go with a new question. It's great." Maybe, I think, my sense of something missing is wrong; she's identifying what she's learning after all. Maybe I'm only imagining an underground, unarticulated frustration she feels with this class, and maybe I just can't see something that really is happening in her writing.

Then at the semester's end Rachel writes her evaluation for the course in a voice I hadn't heard from her before — one of anger, of frustration, and of intense involvement with this writing task: "Supposedly this was a course in composition, but I'll tell you I didn't learn one thing about composition from it."

Mirror-Mirror *or* Revising with Lacan

With Lacan's rereading of Freud and, particularly, his reading of Freud's early thinking on the development of ego in "Narcissism" (Freud 1962b, XIV), that sense of the inevitability of the movement from self to other, individual sensation to social codification, is both reinforced and rendered as troubling. Beginning with the infant in an amorphous and boundaryless state, just a "l'hommelette" or "omelette" (little man, mass of egg), Lacan explores the advent of the largely metaphoric "mirror stage" in which individuals confront and seek to connect with a smooth and consistent reflection of themselves (1977b, p. 197). The mirror images they find can be gratifying — giving a sense of shape and wholeness to what was before a chaotic jumble of needs and sensations — but such images are also a source of discord and anxiety. The outer image of containment and completion is at odds with the inner sensations of fragmentation and incoherence; it leads to conflict between the "Ideal-I" reflected in the mirror and the "turbulent movements that the subject feels are animating him [or her]," and it asks an individual to combat and contain those sensations increasingly in order to assume an identity that's outside, other, and alienating (1977a, p. 2). "It is this moment," Lacan writes, "that decisively tips the whole of human knowledge into mediatization through the desire of the other" (1977a, p. 5). It is at this moment, in other words, when American ego psychology's clear distinctions between individual and society break down, revealing how an individual sense of self, meaning, and reality is thoroughly mediated by social mirrors and the images of wholeness and coherence they reflect.

The story of Lacan's mirror stage helps me to understand why professional writers are so often reluctant to talk about revision and show to others early drafts of their work. Fiction writer Tobias Wolff, for instance, destroys all early versions of his stories, explaining, "They embarrass me, to tell you the truth. . . . I only want people to see my work at its very best" (quoted in Woodruff 1993, p. 23). "When I finish a piece of writing," says Joyce Carol Oates, notorious for her reticence about the subject of her own writing, "I try my best to forget the preliminary stages, which involve a good deal of indecision, groping, tension" (quoted in Woodruff 1993, p. 167). Those early drafts may not match up at all to social mirrors that tell us what a short story ought to look like or what a good writer's sentences ought to sound like. They may even pose a threat to the writer's sense of himself or herself as a good writer at all, a threat to the belief that this draft can ever be finished and published. (This is something against which students in my fiction-writing classes particularly struggle, saying that they want or need to put their story drafts aside "to cool," when, in fact, I suspect that they fear the unsettling images these drafts reflect, images they see not in terms of possibility, but of failure to match up and fit in.) Lacan's analysis of the mirror stage tells me, too, why students often respond in conferences and in peer groups (as Richard Beach observed in a 1986 essay) with "Oh, I feel pretty good [about this draft]" or "I don't feel good about it at all but I don't want to revise it." It makes sense, I think, especially in an environment of evaluation, of grades, to respond to dissonance and disjuncture by insisting, "No, this is clear enough, good enough" or to worry that any intervention might make a sense of misfit and distortion even worse.

In my view, the story of Lacan's mirror stage is the story that underwrites social constructionist understandings of writing and revision. "[I]t is evident," Thomas Recchio (1991) writes, "that we all have to find ways to function in a language [or languages] . . . that have already been configured" (p. 446). "[H]e must become like us," Bartholomae (1983) writes. ". . . He must become someone he is not" (p. 300). Like Lacan, both Recchio and Bartholomae stress how from the very first word, the very first draft, a student in the composition classroom encounters, grapples with, and tries to accommodate an alien, even alienating, way of writing. Both stress that a notion of revision as a clean movement from writer-based to reader-based prose is also fiction, since languages and contexts for writing are already social, already reader based. A writer doesn't create language in isolation and out of thin air, then work toward involving others; one's words are already deeply involved in the work and words of others, come from without rather than from within, and can seem, as Lacan writes, like "the assumption of the armour of an alienating identity . . ." (1977a, p. 4).

This isn't to say that Recchio, Bartholomae, and other social constructionists postulate a writer who has no agency within this armor. Through "orchestrating and subordinating" the multiple social discourses of a text, Recchio (1991) states, a student may "begin to find her own voice" (pp. 452–453). "The person writing," Bartholomae (1990) says, "can be found in the work, the labor, the deployment and deflection . . ." (p. 130). Still, here, as in the usual reading of Lacan, there is that overriding sense of inevitability: We can resist this narrative of being subsumed and written by the assumptions and rituals of a single community — through deployment and deflection, subordination and control — but we cannot fundamentally alter it.[8]

In "Fighting Words: Unlearning to Write the Critical Essay," Jane Tompkins (1988) examines the narratives — of movie westerns, of the biblical David and Goliath — that underwrite traditional forms of academic writing: critics gunning each other's readings down; a graduate student standing up at her first conference with her slingshot-of-a-paper, hoping to smite the big voices in her field so she has the right to speak. That's also the narrative of my first academic publication: Set up this authority, set up that, then tear them down, get on with what you want to say. I was shaken when, one year later, I met one of those authorities face to face. It occurred to me then, and should have occurred to me before, that she was more than the few words on the page I chose to quote: a living breathing person leading a complex life, asking complex questions — who she is and what her work is far exceeding the boundaries I'd drawn.

In this chapter, too, I'm doing it again, choosing quotations from writers whose work exceeds the space I'm giving them and the narrow focus of revision I've selected. This is a problem — one to which I have to keep returning, not skipping over with the gesture of a "However" or "Yet it's easy to see . . . ," creating a text that's problematically concise, simply clear.

The Trouble with Mirrors

Freud and Lacan are not figures I want to dismiss, and I don't think, either, that compositionists can or should shrug off the influence of twentieth-century psychologies. Freud remains appealing to me if for no other reason than because he located his research in narrative. Though he wasn't always a critical reader of his narratives with their traces of sentimental romance, Victorian melodrama, and the mechanistic metaphors of industrial capitalism, he illustrates why forms of narrative research — case studies, ethnographies, autobiographical literacy narratives — are crucial to the making of knowledge in composition: They make visible what is "uncanny" in our thinking and in our practices; they reveal the slips and contradictions that disrupt our broad generalizations (or we might say "wishes") about what's happening in our classrooms and in our discipline. Stories, as Mary Ann Cain (1995) observes, don't merely "mirror" our assumptions and expectations; they "talk back."

Similarly, all the slips and contradictions of a classroom text like Elbow and Belanoff's (1989) *Community of Writers* — with its conflicting id-based and ego-based assertions, "You write for yourself; you write for others" — make visible and talk back to my own slips, my own contradictions when I try to talk with students about revision. As for Lacan, though his theories may appear grim and deterministic, he does tell me why my students and I are sometimes so unsettled when we look back on our early drafts, those drafts distorting what we wished to see, declining to mirror back ideas smooth-surfaced and well-mannered, the gratifying images of a graceful writer, a good teacher. Composition's social constructionists have also worked to disturb the discipline's harmonious image of the writing process as natural, asocial, and apolitical; they stress that no classroom and no piece of writing can ever be free from the problematic encounter between an individual and society, the pressures and desires to see one's text neatly reflect a preplanned intention, a pleasing image, the certainty of one's membership in a closed society.

But no social mirror — and this is what usual readings of Lacan leave out — can ever reflect back to us, whole and complete, an image of ourselves and the true nature of things. There is always something missing, something else, or, as feminist critic Sheila Rowbotham (1973) writes, misfit and distortion as we lumber around "ungainly-like" in "borrowed concepts" that do not "fit the shapes we [feel] ourselves to be" (p. 30). This has to be the case as well for the mirrors that our readings of Freud and Lacan provide. Those mirrors offer some ideas about writing and revision, individual identity and social meaning, that we want and need. Those mirrors ought to make us restless with what they distort, what they miss, what else they imply.

My restlessness begins when I consider how both our Freudian and Lacanian constructions of revision position the teacher as super-ego, the representative of the "us" students must learn to write like or as the regulatory voice in the margins telling students where and how their texts need to adapt and change. As philosopher Michele Le Dœuff (1989) considers, the position of superego sets teachers up for a "tic"-like approach to responding to students' texts: "systematically correcting [any] infidelities" and "castigating the language of the student . . . by writing in red in the margin . . ." (p. 57). That castigation may be overt with insistent commands like "Be specific!" or "Focus!"; it can also take the seemingly benign forms of "Does this paragraph really belong here?" or "Some readers might be offended by this." Either way, this relationship between teacher and student, teacher and text, doesn't set us up for questioning the textual ideals we and our students are writing/responding to match. It doesn't set us up for understanding the encounter between teacher and text as a potentially rich "contact zone" or "borderland" for questioning, speculating, and, possibly, revising the teacher's response. It constructs instead (Le Dœuff's point as she examines the grading of doctoral exams in philosophy) a position of complete submission for the student, of utter mastery for the teacher. Meanwhile, the question doesn't even come up: *Just who or what has mastered the teacher?*

My restlessness increases when I recall that Lacan's thinking about the mirror stage, so influential to social constructionism, began with his reading of Freud's essay on narcissism — suggesting some disturbing answers to that question: Just who or what has mastered the teacher? In Lacan, the experience of the mirror stage sends an individual in a "fictional direction," toward an imaginary idea of an "us," of a community and its practices into which an individual wants to fit. As compositionist Kurt Spellmeyer observed in his 1994 MLA presentation, "Lost in the Funhouse: The Teaching of Writing and the Problem of Professional Narcissism," this fictional direction is also a *narcissistic* one. It can lead us to seek — in our own writing and in others', in academic journal articles, dissertations, and students' compositions — gratifying images of ourselves, and it can lead us to feel frustrated and annoyed when a piece of writing doesn't reflect such an image. These imaginary identifications don't always lead us to question what's being gratified when we write an article that others call graceful, witty, or astute or when we write in the margins of a student's essay "Nice work" or "Very smoothly written." These imaginary identifications don't always lead us to question, either, the longing among compositionists within their departments and institutions to project certain images of themselves to the exclusion and debasement of others — as in "I teach a cultural studies classroom [rather than a mere writing class]" or "I'm in rhetoric [not composition]" or "I'm a post-process theorist [disassociated, that is, from composition's research of the past twenty years]."

Stressing at the start and end of his presentation that our academic lives are carried out under powerful institutional gazes, very often within English departments that value literature over composition, the high and sweeping theoretical over the narrative, detailed, and everyday, Spellmeyer suggests that compositionists do have some means for resistance. We can shift our attention from texts by a Beckett or a Joyce to texts by students; we can, as Spellmeyer demonstrated in his presentation, deploy French terms in ironic tones and with raised eyebrows, calling for light laughter and an edge of skepticism. These forms of resistance aside, however, we cannot fundamentally revise the forms, voices, and subjects of the texts we write — not according to this story of the formation of academic identity.

Here my restlessness is most extreme as social constructionism (slipping into social determinism), which began with a radical intervention in too-smooth notions of "the writing process," ends with a denial of possibilities for further intervention, as it replaces questions with absolute statements of what must be, and so repeats the move of ego psychology, asserting the need to adapt to a prefigured principle of (institutional) reality: *He must learn to write like us; narratives of academic socialization will always be narratives of loss, violence, compromise, and alienation; academic production is the production of anxiety, narcissism, and neurosis — this is just the way things are.*

I thought about Tompkins's (1988) essay "Fighting Words" and my own David-and-Goliath article this past week while reading poems in Prairie Schooner. *I read poems by T. Alan Broughton that meditate on letters written by Vincent Van Gogh to his brother Theo, one by Cornelius Eady written from a photograph of Dexter Gordon, another by Adrienne Su that takes its occasion from a sentence in* Alice's Adventures in Wonderland: *"Everything is queer today." Funny that poets are often charged with sequestering themselves in silent garrets or with suffering the most from the anxiety of influence. These three poets model for me ways of beginning to write, of working with the words of others, and of finding a voice — ways that don't involve setting up and knocking down. They suggest we might revise our usual forms of academic production by remaining at, rather than trying to get past, that border between one's text and others. Maxine Hong Kingston also offers me an example of this border work between one's voice and another's. In* The Woman Warrior *Kingston (1976) creates, continually returns to, and enriches a portrait of her mother, making places in her text for the both of them, even where — or especially where — their voices, their views, aren't at all one and the same.*

"Too Much": Revising to Death

In "Professional Narcissism," Kurt Spellmeyer focuses on the anxious, even neurotic relationships that form between writer and text, text and reader, when we write to adapt to institutional mirrors. Two fictional stories about revision as adaptation — Margaret Atwood's "The Bog Man" (1991) and Paule Marshall's *Praisesong for the Widow* (1984) — also focus on those powers of social mirrors and suggest more chilling consequences still. In "The Bog Man," there is Julie who revises again and again the tale of her long-ago affair with Connor, a married archeology professor who brought her as his "assistant" on an excavation in Scotland. Throughout the story Julie revises Connor, revises herself, even revises the setting where they broke up because "Julie broke up with Connor in the middle of a swamp" sounds "mistier, more haunted" than "Julie broke up with Connor in the middle of a bog" or, the truth, in a pub (p. 77). In her revisions of the story, told "late at night, after the kids were in bed and after a few drinks, always to women," Julie works to shut out any details that might be less than amusing, too hard to figure out (p. 94). She "skims over the grief," "leaves out entirely any damage she may have caused," thinks that this or that fact "does not really fit into the story" (pp. 94–95). Connor, like the bog man they go to Scotland to excavate, "loses in substance every time she forms him in words" (p. 95). In the end, Julie has an ironic, consistent, and lifeless tale of an episode from her life. In the end, Connor is "almost an anecdote" and Julie is "almost old" (p. 95).

Avey, the main character in Paule Marshall's novel *Praisesong for the Widow*, is also "almost old" when she begins, with great restlessness and resistance, to look back on the narrative of middle-class socialization she and her now-dead husband, Jerome, followed as they moved "out" and "up" from a fifth-floor walk-up in Harlem to a suburban house in White Plains, New York. She remembers the "small rituals" they left behind: a coffee ring on Sunday morning, gospel choirs on the Philco, Jerome (who then called himself "Jay," even his name changing with their move) reciting the poetry of Langston Hughes (pp. 124–126). She remembers their "private lives," their lovemaking, that had seemed "inviolable" but that also "fell victim to the strains. . . . Love like a burden [Jerome] wanted to get rid of" (p. 129). And she remembers the dances Jerome led her in across their small living room, "declaring it to be the Rockland Palace or the Renny," in the days before his voice began to change to one that said, "If it was left to me I'd close down every dancehall in Harlem and burn every drum! That's the only way these Negroes out here'll begin making any progress!" (pp. 95, 132).

"Too much!" That's what Avey cries out as she finally lets herself remember and mourn the changes in her husband, in herself, the cost of their "progress." She doesn't romanticize the years on Halsey Street in Harlem and doesn't erase the grim hardship; she does ask herself, "Hadn't there perhaps been another way?" She thinks, "They had behaved, she and Jay, as if there had been nothing about themselves worth honoring" (p. 139).

Julie, Jerome, and Avey are cast within narratives of accommodation and change that point toward the not-always-acknowledged implications of composition's dominant theories and practices of revision. Julie, for instance, strategizes and adapts, alters and omits, so that her story's "effect" matches her "intention." She revises with the aim of better functioning within an already configured language — here, the already configured and even clichéd language of college girls who get into affairs with married professors, of a middle-aged, middle-class woman who makes light of younger, wilder days. While Recchio considers that an individual voice may be formed through the work of orchestration and subordination, coherence and control, Atwood's story dramatizes the opposite case as Julie's orchestrations and subordination lead, in the end, to no voice at all. The same is true and much more disturbing in Marshall's story of Jerome. His work to adapt his life and his words to a single course of action, one proper tone, ends with his lying in a coffin while everyone congratulates his widow "on how well she had held up in the face of her great loss" (pp. 132–133).

In feminist readings of psychoanalysis the revision process involves both *dream-work* (the exploration of identifications and meanings along the border of consciousness) and *death-work* (the critique and dismantling of beliefs and identifications we experience as our selves, making their loss a kind of death). Joining the work of discovering and questioning, dis-orienting and re-orienting, revision becomes that process Winnicott (1971) calls "creative living" and that Kristeva (1986a) calls "dissidence": a process through which one recognizes how he or she has been situated, the process through which one negotiates with reality "out there" to change that situation. In Marshall's depiction of Jerome's brief life, however, there is no room for dream-work, dissidence, and negotiation with reality "out there." While Lacan (1977a) defines death-work as working one's way toward a "new truth" that is "always disturbing" (p. 169), in Marshall's representation of Jerome there is no work, no activity, no confrontation with and reflection on what in these life changes are disturbing; there is only the literal and complete killing off of a whole history, a whole host of attachments, every one of his daily rituals for meaning, as he works to adapt his life to one principle of reality. It's a story not of *re-vision* but of assimilation.

With Julie, Jerome, and Avey's narratives in mind, we might reconsider resistance to revision and that fear Lisa expressed of revision taking the "life" from a piece of writing just as Jerome's process of change literally took the life from him. Lisa, unlike Jerome, is not marginalized by race; however, as an untenured instructor in the university, a Jewish woman in the predominantly Christian and Protestant Nebraskan culture, a woman who came to feminism in her forties and after an impoverishing divorce, Lisa is aware each time she sits down to write of working against the grain of the dominant culture, a working-against she's only recently found the confidence to try. Viewing revision as the work of toning down and fitting in, the work of moving away from, not into, disturbing new positions and truths, she fears the silencing of a voice she's only just begun to use. In some instances at least, Lisa persuades me, a refusal to revise may arise from an intuitive understanding of the intimate link between language and identity, an intuitive understanding that we really can revise a story, revise ourselves, to death.

That is, unless we return to that intersection between a full and excess-ive life and the limits of a particular society, asking, with Marshall's Avey, if there isn't another way.

Sometimes relationships in the classroom — to reading, to other students — can recast, rather than reinforce, the usual social mirrors teachers and students write and respond within. In an intermediate composition class, Scott, a senior in his midtwenties, reads aloud in class a narrative of a ski trip in which he and his friends abandon another friend, new to skiing, on the beginner's slope. In his draft, Scott represents this friend as "whining" and "annoying," comedically clumsy and inept, deserving, so the story implies, to be left behind. The students in class laugh as Scott reads. Except Amanda, Scott's journal partner, who writes to him in her next journal, "What about you? Weren't you a beginner on that trip too? Did you worry about being left?"

Meanwhile, Scott is also reading Tim O'Brien's (1990) semiautobiographical novel The Things They Carried *in which the narrator, Tim, recreates his decision to go to Vietnam, feeling as though there were "an audience" to his life, an audience shouting "Traitor!" and "Pussy!" as he tries to imagine swimming for Canada (p. 60). Later O'Brien's narrator considers what happened when he sent one of his published stories to Norman, a foot soldier who was with him in Vietnam on the night when Kiowa, another foot soldier, was killed in a "shit field." About the story, Norman writes back, "It's not terrible . . . but you left out Vietnam. Where's Kiowa? Where's the shit?" (p. 181). With O'Brien's words in mind, Scott considers the audiences to his own life who expect him to be amusing, to keep it light, to skip the shit. He considers that in his latest draft, about canoeing on the Niobrara River, he's repeated the move that Amanda noticed in his ski trip draft — displacing his confusion and fear onto others, setting them up as comedic and inept, almost writing himself out of the story altogether. During an in-class glossing activity, Scott lists in the margins of his draft, as O'Brien does in his short story "The Things They Carried," some of the events, problems, and questions that he carried on this trip. He writes, "We were all having problems, and I want to bring those out" and "What's really going on here? Where's my trip?"*

With his glosses, Scott begins to revise, adding a scene in which he and his friend Chuck, riding down the Niobrara one afternoon in a slowly meandering canoe, talk seriously about their lives, relationships, and futures — the kind of serious and meandering talk between two men that isn't usually represented in social (and classroom) discourse. This and other revised passages don't present a version of Scott as whole and complete, who he really is, the way it really was. In the margins of the revision and his journal, he continues to write, "I may be using Chuck to say some of how I was feeling and perceived things" and "I'm looking for a voice I can feel comfortable with" and "I need to try this paragraph again." The revision does, though, lead him to a next step: giving the draft to Chuck to read, "fidgeting" while Chuck read "very slowly," and feeling "a great weight lifted" when Chuck responded by asking for a copy to keep. "He didn't ask 'Where's the Niobrara?'" Scott writes. "He didn't complain that I'd left out the shit."

Wrestling with Lacanian Bondage

Like Marshall's Avey, film theorist Joan Copjec (1989) also seeks another way, one out of what she calls the "realtight" bond in contemporary psychoanalytic theory between the "symbolic" and the "imaginary," between individual identity and the social gazes thought to determine, wholly, completely, who we can be and what we can say (p. 227). That real-tight bond seals us off from any consideration of the "real" or of, as Freud (1962b) puts it, that "inch of nature" that exceeds any one construction of our selves (Copjec 1989, pp. 228–229; Freud 1962b, XXI, p. 91). It leads, for instance, to film theorists positing a single (male) gaze that women are positioned within and must take pleasure from as they view a film, with no room for restlessness, resistance, another way of watching.

But this real-tight bond, Copjec writes, is also the result of a *misreading* of Lacan and, in particular, the familiar Lacanian aphorism, "Desire is the desire of the Other" (Copjec 1989, p. 238). In this misreading — one exemplified not only in film theory but also in composition's social-constructionist theories of writing — writers and their texts are viewed as entirely determined by the social mirrors that surround them, by actual and identifiable "Others" to which we can point and say, "Yes, there's the locus of my desire, the mirror I want to match." According to this (mis)reading, Copjec writes, individuals take on social representations as images of their own "ideal being" — that "Ideal I" from Lacan's mirror stage. As we take a "narcissistic pleasure" from such images (because they offer us shape and symmetry), we become "cemented" or "glued" to them, coming to call them (no longer an alienating armor) our selves — or, in the classroom, our definition of good writing, what we want our teaching and our students' texts to reflect (Copjec 1989, p. 229; this is likewise Spellmeyer's point in "Professional Narcissism" [1994]).

The problem with this construction of desire and the formation of identity is that it overlooks the capital "O" Lacan places here on "Other."

In Lacan, there are "others" — small "o" — who are the people, communities, histories, social representations, and social discourses with whom and with which we interact, influence, and are influenced by — that "mediatization" the end of the mirror stage tips us toward, others with identifiable shapes, locations, and limits. There is also a persistent sense of *Otherness* (capital "O") beyond the limits of those people, communities, and discourses, a persistent sense we can't quite see and name that we might call the "real," the "inch of nature" that exceeds, overflows, cannot be contained and copied. "[W]e *have no image* of the Other's desire . . .," Copjec writes, no single representation that can bring "reunion"; there is always "something more, something indeterminate, some question of meaning's reliability" (pp. 236–238, my emphasis).

In Copjec's reading of Lacan, identity is produced "not in conformity to social laws," but "in response to our inability to conform" to social laws and discursive limits (p. 242): with the recognition of limits there's restlessness, movement, a desire that can't be satisfied with determined gazing into the reflection of one social mirror.[9] Copjec's reading takes us back to that intersection between individual and society, between excess and limits, with the understanding that a sense of something missing, something else isn't a mistake to be corrected, isn't an unruly id to be suppressed, but is instead the start of revisionary activity by a self that is neither singular and static nor entirely composed by a fixed set of social determinants.

In an introductory fiction-writing class, the instructor says to me, "Technically, your story is very good. Clear. Logical, Complete. Good details." He pauses. "It's just that — " He smiles, starts again. "I think maybe you haven't found your material yet. You need to let yourself be a little messy." He adds, handing me back my story, handing me another story too, "Read this. Maybe it'll say what I mean." I nod, make my exit, frustrated, angry, ready to write on an end-of-semester evaluation, "Supposedly this was a course in fiction writing, but I'll tell you . . ." My material? What is that? And why were none of the routines I'd followed to write news stories (I was then working for a daily paper) working for me now? How did Mona Simpson, the writer of the story this instructor handed me, manage to make her stuff sound so, well, real? Home now, I head straight to my computer, turn it on, then do something else: turn off the lighted screen. This semester I'm also taking a seminar for writing tutors. We're reading Mikhail Bakhtin (1981), who claims that words hold within them whole lives and histories, the suggestions of relationships, of conflicts, of resolutions that can't last for long. We're also reading Peter Elbow (1987), who advocates shutting off the computer screen, writing in the dark. Do I believe it? Try it? Let the words run along, then reread to see what story is being written there, one I hadn't planned and controlled? I begin to write, thinking that whatever happens will prove to my instructor that a mess is exactly what will come of this, thinking too about the last time I felt this mute, pent-up, and confused — when I

was sixteen years old and running away from home. I write, "In Cincin-
nati the snow turned to rain . . ." Half an hour later I stop, print it out,
and without looking at the pages, mail them to the instructor with an
irritable note, "So. Is this my material?"

"Yes," he said.

This is not the story "How I Came to Discover My Own True Voice."
(The fiction that came from writing in the dark, "The Road from Pros-
perity" [1996], ended up being seven years in the making — seven years
of trusting, doubting, then trying to trust again Elbow and Bakhtin,
seven years of discovering how to read and work with the Otherness of
my own words, the unruliness of my writing.) It's a story instead about
coming up against the limits of my writing, traveling over the curricu-
lar boundaries into another class (a so-called theory class), coming back,
learning to write — maybe for the first time.

Writing in the "Chinks and Cracks"

One way of starting the kind of revision, Copjec's essay suggests, is through exploring practices of "prodigality" that can both highlight and take us beyond a particular community or genre's discursive limits. In an essay that begins with the either/or choice feminists face between "silence and cooptation," Jerry Aline Flieger (1990) considers that beyond the position of "dutiful daughter" to institutional forms of living and writing or that of "illegitimate mother's daughter" who rejects institutions (and voice, power, authority), there is the possibility of another position: that of the "Prodigal Daughter" (pp. 57–59). The prodigal daughter "is a daughter still" who "acknowledges her heritage," but who also "goes beyond the fold of restrictive paternal law" and returns not casti-gated and repentant, ready to settle down and fit in, but "enriched" (pp. 59–60). The prodigal daughter "is lush, exceptional, extravagant, and affirmative"; her participation in one community (like feminism) creates for her an identity that exceeds the limits of another (like psychoanaly-sis). That excess-iveness allows her to take exception to a community's limits and laws; it enables her to introduce new questions and rituals, to "enlarge its parameters" and "recast its meanings," changing the bounds of "what is permissible" (p. 60), changing, indeed, what constitutes that community and the practices of those within it.

Enlarging the parameters and reenvisioning limits also concerns Michele Le Dœuff as she reworks static notions of rationality in phi-losophy into practices of "migration" — writing with and through other social discourses and needs rather than positioning philosophy apart from and above others. "I am seeking the greatest possibility of move-ment," Le Dœuff writes, a practice of writing that migrates into and creates authority from "different fields of knowledge, 'disciplines' or discursive formations, between different periods of thought and between supposedly different 'levels' of thought, from everyday opinions to the original metaphysical system" (1991, p. 51). For Le Dœuff this means bringing her experiences with the Women's Movement in France into her work as a philosopher, rather than choosing a focus on one or the other. In this way Le Dœuff recasts her role from a "precious admirer" of and careful commentator on the texts of male philosophers (1989, p. 120). Migration shows her the limits of those texts, creates new questions and possibilities of projects beyond philosophy's usual bounds: critiques of philosophy's strategy for authority through displacing "theoretical incapacity" onto others in order to create its meanings (1989, p. 126); examination of the "erotico-theoretical transference" that has historically defined women's relationships to philosophy; exploration, too (since the prodigal daughter is also "affirmative"), of "plural work" with other writers and other disciplines that reconnects philosophy to daily social concerns.[10]

Flieger and Le Dœuff's practices of migration and prodigality aren't pendulum swings away from the social and back to the purely private and personal: an uncritical celebration of an untamed id, the mirage of an essentialized female language. Quite the opposite, the experience of migration, Le Dœuff writes, works to "exile" a writer from the conventions of a discipline and the assumptions of doctrinal bases, and by doing so denaturalizes those conventions and assumptions, preventing them from becoming commonplace, essential, the way it must be (1991, p. 222). Similarly, plural work, instead of promising escape and freedom, offers Le Dœuff a "continuing sense" of "limits," "the recognition that 'I do not do everything on my own,'" and that this incompleteness is not a "tragedy," but the opportunity to continue revising along that border of "the unknown and the unthought" (1989, pp. 126, 128). As Julia Kristeva writes, also working with these notions of migration and exile, the experience of traveling beyond disciplinary limits and comfortable ways of knowing and writing can take us out of "the mire of common sense" and enable us to become a "stranger" to the daily communities, discursive formations, and rituals for meaning we would otherwise take for granted, their limits and implications invisible to us (1986a, p. 298). Neither advocating a search for a singular self nor attachment to one social identity, these theorists seek instead the formation and recognition of multiple attachments, bringing *all* of one's identities to the scene of writing, working for a voice of lushness that's a powerful means of critique and creation both.

The writings of Teresa de Lauretis, Trinh T. Minh-ha, and Minnie Bruce Pratt also demonstrate the creative, critical, and socially responsive uses of migration and prodigality. In *Technologies of Gender,* de Lauretis (1987) argues for migration away from a focus on the "positions made available by hegemonic discourses" and toward "social spaces carved in the interstices of institutions," in the "chinks and cracks" where one can find — already in existence, not needing to be longed for, a utopian future not yet come — "new forms of community" and "micropolitical practices of daily life and daily resistances that afford both agency and sources of power . . ." (pp. 25–26). Writing away from the prevailing discourses and the positions they allow is what Trinh (1989) does in *Woman, Native, Other* as she moves away from the word *author* with its implications of a solitary genius and toward the word *storyteller* with its connection to dailiness, community, and collectivity. The essays of poet and lesbian activist Minnie Bruce Pratt (1991) also stress that the work of crossing limits isn't the trivial and apolitical pursuit of an ivory-towered class of writers, without consequence for the better or worse. In claiming her identity as a lesbian, "step[ping] over a boundary into the forbidden," Pratt lost her children to her husband's custody, the court ruling that she had committed a "crime against nature" (p. 24). In claiming that identity, she writes, she also gained the ability to keep crossing boundaries, connect her struggles as a lesbian to those of others subordinated by race, gender, or class, and take her poetry "beyond the bounds of law and propriety into life" (pp. 23–24, 241).

In the here and now, these writers offer examples of writing that seeks to name, understand, and transgress the limits of prefigured texts, understandings, and ways of living. They demonstrate revision not as that one-way movement from writer-based to reader-based prose, but instead as that moment of looking back on a text, asking how it's already reader based, already socialized and reproducing the limits of a given society, and whether there's something missing, something else. Doing so, they radically question Lacanian (and social constructionist) notions that coming into language always and only means compromise and alienation. In these writings there's a refusal to leave the intersection with a quick and uneasy compromise; there's the work of revision as seeking other options and attachments, as expanding one's focus, and as learning to write to excess.

That's true too for Paule Marshall's Avey in *Praisesong for the Widow* (1984) who does not remain within White Plains' bounds of middle-class propriety and within the narrative of loss, violence, and compromise that marked her husband's death. Moving instead into another story of revision, Avey abandons the security and strict itinerary of a middle-class cruise ship. She travels — disoriented, ill, weary from mourning her husband Jay and their early life together — to the island of Carriacou. There, in the company of others making their yearly excursion to this island of their birth and of their ancestors, Avey begins to dance, "[a]ll of her moving suddenly with a vigor and passion she hadn't felt in years," her feet picking up the rhythm of the Carriacou Tramp, "the shuffle designed to stay the course of history" (1984, pp. 249–250). At the novel's end Avey, like Flieger's prodigal daughter, is on her way back to New York — exceptional, extravagant, and prepared now to alter the former limits of her life.

In class, Brandie reads her draft and writes back to her words in the margins. She writes "Spark!" and "I was amazed when I wrote this" next to the first paragraph that ends, "I can't believe that it took me nineteen years, one month, and six days to realize that I, Brandie Marie Anderson, have no idea whatsoever what I want to do with the rest of my life." She writes, "Here is where I start to feel that my ideas scatter . . ."

next to the final paragraph that concludes "I have learned that I can do anything I want in this world, or I can do nothing." In between these paragraphs she's told the story of bringing a college friend, who grew up in a large city, home to visit her family. She's described feeling proud ("I felt like I was the man who invented the whole farming system itself") and defensive ("I wanted to destroy her feelings that my house was like that on Little House on the Prairie*") and confused ("I don't know why I thought my life was the only kind there was. I don't know why I never questioned my future"). In the margins she writes, "But is that really so bad?"*

Then Brandie turns to her journal partner, Meg, and says, "Do you want to trade?" Brandie reads and writes back to Meg's draft, which is about growing up with two families — her mother, stepfather, and their children together; her father, stepmother, and their children together. Meg reads and writes back to Brandie's draft, responding primarily to Brandie's marginal glosses: "I think this paragraph is perfect!" and "Brandie, what exactly was different about your background, and what made you think June's was so exciting? There's the obvious — bigger town, more to do, but tell me in your own words!" and "You ask yourself if that [not questioning the future] is so bad. Can you try to answer the question?" Reading this, Brandie nods and starts to make a list called "Differences" at the bottom of the page. By the end of class when she gives the draft to me, its margins — top, bottom, right, and left — are filled with conversation, arrows, directions, questions. Next to the glosses I write, "Yes," "Yes," and "I'd like to hear about this too," then respond to one sentence near the end that says, "I can really see myself teaching . . . except to teach you have to know everything, and I know I don't." I write: "I'd like to hear more about what you see when you see yourself teaching. What creates the view that a teacher must know everything? . . . Let's talk about this — maybe in a journal?"

Brandie does choose this draft to revise, responding to Meg's questions and her own. There are other kinds of revision taking place, too, of which this particular essay, by itself, is only a part: revision as Brandie strays from writing essays in a consistently upbeat tone with one "positive idea" she wants to "get across"; revision as Brandie and Meg carry their conversation from the margins of each others' drafts into their journals, writing about the differences in their lives and families; revision as Brandie and I write in journals back and forth about the images of teachers we've grown up with and what it can mean to see one's self as a teacher. There's revision too as I no longer reserve the space in the margins for my pen. Have I eliminated teacher as "superego," as regulatory voice? No. But just as Freud didn't posit the id, the ego, and the superego as absolute, distinct realms, I'm trying to blur the boundaries and populate this space with multiple voices, relationships, and tones.

Toward an Excess-ive Theory of Revision

"[A]t every point of *opposition*," writes Gayle Elliott (1994) in an essay about the tensions between feminist theory and creative writing, "is a point — an *opportunity* — of *intersection*" (p. 107, Elliott's emphases). "Limits," Ann Berthoff (1981) writes, "make choice possible and thus free the imagination" (p. 77). These words also apply to that opposition between the fullness of a life and the limits of genre and community. Yes, writers do confront languages already configured for them. Yes, we do write within powerful institutional gazes that can seem as impervious and punishing as the barbed wire that lines this country's southern border, and yes, identities do exceed the bounds of what's called permissible and appropriate in a given genre, discipline, or classroom, creating narratives of loss and of compromise. But Copjec, Fleiger, Pratt, Le Dœuff, Trinh, Marshall, and a great many writers more demonstrate that opposition *can* become intersection, a contact zone populated with activity, meaning, and the kind of revision that comes from working at the borders of community, writing to exceed the limits of a given language and form.

These writers also demonstrate that the first-person narrative, accompanied by practices of re-vision, doesn't necessarily produce "the ideology of sentimental realism" and reification of "a single authoring point of view" — the troubling limits of an "expressivist" conception of composing that David Bartholomae (1995) argues convincingly against (p. 69). When we understand with Joan Copjec that the "real" can't be inhabited, that even the most seemingly "complete" and "authentic" narrative has its limits and inexpressible excesses, we can begin to read at the limits. We can value not so much the "genuine voice" of a personal narrative, or its "candor" or "unique sensibility," but rather the activity of this writer at the border between text and context, between the fullness of experience and the limits of language that can be worked, transgressed, and radically revised.

When I return to composition studies from this migration into psychoanalysis, feminism, philosophy, and fiction, I find plenty of examples of working at the borders and transforming opposition into intersection. Histories of rhetoric, for example, show the historical specificity, the historical *limits*, of conventional forms for teaching writing like the five-paragraph essay and the rhetorical modes. In making visible the boundaries those forms describe, these histories open up the possibility of — and need for — migration.[11] Teachers of creative writing like Gayle Elliott show how the borders separating composition, creative writing, and critical theory can be redrawn, urging the greatest possibility of movement across "creative" and "critical" genres and identities. Alice Gillam (1991) redefines writing centers from a "battleground" (where students must choose between either focusing, cutting, and controlling or leaving a first draft as is) to a site where writers "*flesh out* the contradictions" and "*puzzle over* the off-key shifts in voice," as a way of discovering rather than imposing focus (p. 7, my emphases). In "Dialogic Learning across Disciplines," Marilyn Cooper (1994b), like

Gillam, migrates toward the theories of Mikhail Bakhtin to consider that disciplinary conventions aren't fixed entities to be acquired by students, but are subject to "the forces of unification and the forces of diversification," making it possible for students to participate in the work of diversification as well (p. 532). Min-Zhan Lu (1994) dramatizes how that participation takes place when members of her first-year composition class examine an apparent "error" in a student's text *as* a richly nuanced and meaningful stylistic choice. Through this revision, they create a contact zone between the official codes of school and other languages students bring to this setting; they reconsider academic production as involving "approximating, negotiating, and revising" among contending codes — *including* those traditionally excluded from academic discourse (p. 447).

Lu especially helps me respond to teachers who fear that encouraging an excess-ive understanding of revision will confuse and even harm students both struggling with alien academic discourses and writing for professors who value neatly managed and monovocal meanings. Forces of unification, as well as of diversification, are always present in a classroom as students and teachers bring with them a range of histories, experiences, and assumptions about the limits and possibilities of writing in classrooms.[12] Rather than taking academic conventions as natural or as unquestionably superior to other language practices, rather than ignore these varied histories and varied understandings of just what the limits are, Lu writes that "the process of negotiation encourages students to struggle with such unifying forces" (p. 457) — to resist for a moment the work of subordination, coherence, and control; to pause, reflect, and consider the complexities of their choices; to realize that there *are* choices. Instead of confusing or misleading students, this renaming of error as style to be *puzzled over, thought through* (the same way teachers and students would puzzle over and think through the stylistic choices of a Gertrude Stein) offers those who want to resist a single official style, the community-based practices of revision, reflection, and argumentation they need to do so; it also offers those familiar with the discourses of school a view of that style's limits, as well as a view of the chinks and the cracks through which they might stray.

In composition's process legacy we can also find, I believe, practices of revision and reflection that can guide students and teachers as they consider revision as getting restless with a draft's initial meanings and representations, as seeking alternatives. Ann Berthoff's philosophy and practices, for instance, have always sought to engage the "form-finding and form-creating powers of the mind" in the "possibility of changing" a reality (1981, pp. 85, 92). Her practice of glossing invites students to reflect and revise along the borders of their texts — to "think about their thinking" and "interpret their interpretations," to see the limits and the choices there — while her practice of interpretive paraphrase offers a writer the means to write toward what exceeds. The double-entry notebook creates a visible space of critical exile where one can look back on, name, and rename initial meanings and representations; the question, "What's the opposite case?" encourages migrating from and complicating a first draft's focus.

I could continue — migrating from Berthoff's revisionary pedagogy to considering Elbow and Belanoff's loop writing as prodigality, Sondra Perl's open-ended composing process as creating a contact zone between forces of unification and diversification. But my point is this: These theorists tell me we need to remain at the intersection between "process" and "post-process" conceptions of composing, not quickly push past that intersection, not call one side the "past" and the other the "present." We need more border talk between the classroom practices and detailed case studies of the 1970s and 1980s, and current calls for institutionwide revisions of community, genre, academic discourse, and academic authority. (It's Flower and Hayes, I realize, who first showed me what I could learn about my classrooms through writing and reflecting on case studies; Elbow continues to invite me to turn off the computer screen as I draft.) Investigating the borders, we can refuse the gesture of projecting theoretical incapacity onto others; we resist *that* mirror for establishing authority. At the intersection, process pedagogies can be revitalized through examining how race, class, gender, ethnicity, sexual orientation — students' and teachers' many and varied cultural and personal histories — inform their writing, reading, and revising. And at the intersection teachers can both question and reclaim practices of revision we and our students need if we are to enact our many visions of change, if we are to be able, on a day-to-day basis, to question, intervene, and create; if we are to be able, on a day-to-day basis, to confront confusion, turn opposition into intersection, and create from the experience of limits the experience of choice.

Taking the sentence about her father from her adoption draft, Moira revises, creating another essay that considers her father's beliefs about what her decisions should be. With that draft comes another source of restlessness, though, as Moira considers that her responses, her beliefs, aren't in this writing. In the writing center she places another sheet of paper beside the draft and, asking of each paragraph, "Where am I in this?" she begins to write back to her draft on the new page — a kind of excess-ive version of glossing. "I think," she says after twenty minutes of this writing, "that the thing is this: My father always taught me that the decisions we make should bring us peace. But what we both have to learn is that we may have different ideas about what peace is, what decisions are right for me." It's close to the end of our meeting in the writing center and Moira checks her syllabus to see when her draft is due. She talks about leaving the draft as is or cutting up the paragraphs of both writings seeing what would happen if she tried to put them together. She talks about rewriting the first paragraph with a new emphasis on what she and her father need to learn, and she talks too about taking both pieces of writing to her composition class' next draft workshop, asking her small-group members what they think.

Moira talks too, as she's packing up, about her father's uneasy childhood, how he dropped out of school, why it's so important to him that her life be perfect. "Is that history a part of what you're talking about in your draft?" I ask, and Moira nods. "It should be," she says. "It says why. It tells me why."

Something Missing, Something Else

When Moira, like Brandie, whose words began this chapter, dares to consider that there's something missing in her text, something more, she recognizes the limits of that text and there, at the limit, she imagines what might happen next. What happens next is talking and writing on the borders of a neat and tidy draft, recognizing that its incompleteness isn't a tragedy at all, but a site of choice including the choice to stop for now, including the choice to continue. What happens is Moira and I both know that in a few weeks some of this writing will be graded, that she will decide which. Meanwhile there's time, here and there, in the chinks and cracks of her work and school schedule, for Moira to migrate toward questions other than: *What will get me an A?*

But this kind of work can only happen — *really happen* — within settings like Moira's writing class that promote and support an excessive understanding of revision: one that questions the ideal of the complete, contained, and disciplined body, the complete, contained, and disciplined text; one that takes the double perspective that revision involves both movement toward social goals *and* questioning what's being perpetuated or omitted in the process. Those questions can return a writer to invention as marginal glosses carry into other writings, as an interpretive paraphrase grows into something too big, too complicated to be easily integrated into the paper from which it came. So that students don't feel overwhelmed by the reflections these texts-in-progress mirror back, we also need to situate these practices in relationships that offer challenge and support like Brandie's with her journal partner and Scott with his reading of Tim O'Brien. Because investigating limits and straying from what may have been comfortable boundaries can be disorienting, dismaying, a threat to one's sense of self and to the life of a draft, students need the greatest possibility of choices about when to ask: *Something missing, something else?* In my classes this has meant that some students revise a particular draft by taking the same general topic, migrating into another genre, seeing how an autobiographical narrative, for instance, might look as a poem, a collage, a research project, a letter, or a fictional story. Meanwhile, others revise not by returning to a particular draft but to a journal entry (a kind of revision advocated by Ken Macrorie), seeing its limits and how this writing might be carried on. In one case a student struggling with the idea of revision reread a favorite book from his adolescence; his revision took the form of writing about that experience of rereading. In institutional settings, including my classrooms, revision *does* become another limit, another constraint, a social ideal to which students feel they must adapt.

Around that word *revision*, though, there are borders students and teachers can name, question, negotiate, and rename, creating excess-ive understandings of what revisionary work can mean.

This kind of revision, however, depends on teachers supporting students' work at the intersection. It asks teachers to practice forms of response and evaluation that make sense of such work instead of operating out of a double standard that allows many of us to feel confident reading the excess-ive writings of a Joyce, Dickinson, or Foucault, but dismayed before a student who is writing at the line between what's comfortable and familiar and what's challenging, strange, and new.[13] This kind of revision depends on a teacher's ability to revise as well, to turn that question — Something missing, something else? — back on his or her reading of a student's draft, on what the limits of that reading are, what other ways of reading there might be.

Here, though, I come to the limits of this chapter and of this book, with a recognition that there's a great deal missing, a great deal more. Or I come to an intersection between this project I'm trying to finish and future projects I imagine, including:

- Where and when do teachers begin to feel restless with their ways of responding to students' texts, suggesting an intersection between a full, excess-ive experience of reading and the limits of prefigured forms for response? Where and when do teachers begin to ask, "Something missing, something else?" of their responses?

- What happens when teachers bring their reading of students' texts into dialogue with their reading of other writers whose work pushes against any single "Ideal Text" (to borrow Knoblauch and Brannon's apt and Lacanian phrase)?[14] Or, given that many teachers have argued precisely for such an intersection, what works against this happening or against this happening more?

- What would it mean to bring an excess-ive understanding of revision into dialogue with current research in the use of portfolios and of contract grading? To what extent do these practices of assessment in particular institutional contexts continue to perpetuate the ideal of complete, contained, disciplined texts? To what extent do these practices, again in particular institutional contexts, work to subvert such an ideal, pointing toward the excess-ive instead?

- What would it mean to alter the question, "How is this piece of writing finished?" into "What work does this writing suggest that might be carried on?" and "What are the future projects that might arise from it?"

- What would it mean to consider the literature classroom as a place that's also very much concerned with the investigation of

"Something missing, something else?" Can we locate the work of interpretation in a literature class, as in the composition class, at the intersection between full, excess-ive experiences of reading and the limits of prefigured forms for response?

- What would happen in a fiction workshop if students and their teacher investigated, examined, and revised the limits of cultural notions of who a fiction writer or poet is and how he or she works? What would it mean to create such a workshop that actively seeks to address, as fiction writer Eve Shelnutt puts it, "the myth that works of the imagination and full consciousness are anti-thetical" (1989, p. 5)? What difference would this make to students' writing and to their reading of each others' work?[15]

- And since some ideas about just what "full consciousness" means in contemporary critical and literary theory make me restless, what intersections can I discover between my own excess-ive experiences as a writer of fiction and the limits of the theories through which I make sense of those experiences? How can Le Dœuff's project of working between philosophy and feminism become my own as I migrate between fiction and feminism, teacher and writer?

But all of these questions are, really, various versions of, departures from, and returns to this: What will happen when we begin to read, write, and teach at that tense, problematic, and fascinating boundary between *individual* and *society* — reading, writing, and teaching with an excess-ive and pluralized understanding of these terms and of the intricate braids that make it impossible for us to distinguish between the two? What if we read to see boundaries our texts and our students are getting restless within? What if we learned to watch for places where a text begins to resist, get unruly, and maybe even stray? What will happen when we read with the belief that our students do have, as Ross Winterowd wrote in 1965, *"restless minds"* that we can glimpse and encourage in their writing — if we get restless with static ways of reading, conventional forms of response (p. 93)?

Which suggests yet another question: What will happen when we begin to read to discover not *whether* a student needs to revise (suggesting the responses of no or yes, finished or not, still within that frame that values the complete and the contained), but to discover instead where and how, in or around this writing, he or she *has already started* to revise? That's work we can notice, work we can value, work that might continue within or beyond this not-so-single text. What would this mean for our students' writing? For how teachers and students talk about writing? For how students and teachers understand what revision can be?

As an undergraduate in an advanced composition class (before I migrated over into the fiction workshop, before I'd come up hard against the limits of my writing), I turned in an essay every Friday, got it back every Monday with an A. Especially since I then worked for a daily paper, I was a practiced writer — maybe too practiced and I knew it too. "Wonderfully wrought throughout" the professor wrote beside those A's. "Graceful." "Lovely." I felt gratified by those comments and A's. Restless too. Not so sure these essays really were so perfect and complete. Not sure what to do about it either, what questions to ask and where. At the semester's end the professor told us to return to the essay that received the lowest grade, revise it for a higher one.

"Mine were all A's," I told him after class. "What should I do?"

"You don't have to do anything," he said. "Your work is fine as is."

It wasn't, it isn't, not at all — but that's another story. Or the story of why I'm writing now, still restless, not satisfied.

Notes

1. I've taken these constructions of revision from three current composition textbooks but want to avoid attaching authors' names to them, since I found a dozen other textbooks that offered similar understandings of revision, telling me that none of these constructions can be attributed to a single author.

2. Michele Le Dœuff's (1989) *The Philosophical Imaginary*, which ties philosophy's systematic suppression of its own contradictions to its desire to gain and maintain academic status, also offers a way to read composition's history and particularly its history of teaching revision as the containment, rather than exploration, of dissonance. Likewise Mikhail Bakhtin's (1968) *Rabelais and His World* traces the ideological history of an emphasis on the text as a "classical body" that is "entirely finished, completed, strictly limited" — and, so, seemingly divorced from "living practice and class struggle" (pp. 320, 471).

3. In this chapter, I'll be looking at the most prominent and frequently cited constructions of revision from composition's *expressivist, cognitivist,* and *social constructionist* orientations. There are crucial differences, though, among composition teachers within these orientations and individual voices that have argued for or suggested different constructions of revision. Susan Osborn (1991), for instance, seeks to "provide a context in which revision and revision are explicated as both integral to the writing process and a way of knowing ourselves as readers and writers" (p. 270). Min-Zhan Lu (1994) also stresses "writing as a process of re-seeing" — including re-seeing, negotiating, and revising the conventions of academic discourse (p. 449). Recent articles in the *Writing Center Journal* — by, for instance, Alice Gillam (1991) and Cynthia Haynes-Burton (1994) — likewise work against the grain of revision as a one-way movement from writer-based to reader-based prose. In this chapter, then, I have the double aims of (1) explicating the construction of revision against which these teachers write and (2) writing toward the construction of revision their work suggests.

4. The terms *writer-based* and *reader-based* prose come from Linda Flower's (1979) essay "Writer-Based Prose: A Cognitive Basis for Problems in Writing," and her terms have given compositionists ways of thinking about the

kind of audience for whom a piece of writing might be intended. This book, for instance, is decidedly intended for others to read and so it might be called *reader-based*, while the journal in which I considered the questions, problems, and breakthroughs of this book's writing is decidedly intended for me alone and so might be called *writer-based*. The problem I'm working with in this essay, though, is how these terms have been lifted from their original context, *writer-based* becoming increasingly used as synonymous with *solipsistic*, while *reader-based* is increasingly reduced to meaning *clear, concise, and instantly, easily understandable* and reduced to the single, unquestioned goal of revision.

5. The most thoughtful and searching critique I've found of the psychoanalytic frame, particularly the Lacanian psychoanalytic frame, in the classroom is Ann Murphy's (1989) "Transference and Resistance in the Basic Writing Classroom: Problematics and Praxis." Though I read that essay as underwritten by the assumptions of ego psychology — the need for students and teachers to adapt to and function within a social reality, a belief in stable and socially rewarding roles students can write toward, along with a promise to students that mastery of writing conventions can be "congruent with her or his own needs" (p. 185) — this statement from Murphy remains central to my thinking about revision in this book and in my teaching: "[A] process which seeks further to decenter [students] can be dangerous" (p. 180). Like Murphy's students in basic writing classrooms, the students I meet are already (often in ways that aren't readily apparent) decentered, divided, disoriented. They don't need or want a teacher, from her position of relative security and power, to create decentering experiences for them. What needs to be decentered instead, I think, is the view that learning and writing can ever be safe, neat, and tidy, leading us to be surprised, dismayed, and totally unprepared when we find again and again that no, learning and writing are not safe and neat at all. What needs to be decentered, too, I think, is the view that essays, unlike our lives, should contain nothing of disorientation, uncertainty, and division.

6. In *Dora* (Freud 1962a), for example, Freud contrasts the hysterical patient's "inability to give an ordered history" of her life with that of a patient whose "story came out perfectly clearly and connectedly" and whose case, Freud thus concluded, could not be one of hysteria (p. 31). In other words, Freud equates the unruly, disorderly, and discontinuous with emotional illness, and the clear, calm, and perfectly connected with emotional health. Ironically, Freud's own text might be called hysterical, then, with its many and sometimes acknowledged incompletenesses, contradictions, and omissions.

7. Elizabeth Wright (1989) takes a closer look at the forms of psychoanalysis that have influenced literary studies and theories and (by implication) composition, too.

8. Recently, however, Recchio (1994) suggests a much more dialogic and recursive process of revision in which society shapes individuals' texts, but in which many individuals in turn speak back to and shape society. "Realizing [this] potential of the essay in the Freshman English classroom, however," he writes, "is a thorny problem, for writing pedagogy has been dominated by formalized self-contained systematic thought where play, discovery, and recursiveness are squeezed out of discourse, and subordinated to a misleading formalist consistency and clarity" (p. 224).

9. Copjec's figuring of an unsatisfiable and restless desire runs against the grain of consumer culture that depends on our believing that if we can

acquire the right sweater/car/hand cream/theoretical frame/language/publication/degree we will be satisfied, reunited with our complete being. There is no "Other" that can complete us, no matter what advertisements, textbooks, how-to guides, and academic programs may promise. She suggests to me that a classroom that seeks to understand this and at least question the ideal of the whole, complete, unified, and nothing-left-to-say text is also a classroom that prepares students and teachers to see themselves as critics and creators, rather than frustrated consumers, of culture.

10. For further exploration see Le Dœuff's essay "Long Hair, Short Ideas" in *The Philosophical Imaginary* (1989a) and the "Second Notebook" in *Hipparchia's Choice* (1991).

11. See, for example, Sharon Crowley (1991) and James Berlin (1984).

12. Carrie Leverenz (1994) offers a careful and disturbing examination of such forces of unification at work in students' responses to each others' writing in a composition classroom.

13. I'm indebted to Wendy Bishop and Hans Ostrom (1994a) who made this point in their 1994 MLA presentation, "Letting the Boundaries Draw Themselves."

14. Freud's *Dora* (1962a) or *Interpretation of Dreams* (1962b, IV), with all of their assertions, examples, clarifications, contradictions, caveats, and footnotes that continue for a page or more, strike me as excellent choices for disrupting stable notions of what can constitute "academic" writing. Try reading one of these, then telling someone, "Writing in academia must be clear, consistent, and concise." I don't think such an assertion is possible after Freud.

15. I think of these questions especially because recently a teacher remarked to me that students in her class who name themselves as "Writers" — capital "W" — also produce the most "writer-based" and "egocentric" work she's ever seen. I suspect, though, that the writing of such a student isn't at all writer based, individualistic, divorced from readers and the social realm. Instead, that writing and that writer are probably very much caught up in and overdetermined by those social myths of the solitary, misunderstood, at-odds-with-society poetic genius — "a breath-mist," poet and fiction writer Fred Chappell (1992) writes, that one needs to clear away in order to begin to write (p. 21).

Works Cited

Ahlschwede, Margrethe. 1992. "No Breaks, No Time-Outs, No Place to Hide: A Writing Lab Journal." *Writing on the Edge* 3: 21–40.

Alton, Cheryl. 1993. Comment on "Crossing Lines," *College English* 6: 666–669.

Anzaldua, Gloria. 1987. *Borderlands / La Frontera: The New Mestiza*. San Francisco, CA: Spinsters/Aunt Lute.

Atwell, Nancie. 1987. *In the Middle*. Portsmouth, NH: Boynton/Cook.

Atwood, Margaret. 1991. "The Bog Man." In *Wilderness Tips*. New York: Doubleday.

Bakhtin, Mikhail. 1968. *Rabelais and His World*. Translated by Helene Iswolsky. Cambridge, MA: MIT Press.

———. 1981. *The Dialogic Imagination*. Translated by Caryl Emerson and Michael Holquist. Edited by Michael Holquist. Austin, TX: University of Texas Press.

Bartholomae, David. 1983. "Writing Assignments: Where Writing Begins." In *Forum*. Edited by Patricia L. Stock. Upper Montclair, NJ: Boynton/Cook. 300–312.

———. 1985. "Inventing the University." In *When a Writer Can't Write*. Edited by Mike Rose. New York: Guilford Press. 134–165.

———. 1990. Response to "Personal Writing, Professional Ethos, and the Voice of 'Common Sense.'" *Pre/Text* 11.1–2: 122–130.

———. 1995. "Writing with Teachers: A Conversation with Peter Elbow." *College Composition and Communication* 46: 62–71.

Beach, Richard. 1986. "Demonstrating Techniques for Assessing Writing in the Writing Conference." *College Composition and Communication* 37: 56–65.

Berlin, James. 1984. *Writing Instruction in Nineteenth-Century American Colleges*. Carbondale, IL: Southern Illinois University Press.

Berthoff, Ann E. 1981. *The Making of Meaning*. Portsmouth, NH: Boynton/Cook.

Bigras, Julien. 1978. "French and American Psychoanalysis." In *Psychoanalysis, Creativity, and Literature*. Edited by Alan Roland. New York: Columbia University Press. 11–21.

Bishop, Wendy. 1990. *Something Old, Something New: College Writing Teachers and Classroom Change*. Carbondale, IL: Southern Illinois University Press.

———. 1993. "Writing Is/And Therapy?: Raising Questions about Writing Classrooms and Writing Program Administration." *Journal of Advanced Composition* 13: 503–516.

——— and Hans Ostrom. 1994a. "Letting the Boundaries Draw Themselves: What Theory and Practice Have Been Trying to Tell Us." MLA Convention. San Diego, CA. 29 December.

Bizzell, Patricia. 1984. "William Perry and Liberal Education." *College English* 46: 447–454.

Bleich, David. 1988. *The Double Perspective: Language, Literacy, and Social Relations*. New York: Oxford University Press.

———. 1989. "Genders of Writing." *Journal of Advanced Composition* 9: 10–25.

Bloom, Lynn Z. 1992. "Teaching College English as a Woman." *College English* 54: 818–825.

Brand, Alice. 1991. "Social Cognition, Emotions, and the Psychology of Writing." *Journal of Advanced Composition* 11: 395–407.

Brannon, Lil, and C. H. Knoblauch. 1982. "On Students' Rights to Their Own Texts: A Model of Teacher Response." *College Composition and Communication* 33: 157–166.

Brannon, Lil. 1993. "M[other]: Lives on the Outside." *Written Communication* 10: 457–465.

———. 1994. "Rewriting the Story: Expressivism and the Problem of Experience." Conference on College Composition and Communication, Washington, DC. 23 March.

Bridwell-Bowles, Lillian. 1992. "Discourse and Diversity: Experimental Writing within the Academy." *College Composition and Communication* 43: 349–368.

———. 1995. "Freedom, Form, Function: Varieties of Academic Discourse." *College Composition and Communication* 46: 46–61.

Brodkey, Linda. 1994. "Writing on the Bias." *College English* 56: 527–547.

Brooke, Robert. 1987. "Lacan, Transference, and Writing Instruction." *College English* 49: 679–691.

———. 1988. "Modeling a Writer's Identity: Reading and Imitation in the Writing Classroom." *College Composition and Communication* 39: 23–41.

———, Judith Levin, and Joy Ritchie. 1994. "Teaching Composition and Reading Lacan: An Exploration in Wild Analysis." *Writing Theory and Critical Theory*. Edited by John Clifford and John Schilb. New York: MLA. 159–175.

Broughton, T. Alan. 1993. "Preparing the Way," "On This Side of the Canvas," "Death as a Cloudless Day," and "Refuge." *Prairie Schooner* 67 (Fall): 51–55.

Bruffee, Kenneth A. 1984. "Peer Tutoring and the 'Conversation of Mankind.'" In *Writing Centers: Theory and Administration*. Edited by Gary A. Olson. Urbana, IL: NCTE. 3–15.

Cain, Mary Ann. 1995. *Revisioning Writers' Talk: Gender and Culture in Acts of Composing*. Albany, NY: State University of New York Press.

Chappell, Fred. 1992. "First Attempts." In *My Poor Elephant: 27 Male Writers at Work*. Edited by Eve Shelnutt. Atlanta, GA: Longstreet. 17–29.

Clark, Beverly Lyon, and Sonja Weidenhaupt. 1992. "On Blocking and Unblocking Sonja: A Case Study in Two Voices." *College Composition and Communication* 43: 55–74.

Clark, Irene L. 1993. "Portfolio Grading and the Writing Center." *The Writing Center Journal* 13: 48–62.

Clark, Suzanne. 1994. "Rhetoric, Social Construction, and Gender: Is It Bad to Be Sentimental?" In *Writing Theory and Critical Theory*. Edited by John Clifford and John Schilb. New York: MLA. 96–108.

Con Davis, Robert. 1987. "Pedagogy, Lacan, and the Freudian Subject." *College English* 49: 749–755.

Cooper, Marilyn. 1994a. "Really Useful Knowledge: A Cultural Studies Agenda for Writing Centers." *The Writing Center Journal* 14: 97–111.

———. 1994b. "Dialogic Learning across Disciplines." *Journal of Advanced Composition* 14: 531–546.

Copjec, Joan. 1989. "Cutting Up." In *Between Feminism and Psychoanalysis*. Edited by Teresa Brennan. London: Routledge. 227–246.

Crowley, Sharon. 1991. "A Personal Essay on Freshman English." *Pre/Text* 12.3–4: 156–176.

Daniell, Beth. 1994. "Composing (as) Power." *College Composition and Communication* 45: 238–246.

de Beauvoir, Simone. 1959. *Memoirs of a Dutiful Daughter*. Translated by James Kirkup. Cleveland, OH: World Publishing.

———. 1962. *The Prime of Life*. Translated by Peter Green. Cleveland, OH: World Publishing.

de Lauretis, Teresa. 1987. *Technologies of Gender*. Bloomington, IN: Indiana University Press.

Deletiner, Carole. 1992. "Crossing Lines." *College English* 54: 809–817.

Eady, Cornelius. 1993. "Photo of Dexter Gordon, About to Solo, 1965." *Prairie Schooner* 67 (Fall): 11.

Ebert, Teresa L. 1991. "The 'Difference' of Postmodern Feminism," *College English* 53: 886–904.

Ede, Lisa. 1994. "Reading the Writing Process." In *Taking Stock: The Writing Process Movement in the 90s*. Edited by Lad Tobin and Thomas Newkirk. Portsmouth, NH: Boynton/Cook. 31–43.

Elbow, Peter. 1973. *Writing without Teachers*. New York: Oxford University Press.

———. 1981. *Writing with Power*. New York: Oxford University Press.

————. 1987. "Closing My Eyes As I Speak: An Argument for Ignoring Audience." *College English* 49: 50–69.

———— and Pat Belanoff. 1989. *Community of Writers.* New York: McGraw-Hill.

————. 1990. *What Is English?* New York: MLA.

Elliott, Gayle. 1994. "Pedagogy in Penumbra: Teaching, Writing, and Feminism in the Fiction Workshop." In *Colors of a Different Horse: Rethinking Creative Writing Theory and Pedagogy.* Edited by Wendy Bishop and Hans Ostrom. Urbana, IL: NCTE. 100–126.

Ellsworth, Elizabeth. 1989. "Why Doesn't This Feel Empowering? Working through the Repressive Myths of Critical Pedagogy." *Harvard Educational Review* 59: 297–324.

Faigley, Lester. 1992. *Fragments of Rationality: Postmodernity and the Subject of Composition.* Pittsburgh, PA: University of Pittsburgh Press.

————, and Stephen Witte. 1981. "Analyzing Revision." *College Composition and Communication* 32: 400–414.

Felman, Shoshana. 1987. *Jacques Lacan and the Adventure of Insight: Psychoanalysis in Contemporary Culture.* Cambridge, MA: Harvard University Press.

————. 1993. *What Does a Woman Want?: Reading and Sexual Difference.* Baltimore, MD: Johns Hopkins University Press.

Flax, Jane. 1990. *Thinking Fragments: Psychoanalysis, Feminism, and Postmodernism in the Contemporary West.* Berkeley, CA: University of California Press.

Flieger, Jerry Aline. 1990. "The Female Subject: (What) Does Woman Want?" In *Psychoanalysis and . . .* Edited by Richard Feldstein and Henry Sussman. New York: Routledge. 54–63.

Flower, Linda. 1979. "Writer-Based Prose: A Cognitive Basis for Problems in Writing." *College English* 41: 19–37.

————, John Hayes, Linda Carey, et al. 1986. "Detection, Diagnosis, and the Strategies of Revision." *College Composition and Communication* 37: 16–55.

Freire, Paulo. 1992 (1970). *Pedagogy of the Oppressed.* New York: Continuum.

Freud, Sigmund. 1962a. *Dora: An Analysis of a Case of Hysteria.* New York: Collier/Macmillan.

————. 1962b (1958). *The Standard Edition of the Complete Psychological Works of Sigmund Freud.* Edited and translated by James Strachey. London: Hogarth.

Frey, Olivia. 1990. "Beyond Literary Darwinism: Women's Voices and Critical Discourse." *College English* 52: 507–526.

Fuller, Margaret. 1992. *The Essential Margaret Fuller.* Edited by Jeffrey Steele. New Brunswick, NJ: Rutgers University Press.

Fulwiler, Toby. 1990. "Looking and Listening for My Voice." *College Composition and Communication* 41: 214–220.

Gallop, Jane. 1982. *The Daughter's Seduction: Feminism and Psychoanalysis.* Ithaca, NY: Cornell University Press.

————. 1988. "The Seduction of an Analogy." In *Thinking through the Body.* New York: Columbia University Press.

Gere, Anne Ruggles. 1994. "Kitchen Tables and Rented Rooms: The Extracurriculum of Composition." *College Composition and Communication* 45: 75–92.

Gillam, Alice M. 1991. "Writing Center Ecology: A Bakhtinian Perspective." *The Writing Center Journal* 11: 3–11.

Glass, James M. 1993. *Shattered Selves: Multiple Personality in a Postmodern World*. Ithaca, NY: Cornell University Press.

Gore, Jennifer. 1993. *The Struggle for Pedagogies: Critical and Feminist Discourses as Regimes of Truth*. New York: Routledge.

Harris, Muriel. 1995. "Talking in the Middle: Why Writers Need Writing Tutors." *College English* 57: 27–42.

Haynes-Burton, Cynthia. 1994. "'Hanging Your Alias on Their Scene': Writing Centers, Graffiti, and Style." *Writing Center Journal* 14: 112–124.

Heath, Shirley Brice. 1982. *Ways with Words: Language, Life, and Work in Communities and Classrooms*. Cambridge, MA: Cambridge University Press.

———. 1994. "Finding in History the Right to Estimate." *College Composition and Communication* 45: 97–102.

Helmers, Marguerite H. 1994. *Writing Students: Composition Testimonials and Representations of Students*. Albany, NY: State University of New York Press.

Herzberg, Bruce. 1994. "Community Service and Critical Teaching." *College Composition and Communication* 45: 307–319.

hooks, bell. 1989. *Talking Back*. Boston, MA: South End Press.

Horner, Bruce. 1994. "Mapping Errors and Expectations for Basic Writing: From the 'Frontier Field' to 'Border Country,'" *English Education* 26: 29–51.

Hunter, Ian. 1988. *Culture and Government: The Emergence of Literacy Education*. London: Macmillan.

Jardine, Alice. 1989. "Notes for an Analysis." In *Between Feminism and Psychoanalysis*. Edited by Teresa Brennan. London: Routledge. 73–85.

Jouve, Nicole Ward. 1991. *White Woman Speaks with Forked Tongue: Criticism as Autobiography*. London: Routledge.

Kalpakian, Laura. 1991. "My Life as a Boy." In *The Confidence Woman: 26 Women Writers at Work*. Edited by Eve Shelnutt. Atlanta, GA: Longstreet. 43–57.

Kingston, Maxine Hong. 1976. *The Woman Warrior: Memories of a Girlhood among Ghosts*. New York, NY: Knopf.

Kirsch, Gesa B. 1993. *Women Writing the Academy: Audience, Authority, and Transformation*. Carbondale, IL: Southern Illinois University Press.

Knoblauch, C. H. 1990. "Literacy and the Politics of Education." In *The Right to Literacy*. Edited by Andrea A. Lunsford, Helene Moglen, and James Slevin. New York: MLA. 74–80.

———. 1991. "Critical Teaching and Dominant Culture." In *Composition and Resistance*. Edited by C. Mark Hurlbert and Michael Blitz. Portsmouth, NH: Heinemann. 12–21.

———, and Lil Brannon. 1993. *Critical Teaching and the Idea of Literacy*. Portsmouth, NH: Boynton/Cook.

Kristeva, Julia. 1986a. "A New Type of Intellectual: The Dissident." Translated by Sean Hand. In *The Kristeva Reader*. Edited by Toril Moi. New York, NY: Columbia University Press.

———. 1986b. "Women's Time." Translated by Alice Jardine and Harry Blake. *The Kristeva Reader*. Edited by Toril Moi. New York, NY: Columbia University Press.

———. 1987. *In the Beginning Was Love: Psychoanalysis and Faith*. Translated by Arthur Goldhammer. New York, NY: Columbia University Press.

Lacan, Jacques. 1977a. *Ecrits: A Selection*. Translated by Alan Sheridan. New York: Norton.

———. 1977b. *The Four Fundamental Concepts of Psychoanalysis*. Translated by Alan Sheridan. London: Hogarth.

Lamb, Catherine. 1991. "Beyond Argument in Feminist Composition." *College Composition and Communication* 42: 11–24.

Le Dœuff, Michele. 1989. *The Philosophical Imaginary.* Translated by Colin Gordon. Stanford, CA: Stanford University Press.

———. 1990. "Women, Reason, Etc." *Differences: A Journal of Feminist Cultural Studies* 2: 1–13.

———. 1991. *Hipparchia's Choice: An Essay Concerning Women, Philosophy, etc.* Translated by Trista Selous. Oxford: Blackwell.

———. 1993. "Harsh Times." *New Left Review* 199 (May–June): 127–139.

Leverenz, Carrie Shively. 1994. "Peer Response in the Multicultural Composition Classroom: Dissensus — A Dream (Deferred)." *Journal of Advanced Composition* 14: 167–186.

Lorde, Audre. 1980. *The Cancer Journals.* Argyle, NY: Spinsters.

Lu, Min-Zhan. 1994. "Professing Multiculturalism: The Politics of Style in the Contact Zone." *College Composition and Communication* 45: 442–458.

Lunsford, Andrea. 1991. "Collaboration, Control, and the Idea of a Writing Center." *The Writing Center Journal* 12: 3–10.

———, Helene Moglen, and James Slevin, eds. 1990. *The Right to Literacy.* New York: MLA.

Macrorie, Ken. 1970. *Telling Writing.* Rochelle Park, NJ: Hayden.

Marshall, Paule. 1984. *Praisesong for the Widow.* New York: Dutton.

Miller, Susan. 1994. "Composition as Cultural Artifact: Rethinking History as Theory." In *Writing Theory and Critical Theory.* Edited by John Clifford and John Schilb. New York: MLA. 19–32.

Moi, Toril. 1989. "Patriarchal Thought and the Drive for Knowledge." In *Between Feminism and Psychoanalysis.* Edited by Teresa Brennan. London: Routledge. 189–205.

Morrison, Toni. 1970. *The Bluest Eye.* New York: Washington Square.

Morson, Gary Saul. 1994. *Narrative and Freedom: The Shadows of Time.* New Haven, CT: Yale University Press.

Mortensen, Peter, and Gesa E. Kirsch. 1993. "On Authority in the Study of Writing." *College Composition and Communication* 44: 556–572.

Murphy, Ann. 1989. "Transference and Resistance in the Basic Writing Classroom: Problematics and Praxis." *College Composition and Communication* 40: 175–187.

Murray, Donald M. 1982. "Teaching the Other Self: The Writer's First Reader." *College Composition and Communication* 33: 140–147.

———. 1995 (1991). *The Craft of Revision.* 2nd ed. Fort Worth, TX: Harcourt Brace.

North, Stephen. 1984. "The Idea of a Writing Center." *College English* 46: 433–446.

———. 1990. "Personal Writing, Professional Ethos, and the Voice of 'Common Sense.'" *Pre/Text* 11.1–2: 105–119.

O'Brien, Tim. 1990. *The Things They Carried.* New York: Penguin.

———. 1994. "The Vietnam in Me." *The New York Times Magazine* October 2: 48–57.

O'Connor, Frank. 1988. "Guests of the Nation." In *Fiction 100*, 5th ed. Edited by James H. Pickering. New York: Macmillan. 1227–1235.

Ohmann, Richard. 1976. *English in America: A Radical View of the Profession.* New York: Oxford University Press.

Olsen, Tillie. 1976 (1956). "I Stand Here Ironing." In *Tell Me a Riddle.* New York: Dell.

Osborn, Susan. 1991. "'Revision/Re-Vision': A Feminist Writing Class." *Rhetoric Review* 9: 258–273.

Pontalis, J. B. 1978. "On Death-Work in Freud, in the Self, in Culture." In *Psychoanalysis, Creativity, and Literature.* Edited by Alan Roland. New York, NY: Columbia University Press. 85–95.

Pratt, Mary Louise. 1991. "Arts of the Contact Zone." In *Profession.* New York: MLA. 33–40.

Pratt, Minnie Bruce. 1991. *Rebellion: Essays 1980–1991.* Ithaca, NY: Firebrand.

Quandahl, Ellen. 1994. "The Anthropological Sleep of Composition." *Journal of Advanced Composition* 14: 413–429.

Ragland-Sullivan, Ellie. 1987. *Jacques Lacan and the Philosophy of Psychoanalysis.* Urbana and Chicago, IL: University of Illinois Press.

Recchio, Thomas. 1991. "A Bakhtinian Reading of Student Writing." *College Composition and Communication* 42: 446–454.

———. 1994. "On the Critical Necessity of 'Essaying.'" In *Taking Stock: The Writing Process Movement in the 90s.* Edited by Lad Tobin and Thomas Newkirk. Portsmouth, NH: Boynton/Cook. 219–235.

Rich, Adrienne. 1979. "When We Dead Awaken: Writing as Re-Vision." In *On Lies, Secrets, and Silence.* New York: Norton.

Ritchie, Joy. 1990. "Between the Trenches and the Ivory Towers: Divisions between University Professors and High School Teachers." In *Farther Along: Transforming Dichotomies in Rhetoric and Composition.* Edited by Kate Ronald and Hephzibah Roskelly. Portsmouth, NH: Boynton/Cook. 101–121.

Robinson, Marilynne. 1982. *Housekeeping.* New York: Bantam.

Rorty, Richard. 1991. "Feminism and Pragmatism." *Michigan Quarterly Review* 30 (Spring): 231–258.

Rose, Mike. 1989. *Lives on the Boundary: The Struggles and Achievements of America's Underprepared.* New York: Free Press; London: Collier Macmillan.

Rosenblatt, Louise. 1983 (1938). *Literature as Exploration.* 4th ed. New York: MLA.

———. 1993. "The Transactional Theory: Against Dualisms." *College English* 55: 377–386.

Rowbotham, Sheila. 1973. *Woman's Consciousness, Man's World.* London: Penguin.

Rushdie, Salman. 1990. *Haroun and the Sea of Stories.* New York: Viking.

Schuster, Charles I. 1985. "Mikhail Bakhtin as Rhetorical Theorist." *College English* 47: 594–607.

Severino, Carol. 1994. "Writing Centers as Linguistic Contact Zones and Borderlands." *The Writing Lab Newsletter* 19 (December): 1–5.

Shelnutt, Eve. 1989. *The Writing Room: Keys to the Craft of Fiction and Poetry.* Marietta, GA: Longstreet.

Silko, Leslie Marmon. 1977. *Ceremony.* New York: Viking Press.

Smith, Frank. 1986. *Insult to Intelligence: The Bureaucratic Invasion of Our Classrooms.* New York: Arbor House.

Sommers, Nancy. 1980. "Revision Strategies of Student Writers and Experienced Adult Writers." *College Composition and Communication* 31: 378–388.

Spellmeyer, Kurt. 1994. "Lost in the Funhouse: The Teaching of Writing and the Problem of Professional Narcissism." Division on the Teaching of Writing. MLA Convention. San Diego, CA. 29 December.

Sperling, Melanie, and Sarah Warshauer Freedman. 1987. "A Good Girl Writes Like a Good Girl." *Written Communication* 4: 343–369.

Spivak, Gayatri Chakravorty. 1989. "Feminism and Deconstruction Again: Negotiating with Unacknowledged Masculinism." In *Between Feminism and Psychoanalysis.* Edited by Teresa Brennan. London: Routledge. 206–223.

Stone, Leo. 1984. *Transference and Its Context: Selected Papers on Psychoanalysis.* New York: J. Aronson.

Su, Adrienne. 1993. "Alice Descending the Rabbit-Hole." *Prairie Schooner* 67 (Fall): 34–35.

Sunstein, Bonnie. 1994. *Composing a Culture: Inside a Summer Writing Program with High School Teachers.* Portsmouth, NH: Boynton/Cook.

Tobin, Lad. 1993. *Writing Relationships: What Really Happens in the Composition Class.* Portsmouth, NH: Boynton/Cook.

Tompkins, Jane. 1987. "Me and My Shadow." *New Literary History* 19: 169–178.

———. 1988. "Fighting Words: Unlearning to Write the Critical Essay." *Georgia Review* 42: 585–590.

———. 1992. "The Way We Live Now." *Change* 24 (November/December): 15–19.

Trimbur, John. 1989. "Consensus and Difference in Collaborative Learning." *College English* 51: 602–616.

———. 1994. "Taking the Social Turn: Teaching Writing Post-Process." *College Composition and Communication* 45: 108–118.

Trinh, T. Minh-ha. 1989. *Woman, Native, Other: Writing Postcoloniality and Feminism.* Bloomington, IN: Indiana University Press.

Warnock, Tilly, and John Warnock. 1984. "Liberatory Writing Centers: Restoring Authority to Writers." In *Writing Centers: Theory and Administration.* Edited by Gary A. Olson. Urbana, IL: NCTE. 16–23.

Weesner, Theodore. 1987 (1967). *The Car Thief.* New York: Vintage.

Welch, Nancy. 1993. "Resisting the Faith: Conversion, Resistance, and the Training of Teachers." *College English* 55: 387–401.

———. 1994. "The Cheating Kind." *Other Voices* 20 (Spring): 37–45.

———. 1996. "The Road from Prosperity." *Threepenny Review* 64 (Winter): 14–16.

Winnicott, D. W. 1971. *Playing and Reality.* London: Tavistock.

Winterowd, W. Ross. 1965. *Rhetoric and Writing.* Boston, MA: Allyn and Bacon.

Woodruff, Jay, ed. 1993. *A Piece of Work: Five Writers Discuss Their Revisions.* Iowa City, IA: University of Iowa Press.

Woolbright, Meg. 1992. "The Politics of Tutoring: Feminism with the Patriarchy." *The Writing Center Journal* 13: 16–30.

Wright, Elizabeth. 1989 (1984). *Psychoanalytic Criticism: Theory in Practice.* London: Routledge.

Welch's Insights as a Resource for Your Teaching

1. Welch values a vision of writing that runs counter to mainstream academic discourse. What sorts of practical difficulties might this vision present in your classroom, and how might you imagine handling them?

2. What do you make of Welch's use of psychoanalytic concepts to understand revision? How might some of these tools be helpful in

understanding other phases of the composing process and other aspects of the teaching of writing?

Welch's Insights as a Resource for Your Writing Classroom

1. Ask your students to reconsider a "finished" piece of writing. What sorts of things would they add to it if they were to lengthen it a great deal? What sorts of digressions would they undertake? Help them to realize that they are not simply tacking on more prose but are free to explore digressions that may entirely change the focus and thrust of the paper.

2. Ask your students to reflect on some of the potential digressions they delineated in question 1 as potential topics for future essays. Would they want to pursue any of these further? Which ones, and why?

Teaching Writing with Computers

Computer literacy is no longer optional; writers need computer literacy to succeed at the university and beyond. Today, teaching writing with computers has moved beyond teaching students how to use word processing features — like "cut and paste" — as an alternative to pencil and paper drafting and revising. Students' increasing aptitude and experience with computers prior to coming to the university, as well as increased access to technology, demand that we change the way we think about integrating computers into the writing classroom. Most exciting are the possibilities and opportunities that computers offer us to create interactive classrooms that provide forums for communication and feedback among diverse groups.

Because teacher and student expertise in working in computer-assisted or computer-mediated classrooms may vary greatly, and because technology is changing so rapidly, writing instructors must try to keep up to date by interacting with colleagues — whether at work, at conferences, or online — and by reading professional journals (see the Annotated Bibliography.

Computers and the Writing Classroom: A Look to the Future

Charles Moran

Charles Moran, in this first chapter from Reimagining Computers and Composition, *writes from his extensive experience teaching writing and working with computers in writing classrooms. Answering the question, "What is a writing classroom in 2050 . . . ?," he writes about the necessity for writing teachers to think seriously about present and potential uses of computer-mediated communication and to "begin to build, at least in our imaginations, the writing class of the coming virtual age."*

Moran cites three forces — "national dissatisfaction with schools as they are, the rising energy-cost of such schools, and the decreasing cost of computer and communications technology" — that make it imperative for writing teachers to rethink the experiences possible in the writing class-room of the future. He describes two existing classrooms: "the computer-equipped, brick-and-mortar classroom and the computer-mediated, on-line classroom." From his perspective ("not as a techno-groupie but as a moderately rational writing teacher"), Moran believes that computer technology creates unique opportunities for writing teachers to create, fine-tune, or maintain real interactive writing classrooms.

> The real impact in computers is not the silicon. It's not even the current software. It's the re-thinking.
>
> — Robert Frankston

The college writing classroom of the year 2050 will not be what it is today. But what will this writing classroom look like? What shapes and characteristics will it have? How will it be equipped? As Robert Frankston suggests in the epigraph, the future design of the writing classroom will be less the result of the new technology than it will be the result of the deep, merciless re-thinking that this new technology compels us to undertake. So let us begin the re-thinking here by look-ing at the conventional writing classroom and asking ourselves, "What do these college writing classrooms look like now? Are they now what we want? And what, given the advent of computer technology, are the alternatives?"

The "Real" Writing Classroom

Suddenly the conventional college writing classroom seems an odd place, a "virtual reality" of its own, frozen in time, remarkably similar to the turn-of-the-century urban school classrooms pictured in histories of American education (e.g., Tyack 46, 56). This writing classroom is an expensive, impersonal structure serially inhabited by different classes, none of which leaves any trace in the room. The room serves as a "writ-ing" classroom only when the writers and their teacher appear; at other times, it serves as a classroom for History 102, Economics 312, German 103, Philosophy 201, Management 207. There are no books in the room, except for those that students and teachers bring with them. There is a teacher's desk at the head of the room, a symbol of authority that has in it only the fugitive piece of chalk and perhaps an old blue-book or two. Otherwise, there are no writing materials in this desk, which is a stage device, a prop, and not a workspace. The teacher works at an-other, "real" desk, at home or in a college office, where there are pencils, pens, staplers, paper, stamps, paper-clips, a typewriter and/or a PC, an address-book; and, somewhere near the desk, there are bookshelves, a bulletin-board with reminders and mementos on it, pictures, a telephone, a file cabinet.

Facing the classroom teacher-desk, there are student desks, not often, these days, bolted to the floor, but still set in rows. These desks, like the teacher's classroom desk, are "unreal" workspaces. They are also poor writing places. The writing surface is often irregular, often small, and, for those who are left-handed, awkwardly placed. And if one wants to set up small groups, these pieces of furniture suddenly become awkward and heavy, for they have been built of metal and laminated, wood-grained plastic — to last.

There are other pieces of equipment in this conventional classroom that, given our deconstructive move, now seem as unreal as the unreal desk. Behind the desk is a chalkboard that, in colleges and university classrooms, is usually empty at the beginning of class; a given class meets there so seldom that any messages "saved" on the chalkboard will likely not survive the two-to-four-day interval between classes. On the walls of the classroom there are bulletin boards which, by default, have been taken over by those paid to staple advertising — for vacation travel or magazine subscriptions — on every available open wall-space. These materials have a somewhat hallucinatory connection with the business of the writing class. In an elementary school, where students and teachers spend the full day in one room, the class can post its writing on bulletin boards and thus "publish" on the classroom walls. But here the walls, the furniture, belong to everyone and to no one — as impersonal as a room in a motel.

Reasons for Change

From this perspective, we begin to see that this classroom we inhabit is not an inevitable structure, or even a good one, *for* our purposes. Indeed, to argue *for* the conventional writing classroom is not going to be easy. We would, if we could, redesign these writing rooms, even without the impetus of technological change. We would go to our administrators and schedule writing classes in particular rooms for the entire school day, and we would turn these rooms into writing rooms: equip them with dictionaries, paper, staplers, file cabinets, envelopes, stamps, paper clips, typewriters, copy machines, handbooks, thesauri — anything that a writer might want or need. We might ask for a mix of furniture: some writing desks where a writer could write alone, and some small round tables where writers could read and discuss one another's projects. There might be something like the "author's chair" of some elementary classrooms, a place where, by custom, writers read their work to others, for response and comment.

So we should re-think the writing classroom in any case. But today there are forces that would drive us to re-think the writing classroom in its present form, even if it were now acceptable to us. The first of these forces is the widespread perception that we are not now doing our job very well. We can assign some, and perhaps most, of this public dissatisfaction with higher education to demographic and economic factors, but we are left with an uncomfortable residue — a feeling that we might, somehow, do better. We cannot be long satisfied with the outcome of our teaching if so many others are dissatisfied.

A second force is the cost of the brick-and-mortar classroom. This conventional classroom must be heated and cooled, lighted and swept, secured and re-painted and maintained — and it will be used for two thirteen-week periods during the year — half of the year! — and only for five days/week — 130 days! — and at most fourteen hours/day. There may be occasional, or even systematic, use of the facility in the off-season, and colleges on trimester or quarter systems may make better use of their facilities, but even with a summer-school and a conscientious division of continuing education, it would be hard to imagine a classroom that was used for more than 50 percent of the hours in a given year. The cost of constructing, maintaining, securing, lighting, heating, and cooling this largely unused classroom will, given the inevitable rise in energy cost, force us to consider alternatives.

The third force that will drive change in our classrooms is the precipitous drop in the price of computer technology. Though higher education is not now spending widely, or even wisely, on the acquisition of computer technology (Flynn), it won't be too long before the cost of computer and communications equipment will look like a pleasant alternative to the rising, energy-driven cost of the brick-and-mortar classroom. And we writing teachers are well placed to utilize this technology, because we don't need tremendously expensive systems. One can write now, and perhaps forever, on a simple PC, and one can connect, with this same PC, to other writers on other PC's. Despite the advent of multimedia environments, as writing teachers all we really need to work with is a PC and a wire.

Given these I-think-unarguable facts, I look ahead to the "new" writing classroom not as a techno-groupie but as a moderately rational writing teacher, one who is attempting to see the outlines of a future that is sure to arrive. If we were now, as a nation, satisfied with the products of our existing writing classrooms; if our present system of higher education were not rapidly pricing itself out of the American marketplace; and if the cost of computer technology were not dropping exponentially; then the following sections would be, even in my own eyes, self-indulgent. But it seems clear to me and to others (e.g., Tiffin) that the writing classroom of the next millennium will be radically different from the writing classroom of today. In the sections that follow, I will look at two different but related models: the computer-equipped, brick-and-mortar writing classroom, and the "virtual," online classroom.

The Computer-Equipped Writing Classroom

It is certain that the new will first inhabit the forms of the old. Indeed, much of the old may persist within the new. We still "drive" automobiles, and we speak of their "horsepower." And the fact that neither of the two books emanating from the recent English Coalition (Lloyd-Jones and Lunsford; Elbow) considers our subject suggests that most of us are not eager to contemplate the changes in school design that lie ahead. We will begin therefore by considering the computer-equipped writing classroom — a brick-and-mortar classroom, with all its attendant energy costs, but one with computers in it — a room that students are scheduled into just as they are into conventional classrooms. This facility will not be more cost-effective than the conventional classroom, but we'll assume that for the near-term we will be reluctant to abandon the ways in which our colleges presently operate in space and time. Students will continue to come to brick-and-mortar classrooms, physical spaces within which teaching and learning occur. Given this assumption, we can ask, "What will these new writing-rooms look like? What will their equipment be? And how will it seem to learn, and to teach, in these rooms?"

I describe here my own college-level, computer-equipped classroom, one that operates on a "MWF" and "TuTh" schedule and serves 16–20 different teachers and classes each semester. The room has a few more workstations than students — to minimize the disruption caused by inevitable hardware failure. The workstations are networked. Each class has its own "area" or section of the subdirectory structure on the file-server's hard disk. Each teacher has, as well, his or her own subdirectory — his or her "desk." Given the ability of LAN-software to "map" and to assign "rights," each class "sees" only its own subdirectory structure, one that can be customized according to its needs but which will remain constant throughout the semester — a "virtual" workplace, where assignments, syllabi, prompts, and peer-responding instructions are kept in read-only form; where work-in-progress is saved in read/write form; and where final products are sent to a "turn-in" subdirectory. In a writing classroom that was not computer-equipped, even one as marvelous as the ideal writing classroom we imagined above, we would not have storage space for all of this paper: we would need twenty file drawers for the writing of all the students in the twenty classes that write in this room; we would need bookshelves for multiple copies of hard-bound dictionaries, handbooks, and thesauri; we would need wall space sufficient for multiple, proprietary blackboards and bulletin boards; and we would need a secure place for teachers to store attendance and grade records. In the computer-equipped classroom, all of this material resides in the system's file-server, which is the size of one instructor's briefcase, or, more accurately, it resides on the file-server's hard disk, which is, at the moment of this writing, the size of a pocket-dictionary.

The materials accessible on the classroom's hard disk become a "virtual space," designed and furnished by the teacher and the students together. We live and work in this virtual classroom through an act of imagining, just as we construct the "virtual" worlds created by novels, plays, poems, and computer-games. Through the screen each class accesses its own bulletin board, mail system, virtual filing-and-storage system for student writing, and store of syllabi, schedules, writing prompts, teachers' comments, peer-readers' comments, and attendance records. Teachers may access through the screen their own private files: a "virtual" grade-book, class roster, annotated syllabus, and notes on, let's say, particular students' progress toward particular goals. Given the compression that occurs when you convert print-text into magnetically charged bits of iron oxide, and given a network with a file server with a 300 MB hard disk — trailing-edge technology, as of this writing — there is room in this system for roughly 150,000 pages of double-spaced student writing, or, assuming that we need 60 MB for software and that in a given semester the system will be used by twenty sections of twenty students, the system has the capacity to store some three hundred pages of text per student. Further, students have their own disks, private spaces where they can store hundreds of "pages" of their own material. And all of this electronic text can be made shareable or, to put the matter more accurately, can be copied and re-copied without cost or increase in physical dimension.

In a typical class in this typical computer-equipped writing room, students log in, using their instructor's name and password, and a log-in script invisibly and silently routes them to their class subdirectory structure — their own working environment. What first appears on their screen is a greeting from their instructor, and, let us say, instructions to pick up the day's writing prompt from the Prompt box. Or the instructions may be to read through the final drafts submitted in the Turn-in box, and, opening a second window, to write a response to the author of their, or the teacher's, choice. In one of these "boxes" may also be "magazines" edited by groups of students from work submitted to them in yet another "box." The writers, as they work on their screens, are in their "home room" — a digitized space, a literate environment, filled with writing tools and their own writing.

Where does the teacher fit into this structure? It depends to a considerable degree on the design of the physical and virtual spaces. We could design a computer-equipped classroom that replicated the structure of the conventional classroom — not *my* choice, but a choice nevertheless. To do so, we'd mark a workstation, by position or custom, as the "teacher's place." This workstation could stand at the "head" of the class, facing the students' workstations, in the same layout as that of a conventional classroom, where the teacher's desk faces the students' desks. Or the teacher's workstation could be electronically exalted: through software now available, such as *Real-Time Writer* or *Timbuktu*, the teacher would be given the right to take over student screens, write on them, broadcast to them, or observe them. And the teacher's workstation could have near it an overhead projector, one that permits the teacher's screen to become an electronic chalkboard for purposes of demonstration.

Why would we design a computer-equipped writing classroom in this way? As a small and therefore inefficient lecture hall? Samuel

Johnson argued in 1781 that, given the availability of books and the ability to read, lectures were no longer a necessary mode of education (Boswell 1136). Yet in 1987, more than two centuries later, the English Coalition felt the need to argue that the freshman writing course should not be teacher-centered, but should "stress an *active, interactive theory of learning* (rather than a theory of teaching), one that assumes students do not learn by being passive eavesdroppers on an academic conversation or vessels into which knowledge is being poured" (Lloyd-Jones and Lunsford 27; see also Elbow 32). Apparently a change in available media does not significantly change the ways in which teaching and learning are conducted. All I can say, therefore, is that computer technology *presents us with the opportunity* to break with the past and to create interactive writing classrooms.

Let us therefore re-imagine the classroom and the software in such a way that the teacher becomes a member of an interactive community of writers — distinguished from the student writers by degree of writing experience and training, so still clearly the writing teacher, but otherwise inhabiting the same world as the students. With such a goal we would not distinguish a "teacher's workstation" but would set our workstations in sets of six or eight, in "pods" or islands extending from one of the room's walls. The workstations would be identical, but the teacher, given a log-in and password procedure, could be assigned "rights" that students do not have. For instance, the students could be given full read/write rights to several subdirectories, but read-only rights to others.

I am assuming that the teacher and class have the autonomy to build their own "virtual classrooms" — and I need to note here that this is an assumption and a hope, not an inevitable consequence of the character of computer technology. Indeed, network management is difficult, and once you give the users a measure of autonomy, you multiply network management problems exponentially. System managers' need to standardize applications is in sharp conflict with users' need to choose their own applications. At issue here is the teacher's authority within the larger educational system. In America we have been moving to grant teachers more power in their schools. Electronic classrooms will run easier and cheaper from "dumb" terminals which grant access to a single, managed curriculum. Teacher autonomy will be expensive and will make running the system harder — and schools will be tempted to move, as businesses have, toward the "dumb" terminal and the centralized control which this equipment makes easy. What businesses see as an evil — "hanky-panky on the network" (Lewis, sec. 3:4) — may be, for teachers and for students, the lifeblood of creative teaching and learning.

This computer-equipped classroom will have in it, in addition to networked workstations, a range of online writer's aids: a beginning, simplified word-processing program and a more powerful word-processing program for those who feel the need for such features as complex formatting, sorting, searching, indexing, and the inclusion of graphics with text. There will be an online thesaurus, an online dictionary, and an online spell-checker. There can be online as well style-checkers and a range of programs that function as heuristics, asking the writer questions that are intended to stimulate invention, the generation of ideas. The limit to the number and range of these writers' aids is the teacher's judgment about the extent to which these programs can be helpful to writers.

To the extent that the teacher wants to have students "discuss" online, perhaps as a pre-writing activity, a "chat" program like the Daedalus *Interchange* will permit online, real-time, written exchange of views: a quick e-mail exchange, in effect, or a rapid epistolary exchange, with instantaneous electronic copies for all participants. Such a program will permit group interaction but with the written language as the medium through which the self is presented. The teacher will have to decide on the degree of autonomy students will have in these online, written discussions. Will the teacher begin the session with a prompt? Will the teacher join in the discussion and control "flaming" or discourse that is potentially hurtful to members of the group? Will the teacher direct the formation of sub-conferences or permit students to set up their own? Will the teacher permit students to adopt pseudonyms and thus change their relationship to their written texts? As I have indicated above, the computer-equipped classroom presents us with choices.

A final choice we will have to make in the design of our computer-equipped classroom is the relative value we give to print-text and online text. The computer-equipped writing classroom should have printing facilities in it: ideally quiet, laser- or ink-jet printers. The printers will be available to all workstations, through the network. But what uses should teachers make of these printers? Online text is essentially "free": once the equipment is available, the cost of "printing" a text online is zero. Printers, toner, and paper are expensive. For cost effectiveness, both locally and globally, our classes should operate entirely online: students submit their writing online, and teachers read this writing online.

Yet we now live, and will likely continue to live for some time, in an amphibious condition, one where we function both in the "elements" of print-text and online text. College curricula are still print-based: there are bookstores, printed lecture-note services, written and proctored examinations, and libraries with huge investments in printed books. Our students will, outside our writing classes, be writing for teachers who will read their work in print-text form. To the extent to which this is true, we'll not want to force our writing students to work exclusively in an environment of electronic text. We will, instead, want to help our students manage the transition between electronic text and print in ways that take advantage of the special characteristics of the two media.

For this reason, our computer-equipped classrooms will have graphics programs and desktop publishing programs that will permit student writers to format and to publish their work. In some classrooms, document design will become part of the curriculum. In these classrooms, editing "teams" will work collaboratively, through the network, in assembling documents: flyers, brochures, volumes of essays, all published in printed form through xerography. And, so long as the print-culture of higher education requires students to submit "papers" to their teachers, we will need to have in our classroom at least one workstation with a large-screen, $8^{1}/_{2} \times 11$ black-on-white monitor. With this equipment, we can help our students manage both the rhetorical and formal processes involved in effecting the transition from electronic author to print-text reader.

Beyond Time and Place in the Computer-Equipped Classroom

So far we have been thinking of this computer-equipped classroom as existing in space and time, a function of cinder-blocks, glass, hardware, and wire. We have also, however, considered the extent to which this classroom is a site for the construction of many "virtual" classrooms. The student working in one of these computer-equipped classrooms is physically present but related to a digitized world that is accessed through the class log-in script. In such a networked system that serves many classes, the "reality" that one enters is a function of bricks and mortar, yes, and of the teacher's "live" presence, but this reality is as well a function of one's password, which permits one to enter the virtual world of Prof. Moran's writing class. With another password, you'd enter someone else's class-world, with different software options and a different subdirectory structure, let alone different prompts, messages, journal entries, and files of student writing. In our computer-equipped classrooms at the University of Massachusetts, we see that the computer-equipped classroom begins to break down the physical sense of "the class." When I and my class are scheduled into Bartlett 105, the computer-equipped classroom, I work with my own students, to be sure, but it is likely that there will be in the room also a few students from other sections, logged into their own digitized class environments, and even the occasional teacher, doing class preparation, logged into his or her own subdirectory structure. Our teachers report that on occasion these "visitors" choose to join in, finding the work of the class to their taste. So even in this somewhat retrograde brick-and-mortar computer-equipped classroom, the boundaries of the "class" begin to become permeable, and we begin to see that the "class," defined as a packet of students delivered to a particular place at a particular time, is not a given, unless one accepts the inevitability of the industrial model.

The next step in this deconstruction of the "class" will be to connect our computer-equipped classroom, through bulletin-board or e-mail software, to information sources outside the room. Through telephone lines we can access data bases such as online library catalogues. Through these same telephone lines we can connect with resource persons outside the classroom, bringing their expertise and perspective into our rapidly expanding virtual world. At the 1990 Conference on Computers and Writing in Austin, Texas, we heard of a class that had in this way made contact with a District Attorney and had used this contact to gain direct access to both information and professional opinion relative to a topic the group was writing about. The virtues of this system, as explained by the speaker, were those of an e-mail system: the District Attorney could, on his own schedule, read the communications from the students and write his responses. For him, this situation was feasible. A "live" class visit would not have been possible (Hughes). Or we could connect our writing class with another writing class, as has been happening through networks such as BreadNet, which operates out of Middlebury College in Vermont. We could bring together in an online conference writing classes that were from different cultures — say a northern urban school with a school in the mountains of Kentucky.

But now I begin to anticipate our next move, a move into the writing classroom that exists entirely and solely online. Oh for hypertext!

The Online Classroom

The online class now exists. Indeed, on page 30 of the November 1990 "Education Life" section of the *New York Times,* there is an advertisement for the "American Open University of NYIT," or New York Institute of Technology. The advertisement reads as follows: "The modern way for adults to pursue an undergraduate degree without having to attend traditional classes. Obtain a baccalaureate degree in such areas as business, behavioral sciences, and general studies through computer teleconferencing anywhere in the world." The phrase *open university* connects the NYIT program with a similar program at the Open University in Great Britain, described in the work of Kaye, Mason, and Rumble. Other academic programs delivered solely through computer conferencing are described by Naidu, Mason, Roberts, and McCreary. And in a recent article Romiszowski writes, "In the state of New York alone, more than 100 educational establishments use some form of teleconferencing to supplement, or supplant, face-to-face education" (234). Research into this area brings us into contact with such established conventions as the abbreviations CC (Computer Conferencing) and CMC (Computer-mediated Communication) and such established journals as *Distance Education* and the *American Journal of Distance Education.*

So in imagining an online writing classroom we are not engaging in ungrounded fantasy. There are many online courses now being taught. In England, Canada, and the United States, these courses are generally offered, as the NYIT advertisement suggests, to adults who for one reason or another cannot be in our conventional classrooms M-W-F 10:05 A.M. and who, because of work and parenting schedules, need to work and learn when they can. In other areas, such as Micronesia and northern Canada, where a physical meeting of a class is not economically feasible, "distance learning" is the only alternative, and, with satellite uplinks, computer conferencing "may well be the fastest growing area of applications of technology to communication and education" (Romiszowski 236).

What would an online writing classroom "look" like? It would have three elements, both separable and potentially interactive: (1) a "mail" system; (2) a "filing," or storage-and-retrieval system; and (3) a computer-mediated conferencing system. For the sake of clarity, I will look at these three subsystems separately.

The online mail system makes possible a writing course that is much like the learn-to-write-by-mail services that are advertised in such publications as *Writer's Market* or *Writer's Digest,* or the conference-based writing class envisioned by Lester Fisher and Donald Murray. The essential transaction in this model is that between the writer and the editor. Writers send their writing via a "mail" system; the writing is read, and the editor sends a response by return mail. The editor could be the teacher, or could be students, or both in some mixture and alternation, depending upon the teacher's and students' values and goals.

The virtues of editing online are several: the editors can edit at their convenience, picking up the manuscript at any time of day; the editor will comment in writing and, in so doing, practice both writing and editing skills; and the editor can take the time to reflect and even return to and modify the first response with a subsequent re-vision or re-mailing of the second thoughts. Important here is the fast turnaround made possible by CMC; Kaye notes that in a correspondence course the typical turn-around time is three weeks (Mason and Kaye, 12). During this interval, Kaye notes, the student has most often proceeded to a new piece of the course, so the feedback comes too late to be useful. Online, the turn-around can be rapid and therefore more effective.

The disadvantages of online editing are clear: the difficulty of making comments in a "margin" and the difficulty of drawing arrows and lines — the kinds of editing that we have become so used to on paper do not yet have their equivalent online. Red-lining programs are mildly useful, but they tend to be unwieldly and they produce a text that, with its embedded deletions and additions, is difficult to read. Yet the speed of response may more than compensate for the difficulties we now have in commenting flexibly and economically online on an extended piece of writing. And hypertext holds the promise of an environment where comments-on-text can be more easily made and received.

In addition to the "mail" system, the online classroom would include a virtual storage-and-retrieval system. In this electronic filing cabinet would be all texts produced by the group — more-or-less formal pieces of writing, editors' comments, all mail-messages sent during the semester, texts brought in by members of the group as references, examples, authority. Available also would be transcripts of the online conferences, retrievable by author or topic. Our class storage area would be connected to online, public data bases that students could search as they needed to for their own or their group's writing. We would need to establish protocols that would permit privacy, where appropriate, and access, where appropriate. We can imagine that access to our "classroom's" storage area would be limited to the members of the class itself. It might be important for each member of the class, and here I include the teacher, to have his or her own virtual desk — either housed in memory in the host computer or in the memory of the participant's own workstation — in either case a part of the virtual classroom. The student and teacher would be at their "desks," at school, at home, or wherever, and could log into the "class" at any time.

A third element in our online writing course would be the computer-mediated conference (CMC), a process that may, as some predict, "ultimately emerge as a new educational paradigm, taking its place alongside both face-to-face and distance education" (Kaye, "Computer-Mediated" 3). CMC is seen by some (e.g., Feenberg 26) to hold the "promise that writing will once again become a universal form of expression," as "written," online conferences and e-mail exchanges begin to be used instead of voice communication by telephone.

The computer-mediated conference is a much more flexible medium than the two-way epistolary correspondence. And, whereas the "mail" and "filing" functions are individual in their orientation, CMC is potentially — some would say inevitably — social and interactive. Through the conference, the teacher and students together can design an online classroom that is as full and functional as is the digitized environment stored in the file-server of our computer-equipped writing classroom, described above. That the students are connected to the system by telephone lines, rather than by an Ethernet wire, might seem for most purposes irrelevant. In such a classroom the teacher and students can orchestrate reading-and-writing groups, online, written discussions, brainstorming bulletin-board sessions, and online publication. The response-time in this online classroom would on occasion be slower than it is in a classroom where readers and writers are physically present, but it is not clear that a somewhat relaxed and deliberate cycle of writing-and-response is a disadvantage. And quasi-synchronous conferencing sessions, such as those made possible by Interchange in the computer-equipped classroom, are possible to arrange online, though for these sessions the class would have to agree to be online simultaneously.

Researchers and practitioners have found, too, that CMC is a new and not unproblematic communication medium. Face-to-face communication occurs in a rich context of cues: tone of voice, gesture, facial expression. Andrew Feenberg asserts that "In computer conferencing the only tacit sign we can transmit is our silence, a message that is both brutal and ambiguous" (34). CMC, using as it does just the written word, requires that we pay attention to context-building. This context-building can be the work of the teacher-moderator, whose work, according to Feenberg (35–36), consists of creating an initial context for the discussion, setting norms, setting agenda, recognizing and prompting the participants, "meta-commenting," or dealing with "problems in context, norms, or agenda, clarity, irrelevance, and information overload" (35), and "Weaving," which is "to summarise the state of the discussion and to find unifying threads in participants' comments" (35). Part of the context-building may be one or more face-to-face meetings. All this, Feenberg states, is "an admission of defeat" (37) — the medium is not yet good enough to do what we'd like it to do. Feenberg's teacher-moderator sounds, however, suspiciously like the present classroom teacher who leads and facilitates a classroom discussion. Perhaps Feenberg is right: computer-mediated conferences may require a leader/facilitator. But it is just as likely that we will develop new conventions — such as the "emoticons" of e-mail correspondence — once we have learned to live and work in our virtual classrooms.

The structures of the online classroom can help the participants imagine not just a "virtual classroom" but a "virtual college," a complete educational environment. Lynn Davie carefully constructs a range of "sites" in her computer-mediated conferences: "I may call the main discussion the seminar room; provide a faculty office for advising; provide a small meeting room for informal interactions or help; provide an in-basket for student assignments; or provide workspaces for small group projects, subjects, etc." (79). Davie goes on to say that these metaphors can "help the student learn to navigate" the conference but notes as well that "we need to examine closely the advantages and disadvantages of different metaphors" (79). The context-setting metaphors can be visual and iconic as well as verbal. Alexander and Lincoln have described a graphical-user interface for their Thought Box project, one that permits students to choose from among boxes in the "Courses Building" which consist of "T101 News," "T101 Activities," "T101 Assignments," and "T101 Forum"; from boxes in the "Student Union" which consist of "Book Exchange," "Forum," "Help and Advice," and "Classified Ads": and from icons such as "The Library," in- and out-baskets, newspapers, calendars, calculators, and class notes (90–91). With the graphical interface used by the Open University, we make a full move from the "virtual classroom" to a "virtual university." The "Electronic Campus Map" of the Open University presents the user with a graphic "map," with paths connecting six "buildings" — the Mail Building, the Staff Building, the Courses Building, the Student Union, the Tutorial Building, and the Resource and Information Center (Mason 117). Each building is faced with panels that represent choices that you'd make by "clicking" on the panel with a mouse: the Mail Building, for example, has panels labelled "in tray," "out tray," "your mail," "tutor A's mail," and so on. To the north of the Mail Building is a park-like space, with strolling people in it, labelled "Conversation area."

The "context" of the online classroom can include virtual spaces that stretch or exceed the academic metaphor that seems now to be the norm. Connections to non-academic settings, where students can participate in writing tasks that are being undertaken in worlds outside the college and the university, make possible a virtual "office" space where writers from workplaces join writers from the academy in collaborative writing tasks. In the conventional classroom, the logistics of such an undertaking make it extremely difficult. The working writer does not have time to come to class to explain the context; interaction-at-a-distance is too slow for both sides of this transaction. Online, we can construct a virtual space where the student writers and writers at worksites meet to discuss the writing task in progress.

What Do We Gain? Lose?

But what is lost in this new classroom? I think of Walt Whitman here, who saw the end of writing in the invention of the typewriter (Traubel 314). Will the online classroom be the end of our teaching? Certainly we lose face-to-face contact. But might we not generate another relationship, a different intimacy that might have its own virtues? Might the virtual classroom foster new relationships and new kinds of learning?

Researchers in this field have found that distance learning is often as effective as face-to-face instruction (Chute; George). Barbara Grabowski et al. have summarized the research in the field, conspicuously citing the work of Linda Harasim, who found that students in an online, computer-mediated conference experienced and demonstrated increased initiative and increased responsibility for their own learning, and of Downing et al., who found that in an online engineering course, students "asked more challenging questions, and that students reported high-quality instructor responses to their inquiries" (Grabowski, Pusch, and Pusch). And Starr Hiltz finds that for some learners, CMC is a better learning environment than the brick-and-mortar classroom. In her study, Hiltz finds also that students reacted more favorably to the online environment when the courses were constructed in such a way as to foster collaborative learning. She notes as well that one computer-mediated conference was still going strong a month after the end of the semester, "with over a hundred new entries which continued to discuss the issues raised in the course" (7). Hiltz's findings are supported by Linda Harasim, who argues that "as a medium, it [CMC] is particularly conducive to information-sharing, brainstorming, networking, and group synergy" (61), and by McCreary, who finds that CMC has enriched the entire academic culture at her university, the University of Guelph, Ontario.

Given the research now extant, the proposition that online classrooms are somehow cold and impersonal and therefore in some way dangerous is arguable. Is an epistolary relationship less warm, less personal, less intimate than a "live" relationship? Is a class conducted through a computer-mediated conference less warm, less personal, less intimate than a face-to-face classroom experience? Given the powers of the human imagination, are human warmth and a sense of intimacy necessarily dependent upon physical presence? There is some doubt.

The online writing classroom has much to offer. It has all the virtues of distance education, in that it opens the class to people who cannot, for one reason or another, travel to a particular place at a particular time. The online classroom does not require the heating, cooling, and maintenance of the conventional classroom. And the online classroom does not require travel to a physical place, a factor that is now crucial in areas of low population density, but given that the cost of travel increases at double the rate of inflation (Chute 265), it will become increasingly important in all institutions of higher education. But perhaps more important, because the online classroom offers such wide access, it creates the possibility that classes could be more diverse than they now are: online writing classes could be deliberately composed of writers from different backgrounds, of different ages, and of different cultures. Such classes could become forums for our emerging cultural democracy. Further, the online, computer-mediated conference may be a site that will encourage the emancipating discourse envisioned by Boyd, Cooper, and Selfe, and Flores — discourse in which status is less than it now is a function of race, gender, and class.

Clearly there are differences between online and "live" teaching and learning. These differences may seem to some to be losses. To the extent that students and teachers have experienced agency in "live" teaching situations, both will experience the virtual classroom as change and perhaps discomfort. Shoshana Zuboff has described the dislocation felt by workers at industrial sites as they moved from the foundry floor to the air-conditioned, information-processing booths above the floor. It would be extraordinary to imagine that students and teachers would not feel the sense of loss that attends the change in the nature of their work. To the extent that students and teachers have learned to be "good on their feet" in oral, face-to-face discussion, we'd expect the online environment to seem to them restrictive: impersonal, cold, devoid of human contact. And, so long as the online environment is created by the written language, students with learning disabilities that affect the production and reception of the written language will be at a disadvantage.

But, despite the fact that for some this will be a difficult transition and despite the fact that questions of access and equity remain to be addressed, for the reasons I have laid out above — our national dissatisfaction with schools as they are, the rising energy-cost of such schools, and the decreasing cost of computer and communications technology — we need to begin now to consider the shape that our writing classrooms may take in the second millennium. The two writing rooms I have described — the computer-equipped, brick-and-mortar classroom and the computer-mediated, online classroom — both now exist. From my perspective, writing now in 1991, they will soon, perhaps by the year 2050, seem entirely normal. John Tiffin argues that "the fibre optic telecommunication system will be to the current copper-based telephone system what the railway lines were to a donkey-track." Given the emerging capacity for electronic communication, he argues, "It seems highly unlikely that schools will survive in anything like their present form" (240). I think that Tiffin is right. It is time to begin to build, at least in our imaginations, the writing class of the coming virtual age.

Works Cited

Alexander, Gary, and Ches Lincoln. "The Thought Box: A Computer-Based Communication System to Support Distance Learning." Mason and Kaye 86–100.

Boswell, James. *The Life of Samuel Johnson, LL.D.* Ed. R.W. Chapman. London: Oxford UP, 1960.

Boyd, Gary. "Emancipative Educational Technology." *Canadian Journal of Educational Technology* 16.2 (1987): 167–72.

Chute, Alan G. "Strategies for Implementing Teletraining Systems." *Educational and Training Technology International* 27.3 (1990): 264–70.

Cooper, Marilyn M., and Cynthia L. Selfe. "Computer Conferences and Learning: Authority, Resistance, and Internally Persuasive Discourse." *College English* 52.8 (1990): 847–69.

Davie, Lynn. "Facilitation Techniques for the Online Tutor." Mason and Kaye 74–85.

Elbow, Peter. *What Is English?* New York: MLA, 1990.

Feenberg, Andrew. "The Written World: On the Theory and Practice of Computer Conferencing." Mason and Kaye 22–39.

Fisher, Lester, and Donald Murray. "Perhaps the Professor Should Cut Class." *College English* 35 (1973): 169–73.

Flores, Mary J. "Computer Conferencing: Composing a Feminist Community of Writers." *Computers and Community.* Ed. Carolyn Handa. Portsmouth: Boynton, 1990. 106–17.

Flynn, Laurie. "Funding PC Purchases Is Low Priority on Campus." *InfoWorld* 12.42 (1990): 5.

Frankston, Robert. Interview "Welcome to the *Byte* Summit." *Byte* 15.9 (1990): 271.

George, Judith. "Audioconferencing — Just Another Small Group Activity." *Educational and Training Technology International* 27.3 (1990): 244–48.

Grabowski, Barbara, and Suciati and Wende Pusch. "Social and Intellectual Value of Computer-Mediated Communications in a Graduate Community." *Educational and Training Technology International* 27.3 (1990): 276–83.

Harasim, Linda. "Online Education: A New Domain." Mason and Kaye 50–73.

Hiltz, Starr R. "Collaborative Learning in a Virtual Classroom: Highlights of Findings." Paper presented at the Computer Supported Cooperative Work Conference, June 1988. Revision for CSCW Proceedings. ED 305–895.

Hughes, Bradley. "The Police Chief, the Judge, the District Attorney, and the Defender: Using Networked Writing to Bring Professionals into an Undergraduate Course on Criminal Justice." Paper given at the Sixth Conference on Computers and Writing, Austin, TX, 17–20 May 1990.

Kaye, Anthony. "Computer-Mediated Communication and Distance Education." Mason and Kaye 3–21.

————. "Computer Conferencing for Education and Training: Project Description." Project Report CCET/1. Open University, Walton, Bletchley, Bucks (England). Institute of Technology. 1985. ED 273–60.

Lewis, Peter H. "The Executive Computer," *New York Times* 6 June 1990, sec. 3:4.

Lloyd-Jones, Richard, and Andrea Lunsford. *The English Coalition Conference: Democracy through Language.* Urbana, Ill.: NCTE, 1989.

Mason, Robin. "An Evaluation of CoSy on an Open University Course." Mason and Kaye 115–45.

————. "Computer Conferencing: A Contribution to Self-Directed Learning." *British Journal of Educational Technology* 19.1 (1988): 28–41.

Mason, Robin and Anthony Kaye, eds. *Mindweave.* New York: Pergamon P, 1989.

McCreary, Elaine. "Computer-Mediated Communication and Organisational Culture." Mason and Kaye 101–12.

Moran, Charles. "The Computer-Writing Room: Authority and Control." *Computers and Composition* 7.2 (1990): 61–70.

Naidu, Som. "Computer Conferencing in Distance Education." 1988. ED 310–74.

Roberts, Lowell. "The Electronic Seminar: Distance Education by Computer Conferencing." Paper presented at the Fifth Annual Conference on Non-Traditional and Interdisciplinary Programs, Fairfax, VA, May 1987. ED 291–358.

Romiszowski, Alexander. "Shifting Paradigms in Education and Training: What Is the Connection with Telecommunications?" *Educational and Training Technology International* 27.3 (1990): 233–36.

Rumble, Greville. "The Use of Microcomputers in Distance Teaching Systems." ZIFF Papiere 70, Fernuniversitat, Hagen (West Germany), 1988.

Selfe, Cynthia L. "Technology in the English Classroom: Computers through the Lens of Feminist Theory. *Computers and Community.* Ed. Carolyn Handa. Portsmouth: Boynton, 1990. 118–39.

Tiffin, John. "Telecommunications and the Trade in Teaching." *Educational and Training Technology International* 27.3 (1990): 240–44.

Traubel, Horace. *With Walt Whitman in Camden.* New York: Rowman, 1961.

Tyack, David B. *The One Best System.* Cambridge: Harvard UP, 1974.

Zuboff, Shoshana. *In the Age of the Smart Machine: The Future of Work and Power.* New York: Basic, 1988.

Moran's Insights as a Resource for Your Teaching

1. You may be a novice or you may already have designed your writing classroom to take advantage of computer technology. Look at your experiences, as a student or a writer, with computers and writing and reflect on your practices as you wrote by hand, by computer, or by some mix. In your journal, write entries prompted by these questions: What can I do with my computer-equipped, brick-and-mortar classroom? What if I shifted to a computer-mediated, online classroom? Use that speculation as you design your course syllabus and when you visit with the

support staff on your campus who help faculty use academic computing resources.

2. Moran provides a clear overview of "computer-equipped" and "computer-mediated" writing sites and describes some practices in specific detail. He also provides a useful bibliography containing theoretical perspectives and practical advice that can broaden your understanding of computers and classrooms. You can also use online resources, both local and national. Many public discussions about writing, pedagogy, composition theory, rhetorical theory, and cultural-studies theory foster conversation among teachers and researchers.

   If you haven't listened in yet, try one of the following lists. To subscribe to any that pique your interest, send a note. For example, subscribe to a list for writing program administrators by sending a note to listserv@asuvm.inre.asu.edu.

   LISTPROC@LISTSERV.TTU.EDU   The Alliance for Computers and Writing is open to anyone interested in using computing technologies in their writing classrooms. This professional organization is dominated by young writing instructors and researchers, but you will also find many veteran teachers and researchers like Moran participating in the online conversations.

   LISTSERV@TC.UMN.EDU   The Conference on Basic Writing welcomes novice and veteran instructors and others eager to discuss pedagogical strategies, curriculum initiatives, and administrative challenges related to basic writing programs. Like those of this volume, its discussions are alternately theoretical and practical.

Moran's Insights as a Resource for Your Writing Classroom

1. Moran encourages us to reimagine the classroom and software so that the writing instructor is a member of an interactive writing community. As the pedagogy of Paulo Freire indicates, the instructor would be a "master learner" working collaboratively with "learners" (as opposed to "students," who are acted on rather than agents). However, with computers and writing, some learners would be the "master learners" for the teacher and their peers. This is particularly the case when you equip or mediate a writing classroom with computers. Write a questionnaire or journal prompt to survey the expertise with computers and writing that students bring to your classroom. It's likely that several of your students have gone further in cyberspace than others, and they can be helpful guides and troubleshooters.

2. If you don't have access to a networked classroom or lab, impro-
   vise and set up an electronic conference on e-mail to facilitate
   online written discussions. The electronic conference can enhance
   invention strategies: It provides a "safe" space for writers to ask
   whether a topic or thesis or organization or persona sounds
   "okay" to peers; writers can also eavesdrop on discussions of
   writing and learn how peers might respond to a prompt. The
   conversation is "linear" (as opposed to real-time, with instantaneous electronic copies to all class members), but it is leagues
   beyond the classtime-bound conversations of the traditional
   classroom.

   If you haven't set up such a conference before, you can learn
   how by following the tutorial that accompanies your e-mail
   software. Moran's questions will be helpful as you work with an
   electronic conference. He doesn't pose a question about how
   writers might "contextualize" their contribution and write for
   online readers.

   When participating in e-conferences peers use direct address
   to a specific "speaker" online, restate themes or passages to bring
   the conversation back to the strand they want to follow, and cite
   specific "speakers" and statements, including and acknowledging
   other participants in the discussion. They follow the oral conventions of conversation or jam sessions when they can't see their
   audience and seem, so far, to be writing to their online listeners
   more consciously than they write to readers of their print texts.

Narratives of Self in Networked Communications

Patricia R. Webb

According to the Daedalus Web site, the InterChange *interactive writing
program*

> *facilitates synchronous, or 'real-time,' discussions for whole classes, small
> groups, or both simultaneously. Students compose private messages and send
> them to all the members of a discussion group for immediate viewing.
> Transcripts of these discussions are automatically saved to your file server,
> and can be saved to disk or printed and reviewed at any time.*

Some theorists argue that Daedalus InterChange *and similar programs
herald the birth of a new writing genre. They claim that online discussion
radically transforms the writing process and liberates both student and
teacher from traditional rules and assumptions. In the following essay,
Patricia Webb refutes this theory, suggesting that* InterChange *and other
networked programs can "easily coexist with . . . humanist conceptions of
the author as a unitary genius writing alone in his garret" (p. 181). Webb
believes that students and teachers have much to gain from working with*
InterChange *and related technologies, but she does not propose that*

technology alone can revolutionize the way students think, write, and revise. Webb takes a more cautious approach to online learning, recommending that teachers challenge students' assumptions about online discussion and authorship, and suggests ways to use dialogic technologies to their advantage.

> While electronic discourse explodes the belief in a stable unified self, it offers a means of exploring how identity is multiply constructed and how agency resides in the power of connecting with others and building alliances.
>
> — Lester Faigley (199), discussing his experience with *InterChange*

> I usually don't use other people's writing to write my own piece. I may get a few ideas from other sources but I don't think that only using a few of your own sentences in a piece is a good idea.
>
> — Paula[1] in an *InterChange* discussion about writing processes

The contradictions between Faigley's assertion that authorship is radically changed by Daedalus *InterChange* discussions and Paula's individualistic and traditional description of her writing offered during an actual *InterChange* session in one of my composition courses are striking. They highlight the problematic claims surrounding networked communications used in the classroom. Although it has been argued that the unified stable self is challenged by the inclusion of networked technologies in our classrooms (Barker and Kemp; Batson; Bolter; Faigley; Joyce; Landow; Spender; Turkle), students' own usage of these technologies and their reflective accounts of their interactions in those spaces suggest that, far from being radical, technologies such as *InterChange* easily coexist with and are supportive of humanist conceptions of the author as a unitary genius writing alone in his garret. Unless we emphasize critical use (Hawisher and Selfe) of networked technologies, we will perpetuate the ideas of self and author we are supposedly challenging by including these new technologies in our classrooms.

My experience with using networked technologies in composition courses was that our *InterChange* discussions allowed students to explicitly describe their perceptions of themselves as writers, perceptions that were grounded in humanist notions of the unitary, rational self. Soliciting our students' perceptions and making them a focal point of discussion is an important first step; however, once these ideas are clearly laid out, it is then crucial that we explicitly and concretely illustrate the ways networked technologies can alter these traditional conceptions. This second component is difficult to implement in a climate shaped by technological enthusiasm untempered by theoretical reflection about technologies' implications. This paper highlights ways the unitary self was reasserted throughout the *InterChange* discussions in my two composition courses during the Fall of 1995, explores the necessity of critically using network technologies to question students' assumptions about writing, and points to practical ways of critically integrating technologies into our composition classrooms.

Current Research on Network Technologies' Influences on Student Writers

Since the introduction of computer networking into composition classrooms across the country, instructors who have included networked conversations in their classrooms have acknowledged the changes that occur in students' writing as a result. Not only do these technologies change what students are writing, theorists claim, but they radically change what it means to write. Asserting that real-time conferencing programs allow a heteroglossia of voices, Paul Taylor suggested that "computer conferencing is evolving into a new genre, a new form of communication that has not been possible before now" (145). Echoing this idea of a new genre of communication, M. Diane Langston and Trent Batson found in their research that networks used in composition classrooms help students develop a sense of a "real" audience and interact more with their peers. On the basis of these findings, they argued that network technologies can create a sense of community in the classroom that would otherwise be impossible. Expanding on this notion of community, Thomas Barker and Fred Kemp stated that although "the usual complaint against using computers pedagogically in the classroom is that they isolate students. . . . Actually the opposite occurs when computers are networked and programmed to manage text transactions between class members" (16). And, in their research, Kathleen Skubikowski and John Elder noted that "what surprised us was the degree to which networked corresponding enhanced our creation of a writing community" (104). At the heart of these theorists' arguments and findings, then, is the assertion that networked technologies such as *InterChange* allowed instructors to implement social constructionist ways of thinking in their classrooms, thus challenging traditional notions of what it means to write.

Even students in my composition course touted the great possibilities of networked communication. When asked to reflect on how *InterChange* discussions differed from traditional interactions in a classroom, Lucas wrote that

> in class discussions a person's ideas may be lost because they did not have the chance to respond before the topic was changed. In the *InterChange* everyone got to respond. Whether or not a person wanted to "hear" them was their choice. (journal entry)

To the same question, Erin responded that

> the *InterChange* discussion seems very different from regular classroom discussion. It seems as though everybody offers more ideas on the computer. There is a lot more interaction among students on the

> *InterChange*. . . . I enjoyed giving my opinions and receiving feedback specifically directed back to me. (journal entry)

These student comments echo Trent Batson's claim that "networks create an unusual opportunity to shift away from the traditional writing classroom because they create entirely new pedagogical dynamics" (32). And, like some students who did not like the *InterChange* discussions at first but came to find the discussions useful as the semester progressed, many composition theorists too note the drawbacks of networked technologies only to reach the conclusion that even with the drawbacks, they will still use the technologies because of the overwhelming benefits. Geoffrey Sirc and Thomas Reynolds claimed that after two years of using networked technologies in their classrooms, they were

> happy with the results we see in the transcripts. Students may not always enjoy the reading and writing assignments we give them, but they see the logic of them and, more importantly, they are always willing to discuss ideas and concepts. . . . You can found a course on network interaction, we feel, but you must let it all ride on the *InterChange,* lift off the lid and see for yourself, and let students see for themselves, what sort of exotic things are under there. (156)

Despite the problems they encountered while using computer-mediated communications (CMC) technologies, these theorists clearly still emphasized the benefits over the drawbacks, suggesting that the changes in the concept of authorship created by the technologies were worth the hassles they may have faced.

One of the most persuasive proponents of the claim that networked technologies change traditional notions of writer and writing is Dale Spender. She contended that because we are entering a new phase, one in which print technology and computer technology are beginning to combine, what it means to be an author is radically changing. In *Nattering on the Net*, Spender argued that computer technologies, especially network technologies, allow more people to author texts online. The usual gatekeeping systems of print technology (publishers, editors, and reviewers) seem to have little place in this new online conversation, and thus, Spender contended, authorship is being democratized. The self that produces text online is allowed and even encouraged to be multiple, contradictory, and unstable. As a result, she argued that "we are now on course to see composition as a human skill, the production of information as a human right, within the range of all individuals and not just limited as a privilege of a professional few" (86).

But how different are electronic classrooms? How do they challenge the usual ways of thinking about our students' relationship to writing? The previously described claims seem to suggest that all that is needed to change the traditional view of authorship is to have students write together online or talk to one another about writing online. We all know by now that this is an overly simplistic solution to complex problems writing instructors face today. And, although I admire Spender's (and others') enthusiasm and want to believe her predictions, I am hesitant to accept that network technologies are democratizing or that they change our conception of what it means to be a self writing.

For some composition theorists, the euphoria produced by computer technologies has begun to wear off, and they are now moving toward a more moderate view, arguing for critical and reflective use of these technologies. These voices from within the academy argue that there is nothing inherent in network technologies that assures communication occurring there will challenge the humanist rational self; rather, it is how the technology is used and presented that counts — the pedagogy. Supporting this point, Gail Hawisher and Cynthia Selfe wrote that "if electronic technology is to help us bring about positive changes in writing classes, we must identify and confront the potential problems that computers pose and redirect our efforts" (56). They do not claim that technology is inherently bad, so therefore we should not use it; rather, they caution us to think critically about our use and to pay close attention to the problems that arise as we use network technologies. Their "objections lie not in the use of computer technology and online conferences but rather in the uncritical enthusiasm that frequently characterizes the reports of those of us who advocate and support electronic writing classes" (56). They thus critiqued those who uncritically embrace technologies as the automatic answer to problems of authorship and authority in the classroom. Network technologies *can* help us challenge traditional notions of authorship and authority, they contended, but only if used critically and reflexively.

Because of the enthusiasm for new technologies and because of theorists' promises of change, I chose to include several *InterChange* discussions throughout the semester in my composition class. I integrated the *InterChange* discussions into our other class work even while I made them the basis for discussion. For example, before the first discussion, students read a piece in which an author described his writing process. We then used *InterChange* to discuss the students' responses to the author's unorthodox approach to writing. I then made our *InterChange* discussion the "text" for analysis in the next class period, asking students for responses to the medium. In this way, I attempted to change the shape of my classroom by giving students more of a voice in the initial discussion and then asking them to reflect on how that space felt to them. My goal was to use the technology critically and reflexively. But as I analyzed the transcripts of our many *InterChange* discussions throughout the semester, I realized that though students were using a new medium, they still clung to many of the same rules and expectations of traditional classroom discussion: Students still conceived of themselves as unitary and stable selves who had to come up with their own ideas in order for them to count. If they relied on their discussions with others to generate their essays and if others helped them write their papers, their work did not count — it was not a rightful text unless they had produced it in isolation and could then claim their ideas exclusively as their own. The comments students made during *InterChange* discussions and in journal reflections about *InterChange* discussions suggest that the discussions did not reveal the social nature of writing. Although Langston and Batson contended that "in an electronic, conversational writing environment, the position of individuals in ongoing social dialectics is more obvious and concrete. . . . Collaboration and social context attain a practical reality" (151), my students' comments and reflections seemed to present the opposite view.

Furthermore, *InterChange* discussions were viewed as an extension of class discussions rather than as a text that could be integrated into students' own writing or could help them generate their own writing. They did not see that they were collectively producing a text based on group knowledge, as Barker and Kemp have claimed[2]; instead, they thought they were "talking." And in a composition class, "talking" supposedly does not count.[3] Although Langston and Batson suggested that real-time conversations online effectively help students merge the conversation and the composing process, students in my classes did not make the connection between what they were doing in *InterChange* discussions and what they did when they were composing their papers. What I found, then, is that even though I had incorporated this supposedly "radical" technology into my classroom, students' conceptions of what it meant to write and to be an author were not in the least changed by their experiences with *InterChange*. The narrative of author as singular self is strongly held indeed. These narratives prevailed in my students' reflections about writing (or speaking) in *InterChange* discussions. Although network technologies can offer us opportunities to challenge traditional notions of self, we must first understand how strongly entrenched those narratives are and what shape they take before we can begin to consider disrupting them. Merely introducing technology into the classroom is not, as I found, a guarantee that these narratives will be disrupted.

My experiences with using *InterChange* in my composition classes, then, complicated my notions of what it means to be an online writer and writing teacher in college classrooms. Unabashed enthusiasm or hype about technology in the classroom leads to a further propagation of the humanist view of the writer as single, autonomous individual who must create his work in isolation for it to be considered important work. If we introduce technology without explaining to students the ways it can be used, we are encouraging them to place traditional narratives of self onto new technology. If we do not bring their perceptions of technologies and writing to the foreground and make these perceptions part of class discussion, we make no headway. Once we engage their perceptions and assumptions, we can teach students to use the technology to collaborate with one another, to question their assumptions about writing, and to expand their concept of audience. Relying upon the hype without critiquing it will reproduce the classroom we claim network technologies challenge.

The Self Reiterated: *InterChange* Discussions on Writing

My experience using Daedalus *InterChange* in writing classes suggests that students can adapt to new technologies without challenging their notions of self. Having extensively read the many sides of the debate concerning computer technologies, during the Fall of 1995, I again decided to include *InterChange* discussions in both my writing classes, this time in two sections of the university's introductory first-year composition course. The first session took place in the second week of the semester. It centered on a piece of writing I had asked the students to read for that class period. The piece, written by Michael Greer, a production editor with the National Council of Teachers of English in Urbana, Illinois, explained the process he used to write a book "annotation" that would be printed on the back cover of a book:

> I'll describe here the process I used to produce a single piece of copy, a two-hundred-word annotation that would be used as a jacket blurb and marketing copy, in promotional fliers, and online advertising. The book I had to write this copy for was *Critical Theory and the Teaching of Literature,* edited by James F. Slevin and Art Young; it's a college-level collection of essays by twenty-one different contributors. Given that the book would occupy a crowded field, I had to write marketing copy that would make the book sound new, different, exciting. I had to write a description that would make people want to buy the book. I had a relatively set format and voice in which to write the piece; in other words, the conventions were more or less set for me: I had to work within the parameters defined by "annotation" and "marketing copy." (1)

As part of a unit that focused on writing processes, I asked students to respond to his writing process and to compare it to their own.

My first class was composed of fifteen students, nine women and six men. From the beginning of the semester, they, as a group, were talkative in face-to-face interactions. It was not surprising, then, that the group actively responded to one another during the first *InterChange* session, even though they did not know each other well. In her reflections about her first *InterChange* experience, Ava explained that

> at the beginning many of us did not know each other so it was even less difficult to say what we wanted to say. But we all could get an idea of how the class as a whole felt on a particular subject. . . . Some people decided to have their own conversations, while others remained on the main topic of concern. Others started their own topics by asking their own questions or expressing their opinions. Regardless, every ones "voice" was heard. (journal comments)

Students quickly adapted to the mechanics of the program: they learned that text scrolled by quickly and that they would have to scroll back up to read it; as Ava pointed out, they realized that several conversations could be held concurrently and that maneuvering in this space required different skills than were required in traditional classroom discussions; they learned that they could respond directly to others and ask questions of others without first going through me, the instructor. The first *InterChange* session was different from traditional classroom discussions in that it disrupted the usual initiation, response, evaluation pattern (Mehan). In a journal response, Amy summed the experience up, saying

> *InterChange* discussions are different from in class discussions for many reasons. I can respond whenever I want to and do not have to "wait my turn," I can take my time and think about what others have written before responding, I can talk specifically to one person, I can change the topic if I so desire, I can ignore comments, I can see direct feedback from others about my own ideas and thoughts.

Clarence, the first to post a comment, writes "Hi everyone!" This prompt elicits several responses, all of a chatty, getting-to-know-one-another nature. Just as the students greeted each other when they entered the traditional classroom space, on *InterChange* they also chatted briefly before getting down to business. One student, who was particularly eager in class and who appeared always to be prepared and enthusiastic about class, was the first to compare her writing process with the editor's. In message #6 of this first *InterChange* discussion, Catherine writes: "Thank goodness we don't have as many critics of our writing as this person did!" This response reflects the pattern of the first wave of responses to the editor's writing process. Another student commented that he had never revised that much before; another commented that "this guy's writing process is absolutely nothing like mine. He's way too technical." In addition to responding on the basis of their own experiences, students also began to critique the writer's process. These critiques ranged from accusing the author of plagiarism because he pulled from a variety of sources to write the annotation to the charge that he revised far too much and got advice from too many people. Clearly, the modernist assumption about author as isolated genius was guiding student responses to the editor's writing process.

The student critiques expressed traditional beliefs about writing, which I found both commonplace and odd — commonplace in the sense that they had been taught certain standards of writing and it was not surprising that they used those criteria to judge this person's writing; odd in that they were using what some have called "revolutionary technology" to put forth traditional beliefs about writing. Hawisher and Selfe pointed to this occurrence also, arguing that "given the considerable corporate and community investment accompanying this technology as its use expands within our educational system" (55), we need to closely scrutinize the ways we are using these technologies. Many times, however, new technologies are used to propagate traditional beliefs. Hawisher and Selfe contended that writing instructors "have not always recognized the natural tendency when using such machines, as cultural artifacts embodying society's values, to perpetuate those values currently dominant within our culture and our educational system" (55). The physical setting in which my students posted their responses during the *InterChange* discussion added to this natural tendency. Sitting by themselves at computer terminals posting individual responses to their peers feeds into student perceptions of author as singular entity. Clearly, the material conditions in which we deploy these technologies and the framework of the technologies themselves can counteract our intentions for them to highlight the dialogic nature of writing. As our use of these network technologies increases, so too should our awareness of the ways we are situated in relation to technologies and how these technologies position us in relation to themselves. This awareness must include a consideration of not only the effects that we think technology is having on students, but also student accounts of their use of the technology.

Of the critiques students posed during the *InterChange* discussion, I find the charge of plagiarism most interesting. Brice, who was unafraid to state his position in class and on *InterChange,* was the first to make this accusation: "I really cannot identify with experience. To me it almost sound like the entire piece was a compilation of someone else's words. Can you say PLAGIARISM?" The all caps presentation of the word *plagiarism* not only stresses his disdain in his critique, but also makes his comment stand out from the others. In a visual arena, Brice is the first to explore the possibilities of creating a sense of tone and voice even in the space of a narrow bandwidth technology. Matthew quickly agrees with Brice's accusation of plagiarism, but, interestingly enough, he doesn't remember the name of the person who made the charge: "I agree with whoever accused the author of plagiarism. It seems that he used very little of his own writing." Thus, even as he argues for the importance of individual authorship, Matthew himself does not cite the author of the comment to which he is responding.

Other composition theorists who have studied network communication also discovered this tension. In their study of woman@waytoofast, an online discussion group for the academic women in their study, Gail Hawisher and Patricia Sullivan (1998) noticed that discussion members forgot who had made a comment but still remembered the comment (Gail Hawisher, personal communication, July 15, 1995). For my class, this discrepancy could be explained by the fact that students did not know each other well and could not connect an in-real-life (IRL) face to the name on the screen. Also, though, this seems to support Lee Sproull and Sara Kiesler's assertion that who says the comment is not necessarily as important as what the comment is. To support their point, they cited Shoshana Zuboff, who argued that

> all messages have an equal chance because they all look alike. The only
> thing that sets them apart is their content. If you are a hunchback, a
> paraplegic, a woman, a black, fat, old, have two hundred warts on your
> face, or never take a bath, you still have the same chance. It strips away
> the halo effects from age, sex, or appearance. (370)

In the beginning of the semester this argument seemed to be true. Once
the students got to know each other face to face, however, the situation
changed. They responded directly to each other by name and carried
on sustained conversations with others in the classroom. When calling
people on their arguments, they hailed them by name. In his journal
reflections about his experiences with *InterChange,* Brice wrote

> over the course of the class, our *InterChange* discussion took a lighter
> tone. As we began to know each other we were freer in our comments
> and opinions. We also knew the instructor better and we were less
> fearful of repercussions for comedic remarks. I also think that as time
> went on I learned to focus better on the people that I thought were
> going to contribute something useful to the discussion. (journal com-
> ments)

Likewise, Clarence noted that "at first we didn't know each other. We
. . . were responding to names . . . without actually knowing who that
person was. As time went on, however, and the students began to know
each other, *InterChange* was more productive" (journal comments). Thus,
students noted that when they did not know each other, the self who
said the comment was less important. When they were familiar with
each other's IRL personalities, the IRL self began to matter. By pointing to the ways that external cues have a direct effect on networked
communications, these findings complicate assertions such as Sproull
and Kiesler's.

During the first *InterChange* discussion in class, the argument for
belief in the authority of the author (and that texts can be and should
be owned by individuals) is first introduced with this accusation of
plagiarism, but the theme is continued through much of the discussion. One example of this occurred in the discussion that arose around
the word *montage.* In his description of his writing process, the editor
labeled the finished product a montage. Greer described his work in
this way:

> The text that I wrote was thus a montage or a collection of other
> people's writing more than my own. I picked sentences I found effective
> and began to order them on my own page, and a shape began to emerge.
> This activity was more like building or sculpting than like "writing" in
> our traditional sense. (1)

A discussion ensues about the word *montage* and the view of writing
that it embodies. Elizabeth introduces the topic: "I've never heard or
read the word montage before." Picking up on her message, Brice ex-

presses his frustration with the way the editor presented *montage,* writing "I don't appreciate the fact that it seemed like he thought we wouldn't understand the meaning of a montage, so he had to give us another word to define it." Interestingly, Brice was upset because the author chose to define the term for his audience, while Elizabeth expressed a lack of knowledge about the term. Two different receptions of this one word, then, illustrate the different ways readers approach the text; however, Brice is quick to assume that he speaks for a universal reader, whereas Elizabeth merely expresses her personal confusion. Many messages later, another student, Rachel, re-introduces the topic. "Actually, I heard 'montage' before in art class," she writes. No one responds to her comment, yet she pursues this train of thought, later writing "Isn't 'montage' like 'patchwork'?" No one responds to her, and she herself moves on to other topics.

Even though this discussion of *montage* was brief, it indexes some interesting questions. First, the word *montage,* which means "a single pictorial composition made by juxtaposing or superimposing many pictures or designs" (*American Heritage Dictionary,* 1170), seems to highlight the ways computers are supposed to be changing our writing, but some students didn't know what the term meant. Second, some responded negatively to the editor's use of it. Rachel attempted to define it from the context of her art class, but by that time the class had moved on to another discussion. The editor's writing process — pasting together a variety of sources to construct a coherent annotation — relied on montage. The computer makes this sort of cutting and pasting easier, but it has also been argued that the computer reflects postmodern fragmentation in that it changes our view of text.[4] Instead of seeing the whole product, we now think of the text in terms of the scrolling of screens. We are unable to view all the text at one time, so this has supposedly affected writing methods and argumentation patterns: the traditional essay form with its beginning, middle, and end does not hold up well when we can jump back and forth between screens. In Brice's response to the use of the word *montage,* then, I would contend that he is responding negatively not only to the author's use of another word to define *montage,* but also to the very premise on which montages are based — a piecing together of a variety of things to construct a new "whole." Clearly, Brice perceives texts as constructed and presented in certain ways, and the editor's construction of the annotation does not fit into that pre-existing definition of *text* and *author.* Brice's initial hostility toward the editor continues throughout the discussion. In his eyes, the editor is breaking some cardinal rules of writing, and Brice continually critiques him for that. Underlying Brice's assertions are the assumptions that texts are supposed to be individually produced, that the author of the text is clearly delineated and given credit, and that the author owns the text.

At the heart of this assertion is a narrative of a coherent, stable self grounded in a body. Allucquere Rosanne Stone contended that it is the combination of the psychic self and the body upon which humanist notions of self-determination are based. This notion of a self grounded in a body in turn shapes our view of community. Stone wrote:

> Our commonsense notions of community and of the bodies from which communities are formed take as starting points, among others, that communities are made up of aggregations of individual "selves" and that each self is equipped with a single physical body. I tell inquiring scholars that at the Department of Radio-TV-Film here at the University of Texas at Austin, we refer to these principles as BUGS — a body unit grounded in a self. The notion of the self as we know it, called in various studies the "I" and in others the "subject," that tenacious just-so story that goes on to assure us that there exists an "I" for each body and that while there can be more than one "I" on tap there can only be one present at any time, seems a natural and inevitable part of life. (84–85)

If the basic unit of reality is the self and this self is supposed to be contained within a body, then multiple positions within one body at any one time are not allowed. This rule supposedly applies to writing also. The author who writes a text is supposedly a self grounded in a body. This self may have different roles to play, but at any one time, the author must be firmly grounded in one role. This requirement makes the self appear coherent and stable, rather than recognizing the ways selves are always already multiple, contradictory, and fragmentary. Thus, one way of constructing the self in this way involves the narrative of writing as a solitary, self-based act. My students' assertions about what an author is and is not are based in this narrative.

The narrative of the author as a coherent, stable self grounded in a body was reiterated in my other class' *InterChange* discussion. The other writing class was composed of thirteen students, six men and seven women. From the beginning of the semester, it was clear that this group did not coalesce well. Throughout much of the semester, they did not like to talk in class, they did not actively participate in class discussions, and they did not freely respond to each other's comments or questions. In their first *InterChange* discussion, students were responding to the same assignment — the NCTE editor's discussion of his writing process. They, like my first class, began by addressing the issue of plagiarism. They commented that their writing was different from his because they included original material, rather than just using other people's words. This observation led to an interesting discussion about originality and creativity. As they struggled to define what creativity was, they defined their perception of the writer's role. Even though they were doing so in an online discussion using innovative technology, their definition of an author, like that of the other class, was based on a traditional narrative of author. Using the technology did not radically change their conceptions of themselves and others. The following is a partial transcript of the discussion that ensued around the topic of creativity:

Brandy (Message #10): I use more of my own ideas when I write instead of copying others' ideas

Mark (Message #11): I don't usually get myself involved in compilations. I just write whatever comes into my head.

Dan (Message #12): most of the material in my papers is original that's called plagiarism

Regina (Message #13): I feel that if you pull things from other peoples work, then it's not writing, it merely copying.

Shelly (Message #14): Whatever works for him. He had a deadline he wasn't ready for and had to write something.

Dan (Message #16): it's called creative copying

Paula (Message #17): I don't usually use other people's writing to write my own piece, i may get a few ideas from other sources but i don't think that only using a few of your own sentences in a piece is a good idea.

Eliza (Message #18): TRUE

Bernie (Message #19): I think that good because he gets support from other people, as long as he quotes them.

Jessica (Message #20): My writing process is different because I don't draw sentences and phrases from other works. I use my own sentences. I also don't have that many people revise my work.

Jane (Message #22): Whenever I write a paper I may ask one or two people to read it, but never any more. My friends write totally different and I would literally have to re-write my paper to please all of them.

Mark (Message #24): Copying is boring. You have to just let your ideas flow freely or else you're not going to come out with a product that is satisfying to you.

Regina (Message #29): I agree Jessica: everyone writes different. All papers should include originality.

In this discussion, the students all agree that the editor's work is not original or creative because he merely pieced together sentences from other sources, thus highlighting their perceptions of what it means to be an author. The narrative about writing the editor provides for the students contradicts the dominant narrative of writer as self-contained and writing as owned. Because of this discrepancy, they argue that the annotation is not original and should not be attributed to the author — i.e., the author doesn't own the work because he used other people's ideas. This discussion overlooks the context of the editor's task, however. Students were responding to his writing based upon their own educational experiences — what they've learned, what writing situations they have been in, and what they have been rewarded for. When they argue against using other people's writing in their own texts, they reinforce humanist notions of the individual as coherent, rational, and singular. The students claimed that they may consult other works to help them generate ideas, but the texts they write are reflections of their own thinking. Although theorists such as Landow and Bolter often argue that computers are changing the way we view texts by highlighting the intertextual nature of writing, these students clearly argued against intertextuality in favor of a traditional sense of creativity. They viewed intertextuality and creativity as antithetical to one another. By privileging ahistorical creativity, the students overlooked the fact that all writing, including the NCTE editor's project, is context bound. The situation in which the editor wrote — as the *production editor,* not the *author,* of the book — and the text he was writing — "an annotation that would be used as a jacket blurb and marketing copy," a text, after all, that is not owned or claimed by one single author — were not addressed by the students. The editor relied on other people's works because his situation called for it. The students did not consider that the dynamics of his working space were different from the dynamics under which they operated. Instead of taking these different contextual issues into account, they relied purely on their own experience and condemned the editor for not adhering to those traditional boundaries.

The editor clearly explained that his writing process is different from traditional conceptions of writing. The editor's description of his writing process challenges the students' traditional assumptions, but instead of rethinking their own processes (and realizing how multivocal texts really are, after all, because we are always processing other people's ideas in our writing, no matter who gets to claim the status of author), they judged the editor and decided that what he had done was merely copying. They did not recognize that organizing and selecting the sentences and sculpting them to appear as a coherent text could be considered an original act — a kind of collaboration. This response is in large part dictated by their previous schooling experiences. Grades are given to individuals for their original work. Writing is taught as a process that requires a single individual at the center. Even the texts assigned as writing models emphasize the singularity of the author and the importance of one person's contributions. To assert, as some have, that network technologies provide a space for students to learn about the multivocality of texts is overly simplified. Networks can provide that space, but unless we, as instructors, provide our students with direct instruction about multivocality and the potentials for collaboration that networks offer, they will use new technologies to support old, limiting ideas of author and self.

My experience in using *InterChange* points to a key flaw in the writing class itself: In its current configuration, the writing class is a separate, self-contained entity. Students do not write for any sort of "real world" context other than to get a grade. Lynn Veach Sadler also addressed this point, arguing

> the composition classroom is an artificial construct. English professors will not be one's audience in the after-life of college (except in the few instances in which people become college professors), and we English teachers probably do not spend enough of our precious teaching time on this topic. (158)

Sadler contended that we need to teach students to see the bigger picture — to place their writing situation in the context of their audience's expectations and their own goals as writers. Writers always write in certain contexts and, therefore, they must understand how a piece of writing fits into the history of other writing done in particular contexts. We need to teach our students to assess the context of their writing situations. Networked technologies such as *InterChange* can help this assessment by allowing writers to converse with their audience (other students in this case), but we must teach students to use the technologies in this way. If we assume that they will automatically see the revolutionary potentials *InterChange* has for providing them contact with their audience, we will be disappointed again and again as students use technology to support their usual perceptions of self and of writing.

If we ask our students to write for an ambiguously defined "educated" audience, we are most likely encouraging them to write to us, their teachers. To solve this difficulty, we could ask our students to write for specifically described audiences other than the usual academic, "educated" other. Network technologies can assist us with this goal, but we must be sure that students receive actual feedback from that audience. Often, students are given other, business-oriented audiences to write for, but they rarely receive feedback from their intended audience. In such situations, students still write for the teacher, because the only person reading their work is their teacher. Thus, even though this environment appears to be providing students with concrete audiences, we are still asking them to write in an academic void. Arguing for this point, Susan Miller asserted that

> to date, it is uncommon for either freshmen or advanced students to be asked to discover how much, what kind, and what quality of writing they are responsible for, either as students or as later professionals. It is equally uncommon to ask them to imagine the results they wish from a piece of writing, or to give attention to the realities of deadlines and collaboration that writing situations impose on their individual processes. For instance, few people who write effectively are responsible alone for every element of a text's production. But the roles of the person or situation that creates an actual writing "assignment" or of the person or organization responsible for the text's publishable form are rarely enacted in compositions, even in those that depend heavily on peer group and collaborative processes. (199)

When we add network technologies to our classroom, we do not automatically alleviate the problem students face when asked to write for an abstract "educated" audience with whom they have no contact. Often, assignments are written in ways that encourage the students to place the teacher in the position of "reader" and, therefore, they do not see their peers as part of their audience. Thus, using *InterChange,* students can receive feedback from peers about their writing, but if these discussions are treated as informal conversations with people who are not part of their paper's audience, students will not likely regard very highly the response they get there. Such a structure furthers the modernist notion of the writer as individual whose work is not shaped by interaction with others: Students write papers to get grades and do not really see how their peers, who are after all in the same position as themselves, can help them. If we set up our assignments this way, we are actually hiding the political and social implications of what occurs in our classrooms and the effects our assignments have; again, we are emphasizing the individual writer who places ingenuity first and audience considerations second. When we require students to write in a void, we're actually asking them to replicate the standards of the academy, but instead of foregrounding this goal, we package it as if we are teaching them the essentials, the basics of writing. As David Bartholomae suggested, we often keep secrets from students and fail to adequately explain why their writing will succeed or fail in the academy. The academy, like society at large, is heavily invested in the notion of the single, coherent, rational self and the discourse that sustains it.

The belief in durable, stable boundaries between self and other is demonstrated in my students' definitions of *author.* The narrative of the humanist self is embodied in many classroom practices — grading procedures, classroom designs, process approaches to writing. It is not surprising, then, that this humanist self can also be found when we use new technologies in our classroom because, as Michel Foucault argued in *Discipline and Punish,* the humanist self is at the core of Western identity. Stone extended Foucault's argument when she stated

> the coupling between our bodies and our selves is a powerfully contested site, densely structured, at which governments, industries, scientists, technologists, religious fanatics, religious moderates, media practitioners, and scholars fight for the right to speech, for a profoundly moral high ground, and not incidentally for the right to control the epistemic structures by which our bodies mean. (84)

The struggle to define self is, then, central to all facets of life. What it means to have a self is at the core of power-knowledge relations. It is no wonder, then, that traditional narratives are so pervasive. After all, many people benefit from the status quo. It is also no wonder that so many challenges have been waged against these traditional narratives. The composition classroom is just one site of this struggle, but it is a crucial site; because the acts of writing and reading construct powerful narratives of identity, who gets to control the shape of those endeavors is an important question.

Conclusion

What stories were told during my classes' *InterChange* discussions? The narrative of the stable, coherent, rational self as embodied in the individual author was a narrative told again and again by my students. The narrative my students told does not necessarily contradict the dominant narratives shaping technology; rather, my students' interactions with the technologies seem to be on a completely different but recognizable plane. At the heart of both sides of the argument concerning technology is a belief that network technologies are new and will thus have unpredictable effects. To the young adults in my class, though, computer technologies are not new. They've grown up in a world directly shaped by technology. They've played video games, have home computers, are familiar with the Net. Even if they aren't technocrats, their view of life has been shaped by a certain laissez-faire view of technology. For them technology does not challenge the traditional narrative of self; it merely enacts it more pervasively by situating lone writers at terminals. The claims theorists make, or the uncritical enthusiasm about technology, and the realities that students live in are, thus, very different. To understand what is going on here, we must acknowledge that difference, understand the nature of it, and analyze how it is played out in composition classrooms.

Notes

I thank Gail Hawisher, Paul Prior, and Michael Greer for their insightful comments on various drafts of this article. Gail's encouragement and vision have directly influenced this work. Paul's wonderful suggestions about the shaping of my ideas were offered at just the right time. And Michael's lively conversations and suggestions and his patient editing were extremely helpful.
1. All student names have been changed to pseudonyms, and permission has been granted to the author to use student comments in this paper.
2. Barker and Kemp argued that

    > the essential activity in writing instruction is the textual transactions between students. These transactions should be so managed by the network as to encourage a sense of *group knowledge*, a sense that every *transactor* influences and is influenced by such group knowledge, and a sense that such group knowledge is properly *malleable* (responsive to the influences of each transactor). (15)

    > I did not find that my students developed this sense of group knowledge when they used *InterChange*.

3. Janet Eldred and Ron Fortune argued that analyzing the metaphors we use to describe computer interactions is important because metaphors powerfully shape the way we view our relationship within the world. "Metaphors . . . work from a known or familiar frame of reference to explain some-

thing whose attraction is based in part on its departure and difference from that frame" (59). They contended that often the ways we use metaphors repeat the traditional oral/literacy dichotomy in which oral conversation is devalued over formal writing practices. Oral conversations are used to generate topics, but the actual work of writing takes place alone — between the student and her text. These divisions are played out in online synchronous conferencing as well.

4. In *Writing Space: The Computer, Hypertext, and the History of Writing,* Jay David Bolter argued that hypertext changes the ways we engage with texts — both as readers and as writers. He wrote:

> Writing is the creative play of signs, and the computer offers us a new field for that play. It offers a new surface for recording and presenting text together with new techniques for organizing our writing. In other words, it offers us a new writing space. (11)

References

The American Heritage Dictionary of the English Language. 3rd ed. Boston: Houghton, 1992.

Barker, Thomas, and Fred O. Kemp. "Network Theory: A Postmodern Pedagogy for the Writing Classroom." *Computers and Community: Teaching Composition in the Twenty-First Century.* Ed. Carolyn Handa. Portsmouth: Boynton, 1–27.

Barrett, Edward. *The Society of Text: Hypertext, Hypermedia, and the Social Construction of Information.* Cambridge: MIT P, 1989.

Bartholomae, David. "Inventing the University." In *When a Writer Can't Write.* Ed. Mike Rose. New York: Guilford, 1985. 134–65.

Batson, Trent. "The ENFI Project: A Networked Classroom Approach to Writing Instruction." *Academic Computing* 1 (1988): 32–33.

Bolter, Jay David. *Writing Space: The Computer, Hypertext, and the History of Writing.* Hillsdale: Erlbaum, 1991.

Eldred, Janet, and Ron Fortune. "Exploring the Implications of Metaphors for Computer Networks and Hypermedia." *Re-imagining Computers and Composition: Research and Teaching in the Virtual Age.* Ed. Gail E. Hawisher and Paul LeBlanc. Portsmouth: Boynton, 1992. 58–73.

Faigley, Lester. *Fragments of Rationality: Postmodernity and the Subject of Composition.* Pittsburgh: U Pittsburgh P, 1992.

Foucault, Michel. *Discipline and Punish: The Birth of the Prison.* New York: Vintage, 1979.

Greer, Michael S. "The Writing Process at Work." Manuscript. 1995.

Hawisher, Gail E., and Cynthia L. Selfe. "The Rhetoric of Technology and the Electronic Writing Class." *College Composition and Communication,* 42.1 (1991): 55–67.

Hawisher, Gail E., and Patricia Sullivan. "Women on the Networks: Searching for e-Spaces of Their Own." *Feminism and Composition Studies: In Other Words.* Eds. Susan Jarratt and Lynn Worsham. New York: MLA, 1998.

Joyce, Michael. *Of Two Minds: Hypertext, Pedagogy, and Poetics.* Ann Arbor: U of Michigan P, 1995.

Landow, George P. *Hypertext: The Convergence of Contemporary Critical Theory and Technology.* Baltimore: Johns Hopkins UP, 1992.

Langston, M. Diane, and Trent W. Batson. "The Social Shifts Invited by Working Collaboratively on Computer Networks: The ENFI Project." *Computers and Community: Teaching Composition in the Twenty-First Century*. Ed. Carolyn Handa. Portsmouth: Boynton, 1990.

Mehan, Hugh. *Learning Lessons: Social Organization in the Classroom*. Cambridge: Harvard UP, 1979.

Miller, Susan. *Textual Carnivals: The Politics of Composition*. Carbondale: Southern Illinois UP, 1991.

Peek, Robin P., and Gregory B. Newby, eds. *Scholarly Publishing: The Electronic Frontier*. Cambridge: MIT P, 1996.

Rheingold, Howard. *The Virtual Community: Homesteading on the Electronic Frontier*. New York: Harper, 1993.

Sadler, Lynn Veach. "Preparing for the White Rabbit and Taking It on the Neck: Tales of the Workplace and Writingplace." *Professional Writing in Context: Lessons from Teaching and Consulting in Worlds of Work*. Ed. John Frederick Reynolds, Carolyn B. Matalene, Joyce Neff Magnotto, Donald C. Samson, Jr., and Lynn Veach Sadler. Hillsdale: Erlbaum, 1995. 129–78.

Sirc, Geoffrey, and Thomas Reynolds. "Seeing Students as Writers." *Network-Based Classrooms: Promises and Realities*. Ed. Bertram Bruce, Joy Kreeft Peyton, and Trent Batson. Cambridge: Cambridge UP, 1993. 138–60.

Skubikowski, Kathleen, and John Elder. "Computers and the Social Contexts of Writing." *Computers and Community: Teaching Composition in the Twenty-First Century*. Ed. Carolyn Handa. Portsmouth: Boynton, 1990. 89–105.

Spender, Dale. *Nattering on the Net: Women, Power, and Cyberspace*. North Melbourne, Aust.: Spinifex, 1995.

Sproull, Lee, and Sara Kiesler. *Connections: New Ways of Working in the Networked Organization*. Cambridge: MIT P, 1991.

Stone, Allucquere Rosanne. *The War of Desire and Technology at the Close of the Mechanical Age*. Cambridge: MIT P, 1995.

Taylor, Paul. "Social Epistemic Rhetoric and Chaotic Discourse." *Re-imagining Computers and Composition: Teaching and Research in the Virtual Age*. Ed. Gail Hawisher and Paul LeBlanc. Portsmouth: Boynton, 1992.

Turkle, Sherry. *Life on the Screen: Identity in the Age of the Internet*. New York: Simon, 1995.

Zuboff, Shoshana. *In the Age of the Smart Machine: The Future of Work and Power*. New York: Basic, 1988.

Webb's Insights as a Resource for Your Teaching

1. In your journal, reflect on the ways that students used the *InterChange* discussions in their writing processes. In what ways did using *InterChange* as a part of the writing process help your students to see writing as a collaborative, social activity?

2. Reflect on your own writing practices — both online and off. In what ways do you collaborate? How has your writing changed as a result of using networked computers? Share these reflections with your students and use them to guide your teaching strategies.

Webb's Insights as a Resource for Your Writing Classroom

The following are Patricia Webb's suggestions for using networking programs such as *InterChange* in the classroom:

1. Encourage students to question their traditional definitions of *original* and *creative*. The image of the singular author writing in his garret alone scarcely resembles the ways writers in real-world contexts actually write. Encourage students to adapt such metaphors as *montage* to describe the process of writing.

2. Have students read "real-world" authors' descriptions of their writing processes.[1] Or, if possible, set up real-time conferences with writers in various fields. In these conferences, guest speakers could explain how they write, what writing situations they face, and with whom they write. Students could then ask them questions to get a better sense of real-world writing situations and the types of collaboration that occur there.

3. Create assignments that require students to work together to gather and present information. If students have access to the Internet, require that they use those resources together to track down the information they seek. (Again, make sure their use of the technology is integrated into class goals.) . . .

4. Have students subscribe to listservs and other online conversations so that their writing has a real-world context. Listservs call for a different sort of writing than most students will expect to do in a writing class. Furthermore, other members of the listserv may respond to them, highlighting the ways their writing has real effects.

---

[1] In *The Virtual Community: Homesteading on the Electronic Frontier*, Rheingold (1993) defined cyberspace as a "place" with all the qualities of other important spaces in our life. Because of its ability to link people across time and space, cyberspace, according to Rheingold, is perhaps

> one of the informal public places where people can rebuild aspects of community that were lost when the malt shop became a mall. Or perhaps cyberspace is precisely the wrong place to look for the rebirth of community, offering not a tool for conviviality but a life-denying simulacrum of real passion and true commitment to one another. In either case, we need to find out soon. (26)

He then goes on to show clearly that he supports and favors the first of those two options and fears the second option, which, he claimed, will happen if corporations take control of the Web.

Teaching Visual Literacy

Images surround us — on television, in magazines, on the Web, in cartoons, on billboards, and in myriad other forms. This continuous influx of visual imagery inevitably contributes to shaping and structuring our views of reality; this is particularly true of our younger students. The visual representations that inundate our lives are "texts" in any real sense of the word — we "read" and interact with them to arrive at an understanding. Just as we teach students to actively read print texts, we must teach them to actively "read" and analyze visual texts. Conversely, we should also be aware of how we can use and manipulate visuals in our own process of composing. Not only do we want students to read both print and visual texts critically, but we also want them to think critically about the texts that they themselves produce. In this age of computer awareness and advances, students are expected to be literate in the principles of document design and should know how to enhance or create meaning by designing effective print, electronic, or multimedia documents.

A Conceptual Map of Visual Communication

Sandra E. Moriarty

In exploring the evolving and cross-disciplinary body of visual communication study, of which visual literacy is a part, Sandra Moriarty raises the need for a model that presents the different facets of visual communication as parts of a unified field. To begin to address this need, she develops a preliminary map of the field that more clearly identifies the central theories and areas of study of visual communication. In developing this model, Moriarty consciously attempts to move away from verbal language metaphors and their inherent limitations. Her article ultimately outlines the theoretical underpinnings from which a multidisciplinary program of visual communication research might be structured. The essay following this one, "Teaching Text Design," focuses on practical techniques and approaches to composition that employ the principles of visual communication theory.

The study of visual communication theory is a multi-disciplinary, multi-dimensional effort. People who write on this topic come from mass communication, film and cinema studies, education, art, anthropology, psychology, philosophy, linguistics, semiotics, and architecture and archaeology among other fields.

Although this brings a rich mélange of viewpoints, which is an asset because of the insights that come from cross-fertilization, it causes some problems academically for those who teach visual communication because of the lack of any sense of common theory and the difficulties of interaction. This is not to suggest that there is or should be a central, core theory that organizes the field; however, it would be easier to order a curriculum, as well as a graduate program of study, if there were some notion of at least the important areas and theories that need to be covered in a study of visual communication.

In a recent project undertaken by this author to identify the theoretical roots of visual communication (Moriarty, 1995), one of the respondents observed that "There are no key theories in visual communication." The study concluded, however, that from both a review of the literature and the responses to the survey about theoretical roots, that there is an evolving and well-recognized body of visual communication theory and literature that crosses a variety of disciplines that could provide some sense of a coherent conceptual base. Such work clusters in the areas of visual literacy, visual thinking, visual perception, imagery, and representation. With more attention to this evolving body of literature, visual communication would have more visibility and recognition as an academic field of its own.

Furthermore, that study found that most scholars responding to the survey were frustrated by the verbal language metaphor which drives much of the work in visual communication. While a central theory may be too much to hope for, there is still a need for the development of a more widely accepted model that better addresses the unique characteristics of visual communication. It is the purpose of this paper to address that issue and attempt to develop a map of the field that more clearly identifies the central theories and areas of study of visual communication.

Review

As an introduction to the problem of defining the field of visual communication, let's begin with a review of the evolving literature of visual communication theory. Probably the most important book specifically focused on visual communication theory is Sol Worth's (1981) series of essays which appeared in his landmark book, *Studying Visual Communication*. Worth approaches visual communication from a sociological and anthropological position with insights from semiotics. Other work by Worth and his students at the University of Pennsylvania's Annenberg School is reported in the now defunct journal *Studies in Visual Communication*. Two journals that carry a lot of the material that previously appeared in *Studies in Visual Communication* include *Visual Anthropology* and *Visual Sociology*.

From the mass communication area comes Paul Lester's book *Visual Communication: Images with Messages*. Publications in the mass communication area include the *Visual Communication Quarterly*, a joint publication of the Visual Communication Division of the Association for Education Journalism and Mass Communication and the National Press Photographers Association. It appears as an insert in the *News Photographer* magazine. Other mass communication oriented work can be found in *Journalism Quarterly*, *Journal of Communication Inquiry*, *Critical Studies in Mass Communication*, *Communication*, and *Journal of Communication*, among many others.

Another important work from the visual literacy area is a book of readings called *Visual Literacy* edited by Moore and Dwyer (1994), which comes from the educational media discipline but includes a number of essays that relate to basic visual communication theory. Rune Pettersson's (1993) *Visual Information* is another useful book of readings that focuses more on the nature of visual information processing and comprehension.

Paul Messaris's (1994) book, *Visual "Literacy": Image, Mind and Reality*, looks at visual literacy from the viewpoint of psychology and natural perceptual processes and questions how much of visual perception is really "learned." Another important work is a taxonomy of pictorial theory and imaginal process that has been developed by Levie (1984).

Other important investigations in the visual literacy field include Braden and Hortin's (1982) "Identifying the Theoretical Foundations of Visual Literacy," which traces the history of theoretical development in the area of visual literacy along with John Hortin's review, "The Theoretical Foundations of Visual Learning" in Moore and Dwyer's (1994) book of readings. A work by Braden and Baca (1991), "Toward a Conceptual Map for Visual Literacy Constructs" attempts to map the field of visual literacy in terms of basic concepts, as this report hopes to do for the broader area of visual communication. The visual literacy approach outlined by Hortin begins with verbal language as a fundamental model and focuses on the transactional processes by which we receive and transmit visual meaning.

Visual literacy work is best found in [. . .], *The Journal of Visual Literacy* (formerly titled *The Journal of Visual Verbal Languaging*), and in other education publications such as *Educational Communication and Technology*, and the International Visual Literacy (IVLA) conference proceedings.

Three bibliographies of the visual literacy area have been constructed both accompanied by a taxonomy of key areas of study. The first is the previously mentioned work by W. Howard Levie (1984), which is broader than just visual literacy and has a thorough review of the psychology of pictorial recognition. The other two are by Alice Walker [. . .] which include a seven-year IVLA Bibliography published in 1990 and a second bibliography which includes a schematic model of the field of visual literacy published in 1992.

Key Elements

In order to build a model of a field, which is the intention of this paper, one must first identify the key elements and then develop the structure that depicts their relationships. In order to isolate these elements, let's first look at other models that are relevant to an analysis of the dimensions of visual communication. As Braden and Clark (1991) have observed, "In spite of this growing body of literature, there has been no strong statement of agreement as to what the components of visual literacy actually are." That sentiment applies even more so to the area of visual communication whose scope is even broader.

Domains

The notion of language as a metaphor for how visual communication operates is an important premise in much of the visual literacy work. In an early classic work, Ruesch and Kees (1956) developed a model of nonverbal languages that isolated three types of nonverbal languages or domains — pictorial, action, object.

Mass communication scholar Patsy Watkins (1995) in her response to the theory survey mentioned earlier identified six key domains of visual communication theory: aesthetic, functional, historical, symbolic, perceptual, and cultural.

John Belland (1995), who approaches visual communication from an English/creative writing perspective, structured his analysis of basic theories into four categories in his response to the previously mentioned theory survey: (1) the mechanical-biological eye, or "the eye that sees," (2) the cultural and pictorial eye, or "the eye that frames," (3) the inner eye, or "the eye that creates and imagines," and (4) the cinema/TV eye, or "the moving eye."

Griffin and Whiteside, working from a communication theory approach, proposed three interdependent categories: a theoretical perspective, a visual language perspective, and a presentational perspective. A similar effort in the visual literacy area was undertaken by Roberts Braden (1987) who has identified three domains as: visualization, theory-research-practice, and technology.

In a landmark Delphi study involving 52 visual literacy scholars, Judy Clark-Baca (1990) arrived at 167 statements which were identified as constructs that define, describe, or elaborate upon visual literacy. From this study, a map of visual literacy constructs (Figure 1) was developed by Clark-Baca and Braden (1991). That cluster map has at its center the notion of "purposes," which suggests that at the heart of visual literacy is the notion of goals or objectives. Surrounding that driving concept are the six areas of communication, learning, thinking, constructing meaning, creative expression, and aesthetic enjoyment. Each of the six areas generates its own cluster of categories and activities.

Levie's (1984) visual literacy taxonomy begins with psychology including perception, construction of meaning, memory and learning. Then he moves to mental imagery, and concludes with what he calls miscellaneous topics.

Alice Walker (1992) developed a schematic model of visual literacy based on the titles given to the annual IVLA conferences (Figure 2). Using "Enhancing Human Potential through Visual Literacy" as the

Figure 1. The Purposes of Visual Literacy

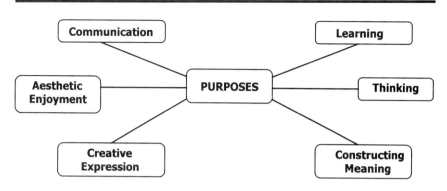

focal point, she arranged Research, Theory, Examining, Extending, and Experiencing around that topic. That cluster leads to "Seeing and Understanding" which is manifested in three ways: Computers and Technology, Arts, and Schools and Curriculum.

Relationships

A number of these scholars have also attempted to diagram or map the relationships between and among these components.

Braden and Hortin (1982) mapped the domains of visual literacy from a language perspective. In their basic Venn diagram of visual literacy constructs (Figure 3), visual literacy overlaps with vision and linguistics. Subsumed within the visual literacy category is the topic of visual language. The relationship with vision and linguistics is an interactive one; in other words, the concerns of visual literacy overlap and interact with those of linguists and perceptual psychologists who study vision.

In a second diagram (Figure 4) Braden and Hortin (1982) focus more closely on the components of visual literacy. Working with an unstated continuum, they identify message and communication areas on the left (visual literacy and graphic arts); creativity and expressions elements (fine art and aesthetics) are on the right. Fine art touches but does not overlap with visual literacy; graphic arts overlap visual literacy. Aesthetics overlap with fine art and graphic arts, but not visual literacy.

Another important work is one by Barbara Seels (1994) that attempts to define the field of visual literacy in terms of three major domains: visual thinking, learning, and communication. In Seels's approach, which reflects her education orientation, visual literacy is the focus and visual communication is a subordinate area. However, in her "Visual Literacy Cube" (Figure 5), visual communication is at the top

Figure 2. Major Divisions in Table of Contents of IVLA Readings: 1982–1991

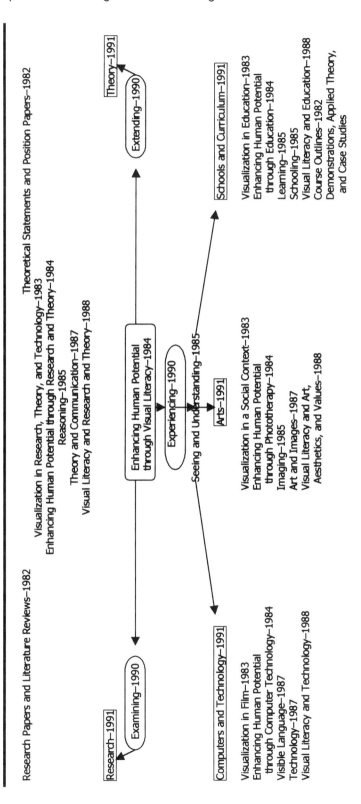

Figure 3. The Interactive Structure of Visual Literacy

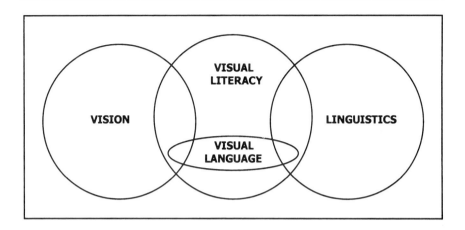

Figure 4. "Related" and "Interactive" Elements of Visual Literacy

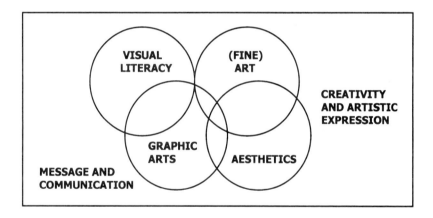

of a three-part construction with visual thinking and visual learning as sides of the structure. Seels's elaborated model (Figure 6) identifies related areas that are subsumed under her three categories.

The analysis of this paper focuses on visual communication as an umbrella area, and would turn Seels's relationships around with visual communication as the central orienting concept and visual literacy as one aspect under that umbrella.

Johns's proposed model (1994) developed from a communication theory approach is anchored in an intentional, one-way transfer of the iconic representation of some stimulus which is encoded for transfer through a medium to a receiver (Figure 7). His contribution to a basic communication model is the notion of life experience which filters or focuses the perception and interpretation of the message as a necessary condition of visual communication.

Figure 5. The Visual Literacy Cube

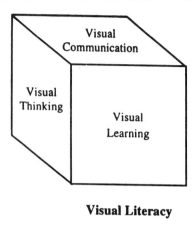

Visual Literacy

Figure 6. Relationships of Areas of Study in Visual Literacy

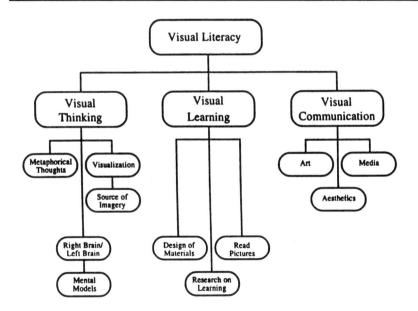

A Conceptual Map of Visual Communication

This paper will attempt to build on this work and map the field of visual communication using communication as the conceptual platform on which to build a model. One place to start mapping the field of visual communication is with the visual communication theory survey mentioned earlier. In that study a total of 16 theoretical areas was mentioned as providing grounding for visual communication study. This illustrates the difference between visual communication and visual lit-

Figure 7. A Proposed Visual Communication Model

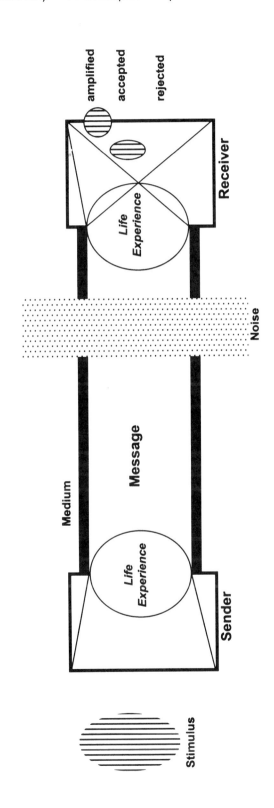

eracy, which is more contained. This list is important because it provides a view of the breadth of the field, as well as the areas deemed to be of more importance by these scholars.

The following chart summarizes and groups the areas in terms of their most frequent mentions. The list below begins with the area followed by the related theories that were mentioned by the respondents. The most important theoretical foundation based on the frequency of mentions by these scholars was psychology. Next came meaning theories such as semiotics. Tied for third were the areas of aesthetics, mass communication theories, and cultural or critical studies. The last four major areas were cinema or film studies, communication theories, literary studies, and education. An outline of these categories ordered in terms of frequency of response would be:

Visual Communication Theoretical Foundations

1. Psychology:
     perception: gestalt perception
     cognitive and information processing: schema theories

2a. Meaning theories:
     semiotics/semiology: signs, symbolism

2b. Visual Communication/Philosophy:
     imagery
     representation
     pictorial perception

3a. Aesthetics:
     graphic design
     fine arts: visual arts

3b. Mass Communication:
     photography
     advertising
     broadcasting
     journalism/news: uses and gratifications

3c. Cultural/Critical Studies:
     ethics/social responsibility
     ideology
     stereotyping: gender (feminist studies), racial

4. Cinema/Film/Video Studies:
     formalists
     movement/kinesthetics

5. Communication Theories:
     rhetoric
     persuasion
     diffusion
     interpersonal

6. Literary Studies:
   postmodern
   reader response
   narrative

7. Education:
   visual literacy: learning theory
   media literacy
   critical viewing
   development

8. Other theoretical approaches:
   historical
   linguistics
   ideation/creativity
   anthropological/ethnography/sociology
   chaos/complex systems

Domains

A second source for ideas to use in mapping the visual communication field is the previous review of domains. Notice that the list of foundation disciplines contains several different types of theoretical sources including intellectual domains (psychology, learning theory, communication, aesthetics, philosophy) and areas of professional practice (education, mass communication, film and cinema, art and graphic design).

A useful model might then organize the intellectual areas around the notion of practice, similar to how Braden and Clark-Baca centered their model on the functional dimension of purpose. The concept of practice in visual communication necessarily includes the media by which a message is communicated. Therefore, in the model in Figure 8, there is a box in the center used to identify areas of media practice which are proposed here as being education technology, mass communication, film/cinema, and art/graphic design. These are areas where visual skills are taught and questions of effectiveness arise and purposes are examined.

Surrounding the area of media practice are the theoretical frameworks of communication theory within which media and professional practice operate. The transactional nature of communication suggests the two basic categories of message production and message reception which are identified in one way or another in most communication models; Schramm's (1954) basic communication model identifies source and receiver, concepts which are easily reinterpreted as production and reception. These terms are also more in keeping with the notion of practice, as well as many approaches to visual literacy which are organized around these same two topics. The social and cultural context within which communication occurs is another important framework, one which is left out of most communication models.

Figure 8. Visual Communication Domains

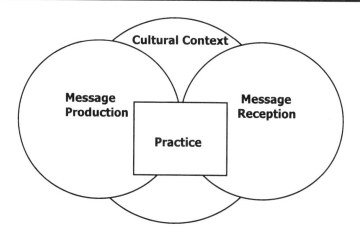

These three categories or frames — production, reception, and context — include almost all of the domains and components identified in the previous review of models and maps. For example, if we elaborate on the production category, we find a cluster of topics such as ideation (creative expression), visualization (visual thinking), and meaning construction which includes an understanding of signs and symbols, a sense of aesthetics, professional skills, and visual literacy. All of these functions cluster around the idea and function of producing a message.

The reception area can be categorized in terms of visual perception, the most basic category of research and theory building, which also includes the optical and physiological reception systems, cognition, which is an aspect of visual thinking that includes the ability to interpret and understand signs and symbols, aesthetic appreciation which permits receivers to appreciate the beauty and skill of the message whether formally trained or not, and visual learning (literacy), which includes critical viewing as well as education directed at aesthetic appreciation, and semiotics which is based on the notion of a system of shared signs and symbols, many of which at least from a Peircian perspective, are visual rather than language based.

Cultural context serves as a frame in which meaning is conveyed and interpreted. Anthropologists, sociologists, and ethnographers study the social uses of visuals as well as the role of visuals in signifying social meaning. Critical studies such as ethics and ideology are the focus of cultural studies as well as the concern of most professional areas of practice. Critical viewing is an important aspect of cultural analysis and the point where cultural context overlaps with visual literacy. The various areas of meaning studies, such as semiotics, help identify the nature of the culturally shared sign and symbol systems used in visual communication.

Intersections

It is important to note that these areas are not independent but intersecting, a notion that Braden and Hortin identified in their models. For example, there are a number of points of intersection between production and reception. Visual thinking — the ability to visualize — is important in both creating (encoding) and interpreting (decoding) a visual. Likewise meaning construction is paralleled by meaning interpretation. And the social uses analyzed by anthropology are similar to the concept of audience uses which are the focus of communication studies. The three areas of intersection noted in the previous paragraph involve intersections from one column to another and they are identified with solid lines.

However, there are other points of intersection that extend across all three of the domains. For example, the concept of shared signs and symbols intersects with all three of the key elements: production, reception, and context. Signs and symbols have to be shared or the transactional nature of communication is violated and the only way they can be shared is socially through a commonly agreed upon code. A sense of aesthetics is important for producing visuals, and also for appreciating them. However, aesthetic appreciation only occurs within a cultural environment. In other words, production and reception overlap with context at these critical points of intersection, which are marked in figure 9 with dotted lines.

The fully elaborated conceptual map of visual communication is depicted in figure 9. Although this details the complexities of the field, it probably doesn't do justice to all the related areas, nor does it effectively illustrate all the possible points of overlap. Nevertheless, it is an initial first step towards circumscribing the field of visual communication as a discipline of its own with its own body of literature, theory, and scholarly work.

Conclusion

People who teach visual communication are housed in different academic departments and that makes it difficult to bring together scholars and researchers who are working on similar questions relating to visual communication. It's probably wishful thinking for most of us who are affiliated with entrenched academic disciplines, but an enlightened approach to this area would be through a cross-discipline program that brings all these viewpoints together.

As mentioned earlier, a number of respondents to the visual theory survey called for a new model of visual communication, something that moves away from the limitations of the verbal language metaphor. Envision a department or college of visual communication that includes people with backgrounds in psychology, philosophy, communication, anthropology, sociology, and education, among others — all working together as members of cross-disciplinary teams that could investigate

Figure 9. A Conceptual Map of Visual Communication

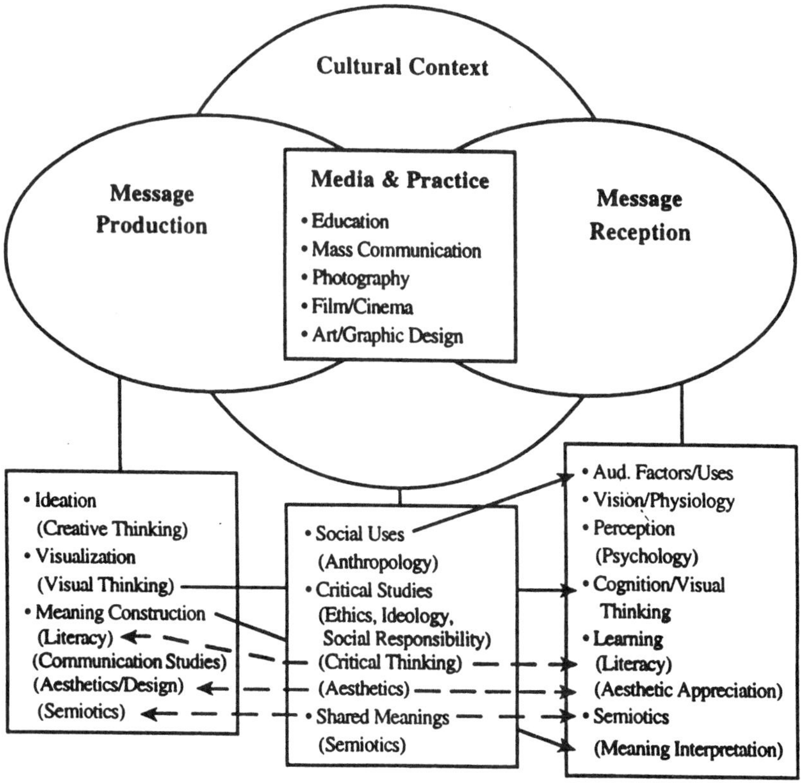

the central research questions in visual communication and develop a new theory of how visual communication works. This map identifies the various areas and foundation theories on which such a program might be built.

References

Belland, J. (1995). Survey comments, in S. Moriarty, Visual communication theory: A search for roots. *Visual Communication, 9.* Flagstaff, AZ, June.

Braden, R., & Hortin, J. (1982). Identifying the theoretical foundations of visual literacy. *Journal of Visual/Verbal Languaging, 2*(2), 37–51.

Braden, R. (1987). High-impact technology and visual literacy: Reacting to change. *Invitational Symposium on Verbo-Visual Literacy.* Stockholm, Sweden.

Braden, R., & Clark-Baca, J. (1991). Toward a conceptual map for visual literacy constructs. In D. G. Beauchamp, J. Clark-Baca, & R. A. Braden (Eds.), *Investigating Visual Literacy.* Rochester, NY: The International Visual Literacy Association, 151–161.

Clark-Baca, J. (1990). *Identification by consensus of the critical constructs of visual literacy: A Delphi study.* Unpublished doctoral dissertation, East Texas State University.

Clark-Baca, J., & Braden, R. (1990). The Delphi study: A proposed method for resolving visual literacy uncertainties. In R. A. Braden, D. G. Beauchamp, & J. Clark-Baca (Eds.), *Perceptions of Visual Literacy.* Rochester, NY: The International Visual Literacy Association.

Hortin, J. (1994). Theoretical foundations of visual learning. In D. M. Moore & F. M. Dwyer, *A Spectrum of Visual Learning.* Englewood Cliffs, NJ: Educational Technology Publications, 5–29.

Johns, J. (1994). *A proposed model for visual communication.* Unpublished paper, Wright State University.

Levie, W. H. (1984). Research and theory on pictures and imaginal processes: A taxonomy and selected bibliography. *Journal of Visual / Verbal Languaging, 12*(2), Fall, 7–41.

Messaris, P. (1994). *Visual "Literacy": Image, mind and reality.* Boulder, CO: Westview Press.

Moore, D. M., & F. M. Dwyer (Eds.). (1994). *Visual literacy: A spectrum of visual learning.* Englewood Cliffs, NJ: Educational Technology Publications.

Moriarty, S. (1995). Visual communication theory: A search for roots. *Visual Communication, 9.* Flagstaff, AZ, June.

Pettersson, R. (1993). *Visual information.* Englewood Cliffs, NJ: Educational Technology Publications.

Ruesch, J., & W. Kees (1956). *Nonverbal communication.* Berkeley, CA: University of California Press.

Schramm, W. (1954, rev. ed. 1971). How communication works. In W. Schramm (Ed.), *The Process and Effects of Mass Communication.* Urbana, IL: University of Illinois Press.

Seels, B. (1994). Visual literacy: The definition problem. In D. M. Moore & F. M. Dwyer, *A Spectrum of Visual Learning.* Englewood Cliffs, NJ: Educational Technology Publications, 97–112.

Walker, A. (1991). Examining visual literacy, 1983–1989. A seven-year IVLA bibliography. In R. A. Braden, D. G. Beauchamp, & J. Clark-Baca, *Perceptions of Visual Literacy.* Rochester, NY: International Visual Literacy Association, 131–160.

Walker, A. (1992). Developing the schemata of visual literacy. *Journal of Visual Literacy, 12*(2), Autumn, 75–87.

Watkins, P. (1995). Survey comments, in S. Moriarty, Visual communication theory: A search for roots. *Visual Communication, 9.* Flagstaff, AZ, June.

Worth, S. (1981). *Studying visual communication.* Philadelphia, PA: University of Pennsylvania Press.

Moriarty's Insights as a Resource for Your Teaching

1. Moriarty describes Braden and Hortin's construct of visual literacy as the domain that overlaps both vision and linguistics, allowing the two to interact as visual language. Do you feel that the verbal language metaphor for visuals is ultimately limiting? If so, how might you circumvent such limitations?

2. Do you think that exploring the multidisciplinary aspect of visual communication theory should be limited to the scope of visual literacy, insofar as it applies to the teaching of composition?

Moriarty's Insights as a Resource for Your Writing Classroom

1. In accounting for the multidisciplinary nature of visual communication studies, Moriarty states that "anthropologists, sociologists, and ethnographers study the *social uses* of visuals" (emphasis added). Contrast this idea of consciously and purposefully manipulating visuals with the traditional method of analyzing and critiquing how visuals actively work on us, as passive objects. How might you engage students in both behaviors?

2. Explain to students Moriarty's contention that, while aesthetics are important for producing and appreciating visuals, aesthetic appreciation only occurs within a cultural environment. Ask students to practice reconciling these points to produce visuals for different specified audiences and purposes.

Teaching Text Design

Robert Kramer and Stephen Bernhardt

*As computer technology grows more and more complex, writers are increasingly able to manipulate the way their writing appears on the page. No longer producing mere blocks of prose to be read, they now can design the text to maximize their readers' visual experience of their work. Besides providing strong advice on how to do this, this article illustrates its points by performing the very techniques it describes. Whether directing us to understand the page as a grid, use active white space, or exploit certain kinds of guiding structures or typesettings, Kramer and Bernhardt continually dramatize their advice in ways that you'll surely enjoy. They refer at several points to the format of the journal in which the article originally appeared (*The Technical Communication Quarterly*), but their remarks could apply to virtually any academic journal, and thereby implicitly raise questions about how journals and journal articles, to say nothing of student work, might come to look in the near future.*

Teaching Text Design

Robert Kramer
New Mexico State University

Stephen A. Bernhardt
New Mexico State University

A growing body of literature defines a rhetoric of visible text based on page layout, typography, and the various design features afforded by page composition tools built into word processors and page design programs. Little has been written, however, about what a writer needs to know about design and in what order. This article describes and demonstrates a scope and sequence of learning that encourages writers to develop their skills as text designers. It introduces relevant literature that is helpful for such learning and it does so in an evolving format that displays visually what the essay discusses verbally.

Since the introduction of personal publishing tools first made available through the coupling of the personal computer and the laser printer, we have found ourselves in possession of the means for not merely typing essays but designing text. In recognition of the power and possibilities of these tools, the fields of rhetoric and technical communication have begun to construct a rhetoric based on the design of texts that display their meanings through visual/verbal integration. In all corners of our culture, visually informative texts are on the ascendancy, and it is crucial that we continue to map the principles of visual design and that we pursue principled methods for learning to become text designers. In this essay, we suggest a scope and sequence of text design skills and knowledge as a contribution toward a curriculum that helps writers become text designers. In a spirit of playfulness that is true to our subject, we attempt to create an object lesson here that demonstrates through display. We will struggle throughout to not only *tell* but *show* the principles we are discussing, beginning with our "student essay" text on the next two pages—then to a designed text.

Winter 1996, Vol. 5, No. 1 (35–60)

Robert Kramer, Stephen A. Bernhardt
Designing Text
English 101

Designing Text

We will begin this article with a visual distinction between designed, rhetorically active text, and the texts that our students are most familiar with: essays.

Students of technical and professional writing often come directly from introductory composition classes, where they may have been expected to do very little work with text design. The prevailing composition aesthetic is a strict, almost puritanical functionalism, meant not for readers but for the teacher who will annotate the text. Students are taught to create pages with flat surfaces: long, double-spaced paragraphs punctuated only by the occasional half-inch or five-space indent; generously wide and symmetrical, one-inch margins all around; and a simply typed page number in the upper right corner of following pages.

Writers would begin to understand the rhetorical design principles of professional documents, as well as increase their software skills, if they were to immediately jettison this clunky design. Changing our perception of the page as a *writing* space to the page as a *design* space propels us to think beyond the confines of the semantic and lexical constructions of words alone and toward the shape of text and our authorial control over its useful readability.

The contrast of these two "school essay" pages with the rest of this journal suggests how much information is communicated through a few simple design elements. The page grid on these facing pages says little except "block of text." The consistent double spacing, desired presumably for interlinear annotation, wastes the potential of white space to convey meaning in active ways. The white space is spread passively, indiscriminately, between every line. Similarly, the monospaced one-inch-all-around margins cause the writer to miss opportunities for using indentation for meaningful effects. In general, there is little in the design that reflects an understanding of the crucial distinction between *active* and *passive* white space.

Headings that would signal text divisions are conspicuous only in their absence, and the particularly unattractive and tiring Courier font make

```
for pages with little appeal.
     Understanding that text is a surface, layered in
its meaning, and most successful when its design is
both helpful and intuitive to the reader are important
starting places for writers as they begin to exercise
control over rhetorical design.
```

We began making a few simple but significant changes at the page break. We reintroduced the facing page headers that identify us as authors on the left (with a somewhat redundant acronym TCQ) and identify the journal on the right with the page numbers on the outside margins where they are most useful. More obviously, we went to single-spaced paragraphs, using space breaks between paragraphs, instead of double spacing every line. Interparagraph space breaks are not the practice in this journal, but it is a style that makes sense for many kinds of memos, reports, and correspondence. The space breaks start to divide the piece into meaningful units instead of spreading ink uniformly across the page.

We then switched fonts to a 10 point Palatino. This change is significant, since it increases the typeset quality by substituting for the monospaced Courier font (where each letter gets the same space, whether an i or an m) a proportional font (where letters take different widths depending on their shape). Since proportional fonts carry intersentential spacing with them (a little extra space break after a period), we went from double-spacing between a period and capital letter to single-spacing (not an easy adjustment for those of us drilled in touch typing). We adjusted the paragraph indents from a one-half inch tab to a one-quarter inch, in keeping with the more modern look of the journal. Finally, we allowed ourselves to introduce a heading on the next page (in a larger, bold, sans-serif font) to begin to further segment the text into meaningful subsections and to provide signposts to busy readers.

Each of these adjustments reflects small but significant changes brought about by the transition from typewriter to desktop tools for producing paper texts. To summarize our changes as design guidelines:

- See the page as a grid.
- Use active white space.
- Use text structures to guide the reader.
- Create a typeset look through appropriate use of proportional fonts and spacing.
- Control the document through features such as style definitions.

We will take up each of these principles in the following sections, moving in each section from basic understandings toward more sophisticated. These guidelines are simple enough to be learned in any class, whether composition or technical writing, whether in English or in the disciplines. Writers can work to gradually refine and advance their understanding of text design and their competence with the tools.

See the Page as a Grid

A first principle of page design is to think of the page as a grid that organizes communicative elements. Lay shows how grids create unity, balance, and proportion in documents (Lay 73). Others have pointed out that page design cues various gestalts: groupings, progressions, beginnings and endings, digressions (Bernhardt; Moore and Fitz). We can think of grids as ways of organizing the space of a page. Readers need to know where they are in a document, where they are going, and how they can get there. They need to know what sort of information is in what predictable place. Grids bring predictability; readers use the grid to know how to read the page.

Pages are spaces comprised of defined areas and boundaries. When a grid overlays a page, text and graphic elements are placed in the resulting rectangular spaces. Page design software and more sophisticated word processors provide grids that are variable in granularity and visible on screen, although they do not print. The alignment of textual and visual elements to a grid insures consistency between parallel text elements, and creates a defined and recognizable look. In highly functional documents, such as computer documentation, a grid helps define and separate explanation, from cautions, from steps in a procedure, from tips for experts. In other documents, such as ads or brochures, a grid contributes to a balanced, aesthetically pleasing page design. Grids are a powerful design tool.

The *TCQ* grid is fairly simple: 4.5" x 7.5" blocks of print. Headers and (first page only) footers break out of the block, and the headings are outdented from the block. Lists and extended quotations are block indented an extra quarter inch. The narrow page width leads to a readable line length (about 65 characters) for a publication that is meant to be read seriously.

We can easily imagine other grids that might inform other texts, page designs derived from making intentional choices of layout for given communicative tasks. A play-script layout, with one-third/two-thirds vertical columns, as on the following pages, proves to be highly pleasing and useful for a wide variety of publications. We have seen grant proposals in this format

The TCQ Grid

Many publications use a "play script" format, with a one-third/two-thirds grid. It is a flexible design that allows marginalia– commentary, headings, graphic elements–to float beside the text.

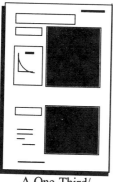

A One-Third/
Two-Thirds Grid

that were simply beautiful, with call-outs, highlight points, and compelling graphs and data displays fitting nicely into the left column. The design prevents long, hard-to-scan lines, and uses plenty of white space to create an open look. Visuals can occupy any of the thirds, spanning the columns to take two-thirds or the whole width of the page.

Grids make great planning tools, as publications can be roughed out with pencil and paper as thumbnails or storyboards before executing the actual design and investing time at the computer. Books on desktop publishing have much to say about designing with grids, and they provide great examples from both popular media and from serious graphic design artists. Some good sources include Shushan and Wright; Brown; Bivens and Ryan; Parker; and White. Planning on the grid also encourages the designer to consider facing pages as the unit of composition, rather than single pages.

As in any art, grids provide stability and constraint. Once the grid is in place, the artist can violate it, break the frame, work to his or her own vision. The temptation for beginning page designers is to imagine grid spaces as symmetrical, rectangular, and right angled to the page orientation. While such thinking makes a good starting point, most experienced designers love to play with the grid, break its constraints, and layer objects across and on top of the spaces of the grid.

An activity that gets writers thinking about grids is to produce a simple essay or review in two-column format. A writer might pre-

Technical Communication Quarterly   41

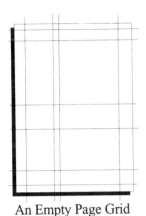

An Empty Page Grid

Use Active White Space

"Any discussion of the rhetoric of practical documents must encompass the language of visual design"
—Kostelnick

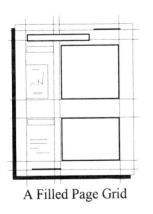

A Filled Page Grid

pare a movie review to look exactly as it would if it appeared in the feature pages of the local paper, complete with headline, teaser, and mug shot. A more complicated task would be to set up a résumé on two different, contrasting grids, perhaps with one purposefully over-designed. Such experiments help a writer learn to contrast serious grids with playful ones and gain control over the rhetoric of design.

Designers begin to use white space actively when they start to see both the positive (ink-filled) and negative (white) spaces on the page. White space conveys a lot about a document: what type it is, how it should be approached, and what must be read and what can be skipped.

White space can be either active or passive: passive white space is defined incidentally by the space left over as the text takes shape. Active white space, in contrast, intentionally defines the shape, organization, progression, and readability of the text itself. Passive is accidental; active is intentional.

We recognize a memo by its heading, perhaps a company logo or letterhead, the arrangement of its To-From-Date-Subject introduction, and its block-style text body and signature. Our recognition is largely a case of recognizing a form as it is defined by the shape of the text. The text shape, in turn, is defined by the page space around it, or its (sometimes not white) white space.

On the following page, the text is set to conform fully to the *TCQ* format, with an indent to mark paragraphs and no space break between paragraphs. To aid readability and signal organization, we might choose to separate paragraphs in a memo with a space break because it makes the paragraphs easier to read as specific points or makes those points distinct from other content and easy to reference. *TCQ* also uses two spaces after a period.

White space can also act as a stylistic tool (Kostelnick 26). The arrangement and style of textual elements on a page can either inhibit or invite readers into a document. An inviting document tends to be open and expansive, with text defined into blocks by white space, headings that are separated by spacing, text that is set with a little extra space between each line, and visual elements that are bordered by white space. Many readers avoid intimidating, dense texts. In a journal such as this, readers are present on their own volition, out of a sense of intellectual curiosity, with plenty of motivation to read pages, even if they are a bit dense (the pages, not the readers) in their ink to white space ratio.

Designers tend to see blocks of text as shapes in space, not necessarily as something to be read. Page design programs frequently provide mumbo-jumbo filler text in a meaningless "Greek" filler (lorum ipsit), so the designer can concentrate on shape and not be distracted by meaning. Text blocks become design elements in balance and juxtaposition with other graphic elements.

In many kinds of text, there really is no need to cover the page with ink. Much designed text has an ink-to-space ratio of less than 50%. As writers develop their design styles, they can become more aware of white and black as defining elements of the page and begin to use white space actively to structure their ideas, invite readers into the text, and show them how it can be read. Writers need to recognize the truth in the huckster's maxim, "If you don't get 'em into the tent, they ain't going to see the show." A visual style, with plenty of white space on an attractive grid, is the ticket.

Use Text Structures to Guide the Reader

Design is functional insofar as it shows readers how to read a text: what the structure and progression is, what can be read or skipped, what is more important or less important. Page composition programs provide a wide range of tools to help writers show structures. Such displayed structures ideally complement the internal, logico-semantic meanings created within the text.

Margins, Justification, and Indentation

The use of white space for margins, justification, and indentation deserves special consideration. The one-third/two-thirds grid that organized the previous facing pages can be thought of as providing a wide left margin, but a special sort of margin that can include visual and textual elements. Some texts, especially those being bound, benefit from a wide, empty inner margin. Other texts benefit from a wide right margin, especially those that will be annotated. Functional design challenges the default settings: one inch all around and a half-inch indent on each paragraph.

Business writing classes have traditionally experimented with block styles, with and without indentation, some with full justification, some with left justification.

This text is **flush left.**

This text is flush right.

This text is centered.

We have set this page to full justify to show the effect. The journal carries a "ragged right" margin, meaning that the text is not flush to the right margin. This is consistent with some marginally compelling research on readability that suggests that readers use the ragged right to track the text and keep their place. It also helps avoid "rivers" of white space that result when the extra word spacings of full justification form noticeable alignments–rivers–of white space that run down the page. Tight hyphenation zones can help control such accidental effects, though for most texts, it is best to keep the hyphenation off or set loose so not too many words are broken at line ends.

Some texts look better and work better in full justified block paragraphs, without any paragraph indent, especially texts with small column width: brochures, newspaper-style columns, and some flyers. Narrow columns of print just cannot support the indentation without the overall look being ragged. Sometimes the design decisions are motivated more by aesthetics than strict criteria of legibility or readability. There's no good reason, for example, to indent a paragraph following a heading; such following paragraphs actually look better without the indent.

Understanding and controlling left, right, center, and full justification is by no means intuitive. Particularly with right justification, writers need to experiment to see how it works, what happens when lines wrap, and how text lines up on a return. A little time might well be spent investigating the ruler bar, which typically offers easy control of margins and indents. Some of the settings are hard for many to grasp, for example, the two little triangles that control the

44   TCQ: Kramer and Bernhardt

left indents on the first and following lines of paragraphs. Distinguishing and manipulating decimal, center, and right tabs can be hard for others to understand. Many relatively advanced users of a program like Word have not necessarily discovered the control of details afforded by the ruler bar. For example, double-clicking on a tab allows the user to set the tab to carry leader dots (as in a table of contents) or a leader line (useful for drawing a rule across a page). The ruler bar from Microsoft Word for Macintosh shown below is the type of tool writers need to develop a skilled awareness of:

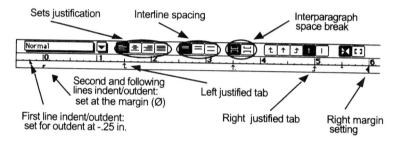

In many kinds of technical texts, the really important information conveyed by indentation is not paragraph breaks, but structural levels in the document hierarchy.

Two or three levels of subordination can be signaled by text that is block indented from the left.

The levels of indent correspond to the patterns of indent in a traditional outline.

Any indent pattern that goes beyond two levels of indent is probably useless to readers.

They are likely to lose track across pages of the level they are on.

A structural cue that is understood by the author and that confuses or is unnoticed by readers is no structural cue at all.

Writers, especially technical writers, need a good understanding of how left block indents signal document structure, and how white space can be used in general to signal divisions and hierarchies.

Tabs and Columns

Nothing is more frustrating than working with a highly formatted document that someone has produced using the space bar and forced returns instead of tabs. Tabs are related to tables, of course, and controlling information in a multiple-columned format is made possible through some combination of tab settings and a page that is set up either in columns or as a table. Tabs, tables, and columns allow the designer to place and manipulate text within the space of the page, rather than simply having text appear within the preset margins.

Every working writer needs to know how to design simple tables for text and data. Doing so is made increasingly simple by word processing software that automates table formatting. Formatting tables still requires that one pay attention to internal margins in the table cells and to the use of borders on cells, and that one understand how a right tab works to keep text or data flush right. There is no excuse for formatting with spaces and forced returns, and as one quickly discovers, with proportional fonts, it is impossible to get text to line up vertically using the space bar. The text may look accurately aligned on the screen, because most fonts display in monospacing, but when the text prints proportionally, columns lined up with the space bar will all be off.

Learning to work with text in columns is an important layout skill. Page composition programs (like PageMaker or Quark or Framemaker) are designed to treat text and graphics as independent blocks, objects that can be moved around and placed on the page. Tabs, margins, and indents can be set independently within the different text blocks that compose the page. Word processors treat text a bit differently and require more finagling with the text to work in columns. Word processors handle columns just fine in newspaper style, when continuous text snakes from the bottom of one column to the top of the next. When the page design requires independent columns of text, as in our one-third/two-thirds pages, a word processor works best when the text is placed inside a table, which is what we did. The two facing pages of our play script format are actually two tables, each with two columns and one row per page and no borders on the cells. We had to futz with the layout a lot to get it to fill the pages and break in the right places, but we were able to do it. Setting tabs is useful any time one needs to line up information in opposing columns of print; creating a table is useful when the text in columns is a bit complicated or when the columns do not correspond line by line.

The ability to handle text (and graphics) as an object that can be placed in a window on a page and moved about is the real advantage of composition programs as opposed to word processors. But the differences are disappearing as programs like Word for Windows 6.0 or WordPerfect 6.0 for Windows incorporate most page composition features, including grids and "snap to grid." In such programs, the writer can place text in a box that can be moved and dropped into place, even over other text or graphic objects. The text can also be made to flow around the frames of graphic objects.

Headers and Footers

Most printed texts use page tops and bottoms for orienting information called *headers* and *footers*. Page numbers, author names, publication information (volume and issue), dates and titles are often found in these areas of the page. These lines of text are separate contextually from the body, riding above and below the running content of the pages themselves, and act as quick reference points, always in the same place, and always saying the same thing in the same way.

TCQ uses alternating headers at the top left and top right of facing pages. The left header has the page number outdented, followed by TCQ: Author Name. The right header spells out Technical Communication Quarterly, followed by a page number that is flush with the right page margin. Both headers are in 9 pt. Helvetica to distinguish them from the body text. Outdenting the even page header follows the *TCQ* grid of outdenting headings from the page margin. Odd page headers are flush right. A footer on the initial page of an article, outdented again, identifies the year, volume, volume number and pages of the article, convenient for keeping track of the source document for photocopies.

We used a different header design on these two pages, placing the page numbers in a footer with alternating author and title lines. The headers have been moved to the inside margins, and the footers to the outside, with the even pages outdented to follow our grid. Whether or not this makes a significant difference is a matter of reading habit. We are used to page numbers in the upper left and right in this type of journal. Magazines place page numbers, if at all, in the footer, often on the inside margins where they are difficult to find. The headers and footers frame the text on the diagonal. Such framing effects are enhanced in some texts by the addition of a rule (a straight printed line in a variable point width) either above or below the header, or by boxing the header and printing the header in inverse (white type on a black background) or with a screen (some ink proportion less than 100% to give a shaded effect). These are small details, but depending on the document and the audience a writer is designing text for, they could become important.

Word processing programs like Microsoft Word and WordPerfect will create headers and footers in separate windows, and then place them in a document in defined areas, automatically appearing on and numbering each page. Content is linked in these text structures, so that changes made to a single header or footer will change all headers and footers on all pages, hence the terms "running head" and "running footer." This is a control feature that allows this part of a text to be set up once, and then essentially ignored, while it adds important orientation to the reader. Students have always been expected to put at least a page number on all following pages of a document. It is good practice to learn to think about information in headers and footers and to make good use of this navigational area of the page.

Headings

Headings break up continuous text into visually coherent parts. They cue the reader to content structure without disrupting the flow of reading, and they partially eliminate the need for paragraph-level transitions. Headings make promises about the content of subsections, and they allow busy readers to find information quickly and to scan documents for information.

When written to be highly specific and directive, headings can carry much more information than paragraph indentations or space breaks. This section is about headings, as indicated by its sub-heading **Headings.** Our entire section on text structures is comprised of a single heading and five subheads. Our headings state topics, but in other documents, headings might ask or answer questions, identify actions, or list steps in a process. Careful attention to heading wording and design can make a document navigable and efficient for readers who come to a text to complete a specific task. Readers can approach the text with varied reading strategies, either to read from beginning to end, or to reference specific points in almost the same way they would look at indexed subjects in a catalogue, reference volume, or hypertext book. Headings are an easy and powerful way to make text less linear and to improve its rhetorical flexibility.

Designers know that headings need to be made visually distinct through some combination of typeface and style features. *TCQ* changes its typeface (to Helvetica from their body type Goudy), point size (to 14 point for a top-level heading in the text and to 12 point for a sub-heading), and type style, going to bold to contrast with the normal body type. Readers have a hard time distinguishing a single point difference in type, but they can usually distinguish a two-point difference, and can certainly do so when the point shift is coupled with other changes (as in normal to bold). The *TCQ* designers add extra spacing around the headings, more before than after, to logically and visually structure the heading with what follows rather than with what came before. The articles don't go below a sub-heading, so there are two levels of descension in the hierarchy. Readers might have trouble with a system of greater subtlety. In headings, designers achieve a lovely melding of form and function, with variables of size, weight, and space signaling the logical hierarchy of the text. A text with problems of global coherence can often be mended with some attention to the structure of sections and their headings. Headings force writer-designers to make promises they actually keep as the document finds a working organization.

Lists

Lists are highly visual and ordered text structures. When buried list structures are extracted from sentences and paragraphs and represented in an indented list, spaced from the body text and numbered or bulleted, they become instantly accessible to the reader. What headers do for whole sections of text, lists do for specific points in a text: they organize parallel ideas into easily referenced and readable forms. We make lists everyday for various purposes, and are accustomed to reading information in list form:

Milk

Olives

Toilet Paper!

Soap

It is hard not to imply precedence through a visual list. Our grocery list has several items, but the user need not purchase milk first, then olives, then toilet paper (though the more obsessive among us order our shopping lists this way, imagining the store layout). The hierarchical arrangement, though, forces the impression of order of importance.

Some lists reflect chronology:

1. lower the blade guard
2. unlatch the blade lock
3. engage the blade with the clutch lever

Visual cues like numbers make the order of the sequence in this list unquestionable.

We used a carefully formatted bulleted list in this article, indenting our bullets one-quarter inch and tabbing the list items another one-quarter inch:

- See the page as a grid.
- Use active white space.
- Use text structures to guide the reader.
- Create a typeset look through appropriate use of proportional fonts and spacing.
- Control the document through features such as style tags, templates, and links.

To keep the look clean, when a bulleted item wrapped at the end of a line, we lined up the following line on the left indent of the first. This list mirrors the order of both first mention of each of these topics in our introduction and the sequence of discussion that structures the whole text. Each item from this initial list became its own section heading.

We indulge a brief confession here. When we first wrote the introductory section where this list of design principles appears, the individual items were buried inside paragraphs and spread across a page. Our design instincts recognized a list buried in the linear prose structure and urged us to pull the separate points out into a vertical list, bullet them, and bring them into parallel verb/complement structures. Once we had done so, we saw them as the structure that could hold the whole essay together and so created section headings from the list. The design of the whole grew from a local design principle: if information is list-like, make it a visible list. This is a liberating moment for writers: when they recognize a list that is buried in a paragraph and decide to make the logical structure visible.

Create a Typeset Look

Typography as a design concept includes the selection of typefaces: family, size, and spacing on a page (Shushan and Wright 14). The writer facing the blank page must be able to make decisions about what sort of typographic design is appropriate given a specific rhetorical situation. Decisions can be based on what type is best suited to the purpose and audience, what is most readable, what styles best cue the content, and what type offers the most aesthetic face without sacrificing legibility.

Type in its simplest clothing is a graphic element comprised of widths and lengths, spacing and subtle shapes, its meaning displayed by the controlled spread of ink on a page. To ignore the visual value of a typeface is to ignore the single most important feature affecting the readability and design of a text.

Page design software and sophisticated word processors grant authorial control over text size, shape, style, color, spacing, width, and proportion. Type treatments such as bold, italics, and underline provide additional levels of meaning to a font without changing its family, an important consideration: font changes in documents should be used to signal new content through structures like headings and call outs. By using different type families and type styles, writers can create multiple levels of meaning and visual cues in a document while contributing to its readability.

Controlling Line Length, Leading, and Kerning

Line length, called *measure,* is a factor in text readability. Generally, shorter lines mean easier tracking for the reader and fewer instances of losing one's place. A rule of thumb that is frequently violated is that lines should be about $1^1/_2$ to 2 alphabets long (≈40–60 characters). A good actual line length for a specific text is dependent on how closely spaced the font is and how large the point size is. With larger point type, lines can be made longer.

Leading (pronounced "ledding" after the name of the metal slugs that separated lines of set type) provides interlinear space. Type can be set tight or open, with very little space from the bottom of the characters on one line to the top of the characters on the next or with extra space to open up the text. All word processors provide gross adjustments to leading through single, space-and-a-half, or double-spaced line settings, a system inherited from the typewriter. Sophisticated word processors allow the type designer to control leading more exactly. This paragraph is set as 10 point Palatino on 14 point leading, a little open.

Leading is measured in points (a point is approximately 1/72 of an inch; 12 points ≈ 1 pica; 6 picas ≈ 1 inch). The leading of a text is described in terms of point size of type on leading. This paragraph is set in Avant Garde 12/20, giving a very open look that might work for ad copy, marketing information, or highly designed annual reports. *TCQ* sets its body type as Goudy 11 point type on 11.5 point leading (expressed "11 on 11.5"). This is a bit tight. Setting the leading to **AUTO** would generally result in 9-point text set 9/11, or 10-point as 10/12, with about two extra points of leading, spread proportionally above and below the line of type. With larger font sizes, less leading is needed. Leading can also be set negatively, so lines of type actually touch or overlap. Shushan and Wright, and Brown both provide technical discussions of these issues and provide good examples.

Kerning is an advanced design tool that allows the typesetter to adjust for the spacing between letters to approximate a hand-set look. Kerning refers to the space between letters, which can be open or tight. All proportional fonts do some automatic kerning, so an A and a V would be set a little tight to accommodate their shapes, which are not strictly rectangular but oblique. A little kerning with the eye on a display text, like a poster or flyer, can make a difference in the professional look. A series of lines beginning with capital letters, for example, will not line up to the eye on the left margin because of the different letter shapes, but can be kerned into an alignment that pleases the eye.

Line length (or measure), leading, and kerning are design tools that allow for careful copy-fitting. While controlling these features is not necessary in many ordinary texts, they can provide for special effects or contribute to the design of texts that must be highly readable.

Understanding the Face of Type

Writers accustomed to writing essays with flat text surfaces and undistinguished type find themselves loose in a candy store when they discover the typographic variation available today on most word processing systems. Our network offers a choice of well over 200 fonts in various styles and the invitation to experiment is irresistible. Any number of fonts may end up in a document as students begin to explore the possibilities of playing with type:

• Now Available •
T Y P O g r A p h y
Hundreds of styles
I n s t a n t   A c c e s s   to
Voice *Tone* Expression
All at your FINGERTIPS
You've Never Seen
Anything Like This!!

While writers discover how to use software to manipulate type features, they also develop awareness of typography's role as both an aesthetic and structural element. As they learn to talk type on its own terms, they gain respect for its influence on the page.

For our sample "essay" pages, we chose Courier, a particularly rigid and underdesigned font that is associated with typewritten text.

52 TCQ: Kramer and Bernhardt

Courier lacks variability in both letter width (it is monospaced, with no kerning) and stroke: the lines that form the characters are of uniform thickness. Courier does have the virtue of being robust under abuse: it can be repeatedly photocopied or faxed and hold its defining shapes well. Courier is a sturdy but boring font.

Typographers have a whole language for talking about type, some of which is displayed in this diagram:

adapted from Shushan and Wright, 1991

A typeface is a graphical image, its details highly refined and carefully designed to be unique from font to font. It is a conditioned habit to look right through the typeface to the words of the text, and not see type as a graphically rich design element. While modern type does not have the graphic texture derived from being stamped onto a page by a small, letter-shaped brick attached to a levered arm, the ink or toner *is* spread precisely as if brushed, and meaning is created by the combination of intricate graphic details forming identifiable design characteristics.

The differences in many of the features indicated in our display of Quiet Elephants (below) are what define different type families. A type family is the sum of all the variations of a single typeface (Shushan and Wright, 21). These variations include widths, *slant*, and styles like **bold**, regular, <u>underline</u>, and light. The most identifiable changes in type families occur in serifs, x-height, and counters. Our Quiet Elephants take on different appearances on these subtle levels when the typeface is changed:

Quiet Elephants	14pt. Palatino
Quiet Elephants	14pt. Times
Quiet Elephants	14pt. Bookman
Quiet Elephants	14pt. Bernhard Modern

These four lines are all set in 14 point type, but vary widely in measure. Bookman has a large counter (the open space in closed letter forms like a, o, p, g, and q) and requires significantly more line length per word. Its x-height is roughly the same as Palatino, yet its counters are horizontally oval rather than round. Font designers find pleasure in adding high detail to certain letters: the Q is highly unique in these faces. (While we are on the subject of Qs, allow yourself to linger on the gorgeous Q on the cover of this journal. It is a fine example of type as a design element.)

Lines in Bookman appear almost stretched lengthwise as they spread across a page; our article would be several pages longer in this font. Bookman is also considerably heavier in stroke than Palatino or Times. Large text bodies like those in this article would not be difficult to read, but the space consumed by this heavy, open font makes it a poor choice for an academic article. It remains a favorite of children's book designers.

Times has a taller x-height than Bookman, but is more compressed, or tighter, on its baseline than Bookman and Palatino. It is a highly efficient typeface for columns and grids that require a great deal of compressed text. Newspapers make excellent use of Times, and some of the many variants of this font family are at use in all sorts of academic texts. Our article would be significantly shorter in this font, but not as easily read. Times is an extremely popular body font, available on all laser printers, and always a good choice for serious text. These four fonts are also called serif or Roman fonts; each point on each letter has a flourishing stroke.

Often, the only way to decipher a type's readability and appropriateness is to see it in action. It is very difficult to distinguish immediately between typefaces like Palatino and Times unless seen side by side; not so difficult with Bernhard Modern. Setting the same text in different typefaces and then discussing the effects is a good way to start to pay attention to type design. A writer might first print a memo in Courier, then in Palatino. Seeing the very obvious differences will begin to train the designer to make sense of the candy store options. Try for a moment to distinguish between *TCQ*'s use of Goudy in this journal, and our use of Palatino. Another useful exercise is to print samples of a variety of fonts and discuss people's impressions about which fonts would be suitable for what types of documents (party invitations, newspapers, lab reports, computer documentation, and so on).

Invitation **Party** brochure **banner**
Newspaper screen document
Posters

Type Styling

Type can be styled to add meaning without changing the font family. Styles can include **bold**, *italic*, CAPS, SMALL CAPS, underlined, double-underlined, s h a d o w, ~~strikethru~~, and hidden.

Both of the following sentences are in 12 point Helvetica. The second has style treatments that add important dimensions to its meaning and effectiveness:

Press the red button prior to initiating the grinding roller.

Press the **red** button <u>PRIOR</u> to initiating the grinding roller.

Writing instructions using one or two fonts are good style assignments. Writers increase their rhetorical skills by using style, instead of point size and different type families, to guide the reader carefully through a text that *could* have serious consequences if not read correctly: like not pressing the **red** button.

The threat of these styles is that novice designers sometimes end up producing texts that look like ransom notes. A careful book designer decides on a specific use for each type style: for example, **bold** for action steps, *italic* for emphasized words, single quotes for words as linguistic examples, underline for titles of published works, and SMALL CAPS for glossary terms. Carefully defining functions for each style and resisting the temptation to overuse the styles leads to effective use.

Choosing for Function: Display/Body/Legibility

Most students would not have trouble discerning which of the two memorandums following would be the more effective document:

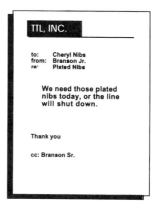

The first memo uses a display font, Castellar MT, for both the memo's letterhead and its body, Courier for its heading, and a script font, Zapf Chancery, for its signature line. It is nearly impossible to get a sense of tone or professionalism from its display, and it is distracting to read. The second memo uses a sans serif font for both heading and body, a successful choice because of the short length of the memo. A larger body might have warranted a serif font like Palatino.

It is important to recognize that some font families were designed for screen displays only and never meant to be printed. Apple Computer created fonts and assigned city names (Geneva, Chicago, Monaco) that would look very large and distinct and readable on screen. But they do not make good choices for printed documents. Within the last couple of years, we have seen the development of font families that erase the distinction between screen font and printer font. The older font families had separate files for each point size and for both screen and printer. The new scalable typefaces are vector-defined, so the whole range of point size is defined mathematically. The newer fonts go by names like TrueType on the Macintosh and ATM (Adobe Type Manager) within Windows.

Sans serif, or Swiss/Gothic typefaces are uniform and do not have finishing strokes at the end of each form. Common sans serif fonts include the standard Helvetica as well as Univers, Futura, and Ariel. Some of these fonts, like the Avant Garde of this paragraph, are so round that they make better display fonts, or at best detract from the "serious" look of a text. Avant Garde usually makes a poor choice for body text.

The bold styles of Helvetica are a favorite of many designers for headings, as is the case in this journal. Nobody, however, would want to read much body text in a bold Helvetica. It is a matter of debate whether sans serif fonts slow readers down. It may just be a matter of our being used to seeing body text set in serif.

The absolute default setting in current practice favors a bold Helvetica font for headings and a Times-Roman font for body type (a look similar to this journal). Such a pairing is undoubtedly conservative, but never wrong. It represents a starting point and type can be designed from there, with various and subtle effects.

Some Fine Points on Type

Gaining control of a few typographic details can lend an element of professional design to a document:

- Since proportional fonts build in extra spacing after end punctuation, it is not necessary to space twice after periods, exclamation points, question marks, and colons. Though not extinct, double spacing is a holdover from the typewriter era.

- Quotation marks and apostrophes are designed elements of a type family (called *typographer's quotes* or *smart quotes*). Some software has a setting to turn on typographer's quotes; in other software, combination keystroke commands will display them. They look much better than the all-purpose variety ("these" vs. " these").

- Dashes and hyphens are distinguishable in typeset text. Dashes are available through certain keystroke combinations or through special character maps. Picky people can further distinguish n-dashes from the slightly longer m-dashes (named for their width, which corresponds to the letters *n* and *m*).

- Advanced word processors have equation editors for writing formulas. Students of science, math, and engineering in particular appreciate learning how to insert $\sqrt{\frac{1}{5}} \geq \bar{x}$.

- Character maps or Key-Caps provide special characters that can be quite useful, beginning with bullets, but also symbols such as ©, ø, ∧ , ✔, and ❻. Where these symbols reside and how they are inserted in documents varies, but they are not difficult to master.

Control the Document

A final design skill involves using the advanced tools of the word processor or composition program to insure consistency in the elements of layout and typography discussed above. Everything we have discussed here can be done "on the fly" with text marked up and formatted as one composes. Indeed, we had to do a lot of formatting on the fly, since we have tried to demonstrate so many variables of layout and typography. For most documents, however, *style sheets* allow for much better design control than designing on the fly. Style sheets (sometimes called *style formats* or *style tags*) allow the text designer to define and tag each structural element of the composition. Style sheets are a sort of mark-up language, similar to SGML (Standardized General Markup Language) used in many kinds of technical publications or HTML (Hypertext Markup Language) used to format hypertexts.

A style sheet for a document defines the various elements of composition. In this text, we have defined our heading levels, headers, body paragraphs, bulleted lists, and bibliographic entries within the style sheet of the word processor. Our style definition for the top level heading in this article stipulates:

Normal + Font: B Helvetica Bold 18 Point, Indent: Left -0.25 in
First 0 in. Space Before 24 pt After 12 pt, Keep With Next

The definition inherits the defining features of Normal (the definition of our body paragraph), but changes the font, indents it negatively (outdents), provides 24 points of white space before the heading (to drop it away from the last line of the previous body paragraph), inserts 12 points of white space below the heading, and keeps the heading with the following paragraph (so as not to widow the heading at the bottom of a page). Not evident in the definition is its singular association with the heading text; after typing it and pressing return, the next paragraph is defined as normal (body text). Any formatting element (tabs, indents, spacing, type style, justification) can be embedded in the style definition.

Style sheets can be created for different types of documents: memos, proposals, personal letters, forms, lab reports. Then a new file can be opened with the template that is governed by the appropriate style sheet. Style sheets can also be used to govern the "look" of a company's documents, so that people working on different projects will produce documents that have a similar corporate identity.

Once defined, any change to a style definition ripples through a document and all the elements with that tag change consistently. Thus, if the designer decides to open up the body paragraph by introducing a little extra leading, going say from 12 auto to 12/14, the change would take place on every other body paragraph in the text. Further, if other elements in the style sheet are "based on" the definition of the body paragraph, those would change, too. So if the designer wanted to change the font from Palatino to Times, and all style definitions were based on the body paragraph definition, then all the definitions would change based on a single change to the font for body paragraphs.

Many word processors provide additional tools for document control. Some allow one to avoid leaving widows (the first line or two of a paragraph or a header that is left behind at a page break) and orphans (a line that is pushed to the next page at the break). Others allow for flexible hyphenation zones. Some allow text to be defined so that it is not separated from what follows, or so that a group of lines stays together, or so it always starts at the top of a column or the beginning of a new page. All such features begin to automate document design and control the design from the top level, so decisions are not made locally.

It is hard to convey why this high-level document control is important until one starts working with long and complexly formatted documents. But as documents grow longer and as formatting grows more complex and subtle, keeping the formatting decisions consistent across the text becomes increasingly difficult. Style sheets provide extremely powerful and reliable tools for doing so. Learning to use style sheets in a word processor also prepares one for using them in other applications: in composition programs, in hypertext authoring languages, or in scripting languages.

Designing Documents

All of the elements discussed above are brought into play as writers design working documents. Writers can begin by thinking of the page as a grid and seeing the space as divisible into areas of ink and white space. The white space itself can be considered an active design element, used to separate content, to open up the page, and to cue the reader to the progress of the document. Areas of the page can be designed to contain orienting information in the form of headers and footers, and the logical organization of the text can be cued through headings that signal the hierarchy and content.

An attractive and readable design can be further encouraged by controlling line length and leading, making sure these elements are in balance with the appropriate font. The font can be chosen and sized with regard for the function of the document and its audience. Internally, the designer can choose body fonts for readability and display fonts for headings. All the elements can be defined and controlled through style sheets, with the careful definitions evolving into templates or master pages for certain documents that are produced more than once.

We have touched on some basics of text design in this article. Any of these elements can be extended, their subtleties played upon, the use of typographic tools developed and refined. We have discussed primarily text, but beyond text lie the important areas of designing and incorporating visuals (Tufte) and architecting whole publications. Developing control over the elements of layout and typographic design leads one naturally to begin thinking about designing documents with multiple pages. The challenge of design becomes an issue of how to lead readers into documents and how to direct their reading processes once the document has their attention. Facing pages can be designed as single design units, information can be emphasized or de-emphasized, and the page can gain texture from elements that are central or peripheral, verbal or visual.

Some may object that the kinds of learning we are describing here are superficial, launching the old challenge that we are modern sophists, more concerned with form than context, with display over truth. But we think not. Seeing is thinking (Arnheim, Horowitz). Thinking about design is thinking about structure, function, and

Technical Communication Quarterly   59

aesthetics. Making decisions about layout and text structures is one powerful way a writer brings organization and coherence to a text. Controlling documents with the sophisticated tools of word processing and page composition is no simple matter, but goes directly to the issue of capable control over hardware and software, a skill increasingly critical for all those of us who are surrounded by machines. Seeing a text at the top level and watching the many design decisions filter down through the actual printing of the text—being in control of the software and the text—grants a powerful feeling of mastery of language and machine. These kinds of learning are worth developing, through the classes we teach and take, and through our personal struggles to control the tools well enough to design the texts we envision.

Works Cited

Arnheim, Rudolf. *Art and Visual Perception*. Berkeley: University of California P, 1954.

———. *Visual Thinking*. Berkeley and Los Angeles: University of California P, 1969.

Bernhardt, Stephen A. "Seeing the Text." *College Composition and Communication* 37 (1986): 66–78.

Bivens, Thomas, and William E. Ryan. *How to Produce Creative Publications: Traditional Techniques and Computer Applications*. Lincolnwood, IL: NTC Business Books, 1991.

Brown, Alex. *inPrint*. New York, NY: Watson-Guptil Publications, 1989.

Horowitz, Mardi Jon. *Image Formation and Cognition*. New York: Appleton-Century-Crofts, 1970.

Kostelnick, Charles. "Visual Rhetoric: A Reader-Oriented Approach to Graphics and Design." *The Technical Writing Teacher* 16 (1989): 77–88.

Lay, Mary. "The Non-Rhetorical Elements of Design." *Technical Writing, Theory and Practice*. New York: MLA, 1989.

Moore, Patrick, and Chad Fitz. "Using Gestalt Theory to Teach Document Design and Graphics." *Technical Communication Quarterly* 2.4 (1993): 389–413.

Parker, Roger. *The Makeover Book: 101 Design Solutions for Desktop Publishing*. Chapel Hill, NC: Ventana P, 1989.

Shushan and Wright. *Desktop Publishing by Design*. 2nd Edition. Redmond, WA: Microsoft Press, 1991.

Tufte, Edward R. *Envisioning Information*. Connecticut: Graphics P, 1990.

White, Jan V. *Graphic Design for the Electronic Age*. New York: Watson-Guptil Publications, 1988.

Kramer and Bernhardt's Insights as a Resource for Your Teaching

1. Kramer and Bernhardt begin by presenting their work in the standard format of the student essay. How would you characterize this format? What, in particular, makes it seem relatively impoverished from a visual perspective?

2. Choose one particular feature of text design that the authors describe, and experiment by using it in the next handout you compose for your students. Reflect on the degree to which students' responses to the handout are affected by the design.

Kramer and Bernhardt's Insights as a Resource for Your Writing Classroom

1. Have your students compose a short paper in the traditional method, then ask them to play with various design possibilities as explored by Kramer and Bernhardt. Ask students to discuss how certain sorts of changes in design might strengthen or weaken the text in question, and why.

2. Browse the Web to find a text that seems particularly well designed, or create your own. Have your class think about its various design features and try to explain why its designers might have made the choices that they did.

3. Reflect on the implications of reconsidering authors as designers. What are the dangers or benefits of thinking about writers and writing in terms of design?

Responding to and Evaluating Student Writing

Careful reflection on classroom practice prompted the articles in Chapter 3 of this volume. Each essay is, of course, informed by philosophical perspectives, but all these readings focus very specifically on practical strategies for working with students at different skill levels in a variety of writing sites. You'll find many connections among the readings and a high degree of "intertextuality." Although you may be tempted to turn to just one of these readings only as a strong need arises, we recommend that you read them all and that you read them against the other pieces in this collection. These articles all resonate with a strong concern for student growth and empowerment.

Teachers' responses to student texts are continuously cited as the most significant influence — positive or negative — on students' concepts of themselves as writers. Although to many students "teacher response" signifies grades and summary comments, teachers may respond to student writing in several other ways: inside and outside the classroom, through structured feedback and spontaneously, and as both ally and gatekeeper. From the essays in this section, you can carry away caveats about ways of responding and strategies to try.

Responding to Student Writing

Nancy Sommers

In the conclusion of this landmark essay, Nancy Sommers describes what continues to be a major responsibility for writing teachers: "The challenge we face as teachers is to develop comments which will provide an inher-

ent reason for students to revise; it is a sense of revision as discovery, as a repeated process of beginning again, as starting out new, that our students have not learned. We need to show our students how to seek, in the possibility of revision, the dissonances of discovery — to show them through our comments why new choices would positively change their texts, and thus to show them the potential for development implicit in their own writing."

Sommers's article reports the findings and the significance to teaching practice of collaborative research on the nature and effects of teachers' comments on first and second drafts. Lil Brannon, Cyril Knoblauch, and Sommers learned that instructor commentary can "appropriate" student texts — that is, distract writers from their own purposes in writing texts and focus them instead on responding to what they perceive the instructor wants in future drafts. They also found that instructor commentary was rarely text-based but rather exemplified the abstract, vague, and generic writing that we ask our students to avoid.

The article prompts writing teachers to analyze how they respond to student writing in all its stages, to adapt their comments on each draft to the needs and purpose of the writer, and to demonstrate through text-based comments the "thoughtful commentary" of attentive readers.

More than any other enterprise in the teaching of writing, responding to and commenting on student writing consumes the largest proportion of our time. Most teachers estimate that it takes them at least twenty to forty minutes to comment on an individual student paper, and those twenty to forty minutes times twenty students per class, times eight papers, more or less, during the course of a semester add up to an enormous amount of time. With so much time and energy directed to a single activity, it is important for us to understand the nature of the enterprise. For it seems, paradoxically enough, that although commenting on student writing is the most widely used method for responding to student writing, it is the least understood. We do not know in any definitive way what constitutes thoughtful commentary or what effect, if any, our comments have on helping our students become more effective writers.

Theoretically, at least, we know that we comment on our students' writing for the same reasons professional editors comment on the work of professional writers or for the same reasons we ask our colleagues to read and respond to our own writing. As writers we need and want thoughtful commentary to show us when we have communicated our ideas and when not, raising questions from a reader's point of view that may not have occurred to us as writers. We want to know if our writing has communicated our intended meaning and, if not, what questions or discrepancies our reader sees that we, as writers, are blind to.

In commenting on our students' writing, however, we have an additional pedagogical purpose. As teachers, we know that most students find it difficult to imagine a reader's response in advance, and to use such responses as a guide in composing. Thus, we comment on student writing to dramatize the presence of a reader, to help our students to become that questioning reader themselves, because, ultimately, we believe that becoming such a reader will help them to evaluate what they have written and develop control over their writing.[1]

Even more specifically, however, we comment on student writing because we believe that it is necessary for us to offer assistance to student writers when they are in the process of composing a text, rather than after the text has been completed. Comments create the motive for revising. Without comments from their teachers or from their peers, student writers will revise in a consistently narrow and predictable way. Without comments from readers, students assume that their writing has communicated their meaning and perceive no need for revising the substance of their text.[2]

Yet as much as we as informed professionals believe in the soundness of this approach to responding to student writing, we also realize that we don't know how our theory squares with teachers' actual practice — do teachers comment and students revise as the theory predicts they should? For the past year my colleagues, Lil Brannon, Cyril Knoblauch, and I have been researching this problem, attempting to discover not only what messages teachers give their students through their comments, but also what determines which of these comments the students choose to use or to ignore when revising. Our research has been entirely focused on comments teachers write to motivate revisions. We have studied the commenting styles of thirty-five teachers at New York University and the University of Oklahoma, studying the comments these teachers wrote on first and second drafts, and interviewing a representative number of these teachers and their students. All teachers also commented on the same set of three student essays. As an additional reference point, one of the student essays was typed into the computer that had been programmed with the "Writer's Workbench," a package of twenty-three programs developed by Bell Laboratories to help computers and writers work together to improve a text rapidly. Within a few minutes, the computer delivered editorial comments on the student's text, identifying all spelling and punctuation errors, isolating problems with wordy or misused phrases, and suggesting alternatives, offering a stylistic analysis of sentence types, sentence beginnings, and sentence lengths, and finally, giving our freshman essay a Kincaid readability score of eighth grade which, as the computer program informed us, "is a low score for this type of document." The sharp contrast between the teachers' comments and those of the computer highlighted how arbitrary and idiosyncratic most of our teachers' comments are. Besides, the calm, reasonable language of the computer provided quite a contrast to the hostility and mean-spiritedness of most of the teachers' comments.

The first finding from our research on styles of commenting is that *teachers' comments can take students' attention away from their own purposes in writing a particular text and focus that attention on the teachers' purpose in commenting.* The teacher appropriates the text from the student by confusing the student's purpose in writing the text with her own purpose in commenting. Students make the changes the teacher wants rather than those that the student perceives are necessary, since the teachers' concerns imposed on the text create the reasons for the subsequent changes. We have all heard our perplexed students say to us when confused by our comments: "I don't understand how you want me to change this" or "Tell me what *you* want me to do." In the beginning of the process there was the writer, her words, and her desire to communicate her ideas. But after the comments of the teacher are imposed on the first or second draft, the student's attention dramatically shifts from "This is what I want to say," to "This is what *you* the teacher are asking me to do."

This appropriation of the text by the teacher happens particularly when teachers identify errors in usage, diction, and style in a first draft and ask students to correct these errors when they revise; such comments give the student an impression of the importance of these errors that is all out of proportion to how they should view these errors at this point in the process. The comments create the concern that these "accidents of discourse" need to be attended to before the meaning of the text is attended to.

It would not be so bad if students were only commanded to correct errors, but, more often than not, students are given contradictory messages; they are commanded to edit a sentence to avoid an error or to condense a sentence to achieve greater brevity of style, and then told in the margins that the particular paragraph needs to be more specific or to be developed more. An example of this problem can be seen in the following student paragraph:

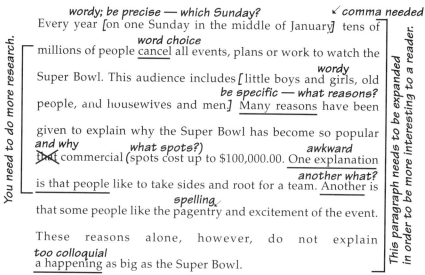

In commenting on this draft, the teacher has shown the student how to edit the sentences, but then commands the student to expand the paragraph in order to make it more interesting to a reader. The interlinear comments and the marginal comments represent two separate tasks for this student; the interlinear comments encourage the student to see the text as a fixed piece, frozen in time, that just needs some editing. The marginal comments, however, suggest that the meaning of the text is not fixed, but rather that the student still needs to develop the meaning by doing some more research. Students are commanded to edit and develop at the same time; the remarkable contradiction of developing a paragraph after editing the sentences in it represents the confusion we encountered in our teachers' commenting styles. These different signals given to students, to edit and develop, to condense and elaborate, represent also the failure of teachers' comments to direct genuine revision of the text as a whole.

Moreover, the comments are worded in such a way that it is difficult for students to know what is the most important problem in the text and what problems are of lesser importance. No scale of concerns is offered to a student, with the result that a comment about spelling or a comment about an awkward sentence is given weight equal to a comment about organization or logic. The comment that seemed to represent this problem best was one teacher's command to his student: "Check your commas and semicolons and think more about what you are thinking about." The language of the comments makes it difficult for a student to sort out and decide what is most important and what is least important.

When the teacher appropriates the text for the student in this way, students are encouraged to see their writing as a series of parts — words, sentences, paragraphs — and not as a whole discourse. The comments encourage students to believe that their first drafts are finished drafts, not invention drafts, and that all they need to do is patch and polish their writing. That is, teachers' comments do not provide their students with an inherent reason for revising the structure and meaning of their texts, since the comments suggest to students that the meaning of their text is already there, finished, produced, and all that is necessary is a better word or phrase. The processes of revising, editing, and proofreading are collapsed and reduced to a single trivial activity, and the students' misunderstanding of the revision process as a rewording activity is reinforced by their teachers' comments.

It is possible, and it quite often happens, that students follow every comment and fix their texts appropriately as requested, but their texts are not improved substantially, or, even worse, their revised drafts are inferior to their previous drafts. Since the teachers' comments take the students' attention away from their own original purposes, students concentrate more, as I have noted, on what the teachers commanded them to do than on what they are trying to say. Sometimes students do not understand the purpose behind their teachers' comments and take these comments very literally. At other times students understand the comments, but the teacher has misread the text and the comments, unfortunately, are not applicable. For instance, we repeatedly saw comments in which teachers commanded students to reduce and condense what was written, when in fact what the text really needed at this stage was to be expanded in conception and scope.

The process of revising always involves a risk. But, too often revision becomes a balancing act for students in which they make the changes that are requested but do not take the risk of changing anything that was not commented on, even if the students sense that other changes are needed. A more effective text does not often evolve from such changes alone, yet the student does not want to take the chance of reducing a finished, albeit inadequate, paragraph to chaos — to fragments — in order to rebuild it, if such changes have not been requested by the teacher.

The second finding from our study is that *most teachers' comments are not text-specific and could be interchanged, rubber-stamped, from text to text.* The comments are not anchored in the particulars of the students' texts, but rather are a series of vague directives that are not text-specific. Students are commanded to "Think more about [their] audience, avoid colloquial language, avoid the passive, avoid prepositions at the end of sentences or conjunctions at the beginning of sentences, be clear, be specific, be precise, but above all, think more about what [they] are thinking about." The comments on the following student paragraph illustrate this problem:

Begin by telling your reader what you are going to write about.
In the sixties it was drugs, in the seventies it was rock and roll.
avoid "one of the"
Now in the eighties, one of the most controversial subjects is
elaborate
nuclear power. The United States is in great need of its own
source of power. Because of environmentalists, coal is not an
be specific
acceptable source of energy. [Solar and wind power have not
avoid "it seems"
yet received the technology necessary to use them.] It seems that
nuclear power is the only feasible means right now for obtaining self-sufficient power. However, too large a percentage of the population are against nuclear power claiming it is unsafe.
Think more about your reader.

be precise
With as many problems as the United States is having concerning energy, it seems a shame that the public is so quick to "can" a very feasible means of power. Nuclear energy should not be given up on, but rather, more nuclear plants should be built.
Thesis sentence needed.

One could easily remove all the comments from this paragraph and rubber-stamp them on another student text, and they would make as much or as little sense on the second text as they do here.

We have observed an overwhelming similarity in the generalities and abstract commands given to students. There seems to be among teachers an accepted, albeit unwritten canon for commenting on student texts. This uniform code of commands, requests, and pleadings demonstrates that the teacher holds license for vagueness while the student is commanded to be specific. The students we interviewed admitted to having great difficulty with these vague directives. The students stated that when a teacher writes in the margins or as an end comment, "choose precise language," or "think more about your audience," revising becomes a guessing game. In effect, the teacher is saying to the student, "Somewhere in this paper is imprecise language or lack of awareness of an audience and you must find it." The problem presented by these vague commands is compounded for the students when they are not offered any strategies for carrying out these commands. Students are told that they have done something wrong and that there is something in their text that needs to be fixed before the text is acceptable. But to tell students that they have done something wrong is not to tell them what to do about it. In order to offer a useful revision strategy to a student, the teacher must anchor that strategy in the specifics of the student's text. For instance, to tell our student, the author of the above paragraph, "to be specific," or "to elaborate," does not show our student what questions the reader has about the meaning of the text, or what breaks in logic exist, that could be resolved if the writer supplied specific information; nor is the student shown how to achieve the desired specificity.

Instead of offering strategies, the teachers offer what is interpreted by students as rules for composing; the comments suggest to students that writing is just a matter of following the rules. Indeed, the teachers seem to impose a series of abstract rules about written products even when some of them are not appropriate for the specific text the student is creating.[3] For instance, the student author of our sample paragraph presented above is commanded to follow the conventional rules for writing a five-paragraph essay — to begin the introductory paragraph by telling his reader what he is going to say and to end the paragraph with a thesis sentence. Somehow these abstract rules about what five-paragraph products should look like do not seem applicable to the problems this student must confront when revising, nor are the rules specific strategies he could use when revising. There are many inchoate ideas ready to be exploited in this paragraph, but the rules do not help the student to take stock of his (or her) ideas and use the opportunity he has, during revision, to develop those ideas.

The problem here is a confusion of process and product; what one has to say about the process is different from what one has to say about the product. Teachers who use this method of commenting are formulating their comments as if these drafts were finished drafts and were not going to be revised. Their commenting vocabularies have not been adapted to revision and they comment on first drafts as if they were justifying a grade or as if the first draft were the final draft.

Our summary finding, therefore, from this research on styles of commenting is that the news from the classroom is not good. For the most part, teachers do not respond to student writing with the kind of thoughtful commentary which will help students to engage with the issues they are writing about or which will help them think about their purposes and goals in writing a specific text. In defense of our teachers, however, they told us that responding to student writing was rarely stressed in their teacher-training or in writing workshops; they had been trained in various prewriting techniques, in constructing assignments, and in evaluating papers for grades, but rarely in the process of reading a student text for meaning or in offering commentary to motivate revision. The problem is that most of us as teachers of writing have been trained to read and interpret literary texts for meaning, but, unfortunately, we have not been trained to act upon the same set of assumptions in reading student texts as we follow in reading literary texts.[4] Thus, we read student texts with biases about what the writer should have said or about what he or she should have written, and our biases determine how we will comprehend the text. We read with our preconceptions and preoccupations, expecting to find errors, and the result is that we find errors and misread our students' texts.[5] We find what we look for; instead of reading and responding to the meaning of a text, we correct our students' writing. We need to reverse this approach. Instead of finding errors or showing students how to patch up parts of their texts, we need to sabotage our students' conviction that the drafts they have written are complete and coherent. Our comments need to offer students revision tasks of a different order of complexity and sophistication from the ones that they themselves identify, by forcing students back into the chaos, back to the point where they are shaping and restructuring their meaning.[6]

For if the content of a student text is lacking in substance and meaning, if the order of the parts must be rearranged significantly in the next draft, if paragraphs must be restructured for logic and clarity, then many sentences are likely to be changed or deleted anyway. There seems to be no point in having students correct usage errors or condense sentences that are likely to disappear before the next draft is completed. In fact, to identify such problems in a text at this early first-draft stage, when such problems are likely to abound, can give a student a disproportionate sense of their importance at this stage in the writing process.[7] In responding to our students' writing, we should be guided by the recognition that it is not spelling or usage problems that we as writers first worry about when drafting and revising our texts.

We need to develop an appropriate level of response for commenting on a first draft, and to differentiate that from the level suitable to a second or third draft. Our comments need to be suited to the draft we are reading. In a first or second draft, we need to respond as any reader would, registering questions, reflecting befuddlement, and noting places where we are puzzled about the meaning of the text. Comments should

point to breaks in logic, disruptions in meaning, or missing information. Our goal in commenting on early drafts should be to engage students with the issues they are considering and help them clarify their
purposes and reasons in writing their specific text.

For instance, the major rhetorical problem of the essay written by
the student who wrote the first paragraph (the paragraph on nuclear
power) quoted above was that the student had two principal arguments
running through his text, each of which brought the other into question. On the one hand, he argued that we must use nuclear power, unpleasant as it is, because we have nothing else to use; though nuclear
energy is a problematic source of energy, it is the best of a bad lot. On
the other hand, he also argued that nuclear energy is really quite safe
and therefore should be our primary resource. Comments on this
student's first draft need to point out this break in logic and show the
student that if we accept his first argument, then his second argument
sounds fishy. But if we accept his second argument, his first argument
sounds contradictory. The teacher's comments need to engage this student writer with this basic rhetorical and conceptual problem in his
first draft rather than impose a series of abstract commands and rules
upon his text.

Written comments need to be viewed not as an end in themselves —
a way for teachers to satisfy themselves that they have done their jobs —
but rather as a means for helping students to become more effective
writers. As a means for helping students, they have limitations; they
are, in fact, disembodied remarks — one absent writer responding to
another absent writer. The key to successful commenting is to have
what is said in the comments and what is done in the classroom mutually reinforce and enrich each other. Commenting on papers assists the
writing course in achieving its purpose; classroom activities and the
comments we write to our students need to be connected. Written comments need to be an extension of the teacher's voice — an extension of
the teacher as reader. Exercises in such activities as revising a whole
text or individual paragraphs together in class, noting how the sense
of the whole dictates the smaller changes, looking at options, evaluating actual choices, and then discussing the effect of these changes on
revised drafts — such exercises need to be designed to take students
through the cycles of revising and to help them overcome their anxiety
about revising: that anxiety we all feel at reducing what looks like a
finished draft into fragments and chaos.

The challenge we face as teachers is to develop comments which
will provide an inherent reason for students to revise; it is a sense of
revision as discovery, as a repeated process of beginning again, as starting out new, that our students have not learned. We need to show our
students how to seek, in the possibility of revision, the dissonances of
discovery — to show them through our comments why new choices
would positively change their texts, and thus to show them the potential for development implicit in their own writing.

Notes

1. C. H. Knoblauch and Lil Brannon, "Teacher Commentary on Student Writing: The State of the Art," *Freshman English News* 10 (Fall 1981): 1–3.
2. For an extended discussion of revision strategies of student writers see Nancy Sommers, "Revision Strategies of Student Writers and Experienced Adult Writers," *College Composition and Communication* 31 (Dec. 1980): 378–88.
3. Nancy Sommers and Ronald Schleifer, "Means and Ends: Some Assumptions of Student Writers," *Composition and Teaching* 2 (Dec. 1980): 69–76.
4. Janet Emig and Robert P. Parker, Jr., "Responding to Student Writing: Building a Theory of the Evaluating Process," paper, Rutgers University.
5. For an extended discussion of this problem see Joseph Williams, "The Phenomenology of Error," *College Composition and Communication* 32 (May 1981): 152–68.
6. Ann Berthoff, *The Making of Meaning* (Upper Montclair: Boynton, 1981).
7. W. U. McDonald, "The Revising Process and the Marking of Student Papers," *College Composition and Communication* 24 (May 1978): 167–70.

Sommers's Insights as a Resource for Your Teaching

1. Sommers clearly advises multiple readings of student writing. She indicates that reading a student text in order to understand its meaning and to provide concrete, substantive commentary can motivate revision that is critical to students' growth as writers. Don't be daunted by the paper load. If you focus your commentary on what happens as you read and respond to the meaning of a text, you'll find that what may have distracted you at the lexical level has disappeared from or changed substantively in the draft submitted for evaluation and grading. You may be spending the same amount of time or even less time overall when you read early and late drafts.

    Revision conferences can provide good opportunities for you to offer thoughtful commentary. They force you to make text-specific comments and steer clear of abstract suggestions or vague generalities. Conferencing with each student for each writing assignment is clearly not feasible; however, staggering revision conferences with students throughout the early to mid part of the semester would provide students with a helpful experience to clarify and inform the written feedback that they will receive throughout the semester.

2. Ask a colleague teaching the same course to work with you reading some early drafts. Trade a set of drafts. Write your comments about revision on a separate sheet of paper; exchange and compare your comments, paying particular attention to the specificity of each comment and to precision of language. You'll

both profit from the discussion and may find your reading of the text enhanced by this "external assessor."

You might also use this technique when you evaluate late drafts. The ensuing conversation about your evaluative comments and criteria for evaluation will certainly give you both perspective on and confidence about your process of evaluating and grading.

3. The increasing access to computer technology provides you new opportunities for assisting writers in their processes of revision. Check out campus resources for networked classrooms where you can read student drafts even as they generate or rework them. Ask students to give you a draft on disk and write marginal or interlinear comments in italics or boldface. Or you may consider using software or Web-based tools that give you and your students read/write access to individual and group texts.

Sommers's Insights as a Resource for Your Writing Classroom

1. Ask students to write from recall about the commentary they have received outside your writing classroom on their writing. Ask them to explain, in journal entries or in fifteen-minute writing sessions, how a comment prompted or inhibited deep-level revising. One caution: Because such an assignment can trigger painful or angry memories, advise the students not to name the person who wrote comments that obstructed revision. Explain that the "text" of the comment can be analyzed for its effect without your having to know the author. If the students want to laud the instructor whose comments motivated them to revise for wholeness, suggest they write that instructor a fan letter.

2. Peer editors will probably fall into these same styles of commentary. Bring in a sampler of peer editing comments, and ask the class as a whole or in groups to analyze how well they do or do not promote substantive revision.

3. Conduct an in-class session analyzing students' evaluative comments. After students have completed a shared writing task, ask them to respond using a peer editing checklist from the class text or one that you've constructed with the class. Ask students to write sentence-length, specific comments about issues of meaning and about attention to audience concerns. Move from writer to writer and read the comments. Tell each peer editor how and why his or her comments would or would not motivate you to revise.

4. Ask class members to identify commentary that has assisted them in deep revision when they write a self-assessment to accompany a submitted draft. Ask a question like "What advice did your peer readers give and what did you do with the advice?"

Bringing Practice in Line with Theory: Using Portfolio Grading in the Composition Classroom

Jeffrey Sommers

Sommers emphasizes that portfolio grading in the composition class-room — an increasingly frequent teaching and learning option — presents a unique opportunity to connect the practice of responding to and evaluating student writing with an individual's beliefs about writing and about teaching writing. He demonstrates that a portfolio assignment encourages students to revise and helps them discover writing as learning.

Sommers argues that portfolio grading will aid both the learner and the instructor only if the reflective teaching practitioner identifies and works out appropriate answers to the hard questions that such an assessment practice prompts. He describes three portfolio models: representative sampling, holistic perspective, and developmental perspective. Sommers speculates about the interconnections among each model and assessment criteria, grading standards, the student-instructor relationship in the writing classroom, and effects on paper load. The essay is one of twenty-three collected in Portfolios: Process and Product *edited by Belanoff and Dickson.*

Portfolio assessment in the composition classroom offers not a methodology but a framework for response. Rather than provide definitive answers to questions about grading criteria and standards, the relationship between teacher and student, and increased paper loads, the portfolio approach presents an opportunity for instructors to bring their practice in responding to student writing in line with their theories of composing and pedagogy. My essay proposes to take an exploratory look at how portfolio evaluation compels instructors to address a number of important, and long-lived, issues underlying response to student writing. When an instructor chooses to use a portfolio system, certain other decisions must inevitably follow, and it is the implications of these decisions that I propose to examine most closely.

As the writing process has become the focus of composition classes over the past three decades, it seems an almost natural evolution for portfolio evaluation to have entered the classroom. Emphasizing the importance of revision to the composing process — regardless of which theoretical view of composing one takes — ought to lead to a classroom practice that permits, even encourages, students to revise. While such

revision can, of course, occur in a classroom in which the writing portfolio is not in use, the portfolio itself tends to encourage students to
revise because it suggests that writing occurs over time, not in a single
sitting, just as the portfolio itself grows over time and cannot be created in a single sitting. Elbow and Belanoff argue that a portfolio system evaluates student writing "in ways that better reflect the complexities of the writing process: with time for freewriting, planning,
discussion with instructors and peers, revising, and copyediting. It lets
students put these activities together in a way most productive for them"
(14).

Additionally, the portfolio approach can help students discover that
writing is indeed a form of learning. Janet Emig has argued that writing "provides [a] record of evolution of thought since writing is epige-
netic as process-and-product" (128). Portfolios provide a record of that
record. Emig also describes writing as "active, engaged, personal — notably, self-rhythmed" (128). The notion that writing occurs over time in
response to the rhythms created by the individual writer — a notion
that makes eminent sense when one considers that no two writers seem
to work at precisely the same pace and that no two pieces of writing
seem to take form at the same pace even for the same writer — is another excellent argument for using portfolios. The portfolio approach
allows writers to assemble an *oeuvre* at their own pace, within the structure of the writing course and its assignments, of course. Nevertheless,
the portfolio by its very nature suggests self-rhythm because some pieces
will require more drafts than others, even if explicit deadlines are
prompting their composition.

For good cause then have portfolio systems of evaluation become
commonplace in composition classrooms. But with these portfolios also
come serious issues about grading standards and criteria, about how
teachers and students relate to one another, about how teachers handle
increased paper loads. Before examining how these issues might be
resolved, perhaps it is time to acknowledge that this essay has yet to
define portfolio. I have deliberately avoided doing so for two reasons:
first, *portfolio* is a familiar-enough term and not really all that mysterious, and thus what I have written so far should be comprehensible to
my readers; second, no consensus exists about just what a *portfolio* is
or should be, however familiar the concept may seem. In fact, two distinctly different models of portfolios exist, each compelling its adher-
ents to address the central issues of response in very different theoretical ways.

The first model is described well by James E. Ford and Gregory
Larkin, who use as an analogy an artist's portfolio. Each student's work
is "collected, like the best representative work of an artist, into a 'portfolio'" (951). We are to see students in the role of free-lance commercial
artists, approaching an art director at an advertising agency with a
large portfolio case containing their "best representative work." Such a
model is easily transferred into the writing classroom. Students in the
writing course produce a certain number of written documents during

the term, agreeing in advance that only a specified number of those documents will be graded by the instructor. Commercial artists would never compile a portfolio that consisted of every piece of work they had done and neither do the students; the idea is to select a representative sampling that shows the creators at their best.

This portfolio model most likely grows out of instructors' concern with grading criteria and standards. Ford and Larkin, as the title of their article suggests, came to the portfolio as a means of guaranteeing grading standards. Instructors are justified in upholding rigorous standards of excellence because their students have been able to revise their work and select their best writing for evaluation. As Ford and Larkin comment, "A student can 'blow' an occasional assignment without disastrous effect" (952), suggesting that the instructor is being eminently fair. Elbow and Belanoff, in the context of a programmatic portfolio-assessment project, make a similar argument, one equally applicable to the individual classroom. "By giving students a chance to be examined on their best writing — by giving them an opportunity for more help — we are also able to demand their best writing" (13). This portfolio system "encourages high standards from the start, thereby encouraging maximum development" (Burnham 137).

To Ford and Larkin, Burnham, and Elbow and Belanoff, a portfolio is a sampling of finished products selected by the student for evaluation. Although the instructor using this model may very well be concerned with the students' development as writers, as Burnham's remark indicates, essentially this portfolio model is grade driven and could be accurately labeled a *portfolio grading system*. It is grade driven because the rationale for using the portfolio framework grows out of an understanding that the student's written work will ultimately be evaluated.

However, portfolio grading, paradoxically, not only grows out of a concern for eroding standards, but also out of a concern for the overemphasis upon grades in writing courses. Christopher Burnham calls the students' "obsession" with grades a "major stumbling block" (125) to effective learning in the composition classroom and turns to portfolio grading as a means of mitigating the students' obsession with grades. Burnham concludes that the portfolio system "establishes a writing environment rather than a grading environment in the classroom" (137).

Thus, by addressing the issue of responding to the student's writing, Burnham wants to change the relationship between the student and the instructor. He wants to create a more facilitative role for the instructor, in accordance with suggestions about response from Donald Murray, Nancy Sommers, and Lil Brannon and C. H. Knoblauch. He not only wants to allow students to retain the rights to their own writing, he wants them to assume responsibility for their writing, asserting that portfolio grading "creates independent writers and learners" (136).

The question then of when and what to grade becomes quite significant. Although grading criteria must be established by instructors who employ portfolio grading, new criteria for grading the final drafts do not generally need to be developed. Presumably, instructors will bring to bear an already developed set of criteria for grading, applying these criteria rigorously to designated papers, thus protecting the integrity of their standards.[1] Nonetheless, a crucial question arises: When will student work receive a grade: at midterm, only at the end of the term, with each submission? Some instructors grade every draft and revision as students submit them, some grade only the revisions, some grade only papers designated as final drafts. In some portfolio-grading systems, the students select a specified number of final drafts at midterm and a second set at end of the term, while in other systems, all grading occurs at the end of the term.

Instructors using portfolio grading must decide when to offer grades. Grading every draft keeps the students informed, but, because even a temporary grade has an air of finality to many students simply because it is a grade, this policy may undercut the idea that each draft may potentially develop into a finished product. Grading revisions only may encourage the grade-obsessed student to revise if only to obtain a grade, thus introducing revision to some students who otherwise lack the motivation to revise, but also reinforcing the primacy of grades.

By deferring grades until the end of the term, instructors can extend the duration of the "writing environment" that Burnham hopes to substitute for the "grading environment" in the course. However, if students are indeed obsessed with grades, as he argues, then it seems likely that for a substantial number of students, or perhaps for all of the students to varying extents, there will always be a grading environment lurking beneath the writing environment of the course. If instructors respond effectively and frequently and confer with students individually, they can keep students informed of their approximate standing in the course, possibly deflecting their grade anxiety, but it is disingenuous to claim that portfolio grading removes grade obsession. If the portfolio ultimately produces an accumulation of individual grades, grade obsession cannot really be eliminated although it certainly can be reduced.

Yet a larger issue arises, an issue related to one's pedagogical assumptions about the significance of grades. Burnham discusses the portfolio system as a means of leading to student development, a development inevitably measured by the final grades earned by the student's portfolio. Inherent in this model is the idea that students can improve the writing, and thus the grade, by revising and selecting their best work. Inevitably, then, instructors using portfolio grading must address the issue of grade inflation. Although one of the motivating forces behind portfolio grading, as we have seen, is protecting grading standards, the system itself is designed to promote better writing by the students, and it stands to reason that many students are going to be submitting portfolios that consist of writing better than they might be able to produce in a classroom employing a traditional grading system. Will instructors raise the standards so high that even the improved writing in the portfolios falls into the usual grading curve? Or, and this seems much more likely, will the grades themselves on the whole be somewhat higher because of the portfolio approach despite higher standards? Should higher grades be of significant concern to instructors? Do higher grades mean "grade inflation"? What is the role of grades in writing courses? Portfolio grading compels instructors to consider these important questions.

Finally, portfolio grading presents problems to instructors in handling the paper load. Since most programs suggest or stipulate a certain number of assignments per term, instructors using the portfolio system must determine how they will count assignments. Will newly revised papers count as new assignments? By doing so, the instructor can keep the paper load from mushrooming. Let's focus on a course that requires seven papers in a semester (the situation at my institution), with the understanding that the portfolio will consist of four final drafts selected by the student. If instructors count revisions of papers 1 and 2 as papers 3 and 4, their paper load will be less because students will still only produce seven drafts for them to read. On the other hand, the students' options at the end of the term will be reduced by this method of counting; they will have to select four final drafts from only five different pieces in progress.

To ensure students the full choice of seven, however, instructors commit themselves to more responding. In our hypothetical case, they will read at least nine drafts, seven first drafts, and revisions of the first two papers. Thus a routine decision actually has important pedagogical implications.

Several methods of controlling the paper load do exist. One is to divide the term in half, asking students to produce two miniportfolios. At midterm, for instance, in the situation already described, students are required to submit two final drafts for grading out of the first four assigned papers. At the end of the term, students must select two of the final three assigned papers for grading. Thus the paper load is under greater control because the students cannot continue work on the first four papers after midterm. On the other hand, Burnham's desire to create a writing environment rather than a grading environment will be affected because grades will become of primary concern not once but twice during the term.

Another method for controlling the paper load is to limit the number of drafts students may write of individual papers. Without such a limit, some students will rewrite and resubmit papers almost weekly, adding greatly to the paper load; of course, one can argue that such students are developing as writers in an important way. Deadlines for revisions of papers can also be used to control the paper load since "real" writers always work under deadlines. They may revise and revise and revise, but ultimately they must conclude. Instructors may allow students to revise a given assignment as often as they wish but within a designated period of time. Another method of controlling the paper is to limit the number of revisions students may submit at one time or to designate specific times when revisions may be submitted. Late in the term, industrious students may have revisions of three or four different assignments ready to be submitted; some limit on the number they may hand in at one time can help instructors manage the course more effectively. Stipulating that revisions can be handed in only on certain days can allow instructors to plan their time for responding more efficiently.

Eventually, the end of the term arrives, and for many instructors using portfolio grading, the paper load explodes. Portfolios of four papers or more per student come in at the end of the term and must be graded quickly in order to submit final grades on time. Holistic grading can make the paper load manageable as instructors offer no comments but just a letter grade on each final draft. Grading portfolios at the end of the term undeniably requires more time than grading a single final exam or final paper would. However mundane these questions of handling the paper load may seem, the answers one supplies affect the entire portfolio grading system because many of these decisions may influence the relationship between students and their instructors, and some may influence, or be influenced by, instructors' grading criteria and standards.

To sum up then, a portfolio grading system defines a portfolio as a sampling of students' finished writing selected by the students for evaluation. Portfolio grading offers instructors a means of keeping their grading standards high while employing their usual grading criteria, it presents one potential method for reducing students' obsession with grades and transforming the classroom environment into one more engaged with writing than grading, and it increases instructors' paper loads. Instructors' decisions about when to grade and how to manage the paper load raise complications because they affect the relationship between instructors and their students. Thus, teachers planning on implementing portfolio grading need to consider carefully how they will do so in a way that will keep their practice in line with their own theoretical assumptions about writing and about composition pedagogy.

The second, newer, portfolio system model I will call the "holistic portfolio." The holistic portfolio is a response to continued theorizing about the nature of the composing process. Louise Wetherbee Phelps argues that theories underlying teaching practices evolve toward greater depth, and she sketches a hierarchy of response models to student writing beginning with one she labels "evaluative attitude, closed text" (49). In this model, the instructor treats the student text as "self-contained, complete in itself. . . . a discrete discourse episode to be experienced more or less decontextually" (50). This concept of response to a text views reading as evaluation; instructors responding in this model may speak of "grading a stack of papers." The next response model described by Phelps is one she calls "formative attitude, evolving text" (51). Instructors read students' drafts as part of a process of evolution, thus entering into and influencing the students' composing process. In this model of response, instructors locate "learning largely in the actual composing process" (53).

Phelps describes a third model of response as "developmental attitude, portfolio of work": "Whereas the first group of teachers reads a 'stack' of papers and the second reads collected bits, scraps, and drafts of the composing process, the third reads a 'portfolio' of work by one student" (53). Phelps elaborates on two ways to work with portfolios, describing first the portfolio grading model we have already examined, which she dubs "the weak form." In this approach, she writes, "teachers continue to read and grade individual papers, attempting to help students perfect each one" (53). As Phelps has described the models of response, we can see that she has first described portfolio assessment used in a programmatic approach to large-scale decision making about student proficiency and placement. Her second model fairly accurately describes the portfolio-grading approach of Ford and Larkin and Burnham, elaborated upon somewhat in her depiction of "the weak form" of her third response model.

In the second method of using portfolios, Phelps also describes a different portfolio system. Some instructors employ portfolios because they wish to respond from a *developmental* perspective." From this perspective, the student writing "blurs as an individual entity" and is treated as a sample "excerpted from a stream of writing stimulated by the writing class, part of the 'life text' each literate person continually produces" (53). Phelps concludes:

> The reader's function is [to read] through the text to the writer's developing cognitive, linguistic, and social capacities as they bear on writing activities. The set of a single writer's texts to which the reader has access, either literally or through memory, is the corpus from which the reader tries to construct a speculative profile of the writer's developmental history and current maturity. (53)

This definition of portfolio no longer serves as an analogy to the commercial artist's carefully assembled portfolio of a representative sampling of her best work. Instead it more closely resembles an archivist's collection of a writer's entire *oeuvre*. Instructors do not deal with selected writings but evaluate the entire output of the student writer. The implications of such a definition are quite different from those of the portfolio grading model defined by Ford and Larkin, Burnham, and Elbow and Belanoff.

While portfolio grading systems are driven by pedagogic concerns with fair grading as well as with composing process theory, the holistic portfolio system is primarily driven by a pedagogical concern with composing process theory. Although Knoblauch and Brannon's polemic *Rhetorical Traditions and the Teaching of Writing* does not discuss portfolio evaluation, its view of the composing process might very readily lead to it. Knoblauch and Brannon describe the "myth of improvement" that has stifled writing instruction by focusing on the kind of evaluation Phelps details in her first model of response (evaluative attitude, closed text). Knoblauch and Brannon suggest that "the most debilitating illusion associated with writing instruction is the belief that teachers can, or at least ought to be able to, control writers' maturation, causing it to occur as the explicit consequence of something they do or ought to do" (165). This illusion is reductionist, leading to a view of the writing course "in minimal functionalist terms" (165). This "myth of improvement" has produced a definition of teaching and curricular success that stresses "trivial but readily demonstrable short-term 'skill' acquisitions" and has led some teachers "to imagine it is fair to 'grade on improvement,' mistaking a willingness to follow orders for real development" (165).

While Knoblauch and Brannon's book remains controversial, their critique of "the myth of improvement" cogently articulates many instructors' reservations about grading practices based on the artificial academic calendar, a system that demands students learn at a given pace, defined by a ten-week quarter, a fourteen-week trimester, or a sixteen-week semester. Knoblauch and Brannon conclude by arguing that "symptoms of growth — the willingness to take risks, to profit from advice, to revise, to make recommendations to others — may appear quickly, even if improved *performance* takes longer" (169).

For instructors whose conception of the composing process is compatible with the developmental schemes underlying Knoblauch and Brannon's book and Phelp's third model of response, the holistic portfolio should have great appeal. It presents these instructors with difficult decisions, however, in the same areas that the portfolio grading system presented its practitioners: grading criteria and standards, the teacher-student relationship, and handling the paper load.

While upholding grading standards was the catalyst for portfolio grading, holistic portfolio systems appear to be less concerned with the notion of grading standards, at least in traditional terms. Because the holistic portfolio system does not focus instructors' attention on specific final drafts, it does present instructors with some major decisions about criteria for the final evaluation.

Several possibilities exist. Instructors may create a grading system that weights final drafts but also grades draft materials, notes, peer commentary, and so on. Counting the number of drafts or the variety of included material is a way to "grade" preliminary materials. However, any counting method might distort the course's emphasis on development by encouraging students to create "phony" drafts, drafts written after the fact simply to pad the portfolio (just as many of us used to compose outlines after completing high school term papers as a way of meeting a course requirement).

Another way to grade the final portfolio is more holistic, and thus probably "purer" in the sense that it avoids treating individual drafts as "collected bits, scraps, and drafts" and portfolios as part of "the life text" (Phelps 53). The instructor looks for "symptoms of growth," to borrow Knoblauch and Brannon's phrase — "the willingness to take risks, to profit from advice, to revise, to make recommendations to others." Those students who demonstrate the greatest growth receive the highest grades, assuming that the instructor has developed a scale that measures growth — no small assumption.

While the holistic portfolio can fit very nicely into a developmental view of the composing process, it presents great difficulties in fitting at all into a traditional academic grading system and poses serious questions for instructors about how they see their writing courses fitting into the academy. This method of evaluation works most readily in a pass/no pass grading situation, indeed is an argument for such a grading system. But pass/no pass writing courses are the exception rather than the rule. Unfortunately, neither Knoblauch and Brannon nor Phelps really addresses the issue of how to grade in a writing course that emphasizes a developmental perspective on writing. It is conceivable that an instructor holistically evaluating a set of portfolios could assign an entire class of industrious students grades of A, having developed grading criteria that emphasize "symptoms of growth"; such an instructor can have rigorous standards in that only those students who have made the effort and demonstrated the growth receive the A's. However, one suspects this instructor would face a one-to-one meeting with a concerned writing program administrator or department chair sometime after submitting the final grades.

Some compromise or accommodation must undoubtedly be made by instructors, perhaps along the lines discussed earlier of weighting final drafts. The important point to make here is that instructors should be aware of how the grading criteria they develop correlate with the theory underlying their use of portfolio evaluation.

Given the problematic nature of grading holistic portfolios, why would instructors adopt this model of the portfolio system? The holistic portfolio system offers distinct advantages in defining a healthy teacher-student relationship. Burnham's hopes of creating a writing environment rather than a grading environment are more readily realized in the holistic portfolio system. Because the final portfolio will not be graded in any traditional sense, because individual grades on drafts do not occur, in theory the classroom using the holistic portfolio can indeed become a writing environment, since there is no reason for it to become a grading environment, and the instructor can truly doff the evaluator's role and don instead the facilitator's role.

Burnham praises portfolio grading for encouraging students to assume responsibility for their learning; portfolio grading "creates independent writers and learners," he concludes (137). His point is that when students know that they can control their grades through extra effort in revising and through the selection process available to them prior to final evaluation, they become more responsible and more independent; in today's terminology, they become "empowered." However, the motivation comes from a concern with grades.

In the holistic portfolio system, the students are also afforded the opportunity to become more responsible, not for their grades so much as for their development. They can indeed become independent learners, independent of traditional grading obsessions as well. The teacher and student can become "co-writers," in Phelps's phrase. The emphasis in the course falls not on improving texts as a means of improving a grade but instead falls on developing as a writer, understanding that this development is more important than grades on individual texts.

Both models of portfolios, then, hope to free students of the tyranny of the grade. The portfolio grading system does so temporarily, but also readily accommodates the traditional institutional need for grades. The holistic portfolio system can indeed free students to become learners and writers for the duration of a writing course but only if instructors have resolved the essential conflict between their course and the institution's demand for traditionally meaningful grades.

In the final area of paper load, it seems most likely that the holistic portfolio system will produce a heavier paper load than the portfolio grading system will. Any schemes to limit students' output would likely conflict with the theoretical assumptions that lead to using the holistic portfolio system. Thus students' portfolios are likely to grow in length as well as in the hoped-for depth of development. At the end of the term, instructors must read not merely a specific number of selected final drafts, but entire portfolios, certainly a slower process. Periodic reading of the growing portfolios — which instructors taking such a developmental perspective will probably wish to do — may reduce the paper load at the end of the course since instructors can scan the familiar materials in the portfolio, but it will not significantly reduce the paper load so much as spread it out over the course of the term.

Instructors contemplating a portfolio system of either sort, or a hybrid version of the two models described, are faced with the need to answer some important questions for themselves before incorporating the system into their writing classes. Louise Weatherbee Phelps concludes her discussion by commenting that her depiction of response models represents an increasing growth on the part of instructors. She argues that "experience itself presses teachers toward increasingly generous and flexible conceptions of the text and the reading task" (59). If she is correct, as I think she is, then the movement in composition classrooms toward portfolio systems of one sort or another will accelerate as the emphasis on the composing process as central to writing courses continues.

As the profession continues to refine its thinking about composition pedagogy, portfolio systems seem destined to proliferate in use and grow in significance. The portfolio system of evaluation has tremendous advantages, which are described throughout the rest of this book, but it also requires great thought on the part of instructors because a portfolio system implemented in a scattershot manner may well undercut the goals of a writing course. The portfolio offers instructors wonderful opportunities to bring their teaching practice in line with their theoretical assumptions about writing and about teaching, but that convergence can only occur if instructors ask themselves the right — and the tough — questions and work out the answers that best provide what both instructors and students need in the writing course.

Note

1. I am assuming that instructors themselves will grade the papers. Ford and Larkin describe a programmatic use of portfolio grading wherein the portfolios are graded by a team of graders not including the students' instructor. My interest in this essay, however, is in the issues faced by individual instructors who do not have the power to implement such grading practice but must conduct their own evaluations.

Works Cited

Belanoff, Pat, and Marcia Dickson, eds. *Portfolios: Process and Product.* Portsmouth: Boynton, 1991.

Brannon, Lil, and C. H. Knoblauch. "On Students' Rights to Their Own Texts: A Model of Teacher Response." *College Composition and Communication* 33 (1982): 157–66.

Burnham, Christopher. "Portfolio Evaluation: Room to Breathe and Grow." *Training the New Teacher of College Composition.* Ed. Charles Bridges. Urbana: NCTE, 1986.

Elbow, Peter, and Pat Belanoff. "State University of New York at Stony Brook Portfolio-Based Evaluation Program." *New Methods in College Writing Programs.* Ed. Paul Connolly and Teresa Vilardi. New York: MLA, 1986. Reprinted in Belanoff and Dickson.

Emig, Janet. "Writing as a Mode of Learning." *College Composition and Communication* 28 (1977): 122–28.

Ford, James E., and Gregory Larkin. "The Portfolio System: An End to Backsliding Writing Standards." *College English* 39 (1978): 950–55.

Knoblauch, C. H., and Lil Brannon. *Rhetorical Traditions and the Teaching of Writing.* Portsmouth: Boynton, 1984.

Murray, Donald. "Teaching the Other Self: The Writer's First Reader." *College Composition and Communication* 33 (1982): 140–47.

Phelps, Louise Wetherbee. "Images of Student Writing: The Deep Structure of Teacher Response." *Writing and Response: Theory, Practice, and Research.* Ed. Chris M. Anson. Urbana: NCTE, 1989.

Sommers, Nancy. "Responding to Student Writing." *College Composition and Communication* 33 (1982): 148–56.

Sommers's Insights as a Resource for Your Teaching

1. Sommers emphasizes the serious inquiry a writing teacher should undertake before and while introducing portfolio grading in a writing classroom. If you've kept a reflective journal, scan it for passages where you've clarified your beliefs about the student-instructor relationship you desire and about assessment criteria and grading standards. Work out your portfolio policy from those stances.

2. Pat Belanoff and Peter Elbow have written collaboratively and frequently about what they learned from a portfolio-based evaluation program at the State University of New York at Stony Brook. They emphasize the collaborative learning and the feeling of community that result when writing instructors trade and evaluate student portfolios. To benefit most from using portfolio grading, work with one or two colleagues. Read the portfolios holistically, writing down general impressions and overall strengths and weaknesses. Then talk about how those features influence your responses and grading systems. Such conversation can help you clarify your teaching philosophy and gain confidence about your ways of responding to student writing.

3. The "teaching portfolio" cited throughout this ancillary is, of course, a "developmental portfolio." You will accrue the same benefits of ownership, empowerment, and autonomous learning from your teaching portfolio as can your students from their writing portfolios.

Sommers's Insights as a Resource for Your Writing Classroom

1. It's possible to combine the representative and developmental portfolio models so that students can "own" the process and also become more able to identify the ways they have grown as writers. Negotiate with the class the minimum number of writing samples that should be submitted. Require that, for each submission and for the arrangement of the portfolio, students describe the entire process that led to the submitted writing, identify its strengths, and discuss why they view the work as "representative." Ask students to write a cover letter for the portfolio that applies shared criteria — such as an analysis of the "reflectiveness" or "growth" of the writer as demonstrated by the portfolio. Ask for a discussion of goal setting for continuous growth as a writer and learner. Such self-assessment can lead even the most grade-conscious writers into some independence.

2. Invite class members to think about the writings they have peer edited and offer advice to the writers about works they would recommend including in a portfolio.

3. Plan a conference or two with individual writers in which each can talk about the works and the decisions being made about submissions. Some students will be apprehensive about a portfolio assignment; some will dive in.

4. Encourage students to look at all they wrote during the term, including writing across the curriculum, in assessing their work and planning submissions.

Why I (Used to) Hate to Give Grades

Lynn Z. Bloom

This essay describes a powerful transformation in the author's perspective on grading student work — how "a tension-filled monologue (myself muttering to myself)" became a "constructive dialogue between students and teacher." Lynn Bloom begins by enumerating the variety of problems associated with grades, including teacher expectations and the inherent shift from intrinsic to extrinsic motivation, and then proposes a solution to these problems with a way of grading that follows the portfolio model but asks students to grade themselves. The rigorous criteria by which they must justify those grades, she contends, actually lends itself to student honesty, as well as increased self-accountability and evidence of active self-reflection on their progress as writers. This method dramatically shifts the focus of the course from the teacher to the students — and students, Bloom reports, will rise to the occasion.

When I was but a sprig on the family tree, growing up in the New Hampshire college town where my father, Professor Zimmerman, taught chemistry and chemical engineering, an emblematic cartoon by William Steig appeared in the *New Yorker*. It depicted a downcast youth glancing surreptitiously at a report card held with distaste by a man in a suit looming bulbously from his armchair. The caption, "B-plus isn't good enough for a Zimmerman" — yes, that really was the name in the cartoon — so succinctly expressed the family methods that my parents made dozens of copies. The cartoon became their Christmas card that year. When my siblings and I were in college, "the B-plus joke," as we had come to call it, would arrive, anonymously, at midterm and final exam times. As the grandchildren arrived they, too, were blessed with copies of their own. "The B-plus joke" has become the subject of long-distance phone calls, impromptu seminars at family reunions, and considerable sardonic mirth.

That a B-plus was in fact *never* good enough for a Zimmerman, however, is my lifelong legacy. Its message will be inscribed on my grave.

Over the years I've filled up a depressing stack of grade books. Their limp, academic-green covers conceal a myriad of cryptic symbols, which in turn embed stories of work and goofing-off, hope and despair, brilliance and just-going-along-for-the-ride. Although I have always — well, usually — looked forward to reading papers, and can even tolerate reading exams, the calculus of giving grades had become, over time, preferable only to doing the income tax. Until last year.

It's easy to understand why giving grades was so grim, as I explain in the first half of this essay. This half focuses on the nature and problems presented by *grading* — the letters, numbers, percents, and other forms of tallies — the characters that appear in grade books, on transcripts, and in other forms of scorekeeping, individually and in the aggregate. When I say *grading* I mean exactly that. I am not confusing *grading* with other ways of responding to student writing — such as extensive comments, oral or written (on screen or hard copy), preferably on early or intermediate drafts.

But when the semester's approaching end made it necessary once again to assign grades it dawned on me, for reasons that will be made clear in this paper's second half, to put not only the burden of proof but the burden of articulating that proof on the students. Who could have a more vested interest in the outcome of grading than the very recipients themselves? The process by which this worked transformed a tension-filled monologue (myself muttering to myself) to a constructive dialogue between students and teacher — a dramatic alteration for the better. With adaptations to course level and type of class, this method has a potentially wide application.

Why Grades Are Misleading

Grades Exist for an Institution's Administrative Convenience

Letters, numbers, and percents can be tallied, averaged, fiddled with, and fudged to satisfy a variety of institutional purposes. Under the guise of fake precision schools, like other advertisers, can announce, "Our students are better [or worse] than _____." Fill in the blanks: *they were last year.* But what about the year before? *yours.* All of yours? in comparison with all of ours, or only selected populations — say, all pre-meds — under certain circumstances — preparing for the MCAT? *students in other school systems.* Which students? Which systems?

Grades Fit Record-Keeping Formats

Grades fill slots on forms. If transcripts didn't exist, registrars would invent them or their equivalent. They'd have to — to accommodate not a rage for precision but an institutional need for shorthand, a way to code, store, and transmit information in a compact way. Grades are an efficient means of reducing complicated information to a simple code that can be interpreted with alleged unambiguity by whoever sees the symbols and knows the context — and many others who know nothing whatever about the context. Does the meaning of the A, or the B+, or the C — in practice our grading scales sink no lower except for no-shows — reside in the mind of the grader? the reader of the transcript? the student who thinks, irrespective of the actual grade, that it should have been better? Why ask — the meaning is crystal clear.

Grades Look Precise

They aren't. As we who have tried for years to convey the nuances of a host of meanings know only too well, the process of grading attempts to put a precise label on an imprecise assessment of a host of disparate components (such as subject, substance, organization, development, style, accuracy and finesse in using sources, grammar and mechanics, ethos — and perhaps format and punctuality). To amalgamate such disparities under a single symbol is comparable to trying to make strawberry jam — pure, elegant, tangy — by combining the strawberries not only with apples and oranges, but bananas, grapes, blueberries. . . . Truth in labeling requires that we call a fruit salad a fruit salad, and list the components in order of importance. What if other ingredients (broccoli, carrots — dare I say baloney?) enter the mixture, and further distort the categories?

Grades Look Objective

They aren't. Each and every grade reflects the cultural biases, values, standards, norms, prejudices, and taboos of the time and culture (with its complex host of subcultures) in which it's given. No teacher, no student (nor anyone else) can escape the tastes of their time — even rebels work against the current grain, in defiance of the echoes of other voices, other rooms. Although many, perhaps most, of these social constructs are present in all our reading and writing, they are seldom acknowledged, rarely articulated. But they inescapably inform our individual teaching of writing — the assignments we give, the range — however broad or narrow — of what we expect the students to write, and how we respond to it, in commenting and in grading.

Does a given paper deserve a good grade because the revision literally incorporates every single suggestion the teacher made on the first draft? Because the student — as we hear time after time after time — worked so hard on it? Because the student is just learning English/returning to school after long absence/plays football/works a forty-hour week/comes from a disadvantaged background/is laboring under insurmountable obstacles? Because the student is — and why not? — such a nice person?

Will a given paper be downgraded because it's late? sloppy? plagiarized? the sixtieth paper we've read on the subject in three weeks? because the author takes a stand that we find reprehensible, offensive, immoral, even criminal? Grading dresses up the art of marking papers in scientists' clothes. But the better the writers, the more they inspire in us as readers — and consequently, as commentators on the work, the passion that makes humanists of us all. As graders we can be fair, but as human beings we can never be objective.

Grades Label Not Only Papers But Their Writers

We say we're only responding to the text, not to the character of the writer behind it, but our students know better. They know from experience what it is to be labeled "An *A* Student." "A *B* Student." "A *C* student." Or worse. When I gave freshman Dewayne (name changed to protect the innocent) a generous B on doggerel verse he had written to honor his — yes — dog, he took umbrage, "*Hero* deserves more than a B. He's the best dog in Bean Blossom Township." Exactly. If the students are in graduate school, "A B+ isn't good enough for a Zimmerman" is their mantra. "Love me love my paper," they cry, and try as we may to look only at the words on the page, we cannot ignore the writer behind as well as in the text, or the stereotypes that cling to the A, the B, or the C student, clad in the velcro grade to which a host of connotations, positive and pernicious, cling.

Why Grades Are Big Trouble

Grades Are Big Trouble Because They Undermine Good Teaching

Current composition theorists agree, in principle anyway, on the importance of dialogic discussions in which all students have a right to speak up and speak out, along with the value of writing workshops and revisions that incorporate the writer's resultant insights. But grades automatically signal who is more equal than all the rest put together. The teacher, who has the power and authority to award the grade, therefore has the power to impose her views on the directions the discussions and the resulting papers should go. But what if the teacher misses the point? What if the teacher's rage for order overrides the student's need to say something important to him, prompted by an assigned reading but tangential to the teacher's conception of the writing assignment?

"Just tell me what you want," our students ask — "and I'll give it to you in order to get a good grade" is the unspoken half of that sentence. "Abandon personal investment all ye who enter here" might be their motto. For when students engage in that transaction they give up both passion and concern. In consequence, they relinquish ownership of their writing and with it commitment to their subject, engagement with its ideas and point of view, and a willingness to rewrite beyond the minimum. If the students tailor their writing to contours of the teacher's views, how can they engage in the critical thinking and tough-minded independent learning we claim to encourage? No wonder such papers are boring; the teacher has already predetermined what they will say.

Grades Are Big Trouble Because They Inhibit, Even Block, Student Discussion and Response to the Course Material

In transactions between teacher and students such as those described above, only the bold, the hyperconfident, or the naive have the courage to speak for themselves instead of becoming their teachers' ventriloquists.

With most writing assignments we give, we expect the resulting papers to fall within a predictable range, however wide or narrow the latitude. Yet we've all had the experience of the paper that's out of bounds — in which the writer marches to a different beat, down a different avenue, even out of the universe established in the classroom. Once we've ruled out plagiarism — the knee-jerk reaction to aberrant papers — how do we respond to a paper when the student has ignored our careful cues? How do we respond to the fairly common paper that begins to discuss, say, the assigned literary text at hand but that incorporates (some would say *wanders to*) an examination of an issue in the writer's life inspired by something analogous in the text? Do we automatically treat the paper's altered direction as a problem in organization, and see the writing as bent out of shape? Or do we acknowledge such a shift in perspective and structure as ways the student has chosen to make the subject her own? What if the assigned literary analysis begins in the detached stance and vocabulary of a literary critic, but alters to a passionate personal voice that reflects the change in focus?

These are not questions that can be answered in the abstract, but only with specific references to the paper at hand. If we expect our students to function as engaged, critical readers and writers, then we should encourage and accommodate writing that is full of, in Annie Dillard's words, "unwrapped gifts" for the teacher and "free surprises" for the authors, writing that they care about. We can provide appropriate encouragement, direction, and critical queries — preferably on early and intermediate drafts — much more effectively in commentary than in grades. If students and teachers alike write early and write often, there should be no major problems of organization, development, tone in the final version of the paper — by which time a grade (if given) should be almost irrelevant.

Grades Are Big Trouble Because They Look Fixed and Permanent

It's a toss-up as to which is worse, a false appearance of permanence, or an actually unchangeable grade. One scenario occurs when the teacher, attempting to be kind as well as to encourage revision, allows the student to rewrite and rewrite and rewrite the paper in anticipation of a better grade. This procedure not only promises to inundate the teacher with revised old papers on top of the unrevised new ones that continue in response to new assignments, it also signals that grades are negotiable, temporary markers on the road that leads ultimately to A's if both teacher and student have sufficient stamina to stay the course. And why not — if the teacher has provided numerous corrections at each stage, at some point she'll be grading her own writing rather than the student's, anyway.

If, on the other hand, the grade given initially can't be changed, why should the student bother to revise the paper? If grades were out of the picture, the real reasons for revising — such as clarity, emphasis, argument, style — would become manifest, and the implication that writers revise essentially to improve their grades would become irrelevant. When Hemingway said he rewrote the last page of *A Farewell to Arms* 39 times, he was "just getting the words right."

Grades Are Big Trouble Because They're Dishonest

Oh, not necessarily in my course, and naturally not in yours, but that nationwide grade inflation is rampant is not news. For practical purposes undergraduate grading scales in most schools have in the past two decades been reduced from five points to three — A to C, with F's reserved for no-shows, and graduate grades reduced from three points to two (A to B).

A Serendipitous Solution

At the beginning of the fall semester this paper, originally titled "Why I Hate to Give Grades," stopped at this point. It dangled over the abyss of the inevitable, inexorable need of my institution — like most others — to assign grades to the work of every student in nearly every course (with the exception of the occasional pass/fail undergraduate course, and continuing credit for graduate students working on dissertations). I didn't know how to end it.

So I took "Why I Hate to Give Grades" to the first meeting of my advanced Writing Workshop in Creative Nonfiction — 15 juniors and seniors selected by portfolio admission. We all wore shorts (it was hot), but I was the only one professing nonchalance under a big-brimmed red straw hat instead of the *chapeau du jour*, a baseball cap on backward. For although I wanted to set the example of how the workshop would operate in reading and commenting on papers ("What works well in this paper? What could be done to make it better?"), I didn't want these still-strangers to see my uncertain face as I read my work-in-progress.

My reading of that paper proved critical, in ways both intentional and inadvertent. I meant to signal that all of us, myself included, were colleagues in a writing community governed by clearheadedness, candor, and courtesy. I meant to affirm that good ideas were the heart of this course, and that revision was its soul. I wanted the students to acknowledge that nearly everything anyone wrote — or rewrote — could be made still better.

My reading also, of course, illustrated that it was appropriate to discuss unfinished work — a good way to raise questions and solve problems. In retrospect, I can see that the appearance of an unfinished work at the outset of the course may have also signaled that it was all right not to finish anything. Because I myself am often working on several papers concurrently, shifting from one to the other as the insight, or the research data emerges, it seemed reasonable to allow my students the same latitude. However, at some point the work must end; either deadlines descend or the writer has done all she can with a paper and has to let it go. Next time, in the interests of smoothing the roughness that exists even after several drafts, I'll require that at least one major paper be brought to closure; the writer can always open it up later on.

Moreover, by explaining "Why I Hate to Give Grades," I conveyed another message whose power I didn't realize until well into the semester — that grades were incidental, that the emphasis was on the writings themselves. "I really do hate to give grades," I told the class when I returned their warm-up papers, "Why I Write," retitled by one writer, "Why I Wrong." "I want you to focus on making your writing better, and not to get hung up on a letter grade. I tell you what," I said, "let me know when you've finished a paper to your satisfaction, and then I'll give you its grade. However," I was compelled to add, "throughout the semester I'll be keeping a running record of your grades, on the originals as well as the revisions. As a fail-safe mechanism, I'll tell you if your grade on any given version is dipping below C level." The grungy green gradebook came to mind — but never to class.

During the semester the students had to write seven papers (some later papers could expand their predecessors), and turn in revisions on alternate weeks. All original versions, and many revisions, were discussed in class, either in small groups or by the class as a whole. I also wrote extensive commentary, usually on the initial version; the author and I each got a copy of the printout. After the second paper I virtually stopped marking the numerous errors of spelling and mechanics and the absence of titles on the papers; by then even the most cavalier students in this freewheeling group (one student's warm-up was "Why I Rant") understood that house rules insisted on the absence of the former and the presence of the latter.

Preoccupation with the texts, and the rhythm of paper-and-revision, paper-and-revision, obscured the fact that after ten weeks into the semester not one student had ever asked me for a grade on any paper, in class or in conference. The class response groups, like their writing, had taken on an extra-curricular life of their own in which a number of the students analyzed each others' work and spurred each other on. That I didn't know about these meetings until the semester's end attests to an ideal shift of focus. For in becoming each others' audience, the students' reciprocal critiques validated their work and bypassed grading.

Amanda's group typifies the entire class, except for the two who disappeared by mid-semester, though one burly lad surfaced briefly, first with pinkeye, later with pink hair. Amanda explained, in her semester's-end commentary: "While I used to keep my writing strictly to myself, working with class peers has loosened me up a bit. Mike and Jeff have been very encouraging throughout the course of my work, exactly what I need to feel comfortable." In order to avoid feeling constrained, even "shut down by strict guidelines," Amanda decided to "find inspiration" in writing for her friends. "And it made a difference," she said, "Jeff's 'Vision Quest' paper encouraged me to write about my Mt. Washington experience. . . . He told me he stayed up all night writing his paper in its entirety. To be honest, I was jealous. And for the next week I tried to do the same thing." She continues, "I attacked my paper with such hopeful energy that I wrote more in the next few weeks" than in the rest of the semester. "I proudly showed my versions to Jeff, acting out the conversations, explaining and unfolding all of the conflicts and interactions in such a way that I explored the subject many times more deeply than I originally had thought. He has been so encouraging, and inspiring in his own writing, that my account of Washington has taken on a deeply personal significance. I see it now as a metaphor for my life experience since last summer."

"Well," I finally said as the semester's end lurked two weeks away, "I have to give you a semester grade, and no one has asked for a grade yet. Does this mean that your works are still in progress?" They nodded. "O.K. Then when you bring in your completed portfolio for our final conference, include a letter to me in which you identify the grade you think you deserve for the semester, and your rationale for this grade, based on your four best papers. What would the odds be that you could write four more of this quality? This letter will contain a critical analysis of your own work and you'll write it as you would any other critical paper, considering such features as" — I distributed the criteria — "significance of topic; organization; nature and solidity of evidence; language, style, tone; creation of authorial persona and ethos; spelling, mechanics, syntax. Moreover," I added, "explain what problems you had as a writer at the beginning of the semester, and what progress you've made in solving them. Also, include an estimate of your contributions to the writers' workshop." They nodded again. "Do you want me to bring my written assessment of your work to conference too?" I thought of the Evergreen State model. Groans and grimaces. "O.K. It's your show."

The students' self-assessment, while claiming preemptive authority, would also require them to shoulder the burden of proof. I did not realize until we discussed their analyses in conference how much of the burden that removed from me. In all instances but one I agreed exactly with the students' analyses of their performances as writers and critics. There was a single exception. Suzy, the best writer in the class, grossly undervalued work that the rest of us considered superb — taut, complex, original, and precise. Thus her paper on anorexia begins, "I see them everywhere I go: the skinny girls with the gaunt faces and matchstick legs, an ass way too flat and underfed, and eyes that are hard with purpose. They carry their bodies forward, holding their hips out before their smile." In conference, I told Suzy how good her work was and, flipping through her portfolio, I showed her why.

Because the other students and I agreed on the substance of their self-evaluations — content, form, style, growth over time — conferences were the easiest I had experienced in three decades of teaching, and the most expeditious. The material was all there, in the portfolios and in the interpretations. Had I disagreed with their analyses, as I did with Suzy's, I'd have said so and explained why. That we were able to agree so consistently reaffirms the tenor of the feedback that the students had been receiving throughout the semester, in every class and on every paper.

We did not, however, always concur on grades. On the whole, my grades were about a half-step lower than the students', because of differences in emphasis. But because our points of agreement were so numerous, it was also easy to tell the students in person why (in most cases) they'd be getting some form of B instead of the A they desired, but didn't necessarily expect. Thus when Cory wrote, "I want an A and I'll understand a B+," it was easy for me to counter with a B and to explain why. Jeff, a student risen from the ashes of his dropout self, his literary aspirations not only rekindled but inspiring Amanda's work, affirmed, "I'm very happy to tell you that I aced this class and confirmed that I am a good writer, good enough to even continue onto graduate school and maybe one day to earn my keep through my writing. I deserve an A+ for this course." "Not quite," I said, "Your writing is tougher and much better; it still needs work" — again the portfolio showed why — "but keep at it."

In conference I could readily acknowledge the students' eagerness for a grade that accommodated their perceived growth, including their newfound willingness to take risks in writing about subjects that came to mean a great deal to them ("true heart felt renditions of a young girl's feelings and emotions"), to experiment with structure and style, and to revise and revise and revise again. In the same conference, when we perused their portfolios together, the students could acknowledge that even though they'd come a long way their writing still had miles to go before they could match the authority and grace of texts like Suzy's. The sole student who suggested an A based on punctiliousness, punctuation, and perfect attendance conceded that depth and development with overriding virtues. In a point of tact but also of truth, we all agreed that with the students' momentum and morale on their current high, if the course could have lasted for another semester, or even eight more weeks. . . . As I filled out the grade sheets in a half-hour instead of my usual day of agonized indecisiveness, I realized that the semester-long communication culminated in grades that were perceived as just and (except for the underconfident Suzy) surprised no one.

But Would This Work Widely?

At my back I can hear the skeptics scoff. Okay, so you could avoid giving grades in that class because they were advanced students in a merit-based elective; the students were highly motivated, working in a community of writers who received continuous feedback on their work, in and out of class. But I'm teaching a subject-matter course in _____ [fill in the blank]; if I had to spend as much time on writing as you did we'd never get anything else done. And what about freshmen — or grad students — who require continuous grades to reassure them that they're not flunking out? What about large lecture courses where to comment so extensively on papers would cause instant teacher meltdown? (I personally will have more answers after I've experimented with this scheme in other, very different types of courses.)

But teachers working with Writing-Across-the-Curriculum programs have already devised solutions that address most of these matters, and more — ways to assign lots of writing and to manage the paper load through a combination of peer feedback, selective teacher commentary, TA support in large lecture courses, and shifting more responsibility onto the students themselves. If each and every writing assignment incorporates not only the key language of its subject, but of its disciplinary-based form, structure, and style, students will understand what the teacher wants and will have the language both to write in and to discuss their work. Whether or not students have received grades throughout the semester, on papers and on tests — where it would probably be much more confusing to eschew grades than to assign them — there's no reason they can't be asked to submit a semester's end progress report. Again, this could be discipline-specific, and (if desired), could be designed to accompany a portfolio of the semester's work. At minimum, it would comprise a critique of the student's work, and rationale for the semester grade as the basis for discussion with the professor (in small classes) or teaching assistants (in larger classes). The instructor could specify in advance that the conference is to be a colloquy, not a last-ditch attempt to lobby for a better grade. If needed, the conference could be abbreviated, or conducted through e-mail commentary on the student's self-critique, though, like Socrates, I think there is considerable virtue in person-to-person dialogue.

Yes, this solution places a great deal of trust in the students. The instructor trusts that they'll understand what the course is about, what they're supposed to have learned and done in it, and what level of proficiency they've attained relative to where they began, their peers, and college standards. This means that teachers have to be clear about course aims and assignments, consistent in responding (or in training assistants to respond) to student work, and to student self-assessments. Fortunately, we are truly blessed to teach in an educational system where the teachers are strong, the papers are good looking, and all the students are above average. So it shouldn't be hard.

Bloom's Insights as a Resource for Your Teaching

1. Review Bloom's list of complaints about grades. Which are the most serious and which are the least? Why? Does she leave out

any problems that you as a teacher have encountered with grading?

2. Consider Bloom's proposed system of grading. What are your most pressing concerns? Do you feel that Bloom neglects potential problems with this system? Does she adequately address those concerns she does anticipate? What added benefits might her "solution" have that Bloom does not mention?

Bloom's Insights as a Resource for Your Writing Classroom

1. Guide your class in brainstorming, developing, and refining student-derived criteria for assessment. Given the purpose of a particular assignment, what specific features are essential to an effective product? What factors are important to, or would strengthen, the assignment? Once you, as a class, have settled upon standards for assessment and their relative degree of importance, draft a clear and specific rubric. Photocopy and distribute this, or visually display it in the classroom, so that students can refer to it as they write and as they evaluate what they write.

2. Assign Bloom's essay to your students to read. Ask them to write a response that weighs their opinions of the relative strengths and weaknesses of her point of view. Ultimately, they should take a position for or against Bloom's proposal, addressing any concerns they raise by proposing how to adapt or modify the system to what they feel may be a more workable version.

Error

Joseph Harris

In this essay, Joseph Harris situates the discussion of error historically, looking closely at the debate between John Rouse and Gerald Graff over the meaning of Mina Shaughnessy's widely known work, Errors and Expectations, *and detailing the broader politics that make this such a heated debate. Harris argues that we are obligated to teach students to write correctly, not because of any naive faith in the transcendent value of the "standard" but because these issues are inextricably linked to the need for authority and credibility that brings students to the university in the first place. Supporting a shift from issues of phrasing and correctness to matters of stance and argument, Harris's beliefs complement David Bartholomae's overall goal — to help students gain the authority in their*

discourse that will provide them access to academic and professional
communities (see "Inventing the University," Chap. 1).

"How Rouse makes his living is none of my business, but I venture
that if he manages a decent livelihood it is only because he has
somewhere or other submitted to enough socialization to equip him to
do something for which somebody is willing to pay him" (852). So thun-
dered Gerald Graff in the pages of *College English* in 1980, as part of a
response to an article John Rouse had published in the same journal a
year before. Not only was Graff's tone here sententious and overbearing, his question was also rhetorical to the point of being disingenuous,
since how Rouse made his living should have been clear to anyone who
had read his article, which was on the teaching of college writing and
included a standard biographical note on its title page identifying him
as "a teacher of English and an administrator in public schools" as well
as the author of previous pieces in *College English* and of a book called
The Completed Gesture: Myth, Character, and Education ("Politics" 1).
So Rouse was a teacher and writer, "managing his livelihood" in much
the same way as Graff, and probably drawing on much the same sort of
skills and "socialization" in order to do so. Except not quite. For what
Graff — who was identified by a similar note on the first page of his
response as the chair of the English department at Northwestern University, as well as the author of articles in several prestigious literary
journals and of a book published by the University of Chicago Press
(851) — was hinting rather broadly at was that he didn't know who
this guy was, that Rouse (schoolteacher rather than professor; articles
in *College English* rather than *Salmagundi*; book published by trade
rather than university press) was not a player in the academic world
that Graff moved about in. And perhaps why this seemed so important
was that Rouse had presumed to criticize the work of someone who
was such a player, someone who by then had in fact become a kind of
revered figure in the literary establishment, its sanctioned representative of the good teacher — and that was Mina Shaughnessy.

Although in many ways, Rouse had seemed to ask for precisely the
sort of response he got from Graff and others.[1] His article on "The Politics of Composition" offered what I still see as a trenchant critique of
Shaughnessy's 1977 *Errors and Expectations*, a book on the teaching of
"basic" or underprepared college writers that had almost immediately
gained the status of a classic. Rouse argued that Shaughnessy's relent-
less focus on the teaching of grammar might in many cases actually
hinder the attempts of anxious and inexperienced students to elaborate their thoughts effectively in writing. I agree. But his criticism was
couched in language that sometimes seemed deliberately aimed to provoke: Rouse failed to acknowledge, for instance, the crucial political
importance and difficulty of the role that Shaughnessy took on in the
late 1960s when she set up the first Basic Writing Program at City
College of New York, and thus found herself in charge of diagnosing

and responding to the academic needs of thousands of newly admitted and severely underprepared open admissions students. He also failed to note the clear sympathy and respect for such students that runs throughout *Errors and Expectations* and which all of her many admirers argue was central to Shaughnessy's work as a teacher and intellectual. And he was either unaware of or did not see the need to mention her tragic and early death from cancer the year before in 1978. Instead, Rouse went ferociously on the attack, arguing that Shaughnessy's "overriding need to socialize these young people in a manner politically acceptable accounts, I think, for her misinterpretations of student work and her disregard of known facts of language learning" (1–2). This rabble-rousing tone led right into Graff's magisterial response, and a much needed argument over teaching aims and strategies became clouded with competing accusations of elitism and pseudoradicalism, as snide guesses about Mina Shaughnessy's psychopolitical needs or John Rouse's means of earning a living were followed by insinuations about who *really* had the best interests of students in mind. "Is this submission with a cheerful smile? 'Mrs. Shaughnessy, we do know our verbs and adverbs,'" sneered Rouse (8). "John Rouse's article . . . illustrates the predicament of the thoughtful composition teacher today," replied Graff, who then went on to explain that it was the very conscientiousness of such teachers that left them "open to attack from critics of Rouse's persuasion" (851).

I want to do two things in this chapter: First, to work through what might actually be at stake in this argument over error and socialization, to sort out what competing views of the aims and practices of teaching are being offered in it, and, second, to try to understand why this particular issue in teaching, more than any other that I know of, seems to spark such strong feeling. I begin by looking more closely at Mina Shaughnessy, who figures in this debate, I think, less as an advocate of a position which many people now find very compelling than as a kind of icon, a model of what it might mean to be, in Graff's words, a "thoughtful composition teacher."

Shaughnessy was an elegant but evidently also rather slow writer. Her entire body of work consists of a few essays and talks along with a single book, *Errors and Expectations*. This has been enough, though, to secure her place in the history of the field. *Errors and Expectations* showed how students who had often been presumed uneducable, hopelessly unprepared for college work, could in fact be helped to compose reasonably correct academic prose — that their problems with college writing stemmed not from a lack of intelligence but from inexperience. As Shaughnessy put it, "BW students write the way they do, not because they are slow or non-verbal, indifferent to or incapable of academic excellence, but because they are beginners and must, like all beginners, learn by making mistakes" (5). The students whom Shaughnessy worked with (she calls them "BWs" or "basic writers"), and whose writings fill the pages of her book, were for the most part blacks and Hispanics who had been given the chance to attend City through its (then) new and controversial program of open admissions for graduates of New York high schools.[2] Shaughnessy's work with these students was thus an intrinsic part of one of the most ambitious democratic reforms of American higher education — as the glowing reviews of her book in popular liberal magazines like *The Nation* and *Atlantic Monthly* attested.

But while politically liberal, the plan of work sketched out in *Errors and Expectations* is in many ways quite intellectually conservative. What people tend to remember and admire about *Errors and Expectations* is Shaughnessy's early defense of the aims of open admissions, her attentiveness throughout to the language of students, and her analysis late in the book of the difficulties students often have in taking on the critical and argumentative stance of much academic writing. What tends to be forgotten or glossed over is that the bulk of *Errors and Expectations* is a primer on teaching for correctness, pure and simple, as the titles of its Chapters 2 through 6 show: Handwriting and Punctuation, Syntax, Common Errors, Spelling, and Vocabulary. And even the much more celebrated seventh chapter on Beyond the Sentence offers what seems to me a distressingly formulaic view of academic writing and how to teach it. For instance, an extraordinarily detailed "sample lesson" on helping students write about reading (251–55) offers students an extended list of quotations culled from the book they are reading (*Black Boy*), followed by a set of procedures (Observation, Idea, and Analysis — the three of which are themselves broken into substeps) that they are to use in analyzing this list of details, and ends up by instructing them to

> Follow the steps given above. Make observations on parts, repetitions, omissions, and connections. Write down the main idea you get from your observations. Develop that main idea into an essay that makes a general statement, an explanation of the statement, an illustration of the statement, and a concluding statement. (255)

Follow the steps given above. I can't imagine a less compelling representation of the work of a critic or intellectual. Students are not asked in this assignment to say anything about what they thought or felt about their reading, or to connect what the author is writing about with their own experiences, or to take a stand on what he has to say; rather, they are simply told to generate and defend "a main idea" about a list of details that their teacher has given them from the book. What is the point of having students read books (like *Black Boy*) that might speak to their situations and concerns if they are not then encouraged to draw on their life experiences in speaking back to it? The tame parody of critical analysis sketched out in this assignment is "academic" in the worst sense: its form predetermined, its aim less to say something new or interesting than to demonstrate a competence in a certain kind of school writing.

Errors and Expectations thus argues for a new sort of student but not a new sort of intellectual practice. It says that basic writers can also do the kind of work that mainstream students have long been expected to do; it doesn't suggest this work be changed in any significant ways. This is a strong part of its appeal. Throughout her writings Shaughnessy offers a consistent image of herself as an *amateur* and a *reformer*. Even as she helped to set up the new field of "basic writing," Shaughnessy identified herself less with composition than with mainstream literary studies. Few of her admirers miss the chance to note how she was the product of a quite traditional education (B.A. in speech from Northwestern, M.A. in literature from Columbia) or to mark her love of Milton and drama.[3] Her method in *Errors and Expectations* is essentially that of the literary critic: a close and careful explication of difficult texts — except that in this case the difficulty springs from the inexperience of students rather than from the virtuosity of professionals. And her list of references and suggested readings at the end of her book has an undisciplined and eclectic quality: some literature, some criticism, some linguistics, some psychology, some work on second language learning and on the writing process — whatever, it seems, that could be found which might help with the task at hand.

This image of the autodidact or amateur was carefully constructed. Shaughnessy often depicts herself and her colleagues as "pioneers" working on a new "frontier," who need to "dive in" and explore previously uncharted waters (the metaphor varies a bit) so they can form a new kind of knowledge and expertise to use in teaching a new kind of college student. In "Mapping Errors and Expectations for Basic Writing," Bruce Horner points to the troubling (indeed, almost unconsciously racist) implications of describing teachers and students in terms of pioneers and natives. I would add that the "frontier" Shaughnessy claimed to stumble upon was already quite well developed, that even though the field of composition was not disciplined or professionalized in the same ways it is now, many teachers and writers had for some time been dealing with much the same sorts of issues.

There is no question that Shaughnessy brought a new sense of urgency to the problem of teaching underprepared writers. But it wasn't a new problem. In 1961, for instance, David Holbrook had written his moving book on *English for the Rejected* (still perhaps the bluntest and most accurate name for "basic" writers); in 1967, John Dixon was writing in *Growth through English* about students like Joan, the third grader with an IQ of 76 who wrote her poem about "the yellow bird." (It is this British and school-based tradition that John Rouse identifies himself with in his response to Shaughnessy.) And in America, in 1977, the same year that *Errors and Expectations* came out, Geneva Smitherman published *Talkin and Testifyin*, a book that urged teachers to spend less time correcting the language of black students and more time responding to what they had to say. And throughout the 1970s, the very time that Shaughnessy was most active in the profession, what remains perhaps the liveliest and most vehement debate in the history of CCCC was going on around the drafting and eventual approval of its 1974 statement on "The Students' Right to Their Own Language," a document which militantly asserted the need for teachers to move beyond a simple concern with having students write standard written English. None of these texts or authors can be placed in easy agreement with the approach taken by Shaughnessy in *Errors and Expectations*, which remains, again, after everything else is said about it, a book on teaching grammar. What Shaughnessy depicts as a sparse and unpopulated frontier of inquiry, then, looks from another perspective (to make use of a competing cliché) more like a marketplace of ideas as contending factions hawk their positions and argue against the views of others.

But this contrast also shows the appeal of the metaphor of the frontier, which allowed Shaughnessy to present herself less as criticizing than *extending* the reach of English studies. (Contrast this with critics, like Rouse, who positioned themselves as outsiders arguing *against* the status quo.) Even at her angriest moments (as in her article on "The English Professor's Malady," in which she complains of her colleagues' unwillingness to take on the hard work of teaching students not already familiar with their preferred ways of reading and writing), Shaughnessy's argument was for the profession to live up to its own stated values. Her message was consistently one of *inclusion* — that we can (and should) teach a kind of student, the "basic writer," who has too often slipped beneath the notice of the professoriate. And not only that, but she also showed how this sort of teaching could draw on precisely the sort of skills that people trained in English were likely to have, as well as to offer them much the sort of intellectual rewards which they most valued. The pleasures of *Errors and Expectations* are strikingly like that of good literary criticism: Passages of student writing that seem almost impossibly convoluted and obscure are patiently untangled and explicated. Shaughnessy thus offered the profession of English studies a useful image of one of its own best selves: The teacher who happily takes on the class of boneheads that the rest of us dread encountering and who patiently teaches them the very "basics" which we want to be able to assume they already know.

But *what* Shaughnessy argues can (and should) be taught to these new students is dismaying. Here, for instance, is the plan she offers for a basic writing course near the end of *Errors and Expectations*:

Weeks 1–5	Combined work on syntax and punctuation, following recommendations in Chapters 2 and 3.
Weeks 6–7	Spelling — principles of word formation, diagnostic techniques. (After this, spelling instruction should be individualized.)
Weeks 8–12	Common errors — verb inflections for number, noun inflections for number, verb tenses, agreement.

> Weeks 13–15   Vocabulary — prefixes, suffixes, roots, abstract-concrete words, precision. (289)

Fifteen weeks and the focus never moves past correctness. Nowhere here (or anywhere else in her book) do we get a sense that the work of a basic writing course might be not only to train students in the mechanics of writing correct sentences but also to engage them in the life of the mind, to offer them some real experience in testing out and elaborating their views in writing. At no point in *Errors and Expectations* does Shaughnessy talk about how teachers might respond to the gist or argument of student writings, or about how to help students use writing to clarify or revise what they think. Indeed, as Rouse pointed out, Shaughnessy does not even seem to notice how many of the students whose work she cites change what they actually have to say in the process of trying to write more correct sentences.[4] Coupled with this is her nearly complete lack of interest in revision. Almost all of the student writings that Shaughnessy analyzes are timed first drafts; her goal in teaching was not to have students go back to edit and revise what they had written but to write new impromptu pieces with fewer mistakes in them. Her measures of good writing, that is to say, centered on fluency and correctness at the almost total expense of meaning. A footnote near the end of her book strikingly shows this mechanistic emphasis. Comparing some pieces written early in the term with those composed later on by the same students, Shaughnessy remarks,

> In all such before-and-after examples, the "after" samples bear many marks of revision (crossed-out words, corrected punctuation, etc.), suggesting that students have acquired the important habit of going back over their sentences with an eye to correctness. (277)

Revision here is pictured simply as a habit of proofreading. *Errors and Expectations* is thus the sort of book that tells you everything but why — as students and teachers labor together to perfect the form of prose whose actual or possible meanings they never seem to talk about.

Compare this to the sort of work that, at precisely the same time, Geneva Smitherman was arguing ought to go on in writing classes. A sociolinguist active in political and legal debates over the schooling of black children, Smitherman was also a strong influence in the framing of the 1974 CCCC statement on the "Students' Right to Their Own Language." (Shaughnessy was conspicuously absent from this debate.) Her 1977 *Talkin and Testifyin* is an impassioned and lucid defense of the richness and complexity of black English. In its final chapter, Smitherman turns to language education, which she argues should center (for both black and white students) on skills in reading and writing that are "intellectual competencies that can be taught in any dialect or language" (228). To teach such a "communicative competence," teachers need to move beyond a fetishizing of correctness and instead focus on the more substantive, difficult, and rhetorical aspects of communication such as content and message, style, choice of words, logical development, originality of thought and expression, and so forth. Such are the real components of language power, and they cannot be measured by narrow conceptions of "correct grammar." While teachers frequently correct student language on the basis of such misguided conceptions, saying something correctly, and saying it well, are two entirely different Thangs. (229)

This emphasis on forming something to say and working to say it well could hardly be more different than Shaughnessy's focus on error. Smitherman continues to drive this emphasis home by comparing her responses to two student pieces: one a vacuous (and stylistically bland) comment on Baraka's *Dutchman* by a white student teacher, and the other a poorly developed paragraph on the evils of war by a black ninth grader. What I find striking is how Smitherman uses much the same strategy in responding to both writers, challenging them to articulate their positions more fully before working to correct their phrasings. To the white student, Smitherman said,

> as kindly as I could, that his "essay" was weak in content and repetitious, and that it did not demonstrate command of the literary critical tools that teachers of literature are supposed to possess, *plus it didn't really say nothing!* (229)

While in responding to the black ninth grader writing on war, she asked things like:

> "Some say . . ." Who is "some"? . . .
> Exactly who are the two sides you're talking about here? What category of people? Name them and tell something about them. . . .
> Give me an example showing when and how such a disagreement leads to war. . . .(230)

While these two responses show some differences in tone (and perhaps appropriately so, given the varying situations of the writers), their aim is quite similar: to get students to think about what they want to say in their writing and about the effects their words have on readers. Smitherman is quick to say that she is not advocating an "off-the-deep-end permissiveness of letting their kids get away with anything," but rather that she is teaching toward a rhetorical and stylistic awareness that is "deeper and more expansive" than that encouraged by a focus on norms of correctness (233). Her position is much the same as that taken by Rouse in his response to Shaughnessy, and indeed something like it has become in recent years the consensus view of the profession, at least as represented in the pages of *CCC* and *College English* and at the annual meetings of CCCC: Students must learn not simply how to avoid mistakes but how to write in ways that engage the attention of educated readers. Teachers need then to respond to what students are trying to say, to the effectiveness of their writing as a whole, and not simply to the presence or absence of local errors in spelling, syntax, or usage. Correctness thus becomes not the single and defining issue in learning how to write but simply one aspect of developing a more general communicative competence.

This shift in focus was given articulate and moving expression by Mike Rose in his 1989 *Lives on the Boundary*, a book which, like *Errors and Expectations*, gained almost immediate acclaim both within and outside the profession. Like Shaughnessy, Rose argues for the intelligence and promise of students who are too often dismissed as unprepared or even unfit for college work, and like her too, his work and writing speaks to the linkings between education and politics, since the underprepared students he works with are so often also (and not coincidentally) people of color or from lower socioeconomic classes. And, certainly, even though the students Rose works with in Los Angeles in the 1980s often seem to live in an almost completely different world than those Shaughnessy worked with in New York in the 1970s, what both groups most need to learn is how to find their way into a system of education that seems at many points purposely designed to exclude them. But rather than assuming, like Shaughnessy, that what such students need is yet more training in the "basics," Rose argues that an unremitting focus on the more routine and dull aspects of intellectual work can instead act to dim their ambitions and limit their chances of success. One of the most telling bits of evidence Rose has to offer for this view comes from his own life, since as a boy he was placed in the vocational track of his local schools and so learned of the boredom and condescension of such classrooms firsthand. He was only retracked into college prep when a teacher noticed he was doing suspiciously well in biology. You don't know what you don't know, Rose suggests: "The telling thing is how chancy both my placement into and exit from Voc. Ed. was; neither I nor my parents had anything to do with it" (30). We can't expect students to grow proficient at kinds of intellectual work that they don't know about, that they've never really been given a chance to try their hands at.

What struggling students need, then, is not more of the basics but a sense of what others find most exciting and useful about books, writing, and ideas. Here's how Rose describes how he began to form his own aims for teaching while working with a group of Vietnam veterans studying to return to college:

> Given the nature of these men's needs and given the limited time I would have with them, could I perhaps orient them to some of the kinds of reading and writing and ways of thinking that seem essential to a liberal course of study, some of the habits of mind that Jack MacFarland and the many [of Rose's own teachers] that followed him helped me develop? . . . I was looking for a methodical way to get my students to think about thinking. Thinking. Not a fussbudget course, but a course about thought. I finally decided to build a writing curriculum on four of the intellectual strategies my education had helped me develop — some

of which, I later learned were as old as Aristotle — strategies that kept emerging as I reflected on the life of the undergraduate: summarizing, classifying, comparing, and analyzing. (138)

The crucial words here are *habits of mind*, a phrasing even older than Aristotle, at least as it is often used to translate the Greek notion of *arete*, those "virtues" or "excellences" required by the citizens of a democracy.[5] There is an admirable hardheadedness in this teaching project that is reminiscent of Shaughnessy; like her, Rose wants to demystify the workings of the academy for his students. But a course on habits or strategies of thinking is in practice quite different from one focused on issues of correctness in language. As Rose outlines his course,

> Each quarter, I began by having the students summarize short simple readings, and then moved them slowly through classifying and comparing to analyzing. . . . I explained and modeled, used accessible readings, tried to incorporate what the veterans learned from one assignment to the next, slowly increased difficulty, and provided a lot of time for the men to talk and write. (143)

Malcolm Kiniry and Rose offer a more elaborate version of such a course in their 1990 *Critical Strategies for Academic Writing*, a text whose aim is to engage students in reading and writing, at a beginning and approximate level, about the kinds of issues and questions that academics in various fields take on. Similarly, in their 1986 *Facts, Artifacts, and Counterfacts*, David Bartholomae and Anthony Petrosky sketch out a plan for a basic writing course that is set up very much like a graduate seminar: Students read, write, and talk together about a particular intellectual issue over the course of a term, coming at the same topic from a number of different angles, reading one another's writings, seeing how the individual concerns they bring to their common subject influence what each of them has to say about it. The trick of such teaching is, of course, to find a set of readings that underprepared students will find accessible, and not only speak to their concerns but also push their ways of understanding and talking about them. (Some of the classes described in *Facts, Artifacts*, for instance, had students read and write on "Growth and Adolescence," or "Work," or "Creativity.") But what's more important is how this sort of teaching signals a shift in focus from *error* to *academic discourse*, from issues of phrasing and correctness to matters of stance and argument.

I support this shift myself, and, again, feel that Shaughnessy's failure to attend in any sustained way to issues beyond the sentence is what now makes her work, less than twenty years after its appearance, seem of merely historical interest rather than of practical use. (There is a dark irony here: The subtitle of *Errors and Expectations* is *A Guide for the Teacher of Basic Writing*, and Shaughnessy is often invoked as a model practitioner whose scholarship was deeply rooted in her day-to-day work with students. And yet I can't now imagine giving *Errors and Expectations* as a guide to a beginning teacher of basic writing, although I still often offer new teachers other writings from the 1960s and 1970s by people like Moffett, Britton, Elbow, and Coles.) Still one can see how this downplaying of error might seem to outsiders simply a way of slipping past the difficulty and drudgery of actually teaching writing. "Students and parents complain that they are being patronized, that the more relaxed, more personalist pedagogy fails to teach anybody how to write" (852), was how Graff (who is no cultural reactionary) put it in 1980. Given his distrust of Rouse and defense of Shaughnessy, it seems clear that for Graff learning "how to write" involves strong attention to issues of correctness, and his complaint about "relaxed" standards has been echoed in countless ways not only by students and parents but also by college faculty and administrators, as well as by writers in the popular press.[6] As one of my colleagues, a biologist, said to me recently after a curriculum meeting in which I argued for a new structuring of introductory writing courses at my college: "The thing is, most of us think that too many students can't write worth a damn, and we wish you'd just do something about it."

It's tempting to dismiss such complaints as misinformed, as in many ways they surely are. But that is also precisely the problem. Again, for some time now, most compositionists have held that a focus on error can often block the attempts of beginning writers to form their thoughts in prose, and indeed that the explicit teaching of grammatical forms usually has little effect on the abilities of students to write fluently or correctly.[7] But ask anyone *outside* the field (and this includes many writing teachers who are not active in CCCC) what they expect students to learn in a composition course, and you are likely to hear a good bit about issues of proper form and correctness. As even someone like the distinguished liberal philosopher Richard Rorty put it, when asked in an interview about what the aims of a writing course might be,

> I think the idea of freshman English, mostly, is just to get them to write complete sentences, get the commas in the right place, and stuff like that — the stuff we would like to think the high schools do and, in fact, they don't. But as long as there's a need for freshman English, it's going to be primarily a matter of the least common denominator of all the jargon. (Olson 6–7)

Although Rorty's interviewer, Gary Olson, expresses surprise at this response (since Rorty's views on language have influenced many progressive composition theorists), it seems to me both familiar and reasonable enough. What I find more distressing has been the ongoing inability of compositionists (myself among them) to explain ourselves to people like Graff and Rorty. Instead we have too often retreated behind the walls of our professional consensus, admonishing not only our students and university colleagues but the more general public as well when they fail to defer to our views on language learning — answering their concerns about correctness by telling them, in effect, that they should not want what they are asking us for.

This is an unfortunate stance for a field that defines itself through its interest in teaching and the practical workings of language. I am not advocating a return to Shaughnessy-like focus on error, but I do think we can learn from her responsiveness to the concerns of people outside our field. Rather than either meekly acceding to or simply dismissing what Smitherman called "the national mania for correctness" (229), we need to argue for a view of literacy that clearly recognizes and includes such concerns but is not wholly defined by them.

A first step might be to reinterpret worries about "grammar" or "correctness" in a more generous and expansive way. Rather than reading them as moves to trivialize the issues involved in learning to write, to turn everything into a simple matter of proofreading, we might see such remarks as somewhat clumsy attempts to voice concerns about how one gains or loses authority in writing. For even if mistakes do not interfere with what a writer has to say, they can still do serious harm to her credibility. Indeed, it is precisely because many mistakes (lapses in spelling or punctuation, for instance) seem so trivial that their appearance in a writer's text can seem to speak of a lack of care or ability. People don't want to be caught out in their writing or to have their students or children caught out. And so many struggling writers speak of their "problems with grammar" as a kind of shorthand for a whole set of difficulties they have with writing that are much harder to name, much as many readers will begin to complain about fairly trivial errors in a text they have grown impatient with for other less easily defined reasons. It is one thing to feel that in a particular classroom your language will not be held up for ridicule; it is another to feel confidence in your abilities to write to an indifferent or even hostile reader — to a different sort of teacher or examiner, perhaps, or to an applications committee or potential employer. Something like this is, I think, what lies behind many worries about "relaxed" or "permissive" forms of teaching. To gloss over such concerns is to dodge questions about the workings of power in language at their most naked.

Not that responding to them is all that easy either. As I've noted before, simply drilling students in proper forms has been shown to have little effect — and besides, the problem of gaining authority is not merely a matter of getting rid of error; students must also and at the same time acquire a rhetorical ease and power, an ability to write persuasively as well as correctly. And standards of correctness vary from one context to the other, along with the readiness of readers to look for mistakes, as Joseph Williams points out in his stunning 1981 article on "The Phenomenology of Error," in which he shows how the authors of writing handbooks often commit the same errors they decry, and sometimes in the very act of stating them — as when, for instance, while inveighing against the use of negative constructions, one text declares that "the following example . . . is not untypical"; or when in "Politics and the English Language" Orwell casts his famous polemic against the passive voice *in the passive voice*; or when yet another handbook advises that "Emphasis is often achieved . . . by the use of verbs in the active rather than in the passive voice" (158). The reason we don't tend to notice such problems, Williams argues, is that we're not looking for them. And, conversely, why we find so many mistakes in student papers is because we expect to, we're on the watch for them. (Williams clinches his case by revealing, at the end of his article, that he has deliberately inserted about a hundred "errors" in his own text. I have never met a reader who claimed to notice more than two or three on a first reading.)

Williams's point is not that we should downplay the significance of error but that we should focus our attention and energies on those mistakes which really count, on those that seriously impugn a writer's authority. (Maxine Hairston added to this line of thinking in a piece that appeared that same year in *College English*, "Not All Errors Are Created Equal: Nonacademic Readers in the Professions Respond to Lapses in Usage.") This makes good sense, but even more important is how Williams locates "error" as something that exists not simply as marks on a page but also as a part of the consciousness of writers, readers, and (in the form of handbooks and such) the culture at large. A mistake is not a mistake unless it's noticed as one, is how the argument goes, and it's a line of thought that sheds light both on why some writers have such difficulty proofreading their work and on the role that readers play in creating a mania of correctness. For what is involved in detecting errors seems to be not only an awareness of rules but a shift in attentiveness: One needs to learn how to read for mistakes as well as meaning.[8] This suggests the need for a kind of double approach to the issue of error, one that deals frankly with the practical politics of the situation: What writers need to learn is how to read their work for those lapses that will send many readers into a tailspin; what readers (and the culture) need to learn is to lighten up, to recognize the writing of reasonably correct prose as a fairly complex intellectual achievement and to be a little less quick to damn a writer for a few mistakes.

In practice one often sees this sort of double approach. In the *Facts, Artifacts* course, for instance, students are asked to revise and edit one of their writings for publication in a class book, a process which requires them to carefully proofread and correct their prose. And while his *Lives on the Boundary* is a plea to reform education in America, to make it more forgiving of error and more willing to work with difference, the picture Mike Rose offers of himself *as a teacher* throughout the book is of someone who wants to help students claim whatever power they can in the system as it stands. As one woman tells him,

> You know, Mike, people always hold this shit over you, make you . . . make you feel stupid with their fancy talk. But now *I've* read it, I've

read Shakespeare, I can say I, *Olga*, have read it. I won't tell you I like it, 'cause I don't know if I do or I don't. But I like knowing what it's about. (223)

While in another context, I might want to quibble with the term *fancy talk*, what is crucial to realize here, I think, is that unless you already feel at home in the workings of critical or intellectual discourse, that's all it's likely to seem to you: fancy talk. And I don't see how you could possibly begin to feel at ease in any sort of fancy talk unless you also felt sure both that what you had to say would be listened to seriously and that you weren't likely to commit any egregious nails-on-the-chalkboard kinds of mistakes (*c'est je*, that sort of thing) in trying to speak or write it. So while we can't teach for correctness alone, we also can't *not* teach for it either. I think of the joke in Calvin Trillin's 1977 novel *Runestruck*, when a lawyer goes out "on a drive to relax from the pressures of a civil liberties case he was arguing in a nearby town — the case of an elementary school teacher of progressive views who claimed that she was fired by the local school board solely because she had refused to teach her students to spell" (23). "Better watch my grammar" versus "won't really teach kids how to write." Some choice. (And Trillin probably actually knew something about the debate over error in the 1970s, since he is married to Alice Trillin, who taught basic writing with Shaughnessy at City College.) We need to make sure that in distancing ourselves from poor practice (a focus on error alone) we don't seem to advocate an equally unconvincing stance (no concern with error at all).

In the mid-1980s, a number of teachers and theorists tried to break out of this rhetorical bind by arguing that the job of writing teachers was to initiate students into the workings of the academic discourse community, to learn the specific conventions of college writing. I comment more about this move in Chapter 5. For now, I simply want to say that the power of this view has much to do with the elasticity of the term *convention* — which can describe almost anything from a critical habit of mind to a preferred form of citing sources to specific usages and phrasings. Using a term like *convention*, you can argue (and indeed I would) that in learning to write at college, students need to work on everything from spelling and punctuation to active verbs to self-reflexivity — and to do all this at once. Nothing can ruin the credibility of an academic piece more than poor proofreading (I know from hard experience as both a writer and journal editor), but errorless typing doesn't make up for a lack of critical insight either. To gain control over academic discourse, writers need to work on several levels at once — as do their teachers.

There is both a conceptual and rhetorical problem, though, I think, with a stress on specifically academic writing. In her 1991 rereading of *Errors and Expectations*, Min-Zhan Lu criticizes Shaughnessy's tendency to pit the ways with words that students bring with them to college against a seemingly neutral "language of public transactions"

(*Errors* 125), a move which Lu argues allows Shaughnessy to gloss over the fact that academic writing is both characterized by the use of certain linguistic forms and often associated with a particular set of political values. We do not teach a contextless Standard Written English, Lu argues, but a specific kind of writing closely tied to the particular aims and needs of university work. We thus need to recognize there are other Englishes, tied to other contexts or communities, which are not simply underdeveloped or less public versions of academic discourse, but that work toward different ends and whose use may express a competing or oppositional politics — as when, for instance, Geneva Smitherman draws on the forms and phrasings of black English throughout *Talkin and Testifyin*. This view of academic discourse as a limited and specific *use* of language, whose characteristic forms and gestures can thus be defined and taught, has proven a powerful tool in sharpening our sense of what might go on in a college writing class. But it can also seem once more to cast its advocates in the role of simply teaching a professional jargon. For instance, when asked by Gary Olson if writing teachers should try to teach students the "normal discourse" of the academic fields they are studying, Richard Rorty replies,

> It strikes me as a terrible idea. . . . I think that America has made itself a bit ridiculous in the international academic world by developing distinctive disciplinary jargon. It's the last thing we want to inculcate in the freshmen. (Olson 6–7)

Rorty's tone here is sneering, but even still the issue he raises is an important one: Is the point of undergraduate study to prepare students to become professional intellectuals? Or to put it another way, even if our aim is to teach students a particular form of writing (and not some neutral "standard"), is that form best described as "academic"? For some time now in composition, *academic* has served as the opposing term to words like *personal* or *expressive*. That is, if one does not ask students to write directly from experience but instead sets them to writing about books and ideas, then, according to common usage, their work is "academic."[9] But I'm not so sure about the usefulness of the term, which at best tends to suggest a stylistic distance or formality and at worst to serve as a shorthand for pretension and bad writing. And I don't think that the sort of writing I usually imagine myself as teaching toward is in any strict sense *academic* (although it is not simply personal either). That is, while I almost always ask undergraduates to write on texts and ideas, I rarely ask them to do the sort of reading through the relevant academic literature that I would routinely require of graduate students (who *are* training to become professional intellectuals), and I don't spend much time on issues of citation, documentation, and the like.[10] (I rarely even teach anything like the "research paper.") I'm more interested in having students read the work of others closely and aggressively, and to use their reading in thinking and writing about issues that concern them. I would like my students to begin to think of themselves as critics and intellectuals. But that is not at all the same as preparing them to become academics.

I think this is more than a fussing over terms. In his 1994 "Travels to the Hearts of the Forest: Dilettantes, Professionals, and Knowledge," Kurt Spellmeyer shows how academics routinely lay claim to expertise by denigrating the knowledge of nonspecialists or amateurs (a kind of sinister version of the critical move defined by David Bartholomae in "Inventing the University"). By way of example, Spellmeyer shows how university ethnographers and art historians labored to assert the authority of their own systematized and restricted bodies of knowledge over the more idiosyncratic works of "mere" travel writers and connoisseurs. But he might just as easily have chosen to talk about how academic literary scholars have over the years differentiated themselves from mere reviewers or how a newly disciplined generation of composition scholars now seek to distinguish themselves from mere classroom practitioners. With Spellmeyer, I believe we need to be wary of an increasingly narrow professionalization of knowledge — and thus that we should resist equating the "critical" with the "academic."

In making this distinction I also think of books like Peter Medway's 1980 *Finding a Language*, in which he reports on his attempts to do something more than simply pass time as the teacher of a set of working-class British youths near the end of their formal schooling, none of whom were likely to go on to university and all of whom had resisted most other attempts to interest them in their course work. Medway had these students define an issue that mattered to them in their lives outside of school (jobs, politics, sports, and so on), and then had them spend the rest of the term reading and writing about it. There's little about the course, as thoughtful as it is, that would be likely to startle an informed American teacher of basic writing; in fact, it seems very much like the sort of course described in *Facts, Artifacts*. But that's precisely my point. Medway's aim was not to help his students enter the academy (there was little realistic hope of doing so for all but one or two of them); his goal was to have them reflect critically on the world they were part of right then. Freed from having to prepare his students to write according to the formal standards of an academy they would never enter, Medway was able instead to think about how to engage their intellectual curiosity and urge them toward a self-reflectiveness.

Of course Medway was only freed from such expectations by working in a culture that is more stratified by social class than ours. His students had little prospect of moving out of the circumstances that they were born into, whatever they did in school. But the promise of America is to be able to do just that — and education has long been advertised as one way of doing it. Underneath all the worries about correctness in writing, then, there is hope — that getting it right will mean getting ahead (or at least allow the chance of getting ahead). But there is fear, too: What is the point of having a standard that includes everyone, a marker that fails to separate? Language is not only a means of communicating but a form of identification, a badge that seems to define its wearer and yet, paradoxically, can be changed. It is the fear and hope of such change that so powerfully charges the debate on error.

Notes

1. *College English* published sharply critical responses to Rouse by Graff, Michael Allen, and William Lawlor, along with a counterstatement by Rouse, "Feeling Our Way Along." That none of Rouse's critics identified themselves with the field of composition studies points to the politically charged quality of the debate about error.

2. City College's experiment with open admissions sparked a remarkable number of accounts from its faculty, both advocates and opponents, radicals and conservatives. Sidney Hook (*Out of Step*) and Irving Howe (*A Margin of Hope*), for instance, have interesting things to say in their memoirs about the struggles of the 1970s at City. And there have also been a number of accounts by people involved in some way with the teaching of English or basic writing, although this did not always mitigate the sententiousness of their prose — as is shown in the titles of Geoffrey Wagner's *The End of Education* and Theodore Gross's *Academic Turmoil*. And for a quick overview of the events of the 1970s at City, see James Traub's *City on a Hill*.

3. Shaughnessy's career has perhaps been documented more thoroughly than any other recent figure in composition studies. Janet Emig briefly traced her work in an obituary appearing in the February 1979 issue of *CCC*, and a series of writers — including E. D. Hirsch, Benjamin DeMott, John Lyons, Richard Hogart, and Sarah D'Eloia — commented on her work in a special issue, "Towards a Literate Democracy," of the *Journal of Basic Writing* in 1980, and then the same journal published still more reminiscences of Shaughnessy in 1994. John Lyons has a detailed and affectionate, although not uncritical, biographical essay on Shaughnessy in Brereton's *Traditions of Inquiry*. And, more recently, James Traub writes respectfully of Shaughnessy in a book, *City on a Hill*, that is more often quite critical of the open admissions experiment at City College.

4. In "Politics," Rouse points to how Shaughnessy's first example of a basic writer in action shows "his desperate effort to find *something* to say about the assigned topic" given him by his teacher, as he changes his position on the prompt no less than four times in an attempt to get his essay started (2). Similarly, in an article written some ten years later on "Redefining the Legacy of Mina Shaughnessy," Min-Zhan Lu analyzes the writings of a student whom Shaughnessy singles out for praise, pointing out that while the student does indeed seem to grow stylistically more fluent, the political positions she expresses in her successive writings also seem to shift significantly — although this attracts no comment from Shaughnessy.

5. There is a gendered subtext here as well that I can only begin to hint at: The Greek view of *arete* is closely connected with manliness, valor (the word is etymologically related to *Ares*, the god of war). It is thus peculiarly suggestive (even if also coincidental) that Rose should begin to form his notion of teaching toward "habits of mind" while working with a set of war veterans, and certainly the kind of teaching that he, David Bartholomae,

and others have been associated with has strong masculinist overtones. ("Reading involves a fair measure of push and shove" is the first sentence of the introduction to Bartholomae and Petrosky's *Ways of Reading*.) On the other hand, the sort of "fussbudget" course that Rose wants to avoid, and that Shaughnessy provides with her emphasis on form and correctness, has a stereotypically feminine and nurturing (or perhaps schoolmarmish) quality. James Catano offers an interesting look into this issue in his 1990 article on "The Rhetoric of Masculinity."

6. A 1994 poll of parents of public school students, for instance, found them strongly suspicious of "new methods of teaching composition" and desirous for a return to "the basics" (Johnson and Immerwahr); more sustained outsider criticisms of progressive language teaching have also appeared in magazines like *The New Republic* (Traub) and *The Atlantic Monthly* (Levine).

7. The first and still most ringing statement of this professional consensus came from Braddock, Lloyd-Jones, and Schoer in their 1963 *Research on Written Composition*: "In view of the widespread agreement of research studies based upon many types of students and teachers, the conclusion can be stated in strong and unqualified terms: the teaching of grammar has a negligible or, because it usually displaces some instruction and practice in composition, even a harmful effect on improvement in writing" (37–38). In 1985, Patrick Hartwell revisited the research on the effectiveness of explicit teaching of rules of correctness and once again concluded (along with virtually everyone he cites) that such teaching has little usefulness and thus that we ought to "move on to more interesting areas of inquiry" ("Grammar, Grammars, and the Teaching of Grammar" 127).

8. Some of the practical difficulties of teaching and learning proofreading are hinted at by the very number of people who have written on its complexities. The first issue of the *Journal of Basic Writing*, founded and edited by Mina Shaughnessy in 1975, was devoted entirely to the topic of error and included pieces by Sarah D'Eloia, Isabella Halstead, and Valerie Krishna. The 1980s saw more work on the subject from David Bartholomae ("Study of Error"), Mary Epes, Glynda Hull, and Elaine Lees; more recently, Bruce Horner ("Editing") and Min-Zhan Lu ("Professing") have written on the problematic relations between "error" and "style."

9. This standoff between the "academic" and the "personal" gets played out in a 1995 *CCC* interchange between David Bartholomae ("Writing with Teachers") and Peter Elbow ("Being a Writer vs. Being an Academic") — although, tellingly, when pushed, Bartholomae ends up defending not "academic" writing but something he calls *criticism*. Kurt Spellmeyer offers a powerful reading of this exchange, which began as a series of talks at CCCC, in the last chapter of *Common Ground*.

10. We do sometimes talk, though, about the rhetorical and stylistic uses of footnotes.

Works Cited

Bartholomae, David. "Inventing the University." *When a Writer Can't Write: Studies in Writer's Block and Other Composing-Process Problems*. Ed. Mike Rose. New York: Guilford, 1985. 134–65.

———. "A Reply to Stephen North." *Pre/Text* 11 (1990): 122–30.

————. "The Study of Error." *CCC* 31 (1980): 253–69.

————. "Writing with Teachers: A Conversation with Peter Elbow." *CCC* 46 (1995): 62–71, 84–87.

Bartholomae, David, and Anthony Petrosky. *Facts, Artifacts, and Counterfacts: Theory and Method for a Reading and Writing Course.* Upper Montclair, NJ: Boynton, 1986.

————. *Ways of Reading: An Anthology for Writers.* 2nd ed. Boston: Bedford, 1990.

"The Basic Issues in the Teaching of English." *PMLA* 74.4 (1959): 1–19.

Britton, James. "The Distinction between Participant and Spectator Role Language in Research and Practice." *Research in the Teaching of English* 18 (1984): 320–31.

————. *Language and Learning.* Harmondsworth: Penguin, 1970.

————. "Response to Working Party Paper No. 1. — What Is English?" *Working Papers of the Dartmouth Seminar.* ERIC, 1966. ED 082 201.

————. "The Spectator as Theorist: A Reply." *English Education* 21 (1989): 53–60.

Britton, James, Tony Burgess, Nancy Martin, Alex McLeod, and Harold Rosen. *The Development of Writing Abilities (11–18).* London: Macmillan, 1975.

Coles, William E., Jr. *Composing: Writing as a Self-Creating Process.* Rochelle Park, NJ: Hayden, 1974.

————. "Literacy for the Eighties: An Alternative to Losing." *Literacy for Life: The Demand for Reading and Writing.* Ed. Richard W. Bailey and Robin Melanie Fosheim. New York: MLA, 1983. 248–62.

————. *The Plural I.* New York: Holt, 1978.

————. *Seeing through Writing.* New York: Harper, 1988.

————. *Teaching Composing.* Rochelle Park, NJ: Hayden, 1974.

————. "An Unpetty Pace." *CCC* 23 (1972): 378–82.

Coles, William E., Jr., and James Vopat. *What Makes Writing Good? A Multiperspective.* Lexington, MA: Heath, 1985.

Dixon, John. "Conference Report: The Dartmouth Seminar." *Harvard Educational Review* 39 (1969): 366–72.

————. *Growth through English: A Record Based on the Dartmouth Seminar 1966.* Reading, England: NATE, 1967.

————. *Growth through English (Set in the Perspective of the Seventies).* 3rd ed. London: NATE, 1974.

Elbow, Peter. "Being a Writer vs. Being an Academic: A Conflict in Goals." *CCC* 46 (1995): 72–83, 87–92.

————. "Forward: About Personal Expressive Academic Writing." *Pre/Text* 11 (1990): 7–20.

————. "The Pleasures of Voice in the Literary Essay: Explorations in the Prose of Gretel Ehrlich and Richard Selzer." *Literary Nonfiction: Theory, Criticism, Pedagogy.* Ed. Chris Anderson. Carbondale, IL: Southern Illinois UP, 1989. 211–34.

————. "Reflections on Academic Discourse: How It Relates to Freshman and Colleagues." *College English* 53 (February 1991): 135–55.

————. *Writing without Teachers.* New York: Oxford UP, 1973.

————. *Writing with Power: Techniques for Mastering the Writing Process.* New York: Oxford UP, 1981.

Graff, Gerald. "The Politics of Composition: A Reply to John Rouse." *College English* 41 (1980): 851–56.

———. *Professing Literature: An Institutional History.* Chicago: U of Chicago P, 1987.

Hairston, Maxine. "Breaking Our Bonds and Reaffirming Our Connections." *CCC* 36 (1985): 272–82.

———. "Not All Errors Are Created Equal: Nonacademic Readers in the Professions Respond to Lapses in Usage." *College English* 43 (1981): 794–806.

———. "The Winds of Change: Thomas Kuhn and the Revolution in the Teaching of Writing." *CCC* 33 (1982): 76–88.

Holbrook, David. *English for Meaning.* New York: Taylor, 1979.

———. *English for the Rejected.* London: Cambridge UP, 1964.

Horner, Bruce. "Mapping Errors and Expectations for Basic Writing: From 'Frontier Field' to 'Border Country.'" *English Education* 26 (1994): 29–51.

———. "Rethinking the 'Sociality' of Error: Teaching Editing as Negotiation." *Rhetoric Review* 11 (1992): 172–99.

Kiniry, Malcolm, and Mike Rose. *Critical Strategies for Academic Writing.* Boston: Bedford, 1990.

Lu, Min-Zhan. "Conflict and Struggle: The Enemies or Preconditions of Basic Writing?" *College English* 54 (1992): 887–913.

———. "Professing Multiculturalism: The Politics of Style in the Contact Zone." *CCC* 45 (1994): 305–21.

———. "Redefining the Legacy of Mina Shaughnessy: A Critique of the Politics of Linguistic Innocence." *Journal of Basic Writing* 10 (1991): 26–40.

Medway, Peter. *Finding a Language: Autonomy and Learning in School.* London: Writers and Readers, 1980.

Moffett, James. *Coming on Center: English Education in Evolution.* Montclair, NJ: Boynton/Cook, 1981.

———. "Liberating Inner Speech." *CCC* 36 (1985): 304–08.

———. *Storm in the Mountains: A Case Study of Censorship, Conflict, and Consciousness.* Carbondale, IL: Southern Illinois UP, 1988.

———. *A Student-Centered Language Arts Curriculum, K–12.* Boston: Houghton, 1968.

———. *Teaching the Universe of Discourse.* Boston: Houghton, 1968.

———. "Writing, Inner Speech, and Meditation." *Coming on Center* 133–81.

Moffett, James, and Kenneth R. McElheny. *Points of View: An Anthology of Short Stories.* New York: Mentor, 1966.

Olson, Gary A. "Social Construction and Composition Theory: A Conversation with Richard Rorty." *Journal of Advanced Composition* 9 (1989): 1–9.

Rose, Mike. *Lives on the Boundary.* New York: Free Press, 1989.

Rosen, Jay. "Making Journalism More Public." *Communication* 12 (1991): 267–84.

Rouse, John. "Feeling Our Way Along." *College English* 41 (1980): 868–75.

———. "The Politics of Composition." *College English* 41 (1979): 1–12.

Shaughnessy, Mina. "The English Professor's Malady." *Journal of Basic Writing* 3.1 (1980): 91–97.

———. *Errors and Expectations: A Guide for the Teacher of Basic Writing.* New York: Oxford UP, 1977.

Smitherman, Geneva. *Talkin and Testifyin: The Language of Black America.* Detroit: Wayne State UP, 1977.

Spellmeyer, Kurt. *Common Ground: Dialogue, Understanding, and the Teaching of Composition.* New York: Prentice Hall, 1993.

———. "Foucault and the Freshman Writer: Considering the Self in Discourse." *College English* 51 (1989): 715–29.

———. "Travels to the Hearts of the Forest: Dilettantes, Professionals, and Knowledge." *College English* 56 (1994): 788–809.

Trillin, Calvin. *Runestruck*. Boston: Little, Brown, 1977.

Williams, Joseph. "The Phenomenology of Error." *CCC* 32 (1981): 152–68.

Harris's Insights as a Resource for Your Teaching

1. Think about conversations you've had about grammar with students, colleagues, and acquaintances. Did they address the sorts of polarities that Harris discusses? Did they reflect the larger politics that interest him? If not, what aspects of the issue has Harris neglected, and how might you use his thinking to address these hidden problems?

2. What do you think of Harris's suggestion that a principal goal of the classroom must be to honor the students' search for a certain kind of identity and sense of authority and credibility? Do you think that this goal might conflict with other agendas? What specific issues might this goal be in conflict with?

Harris's Insights as a Resource for Your Writing Classroom

1. Ask your students to record their initial ideas of, or associations with, grammar. Next, outline Harris's basic principles for students. Ask your students if they had ever thought of grammar not as a fixed standard, but in terms of having social and cultural ramifications, and have them read the powerful last two lines of the article, which identify grammar as a hot-button issue:

   > Language is not only a means of communicating but a form of identification, a badge that seems to define its wearer and yet, paradoxically, can be changed. It is the fear and hope of such change that so powerfully charges the debate on error.

   Have their perceptions of grammar changed after reflecting on these issues? How? How is this awareness important or relevant to their own lives and learning?

2. Outline the basic principles of the Graff-Rouse debate for your students and ask them which position they support, and why. List specific points of support on the board during the ensuing discussion. Consider having students use these points as a basis for developing a paper topic.

The Phenomenology of Error

Joseph M. Williams

In this essay, Williams explores the "deep psychic forces" that affect the ways we approach errors in student writing. Williams claims that no two people have quite the same conception of what error is and that people detect error only when they are explicitly looking for and expect to find it. The implications of these insights are quite profound — and, indeed, not without a certain political significance. If no one really knows what error is and if everyone sees error only when actively looking for it, then perhaps a certain prejudice informs our encounters with student writing — a prejudice that has no coherent intellectual basis.

I am often puzzled by what we call errors of grammar and usage, errors such as *different than, between you and I,* a *which* for a *that,* and so on. I am puzzled by what motive could underlie the unusual ferocity which an *irregardless* or a *hopefully* or a singular *media* can elicit. In his second edition of *On Writing Well* (New York[:HarperCollins], 1980), for example, William Zinsser, an otherwise amiable man I'm sure, uses, and quotes not disapprovingly, words like *detestable vulgarity* (43), *garbage* (44), *atrocity* (46), *horrible* (48), *oaf* (42), *idiot* (43), and *simple illiteracy* (46), to comment on usages like *OK, hopefully,* the affix *-wise,* and *myself* in *He invited Mary and myself to dinner.*

The last thing I want to seem is sanctimonious. But as I am sure Zinsser would agree, what happens in Cambodia and Afghanistan could more reasonably be called horrible atrocities. The likes of Idi Amin qualify as legitimate oafs. Idiots we have more than enough of in our state institutions. And while simple illiteracy is the condition of billions, it does not characterize those who use *disinterested* in its original sense.[1]

I am puzzled why some errors should excite this seeming fury while others, not obviously different in kind, seem to excite only moderate disapproval. And I am puzzled why some of us can regard any particular item as a more or less serious error, while others, equally perceptive, and acknowledging that the same item may in some sense be an "error," seem to invest in their observation no emotion at all.

At first glance, we ought to be able to explain some of these anomalies by subsuming errors of grammar and usage in a more general account of defective social behavior, the sort of account constructed so brilliantly by Erving Goffman.[2] But errors of social behavior differ from errors of "good usage": Social errors that excite feelings commensurate with judgments like "horrible," "atrocious," "oaf(ish)," and "detestable" are usually errors that grossly violate our personal space: We break wind at a dinner party and then vomit on the person next to us. We spill coffee in their lap, then step on a toe when we get up to apologize. It's the Inspector Clouseau routine. Or the error metaphorically violates psychic space: We utter an inappropriate obscenity, mention our painful hemorrhoids, tell a racist joke, and snigger at the fat woman across the table who turns out to be our hostess. Because all of these actions crudely violate one's personal space we are justified in calling them "oafish"; all of them require that we apologize, or at least offer an excuse.

This way of thinking about social error turns our attention from error as a discrete entity, frozen at the moment of its commission, to error as part of a flawed transaction, originating in ignorance or incompetence or accident, manifesting itself as an invasion of another's personal space, eliciting a judgment ranging from silent disapproval to "atrocious" and "horrible," and requiring either an explicit "I'm sorry" and correction, or a simple acknowledgment and a tacit agreement not to do it again.[3]

To address errors of grammar and usage in this way, it is also necessary to shift our attention from error treated strictly as an isolated item on a page, to error perceived as a flawed verbal transaction between a writer and a reader. When we do this, the matter of error turns less on a handbook definition than on the reader's response, because it is that response — "detestable," "horrible" — that defines the seriousness of the error and its expected amendment.

But if we do compare serious nonlinguistic gaffes to errors of usage, how can we not be puzzled over why so much heat is invested in condemning a violation whose consequence impinges not at all on our personal space? The language some use to condemn linguistic error seems far more intense than the language they use to describe more consequential social errors — a hard bump on the arm, for example — that require a sincere but not especially effusive apology. But no matter how "atrocious" or "horrible" or "illiterate" we think an error like *irregardless* or a *like* for an *as* might be, it does not jolt my ear in the same way an elbow might; a *between you and I* does not offend me, at least not in the ordinary sense of offend. Moreover, unlike social errors, linguistic errors do not ordinarily require that we apologize for them.[4] When we make *media* a singular or dangle a participle, and are then made aware of our mistake, we are expected to acknowledge the error, and, if we have the opportunity, to amend it. But I don't think that we are expected to say, "Oh, I'm sorry!" The objective consequences of the error simply do not equal those of an atrocity, or even of clumsiness.

It may be that to fully account for the contempt that some errors of usage arouse, we will have to understand better than we do the relationship between language, order, and those deep psychic forces that perceived linguistic violations seem to arouse in otherwise amiable people.[5] But if we cannot yet fully account for the psychological source of those feelings, or why they are so intense, we should be able to account better than we do for the variety of responses that different "errors" elicit. It is a subject that should be susceptible to research. And indeed, one kind of research in this area has a long tradition: In this century, at least five major surveys of English usage have been conducted to determine how respondents feel about various matters of usage. Sterling Leonard, Albert Marckwardt, Raymond Crisp, the Institute of Education English Research Group at the University of Newcastle upon Tyne, and the *American Heritage Dictionary* have questioned hundreds of teachers and editors and writers and scholars about their attitudes toward matters of usage ranging from *which* referring to a whole clause to split infinitives to *enthuse* as a verb.[6]

The trouble with this kind of research, though, with asking people whether they think *finalize* is or is not good usage, is that they are likely to answer. As William Labov and others have demonstrated,[7] we are not always our own best informants about our habits of speech. Indeed, we are likely to give answers that misrepresent our talking and writing, usually in the direction of more rather than less conservative values. Thus when the editors of the *American Heritage Dictionary* asks its Usage Panel to decide the acceptability of *impact* as a verb, we can predict how they will react: Merely by being asked, it becomes manifest to them that they have been invested with an institutional responsibility that will require them to judge usage by the standards they think they are supposed to uphold. So we cannot be surprised that when asked, Zinsser rejects *impact* as a verb, despite the fact that *impact* has been used as a verb at least since 1601.

The problem is self-evident: Since we can ask an indefinite number of questions about an indefinite number of items of usage, we can, merely by asking, accumulate an indefinite number of errors, simply because whoever we ask will feel compelled to answer. So while it may seem useful for us to ask one another whether we think X is an error, we have to be skeptical about our answers, because we will invariably end up with more errors than we began with, certainly more than we ever feel on our nerves when we read in the ways we ordinarily do.

In fact, it is this unreflective feeling on the nerves in our ordinary reading that interests me the most, the way we respond — or not — to error when we do not make error a part of our conscious field of attention. It is the difference between reading for typographical errors and reading for content. When we read for typos, letters constitute the field of attention; content becomes virtually inaccessible. When we read for content, semantic structures constitute the field of attention; letters — for the most part — recede from our consciousness.

I became curious about this kind of perception three years ago when I was consulting with a government agency that had been using English teachers to edit reports but was not sure they were getting their money's worth. When I asked to see some samples of editing by their consultants, I found that one very common notation was "faulty parallelism" at spots that only by the most conservative interpretation could be judged faulty. I asked the person who had hired me whether faulty parallelism was a problem in his staff's ability to write clearly enough to be understood quickly, but with enough authority to be taken seriously. He replied, "If the teacher says so."

Now I was a little taken aback by this response, because it seemed to me that one ought not have to appeal to a teacher to decide whether something like faulty parallelism was a real problem in communication. The places where faulty parallelism occurred should have been at least felt as problems, if not recognized as a felt difficulty whose specific source was faulty parallelism.

About a year later, as I sat listening to a paper describing some matters of error analysis in evaluating compositions, the same thing happened. When I looked at examples of some of the errors, sentences containing alleged dangling participles, faulty parallelism, vague pronoun reference, and a few other items,[8] I was struck by the fact that, at least in some of the examples, I saw some infelicity, but no out-and-out grammatical error. When I asked the person who had done the research whether these examples were typical of errors she looked for to measure the results of extensive training in sentence combining, I was told that the definition of error had been taken from a popular handbook, on the assumption, I guess, that that answered the question.

About a year ago, it happened again, when a publisher and I began circulating a manuscript that in a peripheral way deals with some of the errors I've mentioned here, suggesting that some errors are less serious than others. With one exception, the reviewers, all teachers at universities, agreed that an intelligent treatment of error would be useful, and that this manuscript was at least in the ballpark. But almost every reader took exception to one item of usage that they thought I had been too soft on, that I should have unequivocally condemned as a violation of good usage. Unfortunately, each of them mentioned a different item.

Well, it is all very puzzling: Great variation in our definition of error, great variation in our emotional investment in defining and condemning error, great variation in the perceived seriousness of individual errors. The categories of error all seem like they should be yes-no, but the feelings associated with the categories seem much more complex.

If we think about these responses for a moment we can identify one source of the problem: We were all locating error in very different places. For all of us, obviously enough, error is in the essay, on the page, because that is where it physically exists. But of course, to be in the essay, it first has to be in the student. But before that, it has to be listed in a book somewhere. And before that in the mind of the writer of the handbook. And finally, a form of the error has to be in the teacher who resonated — or not — to the error on the page on the basis of the error listed in the handbook.

This way of thinking about error locates error in two different physical locations (the student's paper and the grammarian's handbook) and in three different experiences: the experience of the writer who creates the error; in the experience of the teacher who catches it; and in the mind of the grammarian — the E. B. White or Jacques Barzun or H. W. Fowler — who proposes it. Because error seems to exist in so many places, we should not be surprised that we do not agree among ourselves about how to identify it, or that we do not respond to the same error uniformly.

But we might be surprised — and perhaps instructed — by those cases where the two places occur in texts by the same author — and where all three experiences reside in the same person. It is, in fact, these cases that I would like to examine for a moment, because they raise such interesting questions about the experience of error.

For example, E. B. White presumably believed what he (and Strunk) said in *Elements of Style* (New York[: Macmillan], 1979) about faulty parallelism and *which* vs. *that:*

> Express coordinate ideas in similar form. This principle, that of parallel construction, requires that expressions similar in content and function be outwardly similar. (26)

> *That. which. That* is the defining or restrictive pronoun, *which* the non-defining or non-restrictive. . . . The careful writer . . . removes the defining *whiches,* and by so doing improves his work. (59)

Yet in the last paragraph of "Death of a Pig,"[9] White has two faulty parallelisms, and according to his rules, an incorrect *which:*

> . . . the premature expiration of a pig is, I soon discovered, a departure which the community marks solemnly on its calendar. . . . I have written this account in penitence and in grief, as a man who failed to raise his pig, and to explain my deviation from the classic course of so many raised pigs. The grave in the woods is unmarked, but Fred can direct the mourner to it unerringly and with immense good will, and I know he and I shall often revisit it, singly and together, . . .

Now I want to be clear: I am not at all interested in the trivial fact that E. B. White violated one or two of his own trivial rules. That would be a trivial observation. We could simply say that he miswrote in the same way he might have mistyped and thereby committed a typographical error. Nor at the moment am I interested in the particular problem of parallelism, or of *which* vs. *that,* any more than I would be interested in the particular typo. What I am interested in is the fact that no one, E. B. White least of all, seemed to notice that E. B. White had made an error. What I'm interested in here is the noticing or the not noticing by the same person who stipulates what should be noticed, and why anyone would surely have noticed if White had written,

> I knows me and him will often revisit it, . . .

Of course, it may be that I am stretching things just a bit far to point out a trivial error of usage in one publication on the basis of a rule asserted in another. But this next example is one in which the two co-exist between the same covers:

> *Were* (sing.) is, then, a recognizable subjunctive, & applicable not to past
> facts, but to present or future non-facts. (576)
>
> Another suffix that is not a living one, but is sometimes treated as if it
> was, is -al . . . (242)
> H. W. Fowler, A Dictionary of Modern English Usage.
Oxford[: Oxford UP], 1957.

Now again, Fowler may have just made a slip here; when he read these
entries, certainly at widely separate intervals, the *was* in the second
just slipped by. And yet how many others have also read that passage,
and also never noticed?

The next example may be a bit more instructive. Here, the rule is
asserted in the middle of one page:

> In conclusion, I recommend using *that* with defining clauses except
> when stylistic reasons interpose. Quite often, not a mere pair of *that's*
> but a threesome or foursome, including the demonstrative *that,* will
> come in the same sentence and justify *which* to all writers with an ear.
> (68)

and violated at the top of the next:

> Next is a typical situation which a practiced writer corrects for style
> virtually by reflex action. (69)
> Jacques Barzun, Simple and Direct. New York[: Harper], 1976.

Now again, it is not the error as such that I am concerned with here,
but rather the fact that after Barzun stated the rule, and almost immediately violated it, no one noticed — not Barzun himself who must certainly have read the manuscript several times, not a colleague to whom
he probably gave the manuscript before he sent it to the publisher, not
the copy editor who worked over the manuscript, not the proof reader
who read the galleys, not Barzun who probably read the galleys after
them, apparently not even anyone in the reading public, since that
which hasn't been corrected in any of the subsequent printings. To characterize this failure to respond as mere carelessness seems to miss
something important.

This kind of contradiction between the conscious directive and the
unreflexive experience becomes even more intense in the next three
examples, examples that, to be sure, involve matters of style rather
than grammar and usage:

> Negative constructions are often wordy and sometimes pretentious.
> 1. wordy   Housing for married students is not unworthy of consider-
> ation.
>
> concise   Housing for married students is worthy of consideration.
>
> better   The trustees should earmark funds for married students'
> housing. (Probably what the author meant)

2. wordy   After reading the second paragraph you aren't left with an
            immediate reaction as to how the story will end.

   concise   The first two paragraphs create suspense.

The following example from a syndicated column is not untypical:

> Sylvan Barnet and Marcia Stubbs, *Practical Guide to Writing*.
> Boston [: Little, Brown], 1977, 280.

Now Barnet and Stubbs may be indulging in a bit of self-parody here.
But I don't think so. In this next example, Orwell, in the very act of
criticising the passive, not only casts his proscription against it in the
passive, but almost all the sentences around it, as well:

> I list below, with notes and examples, various of the tricks by means of
> which the work of prose construction is habitually dodged. . . . *Operators*
> or *verbal false limbs*. These save the trouble of picking out appropriate
> verbs and nouns, and at the same time pad each sentence with extra
> syllables which give it an appearance of symmetry. . . . the passive voice
> is wherever possible used in preference to the active, and noun construc-
> tions are used instead of gerunds. . . . The range of verbs if further cut
> down . . . and the banal statements are given an appearance of profun-
> dity by means of the *not un* formation. Simple conjunctions are replaced
> by . . . the ends of sentences are saved by . . .
> "Politics and the English Language"

Again, I am not concerned with the fact that Orwell wrote in the passive or used nominalizations where he could have used verbs.[10] Rather,
I am bemused by the apparent fact that three generations of teachers
have used this essay without there arising among us a general wry
amusement that Orwell violated his own rules in the act of stating
them.

And if you want to argue (I think mistakenly) that Orwell was indulging in parody, then consider this last example — one that cannot
possibly be parodic, at least intentionally:

> Emphasis is often achieved by the use of verbs rather than nouns
> formed from them, and by the use of verbs in the active rather than in
> the passive voice.
> *A Style Manual for Technical Writers and Editors,* ed. S. J. Reisman.
> New York[: ?], 1972. 6–11.

In this single sentence, in a single moment, we have all five potential
locations of error folded together: As the rule is stated in a handbook, it
is simultaneously violated in its text; as the editor expresses in the
sentence that is part of the handbook a rule that must first have existed in his mind, in his role as writer he simultaneously violates it.
And in the instant he ends the sentence, he becomes a critical reader
who should — but does not — resonate to the error. Nor, apparently,
did anyone else.

The point is this: We can discuss error in two ways: we can discuss it at a level of consciousness that places that error at the very center of our consciousness. Or we can talk about how we experience (or not) what we popularly call errors of usage as they occur in the ordinary course of our reading a text.

In the first, the most common way, we separate the objective material text from its usual role in uniting a subject (us) and that more abstract "content" of the object, the text, in order to make the sentences and words the objects of consciousness. We isolate error as a frozen, instantiated object. In the second way of discussing error, a way we virtually never follow, we must treat error not as something that is simply on the surface of the page, "out there," nor as part of an inventory of negative responses "in here," but rather as a variably experienced union of item and response, controlled by the intention to read a text in the way we ordinarily read texts like newspapers, journals, and books. If error is no longer in the handbook, or on the page, or in the writer — or even purely in the reader — if instead we locate it at an intersection of those places, then we can explain why Barzun could write — or read — one thing and then immediately experience another, why his colleagues and editors and audience could read about one way of reflexively experiencing language and then immediately experience it in another.

But when I decided to intend to read Barzun and White and Orwell and Fowler in, for all practical purposes, the way they seem to invite me to read — as an editor looking for the errors they have been urging me to search out — then I inform my experience, I deliberately begin reading, with an intention to experience the material constitution of the text. It is as if a type-designer invited me to look at the design of his type as he discussed type-design.

In short, if we read any text the way we read freshman essays, we will find many of the same kind of errors we routinely expect to find and therefore do find. But if we could read those student essays unreflexively, if we could make the ordinary kind of contract with those texts that we make with other kinds of texts, then we could find many fewer errors.

When we approach error from this point of view, from the point of view of our pre-reflexive experience of error, we have to define categories of error other than those defined by systems of grammar or a theory of social class. We require a system whose presiding terms would turn on the nature of our response to violations of grammatical rules.

At the most basic level, the categories must organize themselves around two variables: Has a rule been violated? And do we respond? Each of these variables has two conditions: A rule is violated or a rule is not violated. And to either of those variables, we respond, or we do not respond. We thus have four possibilities [see Figure 1]:

Figure 1

	[+ response]	[− response]
[+ response]		
[− response]		

1a. A rule is violated, and we respond to the violation.

1b. A rule is violated, and we do not respond to its violation.

2a. A rule is not violated, and we do not respond.

2b. A rule is not violated, and we do respond.

Now, our experiencing or noticing of any given grammatical rule has to be cross-categorized by the variable of our noticing or not noticing whether it is or is not violated. That is, if we violate rule X, a reader may note it or not. But we must also determine whether, if we do *not* violate rule X, the same reader will or will not notice that we have violated it. Theoretically, then, this gives us four possible sets of consequences for any given rule. They can be represented on a feature matrix like [Figure 2]. That is, the first kind of rule, indicated by the line marked 1, is of the following kind: When violated, [+V], we respond to the violation, [+R]. When it is not violated, [−V], we do not respond, [−R]. Thus the same rule results in combinations of features indicated by (a–d). Rule type 2 is characterized by a rule that when violated, [+V], we do not notice, [−R]. But when we do not violate it, [−V], we do not notice it either, [−R]. Thus the single rule combines features indicated by (b–d). The other rules follow the same kind of grid relationships. (As I will point out later, the problem is actually much more complex than this, but this will do as a first approximation.)

I do not assert that the particular items I will list as examples of these rules are universally experienced in the way indicated. These categories are based on personal responses, and it is possible that your responses are quite different than mine. But in fact, on the basis of

Figure 2

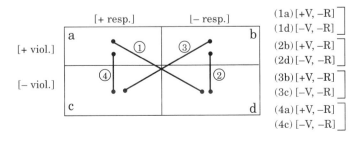

some preliminary research that I shall report later, I would argue that most readers respond in the ways reflected by these categories, regardless of how they might claim they react.

The most obviousest set of rules be those whose violation we instantly notes, but whose observation we entirely ignore. They are the rules that define bedrock standard English. No reader of this journal can fail to distinguish these two passages:

> There hasn't been no trainees who withdrawed from the program since them and the Director met to discuss the instructional methods, if they met earlier, they could of seen that problems was beginning to appear and the need to take care of them immediate. (+V, +R)

> There haven't been any trainees who have withdrawn from the program since they and the Director met to discuss the instructional methods. If they had met earlier, they could have seen that problems were beginning to appear and that they needed to take care of them immediately. (–V, –R)

Among the rules whose violation we readily note but whose observance we do not are double negatives, incorrect verb forms, many incorrect pronoun forms, pleonastic subjects, double comparatives and superlatives, most subject-verb disagreements, certain faulty parallelisms,[11] certain dangling modifiers,[12] etc.

The next most obvious set of rules are those whose observation we also entirely ignore, but whose violation we ignore too. Because we note neither their observation nor their violation, they constitute a kind of folklore of usage, rules which we can find in some handbook somewhere, but which have, for the most part, lost their force with our readers. For most readers, these two passages differ very little from one another; for many readers, not at all:

> Since the members of the committee had discussed with each other all of the questions which had been raised earlier, we decided to conduct the meeting as openly as possible and with a concern for the opinions of everyone that might be there. And to ensure that all opinions would be heard, it was suggested that we not limit the length of the meeting. By opening up the debate in this way, there would be no chance that someone might be inadvertently prevented from speaking, which has happened in the past. (+V, –R)

> Because the members of the committee had discussed with one another all the questions that had been raised earlier, we decided to conduct the meeting in a way that was as open as possible and concerned with the opinion of everyone who might be there. To ensure that all opinions would be heard, someone suggested that we not limit the length of the meeting. By opening up the debate in this way, we would not take the chance that someone might be inadvertently prevented from speaking, something which has happened in the past. (–V, –R)

I appreciate the fact that some readers will view my lack of sensitivity to some of these errors as evidence of an incorrigibly careless mind. Which errors go in which category, however, is entirely beside the point.[13] The point is the existence of a *category* of "rules" to whose violation we respond as indifferently as we respond to their observance.

A third category of rules includes those whose violation we largely ignore but whose observance we do not. These are rules which, when followed, impose themselves on the reader's consciousness either subliminally, or overtly and specifically. You can sense the consequence of observing these rules in this next "minimal pair":

> I will not attempt to broadly defend specific matters of evidence that one might rest his case on. If it was advisable to substantially modify the arguments, he would have to re-examine those patients the original group treated and extend the clinical trials whose original plan was eventually altered. (+V, –R)

> I shall not attempt broadly to defend specific matters of evidence on which one might rest one's case. Were it advisable substantially to modify the arguments, one should have to re-examine those patients whom the original research group treated and extend the clinical trials the original plan of which was eventually altered. (–V, +R)

I appreciate that many of you believe that you notice split infinitives as quickly as you notice a subject-verb error, and that both should be equally condemned in careful prose. At the end of this paper, I will try to offer an argument to the contrary — that in fact many — not all — of you who make that claim are mistaken.

The exceptions are probably those for whom there is the fourth category of error, that paradoxical but logically entailed category defined by those rules whose violation we note, and whose observance we also note. I think that very few of us are sensitive to this category, and I think for those very few, the number of items that belong in the category must, fortunately, be very small. Were the number of items large, we would be constantly distracted by noticing that which should not be noticed. We would be afflicted with a kind of linguistic hyperesthesia, noticing with exquisite pleasure that every word we read is spelled correctly, that every subject agrees with its verb, that every article precedes its noun, and so on. Many of us may be surprised when we get a paper with no mispelled words, but that pleasure does not derive from our noticing that each word in turn is correctly spelled, but rather in the absence of mispelled words.

In my own case, I think I note equally when an infinitive is split, and when it is not. In recent months, I also seem to be noticing when someone uses *that* in the way that the "rule" stipulates, and I notice when a writer uses *which* in the way which the "rule" prohibits. I hope I add no more.

I suspect that some readers put into this category the *regardless / irregardless* pair, *media* as a singular and as a plural, perhaps *disinter-*

ested/uninterested. I offer no pair of contrasting examples because the membership of the category is probably so idiosyncratic that such a pair would not be useful.

Now in fact, all this is a bit more complicated than my four categories suggest, albeit trivially so. The two-state condition of response: [+/−], is too crude to distinguish different qualities of response. Responses can be unfavorable, as the ordinary speaker of standard English would respond unfavorably to

> Can't nobody tell what be happening four year from now.

if it appeared in a text whose conventions called for standard English. A response can be favorable, as in the right context, we might regard as appropriate the formality of

> Had I known the basis on which these data were analyzed, I should not have attempted immediately to dissuade those among you whom others have . . .

(We could, of course, define a context in which we would respond to this unfavorably.)

Since only the category of [+ response] can imply a type of response, we categorize favorable and unfavorable response [+/− favorable], across only [+ response]. This gives us four more simple categories:

> [− violate, − favorable]
>
> [− violate, + favorable]
>
> [− violate, + favorable]
>
> [− violate, − favorable]

The first two I have already illustrated:

> [−v, −f]: He knowed what I meaned.
>
> [−v, + f]: Had I known the basis on which . . . I should not etc.

This leaves two slightly paradoxical categories, which, like Category IV: those rules whose violations we notice and whose observations we notice too, are populated by a very small number of items, and function as part of our responses only idiosyncratically. In the category [− violate, − favorable], I suspect that many of us would place *It is I,* along with some occurrences of *whom,* perhaps.

The other paradoxical category, [+ violate, + favorable] is *not* illustrated by *It's me.* because for most of us, this is an unremarked violation. If it elicits a response at all, it would almost invariably be [− favorable], but only among those for whom the *me* is a bête noir. In fact, I can only think of one violation that I respond to favorably: It is the *than* after *different(ly)* when what follows is a clause rather than a noun:

> This country feels differently about the energy crisis than it did in 1973.

I respond to this favorably because the alternative,

> This country feels differently about the energy crisis from the way it did in 1973.

is wordier, and on principles that transcend idiosyncratic items of usage, I prefer the two less words and the more certain and direct movement of the phrase. My *noticing* any of this, however, is entirely idiosyncratic.

As I said, though, these last distinctions are increasingly trivial. That is why I refrain from pursuing another yet more finely drawn distinction: Those responses, favorable or unfavorable, that we consciously, overtly, knowingly experience, and those that are more subliminal, undefined, and unspecific. That is, when I read

> It don't matter.

I know precisely what I am responding to. When most of us read a *shall* and a shifted preposition, I suspect that we do not consciously identify those items as the source of any heightened feeling of formality. The response, favorable or unfavorable, is usually less specific, more holistic.

Now what follows from all this? One thing that does not follow is a rejection of all rules of grammar. Some who have read this far are undoubtedly ready to call up the underground grammarians to do one more battle against those who would rip out the Mother Tongue and tear down Civilized Western Values. But need I really have to assert that, just because many rules of grammar lack practical force, it is hardly the case that none of them have substance?

Certainly, how we mark and grade papers might change. We need not believe that just because a rule of grammar finds its way into some handbook of usage, we have to honor it. Which we honor and which we do not is a problem of research. We have to determine in some unobtrusive way which rules of grammar the significant majority of careful readers notice and which they do not. One way to do this research is to publish an article in a journal such as this, an article into which have been built certain errors of grammar and usage. The researcher would then ask his readers to report which errors jumped out at them *on the first reading.* Those that you did not notice should then not be among those we look for first when we read a student's paper.

One curious consequence of this way of thinking about error is that we no longer have to worry about defining, rejecting, quibbling over the existence of a rule. We simply accept as a rule anything that anyone wants to offer, no matter how bizarre or archaic. Should anyone re-assert the nineteenth-century rule against the progressive passive, fine. Upon inspection it will turn out that the rule belongs in the category of those rules whose violation no one notices, and whose observation no one notices either. As I said, it may be that you and I will find that for any particular rule, we experience its violation in different ways. But that is an empirical question, not a matter of value. Value becomes a consideration only when we address the matter of which errors we should notice.

Done carefully, this kind of classification might also encourage some dictionary makers to amend their more egregious errors in labeling points of usage. The *AHD,* for example, uses "non-standard" to label

> . . . forms that do not belong in any standard educated speech. Such words are recognized as non-standard not only by those whose speech is standard, but even by those who regularly use non-standard expres-sions. ( )

The *AHD* staff has labeled as non-standard, *ain't, seen* as the past tense of *see,* and *don't* with a singular subject. It has also labeled as non-standard *irregardless, like* for *as, disinterested* for *uninterested,* and *see where,* as in the construction, *I see where.* . . . Thus we are led to believe that a speaker who would utter this:

> I see where the President has said that, irregardless of what happens with the gasoline shortage, he'll still be against rationing, just like he has been in the past. He seems disinterested in what's going on in the country.

would be just as likely to continue with this:

> I ain't sure that he seen the polls before he said that. He don't seem to know that people are fed up.

Indeed, we would have to infer from this kind of labeling that a speaker who said "I ain't sure he seen . . ." would also be sensitive to mistakes such as *disinterested* for *uninterested* or *like* for *as.* In matters such as this, we see too clearly the very slight scholarly basis upon which so much of this labeling rests.

Finally, I think that most of this essay is an exercise in futility. In these matters, the self-conscious report of what should be counted as an error is certainly an unreliable index to the unself-conscious experi-ence. But it is by far a more satisfying emotion. When those of us who believe ourselves educated and literate and defenders of good usage think about language, our zealous defense of "good writing" feels more authentic than our experience of the same items in unreflective expe-rience of a text. Indeed, we do not experience many of them at all. And no matter how wrong we might discover we are about our unreflective feelings, I suspect we could be endlessly lectured on how we do not respond to a *less* in front of a count noun, as in *less people,* but we would still express our horror and disgust in the belief that *less* is wrong when used in that way. It simply feels more authentic when we condemn error and enforce a rule. And after all, what good is learning a rule if all we can do is obey it?

If by this point you have not seen the game, I rest my case. If you have, I invite you to participate in the kind of research I suggested before. I have deposited with the Maxine Hairston of the University of Texas at Austin (Austin, Texas 78712), a member of the Editorial Board of this journal, a manuscript with the errors of grammar and usage that I deliberately inserted into this paper specifically marked. How can I ask this next question without seeming to distrust you? If you had to report right now what errors you noticed, what would they be? Don't go back and reread, looking for errors, at least not before you recall what errors you found the first time through. If you would send your list (better yet, a copy of the article with errors noted on first reading circled in red) to Professor Hairston, she will see that a tally of the errors is compiled, and in a later issue will report on who noticed what.

If you want to go through a second time and look for errors, better yet. Just make clear, if you would, that your list is the result of a deliberate search. I will be particularly interested in those errors I didn't mean to include. There are, incidentally, about one hundred errors.

Notes

1. I don't know whether it is fair or unfair to quote Zinsser on this same matter:

    > OVERSTATEMENT. "The living room looked as if an atomic bomb had gone off there," writes the inexperienced writer, describing what he saw on Sunday morning after a Saturday night party that got out of hand. Well, we all know that he's exaggerating to make a droll point, but we also know that an atomic bomb didn't go off there, or any other bomb except maybe a water bomb. . . . These verbal high jinks can get just so high — and I'm already well over the limit — before the reader feels an overpowering drowsiness. . . . Don't overstate. (108)

2. Erving Goffman, *Frame Analysis: An Essay on the Organization of Experience* (New York: Harper, 1974).

3. Some social errors are strictly formal and so ordinarily do not require an apology, even though some might judge them "horrible": a white wedding gown and a veil on a twice-divorced and eight-month pregnant bride, brown shoes with a dinner jacket, a printed calling card.

4. Some special situations do require an apology: When we prepare a document that someone else must take responsibility for, and we make a mistake in usage, we are expected to apologize, in the same way we would apologize for incorrectly adding up a column of figures. And when some

newspaper columnists violate some small point of usage and their readers write in to point it out, the columnists will often acknowledge the error and offer some sort of apology. I think William Safire in the *New York Times* has done this occasionally.

5. Two other kinds of purely linguistic behavior do arouse hostile feelings. One kind includes obscenities and profanities. It may be that both are rooted in some sense of fouling that which should be kept clean: obscenities foul the mouth, the mouth fouls the name of a deity. The other kind of linguistic behavior that arouses hostility in some includes bad puns and baby talk by those who are too old for it. Curiously, Freud discusses puns in his *Wit and the Relation to the Unconscious* (under "Technique of Wit") but does not in "The Tendencies of Wit" address the faint sense of revulsion we feel at a bad pun.

6. Sterling Leonard, *Current English Usage,* English Monograph No. 1 (Champaign: NCTE, Chicago, 1932); Albert H. Marckwardt and Fred Walcott, *Facts about Current English Usage,* English Monograph No. 7 (Champaign: NCTE, New York, 1938); Raymond Crisp, "Changes in Attitudes toward English Usage," diss., U Illinois, 1971; W. H. Mittins, Mary Salu, Mary Edminson, Sheila Coyne, *Attitudes to English Usage* (London: Oxford UP, 1970); *The American Heritage Dictionary of the English Language* (New York: Dell, 1979). Thomas J. Cresswell's *Usage in Dictionaries and Dictionaries of Usage*, Publication of the American Dialect Society, Nos. 63–64 (University: U Alabama P, 1975), should be required reading for anyone interested in these matters. It amply demonstrates the slight scholarly basis on which so much research on usage rests.

7. William Labov, *The Social Stratification of English in New York City* (Washington, DC: Center for Applied Linguistics, 1966), 455–81.

8. Elaine P. Maimon and Barbara F. Nodine, "Words Enough and Time: Syntax and Error One Year After," in *Sentence Combining and the Teaching of Writing,* ed. Donald Daiker, Andrew Kerek, and Max Morenberg (Akron: U Akron P, 1979) 101–8. This is considered a dangling verbal: *For example, considering the way Hamlet treats Ophelia, there is almost corruptness in his mind.* Clumsy yes, but *considering* is an absolute, or more exactly, meta-discourse. See note 12. This is considered a vague pronoun reference: *The theme of poisoning begins with the death of old King Hamlet, who was murdered by his brother when a leperous distillment was poured into his ear while he slept.* Infelicitous, to be sure, but who can possibly doubt who's pouring what in whose ear (103)? Counting items such as these as errors and then using those counts to determine competence, progress, or maturity would seem to raise problems of another, more substantive, kind.

9. *Essays of E. B. White* (New York: Harper, 1977), 24.

10. Orwell's last rule: *Break any of these rules sooner than say anything outright barbarous,* does not apply to this passage. Indeed, it would improve if it had conformed to his rules:

> I list below, with notes and examples, various of the tricks by means of which a writer can dodge the work of prose construction. . . . such writers prefer wherever possible the passive voice to the active, and noun constructions instead of gerunds. . . . they further cut down the range of verbs. . . . they make their banal statements seem profound by means of the *not un*-formation. They replace simple conjunctions by. . . . they save the ends of sentences. . . .

Should anyone object that this is a monotonous series of sentences beginning with the same subject, I could point to example after example of the same kind of thing in good modern prose. But perhaps an example from the same essay, near the end, will serve best (my emphasis):

> When *you* think of a concrete object, *you* think wordlessly, and then, if *you* want to describe the thing *you* have been visualizing, *you* probably hunt about till *you* find the exact *words* that seem to fit it. When *you* think of something abstract *you* are more inclined to use words from the start, and unless *you* make a conscious effort to prevent it, the existing dialect will come rushing in and do the job for you. . . .

Nine out of ten clauses begin with *you,* and in a space much more confined than the passage I rewrote.

11. Virtually all handbooks overgeneralize about faulty parallelism. Two "violations" occur so often in the best prose that we could not include them in this Category I. One is the kind illustrated by the E. B. White passage: the coordination of adverbials: . . . *unerringly and with immense good will.* The other is the coordination of noun phrases and WH-clauses: *We are studying the origins of this species and why it died out.* Even that range of exceptions is too broadly stated, but to explain the matter adequately would require more space than would be appropriate here.

12. Handbooks also overgeneralize on dangling constructions. The generalization can best be stated like this: When the implied subject of an introductory element is different from the overt subject of its immediately following clause, the introductory element dangles. Examples in handbooks are always so ludicrous that the generalization seems sound:

> Running down the street, the bus pulled away from the curb before I got there.

> To prepare for the wedding, the cake was baked the day before.

Some handbooks list exceptions, often called absolutes:

> Considering the trouble we're in, it's not surprising you are worried.

> To summarize, the hall is rented, the cake is baked, and we're ready to go.

These exceptions can be subsumed into a more general rule: When either the introductory element *or* the subject of the sentence consists of *meta-discourse*, the introductory element will not always appear to dangle. By meta-discourse I mean words and phrases that refer not to the primary content of the discourse, to the reference "out there" in the world, the writer's subject matter, but rather to the process of discoursing, to those directions that steer a reader through a discourse, those filler words that allow a writer to shift emphasis *(it, there, what),* and so on, words such as *it is important to note, to summarize, considering these issues, as you know, to begin with, there is,* etc. That's why an introductory element such as the following occurs so often in the prose of educated writers, and does not seem to dangle (meta-discourse is in [italics]):

> To succeed in this matter, *it is important* for you to support as fully as possible . . .

> Realizing the seriousness of the situation, *it can be seen that* we must cut back on . . .

As I will point out later, the categories I am suggesting here are too broadly drawn to account for a number of finer nuances of error. Some violations, for example, clearly identify social and educational background:

> He didn't have no way to know what I seen.

But some violations that might be invariably noted by some observers do not invariably, or even regularly, reflect either social or educational background. Usages such as *irregardless, like* for *as, different than,* etc. occur so often in the speech and writing of entirely educated speakers and writers that we cannot group them with double negatives and non-standard verb forms, even if we do unfailingly respond to both kinds of errors. The usage note in the *American Heritage Dictionary* (Dell Paperback Edition, 1976; third printing, November 1980) that *irregardless* is non-standard and "is only acceptable when the intent is clearly humorous" is more testimony to the problems of accurately representing the speech and writing of educated speakers. On February 20, 1981, the moderator on *Washington Week in Review,* a Public Broadcasting System news program, reported that a viewer had written to the program, objecting to the use of *irregardless* by one of the panelists. To claim that the person who used *irregardless* would also use *knowed* for *knew* or an obvious double negative would be simply wrong. (I pass by silently the position of *only* in that usage note. See note 13, item 9.) The counter-argument that the mere occurrence of these items in the speech and writing of some is sufficient testimony that they are not in fact educated is captious.

13. Here are some of the rules which I believe belong in this Category II: (1) Beginning sentences with *and* or *but;* (2) beginning sentences with *because* (a rule that appears in no handbook that I know of, but that seems to have a popular currency); (3) *which/that* in regard to restrictive relative clauses; (4) *each other* for two, *one another* for more than two; (5) *which* to refer to a whole clause (when not obviously ambiguous); (6) *between* for two, *among* for more than two. These next ones most readers of this journal may disagree with personally; I can only assert on the basis of considerable reading that they occur too frequently to be put in any other category for most readers: (7) *less* for *fewer;* (8) *due to* for *because;* (9) the strict placement of *only;* (10) the strict placement of *not only, neither,* etc. before only that phrase or clause that perfectly balances the *nor.* The usage of several disputed words must also suggest this category for most readers: *disinterested/uninterested, continuous/continual, alternative* for more than two. Since I have no intention of arguing which rules *should* go into any category, I offer these only as examples of my observations. Whether they are accurate for you is in principle irrelevant to the argument. Nor is it an exhaustive list.

14. The rules that go into Category III would, I believe, include these. Again, they serve only to illustrate. I have no brief in regard to where they *should* go. (1) *shall/will,* (2) *who/whom,* (3) unsplit infinitives, (4) fronted prepositions, (5) subjunctive form of *be,* (6) *whose/of which* as possessives for inanimate nouns, (7) repeated *one* instead of a referring pronoun *he/his/him,* (8) plural *data* and *media,* singular verb after none.

Williams's Insights as a Resource for Your Teaching

1. What is your own definition of *error*? Where does it come from? Make a list of the two or three infractions that are most significant to you, and describe how you came to feel that way about them. How do you respond when you find them in student writing? Does your typical pattern of response to these errors lessen their frequency? What are some other patterns of response you could test in the classroom?

2. What do you make of the surprising turn Williams takes at the end of his essay? Many readers catch only a handful of errors on their first reading and are stunned by the revelation that he has deliberately loaded a hundred into his prose. What are the implications of this surprise with respect to your response to error in student writing? How do you suppose the error got there in the first place?

Williams's Insights as a Resource for Your Writing Classroom

1. Ask your students to discuss their feelings about grammatical correctness. Share with them some of the histrionics that Williams notes in the opening of his essay, and ask them to brainstorm for ideas about where this emotional violence comes from.

2. Explore what you and your students know — and don't know — about error. If Williams is right, you will discover a wide range of disagreement about what *error* means. In class, establish a handful of basic rules that will be considered important criteria of correctness. Then type them up and distribute them to the class. Have the students practice using these rules on their classmates' drafts.

Grammar, Grammars, and the Teaching of Grammar

Patrick Hartwell

This classic essay confronts the enormous complexity of the central "hot-button" issue in our field — the question of error — and negotiates a rich middle ground between those who reject all grammar instruction and those who would organize their classrooms around it. Patrick Hartwell begins by offering five different definitions of grammar; in doing so, he eliminates the confusion generated by competing senses of the term. These five different grammars range from the basic linguistic programming that is an intrinsic feature of human beings, like the opposable thumb, up through the sort of grammar that he calls "metalinguistic," a kind of context-sensitive sophistication about style that one develops after years of careful reflection. By setting forth these different definitions of grammar, Hartwell provides us with a clear way of dealing with this delicate subject.

For me the grammar issue was settled at least twenty years ago with the conclusion offered by Richard Braddock, Richard Lloyd-Jones, and Lowell Schoer in 1963.

> In view of the widespread agreement of research studies based upon many types of students and teachers, the conclusion can be stated in strong and unqualified terms: the teaching of formal grammar has a negligible or, because it usually displaces some instruction and practice in composition, even a harmful effect on improvement in writing.[1]

Indeed, I would agree with Janet Emig that the grammar issue is a prime example of "magical thinking": the assumption that students will learn only what we teach and only because we teach.[2]

But the grammar issue, as we will see, is a complicated one. And, perhaps surprisingly, it remains controversial, with the regular appearance of papers defending the teaching of formal grammar or attacking it.[3] Thus Janice Neuleib, writing on "The Relation of Formal Grammar to Composition" in *College Composition and Communication* (23 [1977], 247–50), is tempted "to sputter on paper" at reading the quotation above (p. 248), and Martha Kolln, writing in the same journal three years later ("Closing the Books on Alchemy," *CCC*, 32 [1981], 139–51), labels people like me "alchemists" for our perverse beliefs. Neuleib reviews five experimental studies, most of them concluding that formal grammar instruction has no effect on the quality of students' writing nor on their ability to avoid error. Yet she renders in effect a Scots verdict of "Not proven" and calls for more research on the issue. Similarly, Kolln reviews six experimental studies that arrive at similar conclusions, only one of them overlapping with the studies cited by Neuleib. She calls for more careful definition of the word *grammar* — her definition being "the internalized system that native speakers of a language share" (p. 140) — and she concludes with a stirring call to place grammar instruction at the center of the composition curriculum: "our goal should be to help students understand the system they know unconsciously as native speakers, to teach them the necessary categories and labels that will enable them to think about and talk about their language" (p. 150). Certainly our textbooks and our pedagogies — though they vary widely in what they see as "necessary categories and labels" — continue to emphasize mastery of formal grammar, and popular discussions of a presumed literacy crisis are almost unanimous in their call for a renewed emphasis on the teaching of formal grammar, seen as basic for success in writing.[4]

An Instructive Example

It is worth noting at the outset that both sides in this dispute — the grammarians and the anti-grammarians — articulate the issue in the same positivistic terms: What does experimental research tell us about the value of teaching formal grammar? But seventy-five years of experimental research has for all practical purposes told us nothing. The two sides are unable to agree on how to interpret such research. Studies are interpreted in terms of one's prior assumptions about the value of teaching grammar: their results seem not to change those assumptions. Thus the basis of the discussion, a basis shared by Kolln and Neuleib and by Braddock and his colleagues — "what does educational research tell us?" — seems designed to perpetuate, not to resolve, the issue. A single example will be instructive. In 1976 and then at greater length in 1979, W. B. Elley, I. H. Barham, H. Lamb, and M. Wyllie reported on a three-year experiment in New Zealand, comparing the relative effectiveness at the high school level of instruction in transformational grammar, instruction in traditional grammar, and no grammar instruction.[5] They concluded that the formal study of grammar, whether transformational or traditional, improved neither writing quality nor control over surface correctness.

> After two years, no differences were detected in writing performance or language competence; after three years small differences appeared in some minor conventions favoring the TG [transformational grammar] group, but these were more than offset by the less positive attitudes they showed towards their English studies. (p. 18)

Anthony Petrosky, in a review of research ("Grammar Instruction: What We Know," *English Journal*, 66, No. 9 [1977], 86–88), agreed with this conclusion, finding the study to be carefully designed, "representative of the best kind of educational research" (p. 86), its validity "unquestionable" (p. 88). Yet Janice Neuleib in her essay found the same conclusions to be "startling" and questioned whether the findings could be generalized beyond the target population, New Zealand high school students. Martha Kolln, when her attention is drawn to the study ("Reply to Ron Shook," *CCC,* 32 [1981], 139–151), thinks the whole experiment "suspicious." And John Mellon has been willing to use the study to defend the teaching of grammar; the study of Elley and his colleagues, he has argued, shows that teaching grammar does no harm.[6]

   It would seem unlikely, therefore, that further experimental research, in and of itself, will resolve the grammar issue. Any experimental design can be nitpicked, any experimental population can be criticized, and any experimental conclusion can be questioned or, more often, ignored. In fact, it may well be that the grammar question is not open to resolution by experimental research, that, as Noam Chomsky has argued in *Reflections on Language* (New York: Pantheon, 1975), criticizing the trivialization of human learning by behavioral psychologists, the issue is simply misdefined.

> There will be "good experiments" only in domains that lie outside the organism's cognitive capacity. For example, there will be no "good experiments" in the study of human learning.
>
> This discipline . . . will, of necessity, avoid those domains in which an organism is specially designed to acquire rich cognitive structures that enter into its life in an intimate fashion. The discipline will be of virtually no intellectual interest, it seems to me, since it is restricting itself in principle to those questions that are guaranteed to tell us little about the nature of organisms. (p. 36)

Asking the Right Questions

As a result, though I will look briefly at the tradition of experimental research, my primary goal in this essay is to articulate the grammar issue in different and, I would hope, more productive terms. Specifically, I want to ask four questions:

1. Why is the grammar issue so important? Why has it been the dominant focus of composition research for the last seventy-five years?

2. What definitions of the word *grammar* are needed to articulate the grammar issue intelligibly?

3. What do findings in cognate disciplines suggest about the value of formal grammar instruction?

4. What is our theory of language, and what does it predict about the value of formal grammar instruction? (This question — "what does our theory of language predict?" — seems a much more powerful question than "what does educational research tell us?")

In exploring these questions I will attempt to be fully explicit about issues, terms, and assumptions. I hope that both proponents and opponents of formal grammar instruction would agree that these are useful as shared points of reference: care in definition, full examination of the evidence, reference to relevant work in cognate disciplines, and explicit analysis of the theoretical bases of the issue.

But even with that gesture of harmony it will be difficult to articulate the issue in a balanced way, one that will be acceptable to both sides. After all, we are dealing with a professional dispute in which one side accuses the other of "magical thinking," and in turn that side responds by charging the other as "alchemists." Thus we might suspect that the grammar issue is itself embedded in larger models of the transmission of literacy, part of quite different assumptions about the teaching of composition.

Those of us who dismiss the teaching of formal grammar have a model of composition instruction that makes the grammar issue "uninteresting" in a scientific sense. Our model predicts a rich and complex interaction of learner and environment in mastering literacy, an interaction that has little to do with sequences of skills instruction as such. Those who defend the teaching of grammar tend to have a model of composition instruction that is rigidly skills-centered and rigidly sequential: The formal teaching of grammar, as the first step in that sequence, is the cornerstone or linchpin. Grammar teaching is thus supremely interesting, naturally a dominant focus for educational research. The controversy over the value of grammar instruction, then, is inseparable from two other issues: the issues of sequence in the teaching of composition and of the role of the composition teacher. Consider, for example, the force of these two issues in Janice Neuleib's conclusion: After calling for yet more experimental research on the value of teaching grammar, she ends with an absolute (and unsupported) claim about sequences and teacher roles in composition.

> We do know, however, that some things must be taught at different levels. Insistence on adherence to usage norms by composition teachers does improve usage. Students can learn to organize their papers if teachers do not accept papers that are disorganized. Perhaps composition teachers can teach those two abilities before they begin the more difficult tasks of developing syntactic sophistication and a winning style. ("The Relation of Formal Grammar to Composition," p. 250)

(One might want to ask, in passing, whether "usage norms" exist in the monolithic fashion the phrase suggests and whether refusing to accept disorganized papers is our best available pedagogy for teaching arrangement.)[7]

But I want to focus on the notion of sequence that makes the grammar issue so important: first grammar, then usage, then some absolute model of organization, all controlled by the teacher at the center of the learning process, with other matters, those of rhetorical weight — "syntactic sophistication and a winning style" — pushed off to the future. It is not surprising that we call each other names: Those of us who question the value of teaching grammar are in fact shaking the whole elaborate edifice of traditional composition instruction.

The Five Meanings of "Grammar"

Given its centrality to a well-established way of teaching composition, I need to go about the business of defining grammar rather carefully, particularly in view of Kolln's criticism of the lack of care in earlier discussions. Therefore I will build upon a seminal discussion of the word grammar offered a generation ago, in 1954, by W. Nelson Francis, often excerpted as "The Three Meanings of Grammar."[8] It is worth re-printing at length, if only to re-establish it as a reference point for future discussions.

> The first thing we mean by "grammar" is "the set of formal patterns in which the words of a language are arranged in order to convey larger meanings." It is not necessary that we be able to discuss these patterns self-consciously in order to be able to use them. In fact, all speakers of a language above the age of five or six know how to use its complex forms of organization with considerable skill; in this sense of the word — call it "Grammar 1" — they are thoroughly familiar with its grammar.
>
> The second meaning of "grammar" — call it "Grammar 2" — is "the branch of linguistic science which is concerned with the description, analysis, and formulization of formal language patterns." Just as gravity was in full operation before Newton's apple fell, so grammar in the first sense was in full operation before anyone formulated the first rule that began the history of grammar as a study.
>
> The third sense in which people use the word "grammar" is "linguistic etiquette." This we may call "Grammar 3." The word in this sense is often coupled with a derogatory adjective: we say that the expression "he ain't here" is "bad grammar." . . .
>
> As has already been suggested, much confusion arises from mixing these meanings. One hears a good deal of criticism of teachers of English couched in such terms as "they don't teach grammar any more." Criticism of this sort is based on the wholly unproven assumption that teaching Grammar 2 will improve the student's proficiency in Grammar 1 or improve his manners in Grammar 3. Actually, the form of Grammar 2 which is usually taught is a very inaccurate and misleading analysis of the facts of Grammar 1; and it therefore is of highly questionable value in improving a person's ability to handle the structural patterns of his language. (pp. 300–301)

Francis' Grammar 3 is, of course, not grammar at all, but usage. One would like to assume that Joseph Williams' recent discussion of usage ("The Phenomenology of Error," *CCC,* 32 [1981], 152–168), along with his references, has placed those shibboleths in a proper perspective. But I doubt it, and I suspect that popular discussions of the grammar issue will be as flawed by the intrusion of usage issues as past discussions have been. At any rate I will make only passing reference to Grammar 3 — usage — naively assuming that this issue has been discussed elsewhere and that my readers are familiar with those discussions.

We need also to make further discriminations about Francis' Grammar 2, given that the purpose of his 1954 article was to substitute for one form of Grammar 2, that "inaccurate and misleading" form "which is usually taught," another form, that of American structuralist grammar. Here we can make use of a still earlier discussion, one going back to the days when *PMLA* was willing to publish articles on rhetoric and linguistics, to a 1927 article by Charles Carpenter Fries, "The Rules of the Common School Grammars" (42 [1927], 221–237). Fries there distinguished between the scientific tradition of language study (to which we will now delimit Francis' Grammar 2, scientific grammar) and the separate tradition of "the common school grammars," developed unscientifically, largely based on two inadequate principles — appeals to "logical principles," like "two negatives make a positive," and analogy to Latin grammar; thus, Charlton Laird's characterization, "the grammar of Latin, ingeniously warped to suggest English" (*Language in America* [New York: World, 1970], p. 294). There is, of course, a direct link between the "common school grammars" that Fries criticized in 1927 and the grammar-based texts of today, and thus it seems wise, as Karl W. Dykema suggests ("Where Our Grammar Came From," *CE,* 22 [1961], 455–465), to separate Grammar 2, "scientific grammar," from Grammar 4, "school grammar," the latter meaning, quite literally, "the grammars used in the schools."

Further, since Martha Kolln points to the adaptation of Christensen's sentence rhetoric in a recent sentence-combining text as an example of the proper emphasis on "grammar" ("Closing the Books on Alchemy," p. 140), it is worth separating out, as still another meaning of *grammar,* Grammar 5, "stylistic grammar," defined as "grammatical terms used in the interest of teaching prose style." And, since stylistic grammars abound, with widely variant terms and emphases, we might appropriately speak parenthetically of specific forms of Grammar 5 — Grammar 5 (Lanham); Grammar 5 (Strunk and White); Grammar 5 (Williams, *Style*); even Grammar 5 (Christensen, as adapted by Daiker, Kerek, and Morenberg).[9]

The Grammar in Our Heads

With these definitions in mind, let us return to Francis' Grammar 1, admirably defined by Kolln as "the internalized system of rules that speakers of a language share" ("Closing the Books on Alchemy," p. 140), or, to put it more simply, the grammar in our heads. Three features of Grammar 1 need to be stressed: first, its special status as an "internalized system of rules," as tacit and unconscious knowledge; second, the abstract, even counterintuitive, nature of these rules, insofar as we are able to approximate them indirectly as Grammar 2 statements; and third, the way in which the form of one's Grammar 1 seems profoundly affected by the acquisition of literacy. This sort of review is designed to firm up our theory of language, so that we can ask what it predicts about the value of teaching formal grammar.

A simple thought experiment will isolate the special status of Grammar 1 knowledge. I have asked members of a number of different groups — from sixth graders to college freshmen to high-school teachers — to give me the rule for ordering adjectives of nationality, age, and number in English. The response is always the same: "We don't know the rule." Yet when I ask these groups to perform an active language task, they show productive control over the rule they have denied knowing. I ask them to arrange the following words in a natural order:

French	the	young	girls	four

I have never seen a native speaker of English who did not immediately produce the natural order, "the four young French girls." The rule is that in English the order of adjectives is first, number, second, age, and third, nationality. Native speakers can create analogous phrases using the rule — "the seventy-three aged Scandinavian lechers"; and the drive for meaning is so great that they will create contexts to make sense out of violations of the rule, as in foregrounding for emphasis: "I want to talk to the French four young girls." (I immediately envision a large room, perhaps a banquet hall, filled with tables at which are seated groups of four young girls, each group of a different nationality.) So Grammar 1 is eminently usable knowledge — the way we make our life through language — but it is not accessible knowledge; in a profound sense, we do not know that we have it. Thus neurolinguist Z. N. Pylyshyn speaks of Grammar 1 as "autonomous," separate from common-sense reasoning, and as "cognitively impenetrable," not available for direct examination.[10] In philosophy and linguistics, the distinction is made between formal, conscious, "knowing about" knowledge (like Grammar 2 knowledge) and tacit, unconscious, "knowing how" knowledge (like Grammar 1 knowledge). The importance of this distinction for the teaching of composition — it provides a powerful theoretical justification for mistrusting the ability of Grammar 2 (or Grammar 4) knowledge to affect Grammar 1 performance — was pointed out in this journal by Martin Steinmann, Jr., in 1966 ("Rhetorical Research," *CE, 27* [1966], 278–285).

Further, the more we learn about Grammar 1 — and most linguists would agree that we know surprisingly little about it — the more abstract and implicit it seems. This abstractness can be illustrated with an experiment, devised by Lise Menn and reported by Morris Halle,[11] about our rule for forming plurals in speech. It is obvious that we do indeed have a "rule" for forming plurals, for we do not memorize the plural of each noun separately. You will demonstrate productive control over that rule by forming the spoken plurals of the nonsense words below:

thole	flitch	plast

Halle offers two ways of formalizing a Grammar 2 equivalent of this Grammar 1 ability. One form of the rule is the following, stated in terms of speech sounds:

a. If the noun ends in /s z š ž č ǰ/, add /ɨ/;
b. otherwise, if the noun ends in /p t k f Ø/, add /s/;
c. otherwise, add /z/.

This rule comes close to what we literate adults consider to be an adequate rule for plurals in writing, like the rules, for example, taken from a recent "common school grammar," Eric Gould's *Reading into Writing: A Rhetoric, Reader, and Handbook* (Boston: Houghton Mifflin, 1983):

> *Plurals* can be tricky. If you are unsure of a plural, then check it in the dictionary.
> The general rules are:
> Add *s* to the singular: *girls, tables*
> Add *es* to nouns ending in *ch, sh, x* or *s; churches, boxes, wishes*
> Add *es* to nouns ending in *y* and preceded by a vowel once you have changed *y* to *i: monies, companies.* (p. 666)

(But note the persistent inadequacy of such Grammar 4 rules: here, as I read it, the rule is inadequate to explain the plurals of *ray* and *tray,* even to explain the collective noun *monies,* not a plural at all, formed from the mass noun *money* and offered as an example.) A second form of the rule would make use of much more abstract entities, sound features:

   a. If the noun ends with a sound that is [coronal, strident], add /ɨ/;
   b. otherwise, if the noun ends with a sound that is [non-voiced], add /s/;
   c. otherwise, add /z/.

(The notion of "sound features" is itself rather abstract, perhaps new to readers not trained in linguistics. But such readers should be able to recognize that the spoken plurals of *lip* and *duck,* the sound [s], differ from the spoken plurals of *sea* and *gnu,* the sound [z], only in that the sounds of the latter are "voiced" — one's vocal cords vibrate — while the sounds of the former are "non-voiced.")

To test the psychologically operative rule, the Grammar 1 rule, native speakers of English were asked to form the plural of the last name of the composer Johann Sebastian *Bach,* a sound [x], unique in American (though not in Scottish) English. If speakers follow the first rule above, using word endings, they would reject (a) and (b), then apply (c), producing the plural as /*baxz*/, with word-final /z/. (If writers were to follow the rule of the common school grammar, they would produce the written plural *Baches,* apparently, given the form of the rule, on analogy with *churches.*) If speakers follow the second rule, they would have to analyze the sound [x] as [non-labial, non-coronal, dorsal, non-voiced, and non-strident], producing the plural as /*baxs*/, with word-final /s/. Native speakers of American English overwhelmingly produce the plural as /*baxɛ*/. They use knowledge that Halle characterizes as "unlearned and untaught" (p. 140).

Now such a conclusion is counterintuitive — certainly it departs maximally from Grammar 4 rules for forming plurals. It seems that native speakers of English behave as if they have productive control, as Grammar 1 knowledge, of abstract sound features (± coronal, ± strident, and so on) which are available as conscious, Grammar 2 knowledge only to trained linguists — and, indeed, formally available only within the last hundred years or so. ("Behave as if," in that last sentence, is a necessary hedge, to underscore the difficulty of "knowing about" Grammar 1.)

Moreover, as the example of plural rules suggests, the form of the Grammar 1 in the heads of literate adults seems profoundly affected by the acquisition of literacy. Obviously, literate adults have access to different morphological codes: the abstract print -*s* underlying the predictable /s/ and /z/ plurals, the abstract print -*ed* underlying the spoken past tense markers /t/, as in "walked," /əd/, as in "surrounded," /d/, as in "scored," and the symbol /Ø/ for no surface realization, as in the relaxed standard pronunciation of "I walked to the store." Literate adults also have access to distinctions preserved only in the code of print (for example, the distinction between "a good sailer" and "a good sailor" that Mark Aranoff points out in "An English Spelling Convention," *Linguistic Inquiry,* 9 [1978], 299–303). More significantly, Irene Moscowitz speculates that the ability of third graders to form abstract nouns on analogy with pairs like *divine: :divinity* and *serene: :serenity,* where the spoken vowel changes but the spelling preserves meaning, is a factor of knowing how to read. Carol Chomsky finds a three-stage developmental sequence in the grammatical performance of seven-year-olds, related to measures of kind and variety of reading; and Rita S. Brause finds a nine-stage developmental sequence in the ability to understand semantic ambiguity, extending from fourth graders to graduate students.[12] John Mills and Gordon Hemsley find that level of education, and presumably level of literacy, influence judgments of grammaticality, concluding that literacy changes the deep structure of one's internal grammar; Jean Whyte finds that oral language functions develop differently in readers and non-readers; José Morais, Jésus Alegria, and Paul Bertelson find that illiterate adults are unable to add or delete sounds at the beginning of nonsense words, suggesting that awareness of speech as a series of phones is provided by learning to read an alphabetic code. Two experiments — one conducted by Charles A. Ferguson, the other by Mary E. Hamilton and David Barton — find that adults' ability to recognize segmentation in speech is related to degree of literacy, not to amount of schooling or general ability.[13]

It is worth noting that none of these investigators would suggest that the developmental sequences they have uncovered be isolated and taught as discrete skills. They are natural concomitants of literacy, and they seem best characterized not as isolated rules but as developing schemata, broad strategies for approaching written language.

Grammar 2

We can, of course, attempt to approximate the rules or schemata of Grammar 1 by writing fully explicit descriptions that model the competence of a native speaker. Such rules, like the rules for pluralizing nouns or ordering adjectives discussed above, are the goal of the science of linguistics, that is, Grammar 2. There are a number of scientific grammars — an older structuralist model and several versions within a generative-transformational paradigm, not to mention isolated schools like tagmemic grammar, Montague grammar, and the like. In fact, we cannot think of Grammar 2 as a stable entity, for its form changes with each new issue of each linguistics journal, as new "rules of grammar" are proposed and debated. Thus Grammar 2, though of great theoretical interest to the composition teacher, is of little practical use in the classroom, as Constance Weaver has pointed out (Grammar for Teachers [Urbana, Ill.: NCTE, 1979], pp. 3–6). Indeed Grammar 2 is a scientific model of Grammar 1, not a description of it, so that questions of psychological reality, while important, are less important than other, more theoretical factors, such as the elegance of formulation or the global power of rules. We might, for example, wish to replace the rule for ordering adjectives of age, number, and nationality cited above with a more general rule — what linguists call a "fuzzy" rule — that adjectives in English are ordered by their abstract quality of "nouniness": adjectives that are very much like nouns, like French or Scandinavian, come physically closer to nouns than do adjectives that are less "nouny," like four or aged. But our motivation for accepting the broader rule would be its global power, not its psychological reality.[14]

I try to consider a hostile reader, one committed to the teaching of grammar, and I try to think of ways to hammer in the central point of this distinction, that the rules of Grammar 2 are simply unconnected to productive control over Grammar 1. I can argue from authority: Noam Chomsky has touched on this point whenever he has concerned himself with the implications of linguistics for language teaching, and years ago transformationalist Mark Lester stated unequivocally, "there simply appears to be no correlation between a writer's study of language and his ability to write."[15] I can cite analogies offered by others: Francis Christensen's analogy in an essay originally published in 1962 that formal grammar study would be "to invite a centipede to attend to the sequence of his legs in motion,"[16] or James Britton's analogy, offered informally after a conference presentation, that grammar study would be like forcing starving people to master the use of a knife and fork before allowing them to eat. I can offer analogies of my own, contemplating the wisdom of asking a pool player to master the physics of momentum before taking up a cue or of making a prospective driver get a degree in automotive engineering before engaging the clutch. I consider a hypothetical argument, that if Grammar 2 knowledge affected Grammar 1 performance, then linguists would be our best writers. (I can certify that they are, on the whole, not.) Such a position, after all, is only in accord with other domains of science: the formula for catching a fly ball in baseball ("Playing It by Ear," *Scientific American,* 248, No. 4 [1983], 76) is of such complexity that it is beyond my understanding — and, I would suspect, that of many workaday centerfielders. But perhaps I can best hammer in this claim — that

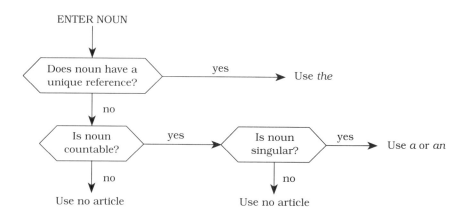

Grammar 2 knowledge has no effect on Grammar 1 performance — by offering a demonstration.

The diagram [above] is an attempt by Thomas N. Huckin and Leslie A. Olsen (*English for Science and Technology* [New York: McGraw-Hill, 1983]) to offer, for students of English as a second language, a fully explicit formulation of what is, for native speakers, a trivial rule of the language — the choice of definite article, indefinite article, or no definite article. There are obvious limits to such a formulation, for article choice in English is less a matter of rule than of idiom ("I went to college" versus "I went to a university" versus British "I went to university"), real-world knowledge (using indefinite "I went into a house" instantiates definite "I looked at the ceiling," and indefinite "I visited a university" instantiates definite "I talked with the professors"), and stylistic choice (the last sentence above might alternatively end with "the choice of the definite article, the indefinite article, or no article"). Huckin and Olsen invite non-native speakers to use the rule consciously to justify article choice in technical prose, such as the passage below from P. F. Brandwein (*Matter: An Earth Science* [New York: Harcourt Brace Jovanovich, 1975]). I invite you to spend a couple of minutes doing the same thing, with the understanding that this exercise is a test case: You are using a very explicit rule to justify a fairly straightforward issue of grammatical choice.

> Imagine a cannon on top of _____ highest mountain on earth. It is firing _____ cannonballs horizontally. _____ first cannonball fired follows its path. As _____ cannonball moves, _____ gravity pulls it down, and it soon hits _____ ground. Now _____ velocity with which each succeeding cannonball is fired is increased. Thus, _____ cannonball goes farther each time. Cannonball 2 goes farther than _____ cannonball 1 although each is being pulled by _____ gravity toward the earth all _____ time. _____ last cannonball is fired with such tremendous velocity that it goes completely around _____ earth. It returns to _____ mountaintop and continues around the earth again and again. _____ cannonball's inertia causes it to

continue in motion indefinitely in _____ orbit around earth. In such a situation, we could consider _____ cannonball to be _____ artificial satellite, just like _____ weather satellites launched by _____ U.S. Weather Service. (p. 209)

Most native speakers of English who have attempted this exercise report a great deal of frustration, a curious sense of working against, rather than with, the rule. The rule, however valuable it may be for non-native speakers, is, for the most part, simply unusable for native speakers of the language.

Cognate Areas of Research

We can corroborate this demonstration by turning to research in two cognate areas, studies of the induction of rules of artificial languages and studies of the role of formal rules in second language acquisition. Psychologists have studied the ability of subjects to learn artificial languages, usually constructed of nonsense syllables or letter strings. Such languages can be described by phrase structure rules:

$$S \Rightarrow VX$$
$$X \Rightarrow MX$$

More clearly, they can be presented as flow diagrams, as below:

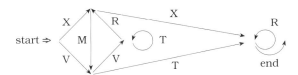

This diagram produces "sentences" like the following:

VVTRXRR.	XMVTTRX.	XXRR.
XMVRMT.	VVTTRMT.	XMTRRR.

The following "sentences" would be "ungrammatical" in this language:

*VMXTT.   *RTXVVT.   *TRVXXVVM.

Arthur S. Reber, in a classic 1967 experiment, demonstrated that mere exposure to grammatical sentences produced tacit learning: subjects who copied several grammatical sentences performed far above chance in judging the grammaticality of other letter strings. Further experiments have shown that providing subjects with formal rules — giving them the flow diagram above, for example — remarkably degrades performance: subjects given the "rules of the language" do much less well in acquiring the rules than do subjects not given the rules. Indeed, even telling subjects that they are to induce the rules of an artificial language degrades performance. Such laboratory experiments are admittedly contrived, but they confirm predictions that our theory of language would make about the value of formal rules in language learning.[17]

The thrust of recent research in second language learning similarly works to constrain the value of formal grammar rules. The most explicit statement of the value of formal rules is that of Stephen D. Krashen's monitor model.[18] Krashen divides second language mastery into *acquisition* — tacit, informal mastery, akin to first language acquisition — and formal learning — conscious application of Grammar 2 rules, which he calls "monitoring" output. In another essay Krashen uses his model to predict a highly individual use of the monitor and a highly constrained role for formal rules:

> Some adults (and very few children) are able to use conscious rules to increase the grammatical accuracy of their output, and even for these people, very strict conditions need to be met before the conscious grammar can be applied.[19]

In *Principles and Practice in Second Language Acquisition* (New York: Pergamon, 1982) Krashen outlines these conditions by means of a series of concentric circles, beginning with a large circle denoting the rules of English and a smaller circle denoting the subset of those rules described by formal linguists (adding that most linguists would protest that the size of this circle is much too large):

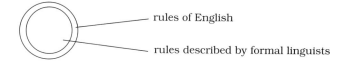

Krashen then adds smaller circles, as shown below — a subset of the rules described by formal linguists that would be known to applied linguists, a subset of those rules that would be available to the best teachers, and then a subset of those rules that teachers might choose to present to second language learners:

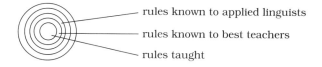

Of course, as Krashen notes, not all the rules taught will be learned, and not all those learned will be available, as what he calls "mental baggage" (p. 94), for conscious use.

An experiment by Ellen Bialystock, asking English speakers learning French to judge the grammaticality of taped sentences, complicates this issue, for reaction time data suggest that learners first make an intuitive judgment of grammaticality, using implicit or Grammar 1 knowledge, and only then search for formal explanations, using explicit or Grammar 2 knowledge.[20] This distinction would suggest that Grammar 2 knowledge is of use to second language learners only after the principle has already been mastered as tacit Grammar 1 knowledge. In the terms of Krashen's model, learning never becomes acquisition (*Principles,* p. 86).

An ingenious experiment by Herbert W. Seliger complicates the issue yet further ("On the Nature and Function of Language Rules in Language Learning," *TESOL Quarterly,* 13 [1979], 359–369). Seliger asked native and non-native speakers of English to orally identify pictures of objects (e.g., "an apple," "a pear," "a book," "an umbrella"), noting whether they used the correct form of the indefinite articles *a* and *an*. He then asked each speaker to state the rule for choosing between *a* and *an*. He found no correlation between the ability to state the rule and the ability to apply it correctly, either with native or non-native speakers. Indeed, three of four adult non-native speakers in his sample produced a correct form of the rule, but they did not apply it in speaking. A strong conclusion from this experiment would be that formal rules of grammar seem to have no value whatsoever. Seliger, however, suggests a more paradoxical interpretation. Rules are of no use, he agrees, but some people think they are, and for these people, assuming that they have internalized the rules, even inadequate rules are of heuristic value, for they allow them to access the internal rules they actually use.

The Incantations of the "Common School Grammars"

Such a paradox may explain the fascination we have as teachers with "rules of grammar" of the Grammar 4 variety, the "rules" of the "common school grammars." Again and again such rules are inadequate to the facts of written language; you will recall that we have known this since Francis' 1927 study. R. Scott Baldwin and James M. Coady, studying how readers respond to punctuation signals ("Psycholinguistic Approaches to a Theory of Punctuation," *Journal of Reading Behavior,* 10 [1978], 363–83), conclude that conventional rules of punctuation are "a complete sham" (p. 375). My own favorite is the Grammar 4 rule for showing possession, always expressed in terms of adding *-'s* or *-s'* to nouns, while our internal grammar, if you think about it, adds possession to noun phrases, albeit under severe stylistic constraints: "the horses of the Queen of England" are "the Queen of England's horses" and "the feathers of the duck over there" are "the duck over there's feathers." Suzette Haden Elgin refers to the "rules" of Grammar 4 as "incantations" (*Never Mind the Trees,* p. 9: see note 3).

It may simply be that as hyperliterate adults we are conscious of "using rules" when we are in fact doing something else, something far more complex, accessing tacit heuristics honed by print literacy itself.

We can clarify this notion by reaching for an acronym coined by technical writers to explain the readability of complex prose — COIK: "clear only if known." The rules of Grammar 4 — no, we can at this point be more honest — the incantations of Grammar 4 are COIK. If you know how to signal possession in the code of print, then the advice to add *-'s* to nouns makes perfect sense, just as the collective noun *monies* is a fine example of changing *-y* to *-i* and adding *-es* to form the plural. But if you have not grasped, tacitly, the abstract representation of possession in print, such incantations can only be opaque.

Worse yet, the advice given in "the common school grammars" is unconnected with anything remotely resembling literate adult behavior. Consider, as an example, the rule for not writing a sentence fragment as the rule is described in the best-selling college grammar text, John C. Hodges and Mary S. Whitten's *Harbrace College Handbook,* 9th ed. (New York: Harcourt Brace Jovanovich, 1982). In order to get to the advice, "as a rule, do not write a sentence fragment" (p. 25), the student must master the following learning tasks:

Recognizing verbs.

Recognizing subjects and verbs.

Recognizing all parts of speech. (*Harbrace* lists eight.)

Recognizing phrases and subordinate clauses. (*Harbrace* lists six types of phrases, and it offers incomplete lists of eight relative pronouns and eighteen subordinating conjunctions.)

Recognizing main clauses and types of sentences.

These learning tasks completed, the student is given the rule above, offered a page of exceptions, and then given the following advice (or is it an incantation?):

> Before handing in a composition, . . . proofread each word group written as a sentence. Test each one for completeness. First, be sure that it has at least one subject and one predicate. Next, be sure that the word group is not a dependent clause beginning with a subordinating conjunction or a relative clause. (p. 27)

The school grammar approach defines a sentence fragment as a conceptual error — as not having conscious knowledge of the school grammar definition of *sentence*. It demands heavy emphasis on rote memory, and it asks students to behave in ways patently removed from the behaviors of mature writers. (I have never in my life tested a sentence for completeness, and I am a better writer — and probably a better person — as a consequence.) It may be, of course, that some developing writers, at some points in their development, may benefit from such advice — or, more to the point, may think that they benefit — but, as Thomas Friedman points out in "Teaching Error, Nurturing Confusion" (*CE,* 45 [1983], 390–399), our theory of language tells us that such advice is, at the best, COIK. As the Maine joke has it, about a tourist asking directions from a farmer, "you can't get there from here."

Redefining Error

In the specific case of sentence fragments, Mina P. Shaughnessy (*Errors and Expectations* [New York: Oxford University Press, 1977]) argues that such errors are not conceptual failures at all, but performance errors — mistakes in punctuation. Muriel Harris' error counts support this view ("Mending the Fragmented Free Modifier," *CCC,* 32 [1981], 175–182). Case studies show example after example of errors that occur *because* of instruction — one thinks, for example, of David Bartholomae's student explaining that he added an *-s* to *children* "because it's a plural" ("The Study of Error," *CCC,* 31 [1980], 262). Surveys, such as that by Muriel Harris ("Contradictory Perceptions of the Rules of Writing," *CCC,* 30 [1979], 218–220), and our own observations suggest that students consistently misunderstand such Grammar 4 explanations (COIK, you will recall). For example, from Patrick Hartwell and Robert H. Bentley and from Mike Rose, we have two separate anecdotal accounts of students, cited for punctuating a *because*-clause as a sentence, who have decided to avoid using *because.* More generally, Collette A. Daiute's analysis of errors made by college students shows that errors tend to appear at clause boundaries, suggesting short-term memory load and not conceptual deficiency as a cause of error.[21]

Thus, if we think seriously about error and its relationship to the worship of formal grammar study, we need to attempt some massive dislocation of our traditional thinking, to shuck off our hyperliterate perception of the value of formal rules, and to regain the confidence in the tacit power of unconscious knowledge that our theory of language gives us. Most students, reading their writing aloud, will correct in essence all errors of spelling, grammar, and, by intonation, punctuation, but usually without noticing that what they read departs from what they wrote.[22] And Richard H. Haswell ("Minimal Marking," *CE,* 45 [1983], 600–604) notes that his students correct 61.1 percent of their errors when they are identified with a simple mark in the margin rather than by error type. Such findings suggest that we need to redefine error, to see it not as a cognitive or linguistic problem, a problem of not knowing a "rule of grammar" (whatever that may mean), but rather, following the insight of Robert J. Bracewell ("Writing as a Cognitive Activity," *Visible Language,* 14 [1980], 400–422), as a problem of metacognition and metalinguistic awareness, a matter of accessing knowledges that, to be of any use, learners must have already internalized by means of exposure to the code. (Usage issues — Grammar 3 — probably represent a different order of problem. Both Joseph Emonds and Jeffrey Jochnowitz establish that the usage issues we worry most about are linguistically unnatural, departures from the grammar in our heads.)[23]

The notion of metalinguistic awareness seems crucial. The sentence below, created by Douglas R. Hofstadter ("Metamagical Themas," *Scientific American,* 235, No. 1 [1981], 22–32), is offered to clarify that notion; you are invited to examine it for a moment or two before continuing.

Their is four errors in this sentence. Can you find them?

Three errors announce themselves plainly enough, the misspellings of *there* and *sentence* and the use of *is* instead of *are.* (And, just to illustrate the perils of hyperliteracy, let it be noted that, through three years of drafts, I referred to the choice of *is* and *are* as a matter of "subject-verb agreement.") The fourth error resists detection, until one assesses the truth value of the sentence itself — the fourth error is that there are not four errors, only three. Such a sentence (Hofstadter calls it a "self-referencing sentence") asks you to look at it in two ways, simultaneously as statement and as linguistic artifact — in other words, to exercise metalinguistic awareness.

A broad range of cross-cultural studies suggest that metalinguistic awareness is a defining feature of print literacy. Thus Sylvia Scribner and Michael Cole, working with the triliterate Vai of Liberia (variously literate in English, through schooling; in Arabic, for religious purposes; and in an indigenous Vai script, used for personal affairs), find that metalinguistic awareness, broadly conceived, is the only cognitive skill underlying each of the three literacies. The one statistically significant skill shared by literate Vai was the recognition of word boundaries. Moreover, literate Vai tended to answer "yes" when asked (in Vai). "Can you call the sun the moon and the moon the sun?" while illiterate Vai tended to have grave doubts about such metalinguistic play. And in the United States Henry and Lila R. Gleitman report quite different responses by clerical workers and Ph.D. candidates asked to interpret nonsense compounds like "house-bird glass": clerical workers focused on meaning and plausibility (for example, "a house-bird made of glass"), while Ph.D. candidates focused on syntax (for example, "a very small drinking cup for canaries" or "a glass that protects house-birds").[24] More general research findings suggest a clear relationship between measures of metalinguistic awareness and measures of literacy level.[25] William Labov, speculating on literacy acquisition in inner-city ghettoes, contrasts "stimulus-bound" and "language-bound" individuals, suggesting that the latter seem to master literacy more easily.[26] The analysis here suggests that the causal relationship works the other way, that it is the mastery of written language that increases one's awareness of language as language.

This analysis has two implications. First, it makes the question of socially nonstandard dialects, always implicit in discussions of teaching formal grammar, into a non-issue.[27] Native speakers of English, regardless of dialect, show tacit mastery of the conventions of Standard English, and that mastery seems to transfer into abstract ortho-

graphic knowledge through interaction with print.[28] Developing writers show the same patterning of errors, regardless of dialect.[29] Studies
of reading and of writing suggest that surface features of spoken dialect are simply irrelevant to mastering print literacy.[30] Print is a complex cultural code — or better yet, a system of code — and my bet is
that, regardless of instruction, one masters those codes from the top
down, from pragmatic questions of voice, tone, audience, register, and
rhetorical strategy, not from the bottom up, from grammar to usage to
fixed forms of organization.

   Second, this analysis forces us to posit multiple literacies, used for
multiple purposes, rather than a single static literacy, engraved in "rules
of grammar." These multiple literacies are evident in cross-cultural studies.[31] They are equally evident when we inquire into the uses of literacy in American communities.[32] Further, given that students, at all
levels, show widely variant interactions with print literacy, there would
seem to be little to do with grammar — with Grammar 2 or with Grammar 4 — that we could isolate as a basis for formal instruction.[33]

Grammar 5: Stylistic Grammar

Similarly, when we turn to Grammar 5, "grammatical terms used in
the interest of teaching prose style," so central to Martha Kolln's argument for teaching formal grammar, we find that the grammar issue is
simply beside the point. There are two fully articulated positions about
"stylistic grammar," which I will label "romantic" and "classic," following Richard Lloyd-Jones and Richard E. Young.[34] The romantic position is that stylistic grammars, though perhaps useful for teachers,
have little place in the teaching of composition, for students must
struggle with and through language toward meaning. This position rests
on a theory of language ultimately philosophical rather than linguistic
(witness, for example, the contempt for linguists in Ann Berthoff's *The
Making of Meaning: Metaphors, Models, and Maxims for Writing Teachers* [Montclair, N.J.: Boynton/Cook, 1981]); it is articulated as a theory
of style by Donald A. Murray and, on somewhat different grounds (that
stylistic grammars encourage overuse of the monitor), by Ian Pringle.
The classic position, on the other hand, is that we can find ways to offer
developing writers helpful suggestions about prose style, suggestions
such as Francis Christensen's emphasis on the cumulative sentence,
developed by observing the practice of skilled writers, and Joseph Williams' advice about predication, developed by psycholinguistic studies
of comprehension.[35] James A. Berlin's recent survey of composition
theory (*CE*, 45 [1982], 765–777) probably understates the gulf between
these two positions and the radically different conceptions of language
that underlie them, but it does establish that they share an overriding
assumption in common: that one learns to control the language of print
by manipulating language in meaningful contexts, not by learning about
language in isolation, as by the study of formal grammar. Thus even
classic theorists, who choose to present a vocabulary of style to stu-

dents, do so only as a vehicle for encouraging productive control of communicative structures.

We might put the matter in the following terms. Writers need to develop skills at two levels. One, broadly rhetorical, involves communication in meaningful contexts (the strategies, registers, and procedures of discourse across a range of modes, audiences, contexts, and purposes). The other, broadly metalinguistic rather than linguistic, involves active manipulation of language with conscious attention to surface form. This second level may be developed tacitly, as a natural adjunct to developing rhetorical competencies — I take this to be the position of romantic theorists. It may be developed formally, by manipulating language for stylistic effect, and such manipulation may involve, for pedagogical continuity, a vocabulary of style. But it is primarily developed by any kind of language activity that enhances the awareness of language as language.[36] David T. Hakes, summarizing the research on metalinguistic awareness, notes how far we are from understanding this process:

> the optimal conditions for becoming metalinguistically competent involve growing up in a literate environment with adult models who are themselves metalinguistically competent and who foster the growth of that competence in a variety of ways as yet little understood. ("The Development of Metalinguistic Abilities," p. 205: see note 25)

Such a model places language, at all levels, at the center of the curriculum, but not as "necessary categories and labels" (Kolln, "Closing the Books on Alchemy," p. 150), but as literal stuff, verbal clay, to be molded and probed, shaped and reshaped, and, above all, enjoyed.

The Tradition of Experimental Research

Thus, when we turn back to experimental research on the value of formal grammar instruction, we do so with firm predictions given us by our theory of language. Our theory would predict that formal grammar instruction, whether instruction in scientific grammar or instruction in "the common school grammar," would have little to do with control over surface correctness nor with quality of writing. It would predict that any form of active involvement with language would be preferable to instruction in rules or definitions (or incantations). In essence, this is what the research tells us. In 1893, the Committee of Ten (*Report of the Committee of Ten on Secondary School Studies* [Washington, D.C.: U.S. Government Printing Office, 1893]) put grammar at the center of the English curriculum, and its report established the rigidly sequential mode of instruction common for the last century. But the committee explicitly noted that grammar instruction did not aid correctness, arguing instead that it improved the ability to think logically (an argument developed from the role of the "grammarian" in the classical rhetorical tradition, essentially a teacher of literature — see, for example, the etymology of *grammar* in the *Oxford English Dictionary*).

But Franklin S. Hoyt, in a 1906 experiment, found no relationship between the study of grammar and the ability to think logically; his research led him to conclude what I am constrained to argue more than seventy-five years later, that there is no "relationship between a knowledge of technical grammar and the ability to use English and to interpret language" ("The Place of Grammar in the Elementary Curriculum," *Teachers College Record,* 7 [1906], 483–484). Later studies, through the 1920s, focused on the relationship of knowledge of grammar and ability to recognize error; experiments reported by James Boraas in 1917 and by William Asker in 1923 are typical of those that reported no correlation. In the 1930s, with the development of the functional grammar movement, it was common to compare the study of formal grammar with one form or another of active manipulation of language; experiments by I. O. Ash in 1935 and Ellen Frogner in 1939 are typical of studies showing the superiority of active involvement with language.[37] In a 1959 article, "Grammar in Language Teaching" (*Elementary English,* 36 [1959], 412–421), John J. DeBoer noted the consistency of these findings.

> The impressive fact is . . . that in all these studies, carried out in places and at times far removed from each other, often by highly experienced and disinterested investigators, the results have been consistently negative so far as the value of grammar in the improvement of language expression is concerned. (p. 417)

In 1960 Ingrid M. Strom, reviewing more than fifty experimental studies, came to a similarly strong and unqualified conclusion:

> direct methods of instruction, focusing on writing activities and the structuring of ideas, are more efficient in teaching sentence structure, usage, punctuation, and other related factors than are such methods as nomenclature drill, diagramming, and rote memorization of grammatical rules.[38]

In 1963 two research reviews appeared, one by Braddock, Lloyd-Jones, and Schorer, cited at the beginning of this paper, and one by Henry C. Meckel, whose conclusions, though more guarded, are in essential agreement.[39] In 1969 J. Stephen Sherwin devoted one-fourth of his *Four Problems in Teaching English: A Critique of Research* (Scranton, Penn.: International Textbook, 1969) to the grammar issue, concluding that "instruction in formal grammar is an ineffective way to help students achieve proficiency in writing" (p. 135). Some early experiments in sentence combining, such as those by Donald R. Bateman and Frank J. Zidonnis and by John C. Mellon, showed improvement in measures of syntactic complexity with instruction in transformational grammar keyed to sentence combining practice. But a later study by Frank O'Hare achieved the same gains with no grammar instruction, suggesting to Sandra L. Stotsky and to Richard Van de Veghe that active manipulation of language, not the grammar unit, explained the earlier results.[40] More recent summaries of research — by Elizabeth I. Haynes, Hillary Taylor Holbrook, and Marcia Farr Whiteman — support similar conclusions. Indirect evidence for this position is provided by surveys reported by Betty Bamberg in 1978 and 1981, showing that time spent in grammar instruction in high school is the least important factor, of eight factors examined, in separating regular from remedial writers at the college level.[41]

More generally, Patrick Scott and Bruce Castner, in "Reference Sources for Composition Research: A Practical Survey" (*CE,* 45 [1983], 756–768), note that much current research is not informed by an awareness of the past. Put simply, we are constrained to reinvent the wheel. My concern here has been with a far more serious problem: that too often the wheel we reinvent is square.

It is, after all, a question of power. Janet Emig, developing a consensus from composition research, and Aaron S. Carton and Lawrence V. Castiglione, developing the implications of language theory for education, come to the same conclusion: that the thrust of current research and theory is to take power from the teacher and to give that power to the learner.[42] At no point in the English curriculum is the question of power more blatantly posed than in the issue of formal grammar instruction. It is time that we, as teachers, formulate theories of language and literacy and let those theories guide our teaching, and it is time that we, as researchers, move on to more interesting areas of inquiry.

Notes

1. *Research in Written Composition* (Urbana, Ill.: National Council of Teachers of English, 1963), pp. 37–38.
2. "Non-magical Thinking: Presenting Writing Developmentally in Schools," in *Writing Process, Development and Communication,* Vol. II of *Writing: The Nature, Development and Teaching of Written Communication,* ed. Charles H. Frederiksen and Joseph F. Dominic (Hillsdale, N.J.: Lawrence Erlbaum, 1980), pp. 21–30.
3. For arguments in favor of formal grammar teaching, see Patrick F. Basset, "Grammar — Can We Afford Not to Teach It?" *NASSP Bulletin,* 64, No. 10 (1980), 55–63; Mary Epes et al., "The COMP-LAB Project: Assessing the Effectiveness of a Laboratory-Centered Basic Writing Course on the College Level" (Jamaica, N.Y.: York College, CUNY, 1979) ERIC 194 908; June B. Evans, "The Analogous Ounce: The Analgesic for Relief," *English Journal,* 70, No. 2 (1981), 38–39; Sydney Greenbaum, "What Is Grammar and Why Teach It?" (a paper presented at the meeting of the National Council of Teachers of English, Boston, Nov. 1982) ERIC 222 917; Marjorie Smelstor, *A Guide to the Role of Grammar in Teaching Writing* (Madison: University of Wisconsin School of Education, 1978) ERIC 176 323; and A. M. Tibbetts, *Working Papers: A Teacher's Observations on Composition* (Glenview, Ill.: Scott, Foresman, 1982).

For attacks on formal grammar teaching, see Harvey A. Daniels, *Famous Last Words: The American Language Crisis Reconsidered* (Carbondale: Southern Illinois University Press, 1983); Suzette Haden Elgin, *Never Mind the Trees: What the English Teacher Really Needs to Know about Linguistics* (Berkeley: University of California College of Education, Bay Area Writing Project Occasional Paper No. 2, 1980) ERIC 198 536; Mike Rose, "Remedial Writing Courses: A Critique and a Proposal," *College English,* 45 (1983), 109–128; and Ron Shook, Response to Martha Kolln, *College Composition and Communication,* 34 (1983), 491–495.

4. See, for example, Clifton Fadiman and James Howard, *Empty Pages: A Search for Writing Competence in School and Society* (Belmont, Cal.: Fearon Pitman, 1979); Edwin Newman, *A Civil Tongue* (Indianapolis, Ind.: Bobbs-Merrill, 1976); and *Strictly Speaking* (New York: Warner Books, 1974); John Simons, *Paradigms Lost* (New York: Clarkson N. Potter, 1980); A. M. Tibbetts and Charlene Tibbetts, *What's Happening to American English?* (New York: Scribner's, 1978); and "Why Johnny Can't Write," *Newsweek,* 8 Dec. 1975, pp. 58–63.

5. "The Role of Grammar in a Secondary School English Curriculum." *Research in the Teaching of English,* 10 (1976), 5–21; *The Role of Grammar in a Secondary School Curriculum* (Wellington: New Zealand Council of Teachers of English, 1979).

6. "A Taxonomy of Compositional Competencies," in *Perspectives on Literacy,* ed. Richard Beach and P. David Pearson (Minneapolis: University of Minnesota College of Education, 1979), pp. 247–272.

7. On usage norms, see Edward Finegan, *Attitudes toward English Usage: The History of a War of Words* (New York: Teachers College Press, 1980), and Jim Quinn, *American Tongue in Cheek: A Populist Guide to Language* (New York: Pantheon, 1980); on arrangement, see Patrick Hartwell, "Teaching Arrangement: A Pedagogy," *CE,* 40 (1979), 548–554.

8. "Revolution in Grammar," *Quarterly Journal of Speech,* 40 (1954), 299–312.

9. Richard A. Lanham, *Revising Prose* (New York: Scribner's, 1979); William Strunk and E. B. White, *The Elements of Style,* 3rd ed. (New York: Macmillan, 1979); Joseph Williams, *Style: Ten Lessons in Clarity and Grace* (Glenview, Ill.: Scott, Foresman, 1981); Christensen, "A Generative Rhetoric of the Sentence," *CCC,* 14 (1963), 155–161; Donald A. Daiker, Andrew Kerek, and Max Morenberg, *The Writer's Options: Combining to Composing,* 2nd ed. (New York: Harper & Row, 1982).

10. "A Psychological Approach," in *Psychobiology of Language,* ed. M. Studdert-Kennedy (Cambridge, Mass.: MIT Press, 1983), pp. 16–19. See also Noam Chomsky, "Language and Unconscious Knowledge," in *Psychoanalysis and Language: Psychiatry and the Humanities,* Vol. III, ed. Joseph H. Smith (New Haven, Conn.: Yale University Press, 1978), pp. 3–44.

11. Morris Halle, "Knowledge Unlearned and Untaught: What Speakers Know about the Sounds of Their Language," in *Linguistic Theory and Psychological Reality,* ed. Halle, Joan Bresnan, and George A. Miller (Cambridge, Mass.: MIT Press, 1978), pp. 135–140.

12. Moscowitz, "On the Status of Vowel Shift in English," in *Cognitive Development and the Acquisition of Language,* ed. T. E. Moore (New York: Academic Press, 1973), pp. 223–260; Chomsky, "Stages in Language Development and Reading Exposure," *Harvard Educational Review,* 42 (1972),

1–33; and Brause, "Developmental Aspects of the Ability to Understand Semantic Ambiguity, with Implications for Teachers," *RTE,* 11 (1977), 39–48.

13. Mills and Hemsley, "The Effect of Levels of Education on Judgments of Grammatical Acceptability," *Language and Speech,* 19 (1976), 324–342; Whyte, "Levels of Language Competence and Reading Ability: An Exploratory Investigation," *Journal of Research in Reading,* 5 (1982), 123–132; Morais et al., "Does Awareness of Speech as a Series of Phones Arise Spontaneously?" *Cognition,* 7 (1979), 323–331; Ferguson, *Cognitive Effects of Literacy: Linguistic Awareness in Adult Non-readers* (Washington, D.C.: National Institute of Education Final Report, 1981) ERIC 222 857; Hamilton and Barton, "A Word Is a Word: Metalinguistic Skills in Adults of Varying Literacy Levels" (Stanford, Cal.: Stanford University Department of Linguistics, 1980) ERIC 222 859.

14. On the question of the psychological reality of Grammar 2 descriptions, see Maria Black and Shulamith Chiat, "Psycholinguistics without 'Psychological Reality,'" *Linguistics,* 19 (1981), 37–61; Joan Bresnan, ed., *The Mental Representation of Grammatical Relations* (Cambridge, Mass.: MIT Press, 1982); and Michael H. Long, "Inside the 'Black Box': Methodological Issues in Classroom Research on Language Learning," *Language Learning,* 30 (1980), 1–42.

15. Chomsky, "The Current Scene in Linguistics," *College English,* 27 (1966), 587–595; and "Linguistic Theory," in *Language Teaching: Broader Contexts,* ed. Robert C. Meade, Jr. (New York: Modern Language Association, 1966), pp. 43–49; Mark Lester, "The Value of Transformational Grammar in Teaching Composition," *CCC,* 16 (1967), 228.

16. Christensen, "Between Two Worlds," in *Notes toward a New Rhetoric: Nine Essays for Teachers,* rev. ed., ed. Bonniejean Christensen (New York: Harper & Row, 1978), pp. 1–22.

17. Reber, "Implicit Learning of Artificial Grammars," *Journal of Verbal Learning and Verbal Behavior,* 6 (1967), 855–863; "Implicit Learning of Synthetic Languages: The Role of Instructional Set," *Journal of Experimental Psychology: Human Learning and Memory,* 2 (1976), 889–94, and Reber, Saul M. Kassin, Selma Lewis, and Gary Cantor, "On the Relationship Between Implicit and Explicit Modes in the Learning of a Complex Rule Structure," *Journal of Experimental Psychology: Human Learning and Memory,* 6 (1980), 492–502.

18. "Individual Variation in the Use of the Monitor," in *Principles of Second Language Learning,* ed. W. Richie (New York: Academic Press, 1978), pp. 175–185.

19. "Applications of Psycholinguistic Research to the Classroom," in *Practical Applications of Research in Foreign Language Teaching,* ed. D. J. James (Lincolnwood, Ill.: National Textbook, 1983), p. 61.

20. "Some Evidence for the Integrity and Interaction of Two Knowledge Sources," in *New Dimensions in Second Language Acquisition Research,* ed. Roger W. Andersen (Rowley, Mass.: Newbury House, 1981), pp. 62–74.

21. Hartwell and Bentley, *Some Suggestions for Using Open to Language: A New College Rhetoric.* (New York: Oxford University Press, 1982), p. 73; Rose, *Writer's Block: The Cognitive Dimension* (Carbondale: Southern Illinois University Press, 1983), p. 99; Daiute, "Psycholinguistic Foundations of the Writing Process," *RTE,* 15 (1981), 5–22.

22. See Bartholomae, "The Study of Error"; Patrick Hartwell, "The Writing Center and the Paradoxes of Written-Down Speech," in *Writing Centers: Theory and Administration,* ed. Gary Olson (Urbana, Ill.: NCTE, 1984), pp. 48–61; and Sondra Perl, "A Look at Basic Writers in the Process of Composing," in *Basic Writing: A Collection of Essays for Teachers, Researchers, and Administrators* (Urbana, Ill.: NCTE, 1980), pp. 13–32.

23. Emonds, *Adjacency in Grammar: The Theory of Language-Particular Rules* (New York: Academic, 1983); and Jochnowitz, "Everybody Likes Pizza, Doesn't He or She?" *American Speech,* 57 (1982), 198–203.

24. Scribner and Cole, *Psychology of Literacy* (Cambridge, Mass.: Harvard University Press, 1981); Gleitman and Gleitman, "Language Use and Language Judgment," in *Individual Differences in Language Ability and Language Behavior,* ed. Charles J. Fillmore, Daniel Kemper, and William S.-Y. Wang (New York: Academic Press, 1979), pp. 103–126.

25. There are several recent reviews of this developing body of research in psychology and child development: Irene Athey, "Language Development Factors Related to Reading Development," *Journal of Educational Research,* 76 (1983), 197–203; James Flood and Paula Menyuk, "Metalinguistic Development and Reading/Writing Achievement," *Claremont Reading Conference Yearbook,* 46 (1982), 122–132; and the following four essays: David T. Hakes, "The Development of Metalinguistic Abilities: What Develops?," pp. 162–210; Stan A. Kuczaj II and Brooke Harbaugh, "What Children Think about the Speaking Capabilities of Other Persons and Things," pp. 211–227; Karen Saywitz and Louise Cherry Wilkinson, "Age-Related Differences in Metalinguistic Awareness," pp. 229–250; and Harriet Salatas Waters and Virginia S. Tinsley, "The Development of Verbal Self-Regulation: Relationships between Language, Cognition, and Behavior." pp. 251–277; all in *Language, Thought, and Culture,* Vol. II of *Language Development,* ed. Stan Kuczaj, Jr. (Hillsdale, N.J.: Lawrence Erlbaum, 1982). See also Joanne R. Nurss, "Research in Review: Linguistic Awareness and Learning to Read," *Young Children,* 35, No. 3 (1980), 57–66.

26. "Competing Value Systems in Inner City Schools," in *Children In and Out of School: Ethnography and Education,* ed. Perry Gilmore and Allan A. Glatthorn (Washington, D.C.: Center for Applied Linguistics, 1982), pp. 148–171; and "Locating the Frontier between Social and Psychological Factors in Linguistic Structure," in *Individual Differences in Language Ability and Language Behavior,* ed. Fillmore, Kemper, and Wang, pp. 327–340.

27. See, for example, Thomas Farrell, "IQ and Standard English," *CCC,* 34 (1983), 470–484; and the responses by Karen L. Greenberg and Patrick Hartwell, *CCC,* 35(1984): 455–478.

28. Jane W. Torrey, "Teaching Standard English to Speakers of Other Dialects," in *Applications of Linguistics: Selected Papers of the Second International Conference of Applied Linguistics,* ed. G. E. Perren and J. L. M. Trim (Cambridge, Mass.: Cambridge University Press, 1971), pp. 423–428; James W. Beers and Edmund H. Henderson, "A Study of the Developing Orthographic Concepts among First Graders," *RTE,* 11 (1977), 133–148.

29. See the error counts of Samuel A. Kirschner and G. Howard Poteet, "Non-Standard English Usage in the Writing of Black, White, and Hispanic Remedial English Students in an Urban Community College," *RTE,* 7 (1973), 351–355; and Marilyn Sternglass, "Close Similarities in Dialect

Features of Black and White College Students in Remedial Composition Classes," *TESOL Quarterly,* 8 (1974), 271–283.

30. For reading, see the massive study by Kenneth S. Goodman and Yetta M. Goodman, *Reading of American Children Whose Language Is a Stable Rural Dialect of English or a Language Other than English* (Washington, D.C.: National Institute of Education Final Report, 1978) ERIC 175 754; and the overview by Rudine Sims, "Dialect and Reading: Toward Redefining the Issues," in *Reader Meets Author / Bridging the Gap: A Psycholinguistic and Sociolinguistic Approach,* ed. Judith A. Langer and M. Tricia Smith-Burke (Newark, Del.: International Reading Association, 1982), pp. 222–232. For writing, see Patrick Hartwell, "Dialect Interference in Writing: A Critical View," *RTE,* 14 (1980), 101–118; and the anthology edited by Barry M. Kroll and Roberta J. Vann, *Exploring Speaking-Writing Relationships: Connections and Contrasts* (Urbana, Ill.: NCTE, 1981).

31. See, for example, Eric A. Havelock, *The Literary Revolution in Greece and Its Cultural Consequences* (Princeton, N.J.: Princeton University Press, 1982); Lesley Milroy on literacy in Dublin, *Language and Social Networks* (Oxford: Basil Blackwell, 1980); Ron Scollon and Suzanne B. K. Scollon on literacy in central Alaska, *Interethnic Communication: An Athabascan Case* (Austin, Tex.: Southwest Educational Development Laboratory Working Papers in Sociolinguistics, No. 59, 1979) ERIC 175 276; and Scribner and Cole on literacy in Liberia, *Psychology of Literacy* (see note 24).

32. See, for example, the anthology edited by Deborah Tannen, *Spoken and Written Language: Exploring Orality and Literacy* (Norwood, N.J.: Ablex, 1982); and Shirley Brice Heath's continuing work: "Protean Shapes in Literacy Events: Ever-Shifting Oral and Literate Traditions," in *Spoken and Written Language,* pp. 91–117; *Ways with Words: Language, Life and Work in Communities and Classrooms* (New York: Cambridge University Press, 1983); and "What No Bedtime Story Means," *Language in Society,* 11 (1982), 49–76.

33. For studies at the elementary level, see Dell H. Hymes et al., eds., *Ethnographic Monitoring of Children's Acquisition of Reading / Language Arts Skills In and Out of the Classroom* (Washington, D.C.: National Institute of Education Final Report, 1981) ERIC 208 096. For studies at the secondary level, see James L. Collins and Michael M. Williamson, "Spoken Language and Semantic Abbreviation in Writing," *RTE,* 15 (1981), 23–36. And for studies at the college level, see Patrick Hartwell and Gene LoPresti, "Sentence Combining as Kid-Watching," in *Sentence Combining: Toward a Rhetorical Perspective,* ed. Donald A. Daiker, Andrew Kerek, and Max Morenberg (Carbondale: Southern Illinois University Press, 1984).

34. Lloyd-Jones, "Romantic Revels — I Am Not You," *CCC,* 23 (1972), 251–271; and Young, "Concepts of Art and the Teaching of Writing," in *The Rhetorical Tradition and Modern Writing,* ed. James J. Murphy (New York: Modern Language Association, 1982), pp. 130–141.

35. For the romantic position, see Ann E. Berthoff, "Tolstoy, Vygotsky, and the Making of Meaning," *CCC,* 29 (1978), 249–255; Kenneth Dowst, "The Epistemic Approach," in *Eight Approaches to Teaching Composition,* ed. Timothy Donovan and Ben G. McClellan (Urbana, Ill.: NCTE, 1980), pp. 65–85; Peter Elbow, "The Challenge for Sentence Combining"; and Donald Murray, "Following Language toward Meaning," both in *Sentence Com-*

bining: Toward a Rhetorical Perspective (Carbondale: Southern Illinois University Press, 1984); and Ian Pringle, "Why Teach Style? A Review-Essay," *CCC*, 34 (1983), 91–98.

For the classic position, see Christensen's "A Generative Rhetoric of the Sentence"; and Joseph Williams' "Defining Complexity," *CE*, 41 (1979), 595–609; and his *Style: Ten Lessons in Clarity and Grace* (see note 9).

36. Courtney B. Cazden and David K. Dickinson, "Language and Education: Standardization versus Cultural Pluralism," in *Language in the USA,* ed. Charles A. Ferguson and Shirley Brice Heath (New York: Cambridge University Press, 1981), pp. 446–468; and Carol Chomsky, "Developing Facility with Language Structure," in *Discovering Language with Children,* ed. Gay Su Pinnell (Urbana, Ill.: NCTE,1980), pp. 56–59.

37. Boraas, "Formal English Grammar and the Practical Mastery of English." Diss. University of Illinois, 1917; Asker, "Does Knowledge of Grammar Function?" *School and Society,* 17 (27 January 1923), 109–111; Ash, "An Experimental Evaluation of the Stylistic Approach in Teaching Composition in the Junior High School," *Journal of Experimental Education,* 4 (1935), 54–62; and Frogner, "A Study of the Relative Efficacy of a Grammatical and a Thought Approach to the Improvement of Sentence Structure in Grades Nine and Eleven," *School Review,* 47 (1939), 663–675.

38. "Research on Grammar and Usage and Its Implications for Teaching Writing," *Bulletin of the School of Education,* Indiana University, 36 (1960), pp. 13–14.

39. Meckel, "Research on Teaching Composition and Literature," in *Handbook of Research on Teaching,* ed. N. L. Gage (Chicago: Rand McNally, 1963), pp. 966–1006.

40. Bateman and Zidonis, *The Effect of a Study of Transformational Grammar on the Writing of Ninth and Tenth Graders* (Urbana, Ill.: NCTE, 1966); Mellon, *Transformational Sentence Combining: A Method for Enhancing the Development of Fluency in English Composition* (Urbana, Ill.: NCTE, 1969); O'Hare, *Sentence-Combining: Improving Student Writing without Formal Grammar Instruction* (Urbana, Ill.: NCTE, 1971); Stotsky, "Sentence-Combining as a Curricular Activity: Its Effect on Written Language Development," *RTE,* 9 (1975), 30–72; and Van de Veghe, "Research in Written Composition: Fifteen Years of Investigation," ERIC 157 095.

41. Haynes, "Using Research in Preparing to Teach Writing," *English Journal,* 69, No. 1 (1978), 82–88; Holbrook, "ERIC/RCS Report: Whither (Wither) Grammar," *Language Arts,* 60 (1983), 259–263; Whiteman, "What We Can Learn from Writing Research," *Theory into Practice,* 19 (1980), 150–156; Bamberg, "Composition in the Secondary English Curriculum: Some Current Trends and Directions for the Eighties," *RTE,* 15 (1981), 257–266; and "Composition Instruction Does Make a Difference: A Comparison of the High School Preparation of College Freshmen in Regular and Remedial English Classes," *RTE,* 12 (1978), 47–59.

42. Emig, "Inquiry Paradigms and Writing," *CCC,* 33 (1982), 64–75; Carton and Castiglione, "Educational Linguistics: Defining the Domain," in *Psycholinguistic Research: Implications and Applications,* ed. Doris Aaronson and Robert W. Rieber (Hillsdale, N.J.: Lawrence Erlbaum, 1979), pp. 497–520.

Hartwell's Insights as a Resource for Your Teaching

1. Make a list of the different ways in which you might "teach grammar" and then try to identify the assumptions that underlie each one. Which methods are most appropriate, given Hartwell's argument? Which are the least appropriate?

2. Hartwell's "Grammar 5" is clearly the sort of grammar and usage that we want our students to master. What types of difficulties might you expect to encounter in striving to teach this approach? How would you prepare for these?

Hartwell's Insights as a Resource for Your Writing Classroom

1. Briefly outline for your students Hartwell's five different types of grammar. Ask them to describe what specific components they think might constitute the all-important "Grammar 5."

2. Ask your students to describe their chief concerns about grammar. Challenge them to address these concerns by following Hartwell's ideas about formal grammar instruction and considering specific methods to engage active language involvement.

Issues in Writing Pedagogy: Institutional Politics and the Other

Check the table of contents of journals like *Rhetoric Review*, *Journal of Teaching Writing*, or *College English*; scan a program of the Conference on College Composition and Communication; use the Internet to subscribe to <listserv@vm.cc.purdue.edu>; browse in the "new acquisitions" section of your library; or pick up the weekly *Chronicle of Higher Education*. You will find vigorous discussion of multiple issues that influence and grow out of the teaching of writing at the college level. One of these issues, the extension of writing as learning across the curriculum, has become part of campus conversations and is quickly becoming a "given" for institutional reform. Of the many issues that challenge and encourage teachers of writing, two currently receive the strongest focus: How might writing teachers acknowledge the diversity of our students' experience? How can we use writing assessment to nourish our teaching?

The readings in Chapter 4 are portals to the larger discussions on diversity, assessment, teaching, and student learning. Each reading provides both an entry to the discussion and reading paths to follow when you decide to broaden and deepen your engagement.

Paradigms of writing, language acquisition, and reading as recursive processes have led to recognition of and respect for the individual engaged in learning. This recognition and respect has in turn informed the discussion, research, and practice in many areas: admissions policies; the teaching of writing, English as a second language, and composition as cultural critique; collaborative learning; whole-language learning; the "feminization" of composition; and assessment. There is also greater awareness of multicultural perspectives on writing, reading, and the gaining of wisdom.

Nouns such as *literacy, diversity, feminism, multiculturalism, social construction, negotiation, discourse communities,* and *postmodernism* resonate in our professional conversations. We simultaneously individualize instruction and "acculturate" students to discourse communities. We attempt to balance recognition of and tolerance for diversity with recognition of and tolerance for common ground and "universal" beliefs and values.

Terms such as *literacy, diversity,* and *multiculturalism* seem descriptive. However, competing definitions are offered daily. We hear national, state, local, and institutional mandates for increasing and enhancing literacy, for acknowledging and respecting diversity, and for broadening our awareness of and inquiry into the multiple perspectives, issues, and cultures (ethnic, regional, social, political, gender-linked, religious, and so on) that make up the mosaic of "America" and of the world community. Equally often, we hear critical voices stipulate alternative definitions for literacy (lowering standards, weakening education), for diversity (exclusivity and prejudice), and for multiculturalism (attempts by the "other" to break down the coherent tradition and value system of the "majority").

The community of writers with whom we work brings together individuals who have traditionally been welcomed to and included in knowledge communities and individuals who have been excluded. We teach these students in times of vigorous debate about how education could and should serve all these learners. The task is daunting and exciting. Look to the Annotated Bibliography for more readings to guide you in reflecting on your practices within this environment.

The Sad Women in the Basement: Images of Composition Teaching

Susan Miller

Susan Miller is interested in the institutional politics that affect writing instruction. While composition courses generate the overwhelming share of the money in English departments, the teachers of these courses are usually the lowest paid and receive no benefits, sabbaticals, or tenure, unlike their colleagues who teach literature and generate less revenue. Historically, the drudgework of teaching writing has been the province of women, while the easier and more lucrative task of teaching literature courses has been the province of men. These injustices inform the entire structure of literate practice in this country.

One of the chief characteristics of composition, at least of composition perceived as teaching, has been that it fills the time that others take to build theories. Creating a process paradigm, despite its incompleteness, has been a monumental achievement because its existence *as* theory historically marks a new era in which composition professionals have room of their own, space to write their own story and become included in "history," not just to pore over student writing to find its faults.

But it remains to speculate about why a space for research and theory building has been filled with assertions that professional teachers of composition, taken and taking themselves seriously, work in a symbol system described as a "paradigm." That specific form takes them even further from the immediate and powerful community around them, their colleagues in literary study. It might be argued that this choice was made because such a model for observing writing lay ready for application and that composition professionals took it up because they agreed that writing is a "behavior" of autonomous individuals. But other models for studying other conceptions of writing were equally available. The choice to describe the past and present in composition as "current-traditional" and "process" paradigms, explanations of writing as a set of observable actions, is very much like the choice of "rhetoric" to explain composition history. Its particular sort of authority also invites interpretation.

We cannot refuse this invitation, for as Gerda Lerner stressed in *The Creation of Patriarchy,* already established symbol systems are provisions that even enslaved and socially powerless males commonly adopt to identify with other males who have power and wealth. She comments that historically, "what was decisive for the individual was the ability to identify him/herself with a state different from that of enslavement or subordination" (222). But as they established their research, composition professionals did not choose to identify their work with the traditions of those who held power in their immediate surroundings. Their choice to risk a move even further from literary studies is, in English studies, both "different" and suspiciously, because overtly, "scientific." Its alienation from root metaphors in literary study can help us further understand the subordinated identity that it was meant to remedy, the established identity of those who teach composition.

At least one contrast between theories presented as a "paradigm" and promoted or objected to as they relate to "science" and early identities of composition teaching is their difference in regard to traditional images of masculinity. Words like *hard* (data, science), *tough-minded,* and *rigorous,* like the word *test,* fall on the right side of our most common images of power. Not "everyone" in composition consciously chose these distinctive metaphors over another symbolic code they might have applied from a broad "English" or from specifically literary study. Many have taken exception to it; many are appalled by its "difference," if not entirely by its symbolic forcefulness. But everyone in composition has in some measure benefitted from this symbolic choice, just as all women have (again, in some measure) benefitted from feminist theories that decisively separate them from earlier, traditional representations.

This choice attaches composition to a form of power that clarifies the more traditional and accepted identity of the composition teacher, an identity deeply embedded in traditional views of women's roles. Apart from self-evident statistics about the "feminization" of composition (Holbrook), many theoretical positions and the self-perceptions of individual composition teachers confirm that composition teaching has been taken to be "worthy" but not "theoretically" based, culturally privileged, work. To overcome this ancillary status, composition professionals have found it entirely reasonable, if not entirely successful, to redefine their hitherto blurred identity in more crisply masculine, scientific, terms.

As the last chapter suggested with the example of "motherhood," individuals are "placed," or given the status of subjects, by ideological constructions that tie them to fantasized functions and activities, not to their actual situations. These ideological constructions mask very real needs to organize societies in particular ways. For example (here, *the* example), the identity of the female person was created as "woman," the opposite, complement, extension, and especially the supplement to male identity. This traducement was first necessary to organize cultures for their survival. A female's particularity or her ignorance of such category formation could not at first, and has not later, excused her from a cultural identity devised to ensure group survival. She responds by virtue of the call for womanhood, not consciously *to* it. This particular "hood" cloaks, suppresses, and finally organizes individual female particularity.

Similarly, when we look at the particularity of people (of both sexes) who teach composition, we may find enormous variations in their interests, education, experience, and self-images as teachers. But when we examine the ideological "call" to create these individuals as a special form of subjectivity for composition teaching, we see them in a definitive set of imaginary relationships to their students and colleagues. Particularities are masked by an ideologically constructed identity for the teacher of composition.

The female coding of this identity is, in fact, the most accurate choice if a choice between sexes is made at all, although the large proportion of women hired to teach composition does not simply cause — or simply result from — cultural associations that link nurturance to teaching "skills" of writing. But we cannot overlook the facts. As Sue Ellen Holbrook infers from her statistical analysis of this "Women's Work," it is likely that about two-thirds of those who teach writing are women (9). In 1980, 65 percent of the participants in the NCTE College Section were women, in comparison to 45 percent women participants in MLA (10). Drops in doctoral enrollments in the 1970s and 1980s have been decreases in *male numbers,* not in numbers of females, so concurrent drops in full-time tenurable appointments have affected women most directly. Women, by and large, fill the temporary jobs teaching composition that are the residue from declines in "regular" appointments.

In composition research, the hierarchy that places women in a subordinate status is maintained: men appear to publish a greater percentage of articles submitted to *College English* (65 percent); books by men dominate in selective bibliographies (approximately 70 percent); male authors overwhelmingly dominate in "theoretical" (as against nurturant, pedagogical) publication categories (Holbrook 12–13). Holbrook's analysis of these demonstrable proportions and of the historical position of women as faculty members in universities gives her good ground for inferring that "men develop knowledge and have higher status; women teach, applying knowledge and serving the needs of others, and have lower status" (7–8).

Economic determiners obviously have had a great deal to do with these dispositions among the actual genders of composition teachers. But imaginary relationships of all teachers of composition to their students and colleagues are complex, not simple results of a one-to-one correspondence between kinds of "work" and patriarchal images of men and women. For instance, no one can take issue with evidence that the origins of English studies required that those who taught composition would contribute to the survival of a whole group. Just as "it was absolutely necessary for group survival that most nubile women devote most of their adulthood to pregnancy" (Lerner 41), it was absolutely necessary that the earliest English departments devote a significant portion of their energy to fulfilling the vision of them Eliot imagined at Harvard and that others took up: offering quasi-religious literary principles *and* a test of composition.

As I have said, we cannot be reductive here: composition teaching is not precisely, at least not only, "imaginary" womanhood, as I will explain. But the inference suggested by evidence of early huge composition classes, of the few people appointed to conduct their teaching, and of "leadership" in composition programs from one person over multitudes of students (like A. S. Hill's at Harvard or of "Miss Dumas and the staff" at Georgia) is that a great deal of delivery from a very small (conceptual) input was required of English departments from the outset.

It is interesting in this regard that we also have heard so much and so often about the "victory" of Francis Child at Harvard in giving over rhetoric for literature when he threatened to leave for Johns Hopkins in 1875 (e.g., Corbett 625–26; Kitzhaber 55; Graff 40–41). A. S. Hill was brought in from his newspaper career to manage composition in 1876 so that others' literary study would not symbolically sink under its weight. His task was to manage the actual "work" that Richard Ohmann has described ("Reading"), in a position that became a symbol of the management of "work" itself. In this regard, it is unlikely that presidents in new, vocationally justified land grant institutions, or anyone else, would have permitted English departments to thrive without well-managed labor from composition teaching. Along with evidence in discussions like William Riley Parker's, Wallace Douglas's, or James Berlin's of "where English departments come from," the small

Relation of Promotion to Field of Specialization

When asked if promotion is related to field of specialization in their departments, sixty-two (71 percent of the eighty-seven who answered this question) replied no. One qualified by stating that "it is, I believe, related to sex." (Four did not answer; seven were unsure.) The fourteen respondents who replied yes (22 percent) included two who stated that composition appears to create a privilege for promotion. Three described their departments as accustomed to differentially evaluating work in "the many mansions" of scholarship; one said that "the department must promote to full professor in five years, no matter what"; and one echoed responses to questions about tenure difficulties with "no, not yet." Four others, however, spoke of various kinds of normal and extraordinary field-related prejudices:

1. Yes, partially due to relative new entry of composition; we have no full professor in composition.

2. Some departments will never change their negative attitude toward composition as a specialty. . . . They [people in composition] have grudgingly been afforded a certain status. The central administration is very aware of our strength in the composition/rhetoric area and is extremely supportive.

3. The Chair debated the authenticity of a national award that a . . . book . . . had won (but not the award won by a poetry book of a colleague). Thus, he denied my promotion but supported that of my colleague.

4. While work in composition is worthwhile, literature is better.

sizes of early departments in comparison to the numbers of students to whom they were required to teach composition point out that this teaching, if only at first, helped justify new English departments. It was loud in their ideological "call."

All of this evidence points toward how a cooperative brotherhood within English studies first *necessarily* separated and subordinated the teacher of composition in those departments that were well enough supported to establish a division of necessary labor. This division would by definition be inequitable, considering the ideological motivations for including composition in literary English that explain its rise. And in smaller settings, where work could not be divided among different people, the work of composition could be compartmentalized from the leisure or "play" of literature. Single individuals, those who have taught both subjects in largely undergraduate institutions, have identified themselves as members of "literature."

Francis Child's rearrangement of his teaching duties to include research and to focus exclusively on literature thus also became part of an emerging symbol system in English. Escaping rhetoric and composition teaching was an early sign of an institution's ardent regard for individuals. Using Lerner's terms, we can describe this privilege as a symbol in the "American Academic Dream," an internalized goal for those who felt themselves enslaved and poor or who accepted the association of composition with all of the "low" qualities that had been meant to apply to its students. But the important point is that, like women in early communities that depended on their production of live births, composition teachers were at first necessarily placed where they would accrue subordinate associations that were no less binding than those still imposed on women.

Obviously, this historically created role for composition teaching also loads the identity of its teachers with larger biases that were first associated with the whole of English literary study. The cultural identity of anyone in English shared the upstart, nonserious, vulgar (as in vernacular), dilettantish, and certainly nonscientific qualities ascribed to their new pursuits. But as performers in a site for illegitimate and transgressive textual activities that are inextricably linked to, but only placed beside, a newly established and unsophisticated community, composition teachers would not have been separately recognized at all in the larger academic world. The students in the course that I have called a course in silence were taught by those for whom a separate and recognized "profession" of composition was "unspeakable." Outsiders to English did not recognize composition as separate, as they still do not. Among insiders, it was a deniable subtext in a new discipline that was inevitably competing for publicity among established fields and hoping to be regarded as the guardian of national "ideals" with a worthy claim on time for academic research.

Consequently, the work of correcting spelling was at least partially uncompetitive with other symbolically constructed functions for English. Its mundane nature overcame any of its potentially positive associations with morality or serious intelligence in the "new" secular university. And this work was actually threatening to the time necessary to compete for symbolic academic rewards. Like any group or individual widely thought to be *nouveau,* literary studies needed to ignore an embarrassing root under a new family tree if that tree was to grow. The Teaching of Writing Division of the inclusive MLA was established only in 1973, well after a distinct insider group of self-identified composition teachers had formed the Conference on College Composition and Communication in 1949.

We have, therefore, at least two historicized identities from which associations with composition teaching would stem. In actuality, composition teaching was work, and work of a particularly subordinate kind that *by definition within English studies* preceded the students' later exposure to cultural ideals in literature. It was literally "ground work." Ideologically, composition teaching had no claim on professional legitimacy, for it was not grammatical instruction in classical languages to transmit the Hegelian "spirit" of the past. The supposed low quality of its students and their writing, and its own mechanistic practices, had been constituted by the ideology of English to be illegitimate counterparts to ideals of content and perfections of execution that increasingly defined literary textuality. Over time, catalogues that describe developing English curricula in this century show that as even faint associations with classical grammatical instruction grew dimmer, composition was increasingly diminished and simplified. Concurrently, literary studies grew and became more complex.

These actual and imagined historical identities for composition teaching and its teachers have entrenched the imaginary identity around composition teachers. Their power over actual activities, like the power of womanhood over females, is not lessened by new facts. Although composition teachers now teach small classes relative to the majority of classes in other college-level subjects, their new ability to compete for research time, their publications, or the comparatively high salaries that some receive among their colleagues in literature do not automatically improve images held over from entirely different historical conditions.

The teacher of composition thus inevitably has at least some attributes of the stigmatized individual whom Erving Goffman describes in *Stigma: Notes on the Management of Spoiled Identity*. Goffman is a sociologist whose analysis focuses on interactions among stigmatized and normal individuals and groups within the same social situations, an arrangement that occurs in one department where ego identities from both literature and composition complexly conflict as privileged and subordinate, or healthy and "spoiled," identities. He is also a structuralist whose system of analysis identifies the stigmatized by their *relationships* with "normals," not by their intrinsic qualities.

The "central feature" of these relationships is, Goffman says, "acceptance," which in fact appears to be the primary issue that current composition professionals identify when they discuss accomplished and hoped-for changes in their status. The stigmatized individual is treated so that "those who have dealings with him fail to accord him the respect and regard which the uncontaminated aspects of his social identity have led them to anticipate extending, and have led him to anticipate receiving" (8–9). The otherwise physical normalcy of the deaf, the apparent masculinity of a male homosexual, and by extension the Ph.D. in literature of a part-time composition teacher will lead their associates and each of them to expect acceptance in the group who share their larger "ego" identity, a "felt" identity (105). But contamination from deafness, sexual practices, or trivialized teaching responsibilities also means that they will receive treatment from others that powerfully contradicts these expectations.

Goffman lists a number of typical responses to such treatment from stigmatized persons: they attempt to correct the flaw; they use the stigma for "secondary gains," such as an excuse for failures in other

---

Research Awards

Respondents overwhelmingly reported that their institutions and/or departments regularly provide one or another sort of support for research. Of 106 responding to the first questions, eighty-five (80 percent) answered yes or "occasionally"; two responded that support comes only from outside the institution. Thirteen respondents (12 percent) were in institutions where research support is unavailable.

The frequency of applications and success of the eighty-nine who answered the three parts of the question about their own applications for research support show that ninety-three applications for research (not all to investigate problems defined as composition topics) had been made by this group in the previous ten years. One additional person indicated that she had "outside funding." Some respondents had applied and been turned down before later success; some had received more than one award. Although no control group from English or another humanistic department was used to measure this level of activity and four of these respondents defined themselves as "in" literature or as receiving grants toward research in it, a two-thirds (66 percent) rate of awards among this group defines them as aware of funding opportunities, active in pursuing them, and capable of competing successfully when they do.

In addition, those responding to these questions appear to believe that research awards in composition are made as often as in other fields.

---

areas; they see the stigma as a disguised blessing; they reassess the value of being "normal"; they avoid "normals"; and they develop anxieties, hostilities, suspicions, and depression. We can find obvious instances of some of these responses from composition teachers who apply for full-time positions in literature, who imitate the elevation of Francis Child by defining themselves as primarily graduate faculty and researchers, or who avoid the Modern Language Association because it remains "irrelevant" to their interests. Naturally, each of these possible and actual strategies for coping colors encounters with normals and their groups.

Applying this analysis, we must emphasize that no feature *intrinsic* to composition teaching urges stigma on its participants. The *discrepancy* between a felt identity and social treatments of those who allow themselves to be perceived as "in" composition causes stigmatized relations. Thus when it is "normal" to teach both composition and literature, as it is for faculty in undergraduate four-year or junior colleges, or normal to teach composition while engaging in graduate stud-

Perceptions of the Relative Status of Fields in English

The survey asked respondents to rank, on a scale of one to nine, eight fields (literature, literary theory, composition, rhetoric, linguistics, feminist studies, film, and folklore) and an open category ("other") according to their perceptions of these fields' relative status in their departments. . . .

The respondents clearly perceived literature to have the highest status in their departments. They most often placed literary theory in second place, and they placed composition or rhetoric (or the two combined) in third place, where it (or they) received thirty-one mentions (34 percent of ninety ranking these fields). . . .

Composition and rhetoric also held sixth place in these rankings. The seventh rank went to film studies, which was placed at that level twelve times. Folklore held eighth place, receiving thirteen mentions (23 percent), and ninth place was held by "other."

Evaluated this way, data from these respondents suggest the following levels of status among fields:

1. Literature
2. Literary theory
3. Composition/rhetoric
4. Literary theory and composition/rhetoric
5. Linguistics
6. Composition/rhetoric
7. Film
8. Folklore
9. Other

That is, below the clear leader (literature), literary theory and composition/rhetoric appear to be vying for position in many settings, but composition/rhetoric has relatively low status (in sixth place) in many others. . . .

We can infer that these respondents recognized composition/rhetoric as a field as often as they did literature and that they appeared to be aware of recent elevations in its status. Rankings from three respondents were excluded from these data because they provided dualistic, past and future, rankings; these rankings commented directly on the changes perceived by the respondents. One only noted, "*I perceive rhetoric and composition highly. The literature people don't.*"

ies in literature or in creative writing, the stigmatic discrepancy need not develop. Even when all graduate students must teach composition and some faculty occasionally take it on, the larger cultural or academic attitude toward composition does not prevent it from being considered a perverse or abnormal endeavor, one marginal to the "true" identity of members of these groups. In these settings, however, some can treat it as a joke, a source of shared good humor and complaints, or as a temporary initiation ritual that "everyone" must endure, a mark of maturation in trial by fire.

It is easy to see, therefore, that only individual composition teachers in a certain relationship to "normalcy" would be seriously stigmatized by this identity. While the entire activity of composition teaching is stigmatized in its historicized relation to literary centralism, many who engage in it can contain it, neutralize it, ignore it, and otherwise make it "all right." Temporary deafness, cross-dressing on Halloween, being assigned one composition course a year, or holding a graduate assistantship while completing a degree in Shakespeare do not permanently disable relations with the normal.

But it is one thing to go to the circus each year for entertainment, or even as part of one's family duty, and another thing entirely to run off to *join* the circus that composition was constituted to be. Openly displaying the signs that associate an individual with stigmatized groups, like openly engaging in any interaction taken to be peripheral to institutional purposes, inevitably disrupts normal social interactions.

We might infer from this distinction between the results of partial and full participation in a stigmatized, transgressive activity that one of the clearest operations of composition teaching is the cultural regulation and repression through stigma of particular kinds of otherwise normal activities — teaching and learning. Composition courses, from all of the evidence we have of their history, of the identity of their students, and of their choice of a research paradigm, *automatically* raise the issue of legitimacy. By this I mean that these courses and their teaching raise the issue of how an *actual* identity can take on imaginary associations that serve either privileged *or* marginalized cultural roles. The actual activities of someone who is learning to write, or of someone who is teaching composition, inevitably become implicated in a relationship to the imaginary perfection of literary texts. Both literary production and literary products are composition's "Other," the second terms in discrepancies between "the raw and the cooked" or "savage and domesticated" texts.

Given this foundational structure, we can extend Lerner's analysis of the operations of patriarchy to agree that a surplus of women or of live births, and perhaps a surplus of English Ph.D.s in literature, can make available human resources that have traditionally been closely regulated to guarantee that their scarcity will dispose them only in competitive and "proper" social circumstances. A surplus of females as slaves may in fact instigate prostitution, wherein commercialized sexual activity can fulfill symbolic (unlicensed, subnormal) cultural needs (see Lerner 133). But such a surplus can instead become the basis for newly normalized relationships, which a culture can afford to leave "unnamed" or even to elevate to the special status of "independence," "freedom," and "self-determination." In either case, permitting actions by this sort of surplus to remain outside established designations for proper and improper activities — that is, not calling its sexual activity prostitution — will mask the *actual* extracultural or extrafamilial situations of this surplus. Excess women, and perhaps excess Ph.D.s, may take on new roles that cloak their real status as surplus.

Consequently, it is even further possible that a surplus Ph.D. or a Ph.D. candidate in literature will take one of two paths: openly to choose the unlicensed, subnormal identity associated with composition, as many recently have, or more covertly to provide this teaching on a part-time, ad hoc basis while implicitly retaining a "normal" ego identity in a claim that "self-determination" or "independence" are his or her motives. This analysis from Goffman is in no way meant to belie the sincerity of such identity claims. But his structuralist model does explain one way that a group of individuals might *actually* derive their identities from composition teaching but also avoid its stigma through new and *imaginary* legitimizations for it.

Additionally, as Goffman points out, an imagined exemption from a stigma like this one can even further affect the actual conditions around stigmatized status. The surplus of Ph.D.s who have taken up composition teaching as one way to engage in transgressive behavior without actually joining the circus now have special professional grants, organizational fee structures, organizations, and support from professional position papers like the Wyoming Conference Resolution on the status of part-time composition teachers (Slevin 50). All show that normal people may respond to a new imaginary identity for the deviant. Dominant, already accepted groups may, that is, provide new *actual* relations that are within a "normal" range. These dispensations and expressions of concern have resulted from imagining normalcy for marginalized groups of part-time, traveling "gypsy" scholars. New institutional structures incorporate purveyors of the carnival into larger cultural systems, so that it always remains outside and suburban to an established city, not an independent force that might become parallel to it or competitive with it.

Such responses do change actual conditions for one kind of composition teacher, just as feminist theories have contributed to actual benefits for women by urging social services and legislation to benefit those who are marginalized by virtue of being single, divorced, or lesbian. As earlier references to Althusser indicate, ideologies emerge from a struggle *between* classes; they are not positions that a class will inevitably take from within itself.

But no new actuality can entirely revise the identity state of those who choose the first path, openly devoting themselves to a deviant identity as composition teachers or further becoming researchers in composition. Again, Goffman helpfully points toward the condition of this person:

> Even while the stigmatized individual is told that he is a human being like everyone else, he is being told that it would be unwise to pass or to let down "his" group. In brief, he is told he is like anyone else and that he isn't — although there is little agreement among spokesmen as to how much of each he should claim to be. This contradiction and joke is

his fate and his destiny. . . . The stigmatized individual thus finds himself in an arena of detailed argument and discussion concerning what he ought to think of himself, that is, his ego identity. To his other troubles he must add that of being simultaneously pushed in several directions by professionals who tell him what he should do and feel about what he is and isn't, and all this purportedly in his best interests. (124–25)

Goffman hereby suggests that we look even more closely at the situation of these individuals who overtly claim to be *in* composition as its teachers and who are academically placed where they could not be imagined before model building, and finally paradigm construction, were undertaken (see Berlin chap. 7). The professionals surrounding these teachers — their colleagues, their (usually male) privileged theorists, and administrators who form and enact institutional structures — all contribute to a particular kind of blurring in their experienced identity, the conflict that Goffman quite accurately describes as both a contradiction and a joke. As Stallybrass and White say of the "Maid and the Family Romance," both "service" and "motherhood" converge in the call to this group from traditional ideology.

But composition teaching is not simple "motherhood," in service to father texts. The social identity of the composition teacher is intricately blurred in a matrix of functions that we can understand through the instructive example of Freud's description of the "feminine," which was formed at about the same time that composition courses and their teaching first achieved presence in the new university. Despite the problematics feminists point out in his work, Freud's description of associations that contain ambivalently situated women can be seen as a reliable account of nineteenth-century sexual mythologies, offering us historical access to early and continuing images of the gender-coding of composition teaching.

Freud dreamed of his family nurse, whom he later transformed into "mother." The nurse in the dream "initiated the young Freud in sexual matters" (Stallybrass and White 157). But later, in Freud's writing about "femininity," "the nurse has been displaced by the mother" (157). In a series of statements, Freud by turns associated seduction and bodily hygiene with motherhood and the maid, at one time calling the maid the most intimate participant in his initiations and fantasies, and at another thinking of these matters in relation to perfect motherhood. Stallybrass and White infer that because the nineteenth-century bourgeois family relegated child care to nurses, the maid both performed intimate educational functions and had power over the child. "Because of his size, his dependency, his fumbling attempts at language, his inability to control his bodily functions" (158), the child could be shamed and humiliated by the maid. But paradoxically, it is more acceptable to desire the mother than the maid, who is "hired help," so that actual interactions with a nurse/maid might be fantasized as having occurred with the mother.

Difficulties with Tenure in Composition

Among the thirty-four who answered that they had perceived problems with tenure related to composition as a field, only one attributed the difficulty to problems with the quality of a particular person's work. . . .

Among responses . . ., twelve respondents explained specific instances of difficulties that they perceive as related to having composition as a field. Very difficult personal situations were revealed: two were promoted before tenure, then suffered from second thoughts of colleagues about actually tenuring people in composition; two people reported results from an institution that, they say, "routinely passes over people who spend too much time on composition"; one reported that she "made changes in the program," then left her position after warnings about receiving tenure; three reported similar difficulties when appointments to administer composition were later not "counted" for tenure; one said that she had, in an unprecedented departmental action, been put up for review two years after the beginning of her appointment; two other less specific cases involved releasing all of the people in composition, or some of them, while retaining others in literature. One person was told at hiring that he would never be promoted or allowed to serve on committees because he had been hired to teach writing courses. But he witnessed changes from this situation in his department to active hiring in composition. Nonetheless, he reported that a more junior colleague in composition had been reviewed first by the usual three outside reviewers, then by three more because the first group was perceived as "too complimentary."

Without stressing prurient comparisons between the "low" work of composition and this representation of intimate bodily and other educational functions (although in nineteenth-century sociopathology they were certainly there to be drawn) it is fair to suggest that this symbolic blurring still encodes the role of teachers of composition. It explains some otherwise troubling contradictions in their habitually conceived identities. The bourgeois mother and maid, that is, both represent comfort and power. The mother was the source Freud turned to for explanatory information about the maid; the mother was also, with the father, an authority. The maid was an ambivalently perceived site for dealing with low, unruly, even anarchic desires and as yet uncontrolled personal development.

Even down to the reported problematic of leaving the "home" language in a requirement to "'forget' the baby-talk of the body" (Stallybrass and White 166), a developmental stage associated with the maid, we can see an oscillation between images of mother and maid. Leaving the maid represents foregoing infantile freedoms for the embarrassments that the mother/power figure is likely to represent, as she did when the child moved on to formal Latin lessons in the process of leaving the governess for the schoolmaster (a process that Freud's Wolf Man found crucial). By the obvious analogy with learning vernacular language again, as a formalized system, the composition student's teacher combines the two images of mother and maid. This powerful but displaced person blurs anxieties over maturation that must inevitably accompany a move toward public language.

Consequently, one figure of a composition teacher is overloaded with symbolic as well as actual functions. These functions include the dual (or even triple) roles that are washed together in these teachers: the nurse who cares for and tempts her young charge toward "adult" uses of language that will not "count" because they are, for now, engaged in only with hired help; the "mother" (tongue) that is an ideal/idol and can humiliate, regulate, and suppress the child's desires; and finally the disciplinarian, now not a father figure but a sadomasochistic Barbarella version of either maid or mother.

By virtue of all the institutional placements of composition teaching that were described earlier, it is clear that the individual composition teacher is a culturally designated "initiator," much like a temple priest/ess who functions to pass along secret knowledge but not to participate freely in a culture that depends on that knowledge. Strict regulations, analogous to those devised to keep "hired help" in its place, prevent those who introduce the young to the culture's religious values and rites from leaving their particular and special status. These mediators between natural and regulated impulses are tied to vows, enclosed living spaces, and/or certain kinds of dress (see Lerner 123–41).

But this initiating role, whether it is described in terms of religious/sexual initiations or as the groundwork under discursive practices, is unstable in any context. It was never worked out in regard to codified culture even in ancient times, when the socially separated *grammaticus* and *rhetor* argued over who should initiate students into rhetorical composition. Thus the teacher of composition is not assigned only the role of initiator, which might involve the care, pedagogic seduction, and practice for adult roles provided by nurses in bourgeois homes. In addition, this teacher must withhold unquestioned acceptance, represent established means of discriminating and evaluating students, and embody primary ideals/idols of language. This initiator, who traditionally has a great deal at stake in the model-correctness of his or her own language, must also *be* the culture to which the student is introduced.

This embodiment in rules and practice exercises, the rituals of language, displaces actual discourse. It requires the student to keep a distance. If there is an Oedipal situation in regard to working out an imagined young student's entitlements to full participation in cultural "principles," the composition teacher is the Jocasta figure, the desired and desiring but always displaced representation of maturity. In the terminology of psychopathology, this teacher is called into an inverted neurotic situation, one that displays the *social* irruption of *psychic* processes, not the more usual "*psychic* irruption of *social* processes" (Stallybrass and White 176).

Some might counter that this structure contains the imaginary identity called for from any teacher of any introductory course claiming to initiate students into "essential" cultural knowledge. But the composition teacher consciously and unconsciously initiates students into the culture's discourse on *language,* which is always at one with action, emotion, and regulatory establishments. This teacher is always engaged in initiations to the textual fabric of society and thus will always be in a particular and difficult relation to the powers that overtly regulate that society. Although the fairs that permeated social life in Europe were broken up and discontinued in the process of regulations like the Fairs Act of 1871 in England (Stallybrass and White 177), actual carnivals do not disappear. "Fragmentation, marginalization, sublimation, and repression" (178) keep them alive. Similarly, the identity first imposed on teachers of composition is held over, even after their mechanistic and very obviously regulatory earliest roles are revised and are in fact contradicted by many stated goals, practices, and actual situations.

Doubts about the plausibility of this explanation of the composition teacher's blurred identity may be lessened by common responses to these teachers, which should reveal its force. Like the carnival, composition teaching still is often acknowledged as "an underground self with the upper hand" (Stallybrass and White 4). It is an employment that in the majority of its individual cases is both demeaned by its continuing ad hoc relation to status, security, and financial rewards, yet given overwhelming authority by students, institutions, and the public, who expect even the most inexperienced composition teacher to critize and "correct" them in settings entirely removed from the academy. The perduring image of the composition teacher is of a figure at once powerless and sharply authoritarian, occupying the transgressive, low-status site from which language may be arbitrated.

Continuing associations of composition teachers with "Miss Grundyism" also reinforce this claim that as an identity, composition teaching codes the individual of either sex as a woman, the inheritor of the "pink sunsets" image of literary initiation that has in the last quarter-century largely been removed from the self-perceptions of literary professionals by their own "theory." In this way also, the existence of composition within English permits literature to displace and translate an older social identity onto only one of its parts. Composition is a site for residues and traces from earlier literary identities that first coded English as "female" among "hard" disciplines.

If we return to the original question I posed in this chapter, the question of why composition professionals would have chosen a "process paradigm" that appears to estrange them from English studies, we may answer that this choice emerges from their blurred identity and from strategies for coping with its nonetheless clear stigma. The choice of a "process" "paradigm" for research appears to, but finally does not, represent a contradiction in terms. On the one hand, associations with "process" extend and in fact enlarge the subjectivity for its own sake that removes students and their teachers from the need to verify, validate, and find significance in "results." "Process" thereby reinforces the composition professional's claim on a "normal" identity among colleagues in literature, expressing a desire that is difficult to shake. But on the other hand, associations with a scientific "paradigm" give value only to verified, valid, significant "results" from research. This member of the pair of terms reveals yet another mechanism for coping with stigma, in the form of a desire to elevate stigmatized status to a place that is imagined to be above the identity of the "normal."

The juxtaposition of these terms does not, I would argue, unconsciously preserve androgyny and thereby give equal privileges to two terms of a pair that is symbolically female and male, yin and yang. Instead, the choice of this seemingly contradictory pair in a new description of composition teaching and theory contains two equal preservations of the historical (traditional, hegemonic) situation of composition. *Process* practices extend and preserve literary subjectivity, while their explanation in a *paradigm* theory extends and preserves the anxiety about status that has always been associated with English studies, both in regard to the perfection of elitist texts and as a professional concern about identity in relation to older, "harder" disciplines.

As in other examples, composition professionals inevitably recreate the conditions that first established their identities. Persistent attempts to change these conditions without changing the basic structure of high and low that sustain them leave composition in new versions of traditional values. Stallybrass and White summarize such moves in a judgment whose importance cannot be overstated: "The point is that the exclusion necessary to the formation of social identity is simultaneously a *production* at the level of the Imaginary, and a production, what is more, of a complex hybrid fantasy emerging out of the very attempt to demarcate boundaries, to unite and purify the social collectivity" (193). They claim, that is, that by separating itself from an objectionable entity — the stigma, for example, of "mere" teachers of composition engaged in "grotesque" untheorized work — a group necessarily produces a "new grotesque."

We see this process in action in regard to composition teaching and theorizing, both of which have appeared to exclude formerly acceptable literary agendas as well as "soft," unorganized theories of composition or interpretations based on work that is not really "in" the field. But the production that occurs simultaneously with this attempt to mark boundaries, unite, and purify a field of composition also is a process of exclusion, the very process that otherwise dedicated teachers of composition object to and take as their motive for change. Consequently, the theories I have applied to the identity of the composition teacher may appear to describe a condition that is past or clearly passing, not one that is held over in a complex set of continuing interactions that slowly move the teacher out of a sweat shop and into respectable professional modes. Nonetheless, the nature of this movement is too clearly implicated in reproducing the conditions it wishes to revise to be celebrated with unqualified assertions that "change" has occurred, as new institutional blurrings of the identity of composition also demonstrate.

Works Cited

Berlin, James. *Rhetoric and Reality: Writing Instruction in American Colleges, 1900–1985.* Carbondale: Southern Illinois UP, 1987.

Corbett, Edward P. J. *Classical Rhetoric for the Modern Student.* New York: Oxford UP, 1971.

Goffman, Erving. *Frame Analysis.* New York: Harper, 1974.

Graff, Gerald. *Professing Literature: An Institutional History.* Chicago: U of Chicago P, 1987.

Holbrook, Sue Ellen. "Women's Work: The Feminizing of Composition." Presentation, CCCC. St. Louis, March 1988.

Kitzhaber, Albert. "Rhetoric in American Colleges, 1850–1900." Diss. U of Washington, 1953.

Lerner, Gerda. *The Creation of Patriarchy.* New York: Oxford UP, 1986.

Ohmann, Richard. "Reading and Writing, Work and Leisure," from *Only Connect: Uniting Reading and Writing.* Ed. Thomas Newkirk. Upper Montclair: Boynton-Cook, 1986.

Slevin, James. "A Note on the Wyoming Resolution and ADE." *ADE Bulletin* 87 (1987): 50.

Stallybrass, Peter, and Allon White. *The Politics and Poetics of Transgression.* Ithaca: Cornell UP, 1986.

Miller's Insights as a Resource for Your Teaching

1. Miller's analysis of writing instruction in American colleges suggests that to teach writing is to work in a ghetto within the university. This injustice varies from institution to institution, but everyone can reflect on the power dynamics at work in his or her institution and explore strategies for diplomatically thematizing the ghettoization of writing instruction in individual classrooms.

2. In a journal, reflect on the ways that your frustration with writing instruction might affect your own day-to-day morale and, in turn, the morale of your students. Can you think of readings to assign that might boost morale and reduce the somber tedium with which most institutions encode the scene of writing instruction? Narratives about the extraordinary joy and power that come from winning literacy are helpful. Consider the *Narrative of the Life of Frederick Douglass, an American Slave,* for example.

Miller's Insights as a Resource for Your Writing Classroom

1. Ask students to freewrite about the differences between their composition class and, say, a class on Shakespeare or Virginia Woolf. By discussing these perceived differences, students can become aware of the special goals of the course that is designed to teach them to write. By becoming more attuned to these goals, they stand a better chance of reaching them.

2. Assign a literary text in your classroom, and then juxtapose this text with texts written by students or with other nonliterary writing, such as journalism, popular fiction, or song lyrics. Ask the students to discuss and write about the cultural dynamics that envelope each of these texts, and explore how the writing process is affected by the institutional norms that perpetuate and entrench those dynamics.

Tutoring ESL Students: Issues and Options

Muriel Harris and Tony Silva

Muriel Harris, a writing center administrator and theorist, and Tony Silva, an English as a Second Language specialist, wrote this piece for colleagues who train tutors to work with ESL writers. However, the essay also provides composition teachers a clear overview of issues and practical teaching strategies for working with ESL writers. The questions that nag new peer tutors and their responses to texts written by ESL students differ only by degree of apprehension from the questions and reading responses of writing teachers. The "tutorial principles" cited are also standard teaching practices of writing instructors. The recommended readings are useful additions to the professional library of a writing instructor. Use this essay as a jumping-in point for thinking about, and planning to work with, students who compose in English as their second — or third or fourth — language.

For students whose first language is not English, the writing classroom cannot provide all the instructional assistance that is needed to become proficient writers. For a variety of reasons, these students need the kind of individualized attention that tutors offer, instruction that casts no aspersions on the adequacy of the classroom or the ability of the student. We should recognize that along with different linguistic backgrounds, ESL students have a diversity of concerns that can only be dealt with in the one-to-one setting where the focus of attention is on that particular student and his or her questions, concerns, cultural presuppositions, writing processes, language learning experiences, and conceptions of what writing in English is all about. Typically, the tutorial assistance available for these students is provided by writing centers, and much of the personal help available there is precisely the same as for any native speaker of English: The goal of tutors who work in the center is to attend to the individual concerns of every writer who walks in the door — writing process questions, reader feedback, planning conversations, and so on. But also typically, tutors, who bring to their work a background of experience and knowledge in interacting effectively with native speakers of English, are not adequately equipped to deal with some additional concerns of non-native speakers of English — the unfamiliar grammatical errors, the sometimes bewilderingly different rhetorical patterns and conventions of other languages, and the expectations that accompany ESL writers when they come to the writing center. Tutors can be reduced to stunned silence when they try to explain why "I have many homeworks to completed" is wrong or why we say "on Monday" but "in June."

Tutors need some perspective on rhetorical approaches other than those they expect to find, such as a direct statement of the topic or discourse with a linear development. When tutors find, instead, an implicitly stated point or when they become lost in a long, seemingly meandering introduction or digressions that appear irrelevant, they flounder, not recognizing that implicitness and digressions may be acceptable rhetorical strategies in the writing of some other cultures. Because the need to learn more about how to work with ESL writers in tutorials is immediate and real, one of the authors of this essay, a writing center director, asked the other author, the coordinator of ESL writing courses at our university, for help. The conversations that ensued are summarized here in terms of the questions that guided our discussion of various issues and options, and our hope is that our exchanges will be of interest to others who train tutors to work with ESL students. We also hope that composition teachers looking for guidance when conferencing with ESL students will find useful suggestions for their own interactions with these students.

Plunging In: How Do We Prioritize among Errors?

In the peer tutor training course in our writing center, peer tutors are especially eager to meet and work with ESL students, but their initial contacts can be somewhat frightening because some unfamiliar concerns crop up. To the untrained tutor's eye what is most immediately noticeable is that a draft written by an ESL student looks so different. Vocabulary choices might be confusing, familiar elements of essays are missing, and sentences exhibit a variety of errors — some we can categorize, some we cannot. Tutors' first concern is often a matter of wanting some guidance about where to plunge in. Where should they start? New tutors who have not yet completely internalized the concept of the tutorial as focusing only on one or two concerns think initially it is their responsibility to help the writer fix everything in the draft in front of them. As tutors learn the pedagogy of the tutorial, they become more comfortable with selecting something to work on for that session, but they still need suggestions for a hierarchy and some sense of what is most important.

When tutors ask how to prioritize among errors, they should be encouraged to begin by looking for what has been done well in the paper, acknowledge that, and go from there. Such a suggestion fits in well with the tutorial principle of beginning all interaction with writers on a positive note and reminds us that ESL writers should not be separated out as different or unlike other students in this regard. And tutors should also be encouraged to let their students know that errors are a natural part of language learning and that most readers will be interested primarily in what writers have to say. So tutors need to distinguish between errors that will interfere with the intended reader's understanding of the text (global errors) and those that will not (local errors) and to give priority to the former. To illustrate for tutors this notion of global vs. local errors at the sentence level, the following example can help. Suppose an ESL student, attempting to describe some classmates as uninspired by a particular lecture, wrote: "Those students are boring" instead of "Those students are bored." This would constitute a global error. On the other hand, a construction such as "Those student are bored" would represent a local error.

Using Research: How Helpful Is It to Look for Patterns?

With our heightened awareness of multiculturalism, we are also more aware of cultural preferences that are reflected in writing, such as the often-cited Asian preference for indirection. The question in working one-to-one with ESL students is how helpful such generalizations really are. Work in contrastive rhetoric would seem to be particularly valuable because it describes patterns of rhetorical preferences in other cultures, patterns which may explain the seemingly inappropriate rhetorical strategies used by ESL students. But to what degree is such knowledge useful? To what extent should we help tutors become aware of such differences? On the one hand, there is a danger that they can begin to use general patterns as givens, expecting all speakers of other languages to fit the models they have learned. On the other hand, without any knowledge of cultural preferences tutors are likely to see differences as weaknesses and to assume that the ESL student needs basic writing help. For example, instead of introducing the American intolerance of digression as culturally appropriate for American discourse, a tutor might treat an ESL student purposefully using digression as an inadequate writer who has problems with organization. If the tutor assumes that student is deficient, the tutor's tendency might be to work on outlining and to leave aside any rationale for why digressions should be avoided. Tutors need to introduce preferences and conventions of American discourse for what they are — alternate conventions and preferences.

However, to consider the extent to which such knowledge is helpful, we have to begin with some background information. The study of first-language transfer at or below the sentence level, typically referred to as "contrastive analysis" (see Brown 153–63 for a concise summary of this work), and the study of differences in rhetorical preferences among various cultures, usually termed "contrastive rhetoric" (see, for example, Grabe and Kaplan; Leki), have given us useful insights into how the writing of ESL students may differ from accepted standards of American discourse. The question of the transfer of first-language (L1) linguistic and rhetorical patterns to second-language (L2) writing has been a central and contentious issue in ESL studies since the beginning of work in this area. In the early days it was believed that L1 transfer (then called interference) was the primary if not exclusive cause of L2 problems. Therefore, it was felt that if one could catalog the differences between a student's L1 and L2, one could anticipate — and thus be prepared to deal with — any problems that student might encounter in the L2. However, research showed that this was not the case. There were many problems that could not be accounted for by L1 interference. Other factors, such as cognitive development, prior language and/or writing instruction, and experience were also implicated. Today, it is generally believed that transfer can be positive or negative and that it is only one of the potential causes of L2 writing problems. Thus we have to approach the question of the use of such knowledge with some hedging. On one hand, being cognizant of typical problems associated with particular groups of ESL students can be helpful — especially if tutors work largely with one or two particular groups. At the very least, this would make tutors very familiar with these problems and perhaps enhance their ability to deal with them. However, tutors need to keep two things in mind: (1) not all members of a particular group may manifest all of the problems or cultural preferences associated with that group; and (2) not all problems will be a result of transfer of L1 patterns.

A related issue is that of culturally conditioned patterns of behavior, some articulated, some not. In the Writing Lab's tutor-training course, we dip into Edward Hall's work to help tutors-to-be become aware of the variety of human behaviors which are conditioned, consciously or unconsciously, by one's culture. Since some of these behaviors can impede communication in a tutorial, it's important to recognize that such differences occur. A few favorite topics among the tutors-in-training are their reactions to the preference for or avoidance of eye contact, the differences among cultures in regard to the amount of space that people expect to maintain between themselves and others, the acceptability of touching between strangers, and so on. The cautionary advice about not doing too much large-scale or whole-group predicting is worth recalling here, but we also have to be aware that we might make unconscious judgments about others based on our expectations about such behaviors. In addition, we have to deal with different cultural assumptions about time, keeping appointments vs.

showing up (if at all) much later, and so on. Understanding and accommodating cultural differences is, to a great extent, what ESL instruction is all about. This is especially true when working with students who are very new to and not very cognizant of the workings of American culture.

Recognizing Differences: How Do We Distinguish Language Learning from Writing Process Needs?

There is a tendency to think about ESL students as if they're all alike when obviously they're not. And in writing centers our focus is on working with individual differences of all kinds. So when the tutor and student negotiate the agenda of what they'll work on, the tutor has to do some assessment about a variety of things, including some sense of what skills the student has or doesn't have — not an easy matter when it might be that the writer's low level of language proficiency, not weak writing skills, is causing the problem. For example, does the thin, undeveloped two-paragraph essay an ESL student brings in indicate the need to talk about how to develop topics or is the student's lack of language proficiency in English keeping her from expressing a rich internal sense of what she wants to write about? As tutors we know that our conversation would take on a somewhat different emphasis depending on our analysis of the situation. The question then becomes one of how to decide whether the student needs help with language or with writing processes.

While the distinction between language proficiency and writing ability is not clear cut, it is crucial to make such a distinction in order to understand and address a given ESL writer's problems (see Barbara Kroll's "The Rhetoric and Syntax Split" for an excellent discussion of this issue). In some cases, a very low level of English proficiency will prevent a student from producing any kind of coherent prose. For such a student some basic language instruction, preceding or accompanying writing instruction, would be indicated. Then there is the student with enough English proficiency to make it unclear whether problems result primarily from rhetorical or linguistic difficulties or from both. There are a number of ways tutors can proceed when trying to ascertain the cause of the problem — assuming they will see the student more than once. They can try to locate the student's results on general English proficiency tests or tests of English writing ability. They can consult with an ESL professional. They can analyze some samples of the student's writing and make a judgment of their own. They can ask the student's opinion about what the basic difficulty is.

Exploring Writing Process Differences: Do ESL Writers Compose Differently?

A rather small but growing body of research, reviewed and synthesized by Silva, compares the composing of ESL and native English-speaking (NES) writers. The findings of this research suggest that while the composing processes of these two groups are similar in their broad outlines, that is, for both groups writing is a recursive activity involving planning, writing, and revising, there are some salient and important differences. The findings (and these should be seen as very tentative) suggest that adult ESL writers plan less, write with more difficulty (primarily due to a lack of lexical resources), reread what they have written less, and exhibit less facility in revising by ear, that is, in an intuitive manner — on the basis of what "sounds" right, than their NES peers. One implication that can be drawn from this research is that those who deal with ESL writers might find it helpful to stretch out the composing process: (1) to include more work on planning — to generate ideas, text structure, and language — so as to make the actual writing more manageable; (2) to have their ESL students write in stages, e.g., focusing on content and organization in one draft and focusing on linguistic concerns in another subsequent draft; and (3) to separate their treatments of revising (rhetorical) and editing (linguistic) and provide realistic strategies for each, strategies that do not rely on intuitions ESL writers may not have.

Confronting Error: Does It Help to Categorize Sentence-Level Concerns?

When working on grammar with native speakers, tutors categorize types of error so that they can address seemingly disparate problems by focusing on a larger language principle at work. While it's useful to know how to do this so that one can figure out what the problem is and explain it in an effective way to the student, such categorization in the writing of ESL students is often difficult. To do such categorizing well, tutors may need to take a course in the grammar of modern English. Or maybe a short in-service seminar or self-study would do the trick. In any case, a merely intuitive understanding of how English works would not be sufficient for helping ESL writers — who do not share the tutor's native speaker intuitions and who often need explicit explanations. We should also remember that the "rules" of English vary in terms of level of usefulness. Most don't work all the time; some have as many exceptions as cases covered by the rule. So knowing the rules can help tutors a lot; but they can't count on the rules solving their problems in every case. Such advice should make tutors feel more comfortable with their role as writing collaborators rather than as grammarians whose function it is to spout rules. Tutors are there to help with the whole spectrum of writing processes, not to be talking grammar handbooks.

Although tutors do not work primarily on grammar and mechanics, some ESL writers — especially those whose first acquaintance with English was as a foreign language taught in classrooms in other countries — have a tendency to want to know rules. For example, in a tutorial with a native speaker of English or a student born in the United

States who spoke another language before entering school, the student might ask "Is this sentence OK?" or "How do I fix this sentence?" But an ESL student who comes to the United States after studying English as a foreign language in another country is more likely to ask "Why is this wrong?" Such students seem to have a strong inclination toward organizing their knowledge of English by rules. Though things are changing, many foreign language classes (and this includes foreign language classes in the United States) privilege the learning of grammatical rules, of learning about the language as an object, and neglect the learning of how to actually communicate, orally or in writing, in the foreign language. Certainly, this can make learners very rule-oriented in their outlook. However, there is something else that may also contribute to an ESL student's seeming preoccupation with rules. It's necessary to keep in mind that non-native speakers of a language (especially ones with lower levels of second language proficiency) simply don't have the intuitions about the language that native speakers do; that is, it is harder for them to recognize when something "sounds good." Therefore, in lieu of these intuitions, these students will have to rely on explicit rules to a certain extent.

Adjusting Expectations: How Do We Withstand the Pressure to Correct Every Error?

ESL writers often come to the writing center seeking an editor, someone who will mark and correct their errors and help them fix the paper. On one hand, as tutors we are collaborators who listen to the student's concerns when setting the tutorial agenda. On the other hand, as tutors we also want to begin with rhetorical concerns before looking at sentence-level matters. This causes delicate negotiating between tutor and student when these differing preferences for the agenda collide. But tutors should be firm about dealing with rhetorical matters before linguistic ones (recognizing that sometimes this distinction is hard to make), a sequence as beneficial for ESL writers as it is for native speakers. Tutors should remind ESL writers that their linguistic options may be determined to a large degree by the rhetorical requirements of their papers and that, correlatively, it doesn't make sense to focus initially on grammatical or mechanical problems which may disappear as a result of rhetorically based revisions.

A related problem is that when ESL students are particularly insistent on having tutors correct all grammatical errors in a paper, tutors are at a loss to explain in meaningful ways why this is not productive. Resisting such pressure is very difficult, especially when ESL students are writing papers for other courses where they think the paper should be "correct." One way to address this is for tutors to adjust expectations. Tutors need to tell ESL writers that it is unrealistic for them to expect to be able to write like native speakers of English — especially when it comes to the small but persistent problems like articles and prepositions. Tutors can explain that even non-native speakers of English who live in an English-speaking area for many years and write regularly in English maintain a written accent. It might help to compare this to a foreign accent in pronunciation and to remind ESL students that most native speakers (their professors included) will probably not penalize them much or at all for minor problems in their writing. It also helps to remind such students to focus on substance and not worry so much about style. But there are faculty who do have unrealistic demands about the level of correctness, who expect non-native speakers of English to write error-free prose — not to have a written accent, so to speak. If an ESL student's teacher has such unrealistic expectations, then the student is justified in seeking out editing help, and a native English-speaking colleague, friend, or tutor is justified in providing such help.

Another way that tutors can deal with students' insistence on having all errors corrected is to explain the role of a tutor. ESL students need to know that tutors are expected to help them with strategies that will make them effective, independent writers. We need to explicitly state that tutors are supposed to be educators, not personal editors. This problem is often a result of a mismatch between the assumptions and expectations of tutors and students, though tutors do tend to hang on to their kind-hearted desire to help the student turn in a good paper. Writing center specialists endlessly quote Steve North's now famous one-liner that the tutor's job "is to produce better writers, not better writing" (438). But we still suffer pangs when the student leaves with less than an "A" paper in hand. Offering editorial services is not a learning experience — except for the editor, of course — and tutors need to resist their impulse to help as much as ESL students need to resist their desire to have every grammatical error corrected.

Setting Goals: What Can We Accomplish?

Since second-language learning is typically a long, slow process, tutors have to confront the realities of the time constraints they face in tutorials. Sometimes tutors meet briefly with ESL writers who are about to hand in a paper, sometimes tutors may have a few more leisurely tutorials with the same student, and sometimes tutors are able to meet over a more extended period of time, including sessions when the student is not working on a particular paper. The question then becomes one of deciding what can reasonably be done in the varying situations tutors find themselves in. In terms of last-minute encounters, a tutor can't do much with a paper that is about to be handed in — except act as a proofreader or offer moral support. And neither of these has much instructional value in the long run. However, dealing with an early or intermediate draft of a paper at one or more short sessions can be very useful if tutors can resist trying to deal with all of a draft's problems at once. It is more realistic and more useful to focus on one or two salient difficulties, the things that strike the tutor as most problematic for the reader. To do more would probably overload and frustrate the student and wind up being counterproductive. Going this slowly will probably not result in great improvements in a particular paper, but is more likely to facilitate real learning and writing improvement over time.

When tutors are able to meet with ESL students over a period of time and meet when the student is not working on a particular paper, there are several kinds of tutorial activities that might be useful in helping the student build language proficiency. To begin this sequence, a tutor should first look at one or more samples of the student's writing to get a feel for what linguistic features need to be addressed and in what order (global first, local later). Then, always working with a text the student has written previously or writes in the tutorial, the tutor can help the student identify and remedy errors or help the student generate lexical and/or syntactic options that would improve the student's text. This sort of procedure would help with building language proficiency and might also help the student develop effective personalized strategies for generating language, revising, and editing. Such an approach also harmonizes with the writing center philosophy that what we do particularly well in the tutorial setting is to help writers develop strategies individually matched to their own preferences and differences. Because the tutorial is also especially well suited to working through writing processes, to engaging in various processes such as planning, organizing, revising, and editing with the writer, working through various texts the ESL writer is drafting and revising is easily accomplished in a one-to-one setting.

Resisting the Urge to "Tell": How Do We Stop Supplying All the Answers?

Since writing center pedagogy has given high priority to working collaboratively and interactively, a major goal of a tutor is to help students find their own solutions. Tutors thus don't see themselves as "instructors" who "tell" things. Yet the ESL student cannot easily come to some of the realizations that native speakers can as a result of tutorial questioning and collaboration. To confound the problem even more, while the tutor is uncomfortable straying from the role of collaborator, ESL writers are likely to find such a situation strange or uncomfortable when they come from cultures/educational systems where teachers are expected to be "tellers," where those who don't "tell" are seen as poor teachers, or where such casual interaction with relative strangers is seen as odd or inappropriate. This means that tutors cannot assume that a pattern of interaction that is common and accepted in their culture will be familiar or comfortable for their ESL students. Therefore, tutors might find it useful to make sure that they and their ESL students understand each other's goals and expectations vis-a-vis their tutoring sessions.

In terms of the tutor's role, there may have to be adjustments in their pedagogical orientation. Tutors who work with ESL students may have to be "tellers" to some extent because they will probably need to provide cultural, rhetorical, and/or linguistic information which native speakers intuitively possess and which ESL students do not have, but need to have to complete their writing assignments effectively. That is, regardless of their level of skill in collaboration or interpersonal interaction, tutors will not be able to elicit knowledge from ESL students if the students don't have that knowledge in the first place. This is not to suggest that "telling" should become a tutor's primary style of interacting with ESL writers; they should use it when they feel it would be necessary or appropriate, just as they assume the role of informant occasionally when working with native speakers of English. Tutors can also make minor accommodations in their tutoring style when working with ESL writers. For example, with non-native students who are used to hearing directive statements from teachers, Judith Kilborn has suggested that where it is appropriate, tutors modify the normal mode of asking questions so that instead of asking "Why . . ." or "How . . . ," tutors can, for example, say, "Please explain. . . ." An answer to a relatively open-ended request for explanation might be more useful and enlightening for both the ESL student and the tutor.

Making Hierarchies: What Aspects of Grammar Are Most Important?

Although tutorials should begin with discussions of larger rhetorical concerns, at some point ESL students will want help with grammatical correctness. When tutors do confront working with grammar, problems with verb endings and tenses, prepositions, and deleted articles often are the most noticeable. But are these the most useful things to start with? One way to define the most important areas is functionally; that is, the ones most important to address are those that most interfere with the reader's understanding of what the writer wants to say (global errors) regardless of their structural characteristics. Research suggests that ESL writers most commonly make the following errors:

Verbs

> Inflectional morphology (agreement with nouns in person, number, etc.)
>
> Verbal forms (participials, infinitives, gerunds)
>
> Verb complementation (the types of clauses or constructions that must follow a particular verb)

Nouns

> Inflection (especially in terms of singular/plural and count/ mass distinctions)

Derivation (deriving nouns from other parts of speech, e.g., *quick — quickness,* which often seems quite arbitrary to non-native speakers)

Articles (related to problems in classifying nouns)

Use of wrong article

Missing article

Use of an article when none is necessary or appropriate

Prepositions (primarily a result of limited lexical resources)

Knowing which one goes with a particular noun, verb, adjective, or adverb

These four error types account for most of the errors made by ESL writers with a fairly high level of English proficiency; ESL writers with lower levels of proficiency may also exhibit more problems with basic sentence, clause, and phrase structure — which (when combined with vocabulary limitations) result in writing that is very difficult to decipher. Article problems can be important, too; that is, they can seriously obscure meaning in some contexts. But they generally do not cause readers any serious difficulties, and because they are so hard to eradicate, they should not be a high priority for tutors. It might help both tutors and ESL writers to think of article problems in writing as akin to a slight foreign accent in writing — something that doesn't pose serious difficulties and disappears only gradually — if at all.

When working with the complicated matter of articles and prepositions and non-rule-governed matters such as idioms, tutors need some new pedagogies as well as guidance for explaining topics not normally discussed in grammar handbooks. But, while we can develop an explanation of article use in English, such an explanation will not be simple by any means. It would involve making sequential decisions about the noun phrase that an article modifies — common or proper, count or non-count, singular or plural, definite or indefinite. Then, of course, there are the several classes of special cases and the many outright exceptions to the rules (Ann Raimes's *Grammar Troublespots* is helpful here; see 85–92). ESL writers could understand such explanations — but it's not clear that this understanding would translate into greatly improved performance in making correct article decisions while actually writing. Article use can improve gradually with increased exposure to English, but it's not realistic to expect that an ESL writer will ever use articles like a native speaker does. ESL students should be encouraged to do the best they can and then get a native speaker to proofread their work — if proofreading is absolutely necessary. As for preposition problems, they are lexical rather than grammatical problems. We either know the correct preposition in a given context or we don't — there are really no rules we can appeal to. Therefore, ESL writers need to learn prepositions the same way they learn other vocabulary items — through study or exposure to the language. Idioms are also a lexical rather than a grammatical matter. Second language learners usually have a keen interest in idiomatic expressions and are eager to learn and use them. Tutors can capitalize on this interest by providing students with idiomatic options for words and expressions they have used in their text. Both tutor and student might find this a useful and enjoyable activity. One proviso: When introducing an idiom, tutors need to also supply information about the appropriate context for the use of that idiom in order to avoid putting the student in a potentially embarrassing situation.

Encouraging Proofreading: What Strategies Work Well?

With native English speakers we are often successful in helping them learn to edit for correctness by reading aloud, something some ESL students can also learn how to do. Some are able to find their own mistakes, even add omitted articles, and it really works. But for other ESL students, this doesn't seem to be an effective strategy. ESL writers who can't successfully edit "by ear" aren't proficient enough in English to have a "feel" for what is correct and what isn't. It follows that those with higher levels of proficiency will have more success with reading aloud, but even the most proficient aren't likely to display native-speaker-like intuitions. Therefore, some recourse to more mechanical rule-based proofreading strategies or to outside help, such as a native speaker reader, will probably be necessary.

Adding Resources: What Are Useful Readings for Tutors?

Since many tutors and directors would like to better prepare themselves to work with ESL students but have limited time to spend, we will limit our suggestions for further reading to a small fraction of the abundant literature produced in recent years on ESL writing and ESL writers. The resources described in this section were chosen on the basis of their timeliness, breadth, and accessibility.

The first resources are book-length treatments of issues in ESL writing and writing instruction. One is Ilona Leki's, *Understanding ESL Writers: A Guide for Teachers*. This introductory book addresses the history of ESL writing instruction, relevant models of second language acquisition, differences between basic writers and ESL writers, personal characteristics of ESL writers, ESL writers' expectations, writing behaviors, and composing processes, contrastive rhetoric, common sentence-level errors, and responding to ESL writing. The second is Joy M. Reid's *Teaching ESL Writing*. This work deals with the special problems and concerns that distinguish first and second language writing instruction, addressing in particular the variables of language and cultural background, prior education, gender, age, and language proficiency. Reid also provides an overview of different ESL composition teaching methodologies and offers specific information on developing curricula, syllabi, and lesson plans for basic, intermediate, and advanced ESL writing classes. Also useful are two collections covering a broad range of issues in ESL writing. The first is Barbara Kroll's *Second Language Writing: Research Insights for the Classroom,* which contains thirteen papers in two major sections. The papers in the first section address theories of L2 writing and provide overviews of research in a number of basic areas of ESL composition. The second section is comprised of reports of empirical research on current issues in L2 writing instruction. The second collection, Donna M. Johnson and Duane H. Roen's *Richness in Writing: Empowering ESL Students,* includes eighteen papers in three sections which deal respectively with contexts for ESL writing, specific rhetorical concerns of L2 writers, and cultural issues in the writing of ESL students.

Two additional resources are the *Journal of Second Language Writing,* a scholarly journal which publishes reports of research and discussions of issues in second and foreign language writing and writing instruction, and *Resources for CCCC Members Who Want to Learn about Writing in English as a Second Language,* a fact sheet of information about professional organizations, conferences, publications, and educational and employment opportunities for those interested in working with ESL writers. (For a copy of the *Resources* fact sheet, write to Tony Silva, Chair, CCCC Committee on ESL, Department of English, Heavilon Hall, Purdue University, West Lafayette, Indiana 47907-1356.)

Conclusion

ESL instructors and writing center people need to keep interacting with and learning from each other. We each have insights, methods, research, and experiences to share. For those of us in writing centers, it's useful to know that writing center tutors can draw on both research and language teaching approaches used in ESL classrooms. Writing center directors can share with ESL teachers one-to-one pedagogies that work in the writing center as well as our perceptions of how individual differences interact with various classroom pedagogies on different students. We can also share our awareness of the kinds of questions students really ask, our first-hand observations of how students cope with writing assignments and teacher responses, and our encounters with non-native differences that interfere with learning how to write in American classrooms. Such information can only serve to illuminate the work of ESL teachers. Similarly, insights from ESL writing theory, research, and practice can help writing centers, and mainstream composition in general, to deal effectively with their increasingly multilingual and multicultural student populations.

Works Cited

Brown, H. Douglas. *Principles of Language Learning and Teaching.* 2nd ed. Englewood Cliffs: Prentice, 1987.

CCCC Committee on ESL. *Resources for CCCC Members Who Want to Learn about Writing in English as a Second Language (ESL).* Urbana: NCTE, 1992.

Grabe, William, and Robert B. Kaplan. "Writing in a Second Language: Contrastive Rhetoric." *Richness in Writing: Empowering ESL Students.* Ed. Donna Johnson and Duane Roen. New York: Longman, 1989. 263–83.

Hall, Edward. *The Silent Language.* New York: Doubleday, 1959.

Johnson, Donna M., and Duane H. Roen, eds. *Richness in Writing: Empowering ESL Students.* New York: Longman, 1989.

Kilborn, Judith. "Tutoring ESL Students: Addressing Differences in Cultural Schemata and Rhetorical Patterns in Reading and Writing." Minnesota, TESOL Conference. St. Paul, 2 May 1992.

Kroll, Barbara. "The Rhetoric and Syntax Split: Designing a Curriculum for ESL Students." *Journal of Basic Writing* 9 (Spring 1990): 40–45.

———, ed. *Second Language Writing: Research Insights for the Classroom.* New York: Cambridge UP, 1990.

Leki, Ilona. "Twenty-Five Years of Contrastive Rhetoric: Text Analysis and Writing Pedagogies." *TESOL Quarterly* 25 (Spring 1991): 123–43.

———. *Understanding ESL Writers: A Guide for Teachers.* Portsmouth: Boynton, 1992.

North, Stephen. "The Idea of a Writing Center." *College English* 46 (Sep. 1984): 433–46.

Raimes, Ann. *Grammar Troublespots: An Editing Guide for Students.* 2nd ed. New York: St. Martin's, 1992.

Reid, Joy M. *Teaching ESL Writing.* Englewood Cliffs: Regents, 1993.

Silva, Tony. "Differences in ESL and Native Speaker Writing." *Writing in Multicultural Settings.* Ed. Johnnella Butler, Juan Guerra, and Carol Severino. New York: MLA, 1997.

Harris and Silva's Insights as a Resource for Your Teaching

1. Harris and Silva's advice that ESL tutors distinguish global errors from local errors is also a rule of thumb for writing teachers. The authors remind us that many ESL students have a product-centered introduction to writing in English and assume "correctness" will be the writing teacher's first criterion for evaluation. Emphasize in your comments on drafts or in your conferences with ESL writers that your first concern is with the message and that you will focus primarily on errors that impede you in understanding what the writer wants to say. Remind them that, as they revise for ideas and structure, some of their global errors will disappear. Remind them to separate revising (rhetorical concerns) from editing (linguistic concerns).

2. Early in the semester, invite all your students to write you letters describing their histories as writers and learners and detailing anything you need to know about them to work with them as writers. In conferences with individual writers, use your reading of and response to an early writing assignment, journal entries, and the letter to initiate a conversation about the ESL student's writing experiences and about his or her confidence and fluency in spoken and written English. Anticipate that some ESL students — perhaps because of their fluency level or lack of proficiency with basic communication skills in English or perhaps because of cultural communication patterns — will need to become comfortable with one-to-one conferences. They may not articulate their concerns and questions clearly in a first conference or may send verbal and nonverbal messages that they comprehend what you say when in fact they don't. Anticipate that some students will be silent in classroom discussions because they fear speaking incorrectly or they lack cognitive readiness.

Harris and Silva's Insights as a Resource for Your Writing Classroom

1. Both ESL students and students with learning disabilities benefit from work that emphasizes planning, pacing of activities, and writing in stages. Guide students through various heuristics in class and in double-entry journals to help them acquire or refine skills in planning texts. Invite all writers to submit drafts in stages: a discovery draft, a draft focused on ideas and organization, a draft revised to attend to audience, and a draft revised for linguistic concerns. (Many ESL students, most students with learning disabilities, some apprehensive students, and some inexperienced writers will respond to the opportunity.) Set up deadlines, and write up your reader's response and "needs" for the first two drafts. Draft three should go to peer critics; draft four may be shared with peer tutors in your writing centers. Direct writers to submit all drafts along with the "finished" text so that you can comment on their drafting and revising process.

2. Collaborative activities are high-risk experiences for some ESL students and familiar experiences for others. To introduce small-group discussions or projects and peer critique, ask class members to write a three-minute letter about their expectations for and fears about working collaboratively. Merge the letters and make a handout for large-group discussion. Ask the class to agree on some shared responsibilities for collaborative activities. On self-assessment protocols afterward, ask students to evaluate

how well these responsibilities were met. (Return the letter and protocols and ask students to keep them to use in conferences when they assess their work in groups later in the semester.)

Dispositions toward Language: Teacher Constructs of Knowledge and the Ann Arbor Black English Case

Arnetha Ball and Ted Lardner

In this award-winning essay examining the questions of "Black English" in the writing classroom, Arnetha Ball and Ted Lardner consider the ways in which we define knowledge in the field of composition and how these different concepts of knowledge carry implicit patterns of emotional response to the all-important differences (social, linguistic) that distinguish our students from each other. Technical knowledge and knowledge-as-lore both obscure the crucial question of the teacher's affective relation to student diversity, which is the decisive factor in whether many students learn to write. This essay confronts the often shielded yet very real issue of institutional racism — *the "subtle, unconscious manifestations" of internalized bias and prejudice that persist as insidious factors in our educational systems.*

So here's our hypothesis: what students learn about writing depends more than anything else on the context in which they write. . . . And if the linguists are right that the social context is the driving force behind literacy acquisition, then *the social context of your English / language-arts classroom is the most powerful and important variable you can experiment with.* More important than what textbook or speller or dictionary to use; more important than what kinds of assignments to give; more important than how to set up cumulative writing folders; more important than the criteria by which you assign kids to peer response groups; more important than "teaching Graves" versus teaching Calkins or Hillocks. More important than anything.
— Steven Zemelman and Harvey Daniels (50–51)

Because composition has been organized as a field in terms of the classroom, the production, transmission, and assimilation of teacher knowledge continues to be a significant theoretical and practical concern. As John Schilb has recently pointed out, though many writing instructors attempt to separate pedagogy from theory, the "field identifies itself with pedagogy" (*Between* 30). In developing its discussion of pedagogical theory (as distinct from rhetorical theory), scholarship in composition studies has generated what we call constructs of teacher knowledge. In this essay we address competing constructs of teacher knowledge, analyzing them from a perspective which takes racially informed language attitudes and their effects on teaching and learning in culturally diverse classrooms as its central concern. In developing this analysis, our point of departure is the 1979 Ann Arbor "Black English" court case. This case focused on the language barriers created by teachers' unconscious negative attitudes toward students' uses of African American English and the negative effect these attitudes had on student learning.

In our reading, the Ann Arbor case is significant for composition studies for two reasons. First, it stands as a legal intervention into the educational process, disrupting business as usual by holding the school system responsible for the educational underachievement of Black students. It associated low educational achievement not with shortcomings within learners, but with inadequate, ineffective curricular and pedagogical routines. Second, in the Ann Arbor case the court held the school district and teachers responsible for rethinking pedagogy and curriculum in light of extant information about African American English. In so doing, it raised then and continues now to pose the question of how educators accomplish the necessary but complicated task of assimilating new knowledge about race and language in order to translate that knowledge into classroom practice. We believe that barriers similar to those identified in Ann Arbor still affect teaching and learning in many secondary-level and college writing classrooms. Similarly, the complex issues surrounding teacher education and changing teachers' attitudes and behaviors in the classroom remain to be explored in the scholarly dialogue of our field.

We begin here with a summary of the Ann Arbor case, highlighting its focus on teacher attitudes and the consequent issue of teacher knowledge and practice. Next, we argue that three distinct constructs of teacher knowledge are evident in writing studies today, each of which is differentially linked to the issue of race reflected in language attitudes raised in the Ann Arbor case. We conclude with some implications for composition as a field, arguing in particular that pedagogical theory in composition needs to more adequately address questions of language diversity and race in order to affect the climate in the writing classroom.

Background: The Court Decision

In 1979, a Federal District Court handed down a decision in favor of eleven African American children, residents of a scatter-site low-income housing project and students at Martin Luther King Jr. Elementary School, holding the Ann Arbor School District Board responsible for failing to adequately prepare the King School teachers to teach children whose home language was African American English. The case drew national and international attention to the role of language variation in the education of Black children. Stating that a major goal of a school system is to teach reading, writing, speaking, and understanding standard English (Memorandum 1391), Judge Charles Joiner wrote that "when teachers fail to take into account the home language" (1380) of their students, "some children will turn off and not learn" (1381). Challenging a pedagogical ethos grounded in the presumption of universalities, Judge Joiner observed that the teachers involved in the case all testified that they treated the plaintiff students just as they treated other students. However, in so doing they may have created a barrier to learning (1379). In the Ann Arbor case, the Court ruled that the teachers' unconscious but evident attitudes toward the African American English used by the plaintiff children constituted a language barrier that impeded the students' educational progress (1381).

Like the recent Oakland School Board resolution on Ebonics, the Ann Arbor case stirred controversy. As in Oakland, the controversy was in part a result of inaccurate reporting in the media, some of which represented the Court as requiring teachers to teach African American English (see Smitherman, "What"). However, outside of the public furor and of much more substantive import, in ordering the defendant school board to invest time and money in a staff development program for King School teachers, the Court in the Ann Arbor case disrupted the institutional status quo by holding the school district accountable for the inadequate educational progress of the Black children involved. From this perspective, the Ann Arbor case can be viewed as a turning point in the history of educational justice for African American children, and the Court's Memorandum Opinion and Order signals this recognition:

> The problem posed by this case is one which the evidence indicates has been compounded by efforts on the part of society to fully integrate blacks into the mainstream of society by relying solely on simplistic devices such as scatter housing and busing of students. Full integration and equal opportunity require much more and one of the matters requiring more attention is the teaching of the young blacks to read standard English. (1381)

As much as the Court's decision can be viewed as an answer to "a cry for judicial help in opening the doors to the establishment" (1381), it must also be recognized that the overriding theme of the Court's ruling was to uphold existing linguistic, educational, and social arrangements. Many educators have viewed the Ann Arbor decision as a step forward on the same road leading from the *Brown v. Topeka* decision in 1954. Keith Gilyard, for example, calls the Ann Arbor decision a precedent-setting case which ought to have an officially established place within the educational environment (10). But while it is important to note such celebrating of the Ann Arbor case, it is also important to note that the elements of the decision which directly address language barriers and African American English have yet to be cited as a precedent in other cases aimed at school policy. Furthermore, the Court's final Memorandum Opinion and Order explicitly and unequivocally positions African American English in a subordinate relationship to the mainstream:

Black English is not a language used by the mainstream of society — black or white. It is not an acceptable method of communication in the educational world, in the commercial community, in the community of the arts and science, or among professionals. (1378)

The Michigan Legal Services attorneys who mounted the case for the plaintiff children in Ann Arbor drew on the testimony of experts in sociolinguistics and education in order to establish two key propositions: that African American English is a rule-governed language system, and that the teachers' failure to recognize this linguistic fact led to negative attitudes toward the children who spoke it, that, in effect, their attitudes constituted a language barrier impeding students' educational progress. Establishing the first proposition, the expert testimony addressed the second by asserting that communicative interference can derive from either structural mismatches among dialects or from nonstructural phenomena. Nonstructural interference phenomena refers to differing attitudes and conflicting values about speech systems and the individuals who use them. Experts testified that negative linguistic attitudes shaped the institutional policies and practices that hindered the education of African American English speaking children. Then as now, research on language attitudes consistently indicates that teachers believe African American English speaking children are "nonverbal" and possess limited vocabularies. Speakers of African American English are often perceived to be slow learners or uneducable; their speech is often considered to be unsystematic and in need of constant correction and improvement.

In the Ann Arbor case, the Court identified teachers' language attitudes as a significant impediment to children's learning. Because the children failed to develop reading skills, they were thereby impeded from full participation in the educational program at King School. The Court enumerated multiple potential causes (absences from class, classroom misbehavior, learning disabilities, and emotional impairment and lack of reading role models [1391]) for their difficulties, but focused on one:

> Research indicates that the black dialect or vernacular used at home by black students in general makes it more difficult for such children to read because teachers' unconscious but evident attitudes toward the home language causes a psychological barrier to learning by the student. (1381)

The Court called for the Ann Arbor School District Board to develop a program to (1) help the teachers understand the problem, (2) provide them with knowledge about the children's use of African American English, and (3) suggest ways and means of using that knowledge in teaching the students to read (1381). In a court-ordered, twenty-hour inservice program for the King School teachers, experts in reading and sociolinguistics furnished teachers with information on these topics.

In spite of the wealth of information delivered to teachers, however, the school district's report of the results of this inservice program concludes that though teacher respondents "felt positively about all substantive issues, they were somewhat less positive about their understanding of the pedagogical issues" (Howard 17).

The nonstructural barriers resulting from negative attitudes were the focus of the Ann Arbor case, and they remain to challenge successful practice and our students' educational progress today. Survey results reported by Balester suggest that this was as true in 1992 as it was in 1979, the year of the Ann Arbor trial, or in the late sixties when scholarship in applied linguistics first took direct aim at many teachers' traditional, prescriptivist orientations. In 1994, Bowie and Bond found that teachers still continue to exhibit negative attitudes toward African American English, often stating that African American English has a faulty grammar system and that children who speak African American English are less capable than children who speak standard English.

Constructs of Teacher Knowledge

It is clear that the outcome of the Ann Arbor case left many questions unanswered, including the most pressing question of how teachers are to respond to the linguistic and cultural diversity of their students. At the heart of the Ann Arbor decision was the recognition of the need for teachers to become sensitive to students' uses of African American English, to move into a way of being in the classroom which is responsive to and informed by recognition of racial and linguistic difference. However, the unresolved pedagogical issues reflected in the King School teachers' responses to their inservice program remain at the center of our reading of the Ann Arbor case in relation to composition studies: How do teachers learn and transform new knowledge into classroom practice? We argue that three competing constructs of teacher knowledge offer divergent ways of responding to this question. The three constructs we wish to describe are the *teacher as technician, teacher knowledge as lore*, and *teacher efficacy*. We distinguish these constructs from one another in terms of their approaches to the underlying issue of racially informed language attitudes: How do they situate teachers in relation to confronting race as an element in classroom climate? How do they bring to the surface for teachers the awareness of unconscious negative language attitudes? How do they dispose teachers to be able to reflect on and move forward into alternative classroom practices?

Teacher as Technician

The teacher as technician is clearly the operative construct evident in the Ann Arbor case. This construct was a necessary feature of the "objectivist rhetoric" which made up the expert testimony in the trial, which was the dominant rhetoric in the Court's Memorandum Opinion and Order, and which continues to be the undergirding rhetoric of current scholarship on African American English in sociolinguistics, education, and literacy studies. Cy Knoblauch has identified "objectivist rhetoric" as empirical discourse which portrays knowledge as derived from unbiased observation and rigorous argumentative procedure. Because of this, the objectivist paradigm has served as a corrective to superstitions, emotional excesses, and prejudices (130). The Ann Arbor case demonstrates just this corrective potential.

One feature of objectivist rhetoric is its organization of knowledge in linear, cause-and-effect terms. A second feature, evident in the discourse of the case, is the trope of application. The Court acknowledged the necessary contributions of the King School teachers' "skill and empathy" (1391) to classroom success. But the chief significance of the trial lies in the way in which it focused on the need for teachers to apply in practice the findings of modern sociolinguistic scholarship. The process and outcome of the case reflects a technical construct of teacher knowledge in that it subordinates teachers' own reflective resources ("skill and empathy") to disciplinary (sociolinguistic) expertise. The case inscribes teachers as needy recipients of already-formed information which would, it was presumed, ameliorate their attitudes and which would (somehow) be translated into new, more effective writing strategies.

The Final Evaluation of the results of the Ann Arbor inservice program stated that a great deal of information was available regarding such topics as the history and structure of African American English and the effect of teacher attitudes on student learning. But there was evidently little if any attention given at the time to the process of applying this knowledge in practice. Its application was apparently presumed to be automatic. Thomas Pietras, the Language Arts Coordinator for the Ann Arbor School District at the time of the King School trial, wrote that disseminating information to teachers about African American English "assumes that teacher knowledge will result in success in language arts" for speakers of African American English (qtd. in Howard et al. 59), but the results of the questionnaire that teachers filled out subsequent to the inservice speak to the disconnection between knowledge and application. The Final Evaluation distinguishes "substantive" issues from "pedagogical" issues, and the content of the inservice program itself virtually ignored questions of pedagogy, assuming perhaps that providing teachers with knowledge would lead by itself to improved student performance. How that improved student performance was (or is) to be achieved was never addressed; the teacher as technician construct doesn't ask that question, because it tends to bypass altogether the responsive decision-making that teachers must engage in.

The objectivist rhetoric exemplified in the Ann Arbor case in the testimony of experts served to move the Court to intervene in an ingrained, discriminatory institutional practice at King School. When

William Labov, one of the leading expert witnesses to testify in Ann Arbor, wrote about the case saying that "negative attitudes can be changed by providing people with scientific evidence" (32), he expressed perfectly the objectivist view in which science serves as a corrective to prejudice. It also reflects a view of teachers as technicians and of pedagogy as the transparent process of translating "substantive" information in the classroom. Unfortunately, as the King School teachers' own evaluation of their training session indicates, introducing sociolinguistic information seems not to have led them to recognize avenues toward more effective classroom practice. Describing the limitations of objectivist rhetoric and the construct of teacher as technician we argue it entails, Knoblauch suggests that educators may speak of "advances" in "our knowledge of the processes of human learning, including the development of literacy" (130), and may thereby evince "a willingness to ground instruction in what we can observe about those processes" (130). However, Knoblauch goes on, "teachers and researchers accept the least advantageous assumptions of a positivist outlook . . . when they encourage [for example] the new knowledge of linguistics . . . to dictate instructional and learning agendas" (131). The practical (non-)consequences of this acceptance of a "positivist outlook" are evident in the King School teachers' responses. As much as they may have wished for it to be so, they seemed to recognize no clear way in which linguistic or sociolinguistic knowledge could "dictate" teaching and learning processes.

Teacher Knowledge as Lore

Such an impasse is perhaps what composition theorists who talk about teacher knowledge as lore might have predicted. Lore is a postmodern, "postdisciplinary" construct that rejects objectivist, linear, cause-and-effect discourse in favor of complex, multifaceted, and improvisational ways of understanding pedagogical interactions to explain how teachers know what to do.

We identify postdisciplinary views of teacher knowledge as lore with work which has emerged in composition in the last ten years — subsequent, that is, to the Ann Arbor case. Variously formulated by scholars ranging from Stephen North to Louise Wetherbee Phelps and Patricia Harkin, this work has complicated the idea of disciplinary knowledge governing a teacher's practice in the classroom. In Harkin's formulation, lore is identified with teachers' informed intuitions about what works in the classroom. At the center of her discussion is the example of Mina Shaughnessy's *Errors and Expectations*. Harkin identifies Shaughnessy's book as exemplary of lore, and goes on to illustrate the disciplinary critique of lore by reference to critiques of Shaughnessy's work. Harkin writes that critics of teacher knowledge as lore see a danger in teachers who "are willfully ignorant of disciplinary knowledge," and who think they should be free . . . to ignore [for example] modern linguistic scholarship, free to invent their own programs as they go along . . . free to ignore evidence or theory, free to rely on their own insight, free, that is, to ignore facts. (130)

Harkin's reply is to turn aside the ethical implications (teachers ignore facts) and to deconstruct the idea of "facts" in itself: "Facts are only facts in the discipline which constitutes them," she asserts (130). Going on, she argues that because the complex scene of teaching cannot be reduced to the linear causality which disciplinary knowledge demands, teachers cannot be expected to obey disciplinary imperatives. Lore, with its improvisational logic, is the more appropriate interpretive framework with which to think about teaching, to think about how we know what to do in the classroom. The construct of teacher knowledge as lore thus turns us in the right direction as it asks directly about the process of discovery, application, and transformation of teacher knowledge in the classroom. Privileging teachers' direct experiences and reflective practice, lore draws our attention to the moment-to-moment process of observing, interpreting, and decision making that is characteristic of engaged teaching.

However, what the construct of teacher knowledge as lore works to resist — the apparent necessity for teachers to attune their practice to, for example, modern linguistic scholarship — lies at the heart of the Ann Arbor case and the intervention it represented into a discriminatory status quo. One unintended effect, then, of the construct of lore, of relying on teachers' informed intuitions, is to displace a direct confrontation with race as it may be manifested in students' strategic uses of African American English. In its effort to disrupt the disciplinary encroachment of, for example, sociolinguistics (we find Harkin's selection of "linguistics" as evidence quite telling), "postdisciplinary" theory substitutes for one problematic construct, the teacher as technician, an equally problematic construct of teacher knowledge as lore produced through "a process of informed intuition" when "practitioners do what works" (Harkin 134). In Ann Arbor, it took two years of legal action to force the school district to acknowledge that whatever its teachers' intuitions were, what was supposed to be working didn't work for a significant number of African American children. The case highlighted facts about language variation, race, language attitudes, and school performance which teachers ultimately were not free to ignore. Another effect of the postmodern construct of lore might thus be to undermine the strategic uses to which the objectivist discourses of the social sciences have been put. Since *Brown v. Topeka*, these discourses have been a chief weapon in the fight for educational justice for African American students. The familiar antifoundationalist critique that denies truth as a transcendent category could thus also deny access to the court of last appeal against racism in the quest for civil rights and educational equity. It is interesting to imagine but difficult to see how a postdisciplinary perspective might have carried the day in the Ann Arbor case.

The Ann Arbor case thus reveals possibilities and limitations of lore. We remain skeptical of the unintended effects of the antifoundationalism upon which lore is premised since this seems to rule out "appeals to truth, objectivity, ethics, and identity that social critics have traditionally made" (Schilb, "Cultural" 174). In terms of the issues of race and literacy highlighted by the Ann Arbor case and at play in composition classrooms today, postdisciplinarity and lore remain susceptible to such criticisms. Whereas scholars in other fields draw on postmodern theory to make race a prominent element in their analyses of cultural transactions (Cornel West, Patricia Williams), in many of composition's important discussions of postmodern theory, race is hardly mentioned. This is a striking oversight. What we are most concerned with, however, is to find ways to raise teachers' awareness of their own processes of pedagogical discovery and change, to help teachers recognize what their own habits of reflection make accessible to them, and what these habits of mind may leave out. The construct of lore moves us a long way toward the goal of seeing teachers' own reflective practice as the nexus of pedagogical theory. Our concern is that this construct does not put enough pressure on the question of "what works," thereby pushing teachers to confront the limitations of their practice — especially when for the majority of students everything seems to be running along smoothly, as was the case in Ann Arbor, where most of the students at King School were doing very well. In reference to issues of race which are raised in writing classes when students speak or draw on African American English in their writing, we see a need for teachers to avail themselves of facts which may seem external or peripheral to their experience of the classroom, but which may carry significance for some students. When lore does not confront practitioners with their own language biases, it works against change.

Teacher Efficacy

The third construct of teacher knowledge we wish to consider is teacher efficacy. It differs in one significant way from each of the first two constructs insofar as it draws attention to affect as an essential — perhaps the essential — component in teaching practice. In a field closely allied with composition, teacher educators such as Henry Giroux, Kenneth Zeichner, and Daniel Liston have offered a construct of teacher knowledge generated through reflective practice where teachers examine classroom routines in light of encompassing social and institutional pressures. We argue that the construct of teacher efficacy pushes beyond this enlarged view of reflective practice. By making affect a central issue in theorizing pedagogy, teacher efficacy moves closest to the largely unspoken dimensions of pedagogical experience when, let's say, white teachers in university writing courses attempt to mediate the discourse practices of African American English speaking students.

Opening up these deeply felt but difficult to name dimensions of interaction, teacher efficacy speaks to the cumulative effect of teachers' knowledge and experience on their feelings about their students and their own ability to teach them.

This was what the Ann Arbor case was really about: the psychological barriers to learning that cause some students to dis-identify with school. Teacher efficacy as a construct of teacher knowledge places affect at the center and in so doing opens up and addresses questions of motivation and stance which are prior to and underlie curricular designs or pedagogical technique. When we speak of affect here, we refer to the emotional tone of classroom interactions. With reference to the Ann Arbor case, insofar as language variation is a factor in educational achievement, language as the medium of instruction is what counts. What is most relevant about Ann Arbor was how it drew attention to language as the medium of instruction and the interference generated by teachers' unconscious negative responses to their students' own language.

Defining affect in terms of "teachers' expectations, their empathy, and their own sense of self-efficacy" (370), Susan McLeod reminds us of the research which demonstrates the variable influence (positive or negative) of teacher affect on students' motivations for learning. Teacher efficacy refers to a teacher's beliefs about the power she or he has to produce a positive effect on students. McLeod points out that a teacher's emotional state or disposition forms one source of this sense of self-efficacy. Another source, and the most influential, is "the cultural beliefs that go to make up the macrosystem of American education," beliefs which inform teachers' common sense assumptions including "conceptions of the learner and the teacher and the role of education" (379). McLeod and others have shown that many variables contribute to teacher efficacy, including prior experience in multicultural settings, available resources, and teachers' visions of themselves as agents of social change. Teachers with high personal teaching efficacy believe that all students can be motivated and that it is their responsibility to explore with students the tasks that will hold their attention in the learning process. Valerie Pang and Velma Sablan propose that teacher efficacy is an especially important construct in the context of multicultural classrooms, and that teachers and teacher educators need to seriously examine what they believe about their ability to teach children from various cultural and linguistic backgrounds, particularly African American students. Pang and Sablan note that "when the overwhelming majority of the teaching force in this country is not from under-represented groups, the need to look at teacher misconceptions of African American culture, customs, history, and values is essential" (16).

Until the lawsuit, institutional custom invited the Ann Arbor School District to explain away African American student failure by attributing it to shortcomings in students rather than to shortcomings in the educational system or to the teachers' own lack of "skills or knowledge to help low achievers" (McLeod 380). Subsequent to the inservice program ordered by the Court, the King School teachers reflected low efficacy, that is, little confidence in their ability to adapt pedagogy to the various strengths and needs of speakers of African American English. Applied to the teaching of literacy that goes on in college writing courses, the question becomes, how do teachers become aware of unconscious negative attitudes (or even the dimly felt sense of unease resulting from lack of experience) they may bring with them to the learning environment? And, what steps can teachers take to communicate their sense of efficacy and high expectations to culturally diverse students?

Among the three constructs of teacher knowledge considered here, only that of teacher efficacy, grounded as it is in the consideration of affect in the classroom, makes these questions of felt sense, of emotional response, available for reflection. The Ann Arbor case focused on the language barrier which resulted from teachers' negative attitudes toward African American English. Racism — unconscious and institutional — was the clear subtext in the trial. Arthur Spears describes the problematic relationships among race, language variety, and school achievement. Citing dialect differences in other countries, Spears notes:

> Greater language differences are overcome elsewhere. Why can't they be overcome in American schools? The answer that comes through in a number of studies of the issue is that the real problems are attitudinal and social. All these problems can be related to the general problem of institutional racism . . . low teacher expectations and disrespect for the home language and culture of inner-city pupils. (53–54)

Though rarely acknowledged as such, racism in the sense reflected here still remains an issue in the current teaching of writing, surfacing in the classroom in a variety of often subtle, unconscious manifestations (see Delpit). Neither of the first two constructs of teacher knowledge described offer adequate approaches to this problem; neither offers a vocabulary within which to directly address teachers' affective responses — low expectations, disrespect — which are the chief means through which institutional racism is manifested. Neither the teacher as technician construct nor lore offers direct access to unconscious negative racial stereotypes as a central issue in pedagogical theory. Our conclusion is that while unconscious attitudes are indeed, as Labov points out, partly a problem of (lack of) knowledge per se, they are more urgently a matter of feeling, the affective domain of racialized classroom experience which neither the technician model nor lore explicitly engages.

Implications for Practice

The question remains, however: If our goal is to move urban youth in cities like Cleveland or Detroit into academic discourse communities, what stands in the way of that happening? In working toward building a sense of efficacy we need to give particular attention to staff development and writing programs in which teachers re-envision their capacity to function as catalysts of positive growth and development in students. In part, this improved sense of efficacy stems from an improved teacher knowledge base concerning the linguistic practices of diverse students. This can be accomplished by reviewing the literature diligently developed over the past four decades to provide a more complex, more complete linguistic profile of African American linguistic behavior. Characteristic features, discourse patterns, and rhetorical modes in African American English had been identified in the literature prior to the Ann Arbor case (Abrahams; Labov; Smitherman, *Talkin*). Research published since the conclusion of the case in 1979 has shed more light on distinctive discourse patterns and rhetorical modes. Much of this work has generated new knowledge of organizational patterns in the oral and written expository language of African American English speakers (Ball, "Expository"), the subtle ways that academically successful students strategically use African American English in their writing (Ball, "Cultural"), and on the assessment of writing produced by African American English speakers (Richardson). Research investigating the teaching practices of exemplary African American teachers working in community-based organizations has shown that these teachers build on the language practices of their African American students. They work explicitly to make students metacognitively aware of their oral and written uses of African American English and of alternative ways of expressing their ideas in academic and in technical, workplace English (Ball, Broussard, and Dinkins; Morgan; Ball, "Community").

Becoming informed about cultural discourse patterns and rhetorical modes is a significant resource that successful teachers can build on. Most interesting, however, is the impact of an awareness of cultural differences in discourse patterns on classroom interactions. The presence of varied patterns of discourse in classrooms can impact instruction in positive as well as in negative ways (Foster, "Effective"). Speech behavior is central to a full understanding of how a community expresses its realities, and research on teacher efficacy suggests that effective teachers develop strong human bonds with their students, have high expectations, focus on the total child, and are able to use communication styles familiar to their students. Exemplary African American teachers in community-based organizations are able to draw, to varying degrees, on primarily the rhetorical modes and discourse-level strategies of African American English in shaping interactive discourse as the medium of instruction with their students (Ball, Broussard, Dinkins; Foster "Educating"). Their practice in this regard stands as a model for other teachers to reflect on as they consider expanding their own pedagogical repertoires. We are not advocating that all teachers need to learn and teach Black English. We are arguing that the practices of exemplary African American teachers show us ways of focusing on participation patterns in interactive discourse as the medium of instruction in order to raise the awareness of teachers of the possible links between their own styles of communication and their students' responsiveness in classroom exchanges. Having high expectations and good intentions is not enough; these intentions and expectations need to be evident to students in observable or, we might say, audible behaviors in the classroom.

But as important as this knowledge base may be, it will not in and of itself activate teachers to change their practice. The cognitive internalization of information is not enough to increase teacher efficacy. The Ann Arbor case suggests that the key to effective uses of language diversity in the classroom relates fundamentally to teachers' dispositions toward literacy — that is, depends upon teachers' affective stance toward themselves, their work environment, and especially their culturally diverse students. More current research seems to confirm this. Addressing disposition as the most important variable, we have begun to push beyond internalization of knowledge about African American English in the teacher-education programs we are involved in. In doing so, we have found ourselves observing the ways preservice teachers encounter and contextualize the pedagogical ramifications of language diversity. Our observations suggest that preservice teachers who attempt to address the complex issues relating to this topic may do so by examining personal experiences of crossing borders from one speech community to another. Given these observations, we have begun to consider occasions for knowledge-making that appear in "extra-professional" sites where teachers become aware of their own culturally influenced dispositions toward literacy. We have begun to explore ways of talking that help teachers connect to parts of their experience that conventional academic, theoretical frameworks seem to silence.

Implications for Pedagogical Theory

In 1991 Ann Dyson and Sarah Freedman challenged writing and composition professionals to take significant and positive steps toward building a more powerful theoretical framework for writing research and instruction by expanding our framework to

> include more analytic attention to how the complex of sociocultural experiences enter into literacy learning experiences that have roots in social class, ethnicity, language background, family, neighborhood, and gender. Without serious attention to the unfolding of this wider cultural frame in literacy learning, our vision of the whole remains partially obscured. (4)

This call addresses the ways we construct theory in our field, how we represent the relationships among literacy processes, pedagogy, interactions within the classroom, and cultural expectations which embed our institutions. The first two constructs — teacher as technician and teacher knowledge as lore — share a *curricular* view of the theory-practice relationship. Both of these views are consistent with extent models of pedagogical theory offered in composition studies (Brannon; Fulkerson). Each of the first two constructs we consider here analyzes the decisions teachers make in terms of the propositions of theory: a view of the writing process, the development of writing ability, the goal of writing and teaching, the ways knowledge is constructed. Each locates teacher authority within professional discourse, and assigns teachers a stable, centered, and professional subjectivity which is monologic, perhaps ungendered, and more to our point, unmarked by race. Both constructs are therefore, for teachers and the profession alike, discourses of control.

The third construct, teacher efficacy, reconfigures the representation of pedagogical theory. In particular, instead of seeing writing pedagogy as determined by a general theory of writing (in whatever versions this general theory might appear), the alternative we propose would place the teacher, the student, and the site of literacy instruction at the center, each exerting its influence on the others, each influencing an orientation toward the activity of the course, each in relationships with the others which are at best dialogical and, as some scholars have pointed out, often contradictory and conflictual (Lu). The construct of teacher efficacy does not subordinate pedagogy to a teacher's "substantive" knowledge, nor does it place teacher knowledge in dialogue with its situation, as the postdisciplinary view would have it. The construct of efficacy locates pedagogical theory in relation to three intersecting points of view: the institutional context of the writing course, the teacher's sense of herself as an actor within that institutional site, and the dialogizing, ambivalent, often resistant perspectives of students. The virtue of this model of pedagogical theory in composition is that by drawing attention to the "complex sociocultural experiences of literacy learning" Dyson and Freedman refer to, it sharpens the kinds of questions practitioners may ask about what works in and what works on the activity sponsored by the writing classroom.

Changing Dispositions

Disposition has two meanings which offer complementary views of the challenges surrounding literacy education in multicultural classrooms. The first meaning is "one's customary manner or emotional response; temperament." In its response to Oakland's Ebonics resolution, the American public's customary manner of emotional response toward African American English became front-page public news. The second meaning of disposition is "the power to control, direct, or dispose." These two meanings of disposition frame the interrelated issues surrounding the Ebonics controversy and the Ann Arbor "Black English" case, and the significance each holds for the field of composition. On the one hand, the Ann Arbor case came to focus on the language barrier which results from teachers' unconscious, negative attitudes toward African American English. On the other, ill-disposed toward their students' use of African American English, the Ann Arbor teachers expected less and their students not surprisingly lived down to these lowered expectations, evidence of the power of self-fulfilling prophecy.

More than twenty years ago, in response to the Ann Arbor case, the Black Caucus of NCTE and CCCC disseminated a carefully prepared "Commentary" regarding African American English. Recently reprinted in response to the Ebonics initiative, the purpose of the "Commentary" was to express the viewpoints of Black linguists and language arts educators on the topic. Briefly summarized, the "Commentary" asserts that the Black language system in and of itself is not a barrier to learning. The barrier is negative attitudes toward that language system, compounded by lack of information about the language system and inefficient techniques for teaching language skills, all of which is manifested in an unwillingness to adapt teaching styles to students' needs. Such barriers, in fact, reflect teachers', and the public's, dispositions toward literacy. In light of the public outcry over Ebonics, we ask: Have those dispositions changed today? The "Commentary" of the Black Caucus went on to say that the language of Black students is actually a strength on which teachers might draw in order to develop effective approaches to teaching. They concluded the statement with a call for thorough, unbiased research on the topic. However, based on the tone of the criticisms and emotional responses to the Ebonics issue, it became evident that society in general does not take such a detailed or objective view on the matter of the representations of diverse languages in the classroom.

After looking closely at the Ann Arbor case, it seems clear that for writing teachers today, many of the same barriers exist in the classroom that stood between the teachers at King School and their students. Because of cultural differences in patterns of language use, and because of differences in styles of interaction used to demonstrate knowledge, many students from diverse social and linguistic backgrounds are entering urban classrooms where teachers still have a difficult time recognizing and fully utilizing the wealth of language resources students use effectively outside school. These are resources that often go unrecognized and unrewarded within classroom settings. In spite of the considerable professional rhetoric over the past twenty years or so, recent research indicates that African Americans and other students of color are still faring very poorly in our nation's urban schools (Quality Education for Minorities Project). In light of the history of failure and miscommunication that marks the educational experiences of many African American English speakers, educators must continue to insist on seeking ways that the barriers created by diversity in language as the medium of instruction can become, instead, bridges between home language practices and academic registers teachers want students to learn. Making a significant place for affect within pedagogical theories is an important step toward this goal.

Acknowledgments

We would like to thank Ralph Stevens, Margaret Marshall, and Thomas Fox for their careful reading and suggestions on this article.

Works Cited

Abrahams, Roger. *Deep Down in the Jungle*. Chicago: Aldine, 1970.
Balester, Valerie. *Cultural Divide*. Portsmouth: Boynton, 1993.
Ball, Arnetha. "Community-Based Learning in Urban Settings as a Model for Educational Reform." *Applied Behavioral Science Review* 3 (1995): 127–46.
———. "Cultural Preference and the Expository Writing of African-American Adolescents." *Written Communication* 9 (1992): 501–32.
———. "Expository Writing Patterns of African-American Students." *English Journal* 85 (1996): 27–36.
Ball, Arnetha F., Kimberley C. Broussard, and Delvin M. Dinkins. "Investigating Interactive Discourse Patterns of African American Females in Community-Based Organizations." American Educational Research Association. New Orleans, 1994.
Bowie, R., and C. Bond. "Influencing Future Teachers' Attitudes toward Black English: Are We Making a Difference?" *Journal of Teacher Education* 45 (1994): 112–18.
Brannon, Lil. "Toward a Theory of Composition." *Perspectives on Research and Scholarship in Composition*. Ed. Ben McLelland and Timothy R. Donovan. New York: MLA, 1985. 6–25.
"Commentary." *Black Caucus Notes*. Urbana: NCTE. March, 1997.
Delpit, Lisa. "Education in a Multicultural Society: Our Future's Greatest Challenge." *Journal of Negro Education* 61 (1992): 237–49.
Dyson, A. H., and S. W. Freedman. *Critical Challenges for Research on Writing and Literacy: 1990–1995*. Technical Report No. 1–B. Berkeley, CA: Center for the Study of Writing, 1991.
Foster, Michelle. "Educating for Competence in Community and Culture: Exploring the Views of Exemplary African-American Teachers." *Urban Education* 27 (1993): 370–94.
———. "Effective Black Teachers: A Literature Review." *Teaching Diverse Populations Formulating a Knowledge Base*. Ed. Etta Hollins, Joyce King, and W. Hayman. Albany: State U of New York P, 1994. 225–42.
Fulkerson, Richard. "Composition Theory in the Eighties: Axiological Consensus and Paradigmatic Diversity." *CCC* 41 (1990): 409–29.
Gilyard, Keith. *Voices of the Self*. Detroit: Wayne State UP, 1992.
Giroux, Henry. *Teachers as Intellectuals toward a Critical Pedagogy of Learning*. New York: Bergin, 1988.
Harkin, Patricia. "The Postdisciplinary Politics of Lore." *Contending with Words*. Ed. Patricia Harkin and John Schilb. New York: MLA, 1991. 124–38.
Howard, Harry, Lee H. Hansen, and Thomas Pietras. *Final Evaluation: King Elementary School Vernacular Black English Inservice Program*. Ann Arbor: Ann Arbor Public Schools, 1980.
Knoblauch, C. H. "Rhetorical Constructions: Dialogue and Commitment." *College English* 50 (1988): 125–40.
Labov, William. "Recognizing Black English in the Classroom." *Black English Educational Equity and the Law*. Ed. John W. Chambers. Ann Arbor: Karoma, 1983. 29–55.

Lu, Min-zhan. "Conflict and Struggle: The Enemies or Preconditions of Basic Writing?" *College English* 54 (1992): 887–913.

McLeod, Susan H. "Pygmalion or Golem? Teacher Affect and Efficacy." *CCC* 46 (1995): 369–86.

Memorandum Opinion and Order. Martin Luther King Elementary School Children v. Ann Arbor School District Board. Civil Action No. 7–71861. 473 F. Supp. 1371 (1979).

Morgan, Marcyliena. "Indirectness and Interpretation in African American Women's Discourse." *Pragmatics* 1 (1991): 421–51.

North, Stephen. *The Making of Knowledge in Composition.* Portsmouth: Boynton, 1987.

Pang, Valerie O., and Velma Sablan. "Teacher Efficacy: Do Teachers Believe They Can Be Effective with African American Students?" San Francisco: American Educational Research Association, 1995.

Phelps, Louise Wetherbee. "Practical Wisdom and the Geography of Knowledge in Composition." *College English* 47 (1992): 338–56.

Quality Education for Minorities Project. *Education That Works: An Action Plan for the Education of Minorities.* Cambridge: MIT P, 1990.

Richardson, Elaine. *Where Did That Come From? Black Talk for Black Student Talking Texts.* MA Thesis. Cleveland State U, 1993.

Schilb, John. *Between the Lines Relating Composition Theory and Literary Theory.* Portsmouth: Boynton, 1996.

———. "Cultural Studies, Postmodernism, and Composition." *Contending with Words.* Ed. Patricia Harkin and John Schilb. New York: MLA, 1991. 173–88.

Shaughnessy, Mina. *Errors and Expectations.* New York: Oxford UP, 1977.

Smitherman, Geneva. *Talkin and Testifyin.* Detroit: Wayne State UP, 1977.

———. "'What Go Round Come Round': *King* in Perspective." *Harvard Educational Review* 51 (1981): 40–56.

Spears, A. K., "Are Black and White Vernaculars Diverging?" *American Speech* 62 (1987): 48–55, 71–72.

West, Cornel. *Race Matters.* Boston: Beacon, 1993.

Williams, Patricia J. *The Alchemy of Race and Rights.* Cambridge, MA: Harvard UP, 1991.

Zeichner, Kenneth M. "Alternative Paradigms in Teacher Education." *Journal of Teacher Education* 34 (1983): 3–9.

Zeichner, Kenneth, and Daniel Liston. "Teaching Student Teachers to Reflect." *Harvard Educational Review* 57 (1987): 23–48.

Zemelman, Steven, and Harvey Daniels. *A Community of Writers.* Portsmouth: Boynton, 1988.

Ball and Lardner's Insights as a Resource for Your Teaching

1. Reflect on instances in which assumptions you have held or encountered have unconsciously affected your teaching. On what model are your expectations of student behavior and response based? How might your expectations or standards be culturally informed? Question your current practices to see whether your teaching values one pattern of cultural discourse over another. If

so, what modifications will you need to make to adapt your teaching to various discourse styles?

2. Identify the particular features that distinguish what Ball and Lardner might call the affective atmosphere toward diversity at the institution where you teach. How might these impact the ways you address issues of race, diversity, and diverse literacy backgrounds with your class?

3. Consider Ball and Lardner's sense of the ways in which teachers construct knowledge. Which most closely fits your own? Which most closely fits the expectations of your students? Which, in your experience, is the most important knowledge to cultivate?

Ball and Lardner's Insights as a Resource for Your Writing Classroom

1. Ask students what associations come to mind from the phrase "mainstream American culture," and record examples on the board. How and why have they selected these examples? Challenge them to question their perceptions of "mainstream." On what have they based their ideas? Are their notions culturally founded? Do these notions exclude any societal groups?

2. Can students identify examples of institutional racism? What are the implications of this awareness for schools? For other institutions?

3. Outline for your students the three different types of teacher knowledge that Ball and Lardner discuss, and ask them how they feel about these types of knowledge. Can they identify past experiences with these and recognize how the principles governing each may have influenced their learning?

The Costs of Caring: "Femininism" and Contingent Women Workers in Composition Studies

Eileen E. Schell

In this selection, Eileen Schell elaborates on a feminist discourse about teaching that is rooted in an explicitly "feminine" system of caring and nurturing rather than judging and criticizing, in connectedness and empathy rather than abstractions and edicts. This maternalistic mode, however, often conflicts with the desires of women to be taken seriously as teachers and intellectuals. Moreover, it directly corroborates the gender inequities that push women toward lower-paying and less secure jobs than their male colleagues. Women have less time to devote to scholarly activity and reflective inquiry into their practice. As a result, the body of knowledge generated about writing instruction is a distinctly masculine one.

Lorie Goodman Batson contends that when we speak of women in composition studies — their varying interests, desires, motivations, and political affiliations —we often appeal to a common female identity that levels differences and creates alliances where there may be divergences (207–08). As identity categories become increasingly fragmented and contested in postmodern thought, it is important for feminists in composition "to begin challenging the privileging of singular political identities" (Wicke and Ferguson 7). Poststructuralist and postmodern critiques of identity politics necessitate that we reexamine previously unchallenged assumptions about women students and women teachers.

In particular, the argument that feminists in composition should favor what Elizabeth Flynn refers to as "femininist" principles or the "recuperation of those modes of thinking within the field that are compatible with a feminine epistemology" ("Studies" 143) needs to be reexamined. According to Flynn, a feminine epistemology is an approach to language study "characterized by modalities of relatedness and mutuality, indistinct boundaries, flexibility, and non-oppositional styles" (147). In this essay, I examine the limits of femininist thought; I critique arguments that advocate a feminist pedagogy based on an "ethic of care," which is a set of principles that Nel Noddings refers to as a reliance on an ethical subject's "feelings, needs, situational conditions," as a "personal ideal rather than universal ethical principles and their application" (96). It is my contention that femininist pedagogy, although compelling, may reinforce rather than critique or transform patriarchal structures by reinscribing what Magda Lewis calls the "woman as caretaker ideology," the "psychological investment women are required to make in the emotional well-being of men [and others] — an investment that goes well beyond the classroom into the private spaces of women's lives" (174). While I do not wish to discredit femininist pedagogy, I do wish to question the ways that an ethic of care may prevent feminists from addressing one of the most serious gender problems we face in composition studies: the relegating of women to contingent (part-time and non-tenure-track) writing instructorships.

"Femininism" in Composition Studies

Beginning in the latter half of the 1980s, feminists in composition have created a discourse on pedagogy that perpetuates feminine values and principles (Caywood and Overing; Phelps and Emig; Flynn,

"Composing" and "Studies"; Frey, "Equity"; Rubin). In 1987, Cynthia Caywood and Gillian Overing coedited the anthology *Teaching Writing: Pedagogy, Gender, and Equity,* the first book-length work on feminist writing pedagogy. Drawing on the work of feminists Nancy Chodorow, Carol Gilligan, and Sara Ruddick, several volume contributors (Daumer and Runzo; Frey; Goulston; Stanger) advocate a pedagogical approach rooted in Nodding's ethic of care: a process of ethical decision making based on interrelationships and connectedness rather than on universalized and individualized rules and rights.[1] Weaving together strands of liberal and cultural feminisms, the editors contend that feminist pedagogy revalues the experience of women students and encourages individual voice and personal growth in the writing classroom (Caywood and Overing xi). In "Transforming the Composition Classroom," Elisabeth Daumer and Sandra Runzo urge feminist teachers to help their students "unearth" their authentic voices by encouraging them to "search out untraditional sources, often the forms of writing which have not been granted the status of literature because they are either personal (journals, letters, diaries) or community-based (Blues, spirituals, work songs)" (56). In this formulation, female students' subjectivities are represented as buried treasure, which must be brought to light with the assistance of the feminist teacher. Thus the theory of subjectivity in *Teaching Writing* is grounded in Enlightenment notions of the self-governing, autonomous individual.

Cultural feminism, as represented in *Teaching Writing,* entails a radical transformation of pedagogical relationships. "Cultural feminism," writes Linda Alcoff, "is the ideology of a female nature or female essence reappropriated by feminists themselves in an effort to revalidate undervalued female attributes" ("Feminism" 408). Following nineteenth-century ideals of femininity, cultural feminists argue that feminine values have been denigrated and superseded by masculine values such as aggressiveness, confrontation, control, competition, domination, and physical violence. To reverse the perpetuation of harmful masculine values, cultural feminists contend that all people — men and women alike — should emulate feminine values: nurturance, supportiveness, interdependence, and nondominance. In addition, cultural feminists deemphasize a model of communication based on argumentation and endorse a rhetoric of mediation, conciliation, and shared authority. Alcoff warns that, although many women have developed invaluable skills and abilities in response to patriarchal restrictions, feminists should be wary of advocating "the restrictive conditions that give rise to those attributes: forced parenting, lack of physical autonomy, dependency for survival on mediation skills" (414). Furthermore, Devoney Looser cautions that theories of gender identity that presume "a stable and/or recoverable homogenized" female subject "present costs that feminist compositionists may not be ready to pay" (55).

The happy marriage between cultural feminism and expressivist composition studies, however, is evident in many of the essays in *Teaching Writing.* As Wendy Goulston indicates, process theories of composing rely on qualities associated with a "female style" (25). In fact, Caywood and Overing locate their volume at the "recurrent intersection" between feminist theory and expressivist writing theory: the privileging of process over product; the encouragement of inner voice, exploratory or discovery writing; collaboration; and the decentering of teacherly authority (xii–xiii). Caywood and Overing find that "the process model, insofar as it facilitates and legitimizes the fullest expression of individual voice, is compatible with the feminist revisioning of hierarchy, if not essential to it" (xiv).

Unlike expressivist pedagogy, femininist pedagogy consciously embraces "maternal thinking," a term borrowed from Sara Ruddick's landmark essay "Maternal Thinking" (Daumer and Runzo 54). According to Ruddick, feminists should strive to bring the patterns of thinking characteristic of the social practices and intellectual capacities of the mother "in[to] the public realm, to make the preservation and growth of all children a work of public conscience and legislation" (361). In Ruddick's theory of ethics, maternal thinking is governed by three interests: preserving the life of the child, fostering the child's growth, and shaping an acceptable child (348–57). To accomplish these maternal interests, the mother must exercise a capacity for "attentive love," the supportive love and caring that allows a child to persevere and grow (357–58). Applied broadly to human relations, maternal thinking offers a radical alternative to a theory of ethics based on a concept of individual rights (see Perry).

Applied broadly to the feminist writing classroom, maternal thinking encourages writing teachers to create a supportive, nonhierarchical environment responsive to students' individual needs and cultural contexts (Daumer and Runzo 50). The maternal writing teacher "empowers and liberates students" by serving as a facilitator, a midwife to students' ideas; she individualizes her teaching by fostering "self-sponsored writing"; she decenters her authority by encouraging collaborative learning among peers (49). In "The Sexual Politics of the One-to-One Tutorial Approach," Carol Stanger borrows Gilligan's theory of women's moral development to argue for a model of collaborative learning that encourages students to build knowledge through consensus, not competition (41). In "Equity and Peace in the New Writing Classroom," Olivia Frey, like Stanger, endorses a "peaceful classroom" based on "understanding and cooperation," not on competition and aggression: "Group work and peer inquiry . . . discourage harmful confrontation since through cooperative learning students discover how to resolve conflict creatively and effectively" (100). Both Stanger and Frey eschew hierarchical forms of discourse in favor of discourses grounded in mediation and negotiation.

Overall, contributors to *Teaching Writing* suggest that a classroom based on an ethic of care can counteract patriarchal pedagogy's "emphasis on hierarchy, competition, and control" (Gore 70). They also appear to agree with the premise that feminists are better equipped to achieve a nonhierarchical and noncompetitive classroom because they possess the nurturing, maternal qualities to facilitate such a change (70). Yet will the maternal stance work for all women teachers and students, including those who are white and working-class, African American, Latina, or Asian? Caywood and Overing admit that their volume "may not meet some of the particular needs of minority students" (xv), implying that maternal teaching is best suited for white middle-class women. Although the volume omits the important perspectives of minority women and teachers, it nevertheless has served as the starting point for conversation about feminist pedagogy in composition studies (xv) and an inspiration for further feminist pedagogical models based on an ethic of care.

But what are the ethical, emotional, and material costs of a pedagogy based on an ethic of care? If teaching writing is considered women's work — underpaid and underrecognized — how might feminist pedagogy make it difficult for feminists in composition to address gender inequities in academic work, particularly the preponderance of women in part-time and non-tenure-track positions?

The Hidden Costs of an Ethic of Care

Ethnographic studies and surveys of feminist classrooms demonstrate that students, both male and female, expect their women teachers to act as nurturing mother figures (Friedman, "Authority" 205). There is often conflict between that expectation and the teacher's need to be taken seriously as a teacher and intellectual (205). Research on gender bias in student rating of women teachers, conducted by Diane Kierstead, Patti D'Agostino, and Heidi Dill, reveals that

> if female instructors want to obtain high student ratings, they must be not only highly competent with regard to factors directly related to teaching but also careful to act in accordance with traditional sex-role expectations. In particular . . . male and female instructors will earn equal student ratings for equal professional work only if the women also display stereotypically feminine behavior. (Kierstead et al. qtd. in Koblitz)

If a feminist teacher adopts a maternal stance, she may better conform to her students' expectations. But what if her pedagogy favors critical challenge and intellectual rigor, not overt encouragement and nurturance (Friedman, "Authority" 207)? Neal Koblitz reports that if women teachers give challenging assignments and exams and follow rigorous grading policies, students are more inclined to give them lower ratings. A study of teaching evaluations at the University of Dayton indicates that "college students of both sexes judged female authority figures who engaged in punitive behavior more harshly than they judged punitive males" (Elaine Martin qtd. in Koblitz).

The research that Koblitz cites shows that for women teachers caring is not merely a natural instinct or impulse, it is a socially and historically mandated behavior. "Caring," writes the feminist philosopher Joan C. Tronto, "may be a reflection of a survival mechanism for women or others who are dealing with oppressive conditions, rather than a quality of intrinsic value on its own" ("Women" 184). Women who do not occupy positions of power often adopt a posture of attentiveness or caring accompanied by "deferential mannerisms (e.g., differences in speech, smiling, other forms of body language, etc.)" as a way to appease and anticipate the needs of those in power (184).[2] Rather than view caring as solely a natural act, we can productively view it as a form of "emotional labor," a category that the feminist philosopher Sandra Bartky defines as the "emotional sustenance that women supply to others." It is the labor of "feeding egos" and "tending wounds": "The aim of this supporting and sustaining is to produce or to maintain in the one supported and sustained a conviction of the value and importance of his own chosen projects, hence of the value and importance of his own person" (102). Bartky characterizes emotional labor as a continuum occupied on the one end by commercial caregivers, who perform "perfunctory and routinized [caregiving] relationships," and on the other end by "sincere caregivers," who direct "wholehearted acceptance" and emotional support toward the objects of their caregiving (116).

Not surprisingly, academic women often feel compelled to direct their energy into caring labor: teaching, advising students, and performing lower-level administrative duties. As one tenured woman faculty member observes in Angela Simeone's study of academic women:

> I think the great trap of young women today is that there is a sort of subtle pressure to be compliant, to not assert themselves intellectually, to spend . . . more time with students than the men do, to be motherly and nurturing, to be on a million committees, not to be a power within the university but to just do the drudgery that has to be done, to be compliant in every way. And then they don't get tenure and they fail. They don't say no to these demands, and these demands are demands that are much more put on women. (36)

Many administrators and full-time faculty members believe that women make ideal candidates for teaching writing because the same qualities necessary for motherhood — patience, enthusiasm, and the ability to juggle multiple tasks — are qualities that effective writing teachers possess (Holbrook 207). The belief that women's essential nature is to marry and mother is reinforced consciously and unconsciously throughout the institutions of hegemonic culture: the schools, government, religion, and family life. These institutions — or ideological state apparatuses, to use Louis Althusser's term — structure the social relations that interpellate human subjects (81). Through sexual-role socialization in the family, schools, and churches, women learn to channel their energies into nurturing forms of labor: teaching, nursing, social work, and mothering.

This sexual division of labor charts a predetermined pattern for many women's lives, what Nadya Aisenberg and Mona Harrington call the "marriage plot": "The central tenet of the plot, of course, is that a proper goal is marriage, or, more generally, the woman's sphere is private and domestic. Her proper role within the sphere is to provide support for the male at the head of the household of which she forms a part" (6). The marriage plot carries over into the public sphere, where a woman's proper role "is still to be supportive — either to an employer . . . or in some cases to a cause" (6). The marriage plot requires that women's roles, even in academic work, be supportive and nurturing. Women should be satisfied and fulfilled by low-paying, low-status teaching jobs.

The marriage plot is particularly pervasive in composition studies, where a large group of contingent women workers "nurture" beginning writers for salaries that rival those of underpaid waitresses. Sue Ellen Holbrook's history "Women's Work: The Feminizing of Composition Studies" and Susan Miller's "The Feminization of Composition" and *Textual Carnivals* call attention to the prevalence of this caretaker ideology. Miller's metaphorical analysis of the hierarchical, gendered constructions of teaching illuminates how institutional scripts cast women teachers as nurturers (*Carnivals* 137), thus making it problematic for feminists to continue advocating nurturant behavior as a form of empowerment.

According to Judith Gappa and David Leslie, women make up only 27 percent of all full-time, tenure-track faculty members in American colleges and universities, yet they make up 67 percent of all part-time faculty members. In the humanities, 67 percent of part-time positions are filled by women, whereas 33 percent of full-time positions are filled by women (25; see also Burns 21). Bettina Huber reports that of a cohort of 1,674 women who received Ph.D.s in English between 1981 and 1986, 56 percent found tenure-track appointments by 1987, whereas of a cohort of 1,475 men, 77.8 percent did (62). Some women choose to teach part-time because it affords them the flexibility to raise a family or care for aging parents, to pursue a writing or artistic career, or to run a home business. Others are less than happy with their contingent status. Some women turn down full-time employment to avoid relocating a family or a partner already holding a full-time job. Others seek part-time work (often several part-time jobs pieced together) because they cannot find full-time work in an overcrowded job market.

Although conditions of employment vary, universities and colleges often hire contingent writing faculty members on a semester-to-semester basis through "informal interviewing and appointment procedures" and without the benefit of contractual job security (Wallace 11). Many administrators hire contingent faculty members a few weeks or even days before the semester begins, as soon as enrollment numbers materialize for first-year composition. When part-time faculty members are hired, their "research, creativity," or previous academic employment is often not valued (11). Once hired, these teachers may receive little or no training or work orientation. And the criteria for assessing their teaching are often ill-defined (13).

Keeping in mind these grim facts about the gendered nature of contingent writing instruction, we need to assess how theories of femininist pedagogy based on an ethic of care may reinforce the labor patterns that feminists critique. Socialist feminist analyses of women's work in nurturant occupations may help in that assessment.

Socialist Feminism and Sex-Affective Production

Like cultural feminists and liberal feminists, socialist feminists examine how patriarchal socioeconomic relations subordinate women's interests to the interests of men. Unlike cultural and liberal feminists, however, socialist feminists (Michele Barrett, Sandra Lee Bartky, Zillah Eisenstein, Ann Ferguson, Heidi Hartmann, Alison Jaggar) argue that sex, class, and racial oppression maintain the gendered division of labor. Moreover, socialist feminists critically examine women's labor, analyzing the costs and benefits of the ideology of nurturance. The socialist feminist philosopher Ann Ferguson has argued that contemporary American women, despite differences of race, class, and sexual orientation, have in common "a sex/class connection organized by the sexual division of unpaid labor in the family household as well as wage labor, the gender bias of the patriarchal state, the mass media and the public/private split of family household and economy" (8). Although Ferguson seemingly essentializes women's labor, she emphasizes that class identity highlights differences among women, since individual women belong to overlapping classes that are often in conflict with one another: family class, sex class (organized around the gendered division of labor), race class, and economic class (119). Within these different class positions, women are expected to engage in forms of labor that involve the function of caring or sex-affective production, "that human physical and social interaction which is common to human sexuality, parenting, kin and family relations, nurturance and social bonding" (7–8).

Sex-affective production is characterized by "unequal exchange," in which women often receive "less of the goods produced than men" although they work harder and spend more time producing those goods: "The relations between men and women can be considered exploitative because the men are able to appropriate more of women's labor time for their own uses and also receive more of the goods produced" (132). Since sex-affective modes of production are largely unpaid, underpaid, and underrecognized forms of labor — such as mothering, nursing, and teaching — they are essential to the successful functioning of a late-capitalist economy. Moreover, women's involvement in nurturant labor is made to seem natural by discourses on gender and work claiming that women choose "inferior work status" (Bergmann, "Feminism" 23). The feminist economist Barbara Bergmann explains:

> If a person doing the [career] choosing is female, the person's choices are seen as powerfully conditioned by her "home responsibilities." This line of thinking leads to the view of women's inferior position in paid work as a benign and necessary adaptation to biological and social realities, and in no way due to biased and malign behavior on the part of employers. (23)

Maria Markus describes a "second tier" of work for women in the "less attractive, less creative, and usually less well-paid branches" of the professions. Women who end up in the second tier tend to be "'accused' of not 'planning their careers,' of not 'keeping their eyes open to the next step' but instead of burying themselves in the current tasks and awaiting 'natural justice' to reward them for working hard." Furthermore, women's lesser "agility" in professional careers includes their "lower mobility" as a result of family attachments and women's tendency to focus on human relations (105, 106).

In English studies, a second tier of work exists for women in the form of contingent writing instructorships, and such positions epitomize the paradox of sex-affective production. On the one hand, emotional rewards — a "psychic income"[3] — keep women invested in teaching; on the other hand, many contingent women writing instructors recount experiences of exploitation and express feelings of alienation. This paradox supports Bartky's claim that women may be epistemically and ethically disempowered by providing nurturance for others while they receive little compensation — emotional and material — in return (117). Women's so-called innate, instinctual desire to nurture and care for others brings them a psychic income — personal fulfillment and satisfaction — yet that psychic income is "the blood at the root" (A. Ferguson) of women's exploitation as underpaid workers.

To understand the costs as well as benefits of an ethic of care in feminist writing pedagogy, I conducted primary research on contingent women writing instructors' attitudes toward their work, exploring the contradictory forces that surround their involvement in writing instruction. My research reveals that a pedagogy based on an ethic of care is simultaneously empowering and disempowering: it offers psychic rewards while exacting a distinct emotional and material price from women workers.

Contingent Labor as Sex-Affective Production

In the fall of 1992 and spring of 1993, I interviewed a dozen lecturers (both full- and part-time) who held semester-to-semester teaching contracts in the first-year writing program at the University of Wisconsin, Milwaukee, where I worked as a teaching assistant and assistant writing program coordinator. The interviewees were white women ranging in ages from twenty-five to fifty-five; most had master's degrees in literature or education, and some had completed credits toward the doctoral degree. The women of ages twenty-five to thirty-five had five to seven years of teaching experience in community colleges or state universities; the women of ages thirty-five to fifty-five had taught for ten to fifteen years in community colleges, state universities, or public and private elementary and secondary schools. I conducted the interviews in an open-ended manner, allowing the responses to determine the order of the questions. Each interview lasted approximately ninety minutes and was taped and partially transcribed. To allow these women to speak candidly and without fear of institutional reprisal, I have omitted their identities. (I also surveyed essays and articles on women's experiences as part-time and non-tenure-track faculty members to broaden the perspective of my interview project. And as a former part-time faculty member, I drew on my own experiences.)

In the interviews, I investigated how contingent women faculty members describe the costs and benefits of their work, and I paid particular attention to their "workplace emotions," a term used by Carol Stearns and Peter Stearns, who research "emotionology," the history and sociology of the emotions (7–8). Stearns and Stearns define emotions as socially constructed, historically specific responses rather than as transhistorical and transcultural essences. In a separate essay, Peter Stearns describes how nineteenth-century industrialization brought technological displacement, inflation, management impersonality, white-middle-class downward mobility, and the increasing isolation of unskilled workers (149–50). In the early twentieth-century office, management began to suppress anger and impose a standard of surface friendliness, particularly among white-collar workers and those who worked "in a variety of service industries including the airlines and branches of social work" (156). Because of societal expectations and management policies that mandate friendliness and nurturant behavior, workers in caring professions increasingly experience emotions like anger, cynicism, and frustration in response to a loss of autonomy, increased work hierarchies, management domination and surveillance, job instability, lack of promotion, and specific forms of workplace discrimination.[4]

In my interviews with part-time women writing instructors, the concept of workplace emotion helped illuminate a split between the instructors' feelings about their classrooms and their feelings about the institutions that employed them. Both the interviewees and the writers of published narratives revealed that while they liked, even loved, to teach, they nearly all had negative feelings about their working conditions and their relation to the institution at large. In the classroom, they felt in control, valued, and alive; in the institution, they often felt invisible and alienated.

The separation between institutional space and classroom space mirrors the attitude that teaching is a private or individual activity and research a public activity. In an account of her experiences as a part-time writing instructor at the State University of New York, Stony Brook, Clare Frost characterizes this public-private split: "I may be a misfit in the academy but not in my classroom. For me it's not a job, it's a calling. The pain of being an adjunct is not inflicted in the classroom, but in the hallowed halls of academe. My struggle to be seen and heard in this discipline is also a struggle to have faith in myself and what I'm doing" (66).

In both the published narratives and the interviews I conducted, women writing instructors reported passionate feelings about teaching and described a sense of connection and satisfaction; they identified their teaching roles as supportive, nurturing, and facilitative. One interviewee characterized herself as a midwife: "I think they've got little baby writers in them that are going to be born. I'm helping the student who has had x number of bad encounters with writing give birth to that infant writer inside." Many of the interviewees remarked that they continue to endure exploitative working conditions because they enjoy teaching. Frost writes:

> I love the teaching of composition. I enjoy seeing my students use writing to tap into themselves, some for the first time in their lives. I glow when some of their final evaluations say that the course was better than they expected it or that their attitudes about writing have improved. For me, getting to know a new group of young people each semester and seeing what they can accomplish in a few short months is exhilarating. I don't find their writing boring, because I don't find them boring. (66)

One woman, in her late forties and with over ten years of teaching experience, argued that the students, not the institutional setting, offered her psychic rewards: "The students give a lot back to me. The institution doesn't give me much. I get a paycheck, I get an office, I get a nine-year-old computer. I don't get much support from the institution." The attachment to teaching is bittersweet because many contingent teachers are isolated from professional networks. Nancy Grimm, a formerly part-time writing teacher at Michigan Technological University, describes the unstable nature of part-time labor:

> For seven years I have taught part-time. I give conference presentations. I publish a little. I even direct the local site of the National Writing Project — one of the department's few graduate level offerings. But at this university I will never be full-time, and I will never be hired for more than a year at a time. My part-time teaching load fluctuates each year. More than once, I have made less money than I made the year before. My teaching load — and consequently my salary — depends on how many gaps the department has to fill. I am going nowhere, but to work effectively I can't let myself confront the issue too often. (14)

The key issue for contingent women faculty members who wish to participate in research and scholarship is "work time" — the way in which students and teachers circulate in the organizational structure of English (Watkins 4–6). In composition studies, the work time of intellectuals (specialists, practitioners) is directly affected by the research-teaching division, a split predicated on the difference between the creation of knowledge and the perpetuation of already existing knowledge or know-how. Teachers perpetuate what Antonio Gramsci has characterized as the "pre-existing traditional, accumulated intellectual wealth," whereas scholars create new forms of knowledge (307). Scholars, Evan Watkins writes, are classified as professionals "understood to work at the very frontiers of knowledge, at the edge of a 'heart of darkness' where expertise . . . [is] tested in the most demanding situations" (104).

Teaching writing, of course, resides on the low end of the research-teaching binary. Not only is writing instruction devalued, but it also requires substantial time and emotional energy from the teacher. The CCCC "Statement on Principles and Standards for the Postsecondary Teaching of Writing" acknowledges that writing instruction is labor-intensive:

> The improvement of an individual student's writing requires persistent and frequent contact between teacher and student both inside and outside the classroom. It requires assigning far more papers than are usually assigned in other college classrooms; it requires reading them and commenting on them not simply to justify a grade, but to offer guidance and suggestions for improvement; and it requires spending a great deal of time with individual students, helping them not just to improve particular papers but to understand fundamental principles of effective writing that will enable them to continue learning throughout their lives. (335)

The labor-intensive nature of writing instruction makes it difficult for contingent faculty members in composition to take part in scholarly conversations. Mary Kupiec Cayton argues, "The material conditions of participating in the conversation that is academic scholarship include the ability to devote oneself to it wholeheartedly — at least at certain points in time." Borrowing Kenneth Burke's metaphor that scholarship resembles a parlor conversation, Cayton likens contingent faculty members to parlor maids who are busy "attending to the necessary chores that will free the guests for conversing." Because their teaching responsibilities — and often family responsibilities — remove them from the parlor conversation that is academic scholarship, contingent women faculty members often "play a supporting role rather than the role of the participant," and as a result they hear and understand less "of what is transpiring inside the parlor" (655). Frost attests to the difficult choices they must make regarding their work time:

> After family responsibilities and more than thirty hours a week spent directly on the teaching of three sections of composition, I have to think carefully and pragmatically about how I'm going to spend the precious remaining time. . . . For the sad truth is that even if I become more knowledgeable — read theorists, attend conferences, present papers, take additional courses — I will receive no additional institutional

recognition of any sort. I will not receive a penny more in remuneration for the courses I currently teach, nor will I become eligible for a full-time position or additional employee benefits. In fact, no practical or professional benefit will result. (63–64)

One of the interviewees, an experienced instructor with a background in ESL and teaching experience at several institutions, commented that, while she felt the writing program administrator and his assistant valued and respected her work as a teacher, she was invisible to the rest of the university: "As far as the rest of the school goes, I don't even think they know who I am. I'm just someone filling a hole, and they don't know about my experiences, they don't know about my ideas, I know they don't know who I am, they don't care who I am, they just want someone in there teaching classes."

She referred to herself as an interchangeable part, "not even a person — just a cog" in the university machine. Another interviewee described the university as a machine that consumes human labor: "A friend of mine once said the institution wants to chew you up and when they're done with you, they'll spit you out." She commented on her expendability: "You know there will be five more people standing in line to do what I do, and they'll love doing what they're doing just like I love doing what I'm doing."

For those interviewees who had been working for many years as contingent writing instructors, the overwhelming response to their professional situation was a growing and hardening cynicism. One woman stated that she had learned not to expect any rewards or recognition from the university: "I think I'm just very hard-nosed and resigned. I just say 'I like my job, I'm good at my job,' but I don't have any expectations. I don't expect any recognition. I'm just jaded and sort of hardened to anything like that." As Cynthia Tuell relates, contingent faculty members are like handmaids:

> We clean up the comma splices. We organize the discourse of our students as though straightening a closet. When it's straight the "regular" professors teaching "regular" courses don't have to pick through the clutter and can quickly find the suit that suits them. When we can't manage to scrub them clean, we are called on to flunk out the great unwashed before they sully the orderly classrooms of the upper divisions. As handmaids, we are replaceable and interchangeable. . . . As handmaids, we serve the needs of our masters, not the vision we may have of ourselves, of our work, or of our students. (126)

For many women, the cycle of contingent teaching constitutes a form of exploitation sweetened by emotional or psychic rewards.

Although teaching composition has been thought of as women's work for the past seventy years, we have only begun to question the larger socioeconomic structures that channel women into contingent work.[5] As feminists in composition studies, we need to understand how femininist arguments for an ethic of care may reinforce the cycle of sex-affective production, in which women work hard but appropriate few professional rewards for themselves. By studying women's work narratives, we can gain alternative visions of our disciplinary realities and begin to rethink fundamental assumptions about our disciplinary identities and the structure of academic work. Ultimately, we can work on multiple levels — national and local — to organize coalitions that improve the working conditions of our colleagues who are non-tenure-track writing instructors.

Addressing Professional Inequities

Although we — feminist teachers and intellectuals — may exercise an ethic of care in our writing classrooms, we may fail to exhibit an analogous ethic in our relations with non-tenure-track faculty members. Unlike Susan Miller's "sad women in the basement" (*Carnivals* 121), some of us work on the first floors of English departments, where we serve as writing program administrators and as directors of writing centers, writing-across-the-curriculum programs, and graduate programs in rhetoric and composition. Many of us train and supervise graduate teaching assistants and serve as dissertation advisers, holding power and prestige unimaginable to women writing teachers of previous generations.

But our privilege does not mean that we are exempt from the threat of sexual discrimination and sexual harassment. Some of us on the tenure track feel exploited and underappreciated; some of us have been denied tenure and feel that our work in writing pedagogy and rhetorical theory has been undervalued; some of us have been pushed into administering writing programs as untenured assistant professors and must fight to maintain time for our scholarly work. Our experiences resonate with those of the women scholars who pioneered composition studies and who tell us of the great personal and professional price they paid to achieve professional recognition in a fledgling subdiscipline (see Crowley, "Three Heroines").

Empowered financially and professionally yet subject to sexual discrimination and sexual harassment, women academics occupy contradictory roles (see Luke and Gore, "Women"). Evelyn Fox Keller and Helene Moglen find that academic women, because of their historically marginal positions in higher education, "continue to feel the oppression of past struggles and the ongoing burdens of tokenism" (26). Uncomfortable with newly won power and embattled by the criticisms of hostile colleagues, they may not realize the privileges or advantages they do have (28). Nor are they "immune to the problem of competition"; in an economy of scarce resources, where "influence and power are by definition in limited supply," women must compete with one another for positions, committee and teaching assignments, teaching awards, and book contracts (22). Academic women also directly and indirectly benefit from the exploitation of other women's labor, particularly the labor of non-tenure-track faculty members. Even as I write this essay, I am benefiting from the exploitation of contingent faculty members at my institution. My research load — and the research load of three dozen other tenure-track faculty members — is made possible by the labor of approximately forty part-time and full-time non-tenure-track writing faculty members, two-thirds of whom are women. I call attention to this issue to illustrate the deep contradictions — tensions and discontinuities — of academic life. While many of us work to alleviate inequities in our classrooms, we are nevertheless complicit in gendered inequities that are often invisible or appear natural to us. Feminist research in composition studies, however, can serve as a site for exposing, questioning, and changing academic hierarchies that are considered natural. The continuing presence of women in contingent writing instructorships can become a site of activism for feminists in composition.

I am not alone in calling for better working conditions for contingent writing instructors. The CCCC has addressed the problem of contingent labor through its 1989 "Statement of Principles and Standards for Postsecondary Writing Instruction." Adapted from the 1986 "Wyoming Conference Resolution" — a grass-roots petition calling for improvements in the working conditions for exploited writing faculty members — the CCCC statement is "based on the assumption that the responsibility for the academy's most serious mission, helping students to develop their critical powers as readers and writers, should be vested in tenure-line faculty" (330).[6]

Although the statement acknowledges that "most teachers of writing are women and that many more of them are people of color than are tenure-line faculty" (CCCC Committee 336), it does not address the specific barriers to success women face in academic work: racial and sexual discrimination, sexual harassment, and the gendered division of labor.[7] Neither the "Wyoming Conference Resolution" nor the CCCC statement deals with the larger social and economic structures that channel women into contingent labor. The problem of contingent labor in composition studies is not just a professional issue that we can correct by eliminating contingent positions and hiring more full-time faculty members; it is a gender issue, and thus a feminist issue, tied to larger systems of exploitation. To ignore this problem is to ignore one of the largest gender inequities in English studies.

Feminists in composition must find ways to alleviate this problem through collective action. Two groups in the CCCC, the Committee on the Status of Women in the Profession and the Coalition of Women Scholars in the History of Rhetoric and Composition, offer sites for promoting the professional development and equitable treatment of women faculty members in composition. In addition, the yearly CCCC feminist workshop offers a forum for women to meet and discuss feminist research, pedagogy, and professional issues. At the 1995 CCCC feminist workshop, Women in the Academy: Can a Feminist Agenda Transform the Illusion of Equity into Reality?, presenters spoke about family and partner choices, part-time labor, administrative work, ageism, sexual orientation, race, ethnicity, and class issues. Workshop leaders Jody Millward and Susan Hahn distributed a mission statement entitled "Other Choices, Other Voices: Solutions to Gender Issues" and proposed that the CCCC, NCTE, American Association of University Women, and MLA conduct an investigative survey of the employment, underemployment, and professional choices of women in ESL, essential skills, and composition. They urged the organizations to establish an ethical code of hiring that would consider the traditional practice of hiring from the outside rather than promoting from within; the high teaching load and lack of institutional support for nonliterary fields; the overreliance of institutions on temporary contracts and part-time positions; recommendations for health and retirement benefits; recommendations for flexible careers, including job sharing, part-time tenure, and flexibility of tenure deadlines; maternal-leave policies and spousal hiring; the establishment and enforcement of sexual harassment policies; the enforcement of policies to prohibit discrimination based on ethnicity, age, marital status, sexual orientation, and number of children. In addition, members of the workshop drafted a statement on affirmative action to be presented to the CCCC Executive Committee.

Efforts to combat the problem of gender and contingent labor on a national level emphasize consciousness-raising and general organizing strategies, but local organizing may be a better way to change specific institutional climates. On university campuses across the country, faculty women's coalitions have offered many academic women the opportunity to act collectively and speak out against sex discrimination, sexual harassment, and the general exploitation of women faculty members.[8] For instance, on nonunionized campuses a local departmental or university-wide women's coalition could conduct a study of the working conditions of non-tenure-track women faculty members across campus, offering both a statistical analysis and testimonial accounts of hiring practices, salaries, evaluation procedures, contract renewal, fringe benefits, and professional development opportunities. Armed with such a report and a comparative analysis of working conditions at peer institutions, a women's coalition could influence departmental and university administrators to improve the working conditions, salary, benefits, and professional development opportunities for non-tenure-track women. Moreover, faculty women's coalitions provide psychological support for women, a designated space for women to meet and receive professional advice and mentoring (for coalition models see Childers et al.).

A major obstacle confronting women's coalition building is the meritocracy ideal — the individualist "work hard and you will succeed" mentality that fails to acknowledge power relations and hierarchies among women. Many powerful women faculty members see their achievements as individual efforts and hesitate to help other women, particularly non-tenure-track faculty members. Bernice Johnson Reagon characterizes the problem: "Sometimes you get comfortable in your little barred room and you decide you in fact are going to live there and carry out all of your stuff in there. And you gonna take care of everything that needs to be taken care of in the barred room" (358). For women the academy can operate as a barred room where a few enter while others are left outside. As we feminists in composition studies gain intellectual capital and institutional clout, we must not merely advance our individual careers and unquestioningly perpetuate the hierarchies and inequities of disciplinary culture; we must find ways to critique and transform the inequitable labor situation for non-tenure-track women faculty members, many of whom are our former students. While working at the material level — in local university and college settings and through professional organizations — we also need to reassess the theories that guide our feminist practices. Although femininist writing pedagogy deserves recognition and praise, we must ask if an ethic of care will enable us to improve and transform the working conditions and material realities of writing teachers. We need models of feminist thought that reassess rather than reinscribe the costs and benefits of the ideology of nurturance. Socialist feminist analyses enable us to see the costs of nurturant labor and help us make self-conscious choices about our investment in femininist pedagogies. Without acknowledging differences among women, the costs of maternal pedagogy, and the gendered constructions of teaching, theories of femininist pedagogy may reinscribe the woman-teacher-as-caretaker ideology, a time-honored role that has often limited and circumscribed women's mobility and creativity.

Notes

I thank Lynn Worsham for the term "contingent workers" and for her intellectual guidance in the formulation of this essay.

1. See Mary Field Belenky, Blythe McVicker Clinchy, Nancy Rule Goldberger, and Jill Mattuck Tarule's description of a "caring" or "connected" pedagogy in chapter 10 of *Women's Ways of Knowing* ("Connected Teaching"). See also Noddings.
2. See also Tronto's analysis of an ethic of care in *Moral Boundaries*. For a general overview of the philosophical and political debates over an "ethic of care," see Larrabee.
3. "Psychic income" is a term used in economic theory to describe the non-monetary rewards of labor. For a feminist assessment of the psychic costs of a psychic income, see Gillam.
4. For an insightful discussion of pedagogy and schooling as a site for the education of emotion, see Worsham, "Emotion and Pedagogic Violence."
5. For an informative survey of the problem of part-time labor in composition studies, see Slevin. For general accounts of contingent academic employment across the disciplines, see Emily Abel; Gappa and Leslie; Leslie, Kellams, and Gunne; Tuckman and Tuckman; Tuckman, Vogler, and Caldwell.
6. The CCCC statement advises that no more than ten percent of a department's course sections be staffed by part-time faculty members (CCCC

Executive Committee 333). The statement, however, has been criticized by part-time teachers who object to the recommendation that departments transform part-time lines into tenure-track positions and impose "severe limits on the ratio of part-time to full-time faculty" (333). Part-time faculty teachers accused the statement of favoring research faculty members and discrediting practitioners, "those whose expertise has developed outside the typical, traditional scholarly track" (Gunner, "Fate" 117). They argue that the Wyoming resolution has been transformed from an argument for improved working conditions for contingent faculty members to an argument for hiring Ph.D.s in rhetoric and composition. But neither side has fully examined the implications of the relation between gender and part-time status, and this is where feminists can make an important intervention.

7. Regardless of my criticisms of the CCCC "Statement," I would like to acknowledge the important work of Sharon Crowley, James Slevin, and other former members of the CCCC Committee on Professional Standards who have brought the issue of non-tenure-track labor to the attention of tenured faculty and administrators.

8. Faculty members who wish to address the problem of gender and part-time labor should consult the professional statements about reasonable contingent working conditions: Modern Language Association; AAUP Committee; AAUP Subcommittee; CCCC Executive Committee; CCCC Committee; Robertson, Crowley, and Lentricchia (on the "Wyoming Conference Resolution"); Wyche-Smith and Rose (on the "Wyoming Conference Resolution"). General guides to improving the working conditions of part-time faculty members through organizing efforts can be found in Gappa; Gappa and Leslie; Tuckman and Biles; Wallace. Journals and newsletters devoted exclusively to contingent instructors and the improvement of their working conditions are the *Adjunct Advocate, Professing: An Organ for Those Who Teach Undergraduates,* and *Forum: The Newsletter of the Part-Time Faculty Forum for the CCCC.* Helpful general guides to organizing women's coalitions are Bannerji et al.; DeSole and Hoffmann.

Works Cited

Aisenberg, Nadya, and Mona Harrington. *Women of Academe: Outsiders in the Sacred Grove.* Amherst: U of Massachusetts P, 1988.

Alcoff, Linda. "Cultural Feminism versus Post-structuralism: The Identity Crisis in Feminist Theory." *Signs: Journal of Women in Culture and Society* (1988): 405–36.

Althusser, Louis. "Ideology and Ideological State Apparatuses." *Contemporary Critical Theory.* Ed. Dan Latimer. San Diego: Harcourt, 1989. 61–102.

Bartky, Sandra Lee. *Femininity and Domination: Studies in the Phenomenology of Oppression.* New York: Routledge, 1990.

Batson, Lorie Goodman. "Defining Ourselves as Women (in the Profession)." *Pre/Text: A Journal of Rhetorical Theory* (1988): 207–09.

Bergmann, Barbara R. "Feminism and Economics." *Academe* (Sept.-Oct. 1983): 22–25.

Burns, Margie. "Service Courses: Doing Women a Disservice." *Academe* (May-June 1983): 18–21.

Cayton, Mary Kupiec. "Writing as Outsiders: Academic Discourse and Marginalized Faculty." *College English* 53 (1991): 647–60.

Caywood, Cynthia L., and Gillian R. Overing. Introduction. Caywood and Overing, *Teaching* xi–xvi.

Childers, Karen, et al. "A Network of One's Own." DeSole and Hoffmann 117–227.

Crowley, Sharon. "Three Heroines: An Oral History." *Pre/Text: A Journal of Rhetorical Theory* (1988): 202–06.

Daumer, Elisabeth, and Sandra Runzo. "Transforming the Composition Classroom." Caywood and Overing, *Teaching* 45–62.

Ferguson, Ann. *Blood at the Root: Motherhood, Sexuality, and Male Dominance.* London: Pandora, 1989.

Flynn, Elizabeth A. "Composing as a Woman." *College Composition and Communication* 39 (1988): 423–35.

Friedman, Susan Stanford. "Authority in the Feminist Classroom: A Contradiction in Terms." *Gendered Subjects: The Dynamics of Feminist Teaching.* Ed. Margo Culley and Catherine Portugues. New York: Routledge, 1985. 203–08.

Frost, Clare. "Looking for a Gate in the Fence." Fontaine and Hunter 59–69.

Frye, Marilyn. "On Being White: Thinking toward a Feminist Understanding of Race and Race Supremacy." *The Politics of Reality.* Freedom: Crossing, 1983. 110–27.

Gappa, Judith, and David Leslie. *The Invisible Faculty: Improving the Status of Part-Timers in Higher Education.* San Francisco: Jossey-Bass, 1993.

Gore, Jennifer M. *The Struggle for Pedagogies: Critical and Feminist Discourses as Regimes of Truth.* New York: Routledge, 1993.

Goulston, Wendy. "Women Writing." Caywood and Overing. *Teaching* 19–30.

Gramsci, Antonio. *An Antonio Gramsci Reader: Selected Writings*, 1916–1935. Ed. David Forgacs. New York: Schocken, 1988.

Grimm, Nancy. Account. "The Part-Time Problem: Four Voices." By Elizabeth A. Flynn, John F. Flynn, Nancy Grimm, and Ted Lockhart. *Academe* (Jan-Feb. 1986): 14–15.

Holbrook, Sue Ellen. "Women's Work: The Feminizing of Composition Studies." *Rhetorical Review* 9 (1991): 201–29.

Huber, Bettina. "Women in the Modern Languages, 1970–90." *Profession* 90. New York: MLA, 1990. 58–73.

Keller, Evelyn Fox, and Helene Moglen. "Competition: A Problem for Academic Women." Miner and Longino 21–37.

Koblitz, Neal. "Bias and Other Factors in Student Ratings." *Chronicle of Higher Education* 1 Sept. (1993): B3.

Lewis, Magda. "Interrupting Patriarchy: Politics, Resistance, and Transformation in the Feminist Classroom." Luke and Gore, *Feminisms* 167–91.

Looser, Devoney. "Composing as an 'Essentialist'? New Directions for Feminist Composition Theories." *Rhetoric Review* 12 (1993): 54–69.

Luke, Carmen, and Jennifer Gore, eds. *Feminisms and Critical Pedagogy.* New York: Routledge, 1992.

Markus, Maria. "Women, Success, and Civil Society: Submission to, or Subversion of, the Achievement Principle." *Feminism as Critique: Essays on the Politics of Gender in Late-Capitalist Societies.* Ed. Seyla Benhabib and Drucilla Cornell. Cambridge: Blackwell, 1987. 96–109.

Miller, Susan. "The Feminization of Composition." Bullock and Trimbur 39–53.

Noddings, Nel. *Caring: A Feminine Approach to Ethics and Moral Education.* Berkeley: U of California P, 1984.

Perry, William G. *Forms of Intellectual and Ethical Development in the College Years.* New York: Holt, Rinehart, 1970.

Phelps, Louise Wetherbee. "A Constrained Vision of the Writing Classroom." *Profession* 93. New York: MLA, 1993. 46–54.

Reagon, Bernice Johnson. "Coalition Politics: Turning the Century." B. Smith, *Girls* 356–68.

Rubin, Donnalee. *Gender Influences: Reading Student Texts.* Carbondale: Southern Illinois UP, 1993.

Simeone, Angela. *Academic Women: Working towards Equality.* Boston: Bergin, 1987.

Stanger, Carol. "The Sexual Politics of the One-to-One Tutorial Approach and Collaborative Learning." Caywood and Overing, *Teaching* 31–44.

Stearns, Carol Zisowitz, and Peter N. Stearns. Introduction. *Emotion and Social Change: Toward a New Psychohistory.* Ed. Stearns and Stearns. New York: Homes, 1988. 1–21.

Tronto, Joan C. *Moral Boundaries: A Political Argument for an Ethic of Care.* New York: Routledge, 1993.

Tuell, Cynthia. "Composition Teaching as 'Women's Work': Daughters, Handmaids, Whores, and Mothers." Fontaine and Hunter 123–39.

Wallace, M. Elizabeth. "Who Are These Part-Time Faculty Anyway?" *Part Time Academic Employment in the Humanities.* Ed. Wallace. New York: MLA, 1984. 3–29.

Watkins, Evan. *Work Time: English Departments and Circulation of Cultural Value.* Stanford: Stanford UP, 1989.

Wicke, Jennifer, and Margaret Ferguson. "Introduction: Feminism and Postmodernism; or The Way We Live Now." *Feminism and Postmodernism.* Ed. Wicke and Ferguson. Durham: Duke UP, 1994. 10–33.

Schell's Insights as a Resource for Your Teaching

1. In your journal, consider how sexual-identity politics inform your own classroom practice. Reflect on the tension between a "maternalistic" process and its masculine opposite. Which process predominates in your classroom? Which do the students seem to solicit? Which does your institution solicit? How do these solicitations work out in your day-to-day practice?

2. Schell suggests that there is a strong, though incomplete, link between what James Berlin (p. 53) calls the expressivist approach and her description of maternalistic processes. How might you modify Schell's claims about the particular ideologies that inform the gender dynamics of the composition classroom?

Schell's Insights as a Resource for Your Writing Classroom

1. Discuss with your students gender stereotypes that surround the study of literate practices. Broadly speaking, girls are supposed to be good at English, whereas boys are supposed to be good at science — and yet the standard conception of the great writer is typically male. Have them explore these stereotypes, and use Schell's arguments to organize questions for students.

2. Ask your students to write in their journals and then discuss in small groups their understanding of the role of writing instruction within the larger curriculum of their school. Ask them to consider the importance of writing with respect to their chances of success or failure in the world. What role does writing play in one's career? How significant is one's gender? How important is writing within the curriculum of your school? Do gender dynamics govern writing instruction? Are there inequities to discuss?

Becoming a Writerly Self: College Writers Engaging Black Feminist Essays

Juanita Rodgers Comfort

This article describes a method for enabling student writers to connect their personal and social identities in ways that will enhance their writing while avoiding the "self-indulgence" teachers typically fear when introducing the personal into writing. Juanita Rodgers Comfort argues, "Writing instruction should enable students to recognize the writerly self as a persuasive instrument *that can be strategically deployed and to learn to make effective use of their own multiple locations to take personal stands on public issues* that transcend the confessional." *Black feminist writers, she feels, have mastered this effective juxtaposition with essays that go beyond the mere narrative while still invoking the self, and thus serve as excellent models of authoritative* and *contextualized writing.*

> My work requires me to think about how free I can be as an African-American woman writer in my genderized, sexualized, wholly racialized world. To think about (and wrestle with) the full implications of my situation leads me to consider what happens when other writers work in a highly and historically racialized society. For them, as for me, imagining is not merely looking or looking at; nor is it taking oneself intact into the other. It is for the purposes of the work, *becoming.*
> — Toni Morrison, *Playing in the Dark*

Whenever I tell people that I am studying the rhetoric of contemporary black feminist essayists, I'm inevitably asked why rhetoricians should pay attention to the writings of African American women. I'm asked to account for what makes their discursive situations "noteworthy"; after all, my questioners reason, isn't the struggle for personal power, for voice, for credibility, shared by *all* writers? Then why focus on *black women's writing*, specifically — what can *they* show *us*? This question always echoes in my ears for days after each encounter with it. Despite my sense that most of the time it is asked out of intellectual curiosity and in a spirit of goodwill, it has always felt like a trick question to me, designed to somehow betray me as an academic "outsider," to put me in my place and, perhaps, out of the business of locating black women's voices more centrally within the discipline. I've always managed to give what I hoped was an acceptably distanced, "scholarly" response (one that I always hope does not saddle me with the burden of defending my well-considered standpoint as a black feminist rhetorician or the contributions of African American women's writing to "mainstream" scholarly projects):

> I study these works *as I think any rhetorician would*, in order to gain more insight into the challenges faced by all speakers and writers in negotiating an influential ethos for themselves. I examine the writing of African American women, specifically, because *their* texts document the authoritative spaces *they* have created for *themselves* within and against particular configurations of social, cultural, political, and economic power. This work represents *one scholarly direction to take among many*, but it is of vital importance because it contributes to *a useful culturally grounded theory* of rhetorical power.

This answer, for the most part, has satisfied my interlocutors. But I am usually left wondering how my answer, in positioning my black female self as critically distant from the issues involved, removes me from my own work and somehow impoverishes the meaning of that work. As I reread this answer, I see that several strategies of disengagement are apparent (and in fact work to negate the "I" that I have used twice): I locate myself in a mainstream — "as any rhetorician would" — that historically has been populated by white men. I exclude myself from the world of African American writers, obscuring the fact that I happen to be one, eschewing the self-inclusive pronouns "our," "we," and "ourselves" in favor of their self-excluding counterparts "their," "they," and "themselves." I assign myself almost anonymous status among a cohort of scholars. I choose to reduce my conclusions to the neutral terms of "*a* (generic) theory" instead of the "*my* (personally located) theory." And I choose not to articulate at all what is perhaps the most important part of my answer: *I'm doing this work because what "I" (a black woman who is also, ostensibly, an academic "insider") have to say about the African American women's discursive practices contributes to making those practices matter.*

I invoke this brief self-analysis to frame my vision of how literary essays by black feminist writers can be used by college writers at both the first-year and advanced levels to gain valuable insight into writing as a self-defining activity. Displayed through features comprising specific texts as well as through a rhetor's general reputation (whether that rhetor is a professional or student writer), her image in the minds of her audiences can be one of the most powerful influences on their judgments of her work. The enfranchisement of African American women as makers of knowledge in situations where forces work toward muting or silencing us may very well hinge on the task of distinguishing ourselves to audiences (for whom white male perspectives are the norm) specifically as black and female in our grounding assumptions, strategies of argument, and writing style, while simultaneously eliciting from those audiences a favorable impression of our perceived characters. Like all rhetors (student writers included), black feminist essayists must invent effective ways to answer readers' fundamental question: Who is this person and why should I believe what she says?

Cornel West's description of the struggle of the black diaspora to obtain and maintain status and credibility within a Eurocentric (masculinist) cultural framework invokes for me a similar struggle engaged in by student writers within the cultural framework of the academy. West analyzes the problematic of *invisibility* and *nameless-ness*, enacted by cultural authorities, which "promoted Black inferiority and constituted the European background against which Black diaspora struggles for identity, dignity . . . and material resources took place" (102). Perhaps because of my own search for a writerly self that is at once influential in the academic arena, representative of the places I come from outside the academy, and comfortable as a self-image, questions about the writerly self condition everything I write. Over the ten years that I have been teaching composition and rhetoric courses, I've observed that my most insightful students have generally sought to use their writing assignments as tools to help themselves mature as thinking individuals and become more powerful as social beings. Through their writerly eyes, I've come to see that successful college writing demands, and ultimately achieves, something more personally enriching than merely "inventing the university," as David Bartholomae would say. The most successful student writers in my experience learn how to move beyond merely imitating the prose styles and interpretive schemes of disciplinary discourses. They animate those discourses by inventing complex and versatile writerly selves who are able to place their extra-academic worlds into a carefully constructed relationship with those discourse communities.

Universities are, of course, part of the genderized, racialized society that Morrison speaks of. A genderized, racialized society is one in which the statuses and roles of the people in its institutions (educational, military, economic, governmental . . .) and communities (neighborhood, social, religious . . .) — and even the very structures of those institutions and communities — are influenced, even dictated on some level, by gender and race. Racial and gender groups, of course, must be understood not merely in terms of differential physical attributes, but also in terms of discursive habits and social practices, along with perceptions of intelligence, morality, values, and so forth that are typically associated with those attributes, habits, and practices.

The discourses of the university are heavily invested with markers of white race, male gender, and middle and upper socioeconomic classes. As an African American woman who studies and teaches rhetoric and composition at a university, I am keenly aware of the ways in which language constructs the person who knows as much as it defines what one knows. And I am unwilling to pretend that disciplinary discourses are value-neutral enclaves where race, gender, class, spirituality, and other cultural issues don't matter. And so, echoing Morrison, I think it's important for rhetoricians and composition specialists to ask important questions about what happens when *student writers* of any gender or any race work in a genderized, racialized society. If imagining, through composing, is something more significant to students than exercises in critical detachment, and if we do not expect them to remain essentially unchanged by their encounters with the ideas they write about, then composing text must be for the purposes of these students' education, *becoming* insurgent intellectuals (to use a term coined by West and bell hooks) who are personally invested in the world of ideas.

The rhetorical implications of writing one's way toward becoming in a racialized society came into particular focus for me last year, after teaching a graduate seminar on contemporary African American women essayists. The course employed methods of rhetorical criticism to draw insights from literary essays by black feminist writers June Jordan, Alice Walker, bell hooks, Nikki Giovanni, and Pearl Cleage. As I led the class of nine students through the semester (seven black women and two white women, along with several others who sat in on occasional sessions), we all felt strongly attracted to — and sometimes troubled by — the range of essayistic voices that were speaking to us. We raised numerous questions and engaged in more than a few debates about merits of the essayists' personal approaches to public issues. Class discussions defined spaces where issues of identity, location, and meaning emerged from a wide range of experiences with work, family, community, spirituality, and often, the academy. Our encounters with the diversity of these essayists' world views certainly complicated the taken-for-granted, almost stereotypical notions of "black" and "female" identity that were initially prevalent in the class. Regardless of the direction of our critiques, however, none of us doubted the powerful *presence* of these women in their works. As we moved through our reading list, it became increasingly evident to us that who these writers portray themselves to be as African American women had great bearing on their ability to entice us to entertain their positions, share their social agenda, or accept their conclusions. And their self-portrayals as distinctively raced and gendered beings posed a challenge to my students, both black and white, to reconsider what they themselves were about.

An extended example underscores this point. One of my students, a middle-aged white woman, whom I'll call Eleanor, was deeply troubled by the way June Jordan's essay "Requiem for the Champ" (which we read from her collection, *Technical Difficulties*) seemed to defend the aberrant personal behavior of heavyweight boxer Mike Tyson. On the day students presented proposals for their semester projects, Eleanor told the class that because she had always felt connected to Jordan, a renowned poet and political activist, as a "feminist thinker," she could not comprehend why the essayist would stoop to dignify Tyson with what she called an apology, and so she was planning to write a paper arguing for her misgivings. I don't think she realized it at the time she developed her proposal, but Eleanor was beginning an important journey toward a racialized consciousness made possible by Jordan's writing self.

Let me give some background about the essay. In "Requiem," Jordan outlines the horrific conditions of poverty and oppression under which Mike Tyson learned the life rules that have governed his personal behavior as an adult. In keeping with the theme identified by the subtitle of *Technical Difficulties* — "African-American Notes on the State of the Union" — she asks of readers to consider the attitudes of politicians, military personnel, filmmakers, recording artists, and others who authorize, carry out, and applaud both acts of violence and the objectification of women (226). She indicts those who might share responsibility for maintaining the kind of social order that could dehumanize not only Tyson, but even someone as apparently different from him as Jordan herself. It is upon this point that she makes a crucial connection between herself and Tyson, designed to disrupt readers' easy categorizations of either one of them.

The message in Jordan's essay is especially powerful because of its "self-disclosures" — bits of information about herself that Jordan endows with salience, places in specific locations in the essay, packages with other images, flags as revelatory, and connects to the essay's central message. Rhetorically, self-disclosures foreground the embodied nature of the self, which, through selective, insightful sharing, can build connections between writers and readers that authorize the writer to make claims and ensure the acceptability of those claims.

Jordan opens the essay with an assertion of physical proximity to Tyson:

> Mike Tyson comes from Brooklyn. And so do I. Where he grew up was about a twenty-minute bus ride from my house. (221)

Then, she confesses that it took her most of her own life to learn the social lessons that Tyson apparently had not, emphasizing that she was, *for most of her life*, very much like Tyson is now:

Mike Tyson comes from Brooklyn. And so do I. In the big picture of America, I never had much going for me. And he had less. *I only learned, last year*, that I can stop whatever violence starts with me. *I only learned, last year*, that love is infinitely more interesting, and more exciting, and more powerful, than really winning or really losing a fight. *I only learned, last year*, that all war leads to death and that all love leads you away from death. (223, italics mine)

It is difficult to overlook that in the middle of this passage, Jordan speaks words that could easily have come from Tyson (which I indicate here in boldface):

I am more than twice Mike Tyson's age. And I'm not stupid. Or slow. **But I'm Black. And I come from Brooklyn. And I grew up fighting. And I grew up and I got out of Brooklyn because I got pretty good at fighting. And winning.** Or else, intimidating my would-be adversaries with my fists, my feet, and my mouth. And I never wanted to fight. *I never wanted anybody to hit me. And I never wanted to hit anybody.* But the bell would ring at the end of another dumb day in school and I'd head out with dread and a nervous sweat because I knew some jackass more or less my age and more or less my height would be waiting for me because she or he had nothing better to do than to wait for me and hope to kick my butt or tear up my books or break my pencils or pull hair out of my head. (223, italics mine)

Then a little later in the essay, she identifies herself with Tyson again, and this time the connection moves beyond Tyson to identify Jordan with African Americans generally:

I'm Black. Mike Tyson is Black. And neither one of us was ever supposed to win anything more than a fight between the two of us. And if you check out the mass-media material on *"us,"* and if you check out the emergency-room reports on *"us,"* you might well believe we're losing the fight to be more than our enemies have decreed. . . . (224, italics mine)

These passages illustrate two ways that self-disclosures function as a persuasive element. First, as a matter of strategy, Jordan provides specially chosen personal information in order to place herself directly — almost physically — between her readers and Mike Tyson. For the space of reading this essay, Jordan insists that readers perceive of her and Tyson not separately, but together, and as explicitly raced beings. The physical identification becomes a point of *stasis:* If Jordan is so much like Tyson, then we should either dislike Jordan as much as we dislike Tyson, or (the preferred reading) translate our respect for Jordan into a greater valuing of Tyson.

Second, the psychological power of Jordan's disclosures relies on her readers' sense that a defining relationship is taking place between the essayist and her subject. I'm drawn to Sharon Crowley's explanation for this phenomenon, that the writing subject is enmeshed in multiple relations, but when writing, the "writer becomes audience" as well

(34). So, in the process of working through the problems posed by as-suming a personal association with Tyson, Jordan constructs a self who speaks back to her from the pages of her work-in-progress. Having written part of Tyson's life into her own, and then reading reflexively what she has written from the subject position she created for herself, Jordan presumably has on some level become self-identified as "June Jordan, sister of Mike Tyson." So, in a sense, this is a "real" June Jordan who speaks to readers, not a mechanistically crafted persona. And as readers become familiar with the person in the essay who asserts a similar background to Tyson's but demonstrates a decidedly different outcome, Jordan can hope that readers will better understand her stance on the fallen Tyson and why a requiem for him might be justified.

These effects of self-disclosure can shed light on the challenge that Eleanor was faced with. Until she encountered "Requiem," she seems to have been comfortable in a relationship with the essayist that foregrounded gender solidarity over race division. As long as race can be ignored, the two of them can be kindred spirits. "Although I can't share her experience as a black person," Eleanor could reason, "I can certainly share her experiences as a woman, and I can feel good about that." The feminist values that she believed she already shared with Jordan should have precluded either of them from having sympathies for people like Tyson. But the Tyson/Jordan connection in "Requiem," in both its textual strategy and psychological implications, confounded her: How is it possible that Jordan and Tyson can co-exist on the same moral or intellectual plane?

As the essay unfolds, Tyson's rape conviction and its underpinnings of misogyny and violence, about which Eleanor expected Jordan to have an overriding outrage, seem far less of an issue for the essayist than the implications of their shared oppression as black people. Even though Jordan clearly states at one point that she *does not* condone Tyson's behavior, the essay's rhetoric of black identification seems to counter that disclaimer. Eleanor witnesses her woman-to-woman connection with Jordan disrupted by Jordan's identification as a *black* woman, something that Eleanor herself can never be. Therefore, Eleanor must decide how to establish a new relationship with the person that Jordan becomes in the essay, so that she can begin to understand Jordan's message.

As I read Eleanor's semester-project essay, "Down for the Count: The Selection of Metaphor in 'Requiem for the Champ,'" I saw that Jordan's self-disclosures had inspired Eleanor to measure herself against the emergent image of Jordan and to decide what it meant for her to identify with a feminist thinker who claimed the violent sensi-bility of a Mike Tyson. Her essay dealt with the challenge to her own self-identity by emulating Jordan's strategy of self-disclosure. Her struggle to accomplish this illustrates a theory of modern rhetoric that is, in the words of Michael Halloran, "distinguished by its emphasis on the responsibility of speakers to articulate their own worlds, and thereby their own selves" (342–43). "It is no longer valid," asserts Halloran, "to assume that speaker and audience live in the same world and to study the techniques by which the speaker moves his audience to act or think in a particular way. One must turn instead to the more fundamental problem of why the gap between the speaker's and audience's worlds is so broad and how one might bridge it smoothly" (336). Jordan forces Eleanor to take on the responsibility of first acknowledging and then attempting to bridge the racial gap between their feminist worlds.

Eleanor uses Jordan's self-representational strategies to help her interrogate Jordan's position, placing herself between her own readers (her classmates and me) and the June Jordan and Mike Tyson who are the joint subjects of her essay.

Eleanor opens her essay with a disclosure about her eyesight that becomes a metaphor for her struggle to gain insight into Jordan's message:

> The truth is that at age fifty-three, I see less clearly than I did at thirty-three. I now wear glasses most of the time so that my field of vision will not be so limited and the words on the page in front of me will be large enough for me to see without hyper-extending my arms. So you see, I have done my best to correct my vision. . . . so why am I having so much trouble "seeing" what June Jordan wants me to see? For the life of me, I just can't go along with her *apologia* for the troubled life of Mike Tyson, former heavyweight champion and lost soul. Or at least what I see as her defense of the fallen champ.

She answers her own question in a way that discloses her status as a white person:

> . . . but perhaps I am constitutionally incapable of seeing or hearing what you **are** saying. Perhaps it is, as my African American classmates suggest, the myopia that accompanies white skin. This is my limitation, my visual impairment.

And later, responding to, and echoing Jordan's disclosures about encountering the war-like devastation of the neighborhood where Tyson grew up, Eleanor offers her own growing-up story:

> I've never been to Brooklyn and I have not seen war up close and personal. I've never been in combat nor did I grow up in a war zone. I have only seen TV wars. I have not known the ugliness of racism and poverty, and I grew up in a neighborhood where you could buy tulips and ribbons for a girl.[1] . . . And mostly, *I have never been seen as "other"* the way Mike Tyson and June Jordan have. Maybe this is why I cannot see her point; but I can see that she has one. (my emphasis)

Jordan's assertion of a shared identity with Tyson became the catalyst for Eleanor to confront her feminist perspective *with her own whiteness.* I am defining "whiteness" here as a cultural construction of individual and group identity that is associated with the images of race that underpin the structure of our society. The cultural construction of whiteness may be one possible answer to bell hooks' question, "from what political perspective do we dream, look, create, and take action?" (4). In a culturally pluralistic society like America, whiteness does not exist in isolation from non-white cultural constructions such as "blackness"; it must exist in juxtaposition against those other constructions. Whiteness has been a locus of (often abusive) power and privilege for those in society who can claim it and a source of subjugation for those who cannot. Certainly, part of the advantage vested in whiteness lies in its ability to mask its own power and privilege — to render them normative, even invisible, in the minds of most whites, in order to maintain the framework of white supremacy. This dynamic is often painfully visible to those who cannot claim the power and privilege of whiteness.

What June Jordan's essay did for Eleanor, I think, was to force upon her a representation of whiteness that could only be conveyed from the vantage point of Jordan's blackness. The essay's intention and effect were to make uncomfortably visible the taken-for-granted privilege of whiteness, along with its potential to dominate the non-white. It disallowed Eleanor's attempt to claim a "sameness" of perspective with Jordan based on gender solidarity. She responded in her course paper with a set of personal disclosures that certainly cannot be dismissed as merely confessional or self-indulgent, but are in fact essential to the problem of race that Jordan has challenged her to resolve.

The kind of critical engagement exhibited by Eleanor and her classmates at the graduate level has led me to envision the *undergraduate* composition classroom as a place where students can learn strategies for expressing themselves meaningfully within the context of academic discourse. Because first-year and advanced composition courses are a large part of my teaching load, the essayist course enabled me to view authorship issues in student writing in a more focused way. I was particularly able to see that the experiences of my master's-level students, reflected in their class discussions and course papers, displayed important similarities to those of my undergraduate writers. They both seemed to share a strong desire to call upon the resources of their personal lives in order to make sense of their subject matter and to negotiate their stances relative to the conventional demands of academic discourse. While the writing of my master's students was somewhat more proficient, in a technical sense, than that of my undergraduates, the ability to effectively integrate personal stances into academically oriented discussions seemed about the same at both levels.

I further saw that the range of experiences that my undergraduate students — white and non-white, female and male — bring to their classrooms resonates strongly with experiences asserted in the black feminist essays from the seminar. Significant parallels exist between the lives of my students and those of the essayists, in their relationships with spouses/lovers, in their child-rearing responsibilities, in their religious and political affiliations, in their work situations, and in the depth of their community involvement. These students have taken on numerous sophisticated roles, such as parents of children with disabilities, litigants in major lawsuits, career military members, entrepreneurs and businesspeople, and caregivers for relatives with disabilities and catastrophic illnesses. Many of the social, political, and humanistic issues that they expressed a personal stake in resolving in their course papers were the same issues raised by the essayists that my graduate students studied. So whenever I was able to suggest the idea of infusing their school papers with personal stances (using excerpts from essayists to illustrate self-disclosure techniques), my writing students were as attentive as my seminar students. And anxious as well, since few of them felt that they had been given meaningful opportunities to express personal standpoints, and fewer still had been given explicit instruction in how to do so effectively.

What is most memorable about both the professional essayists and my students is what I believe most college writers can be convinced of — that, as Halloran asserts, "the rigor and passion with which they *disclose their world* to the audience, is their *ethos*" (343). Yet I am aware that many composition teachers have considerable difficulty in granting their student writers that *ethos*. Even while assigning compositions they call "essays," these teachers have largely denied to academic writing the essay's invitation to *explicit* personal engagement with its subject matter, viewing most attempts to assert such a personal relationship as incompatible with the critical detachment valued in much disciplinary discourse. I've heard teachers routinely insinuate, and sometimes even state outright, the criticism that Kurt Spellmeyer has described, that students are no more than incomplete knowers whose "right to speak must be learned — or perhaps more accurately, earned — through what is essentially the effacement of subjectivity" (265).

Anxiety over the disclosure of personal information has occasionally been expressed in our professional journals. In a *College English* article, for example, Gordon Harvey suggests that the overt "personal" gesture is often construed by academic readers as irrelevant, inconsequential, and counterproductive. He tries to resolve some of that anxiety by considering ways in which academic writing can be "*informed* by personal experience without injecting personal *information*" (649). Such a dance around the embodied self may well be based on an assumption that one's subjectivity is an element separate from the world being written about, and — especially when expressed through personal disclosures — somehow interferes with clear, logical, critical thinking. However, I am concerned that this attitude can hinder efforts of student writers to integrate disciplinary knowledge with other aspects of their lives, in order to define themselves as distinctive intellectual agents in academic and professional situations and thereby locate meaningful vantage points from which to interpret and apply the information they are learning. Such wholesale dismissal of college students' capability to assert credible knowledge created through placing one's knowledge about a subject within the framework of one's life experiences, which is reflected in the rather cynical teacherly question, "What do *students* know?" perverts the powerfully heuristic question, *Que sais je?* — what do *I* know? — that has driven the development of the essay genre from the time of Montaigne.

Harvey seems to reduce the territory of personal disclosure, advocated mainly by feminist theorists and scholars of the familiar essay, to narrative and autobiography motivated by a desire to make the public voice of academic discourse more connected with lived experience and empathetic to others, less abstract, and less competitive. In Harvey's view, the impulse toward personal disclosure, so defined, often produces bad writing by both college students and professional academic writers. He cites, in particular, the difficulty of contextualizing close analysis of primary texts with personal report; the analytical and the personal (which he admits is an arbitrary distinction), when treated as separate entities, are much like oil and water for most of his student writers.

> The students devote their energy to finding whatever personal connections they can, not to wrestling the issues out of the text or finding things to say besides summaries and platitudes. For students who can't yet manage an extended development of an idea in a "linear" fashion, the invitation to jump back and forth is added disincentive to extending thinking. The textual and the personal sections, sometimes jarringly different in style, are only very roughly stitched together — prompting one teacher I know to call these "Frankenstein" papers. But the assignment also provides an excuse to avoid even the more basic work of focusing closely and describing accurately. The picture given of the text in these essays is distorted, reductive, fudged to fit. (645)

Key for me in this statement is that students are often, at least implicitly, invited to invoke the personal, but not given any explicit rhetorical insight regarding its effective use. Jumping back and forth between personal and analytical is, as even Harvey later acknowledges, arbitrary. That the personal can be analytical, that the analytical can be usefully located from a personal vantage point, seems impossible not only for the student writer to manage but for the teacher to work from as well.

The idea that the essay might be faulted for being "personal" in the ways advanced by Harvey might be attributed, at least in part, to critics' reliance on the notion that identities are the private property of the individuals — as Celia Kitzinger asserts, "freely created products of introspection or the unproblematic reflections of the private sanctum of the 'inner self'" (82). The questionable relevance of the "personal" may stem from viewing the essay's subjectivity as an element separate from the world being written about that can cloud or detract from that world. From this perspective, the "personal" gesture is often construed as irrelevant, inconsequential, and counterproductive, as Harvey suggests. However, looking at the personal dimension from the perspective of black feminist writers, for example, can show how subjectivity is indeed inseparable from the world of ideas — from their interpretation and analysis — and thus essential for ideas to be properly developed by writers and understood by readers.

The problems that Harvey has encountered in many student compositions certainly should not be discounted. Engaging the overt personal gesture is indeed a strategy mishandled in much student writing. Many would agree, I think, that we would like students to go beyond writing that is personal, as Wendell Harris would say, "merely by virtue of narrating a personal experience" (941). Harvey does have an answer, in terms of his concept of "presence" that incorporates, among other things, a sense of motive or why a text needs writing; a development that allows the writer to explore and shape a topic as ideas dictate rather than as a thesis-plus-three ideas formula; use of details such as original metaphors, non-academic analogies; opening up larger questions and issues; and elaborating on reasons for judgments (651–53).

However, I disagree with Harvey's attempt to render *embodied* writers invisible — particularly student writers who, in his eyes, merely "drag in their personal experiences" or allow personal narrative to "infiltrate" traditional academic analysis. I am convinced that significant problems arise with student writing precisely when they have not defined and located themselves as effectively self-authorized knowers for their evaluative audiences. The problem I identify in much personal writing by students is a lack of skill in articulating a self that genuinely contributes to the rhetorical power of their compositions. But identifying a student's lack of skill in this area does not invalidate the *concept* of personal engagement of his or her subject matter as a potentially powerful strategy, which is what I believe happens too often. Dismissing the self-disclosure strategies themselves because students have not yet mastered those strategies seems senseless if the strategies are not being taught to them in the first place. The problematic *ethos* of student writers, which often seems to trigger their instructors' denial of their right to ask (heuristically) and then answer the question "what do I know" from all of their intellectual resources, strongly resonates with the struggle of many African American women writers to do the same. It is this connection between these two groups that allows me, as a composition instructor, to investigate how black feminist essayists attempt to solve the problematic, described by Cornel West, of "present[ing] themselves to themselves and others as complex human beings" (102), and to investigate what students might learn from studying their essays.

Pamela Klass Mittlefehldt's work provides considerable insight on issues involved in the construction of self-identity that black feminist writers typically bring to the essay form. For Mittlefehldt, the essay's focus on the author's voice, the visible process of contemplation, its grounding in particular experience, the reconsideration of and resistance to the orthodox, "make it a useful genre for Black feminists who are writing to change their worlds" (198). The essay's rhetorical edge, rather than the dispassionate contemplation that has characterized Western male essay traditions, is the attraction for black feminist writers. Essays by black feminist writers deal with the dynamic of social identity in provocative ways. Mittlefehldt explains that in the essay, "the author matters intensely. When that author is a black woman, the voice that comes through is one of radical import, for it is a voice that has been traditionally obliterated in Western thought and literature" (198). Having moved from the margins and established a space for their voices by virtue of their success as writers, black women find the essay to be an important space for continually re-forming, re-visioning, and renegotiating personal identity in light of the past and ongoing experiences that shape their lives.

In fact, it becomes even more important for these essayists to allow readers to enter their lives, after they have become more centrally located. Kevin Murray states: "Whereas social identity is a problem for marginal individuals . . . personal identity becomes difficult for people who have achieved a successful moral career to the point where it is hard to distinguish oneself from the official social order" (181). In ways not unlike black women in American society at large, college students constitute a social and cultural category within an institutional hierarchy that includes professors, administrators, support staff, and other members of the college/university community. In light of the diversity of our student populations (in terms of race, ethnicity, class, age, gender/sexual orientation, literacies, and so forth), it is all the more striking that college students, like members of other hierarchies in our society, are subject to the same kinds of invisibility and namelessness.

Black feminist essays teach many possibilities for negotiating self-identity and promoting *ethos* given *the multiple locations from which the authors speak as African American women* (gendered, cultural, economic, generational, spiritual). It is the skillful interweaving of those locations into the subject matter under discussion that allows African American women writers to claim authoritative voices. Two concepts related to this notion of *ethos* are of great import for writing instruction. The first, as expressed by Patricia Hill Collins, concerns the development of an "ethic of personal accountability," wherein individuals place themselves in positions of direct responsibility for their own knowledge claims. For Collins and other black feminist theorists,

> Assessments of an individual's knowledge claims simultaneously evaluate an individual's character, values, and ethics. African Americans reject the Eurocentric, masculinist belief that probing into an individual's personal viewpoint is outside the boundaries of discussion. Rather, all views expressed and actions taken are thought to derive from a central set of core beliefs that cannot be other than personal. . . . Knowledge claims made by individuals respected for their moral and ethical connections to their ideas will carry more weight than those offered by less respected figures. (218)

The second concept is a suggestion that black women's essays can in fact model for student writers those strategies that would enable them to create a distinctive place for themselves in a given discourse community. Mittlefehldt asserts that black women's essays

> . . . are a resistance, a refusal to be silenced, a refusal to be *said*. By telling the stories of their own and other Black women's lives, [the essays] counter the attempts to erase and deny the experiences of Black women in American culture. At the same time, they also challenge the seductive ease of connection by engaging in dialectic tensions of difference. (199)

These two concepts contribute to an understanding of the strategic nature of the essay as a means of knowledge-making grounded in the creation and manifestation of a writerly self. Writing instruction should enable students to recognize the writerly self as a *persuasive instrument* that can be strategically deployed and to learn to make effective use of their own multiple locations to take personal stands on public issues *that transcend the confessional*. A large part of what writing does for people is to help with their personal growth; as writers develop and then read their own work, they place themselves in subject positions relative to their texts and adapt to the role they have laid out for themselves in relation to the subject under discussion. Every text that is produced (in college or elsewhere) contributes to this re-visioning of the self that has been constructed for the writer and includes that self in the social dynamic that is writing. As Stuart Hall asserts:

> we . . . occupy our identities very retrospectively: having produced them, we then know who we are. We say, "Oh that's where I am in relation to this argument and for these reasons." So, it's exactly the reverse of what I think is the common sense way of understanding it, which is that we already know our "self" and then put it out there. Rather, having put it into play in language, we *then* discover what we are. I think that only then do we make an investment in it, saying, "Yes, I like that position, I am that sort of person, I'm willing to occupy that position." (qtd. in Drew 173)

This reciprocal movement between writer and text, I believe, must be as much a part of a writing student's rhetorical education as the movement between writer and reader. Since every text represents a cultural position, drawing texts by African American women into writing instruction may serve to make student writers more keenly aware of how their own (and other) texts are constructing them, so that they can exercise greater influence over the Eurocentric masculinist vantage point that has been promoted as objectivity, even though it reinscribes Eurocentric masculinist scientist vision and values.

Judicious use of these essays may also avoid another significant danger, articulated in Gesa Kirsch and Joy Ritchie's critique of the essay's invitation to the personal. They charge that the essayistic writing that has become popular in feminist scholarship offers essentialist renderings of a confessional voice leading to more master narratives (8). A sophisticated understanding of self-disclosure as rhetorical strategy can, I believe, be a way out of such a trap. According to Mittlefehldt, "The self that is constructed in [black feminist] essays emerges from the complexity of each writer's personal experiences as a Black woman. It is strikingly apparent that for these women, that self is multi-voiced and in constant dialogue with others" (201). The multi-layered voice of the writing self that speaks in the essays offers new angles of vision, unique juxtapositions of understanding and accountability. There is a passionate sense of connection in these writings, a clear impression that these words are directed towards others and that they invite response. The self that emerges here is one "grounded in a community. . . . It includes a spectrum of relationships, including ancestors, family, Black women, Black people, women, all living beings" (201–02).

The way a writer uses language to describe, report, narrate, or argue actually shapes a particular self-image both for the writer and the readers. This "rhetorical identity" — the presence invested in the text, developed by the writer to accomplish particular persuasive effects in the minds of readers, not only contributes to the writer's authority/credibility but also helps build a mutual relationship to readers as fellow scholars. Effective rhetorical identity defines a textual voice that is at once distinctive and strongly resonant with readers. My essayist course afforded my students a measure of comfort and a greater sense of strategy in developing their own ideas, which I think can be transferred effectively to the undergraduate writing classroom. The results in my courses, in terms of the rhetorical impact of the writing produced, validated for me the claims of Kurt Spellmeyer, W. Ross Winterowd, William Zieger, and other composition scholars, summarized by Janis Forman, that critical reading of and writing essays in composition classes "open up for students ways of knowing that are too often underrepresented in the curriculum — a willingness to value ambiguity, to invent, to suspend closure, to situate the self in multiple and complex ways through discourse" (5).

What do writing teachers need to consider in helping student writers to develop a more sophisticated approach to personal disclosure, with help from black feminist essayists? One approach would be to consider how these essayists can increase our sensitivity to the situational factors that generate a writer's *ethos*, to compare the constraints of school writing with those traditionally imposed upon African American women writers, and ultimately to draw conclusions regarding the contribution of *ethos*, in turn, to the evolution of the essayist and the student writer alike as an intellectual, as a professional communicator, as an enlightened self.

Having seen personal power at work in the essays by black feminist writers that we studied, Eleanor and the other students in my essayist course managed to enhance the rhetorical force of their own writing. They were able to recognize more circumstances that invite writers to invoke personal statements, to use specific kinds of words, images, and signals that construct a personal perspective; to see how distinctions between spiritual and secular, or between blackness and whiteness, can be manipulated for various reasons; and to learn how these discursive actions taken by essayists make considerable difference in how readers think about a given topic. And sometimes, as happened with Eleanor, students followed up on their observations by taking the risk of asserting their writerly selves more explicitly in their papers. Reflecting on Eleanor's project and the rest of that semester's work, I have come to see that the questions and concerns — even complaints — raised in that class regarding self-portrayal and authorization to speak demand closer examination, not only in seminars on the essay, but also in first-year and advanced composition classes, as well as in writing-intensive courses across disciplines, where student writers are struggling for the kind of credibility born out of rhetorically meaningful self-representations, the kind of credibility that these essayists, at their best, were able to achieve.

One important goal of writing instruction, of course, is to help students become effective communicators in academic and professional situations, where the expectations of audiences constrain what and how something should be said. In a society that is so culturally diverse, technologically sophisticated, and hierarchically complex, finding a vantage point, a place to stand, and a locus of authority, respect, influence, and power cannot be ignored as a teachable subject in rhetoric and composition courses. What many student writers seem to long for, even without knowing exactly how to articulate it, is meaningful instruction in using writing to assess, define, and assert who they are becoming as knowing beings. I think these students would find black feminist essayists useful for their ability to reconcile social and personal identities and for directing those identities toward rhetorically useful ends.

Notes

1. Here Eleanor is responding to the question posed by Jordan in describing Tyson's desolate environment: "In his neighborhood, where could you buy ribbons for a girl, or tulips?" (223).

Works Cited

Collins, Patricia Hill. *Black Feminist Thought: Knowledge, Consciousness, and the Politics of Empowerment.* New York: Routledge, 1990.

Crowley, Sharon. *A Teacher's Introduction to Deconstruction.* Urbana, IL: NCTE, 1989.

Drew, Julie. "Cultural Composition: Stuart Hall on Ethnicity and the Discursive Turn." *JAC* 18 (1998): 171–96.

Forman, Janis, ed. *What Do I Know: Reading, Writing, and Teaching the Essay.* Portsmouth, NH: Heinemann-Boynton/Cook, 1996.

Halloran, S. Michael. "On the End of Rhetoric, Classical and Modern." *Professing the New Rhetorics: A Sourcebook*. Eds. Theresa Enos and Stuart C. Brown. Englewood Cliffs, NJ: Blair/Prentice, 1994. 331–43.

Harris, Wendell. "Reflections on the Peculiar Status of the Personal Essay." *College English* 58 (1996): 934–53.

Harvey, Gordon. "Presence in the Essay." *College English* 56 (1994): 642–54.

hooks, bell. *Black Looks: Race and Representation*. Boston: South End, 1992.

Jordan, June. "Requiem for the Champ." *Technical Difficulties: African-American Notes on the State of the Union*. Ed. June Jordan. New York: Vintage/Random, 1994. 221–26.

Kirsch, Gesa E., and Joy S. Ritchie. "Beyond the Personal: Theorizing a Politics of Location in Composition Research." *College Composition and Communication* 46 (1995): 7–29.

Kitzinger, Celia. "Liberal Humanism as an Ideology of Social Control: The Regulation of Lesbian Identities." Shotter and Gergen 83–98.

Mittlefehldt, Pamela Klass. "A Weaponry of Choice: Black American Women Writers and the Essay." *Politics of the Essay: Feminist Perspectives*. Eds. Ruth-Ellen Boetcher Joeres and Elizabeth Mittman. Bloomington: Indiana UP, 1993. 196–208.

Morrison, Toni. *Playing in the Dark: Whiteness and the Literary Imagination*. Cambridge, MA: Harvard UP, 1992.

Murray, Kevin. "Construction of Identity in the Narratives of Romance and Comedy." Shotter and Gergen 177–205.

Shotter, John, and Kenneth J. Gergen. *Texts of Identity*. London: Sage, 1989.

Spellmeyer, Kurt. "A Common Ground: The Essay in the Academy." *College English* 51 (1989): 262–76.

West, Cornel. "The New Cultural Politics of Difference." *October* 53 (Summer 1990): 93–109.

Comfort's Insights as a Resource for Your Teaching

1. Comfort offers a pedagogy that tightly braids the personal and the political to improve student writing. How can you realistically ensure that in introducing the personal you do not invite the confessional? What other challenges do you anticipate this pedagogy presenting, and how would you meet them?

2. If you are to introduce this pedagogy or aspects of it, it is crucial to provide students with a variety of solid models to analyze. Discuss with your students how the writer juxtaposes the personal and the public. What other writers or essays would provide a solid model like June Jordan's?

Comfort's Insights as a Resource for Your Writing Classroom

1. Comfort's essay offers a powerful tool for teaching students about the bottomless complexity of the idea of "ethos" (the persona or worldview evinced by an author in his or her writing). Try using some of Comfort's ideas in a lesson or series of lessons on "ethos."

2. Using essays that explicitly question the dominant culture provides an especially powerful means to enhance students' skills as critical thinkers. Consider how Comfort's use of the Jordan essay in her class might provide a model for your own attempts to enhance students' capacity for critique.

"So What Do We Do Now?" Necessary Directionality as the Writing Teacher's Response to Racist, Sexist, Homophobic Papers

David Rothgery

David Rothgery meditates on a quandary familiar to all teachers of writing or literature courses and particularly those who have learned to analyze texts rhetorically with the insights of contemporary theory. Contemporary "anti-foundational" theorists like Bakhtin and Derrida posit that humans cannot gain certainty about their existence, behavior, perspectives, or knowledge from universal principles or transcending truths. Any certainty about human experience comes from looking at the situation and examining the conditions of the historical moment, the institutional site, the power structure, the culture within which an event or phenomenon happens. Any "truth" is situational and judged as appropriate, functional, understandable, and reasonable within that situation; foundational moral certainty is illusive and moral pluralism is safe ground.

When teachers read student or professional texts that seem to them morally reprehensible, analysis of "discursive formation" of the text seems insufficient. Rothgery finds no satisfaction in the suggestion that "usable" truths may exist even though transcendent truths do not. He believes there is a continuum by which teachers, learners, and other citizens can measure moral convictions and arrive at a "sense of a necessary direction — one of less cruelty to ourselves and the rest of humankind."

> Then he waited, marshaling his thoughts and brooding over his still untested powers. For though he was master of the world, he was not quite sure what to do next.
>
> But he would think of something. (221)

S o ends Arthur Clarke's classic *2001: A Space Odyssey,* and, as David Bowman contemplates with some dismay his seeming mastery of the universe, his unstated question is one the contemporary writing or literature teacher might well appropriate for his or her own contemporary pedagogical dilemma: So what do I do now with my students? It is the question a high-school English teacher once asked me as she read some Derrida and Nietzsche as part of a required Contemporary Theory and Pedagogy class I was teaching. Her pedagogical quandary was not an isolated one. I answered her with another question: "What if a student in your freshman writing class submits to you a rough draft of a paper which you consider to be racist — very racist? Would you, or should you, with that paper — or perhaps one that asserts that it is the duty of Christians to ferret out every gay and 'beat some sense into him' — mark it as any other paper?"

She seemed to squirm in her seat. She had, in fact, once gotten a racist paper, and her response had been unequivocal: she did not allow the paper and "sat the student down and set him right." Whatever truth there is to Foucault's assertion that each "society has its régime of truth, its 'general politics' of truth — i.e., the types of discourse which it accepts and makes function as true" ("Truth" 131), and whatever personal power agendas are working subtly at the heart of any particular discourse, still, to that teacher that morning, there were some things you could be *certain* about. In the case of a racist paper, some seemingly universal principle far beyond "political correctness," beyond situational truths, was at issue.

Still, as she struggled through some of the assigned readings for the course, it was clear she was having some difficulty reconciling her own moral fervor with what Bakhtin, Derrida, and other theorists of the "anti-foundational" persuasion were arguing: that the human condition does not permit certainty regarding any "Transcendent Truths" as our moral underpinnings, but rather some "truth" in a far less fundamental sense, no matter what we may "feel."

Patricia Bizzell, in restating the dilemma, points to a resolution which works for her and which has implications for any classroom teacher:

> We have not yet taken the next, crucially important step in our rhetorical turn. We have not yet acknowledged that if no unimpeachable authority and transcendent truth exist, this does not mean that no *respectable* authority and no *usable* truth exist. (665; emphasis added)

She implies that teachers must proceed by these "usable" truths and center pedagogical discussions not so much on how one piece of discourse can be made less value-laden, but rather on how all discourse *is* value-laden and therefore political. Dale Bauer, sensitive to a too "authoritative rhetoric" in the classroom, one necessarily tied to a "political position" (391), directs students' attention to "how signs can be manipulated" (391) so as to insure a "mastery that is not oppressive"

(395). On the surface, just as foundationalism in its search for the objective principle is an appealing way to go, so too the kind of anti-foundationalism represented by Bizzell and Bauer — with its recognition that we really can't be certain that any principle is "objective" beyond our saying it is — is appealing in a post-Nietzschean world wherein we have become acutely aware of the linguistic fictional nature of our "non-fictional truths" (consider, e.g., the Margaret Mead version of Samoa). It's all part of the same game. We knock out the big "T" (Truth or Transcendent Truth) but remain, nevertheless, committed to a "respectable authority," a "reasonable truth," an analysis of how power agendas "manipulate signs," and, while showing how our deep-seated aversions to racism, sexism, and homophobia can be subjected to the same process, we, nevertheless, push forward with our convictions. Surely we can and will do this. We will continue to evaluate student papers as to mechanics/usage, style, organization, thesis, and by way of thesis development we will surely "do in" our dangerously myopic, intellectually backward students with appropriately low grades. Our "situational truth" is, if not transcendently valid, certainly more valid than the kind of truth such students promote.

Something about this approach, however, smacks too much of "having our cake and eating it too": There are no Transcendent Truths, but rather "usable truths," which we, as teachers, will make serve as our moral underpinnings. I am uncomfortable. And if I refuse to buy off entirely on the anti-foundationalist argument, I do not believe that makes me a victim of wishful thinking, of a refusal to accept in some way the reality of our essential rhetoricity. Admittedly, the fundamental "situatedness" of the human condition does not allow for the certainty of Transcendent Principles emblazoned across the sky, but neither does it allow for the certainty of there *not* being universals which suggest a direction.

Again and again I have heard professors admit (not in these terms of course, for it is not quite academic to make such admissions) that pedagogical *practice* and contemporary *theory* have to be inconsistent. That is, if it is true we must now discard forever notions of universal principles, it is also true we cannot live (and teach) as though no universal principles underlie anything. In the classroom we encourage a healthy conviction because it leads to the purposefulness which, in turn, increases the probabilities for more creative and powerful rhetoric. This inconsistency is to me, though, as indefensible as an auto manufacturer's claim that it "builds the strongest car possible" when in fact it does not.

On the one hand, the teacher who received the racist paper could have evaluated the rough draft by way of the usual criteria: thesis or essential argument, validity and relevance of supporting evidence, logic and hierarchy of ideas. What better approach than letting the student demonstrate for himself or herself the untenable nature of racist arguments? Such an approach surely works with the arguments, untenable or not, set forth in any paper from "American Management Styles: Finest in the World" to "Survival of Our Wetlands: More Priority, Please."

After all, even with these papers we could argue that, in each case, something bordering on "fundamental" is at work: in the first paper, respect for the laborer perhaps; in the second, concern for our children's children. Still, teachers are not likely, with such papers, to react as our teacher did to the racist paper, which she regarded as a paper of an entirely different species. I suppose we could include in that extreme "different species" category (whether we ever receive them or not) papers which argue that we burn epileptics as devils, raze gay bars, lynch Blacks who dare to date White women, burn cats in satanic rites, or return women to their proper roles as child-rearers and sex toys.

My point in invoking these extreme examples is that, indeed, there is a *continuum,* a "more fundamental" at work, a sense of directionality. I take issue with those who believe we can buy into a universe of "situational ethics" or "usable" truths — that is, until we are willing to grant there is nothing to be gained in striving toward "fundamental" or "transcendent" principles which such papers violate in promoting cruel behavior towards humankind and the other creatures which populate the earth. Burning epileptics at the stake, abusing children, promoting by willful neglect the extinction of an animal species — such acts don't properly merit some gradation of ethical value relative to a particular culture or period of time.

Rarely do we come across extremely reprehensible papers — such as those which do openly promote cruel behavior. But our writing classes do become the setting for argument about capital punishment, euthanasia, abortion, women's rights. If we regard these discussions as having at most only "situational" weight — a "this time and place" payoff — then the dynamics of shared ideas is not allowed its proper role in the *necessary directionality* for the human condition and the condition of the planet we inhabit — that of alleviating suffering and cruelty, physical, mental, and spiritual — no matter which status the cosmic deities or demons accord such cruelty.

What is this "continuum," this "necessary directionality"? Consider the subject of racism. At one end of the continuum are non-racist papers arguing the merits of affirmative action, and at the other end are Skinhead-oriented papers arguing the supremacy of the White race. In between are many kinds of papers, such as one I once received which questioned why White students must be forced to mingle in small-group discussions with Hispanics and Blacks. Surely, for most teachers, something *more* fundamental is at stake in the Skinhead paper, and something *less* fundamental is at stake in the paper on classroom grouping. But this "more"/"less" continuum is, for the teacher, a different vision of ethics than "usable truth," which by its very nature admits of no true sense of continuum. My point is "more fundamental" and "usable" cannot inhabit the same world. At what point, for example, does the seemingly fundamental truth about cruelty and insensitivity to those of different color become the "usable" truth of arrangement of students within classroom groups or the "reasonable" and "situational ethic" of "Does Affirmative Action Succeed in Its Goals?"?

I am certainly *not* arguing that a teacher could not legitimately deal with papers presenting reprehensible ideas by way of the usual criteria of structure, logic, grammar, and style. The question I pose is this: Has contemporary theory, with its insights into the "situatedness" of our existence and perspectives, left us any sense of a valid — indeed, a *necessary,* "we-can-no-longer-go-back-to-that" — directionality by way of shared ideas? Can we indeed go back to treating women as objects, African Americans as possessions, homosexuals as freaks, epileptics as devils?

Stanley Fish argues, in *Doing What Comes Naturally,* that

> questions of fact, truth, correctness, validity, and clarity can neither be posed nor answered with reference to some extracontextual, ahistorical, nonsituational reality, or rule, or law, or value; rather, anti-foundationalism asserts, all these matters are intelligible and debatable only within the precincts of the contexts or situations or paradigms or communities that give them their local and changeable shape. (344)

Fish speaks only of what he can be certain. He cannot be certain of Transcendent Truths. Nor can we. But does this mean we cannot be committed to moving toward truths which are *so comprehensive* that their force cannot be ignored?

Necessary Direction away from cruelty is just such a truth. The question is not so much whether or not we must assign to these "truths" the status of "undeniable absolutes," but whether we must assign to them some essence which is *so fundamental,* so clearly pointing to a necessary direction, that *we must insist that, pedagogically, an unqualified moral conviction must assert itself.* As long as "better" is given its proper "transcendent" due, a true moral purpose remains, and a true moral conviction in the classroom can continue. The confrontation of values, of situational ethics, that defines any composition classroom dynamics is not a naive affective or fictional game that we as teachers must continue to play to produce what Stanley Fish calls the "small . . . yield" of a "few worn and familiar bromides" (355); on the contrary, it is a confrontation founded in our sense of a *necessary* direction — one of less cruelty to ourselves and the rest of humankind.

This is not a starry-eyed meliorism or naive social evolutionism. Surely we do need in our classrooms the kind of discursive analysis the anti-foundationalists call for. A deconstructionist reading of *Mein Kampf* could not have been all bad. But Fish and Bizzell leave us too precarious an anchoring. Without that sense of a *necessary direction,* hate crimes such as the burning of crosses will necessarily be prosecuted only as vandalism, and the Andersonville and Auschwitz behavior will be defended by way of "following orders." We have moved *beyond* that. Indeed, humankind's condition seems to be defined in great measure by "situatedness." But what is functional and reasonable for one time and place must always push against other times and places — other situations on a greater scale. Racist and sexist behavior of any sort that promotes unnecessary cruelty must never be afforded the justification a too-unexamined moral pluralism may allow.

Otherwise, the kind of phenomena I experienced in my Writing Theory class in the spring of 1992 will be the norm. We were discussing Michel Foucault's *The Archaeology of Knowledge.* I had written on the board the sentence "Saddam Hussein is a Hitler." On the one hand, I recognized, as did the students, that the politically "correct" position on this (or on Hussein and the Gulf War in general) would vary greatly from campus to campus. Furthermore, Fish's comment that anti-foundationalism's super-self-consciousness is not a way out, that

> any claim in which the notion of situatedness is said to be a lever that allows us to get a purchase on situations is finally a claim to have *escaped situatedness,* and is therefore nothing more or less than a reinvention of foundationalism by the very form of thought that has supposedly reduced it to ruins (348–49 emphasis added),

still seemed valid here. Thus, the immediate reaction to the "Saddam Hussein is a Hitler" sentence in my class of relatively sophisticated rhetorical-theory students was in line with Foucault (and Fish): that we had to look at who said it and other dimensions of the "enunciative modalities," what "institutional sites" were being represented, and so on. The students suggested several such "sites" each with its own particular "political" baggage, its own appropriation of the statement, and I put them on the board:

Bush Hussein *NY Times* Editors Soldier's Mother

"SADDAM HUSSEIN IS A HITLER." — REALITY?

W.W. II Veteran Berkeley Anti-War Activist Kurds

Our "situating" of a bit of discourse was, for a while, only an *academic* exercise — much as composition classes, I fear, tend to be for anti-foundationalist teachers. But when we finished congratulating ourselves on the incisiveness of our dissection, I put the chalk down and took a different approach. "But what if Hussein really *is* a kind of Hitler?" I asked. "What of the *very real possibility* that Hussein was *greatly* responsible for the unnecessary and perhaps cruel deaths of thousands of Kurds? What then? That is, what do we do now beyond analyzing the 'discursive formation' of that sentence?"

The students were literally unable to speak for almost a minute. It had not occurred to any of the students, all of them very bright, that *even in the classroom* there are questions that require more than being asked — that must be *answered.* I was not asking my students to take arms against Hussein but to sort out for themselves the truths regarding the possibility of a very real atrocity.

The classroom may be a laboratory, but it is a laboratory for the world we live in. Analysis and determination of power zones is of course essential, and too little of that has been done in our classrooms in the past. But when the *only* result for the classroom of anti-foundationalist and post-modernist insights is a discursive analysis which takes on the character of some linguistic Rubic's Cube, then we have plunged into the same idiocy that allowed learning theory to transform classrooms into robotical M and M dispenser systems.

As writers and teachers of writing, we must continue to grope in the recognition that our moral convictions do not translate as self-contained situational ethics alone, that they will continue to be measured along greater and greater scales — scales so large we must of necessity grant *some* of them a "highest order" status. "Better" — though it may and will be misappropriated and misapplied by the inexperienced, the uneducated, the cowardly, the wicked — must continue to be an operational term. We must continue to act, to "do," to "write" not only *as though* our writing is just one more version of Foucault's "discursive formations," emanating from this "institutional site" or that, but indeed *because* some of our convictions *are* more true, *are* better — because we can now discard *forever* some situational ethics.

What is the "new pedagogy" for our composition classrooms? Can it reside in "style," in anti-foundationalist situational truths which do not even consider the possibility of necessary directions (i.e., directions defined by *what can no longer be acceptable*)? That is indeed a "small yield," and the resulting classroom environment will produce too many students with a "small yield" attitude about not only their papers but the convictions which underlie them. Whatever naiveté there may be in the persistent groping in the dark for "first" principles to understand our universe, the real force of the greatest literature, or of that "one in a hundred" student composition, lies in that *groping* beyond the imprisonment of our situatedness. And a pedagogy that chooses to ignore the moral sweat, if you will, does a disservice of the profoundest order to the appreciation of good writing, of great writing. Yes, the groping between student and teacher may clash, but in the areas of racism, sexism, homophobia, the clash should be loud and morally meaningful in recognition that Necessary Directionality remains a valid concept.

Works Cited

Bauer, Dale. "The Other 'F' Word: The Feminist in the Classroom." *College English* 52 (Apr. 1990): 385–96.

Bizzell, Patricia. "Beyond Anti-Foundationalism to Rhetorical Authority: Problems Defining Cultural Literacy." *College English* 52 (Oct. 1990): 661–75.

Clarke, Arthur C. *2001: A Space Odyssey.* New York: Signet, 1968.

Fish, Stanley. *Doing What Comes Naturally: Change, Rhetoric, and the Practice of Theory in Literary and Legal Studies.* Durham: Duke UP, 1989.

Foucault, Michel. *The Archaeology of Knowledge.* Trans. A. M. Sheridan Smith. New York: Pantheon, 1972.

———. "Truth and Power." *Power / Knowledge: Selected Interviews and Other Writings, 1972–77.* Trans. Colin Gordon, Leo Marshall, John Mepham, and Kate Soper. Ed. Colin Gordon. New York: Pantheon, 1980. 109–33.

Rothgery's Insights as a Resource for Your Teaching

1. Without a clear definition of *necessary directionality,* it can be difficult to distinguish what causes a personal reaction against the moral reasoning of a text. Whatever beliefs teachers hold about controversial issues such as abortion, capital punishment, or animal rights, censoring those issues as paper topics clearly denies students opportunities for discovering or defining their own beliefs and for learning how to present their beliefs to an audience that may disagree. Share Rothgery's essay with teaching colleagues and suggest a "brown bag" discussion. Ask colleagues how they work with texts and students to accommodate not only multiple perspectives but also shared convictions or perspectives "we cannot go back to."

2. Rothgery acknowledges that a teacher might evaluate reprehensible texts more rigorously than other texts, using only rhetorical analysis to define the quality of those papers. If you receive a text that repulses you, first draft a letter in which you describe all the strengths of the paper and any problems with it. Put the letter aside and ask three or four veteran instructors to read the text "holistically," citing strengths and weaknesses they find in the "discursive formation." Compare your letter with their feedback as a way to provide the student with a "fair" reading of the text. Then ask those colleagues how/if/why they would deal with what makes the essay reprehensible to you.

Rothgery's Insights as a Resource for Your Writing Classroom

1. Texts that are reprehensible to you will also disturb many of your students. Before you model peer criticism, bring in a text that triggers moral repulsion and pose the question, "If a peer wrote a text that was intentionally or unintentionally stepping beyond what you believe 'must not happen,' how would you help that writer understand your reaction?" Organize small groups of three or four and follow up with reports to the large group. Ask class members to identify common themes from the discussions and to write in their journals about those themes.

2. Swift's "A Modest Proposal" is "canonical" in composition texts partly because the satire deliberately triggers what to Swift was a "transcendent truth" and what Rothgery would describe as a "necessary directionality." Many students will not have read the satire and will be repulsed, sometimes missing the ironic juxtaposition of the two voices in the text. Organize a class discussion

of the text in terms of the traditional argument: demonstration of a problem, formal statement of solution, explanation of the solution, and refutation of alternative solutions. Use the chalkboard to outline the satire twice, side by side: first from the voice of the "modest proposal" and then from the covert voice of Swift as it undercuts and broadens the description of the problem and solutions. Expect that class members will be able to think about how Swift manipulated their early reactions (e.g., "This is sick").

The class conversation will come to focus on the proposer's criteria of evaluation ("fair, cheap, and easy") against the implied criteria of Swift. Assign follow-up journal entries, asking students to analyze the use of "fair, cheap, and easy" criteria in modern or contemporary world events and comment on the moral criteria that perhaps are used or could be used on a "larger scale" over time, across concepts of nation, race, gender, and so on.

Sponsors of Literacy

Deborah Brandt

This essay connects the idea of literacy as an individual development with the idea of literacy as an economic development by exploring how various agents enable, support, regulate, or suppress the development of literacy. Deborah Brandt reports on her findings from one hundred in-depth interviews with people around the country and concludes that we, as teachers of composition, are powerful enough to sponsor literacy on our own terms. We also, however, serve as "conflicted brokers between literacy's buyers and sellers," and Brandt emphasizes that we must sensitize ourselves to the ways patterns of sponsorship also follow patterns of social stratification.

In his sweeping history of adult learning in the United States, Joseph Kett describes the intellectual atmosphere available to young apprentices who worked in the small, decentralized print shops of antebellum America. Because printers also were the solicitors and editors of what they published, their workshops served as lively incubators for literacy and political discourse. By the mid-nineteenth century, however, this learning space was disrupted when the invention of the steam press reorganized the economy of the print industry. Steam presses were so expensive that they required capital outlays beyond the means of many printers. As a result, print jobs were outsourced, the processes of editing and printing were split, and, in tight competition, print apprentices became low-paid mechanics with no more access to the multiskilled environment of the craftshop (Kett 67–70). While this shift in working conditions may be evidence of the deskilling of workers induced by the Industrial Revolution (Nicholas and Nicholas), it also offers a site for reflecting upon the dynamic sources of literacy and literacy learning. The reading and writing skills of print apprentices in this period were the achievements not simply of teachers and learners nor of the discourse practices of the printer community. Rather, these skills existed fragilely, contingently within an economic moment. The pre-steam press economy enabled some of the most basic aspects of the apprentices' literacy, especially their access to material production and the public meaning or worth of their skills. Paradoxically, even as the steam-powered penny press made print more accessible (by making publishing more profitable), it brought an end to a particular form of literacy sponsorship and a drop in literate potential.

The apprentices' experience invites rumination upon literacy learning and teaching today. Literacy looms as one of the great engines of profit and competitive advantage in the twentieth century: a lubricant for consumer desire; a means for integrating corporate markets; a foundation for the deployment of weapons and other technology; a raw material in the mass production of information. As ordinary citizens have been compelled into these economies, their reading and writing skills have grown sharply more central to the everyday trade of information and goods as well as to the pursuit of education, employment, civil rights, status. At the same time, people's literate skills have grown vulnerable to unprecedented turbulence in their economic value, as conditions, forms, and standards of literacy achievement seem to shift with almost every new generation of learners. How are we to understand the vicissitudes of individual literacy development in relationship to the large-scale economic forces that set the routes and determine the wordly worth of that literacy?

The field of writing studies has had much to say about individual literacy development. Especially in the last quarter of the twentieth century, we have theorized, researched, critiqued, debated, and sometimes even managed to enhance the literate potentials of ordinary citizens as they have tried to cope with life as they find it. Less easily and certainly less steadily have we been able to relate what we see, study, and do to these larger contexts of profit making and competition. This even as we recognize that the most pressing issues we deal with — tightening associations between literate skill and social viability, the breakneck pace of change in communications technology, persistent inequities in access and reward — all relate to structural conditions in literacy's bigger picture. When economic forces are addressed in our work, they appear primarily as generalities: contexts, determinants, motivators, barriers, touchstones. But rarely are they systematically related to the local conditions and embodied moments of literacy learning that occupy so many of us on a daily basis.[1]

This essay does not presume to overcome the analytical failure completely. But it does offer a conceptual approach that begins to connect literacy as an individual development to literacy as an economic development, at least as the two have played out over the last ninety years or so. The approach is through what I call sponsors of literacy. Sponsors, as I have come to think of them, are any agents, local or distant, concrete or abstract, who enable, support, teach, model, as well as recruit, regulate, suppress, or withhold literacy — and gain advantage by it in some way. Just as the ages of radio and television accustom us to having programs *brought* to us by various commercial sponsors, it is useful to think about who or what underwrites occasions of literacy learning and use. Although the interests of the sponsor and the sponsored do not have to converge (and, in fact, may conflict), sponsors nevertheless set the terms for access to literacy and wield powerful incentives for compliance and loyalty. Sponsors are a tangible reminder that literacy learning throughout history has always required permission, sanction, assistance, coercion, or, at minimum, contact with existing trade routes. Sponsors are delivery systems for the economies of literacy, the means by which these forces present themselves to — and through — individual learners. They also represent the causes into which people's literacy usually gets recruited.[2]

For the last five years I have been tracing sponsors of literacy across the twentieth century as they appear in the accounts of ordinary Americans recalling how they learned to write and read. The investigation is grounded in more than 100 in-depth interviews that I collected from a diverse group of people born roughly between 1900 and 1980. In the interviews, people explored in great detail their memories of learning to read and write across their lifetimes, focusing especially on the people, institutions, materials, and motivations involved in the process. The more I worked with these accounts, the more I came to realize that they were filled with references to sponsors, both explicit and latent, who appeared in formative roles at the scenes of literacy learning. Patterns of sponsorship became an illuminating site through which to track the different cultural attitudes people developed toward writing vs. reading as well as the ideological congestion faced by late-century literacy learners as their sponsors proliferated and diversified (see my essays on "Remembering Reading" and "Accumulating Literacy"). In this essay I set out a case for why the concept of sponsorship is so richly suggestive for exploring economies of literacy and their effects. Then, through use of extended case examples, I demonstrate the practical application of this approach for interpreting current conditions of literacy teaching and learning, including persistent stratification of opportunity and escalating standards for literacy achievement. A final section addresses implications for the teaching of writing.

Sponsorship

Intuitively, *sponsors* seemed a fitting term for the figures who turned up most typically in people's memories of literacy learning: older relatives, teachers, priests, supervisors, military officers, editors, influential authors. Sponsors, as we ordinarily think of them, are powerful figures who bankroll events or smooth the way of initiates. Usually richer, more knowledgeable, and more entrenched than the sponsored, sponsors nevertheless enter a reciprocal relationship with those they underwrite. They lend their resources or credibility to the sponsored but also stand to gain benefits from their success, whether by direct repayment or, indirectly, by credit of association. *Sponsors* also proved an appealing term in my analysis because of all the commercial references that appeared in these twentieth-century accounts — the magazines, peddled encyclopedias, essay contests, radio and television programs, toys, fan clubs, writing tools, and so on, from which so much experience with literacy was derived. As the twentieth century turned the abilities to read and write into widely exploitable resources, commercial sponsorship abounded.

In whatever form, sponsors deliver the ideological freight that must be borne for access to what they have. Of course, the sponsored can be oblivious to or innovative with this ideological burden. Like Little Leaguers who wear the logo of a local insurance agency on their uniforms, not out of a concern for enhancing the agency's image but as a means for getting to play ball, people throughout history have acquired literacy pragmatically under the banner of others' causes. In the days before free, public schooling in England, Protestant Sunday Schools warily offered basic reading instruction to working-class families as part of evangelical duty. To the horror of many in the church sponsorship, these families insistently, sometimes riotously demanded of their Sunday Schools more instruction, including in writing and math, because it provided means for upward mobility.[3] Through the sponsorship of Baptist and Methodist ministries, African Americans in slavery taught each other to understand the Bible in subversively liberatory ways. Under a conservative regime, they developed forms of critical literacy that sustained religious, educational, and political movements both before and after emancipation (Cornelius). Most of the time, however, literacy takes its shape from the interests of its sponsors. And, as we will see below, obligations toward one's sponsors run deep, affecting what, why, and how people write and read.

The concept of sponsors helps to explain, then, a range of human relationships and ideological pressures that turn up at the scenes of literacy learning — from benign sharing between adults and youths, to euphemized coercions in schools and workplaces, to the most notorious impositions and deprivations by church or state. It also is a concept useful for tracking literacy's materiel: the things that accompany writing and reading and the ways they are manufactured and distributed. Sponsorship as a sociological term is even more broadly suggestive for thinking about economies of literacy development. Studies of patronage in Europe and *compradrazgo* in the Americas show how patron-client relationships in the past grew up around the need to manage scarce resources and promote political stability (Bourne; Lynch; Horstman and Kurtz). Pragmatic, instrumental, ambivalent, patron-client relationships integrated otherwise antagonistic social classes into relationships of mutual, albeit unequal dependencies. Loaning land, money, protection, and other favors allowed the politically powerful to extend their influence and justify their exploitation of clients. Clients traded their labor and deference for access to opportunities for themselves or their children and for leverage needed to improve their social standing. Especially under conquest in Latin America, *compradrazgo* reintegrated native societies badly fragmented by the diseases and other disruptions that followed foreign invasions. At the same time, this system was susceptible to its own stresses, especially when patrons became clients themselves of still more centralized or distant overlords, with all the shifts in loyalty and perspective that entailed (Horstman and Kurtz 13–14).

In raising this association with formal systems of patronage, I do not wish to overlook the very different economic, political, and educational systems within which U.S. literacy has developed. But where we find the sponsoring of literacy, it will be useful to look for its function within larger political and economic arenas. Literacy, like land, is a valued commodity in this economy, a key resource in gaining profit and edge. This value helps to explain, of course, the lengths people will go to secure literacy for themselves or their children. But it also explains why the powerful work so persistently to conscript and ration the powers of literacy. The competition to harness literacy, to manage, measure, teach, and exploit it, has intensified throughout the century. It is vital to pay attention to this development because it largely sets the terms for individuals' encounters with literacy. This competition shapes the incentives and barriers (including uneven distributions of opportunity) that greet literacy learners in any particular time and place. It is this competition that has made access to the right kinds of literacy sponsors so crucial for political and economic well-being. And it also has spurred the rapid, complex changes that now make the pursuit of literacy feel so turbulent and precarious for so many.

In the next three sections, I trace the dynamics of literacy sponsorship through the life experiences of several individuals, showing how their opportunities for literacy learning emerge out of the jockeying and skirmishing for economic and political advantage going on among sponsors of literacy. Along the way, the analysis addresses three key issues: (1) how, despite ostensible democracy in educational chances, stratification of opportunity continues to organize access and reward in literacy learning; (2) how sponsors contribute to what is called "the literacy crisis," that is, the perceived gap between rising standards for achievement and people's ability to meet them; and (3) how encounters with literacy sponsors, especially as they are configured at the end of the twentieth century, can be sites for the innovative rerouting of resources into projects of self-development and social change.

Sponsorship and Access

A focus on sponsorship can force a more explicit and substantive link between literacy learning and systems of opportunity and access. A statistical correlation between high literacy achievement and high socioeconomic, majority-race status routinely shows up in results of national tests of reading and writing performance.[4] These findings capture yet, in their shorthand way, obscure the unequal conditions of literacy sponsorship that lie behind differential outcomes in academic performance. Throughout their lives, affluent people from high-caste racial groups have multiple and redundant contacts with powerful literacy sponsors as a routine part of their economic and political privileges. Poor people and those from low-caste racial groups have less consistent, less politically secured access to literacy sponsors — especially to the ones that can grease their way to academic and economic success. Differences in their performances are often attributed to family background (namely education and income of parents) or to particular norms and values operating within different ethnic groups or social classes. But in either case, much more is usually at work.

As a study in contrasts in sponsorship patterns and access to literacy, consider the parallel experiences of Raymond Branch and Dora Lopez, both of whom were born in 1969 and, as young children, moved with their parents to the same, mid-sized university town in the Midwest.[5] Both were still residing in this town at the time of our interviews in 1995. Raymond Branch, a European American, had been born in southern California, the son of a professor father and a real estate executive mother. He recalled that his first grade classroom in 1975 was hooked up to a mainframe computer at Stanford University and that, as a youngster, he enjoyed fooling around with computer programming in the company of "real users" at his father's science lab. This process was not interrupted much when, in the late 1970s, his family moved to the Midwest. Raymond received his first personal computer as a Christmas present from his parents when he was twelve years old, and a modem the year after that. In the 1980s, computer hardware and software stores began popping up within a bicycle-ride's distance from where he lived. The stores were serving the university community and, increasingly, the high-tech industries that were becoming established in that vicinity. As an adolescent, Raymond spent his summers roaming these stores, sampling new computer games, making contact with founders of some of the first electronic bulletin boards in the nation, and continuing, through reading and other informal means, to develop his programming techniques. At the time of our interview he had graduated from the local university and was a successful freelance writer of software and software documentation, with clients in both the private sector and the university community.

Dora Lopez, a Mexican American, was born in the same year as Raymond Branch, 1969, in a Texas border town, where her grandparents, who worked as farm laborers, lived most of the year. When Dora was still a baby her family moved to the same Midwest university town as had the family of Raymond Branch. Her father pursued an accounting degree at a local technical college and found work as a shipping and receiving clerk at the university. Her mother, who also attended technical college briefly, worked part-time in a bookstore. In the early

1970s, when the Lopez family made its move to the Midwest, the Mexican-American population in the university town was barely one percent. Dora recalled that the family had to drive seventy miles to a big city to find not only suitable groceries but also Spanish-language newspapers and magazines that carried information of concern and interest to them. (Only when reception was good could they catch Spanish-language radio programs coming from Chicago, 150 miles away.) During her adolescence, Dora Lopez undertook to teach herself how to read and write in Spanish, something, she said, that neither her brother nor her U.S.-born cousins knew how to do. Sometimes, with the help of her mother's employee discount at the bookstore, she sought out novels by South American and Mexican writers, and she practiced her written Spanish by corresponding with relatives in Colombia. She was exposed to computers for the first time at the age of thirteen when she worked as a teacher's aide in a federally funded summer school program for the children of migrant workers. The computers were being used to help the children to be brought up to grade level in their reading and writing skills. When Dora was admitted to the same university that Raymond Branch attended, her father bought her a used word processing machine that a student had advertised for sale on a bulletin board in the building where Mr. Lopez worked. At the time of our interview, Dora Lopez had transferred from the university to a technical college. She was working for a cleaning company, where she performed extra duties as a translator, communicating on her supervisor's behalf with the largely Latina cleaning staff. "I write in Spanish for him, what he needs to be translated, like job duties, what he expects them to do, and I write lists for him in English and Spanish," she explained.

In Raymond Branch's account of his early literacy learning we are able to see behind the scenes of his majority-race membership, male gender, and high-end socioeconomic family profile. There lies a thick and, to him, relatively accessible economy of institutional and commercial supports that cultivated and subsidized his acquisition of a powerful form of literacy. One might be tempted to say that Raymond Branch was born at the right time and lived in the right place — except that the experience of Dora Lopez troubles that thought. For Raymond Branch, a university town in the 1970s and 1980s provided an information-rich, resource-rich learning environment in which to pursue his literacy development, but for Dora Lopez, a female member of a culturally unsubsidized ethnic minority, the same town at the same time was information- and resource-poor. Interestingly, both young people were pursuing projects of self-initiated learning, Raymond Branch in computer programming and Dora Lopez in biliteracy. But she had to reach much further afield for the material and communicative systems needed to support her learning. Also, while Raymond Branch, as the son of an academic, was sponsored by some of the most powerful agents of the university (its laboratories, newest technologies, and most educated personnel), Dora Lopez was being sponsored by what her parents could pull from the peripheral service systems of the university (the mail room, the bookstore, the second-hand technology market). In these accounts we also can see how the development and eventual economic worth of Raymond Branch's literacy skills were underwritten by late-century transformations in communication technology that created a boomtown need for programmers and software writers. Dora Lopez's biliterate skills developed and paid off much further down the economic-reward ladder, in government-sponsored youth programs and commercial enterprises, that, in the 1990s, were absorbing surplus migrant workers into a low-wage, urban service economy.[6] Tracking patterns of literacy sponsorship, then, gets beyond SES shorthand to expose more fully how unequal literacy chances relate to systems of unequal subsidy and reward for literacy. These are the systems that deliver large-scale economic, historical, and political conditions to the scenes of small-scale literacy use and development.

This analysis of sponsorship forces us to consider not merely how one social group's literacy practices may differ from another's, but how everybody's literacy practices are operating in differential economies, which supply different access routes, different degrees of sponsoring power, and different scales of monetary worth to the practices in use. In fact, the interviews I conducted are filled with examples of how economic and political forces, some of them originating in quite distant corporate and government policies, affect people's day-to-day ability to seek out and practice literacy. As a telephone company employee, Janelle Hampton enjoyed a brief period in the early 1980s as a fraud investigator, pursuing inquiries and writing up reports of her efforts. But when the breakup of the telephone utility reorganized its workforce, the fraud division was moved two states away and she was returned to less interesting work as a data processor. When, as a seven-year-old in the mid-1970s, Yi Vong made his way with his family from Laos to rural Wisconsin as part of the first resettlement group of Hmong refugees after the Vietnam War, his school district — which had no ESL programming — placed him in a school for the blind and deaf, where he learned English on audio and visual language machines. When a meager retirement pension forced Peter Hardaway and his wife out of their house and into a trailer, the couple stopped receiving newspapers and magazines in order to avoid cluttering up the small space they had to share. An analysis of sponsorship systems of literacy would help educators everywhere to think through the effects that economic and political changes in their regions are having on various people's ability to write and read, their chances to sustain that ability, and their capacities to pass it along to others. Recession, relocation, immigration, technological change, government retreat all can — and do — condition the course by which literate potential develops.

Sponsorship and the Rise in Literacy Standards

As I have been attempting to argue, literacy as a resource becomes available to ordinary people largely through the mediations of more powerful sponsors. These sponsors are engaged in ceaseless processes of positioning and repositioning, seizing and relinquishing control over meanings and materials of literacy as part of their participation in economic and political competition. In the give and take of these struggles, forms of literacy and literacy learning take shape. This section examines more closely how forms of literacy are created out of competitions between institutions. It especially considers how this process relates to the rapid rise in literacy standards since World War II. Resnick and Resnick lay out the process by which the demand for literacy achievement has been escalating, from basic, largely rote competence to more complex analytical and interpretive skills. More and more people are now being expected to accomplish more and more things with reading and writing. As print and its spinoffs have entered virtually every sphere of life, people have grown increasingly dependent on their literacy skills for earning a living and exercising and protecting their civil rights. This section uses one extended case example to trace the role of institutional sponsorship in raising the literacy stakes. It also considers how one man used available forms of sponsorship to cope with this escalation in literacy demands.

The focus is on Dwayne Lowery, whose transition in the early 1970s from line worker in an automobile manufacturing plant to field representative for a major public employees union exemplified the major transition of the post-World War II economy — from a thing-making, thing-swapping society to an information-making, service-swapping society. In the process, Dwayne Lowery had to learn to read and write in ways that he had never done before. How his experiences with writing developed and how they were sponsored — and distressed — by institutional struggle will unfold in the following narrative.

A man of Eastern European ancestry, Dwayne Lowery was born in 1938 and raised in a semi-rural area in the upper Midwest, the third of five children of a rubber worker father and a homemaker mother. Lowery recalled how, in his childhood home, his father's feisty union publications and left-leaning newspapers and radio shows helped to create a political climate in his household. "I was sixteen years old before I knew that god-damn Republicans was two words," he said. Despite this influence, Lowery said he shunned politics and newspaper reading as a young person, except to read the sports page. A diffident student, he graduated near the bottom of his class from a small high school in 1956 and, after a stint in the Army, went to work on the assembly line of a major automobile manufacturer. In the late 1960s, bored with the repetition of spraying primer paint on the right door checks of 57 cars an hour, Lowery traded in his night shift at the auto plant for a day job reading water meters in a municipal utility department. It was at that time, Lowery recalled, that he rediscovered newspapers, reading them in the early morning in his department's break room. He said:

> At the time I guess I got a little more interested in the state of things within the state. I started to get a little political at that time and got a little more information about local people. So I would buy [a metropolitan paper] and I would read that paper in the morning. It was a pretty conservative paper but I got some information.

At about the same time Lowery became active in a rapidly growing public employees union, and, in the early 1970s, he applied for and received a union-sponsored grant that allowed him to take off four months of work and travel to Washington, D.C. for training in union activity. Here is his extended account of that experience:

> When I got to school, then there was a lot of reading. I often felt bad. If I had read more [as a high-school student] it wouldn't have been so tough. But they pumped a lot of stuff at us to read. We lived in a hotel and we had to some extent homework we had to do and reading we had to do and not make written reports but make some presentation on our part of it. What they were trying to teach us, I believe, was regulations, systems, laws. In case anything in court came up along the way, we would know that. We did a lot of work on organizing, you know, learning how to negotiate contracts, contractual language, how to write it. Gross National Product, how that affected the Consumer Price Index. It was pretty much a crash course. It was pretty much crammed in. And I'm not sure we were all that well prepared when we got done, but it was interesting.

After a hands-on experience organizing sanitation workers in the West, Lowery returned home and was offered a full-time job as a field staff representative for the union, handling worker grievances and contract negotiations for a large, active local near his state capital. His initial writing and rhetorical activities corresponded with the heady days of the early 1970s when the union was growing in strength and influence, reflecting in part the exponential expansion in information workers and service providers within all branches of government. With practice, Lowery said he became "good at talking," "good at presenting the union side," "good at slicing chunks off the employer's case." Lowery observed that, in those years, the elected officials with whom he was negotiating often lacked the sophistication of their Washington-trained union counterparts. "They were part-time people," he said. "And they didn't know how to calculate. We got things in contracts that didn't cost them much at the time but were going to cost them a ton down the road." In time, though, even small municipal and county governments responded to the public employees' growing power by hiring specialized attorneys to represent them in grievance and contract negotiations. "Pretty soon," Lowery observed, "ninety percent of the people I was dealing with across the table were attorneys."

This move brought dramatic changes in the writing practices of union reps, and, in Lowery's estimation, a simultaneous waning of the power of workers and the power of his own literacy. "It used to be we got our way through muscle or through political connections," he said. "Now we had to get it through legalistic stuff. It was no longer just sit down and talk about it. Can we make a deal?" Instead, all activity became rendered in writing: the exhibit, the brief, the transcript, the letter, the appeal. Because briefs took longer to write, the wheels of justice took longer to turn. Delays in grievance hearings became routine, as lawyers and union reps alike asked hearing judges for extensions on their briefs. Things went, in Lowery's words, "from quick, competent justice to expensive and long-term justice."

In the meantime, Lowery began spending up to seventy hours a week at work, sweating over the writing of briefs, which are typically fifteen- to thirty-page documents laying out precedents, arguments, and evidence for a grievant's case. These documents were being forced by the new political economy in which Lowery's union was operating. He explained:

> When employers were represented by an attorney, you were going to have a written brief because the attorney needs to get paid. Well, what do you think if you were a union grievant and the attorney says, well, I'm going to write a brief and Dwayne Lowery says, well, I'm not going to. Does the worker somehow feel that their representation is less now?

To keep up with the new demands, Lowery occasionally traveled to major cities for two- or three-day union-sponsored workshops on arbitration, new legislation, and communication skills. He also took short courses at a historic School for Workers at a nearby university. His writing instruction consisted mainly of reading the briefs of other field reps, especially those done by the college graduates who increasingly were being assigned to his district from union headquarters. Lowery said he kept a file drawer filled with other people's briefs from which he would borrow formats and phrasings. At the time of our interview in 1995, Dwayne Lowery had just taken an early and somewhat bitter retirement from the union, replaced by a recent graduate from a master's degree program in Industrial Relations. As a retiree, he was engaged in local Democratic party politics and was getting informal lessons in word processing at home from his wife.

Over a twenty-year period, Lowery's adult writing took its character from a particular juncture in labor relations, when even small units of government began wielding (and, as a consequence, began spreading) a "legalistic" form of literacy in order to restore political dominance over public workers. This struggle for dominance shaped the kinds of literacy skills required of Lowery, the kinds of genres he learned and used, and the kinds of literate identity he developed. Lowery's rank-and-file experience and his talent for representing that experience around a bargaining table became increasingly peripheral to his ability to prepare documents that could compete in kind with those written by his formally educated, professional adversaries. Face-to-face meetings became occasions mostly for a ritualistic exchange of texts, as arbitrators generally deferred decisions, reaching them in private, after solitary deliberation over complex sets of documents. What Dwayne Lowery was up against as a working adult in the second half of the twentieth century was more than just living through a rising standard in literacy expectations or a generalized growth in professionalization, specialization, or documentary power — although certainly all of those things are, generically, true. Rather, these developments should be seen more specifically, as outcomes of ongoing transformations in the history of literacy as it has been wielded as part of economic and political conflict. These transformations become the arenas in which new standards of literacy develop. And for Dwayne Lowery — as well as many like him over the last twenty-five years — these are the arenas in which the worth of existing literate skills become degraded. A consummate debater and deal maker, Lowery saw his value to the union bureaucracy subside, as power shifted to younger, university-trained staffers whose literacy credentials better matched the specialized forms of escalating pressure coming from the other side.

In the broadest sense, the sponsorship of Dwayne Lowery's literacy experiences lies deep within the historical conditions of industrial relations in the twentieth century and, more particularly, within the changing nature of work and labor struggle over the last several decades. Edward Stevens Jr. has observed the rise in this century of an "advanced contractarian society" (25) by which formal relationships of all kinds have come to rely on "a jungle of rules and regulations" (139). For labor, these conditions only intensified in the 1960s and 1970s when a flurry of federal and state civil rights legislation curtailed the previously unregulated hiring and firing power of management. These developments made the appeal to law as central as collective bargaining for extending employee rights (Heckscher 9). I mention this broader picture, first, because it relates to the forms of employer backlash that Lowery began experiencing by the early 1980s and, more important, because a history of unionism serves as a guide for a closer look at the sponsors of Lowery's literacy.

These resources begin with the influence of his father whose membership in the United Rubber Workers during the ideologically potent 1930s and 1940s grounded Lowery in class-conscious progressivism and its favorite literate form: the newspaper. On top of that, though, was a pragmatic philosophy of worker education that developed in the U.S. after the Depression as an anti-communist antidote to left-wing intellectual influences in unions. Lowery's parent union, in fact, had been a central force in refocusing worker education away from an earlier emphasis on broad critical study and toward discrete techniques for organizing and bargaining. Workers began to be trained in the discrete bodies of knowledge, written formats, and idioms associated with those strategies. Characteristic of this legacy, Lowery's crash course at the Washington-based training center in the early 1970s emphasized technical information, problem solving, and union-building skills and methods. The transformation in worker education from critical, humanistic study to problem-solving skills was also lived out at the school for workers where Lowery took short courses in the 1980s. Once a place where factory workers came to write and read about economics, sociology, and labor history, the school is now part of a university extension service offering workshops — often requested by management — on such topics as work restructuring, new technology, health and safety regulations, and joint labor-management cooperation.[7] Finally, in this inventory of Dwayne Lowery's literacy sponsors, we must add the latest incarnations shaping union practices: the attorneys and college-educated co-workers who carried into Lowery's workplace forms of legal discourse and "essayist literacy."[8]

What should we notice about this pattern of sponsorship? First, we can see from yet another angle how the course of an ordinary person's literacy learning — its occasions, materials, applications, potentials — follows the transformations going on within sponsoring institutions as those institutions fight for economic and ideological position. As a result of wins, losses, or compromises, institutions undergo change, affecting the kinds of literacy they promulgate and the status that such literacy has in the larger society. So where, how, why, and what Lowery practiced as a writer — and what he didn't practice — took shape as part of the post-industrial jockeying going on over the last thirty years by labor, government, and industry. Yet there is more to be seen in this inventory of literacy sponsors. It exposes the deeply textured history that lies within the literacy practices of institutions and within any individual's literacy experiences. Accumulated layers of sponsoring influences — in families, workplaces, schools, memory — carry forms of literacy that have been shaped out of ideological and economic struggles of the past. This history, on the one hand, is a sustaining resource in the quest for literacy. It enables an older generation to pass its literacy resources onto another. Lowery's exposure to his father's newspaper-reading and supper-table political talk kindled his adult passion for news, debate, and for language that rendered relief and justice. This history also helps to create infrastructures of opportunity. Lowery found crucial supports for extending his adult literacy in the educational networks that unions established during the first half of the twentieth century as they were consolidating into national powers. On the other hand, this layered history of sponsorship is also deeply conservative and can be maladaptive because it teaches forms of literacy that oftentimes are in the process of being overtaken by new political realities and by ascendent forms of literacy. The decision to focus worker education on practical strategies of recruiting and bargaining — devised in the thick of Cold War patriotism and galloping expansion in union memberships — became, by the Reagan years, a fertile ground for new forms of management aggression and cooptation.

It is actually this lag or gap in sponsoring forms that we call the rising standard of literacy. The pace of change and the place of literacy in economic competition have both intensified enormously in the last half of the twentieth century. It is as if the history of literacy is in fast forward. Where once the same sponsoring arrangements could maintain value across a generation or more, forms of literacy and their sponsors can now rise and recede many times within a single life span. Dwayne Lowery experienced profound changes in forms of union-based literacy not only between his father's time and his but between the time he joined the union and the time he left it, twenty-odd years later. This phenomenon is what makes today's literacy feel so advanced and, at the same time, so destabilized.

Sponsorship and Appropriation in Literacy Learning

We have seen how literacy sponsors affect literacy learning in two powerful ways. They help to organize and administer stratified systems of opportunity and access, and they raise the literacy stakes in struggles for competitive advantage. Sponsors enable and hinder literacy activity, often forcing the formation of new literacy requirements while decertifying older ones. A somewhat different dynamic of literacy sponsorship is treated here. It pertains to the potential of the sponsored to divert sponsors' resources toward ulterior projects, often projects of self-interest or self-development. Earlier I mentioned how Sunday School parishioners in England and African Americans in slavery appropriated church-sponsored literacy for economic and psychic survival. "Misappropriation" is always possible at the scene of literacy transmission, a reason for the tight ideological control that usually surrounds reading and writing instruction. The accounts that appear below are meant to shed light on the dynamics of appropriation, including the role of sponsoring agents in that process. They are also meant to suggest that diversionary tactics in literacy learning may be invited now by the sheer proliferation of literacy activity in contemporary life. The uses and networks of literacy crisscross through many domains, exposing people to multiple, often amalgamated sources of sponsoring powers, secular, religious, bureaucratic, commercial, technological. In other words, what is so destabilized about contemporary literacy today also makes it so available and potentially innovative, ripe for picking, one might say, for people suitably positioned. The rising level of schooling in the general population is also an inviting factor in this process. Almost everyone now has some sort of contact, for instance, with college-educated people, whose movements through workplaces, justice systems, social service organizations, houses of worship, local government, extended families, or circles of friends spread dominant forms of literacy (whether wanted or not, helpful or not) into public and private spheres. Another condition favorable for appropriation is the deep hybridity of literacy practices extant in many settings. As we saw in Dwayne Lowery's case, workplaces, schools, families bring together multiple strands of the history of literacy in complex and influential forms. We need models of literacy that more astutely account for these kinds of multiple contacts, both in and out of school and across a lifetime. Such models could begin to grasp the significance of re-appropriation, which, for a number of reasons, is becoming a key requirement for literacy learning at the end of the twentieth century.

The following discussion will consider two brief cases of literacy diversion. Both involve women working in subordinate positions as secretaries, in print-rich settings where better educated male supervisors were teaching them to read and write in certain ways to perform their clerical duties. However, as we will see shortly, strong loyalties outside the workplace prompted these two secretaries to lift these literate resources for use in other spheres. For one, Carol White, it was on behalf of her work as a Jehovah's Witness. For the other, Sarah Steele, it was on behalf of upward mobility for her lower middle-class family.

Before turning to their narratives, though, it will be wise to pay some attention to the economic moment in which they occur. Clerical work was the largest and fastest growing occupation for women in the twentieth century. Like so much employment for women, it offered a mix of gender-defined constraints as well as avenues for economic independence and mobility. As a new information economy created an acute need for typists, stenographers, bookkeepers, and other office workers, white, American-born women and, later, immigrant and minority women saw reason to pursue high school and business-college educations. Unlike male clerks of the nineteenth century, female secretaries in this century had little chance for advancement. However, office work represented a step up from the farm or the factory for women of the working class and served as a respectable occupation from which educated, middle-class women could await or avoid marriage (Anderson, Strom). In a study of clerical work through the first half of the twentieth century, Christine Anderson estimated that secretaries might encounter up to ninety-seven different genres in the course of doing dictation or transcription. They routinely had contact with an array of professionals, including lawyers, auditors, tax examiners, and other government overseers (52–53). By 1930, 30 percent of women office workers used machines other than typewriters (Anderson 76) and, in contemporary offices, clerical workers have often been the first employees to learn to operate CRTs and personal computers and to teach others how to use them. Overall, the daily duties of twentieth-century secretaries could serve handily as an index to the rise of complex administrative and accounting procedures, standardization of information, expanding communication, and developments in technological systems.

With that background, consider the experiences of Carol White and Sarah Steele. An Oneida, Carol White was born into a poor, single-parent household in 1940. She graduated from high school in 1960 and, between five maternity leaves and a divorce, worked continuously in a series of clerical positions in both the private and public sectors. One of her first secretarial jobs was with an urban firm that produced and disseminated Catholic missionary films. The vice-president with whom she worked most closely also spent much of his time producing a magazine for a national civic organization that he headed. She discussed how typing letters and magazine articles and occasionally proofreading for this man taught her rhetorical strategies in which she was keenly interested. She described the scene of transfer this way:

> [My boss] didn't just write to write. He wrote in a way to make his letters appealing. I would have to write what he was writing in this magazine too. I was completely enthralled. He would write about the people who were in this [organization] and the different works they were undertaking and people that died and people who were sick and about their personalities. And he wrote little anecdotes. Once in a while I made some suggestions too. He was a man who would listen to you.

The appealing and persuasive power of the anecdote became especially important to Carol White when she began doing door-to-door missionary work for the Jehovah's Witnesses, a pan-racial, millenialist religious faith. She now uses colorful anecdotes to prepare demonstrations that she performs with other women at weekly service meetings at their Kingdom Hall. These demonstrations, done in front of the congregation, take the form of skits designed to explore daily problems through Bible principles. Further, at the time of our interview, Carol White was working as a municipal revenue clerk and had recently enrolled in an on-the-job training seminar called Persuasive Communication, a two-day class offered free to public employees. Her motivation for taking the course stemmed from her desire to improve her evangelical work. She said she wanted to continue to develop speaking and writing skills that would be "appealing," "motivating," and "encouraging" to people she hoped to convert.

Sarah Steele, a woman of Welsh and German descent, was born in 1920 into a large, working-class family in a coal mining community in eastern Pennsylvania. In 1940, she graduated from a two-year commercial college. Married soon after, she worked as a secretary in a glass factory until becoming pregnant with the first of four children. In the 1960s, in part to help pay for her children's college educations, she returned to the labor force as a receptionist and bookkeeper in a law firm, where she stayed until her retirement in the late 1970s.

Sarah Steele described how, after joining the law firm, she began to model her household management on principles of budgeting that she was picking up from one of the attorneys with whom she worked most closely. "I learned cash flow from Mr. B____," she said. "I would get all the bills and put a tape in the adding machine and he and I would sit down together to be sure there was going to be money ahead." She said that she began to replicate that process at home with household bills. "Before that," she observed, "I would just cook beans when I had to instead of meat." Sarah Steele also said she encountered the genre of the credit report during routine reading and typing on the job. She figured out what constituted a top rating, making sure her husband followed these steps in preparation for their financing a new car. She also remembered typing up documents connected to civil suits being brought against local businesses, teaching her, she said, which firms never to hire for home repairs. "It just changes the way you think," she observed about the reading and writing she did on her job. "You're not a pushover after you learn how business operates."

The dynamics of sponsorship alive in these narratives expose important elements of literacy appropriation, at least as it is practiced at the end of the twentieth century. In a pattern now familiar from the earlier sections, we see how opportunities for literacy learning — this time for diversions of resources — open up in the clash between long-standing, residual forms of sponsorship and the new: between the lingering presence of literacy's conservative history and its pressure for change. So, here, two women — one Native American and both working-class — filch contemporary literacy resources (public relations techniques and accounting practices) from more educated, higher-status men. The women are emboldened in these acts by ulterior identities beyond the workplace: Carol White with faith and Sarah Steele with family. These affiliations hark back to the first sponsoring arrangements through which American women were gradually allowed to acquire literacy and education. Duties associated with religious faith and child rearing helped literacy to become, in Gloria Main's words, "a permissible feminine activity" (579). Interestingly, these roles, deeply sanctioned within the history of women's literacy — and operating beneath the newer permissible feminine activity of clerical work — become grounds for covert, innovative appropriation even as they reinforce traditional female identities.

Just as multiple identities contribute to the ideologically hybrid character of these literacy formations, so do institutional and material conditions. Carol White's account speaks to such hybridity. The missionary film company with the civic club vice president is a residual site for two of literacy's oldest campaigns — Christian conversion and civic participation — enhanced here by twentieth-century advances in film and public relations techniques. This ideological reservoir proved a pleasing instructional site for Carol White, whose interests in literacy, throughout her life, have been primarily spiritual. So literacy appropriation draws upon, perhaps even depends upon, conservative forces in the history of literacy sponsorship that are always hovering at the scene of acts of learning. This history serves as both a sanctioning force and a reserve of ideological and material support.

At the same time, however, we see in these accounts how individual acts of appropriation can divert and subvert the course of literacy's history, how changes in individual literacy experiences relate to larger scale transformations. Carol White's redirection of personnel management techniques to the cause of the Jehovah's Witnesses is an almost ironic transformation in this regard. Once a principal sponsor in the initial spread of mass literacy, evangelism is here rejuvenated through late-literate corporate sciences of secular persuasion, fund-raising, and bureaucratic management that Carol White finds circulating in her contemporary workplaces. By the same token, through Sarah Steele, accounting practices associated with corporations are, in a sense, tracked into the house, rationalizing and standardizing even domestic practices. (Even though Sarah Steele did not own an adding machine, she penciled her budget figures onto adding-machine tape that she kept for that purpose.) Sarah Steele's act of appropriation in some sense explains how dominant forms of literacy migrate and penetrate into private spheres, including private consciousness. At the same time, though, she accomplishes a subversive diversion of literate power. Her efforts to move her family up in the middle class involved not merely contributing a second income but also, from her desk as a bookkeeper, reading her way into an understanding of middle-class economic power.

Teaching and the Dynamics of Sponsorship

It hardly seems necessary to point out to the readers of *CCC* that we haul a lot of freight for the opportunity to teach writing. Neither rich nor powerful enough to sponsor literacy on our own terms, we serve instead as conflicted brokers between literacy's buyers and sellers. At our most worthy, perhaps, we show the sellers how to beware and try to make sure these exchanges will be a little fairer, maybe, potentially, a little more mutually rewarding. This essay has offered a few working case studies that link patterns of sponsorship to processes of stratification, competition, and reappropriation. How much these dynamics can be generalized to classrooms is an ongoing empirical question.

I am sure that sponsors play even more influential roles at the scenes of literacy learning and use than this essay has explored. I have focused on some of the most tangible aspects — material supply, explicit teaching, institutional aegis. But the ideological pressure of sponsors affects many private aspects of writing processes as well as public aspects of finished texts. Where one's sponsors are multiple or even at odds, they can make writing maddening. Where they are absent, they make writing unlikely. Many of the cultural formations we associate with writing development — community practices, disciplinary traditions, technological potentials — can be appreciated as make-do responses to the economics of literacy, past and present. The history of literacy is a catalogue of obligatory relations. That this catalogue is so deeply conservative and, at the same time, so ruthlessly demanding of change is what fills contemporary literacy learning and teaching with their most paradoxical choices and outcomes.[9]

In bringing attention to economies of literacy learning I am not advocating that we prepare students more efficiently for the job markets they must enter. What I have tried to suggest is that as we assist and study individuals in pursuit of literacy, we also recognize how literacy is in pursuit of them. When this process stirs ambivalence, on their part or on ours, we need to be understanding.

Acknowledgments

This research was sponsored by the NCTE Research Foundation and the Center on English Learning and Achievement. The Center is supported by the U.S. Department of Education's Office of Educational Research and Improvement, whose views do not necessarily coincide with the author's. A version of this essay was given as a lecture in the Department of English, University of Louisville, in April 1997. Thanks to Anna Syvertsen and Julie Nelson for their help with archival research. Thanks too to colleagues who lent an ear along the way: Nelson Graff, Jonna Gjevre, Anne Gere, Kurt Spellmeyer, Tom Fox, and Bob Gundlach.

Notes

1. Three of the keenest and most eloquent observers of economic impacts on writing teaching and learning have been Lester Faigley, Susan Miller, and Kurt Spellmeyer.
2. My debt to the writings of Pierre Bourdieu will be evident throughout this essay. Here and throughout I invoke his expansive notion of "economy," which is not restricted to literal and ostensible systems of money making but to the many spheres where people labor, invest, and exploit energies — their own and others' — to maximize advantage. See Bourdieu and Wacquant, especially 117–120 and Bourdieu, Chapter 7.
3. Thomas Laqueur (124) provides a vivid account of a street demonstration in Bolton, England, in 1834 by a "pro-writing" faction of Sunday School students and their teachers. This faction demanded that writing instruction continue to be provided on Sundays, something that opponents of secular instruction on the Sabbath were trying to reverse.
4. See, for instance, National Assessments of Educational Progress in reading and writing (Applebee et al.; and "Looking").
5. All names used in this essay are pseudonyms.
6. I am not suggesting that literacy that does not "pay off" in terms of prestige or monetary reward is less valuable. Dora Lopez's ability to read and write in Spanish was a source of great strength and pride, especially when she was able to teach it to her young child. The resource of Spanish literacy carried much of what Bourdieu calls cultural capital in her social and family circles. But I want to point out here how people who labor equally to acquire literacy do so under systems of unequal subsidy and unequal reward.
7. For useful accounts of this period in union history, see Heckscher; Nelson.
8. Marcia Farr associates "essayist literacy" with written genres esteemed in the academy and noted for their explicitness, exactness, reliance on reasons and evidence, and impersonal voice.
9. Lawrence Cremin makes similar points about education in general in his essay "The Cacophony of Teaching." He suggests that complex economic and social changes since World War Two, including the popularization of schooling and the penetration of mass media, have created "a far greater range and diversity of languages, competencies, values, personalities, and approaches to the world and to its educational opportunities" than at one time existed. The diversity most of interest to him (and me) resides not so

much in the range of different ethnic groups there are in society but in the different cultural formulas by which people assemble their educational — or, I would say, literate — experience.

Works Cited

Anderson, Mary Christine. "Gender, Class, and Culture: Women Secretarial and Clerical Workers in the United States, 1925–1955." Diss. Ohio State U, 1986.

Applebee, Arthur N., Judith A. Langer, and Ida V. S. Mullis. *The Writing Report Card: Writing Achievement in American Schools.* Princeton: ETS, 1986.

Bourdieu, Pierre. *The Logic of Practice.* Trans. Richard Nice. Cambridge: Polity, 1990.

Bourdieu, Pierre, and Loic J. D. Wacquant. *An Invitation to Reflexive Sociology.* Chicago: Chicago UP, 1992.

Bourne, J. M. *Patronage and Society in Nineteenth-Century England.* London: Edward Arnold, 1986.

Brandt, Deborah. "Remembering Reading, Remembering Writing." *CCC* 45 (1994): 459–79.

———. "Accumulating Literacy: Writing and Learning to Write in the Twentieth Century." *College English* 57 (1995): 649–68.

Cornelius, Janet Duitsman. *'When I Can Read My Title Clear': Literacy, Slavery, and Religion in the Antebellum South.* Columbia: U of South Carolina, 1991.

Cremin, Lawrence. "The Cacophony of Teaching." *Popular Education and Its Discontents.* New York: Harper, 1990.

Faigley, Lester. "Veterans' Stories on the Porch." *History, Reflection and Narrative: The Professionalization of Composition, 1963–1983.* Eds. Beth Boehm, Debra Journet, and Mary Rosner. Norwood: Ablex, in press.

Farr, Marcia. "Essayist Literacy and Other Verbal Performances." *Written Communication* 8 (1993): 4–38.

Heckscher, Charles C. *The New Unionism: Employee Involvement in the Changing Corporation.* New York: Basic, 1988.

Hortsman, Connie, and Donald V. Kurtz. *Compradrazgo in Post-Conquest Middle America.* Milwaukee: Milwaukee-UW Center for Latin America, 1978.

Kett, Joseph F. *The Pursuit of Knowledge under Difficulties: From Self Improvement to Adult Education in America 1750–1990.* Stanford: Stanford UP, 1994.

Laqueur, Thomas. *Religion and Respectability: Sunday Schools and Working Class Culture 1780–1850.* New Haven: Yale UP, 1976.

Looking at How Well Our Students Read: The 1992 National Assessment of Educational Progress in Reading. Washington: U.S. Dept. of Education, Office of Educational Research and Improvement, Educational Resources Information Center, 1992.

Lynch, Joseph H. *Godparents and Kinship in Early Medieval Europe.* Princeton: Princeton UP, 1986.

Main, Gloria L. "An Inquiry into When and Why Women Learned to Write in Colonial New England." *Journal of Social History* 24 (1991): 579–89.

Miller, Susan. *Textual Carnivals: The Politics of Composition.* Carbondale: Southern Illinois UP, 1991.

Nelson, Daniel. *American Rubber Workers and Organized Labor, 1900–1941.* Princeton: Princeton UP, 1988.

Nicholas, Stephen J., and Jacqueline M. Nicholas. "Male Literacy, 'Deskilling,' and the Industrial Revolution." *Journal of Interdisciplinary History* 23 (1992): 1–18.

Resnick, Daniel P., and Lauren B. Resnick. "The Nature of Literacy: A Historical Explanation." *Harvard Educational Review* 47 (1977): 370–85.

Spellmeyer, Kurt. "After Theory: From Textuality to Attunement with the World." *College English* 58 (1996): 893–913.

Stevens, Jr., Edward. *Literacy, Law, and Social Order.* DeKalb: Northern Illinois UP, 1987.

Strom, Sharon Hartman. *Beyond the Typewriter: Gender, Class, and the Origins of Modern American Office Work, 1900–1930.* Urbana: U of Illinois P, 1992.

Brandt's Insights as a Resource for Your Teaching

1. Reflect on the patterns of sponsorship by which you came to reading and writing, and see if you can delineate points of contrast or overlap with those of your students.

2. How might you define your own mission in the classroom in terms of Brandt's idea of sponsorship?

Brandt's Insights as a Resource for Your Writing Classroom

1. Outline Brandt's idea of sponsorship for your students and ask them to identify the primary sponsor of their literacy. What do they make of the fact that their literacy was sponsored the way it was?

2. Ask your students to imagine how they might serve as a literacy sponsor in the future. How might they imagine this project? How will they inhabit that role? Why one way rather than another?

Annotated Bibliography

Research and reflection about writers, writing, and our practices of working with writers have proliferated over the last two decades. Ph.D. programs in rhetoric and composition theory have increased. You can find multiple resources to assist you as you teach yourself more about working with writers: Many sourcebooks and introductions to teaching writing are available; journals and NCTE (National Council of Teachers of English, <http://www.ncte.org>) anthologies offer additional theoretical and pedagogical perspectives on the range of topics addressed in this ancillary. Supplementing the works cited in the individual readings, this brief and selective bibliography offers you a starting point for broadening and deepening your thinking about writers and about ways to work with writers.

Bruffee, Kenneth A. *Collaborative Learning: Higher Education, Interdependence and the Authority of Knowledge.* Johns Hopkins UP, 1993. Bruffee presents a tightly woven analysis. He argues for change in higher education through collaborative learning. Specific analyses of collaborative practice across disciplines provide additional insights and advice to writing teachers who foster collaborative learning.

———. *A Short Course in Writing: Composition, Collaborative Learning, and Constructive Reading.* 4th ed. New York: Harper, 1995. This textbook with prompts for creative and transactional writing can be used in classrooms or by an individual for self-teaching. Bruffee's introduction offers a clear description of the relationships among writing, reading, teaching, and social construction as a needed direction in higher education.

Ede, Lisa, ed. *The Braddock Essays, 1975–1998.* Boston: Bedford/St. Martin's Press, 1999. This book collects nearly twenty-five years of articles that won composition's most prestigious award. It offers not only, then, the best composition scholarship of the last three decades, but a rich historical perspective on the ways the field's interests and methods have evolved.

Enos, Theresa, ed. *A Sourcebook for Basic Writing Teachers.* Manchester, NJ: McGraw, 1987. Thirty-nine essays extend the discussion of basic writing. The collection focuses on the sociolinguistic dimensions of literacy and shows the range of contemporary research, theory, and practice, building on the foundation laid by Mina Shaughnessy in *Errors and Expectations.*

Freire, Paulo. *Pedagogy of the Oppressed.* Trans. Myra Bergman Ramos. New York: Herder, 1972. Freire argues that literacy empowers the individual and that through the process of "naming his world," a person becomes free. His discussion of learner and master-learner collaborating in dialogue and action provides a useful model for writing as process pedagogy.

Gotswami, Dixie, ed. *Reclaiming the Classroom: Teacher Research as an Agency of Change.* Upper Montclair: Boynton, 1987. This book of essays describes reasons for and methods of conducting research in the classroom. Its scope is impressive, both in variety of research projects and methodologies and in discussions of the effects on instructors and students. The editor has pulled together important — and often original — essays by the leading teacher-scholars in composition and rhetoric.

Graves, Richard. *Rhetoric and Composition: A Sourcebook for Teachers and Writers.* 3rd ed. Upper Montclair: Boynton, 1990. Graves organized this sourcebook for writing teachers of all levels. The thirty-eight selections by well-known theorists and researchers document the energetic growth in the discipline of writing since 1963. Five chapters introduce the novice instructor to and update the veteran instructor about the growth and health of the scholarly discipline; practicing teachers' reports and "lore"; strategies to motivate student writers; questions about style; and "new perspectives, new horizons."

Irmscher, William F. *Teaching Expository Writing.* New York: Holt, 1979. The first text written for teachers of writing, this book poses the central questions every new teacher has. Irmscher writes from all the writer's resources: recall of his decades of teaching writing and his status as the "most senior" director of a composition program; humanistic observation of students as writers; conversation with writers and writing specialists; continuous reading in the discipline; and a lively imagination.

Lindemaɪ·n, Erika. *A Rhetoric for Writing Teachers.* 3rd ed. New York: Oxford UP, 1995. Lindemann does not supplant Irmscher but enriches the reading about teaching writing. Her text reports both theory and practice.

Myers, Miles. *The Teacher-Researcher: How to Study Writing in the Classroom.* Urbana: NCTE, 1985. An introduction to classroom writing assessment and research into writing processes, this book reviews procedures for teacher research and theoretical frameworks. It shows teachers — from kindergarten through college — ways to study writing in the classroom using specific examples of research.

Pytlik, Betty, and Sarah Liggett, eds. *Preparing College Teachers of Writing: Histories, Theories, Programs, Practices.* Oxford: Oxford UP, 2002. This book assembles essays from nearly forty teachers from twenty-eight institutions to discuss what new teachers of writing at the college-level need to learn in order to teach well and what sorts of programs are most able to foster the intellectual and professional development of these teachers. It offers rich historical and theoretical contexts for thinking about teacher preparation, as well as insights into institutional, departmental, and programmatic structures, policies, and politics.

Shaughnessy, Mina P. *Errors and Expectations: A Guide for the Teacher of Basic Writing.* New York: Oxford UP, 1979. Shaughnessy was the first to demonstrate an understanding of the processes that "basic writers" experience. This landmark study helps clarify the philosophy of teaching basic writers and design curriculum and classroom practice to assist these writers to develop into mature writers.

Skon, Linda, David W. Johnson, and Roger T. Johnson. "Cooperative Peer Interaction versus Individual Competition and Individualistic Efforts: Effects on the Acquisition of Cognitive Reasoning Strategies." *Journal of Educational Psychology* 73 (1981): 83–92. The researchers compared the effects of cooperative, competitive, and individualistic goal structures on what students achieve and what higher-order cognitive reasoning strategies they learned. The results indicate that cooperative goal structures and the resulting collaboration prompt higher achievement and more discovery of higher-order cognitive reasoning strategies.

Tate, Gary, and Edward P. J. Corbett, eds. *The Writing Teacher's Sourcebook.* 3rd ed. New York: Oxford UP, 1994. With each edition, the editing team adds new articles to a "canon" of essential discussions. These new articles extend theory and perspective or, as with readings about writers and computers, introduce the teaching strategies that had been considered on the "borders" or not central to teaching practice and have now become necessary strategies.

Trimbur, John. "Consensus and Difference in Collaborative Learning." *College English* 51 (Oct. 1989): 602–17. Trimbur extends the conversation about Bruffee's writing on collaborative learning and responds to critical counter-claims by emphasizing the practical realities of collaborative learning.

Villanueva, Victor, ed. *Cross Talk in Comp Theory: A Reader.* Urbana: NCTE, 1997. This massive collection of articles represents an overview of the last thirty years of composition theory, a veritable "who's who" of the emerging discipline and offers a kind of chronology of the field's major interests, as the editor puts it, from "process to cohesion to cognition to social construction to ideology." The book contains forty-one essays, including the major, historical statements by Janet Emig, James Berlin, Mike Rose, Mina Shaughnessy, and others.

Wiener, Harvey S. *The Writing Room: A Resource Book for Teachers of English.* New York: Oxford UP, 1981. Like Irmscher and Lindemann, Wiener offers advice about teaching writing from day one. His focus is the basic writing classroom and his discussion is informed — like Shaughnessy's — by his classroom experiences in an open-doors writing program.

Teaching Writing: Key Concepts and Philosophies for Reflective Practice

Berthoff, Ann E. *Reclaiming the Imagination: Philosophical Perspectives for Writers and Teachers of Writers.* Upper Montclair: Boynton, 1983. Berthoff's theme of "reclaiming the imagination" reflects her philosophy and practice of encouraging writing as dialectical and reflective action.

Blitz, Michel, and Mark Hulbert. *Letters for the Living: Teaching Writing in a Violent Age.* Urbana: NCTE, 1998. By examining closely their students' accounts of life in New York City and in the mining and steel towns of western Pennsylvania, the authors argue that not only is violence a defining feature of many students' experience but that composition can be understood and even taught as an activity of peacemaking. The students in Blitz and Hulbert's classes wrote letters to each other about the diverse circumstances of their lives, and Blitz and Hulbert include this correspondence in the book and accompany it with their own e-mail correspondence to raise difficult questions about the stakes of our mission as teachers of writing.

Bruffee, Kenneth A. "Social Construction, Language, and the Authority of Knowledge: A Bibliographical Essay." *College English* 48 (Dec. 1986): 773–90. This introduction to social constructivist thought in literary criticism and history with its connections to composition studies lays out a foundation of a "social-epistemic" approach to teaching writing. Bruffee provides a bibliography to help other writing teachers explore these philosophical underpinnings.

Emig, Janet. "Writing as a Mode of Learning." *College Composition and Communication* 28.2 (May 1977): 122–27. Emig asserts a "first principle" that informs both contemporary practice in composition classrooms and writing-across-the-curriculum initiatives and programs.

Freire, Paulo. *Pedagogy of the Oppressed.* Trans. Myra Bergman Ramos. New York: Continuum, 1990. Among the most important books written about education in the twentieth century, this book sketches Freire's fundamental insights into the ways classrooms are configured either to alienate students and prepare them for lives of servitude in oppressive regimes or to liberate them through an ongoing practice of critical reflection, dialogue, collaboration, and what he calls "problem-posing." The pedagogy that Freire favors moves beyond the binary opposition of teacher versus student and encourages a more egalitarian dynamic in which everyone plays both roles.

Fulkerson, Richard. "Four Philosophies of Composition." *College Composition and Communication* 30 (Dec. 1979): 342–48. Fulkerson proposed the terms *expressive, mimetic, rhetorical,* and *formalist* to describe philosophies of composition current in the late 1970s and has continued to reflect on and discuss philosophies and concepts that have evolved further. The piece is not dated because of the range of assumptions and practices that students, new instructors, and veteran instructors bring to the writing classroom.

Hillocks, George, Jr. "What Works in Teaching Composition: A Meta-Analysis of Experimental Treatment Studies." *American Journal of Education* 93 (Nov. 1984): 133–70. Hillocks reviews experimental treatment studies of the teaching of composition over twenty years. While assessing effectiveness of different modes and focuses of instruction, he found that a writing-as-process focus within an "environmental mode" was more effective than other approaches to composition. His discussion of the implications of the research is especially useful.

Myers, Miles, and James Gray. *Theory and Practice in the Teaching of Composition.* Urbana: NCTE, 1983. The text has a double audience: it shows teachers how their strategies for teaching writing connect to and reflect an area of research, and it shows researchers that what teachers do intuitively can often be validated by research. The organization of readings by the teaching methods of processing, distancing, and modeling is especially useful.

North, Stephen. *The Making of Knowledge in Composition: Portrait of an Emerging Field.* Upper Montclair: Boynton, 1987. North discusses the place of "practitioner's lore" and the development of new research methodologies to study questions generated by reflection on the writing experiences of diverse students.

Raymond, James C. "What Good Is All This Heady, Esoteric Theory?" *Teaching English in the Two-Year College* (Feb. 1990): 11–15. Raymond answers this question (often posed by writing teachers who are busy with the daily tasks of working with writers). He "translates" poststructural theory into practical applications.

Smith, Frank. "Myths of Writing." *Language Arts* 58.7 (Oct. 1981): 792–98. Smith describes and clarifies twenty-one misconceptions that students, faculty, and the public hold about what writing is, how it is learned, and who can teach it.

Tate, Gary, and Amy Rupiper and Kurt Shick, eds. *A Guide to Composition Pedagogies.* Oxford: Oxford UP, 2001. This book surveys today's major approaches to the teaching of writing. Each chapter is devoted to a different approach and is written by a leading figure in the field. For example, Susan Jarratt discusses feminist approaches to teaching writing, and William Covino discusses rhetorical approaches. Other contributors include Chris Burnham on expressivism, Laura Julier on community-oriented pedagogy, and Susan McLeod on writing across the curriculum.

Thinking about the Writing Process

Generating a Draft

Fulwiler, Toby. *The Journal Book.* Portsmouth, NH: Boynton, 1987. Forty-two essays discuss the use of journals for discovery and invention in writing classrooms and in other disciplines across the curriculum.

Hilbert, Betsy S. "It Was a Dark and Nasty Night It Was a Dark and You Would Not Believe How Dark It Was a Hard Beginning." *College Composition and Communication* 43.1 (Feb. 1992): 75–80. Hilbert writes from lengthy experience as a writing instructor about beginning a new semester with new writers and predictable difficulties. The essay is tonic and a healthy reminder to us about staying focused on why we teach writing as we enter or return to the classroom.

Johnson, T. R. "School Sucks." *College Composition and Communication* 52:4 (June 2001): 620–50. This essay explores the sources, incarnations, and resistances to pedagogies that emphasize writing as a process. Occasioned by the recent epidemic of school shootings and the author's memory of violent schoolyard rhymes, the essay ranges from rhetoric's historical discussion of the pleasures of writing to composition's more recent interest in academic professionalism to Gilles Deleuze's theory of masochism to the problem of teaching and learning in a consumer culture.

Perl, Sondra. *Landmark Essays on Writing Process.* Davis, CA: Hermagoras Press, 1994. This volume collects more than a dozen essays as well as a bibliography for further study on the central, even founding insight of contemporary composition — that is, the idea that composing is a process. The book features work by the leading figures in the field, work that articulated, substantiated, and disseminated the crucial new pedagogy that began to capture the attention of many writing teachers in the 1970s and that continues to focus our field in primary, pervasive ways.

Rose, Mike. *When a Writer Can't Write: Studies in Writer's Block and Other Composing-Process Problems.* New York: Guilford, 1985. Eleven essays identify and analyze cognitive and affective dimensions of writing apprehension. The range of discussion emphasizes the effects of the environment and writing situations on the writer: Novice writers, ESL writers, graduate students, and professional writers are all affected by writing apprehension at various times.

———. *Writer's Block: The Cognitive Dimension.* Carbondale: Southern Illinois UP, 1984. This landmark book researching and analyzing writer's block emphasizes that a variety of cognitive difficulties are behind the problem. Case studies and the report of research results offer useful insights about ways to teach writing that will enable writers to get beyond blocks.

Revising a Draft

Bartholomae, David. "The Study of Error." *College Composition and Communication* 31 (Oct. 1980): 253–69. Bartholomae encourages a study of how students revise texts as they speak aloud about them. He connects the phenomenon to his definition of basic writing as a kind of writing produced as students learn the knowledge of a new discourse community.

Flower, Linda, John R. Hayes, Linda Carey, Karen Schriver, and James Stratman. "Detection, Diagnosis, and the Strategies of Revision." *College Composition and Communication* 37 (Feb. 1986): 16–55. This article, produced through collaborative research and writing, describes some of the important intellectual activities that underlie and affect the process of revision. The article presents a working model for revision, for identifying "problems," and for generating solutions.

Harris, Muriel. "Composing Behaviors of One- and Multi-Draft Writers." *College English* 51 (Feb. 1989): 174–91. This study of eight experienced writers who described themselves as one-draft or multidraft writers provides useful materials for individualizing the processes of rewriting for students.

Sommers, Nancy. "Between the Drafts." *College Composition and Communication* 43 (Nov. 1992): 23–31. Nancy Sommers models the use of personal narrative as another kind of "evidence" to support or argue points in academic writing. She suggests that we should encourage and help students to use personal narrative in academic writing when they can. Use of personal narrative along with the traditional sources is a recurring theme in discussions of assisting writers as they rethink purpose, readership, and identity during the process of revising and re-visioning text.

Sudol, Ronald A., ed. *Revising: New Essays for Teachers of Writing.* Urbana: NCTE, 1982. Useful essays describing both the practice and the theory of revising strategies and processes.

Teaching Critical Reading and Writing

Berthoff, Ann. "Is Teaching Still Possible? Writing, Meaning, and Higher-Order Reasoning." *College English* 46.6 (Dec. 1984): 743–55. Berthoff surveys and evaluates models of cognitive development and their connections to positivist perspectives on language. She discusses alternative perspectives on language and learning that emphasize reading and writing as interpretation and as the making of meaning.

Elbow, Peter. "Teaching Thinking by Teaching Writing." *Change* 15.6 (Sept. 1983): 37–40. Elbow's argument that "first-order creative, intuitive thinking and second-order critical thinking" can and should be encouraged in writing instruction, could be used for writing-across-the-curriculum initiatives.

Flower, Linda, and John R. Hayes. "The Cognition of Discovery: Defining a Rhetorical Problem." *College Composition and Communication* 31.1 (Feb. 1980): 21–32. The researchers used protocol analysis to study the differences between writers engaged in problem-solving cognitive processes.

Karbach, Joan. "Using Toulmin's Model of Argumentation." *Journal of Teaching Writing* 6.1 (Spring 1987): 81–91. This article illustrates the use of Toulmin's three-part model of argumentation: data, warrant, and claim. While describing heuristic procedures, Karbach proposes this informal logic as a strategy for teaching inductive and deductive logic within any writing assignment.

Kneupper, Charles. "Argument: A Social Constructivist Perspective." *Journal of the American Forensic Association* 17.4 (Spring 1981): 183–89. A communication specialist analyzes argumentation theory from the perspective of social constructionism. He examines uses and connections between argument as structure and argument as process along with their social-epistemic implications.

Lunsford, Andrea. "Cognitive Development and the Basic Writer." *College English* 41 (Sept. 1979): 39–46. After reviewing theories of cognitive development, Lunsford demonstrates that many basic writers operate below the stage of forming concepts and have difficulty in "decentering." She recommends strategies and writing assignments to help basic writers practice and acquire more complex cognitive skills.

———. "The Content of Basic Writers' Essays." *College Composition and Communication* 31.3 (Oct. 1980): 278–90. Lunsford reports that three factors affect word choice and linguistic flexibility of basic writers: the level of writing skill they bring to a classroom, their stages of cognitive development, and their self-concepts.

Shor, Ira. *Critical Teaching and Everyday Life.* Chicago: U Chicago P, 1987. Influenced by Paulo Freire's pedagogical theories, Shor emphasizes learning through dialogue. His analysis of education is inclusive: open admissions teaching of writing, traditional and nontraditional students and learning environments, elite and nonelite educational missions, and "liberatory" teaching modes that challenge social limits of thought and action and encourage cultural literacy. Cognitive skills are acquired and enhanced through collaborative problem solving and reflection leading to action.

Wink, Joan. *Critical Pedagogy: Notes from the Real World.* New York: Longman, 2000. This analyzes the often-difficult rhetoric of critical pedagogy to push to new, deeper perspectives on the dynamics of the classroom and the community. The book is rooted in powerful, personal narratives and written in a lively, even informal voice. It brings otherwise abstract ideas to life and constantly tests those ideas against the author's own experience of many years in the classroom.

Teaching Writing with Computers

Blair, Kristine, and Pamela Takayoshi, eds. *Feminist Cyberscapes: Mapping Gendered Academic Spaces.* Stamford, CT: Ablex Publishing, 1999. This collection of essays explores varying contexts (virtual and physical, institutional and cultural) that shape electronic space for women. Although issues of gender and cyberspace have most often been relegated to the margins, the editors of this collection hope to bring into the mainstream of composition studies a rich array of concerns about the relationship between women and technology as a way of understanding women's participation in and resistance to systems of inequality. The contributors to the collection rely on materialist feminism, feminist critiques of technology design and its uses, and feminist pedagogy to examine computerized classrooms, Internet technologies (including e-mail, listservs, and MOOs), and professional development opportunities for women working in computers and composition.

Bruce, Bertram, Joy Kreefy Peyton, and Trent Batson. *Network-Based Classrooms: Promises and Realities.* New York: Cambridge UP, 1993. The collaborative technology of "electronic networks for interaction" accommodates and prompts the social construction of knowledge. The collection ranges from descriptions of "how to" to "effects." Caveat: The rapid development and redesign of the technology and the advent of the World Wide Web may make the nuts and bolts obsolete, so focus on themes, issues, and significance to writing improvement.

Hawisher, Gail, and Paul LeBlanc, ed. *Re-Imagining Computers and Composition: Teaching and Research in the Virtual Age.* Portsmouth, NH: Boynton, 1992. The editors selected twelve essays to describe and speculate about theoretical, research, and pedagogical implications of the dramatically increased use of electronic technology for composition.

Hawisher, Gail E., and Charles Moran. "Electronic Mail and the Writing Instructor." *College English* 55.6 (Oct. 1993): 627–43. The writers describe advantages and effects of introducing electronic communication to a composition course. The essay gives practical advice to newcomers.

Lanham, Richard. *The Electronic Word: Democracy, Technology, and the Arts.* Chicago: U of Chicago P, 1993. In a reader-based study, rhetorician Lanham analyzes the creative potential of electronic writing for coming closer to these long-standing goals: access, unfettered imagination, and effective communication. He views the electronic word as dramatically and healthily changing the construction and experience of "knowledge."

Responding to and Evaluating Student Writing

Anson, Chris. *Writing and Response: Theory, Practice, and Research.* Urbana: NCTE, 1989. The essays include discussion of responding to student journal writing, responding via electronic media, and responding in conferences. Theoretical perspectives and instructional practice are intermixed.

Belanoff, Patricia, and Marcia Dickson, eds. *Portfolios: Process and Product.* Portsmouth, NH: Boynton, 1991. In the first comprehensive collection of writings on using portfolios for classroom and portfolio assessment, the editors called for "practitioners' lore" and research. This is the book to start with when considering use of writing portfolios.

Berthoff, Ann. *Thinking, Writing: The Composing Imagination.* Portsmouth, NH: Heinemann, 1982. Berthoff focuses on the reading-writing relationship within a course organized around the central task of teaching composition. Insights and practical suggestions abound.

Black, Laurel, Donald Daiker, Jeffrey Sommers, and Gail Stygall, eds. *New Directions in Portfolio Assessment: Reflective Practice, Critical Theory, and Large-Scale Scoring.* Portsmouth, NH: Boynton-Cook, 1994. This collection moves readers beyond the merely introductory discussion of portfolios to critical questions of practice and theory: How do changing notions of literacy intersect with the growing interest in portfolios? How can we apply the portfolio approach to large-scale projects of assessment, involving not simply individual classrooms, but whole programs and schools? How do gender and cultural expectations affect readers of portfolios? This collection addresses these and other challenging questions for the reader already versed in the basics of portfolio assessment.

Brooke, Robert E. *Writing and Sense of Self: Identity Negotiation in Writing Workshops.* Urbana: NCTE, 1991. Brooke describes the effects of responding in the context of writing through workshops: effects on the kinds of writing projects students risked and effects on their processes of negotiating identities as writers.

Cooper, Charles R., and Lee Odell, eds. *Evaluating Writing: Describing, Measuring, Judging.* Urbana: NCTE, 1977. With its comprehensive survey of ways teachers can describe writing and measure the growth of writing, this remains a useful sourcebook. The discussion of involving students in the evaluation of writing includes individual goal setting, self-evaluation, and peer evaluation. Multiple responses to multiple processes and features of the writing are implicitly recommended.

Flower, Linda, and Thomas Hucking. "Reading for Points and Purposes." *Journal of Advanced Composition* 11.2 (Fall 1991): 347–62. By researching how undergraduate and graduate students use point-driven or purpose-driven reading strategies, the authors conclude that readers who use a point-driven strategy tend to stay at a less complex level of interpretation.

Freire, Paulo. *Education for Critical Consciousness.* New York: Seabury, 1973. Freire's argument for educational reform focuses on the need for the development of "critical consciousness" in learners, who thus become the agents rather than the subjects of their education. Freire's focus is congenial with social-epistemic rhetoric and emphasizes the social construction of knowledge through collaborative work.

Hamp-Lyons, Liz, ed. *Assessing Second Language Writing in Academic Contexts.* Norwood, NJ: Ablex, 1991. Twenty-one essays examine the multiple issues of assessing second language writing. Many of the articles focus on assessment design and decision making that affect ESL writers in an assessment program, but the principles of good assessment practices for diverse populations are clearly defined.

Hillocks, George, Jr. "The Interaction of Instruction, Teacher Comment, and Revision in Teaching the Composing Process." *Research in the Teaching of English* 16 (Oct. 1982): 261–82. An early study of the effects of instructor response on student revision and attitudes toward writing. The article points out that helpful commentary or conference discussion promotes a writer's growth.

Huot, Brian, and Michael Williamson, eds. *Validating Holistic Scoring for Writing Assessment: Theoretical and Empirical Foundations.* Cresskill, NJ: Hampton Press, 1993. While research into composing processes and the cultural contexts that shape them have boomed in recent decades, inquiry into how we assess student writing has proceeded at the same pace. This collection takes up the issue of assessment from diverse angles: the history of holistic scoring, the question of reliability, placement exams, and ESL programs. An important, thorough, expansive set of essays on a much neglected composition issue with which every teacher must grapple.

Newkirk, Thomas, ed. *Only Connect: Uniting Reading and Writing.* Upper Montclair: Boynton, 1986. The fifteen articles in this collection by major scholars in the discipline of "English" explore the relationships of reading and literary study to composition.

Noguchi, Rei R. *Grammar and the Teaching of Writing: Limits and Possibilities.* Urbana: NCTE, 1991. Beginning with the shared conviction that grammar must be taught within the context and processes of drafting and revising, Noguchi helps writing teachers identify the sites where grammar and writing overlap and suggests productive ways to integrate grammar instruction with issues of meaning, organization, and style.

Odell, Lee. "Defining and Assessing Competence in Writing." *The Nature and Measurement of Competency in English.* Ed. Charles R. Cooper. Urbana: NCTE, 1981. Practical advice about clarifying what an instructor defines as writing competence along with descriptions of holistic and other assessment measures for both classroom and large-scale assessment.

Roseberry, Ann S., Linda Flower, Beth Warren, Betsy Bowen, Bertram Bruce, Margaret Kantz, and Ann M. Penrose. "The Problem-Solving Processes of Writers and Readers." *Collaboration through Writing and Reading: Exploring Possibilities.* Ed. Anne Haas Dysott. Urbana: NCTE, 1989. 136–64.

Welch, Nancy. "One Student's Many Voices: Reading, Writing, and Responding with Bakhtin." *Journal of Advanced Composition* 13.2 (Fall 1993): 493–502. Welch demonstrates a "Bakhtinian" reading of a student text to argue that teachers should respond to the many voices in a student text.

White, Edward M. *Assigning, Responding, Evaluating: A Writing Teacher's Guide.* New York: St. Martin's, 1992. For the "state of the art" in writing assessment, White surveys and evaluates the designs and applications of writing assessments and helps writing instructors use the information garnered through assessment to improve classroom instruction.

———. *Teaching and Assessing Writing.* San Francisco: Jossey, 1985. The publisher here is significant: In this first major discussion of the symbiosis of writing assessment and classroom teaching, the preeminent publisher of discourse in higher education agreed that this would be an important test. This should be the first book a new writing teacher uses to learn about contemporary research and practice in understanding, evaluating, and improving students' writing performance.

Yancey, Kathleen Blake, ed. *Portfolios in the Writing Classroom: An Introduction.* Urbana: NCTE, 1992. This collection focuses on the use of writing portfolios in secondary and higher education courses across the curriculum. The articles describe objectives and designs for the use of portfolios. This is a very useful introduction to the field.

Issues in Writing Pedagogy

Fostering Literacy

Brandt, Deborah. *Literacy as Engagement: The Acts of Writers, Readers, and Texts.* Carbondale: Southern Illinois UP, 1990. This book explores the ways literacy is commonly understood and criticizes, in particular, the dominant theory that becoming literate hinges on a withdrawal from the immediate social world. Brandt suggests that the move from oral to literate modes of action does not significantly reconfigure the fundamental terms of the interpretive dynamic — context, reference, and meaning.

Dyson, Anne Haas, ed. *Collaboration through Reading and Writing: Exploring Possibilities.* Urbana: NCTE, 1989. The discussion of the interrelationships of reading, writing, and learning was first generated at a conference of researchers and theorists concerned with literacy teaching and training.

Heath, Shirley Brice. "An Annotated Bibliography on Multicultural Writing and Literacy Issues." *Quarterly of the National Writing Project and the Center for the Study of Writing and Literacy* 12.1 (Winter 1990): 22–24. This bibliography lists and annotates sixteen books and articles that focus on multicultural writing and literacy issues, including bilingual education, ESL, writing instruction, literacy, and multicultural education.

Many, Joyce. *Handbook of Instructional Practices for Literacy Teacher-Educators.* London: Erlbaum, 2001. This book offers accounts by well-known literacy researchers of how they approach literacy instruction and what they have learned from their actual classroom experiences. Divided into specific areas within literary studies, this book offers a strong starting point for those interested in questions of literacy.

Smith, Frank. *Essays into Literacy.* Portsmouth, NH: Heinemann, 1983. Smith's theory about literacy as the ability to make use of all available possibilities of written language informs thirteen essays written over a ten-year period. The research into and reflection on elementary and secondary reading and writing experiences produced insights that transfer easily to discussion of college-level literacies.

Fostering Diversity

Berlin, James, and Michael Vivion, eds. *Cultural Studies in the English Classroom.* Portsmouth, NH: Boynton, 1993. Berlin offers a comprehensive discussion of cultural critique as a purpose for writing and reading coursework, reminding readers that all pedagogic choices are political, whether they are foregrounded or implicit in course design and activities. Cultural critique necessarily examines and analyzes the power relationships within the multiple cultures of a dominant culture.

Eichorn, Jill, Sara Farris, Karen Hayes, Adriana Hernandez, Susan C. Jarratt, Karen Powers-Stubbs, and Marian M. Schiachitano. "A Symposium on Feminist Experiences in the Composition Classroom." *College Composition and Communication* 43 (Oct. 1992): 297–332. In describing their experiences using feminist composition pedagogies, the writers illustrate ways of respecting diversity within a writing community.

Flynn, Elizabeth A. "Feminist Theories/Feminist Composition." *College English* 57.2 (Feb. 1995): 201–12. Flynn reviews four book-length studies in "feminist composition," connecting them to theoretical perspectives and demonstrating the vigorous dialogue from many directions that feminist pedagogues and theorists have engendered.

Herrington, Anne. "Basic Writing: Moving the Voices on the Margin to the Center." *Harvard Educational Review* 60.4 (Nov. 1990): 489–96. Herrington describes the redesign of a basic writing course to give voice to marginalized minority students. After a shift to reading works by mostly nonwhite authors, students were encouraged to reflect in writing on those readings and on their experiences of marginalization.

Rose, Mike. *Lives on the Boundary: The Struggles and Achievements of America's Underprepared.* New York: Free, 1989. Through personal narrative and incisive analysis, Rose describes the underclass of students representing diverse cultures and subcultures who are considered underachieving, remedial, or illiterate. Rose speculates about the nature of literacy and learning curricula that could empower these marginalized writers and learners.

Teaching ESL Students

Carson, Joan G., and Gayle L. Nelson. "Writing Groups: Cross-Cultural Issues." *Journal of Second Language Writing* 3.1 (1994): 17–30. Citing the dearth of research on communication assumptions and behaviors of Asian students in collaborative writing communities, Carson and Nelson call for additional studies of ways in which culturally specific beliefs and behaviors might affect cooperation and interaction in peer response groups and collaborative writing projects.

Kasper, Loretta, ed. *Content-Based College ESL Instruction*. London: Erlbaum, 2001. This book is designed to train teachers in a particular approach to ESL students: pedagogy rooted in actual cultural contents. It offers clear descriptions of classroom practices, as well as for assessing student progress, and even delineates means for incorporating technology.

Leki, Ilona. *Understanding ESL Writers: A Guide for Teachers*. Portsmouth, NH: Boynton, 1992. This is an excellent handbook for learning about the concerns, expectations, and errors of ESL students. Written for the double audience of ESL instructors and writing teachers, it provides useful advice about responding to the texts of ESL writers.

Raimes, Ann. "Language Proficiency, Writing Ability, and Composing Strategies: A Study of ESL College Student Writers." *Language Learning* 37.3 (Sept. 1987): 439–68. Raimes analyzed the writing strategies of ESL student writers from different levels of ESL instruction. She found that ESL learners were less inhibited by attempts to correct their work.

Reid, Joy, and Barbara Kroll. "Designing and Assessing Effective Writing Assignments for NES and ESL Students." *Journal of Second Language Writing* 3.1 (1995): 17–41. Reid and Kroll emphasize the need to design fair writing assignments that encourage students to learn from writing experiences as they demonstrate what course material they know and understand. They analyze successful and flawed writing prompts and assignments from the perspective of ESL writers; the practical advice they offer is also pertinent to mainstream composition teaching.

Writing across the Curriculum

Anson, Chris, John Schwiebert, and Michael M. Williamson. *Writing across the Curriculum: An Annotated Bibliography*. Westport, CT: Greenwood, 1993. This very useful bibliography describes both scholarship in and pedagogic strategies for extending and using writing across the curriculum, whether the model is "writing as learning" or "writing in the discipline."

Duke, Charles, and Rebecca Sanchez, eds. *Assessing Writing Across the Curriculum*. Durham: Carolina Academic Press, 2001. This book offers guidelines for effective assessment of student writing and tools to improve writing in diverse content areas. It also offers ways to rethink particular methods of instructing and grading and ways to craft assignments more effectively.

Fulwiler, Toby, and Art Young, eds. *Language Connections: Writing and Reading across the Curriculum*. Urbana: NCTE, 1982. This text, aimed at all college and university instructors, offers theoretical perspectives and practical activities to prompt writing as learning. The text encourages peer evaluation, conferences between instructors and students, and shared evaluation and includes a bibliography on cross-curricular language and learning.

Herrington, Anne. "Writing to Learn: Writing across the Disciplines." *College English* 43 (Apr. 1981): 379–87. This essay focuses on the design of writing assignments that can be connected to course objectives, whatever the discipline. Herrington encourages instructors to emphasize writing as discovery and learning in their responses to student writing.

Acknowledgments (continued from page ii)

Deborah Brandt. "Sponsors of Literacy." *College Composition and Communication* 49 (1998). Copyright © 1998 by the National Council of Teachers of English. Reprinted with permission.

Robert Brooke. "Underlife and Writing Instruction." *College Composition and Communication* 38 (1987). Copyright © 1987 by the National Council of Teachers of English. Reprinted with permission.

Kenneth Bruffee. "Toward Reconstructing American Classrooms: Interdependent Students, Interdependent World." *Collaborative Learning* by Kenneth Bruffee (Chapter Four). Copyright © 1993. Reprinted by permission of the Johns Hopkins University Press.

Juanita Rodgers Comfort. "Becoming a Writerly Self: College Writers Engaging Black Feminist Essays." *College Composition and Communication,* June 2000. Copyright © 2000 by the National Council of Teachers of English. Reprinted with permission.

Lisa Ede and Andrea A. Lunsford. "Audience Addressed/Audience Invoked: The Role of Audience in Composition Theory and Pedagogy." *College Composition and Communication,* May 1984. Copyright © 1984 by the National Council of Teachers of English. Reprinted with permission.

Peter Elbow. "Closing My Eyes As I Speak: An Argument for Ignoring Audience." *College English,* January 1987. Copyright © 1987 by the National Council of Teachers of English. Reprinted with permission.

Michael S. Greer. Excerpts from *The Writing Process at Work* by Michael Greer (Manuscript, 1995). Copyright © 1995 by Michael S. Greer. Reprinted with the permission of the author.

Joseph Harris. "Error." Chapter 4 from *A Teaching Subject: Composition Since 1966* by Joseph Harris. Copyright © 1997 by Joseph Harris. Reprinted by permission of Pearson Education, Inc., Upper Saddle River, N.J.

Muriel Harris and Tony Silva. "Tutoring ESL Students: Issues and Options." *College Composition and Communication,* December 1993. Copyright 1993 by the National Council of Teachers of English. Reprinted with permission.

Patrick Hartwell. "Grammar, Grammars, and the Teaching of Grammar." *College English* 47.2, February 1985: 105–27. Copyright © 1985 by the Natinal Council of Teachers of English. Reprinted with permission.

George Hillocks. "Some Basics for Thinking about Teaching Writing." Excerpt (pp. 224–38) from *Teaching Writing as a Reflective Practice* by George Hillocks Jr. Copyright © 1995 by Teachers College, Columbia University. Reprinted with permission. All rights reserved.

Robert Kramer and Stephen Bernhardt. "Teaching Text Design." From *Technical Communication Quarterly* 5.1 (1996): 35–60. Copyright © 1996 by Robert Kramer and Stephen Bernhardt. Reprinted with permission of the Association of Teachers of Technical Writing and the authors. [ATTW, Att. Billie J. Wahlstrom, coeditor *Technical Communication Quarterly,* Dept. of Rhetoric, University of Minnesota, 64 Classroom Office Building, 1994 Buford Ave., St. Paul, MN 55108]

Susan Miller. "The Sad Women in the Basement: Images of Composition Teaching." From *Textual Carnivals.* Copyright © 1991 Board of Trustees, Southern Illinois University. Reprinted with permission of Southern Illinois University Press.

Charles Moran. "Computers and the Writing Classroom: A Look to the Future." From *Reimagining Computers and Composition: Teaching and Research in the Virtual Age* edited by Gail E. Hawisher and Paul LeBlanc. Copyright © 1992. Reprinted with permission of Heinemann-Boynton/Cook Publishers, a subsidiary of Reed Elsevier, Inc., Portsmouth, N.H.

Sandra Moriarty. "A Conceptual Map of Visual Communication." From *Journal of Visual Literacy* 17.2 (1997): 9–24. Copyright © 1994. International Visual Literacy Association, Inc., 363 Bluemont Hall, 1100 Mid-Campus Drive, Kansas State University, Manhattan, KS 66506–5305. (p) 614-292-4872. R&P — John Clark Belland.

Sondra Perl. "Understanding Composing." *College Composition and Communication,* December 1990. Copyright 1990 by the National Council of Teachers of English. Reprinted with permission.

Nedra Reynolds. "Composition's Imagined Geographies: The Politics of Space in the Frontier, City, and Cyberspace." *College Composition and Communication,* September 1998. Copyright © 1998 by the National Council of Teachers of English. Reprinted with permission.

Mike Rose. "I Just Wanna Be Average." From *Lives on the Boundary: The Struggle and Achievements of America's Underprepared* by Mike Rose. Copyright © 1989 by Mike Rose. Reprinted by permission of The Free Press, an imprint of Simon & Schuster, Inc. Reprinted with permission. "Rigid Rules, Inflexible Plans, and the Stifling of Language: A Cognitivist Analysis of Writer's Block." *College Composition and Communication,* October 1980. Copyright © 1980 by the National Council of Teachers of English. Reprinted with permission.

David Rothgery. "'So What Do We Do Now?' Necessary Directionality as the Writing Teacher's Response to Racist, Sexist, Homophobic Papers." *College Composition and Communication,* May 1993. Copyright © 1993 by the National Council of Teachers of English. Reprinted with permission.

Eileen E. Schell. "The Costs of Caring: 'Feminism' and Contingent Women Workers in Composition Studies." *Feminism and Composition,* edited by Susan Jarrat and Lynn Worsham, 1998. Reprinted by permission of the Modern Language Association of America.

Jeffrey Sommers. "Bringing Practice in Line with Theory: Using Portfolio Grading in the Composition Classroom." From *Portfolios, Process, and Product* edited by Pat Belanoff and Marcia Dickson. Copyright © 1991. Reprinted with permission of Heinemann/Boynton/Cook Publishers, a subsidiary of Reed Elsevier Inc., Portsmouth N.H.

Nancy Sommers. "Revision Strategies of Student Writers and Experienced Adult Writers." *College Composition and Communication,* December 1980. Copyright © 1980 by the National Council of Teachers of English. Reprinted with permission. "Responding to Student Writing." *College Composition and Communication,* May 1982. Copyright © 1982 by the National Council of Teachers of English. Reprinted with permission.

Patricia R. Webb. "Narratives of Self in Networked Communications." From *Computers and Composition,* Volume 14, Number 1, 1997. Copyright © 1997 by Ablex Publishing Corporation. Reprinted with permission. [Division of JAO Press Inc., Subsidiary of Elsevier Science Inc. P.O. Box 811, 100 Prospect St., Stamford, CT 06904-0811]

Nancy Welch. "Toward an Excess-ive Theory of Revision." From *Getting Restless: Rethinking Writing and Revision.* Copyright © 1997. Heinemann-Boynton/Cook Publishers, Portsmouth, N.H.

Joseph M. Williams. "The Phenomenology of Error." *College Composition and Communication* 1981. Copyright © 1981 by the National Council of Teachers of English. Reprinted with permission.